Baseball america's

The Baseball

Autograph

Collector's

Handbook

Number 10

By Jack

D1510737

BASEBALL AMERICA, INC.

BASEBALL AMERICA is a registered trademark

BASEBALL AMERICA, INC.
600 SOUTH DUKE STREET
DURHAM, NORTH CAROLINA 27701

Manufactured in the United States of America

ISBN 0-945164-10-6

Cover Photos: Stan Honda.
Production/Cover Design: Valerie Holbert

Baseball America's
The Baseball Autograph Collector's Handbook
Number 10

Contents

Smalling Family Autographs

"One of the Top Ten most influential autograph experts... as sincere and honest as they come."

-John L. Raybin, Encyclopedia of Sports Memorabilia and Price Guide, July 1995

Thank you for purchasing our book! We are a family owned and operated autograph business specializing in baseball autographs, more specifically, signed gum cards, 3x5 cards, and post cards. We have been a trusted autograph dealer since 1962. Your business means a great deal to us!

SELLING AUTOGRAPHS IN LOTS

All autographs are believed to be original and authentic. Please add $2 for shipping.

Deceased players 3x5 cards
(The deceased player lots are assembled by picking the most recently deceased players first, consequently as the quantity increases, the price increases at a greater rate to reflect the higher priced 3x5 cards.)

Price / 25	$17.50
Price / 50	$35.00
Price / 100	$80.00
Price / 200	$175.00
Price / 350	$360.00
Price / 500	$575.00

Living players 3x5 cards
(Multiples of 100 are available.)

Debut years	1910-50	1951-96
Price / 100	$45.00	$30.00

START YOUR AUTOGRAPH COLLECTION TODAY!
Buying lots is a great way to start a collection. Buy them for a child, friend, or any collecting fanatic!

Signed baseball cards
(Multiples of 100 are available.)
Major League cards

Card years	1977-98
Price / 25	$17.50
Price / 50	$32.50
Price / 100	$60.00

BUYING COLLECTIONS

Buying collections
We are interested in buying baseball autograph collections. If you really want to sell, send us your collection along with your phone number. We're particularly looking for collections of 3x5 cards, signed gum cards, and post cards. We can generally agree on a fair price with the sender.

Buying in lots
Baseball 3x5 cards: We'll pay $15.00 per 100 cards for lots. Send 100 or 10,000. Signed baseball gum cards: We'll pay $20.00 per 100 cards for lots. They must be signed on the front. Please do not send minor league cards.

WORLDWIDE ACCESS

If you have access to the internet, check out The Smalling Family, homepage at:
http://www.public.iastate.edu/~dsmallng
it contains family pictures, information about our family, and links to other homepages.
Also, a copy of our current price list can be downloaded in Word format.

Contact us today to receive our complete 64-page catalog!

It contains individually autographed 3x5 card, gum card, and post card prices.
The catalog also includes auctions filled with quality items.

Smalling Family Autographs
R. J. "Jack" Smalling
2308 Van Buren Avenue
Ames, Iowa 50010-4598

Phone: 515-232-7599
Fax: 515-232-7746
E-mail: smalling@ames.net
Homepage address:
http://www.public.iastate.edu/~dsmallng

Smalling Family Autographs

HALL OF FAME SIGNATURES

PLAYER	A 3x5	B 3x5	C 3x5	D 3x5	CUT	PLAQ
APARICIO	15.00					
APPLING	8.00	6.40	5.60			15.00
ASHBURN	12.00	9.60	8.40	7.20	6.00	
AVERILL	15.00		10.50		7.00	20.00
BARLICK	10.00	8.00	7.00	6.00	5.00	15.00
BELL	10.00			6.00	5.00	
BERRA	10.00	8.00	7.00		5.00	
BOUDREAU	5.00	4.00	3.50	3.00	2.50	5.00
BUNNING	8.00	6.40	5.60		4.00	
CAREY	30.00	24.00	21.00			
CHANDLER	10.00	8.00	7.00	6.00		15.00
CONLAN	10.00		7.00			
COVELESKI	6.00					15.00
CRONIN	30.00	24.00	21.00		15.00	
DANDRIDGE		24.00			15.00	25.00
DICKEY	40.00				20.00	
DIMAGGIO			63.00			
DOERR	5.00		3.50		2.50	6.00
DRYSDALE					7.50	
DUROCHER	30.00	24.00	21.00		15.00	
FELLER	6.00		4.20		3.00	
FERRELL	8.00		5.60	4.80	4.00	10.00
GEHRINGER	8.00		5.60	4.80	4.00	15.00
GOMEZ	20.00	16.00	14.00		10.00	
GREENBERG		32.00	28.00		20.00	
GRIMES	20.00	16.00	14.00			
HAINES	40.00	32.00	28.00			
HARRIS			28.00		20.00	
HERMAN	8.00		5.60		4.00	12.00
HOYT	10.00		7.00		5.00	
HUBBELL	10.00		7.00		5.00	
HUNTER	6.00		4.20		3.00	6.00
IRVIN	6.00	4.80	4.20	3.60	3.00	
T. JACKSON	15.00	12.00	10.50	9.00		
J. JOHNSON	20.00		14.00	12.00		
KALINE	12.00	9.60				

	PLAYER	A 3x5	B 3x5	C 3x5	D 3x5	CUT	PLAQ
X	KELL	5.00	4.00	3.50	3.00	2.50	6.00
X	G. KELLY	15.00	12.00	10.50	9.00	7.50	25.00
X	KILLEBREW	10.00	8.00	7.00			
X	KINER	12.00		8.40	7.20	6.00	
X	LEMON	5.00	4.00	3.50	3.00	2.50	6.00
X	LEONARD	10.00		7.00	6.00		15.00
X	LINDSTROM	35.00	28.00	24.50		17.50	
X	LOPEZ	12.00		8.40	7.20	6.00	
X	LYONS	10.00		7.00		5.00	
X	MACPHAIL	8.00					
X	MARQUARD	25.00	20.00				30.00
X	MATHEWS	8.00		5.60	4.80		
X	MAYS					15.00	12.50
X	J. MCCARTHY	25.00	20.00	17.50	15.00	12.50	
X	MIZE	12.00		8.40	7.20	6.00	
X	MUSIAL	12.00	9.60	8.40	7.20	6.00	
X	NEWHOUSER	12.00		8.40		6.00	
X	NIEKRO			6.40		4.80	
X	PERRY	10.00					
X	REESE	15.00		10.50	9.00		
X	RIZZUTO	10.00		7.00	6.00	5.00	
X	ROBERTS	6.00	4.80	4.20	3.60	3.00	6.00
X	B. ROBINSON	5.00		3.50		2.50	
X	ROUSH	10.00		7.00		5.00	20.00
X	SCHOENDIENST	10.00	8.00	7.00			
X	SEWELL	12.00	9.60	8.40		6.00	
X	SLAUGHTER	4.00	3.20	2.80	2.40	2.00	6.00
X	SNIDER	10.00		7.00			10.00
X	SPAHN	6.00		4.20		3.00	
X	TERRY	12.00		8.40			20.00
X	TRAYNOR	115.00					
X	L. WANER	20.00	16.00	14.00		6.00	25.00
X	WEAVER	10.00	8.00				
X	WILHELM	10.00					
X	B. WILLIAMS	10.00					
X							

Key

A - Blank side signed, no other marks, B - Lined side signed, no other marks, C - Lined or blank side with typing or other marks. D - Dedicated to some particular person, Cut - A signature cut from a letter, sheet of paper, return address, etc., PLAQ - Gold Hall of Fame issued plaque (post card)

Contact us today to receive our complete 64-page catalog!

It contains individually autographed 3x5 card, gum card, and post card prices.
The catalog also includes auctions filled with quality items.

Smalling Family Autographs
R. J. "Jack" Smalling
2308 Van Buren Avenue
Ames, Iowa 50010-4598

Phone: 515-232-7599
Fax: 515-232-7746
E-mail: smalling@ames.net
Homepage address:
http://www.public.iastate.edu/~dsmallng

Smalling Family Autographs

**"One of the Top Ten most influential autograph experts...
as sincere and honest as they come."**

-John L. Raybin, Encyclopedia of Sports Memorabilia and Price Guide, July 1995

UPDATE ADDRESS LIST (UPDATED MONTHLY)

The database for the Baseball America Baseball Address List is constantly being updated. These updates average out to 80 per month. This updated address list is available for $20.50 priority mail postpaid. It is printed on 8.5x11 three-hole punched bond paper by a laser printer. There are no pictures, just raw data.

ADDRESS LIST ADHESIVE LABELS

The Baseball America Baseball Address List in the form of adhesive labels is available for $300.00 postpaid. These labels will be the latest addresses available from our files. We make corrections and additions monthly. These labels will reflect these changes. These labels can also be coded to your specifications and will come in zip code order unless specified otherwise.

DEBUT LISTS

The debut year and number are found in the address book. Individual debut lists from 1910-1998 are $0.12 each postpaid or all 89 for $8.00 postpaid.

PREVIOUS EDITIONS OF THE BASEBALL ADDRESS LIST

Year Published	Edition	Price
1984	3	$4.50 plus shipping
1980	1	$2.00 plus shipping

Shipping costs (one or more books): Priority mail - $3.20 / 4th class book rate - $1.55

BAD ADDRESSES

Updates and corrections to addresses shown to be valid in edition #10 will be provided on the following basis only: 1) Send front of returned envelope or copy thereof 2) Request no more than five at a time 3) Send a SASE 4) Corrections are not provided for editions previous to #10 5) Please allow 4-12 weeks for reply; corrections are made after filling orders 6) Corrections are available by regular mail only, not by e-mail

Contact us today to receive our complete 64-page catalog!

It contains individually autographed 3x5 card, gum card, and post card prices.
The catalog also includes auctions filled with quality items.

Smalling Family Autographs
R. J. "Jack" Smalling
2308 Van Buren Avenue
Ames, Iowa 50010-4598

Phone: 515-232-7599
Fax: 515-232-7746
E-mail: smalling@ames.net
Homepage address:
http://www.public.iastate.edu/~dsmallng

Preface

This book concentrates on the personal signatures or autographs of baseball players. It attempts to provide the background, explanations, and wherewithal for a collector to begin or augment his collection. Many illustrations are taken from what are believed authentic signatures. Some helpful hints are provided so that your autograph hunting pursuits may be simplified and fruitful.

When reading and using this book, please keep in mind the moral and legal rights of the ballplayers. Some are more cooperative than others, some have more time to comply with your requests than others, but all are entitled to respect, privacy and the right to affix or not affix his signature based on his own personal thoughts or moods.

There might be nothing more distinctive and personal that a person may do throughout his life than write his own name. This signature, how it changes from childhood to senility, its thin or broad stroke, its clarity, neatness and readability is a reflection of the character, mood and personality of the signer. Perhaps for these reasons, a person's signature has become his universally accepted mark for identification, acknowledgment and legal contractual agreement.

As these addresses are under constant update because of the transient nature of the society in which we live, I would appreciate any information you can provide concerning the validity of the information and addresses contained herein. Please send all correspondence concerning address corrections, changes of address or death notices to:

R.J. "Jack" Smalling
2308 Van Buren Avenue
Ames, Iowa 50010

I hope this edition of *The Baseball Autograph Collector's Handbook* provides a useful, interesting and enjoyable tool for your autograph and baseball historical pursuits.

Sincerely,

Jack Smalling

Jack Smalling

Authenticity

One of the enjoyable features of collecting autographs is knowing that one possesses an original mark made by another human being, who for one reason or another has distinguished him or herself in the eyes of the collector. Facsimile autographs, autographs signed by someone other than the one whose name appears on the autograph or photographs or copies of autographs do not comply with the definition of a true autograph; hence, they are of no value to the collector.

The only way one can be absolutely sure that an autograph is authentic is to personally witness the signer as he affixes his autograph. Practically speaking, were directly obtained autographs the only ones collected, logistic problems would prevent anyone from having but a modest collection. While authenticity can only be assured by directly obtaining autographs, many sources offer a high probability that an autograph is valid.

Knowing how a person's signature is supposed to look is a first step toward ascertaining authenticity. Facsimile autographs to compare with ones you are attempting to validate can be found on baseball cards, in books or magazines, or quite possibly, from the many facsimile autographs found in the text of this book. The reputation of the secondary source (dealer, friend, other collector) from whom you are obtaining the autograph is of utmost importance. Unfortunately, even the most reputable source may be unaware that he possesses a non-legitimate autograph.

Obtaining an autograph from a logical source increases the probability that an autograph is authentic. Other variables being equal, a resident of Boston is more likely to have a valid autograph of a Red Sox player than is a resident of Butte, Mont. A 70-year old is much more likely to possess an autographed Babe Ruth ball than is a 12-year old. Autographs obtained from the estate or from personal friends of the autographer are highly likely to be authentic. Autographs from financial or legal documents, such as cancelled checks or contracts, or any notarized communications can be considered authentic.

How to Obtain Autographs

Although the text of this book is intended to provide the information necessary to obtain autographs through the mail, there are other ways to obtain autographs of ballplayers. There are basically two general categories by which you can obtain an autograph—firsthand or directly, where you actually watch the ballplayer affix his signature, and secondhand or indirectly, where you are not present at the time the ballplayer signs the autograph. As autograph collectors place such a high concern on authenticity, obtaining autographs firsthand is preferential. Practically speaking, some autographs are impossible to obtain firsthand, while many others are near impossible or at best very difficult to obtain firsthand; hence, most collectors obtain a considerable portion of their collections via the indirect method.

Obtaining Autographs Firsthand

The most obvious place to obtain a ballplayer's autograph is at the ballpark. The traditional crowd around the clubhouse awaiting the departure of their favorite players after the game, pens and papers in hand, is still perhaps the most viable means to obtain autographs. Many clubs provide special nights at the ballpark where, before the game, fans are encouraged to chat, photograph and obtain autographs from the local team members who are available for these activities for the time periods specified.

Local merchants sometimes sponsor promotional activities at their establishments and feature a ballplayer as the guest celebrity. The ballplayer is normally available to sign autographs, and the merchants might well provide a medium (photo, postcard, etc.) for obtaining the autograph.

Other opportunities arise at hotels, airports, celebrity dinners or other public places where a ballplayer might chance to be during the course of his normal routine. However, I must emphasize again the necessity for patience and politeness when requesting an autograph in person from a ballplayer. Quite often, time may allow only a few or no signatures to be signed before the ballplayer's schedule requires him to halt the autograph activities.

More and more over the past few years, the many sports collectibles conventions and shows held across the country have been featuring guest baseball players. These shows provide excellent opportunities for obtaining autographs from some of the most popular ballplayers.

Each year the Baseball Hall of Fame in Cooperstown, NY, holds induction ceremonies for newly elected members. Not only do the newly elected members attend, but also many of the members who have been previously elected are in attendance. There is probably no other time or place during the year when one can obtain, in person, as many living HOFer autographs as on induction day in Cooperstown.

Obtaining Autographs Indirectly

Most collectors, by necessity, obtain the bulk of their collections indirectly. Trading with other collectors, purchasing from dealers, purchasing from private parties, bidding at auction from estate liquidations, hobby paper ads, or sports collectibles conventions are the most prevalent methods which do not involve the sports personality himself. The most common way to obtain an autograph from the sports personality without the presence of the sports personality is through the mail. It is for this purpose that The Baseball Autograph Collector's Handbook is most useful.

Autograph collecting is a reasonably popular hobby. It is not uncommon to find other collectors with autograph interests similar to yours. It is also not uncommon to find collectors who posses, more than one autograph of the same player; a duplicate which they can be convinced to part with in exchange for an autograph which they desire but do not possess – one which you yourself may have in duplicate. These conditions form the basis for trade negotiations from which both parties can obtain satisfaction. Most trading is not quite this simple; however, the underlying motives of all tradings are to obtain something you do not possess and desire to have, for something you have but do not place such a high value on as you do the item you desire to obtain.

Dealers in autographed material exist just as they do for any collectible. Many specialize in particular types of autographs. In any event, these dealers have acquired autograph material and are willing to sell it at a given price (a price which may or may not be negotiable). These dealers can be found at sports collectibles conventions, at local flea markets and from advertisements in the hobby papers or autograph oriented periodicals (including this book).

A check of your local newspaper, particularly the auction section of the Sunday edition, is an excellent way to become aware of estate and private party autograph sales and auctions. The auction method offers you the opportunity to obtain autographs you desire for amounts less than you might pay to a dealer. In fact, because of the scarcity of certain autographs, the auction method may be the only available way to obtain a particular autograph. In such cases a fair market value might not be known, and the auction offers a means to arrive at a price based on the value of the autograph to the collector.

Obtaining Autographs Through the Mail

A large number of active and retired baseball players honor autograph requests made through the mail. One of the prime purposes of compiling this book is to provide the collector with the wherewithal to obtain autographs he or she desires through the mail. The author does not profess to know all players who will comply with your autograph requests, nor those who will not comply. The author does not promote or sanction any harassment or excessive requests on your part of the ballplayers contacted through the addresses found in this Address List. To the contrary, I emphatically suggest a polite, patient and respectful course in obtaining autographs through the mail.

Ballplayers, particularly active players during the baseball season, have schedules much tighter and more regimented than the normal 9 to 5 worker. Mail they receive may not be opened for lengthy periods. Many schedule limited time periods that they devote to autograph requests. Quite possibly, dependent on the number of autograph requests a particular player receives, your autograph request might not be answered for a considerable period of time. Be patient. The author knows of cases where years have elapsed before an autograph request was returned.

Like everyone else, ballplayers are human beings and appreciate politeness. Words such as "please" and "thank you" are as pleasantly received and as revered by ballplayers as they are by parents of teenagers (fortunately, ballplayers hear them much more often). Excessive requests, imperative tones and impoliteness are justifiably scorned.

Some ballplayers do not honor autograph requests, either in person or through the mail. Some do not even accept mail, and your letter may come back marked "refused." Some change their autographing philosophies over the years, becoming more liberal or conservative in their autographing habits. Whatever a player's thoughts or ideas are on accepting or refusing autograph requests, they should be respected.

The mechanics of obtaining autographs through the mail are quite simple. Send the request, postpaid, to the ballplayer, including a politely written request outlining what you are asking of the ballplayer, any material that you wish to have autographed and an SASE (self-addressed stamped envelope) large enough to contain the material you wish to be autographed and returned to you. Never send an autograph request postage due. To do so is presumptuous, in poor taste and completely uncalled for.

Do not send an unreasonable amount of material for autographing. A limit of three items per request has become the accepted practice of collectors. An exception to this limit is considered permissible if you have duplicates of the item you wish to have autographed, and you would like to give the ballplayer the opportunity to keep one of the duplicates for his own enjoyment. Ballplayers, like most of us, enjoy seeing and having interesting photos or other material concerning themselves, particularly if the item is novel or the ballplayer has never before seen it. Many collectors use this method as a gesture of good faith and intent when requesting autographs through the mail. However, the limit of three items you wish to have signed and returned to you, exclusive of the items you wish to present to the ballplayer at his option to keep, is still the accepted standard.

It is not considered unreasonable to request a short personalization with an autograph; for example, "To John from . . . ," or "Best Wishes to Gayle from . . . ," etc. Requesting a two-page letter or an answer to a question that requires a dissertation is unreasonable. Do not do it.

Always include an SASE with sufficient postage to cover the material you expect might be returned to you. The SASE alleviates the need for the ballplayer to package and address your reply himself; it enables you to pay, as you should, for return postage; and it assures that the reply will be sent to the party requesting it (assuming you can competently write your own address on an envelope).

Values

Like other collectibles, there is a definite price structure for the autographs of ballplayers. I would like to present a discussion of values within a context of scarcity and desirability, which, when all results are in, are the prime determinants of value for any collectible.

Living or Deceased

Like artists and martyrs, the values of whose accomplishments during their lifetimes are magnified and glorified after death, the value of ballplayers' autographs increases considerably after death. The deceased ballplayer can no longer, of course, sign autographs; hence, the supply of the autographs of this ballplayer ceases at this point in time. All autographs of deceased ballplayers must be obtained secondhand after death, making authenticity questionable.

Hall of Fame Members

The pinnacle of success for a ballplayer is election to baseball's Hall of Fame. This honor is limited to the most skillful and proficient players and those others who have made the most significant contributions to the game. The autographs of these men are among the most desirable and have, other factors being equal, the highest value to collectors.

Popularity and Notoriety

While popularity can generally be measured by ballplaying skills, there are certainly exceptions. Many ballplayers whose skills on the field were limited have achieved success and notoriety in other walks of life (William A. "Billy" Sunday, Joe Garagiola, Chuck Connors, Jim Thorpe, to name a few). The more popular the ballplayer, whether his popularity was derived by playing skills or by some other means, the higher the value placed on his autograph.

Condition and Type of Autograph

Autographs, like other collectibles, exist in various physical conditions – from the weakest, broken pencil autograph to the boldest, unbroken, indelible ink signature. The higher value is placed on the better condition autograph of the same person. Many types of media are available on which to obtain autographs. There are the relatively bland cuts and 3 x 5 varieties at one end of the spectrum and the most elaborate pieces of one-of-a-kind items autographed by the player at the other end. In between there are myriad possible forms and designs that the autograph medium may take. The same autograph has a higher value based on the more interesting, enjoyable and attractive medium on which the autograph is written.

New in This Edition of the Address List

The Address List contains more than 12,250 entries. The players new to the big leagues in 1996 and 1997 have been added with their corresponding debut years and numbers. Address corrections have been made and obituary data has been supplied for those who have died since the last edition. In total, nearly 3,000 additions or corrections have been made.

Major League Team Addresses

BASEBALL COMMISSIONER'S OFFICE
245 Park Avenue • New York, NY 10167 • (212) 931-7800

AMERICAN LEAGUE OFFICE
Gene Budig, President
350 Park Avenue, 18th Floor
New York, NY 10022
(212) 339-7600

ANAHEIM ANGELS
Michael Eisner, Chairman/CEO
Edison International Field of Anaheim
PO Box 2000
Anaheim, CA 92803
(714) 940-2000

BALTIMORE ORIOLES
Peter Angelos, Principal Owner
Oriole Park at Camden Yards
333 West Camden Street
Baltimore, MD 21201
(410) 685-9800

BOSTON RED SOX
John Harrington, CEO
Fenway Park
4 Yawkey Way
Boston, MA 02215
(617) 267-9440

CHICAGO WHITE SOX
Jerry Reinsdorf, Chairman
Comiskey Park
333 West 35th Street
Chicago, IL 60616
(312) 674-1000

CLEVELAND INDIANS
Richard E. Jacobs, Chairman/CEO
Jacobs Field

2401 Ontario Street
Cleveland, OH 44115
(216) 420-4200

DETROIT TIGERS
John McHale, Jr., President/CEO
Tiger Stadium
2121 Trumbull Avenue
Detroit, MI 48216
(313) 962-4000

KANSAS CITY ROYALS
David D. Glass, Chairman/CEO
Kauffman Stadium
PO Box 419969
Kansas City, MO 64141
(816) 921-2200

MINNESOTA TWINS
Carl R. Pohlad, Owner
Jerry Bell, Jr., President
Hubert H. Humphrey Metrodome
34 Kirby Puckett Place
Minneapolis, Minnesota 55415
(612) 375-1366

NEW YORK YANKEES
George M. Steinbrenner, Principal
Owner
Yankee Stadium
161st Street and River Avenue
Bronx, NY 10451
(212) 293-4300

OAKLAND ATHLETICS
Ken Hofmann, Principal Owner
Steve Schott, Principal Owner

Sandy Alderson, President
Oakland-Alameda County Coliseum
PO Box 2000
Oakland, CA 94621
(415) 638-4900

SEATTLE MARINERS
John Ellis, Chairman & CEO
Chuck Armstrong, President
Kingdome
PO Box 4100
Seattle, WA 98104
(206) 628-3555

TAMPA BAY DEVIL RAYS
Vincent J. Naimoli, General
Partner/CEO
Tropicana Field
One Tropicana Drive
Saint Petersburg, FL 33705
(813) 825-3137

TEXAS RANGERS
Thomas Schieffer, President
The Ballpark in Arlington
PO Box 90111
Arlington, TX 76004
(817) 273-5222

TORONTO BLUE JAYS
Sam Pollock, Chairman/CEO
Skydome
One Blue Jays Way #3200
Toronto, Ontario, Canada M5V 1J1
(416) 341-1000

NATIONAL LEAGUE OFFICE
Leonard Coleman, President
350 Park Avenue, 18th Floor
New York, NY 10022
(212) 339-7700

ARIZONA DIAMONDBACKS
Gerald Colangelo, Principal Owner
Richard H. Dozer, President
Bank One Ballpark
PO Box 2095
Phoenix AZ 85001
(602) 462-6500

ATLANTA BRAVES
William C. Batholomay, Chairman
Stanley H. Kasten, President
Turner Field
PO Box 4064
Atlanta, GA 30302
(404) 522-7630

CHICAGO CUBS
Andrew B. MacPhail, President/CEO
Wrigley Field
1060 West Addison Street
Chicago, IL 60613
(312) 404-2827

CINCINNATI REDS
John Allen, Managing Executive
Cinergy Field
100 Cinergy Field
Cincinnati, OH 45202
(513) 421-4510

COLORADO ROCKIES
Jerry McMorris, President/CEO
Coors Field
2001 Blake Street
Denver, CO 80205

(303) 292-0200

FLORIDA MARLINS
John Henry, President
Pro Player Stadium
2267 NW 199th Street
Miami, FL 33056
(305) 626-7400

HOUSTON ASTROS
Drayton McLane, Chairman/CEO
Tal Smith, President
The Astrodome
PO Box 288
Houston, TX 77001
(713) 799-9500

LOS ANGELES DODGERS
Bob Graziano, President
Dodger Stadium
1000 Elysian Park Avenue
Los Angeles, CA 90012
(213) 224-1500

MILWAUKEE BREWERS
Wendy Selig-Prieb, President
Milwaukee County Stadium
PO Box 3099
Milwaukee, WI 53201
(414) 933-4114

MONTREAL EXPOS
Claude R. Brochu, President
Olympic Stadium
PO Box 500, Station 'M'
Montreal, Quebec, Canada H1V 3P2
(514) 253-3434

NEW YORK METS
Nelson Doubleday, Chairman
Fred Wilpon, President/CEO
William A. Shea Stadium

123-01 Roosevelt Avenue
Flushing, NY 11368
(718) 507-6387

PHILADELPHIA PHILLIES
William Y. Giles, President
Veterans Stadium
PO Box 7575
Philadelphia, PA 19101
(215) 463-6000

PITTSBURGH PIRATES
Kevin McClatchy, CEO
Three Rivers Stadium
PO Box 7000
Pittsburgh, PA 15212
(412) 323-5000

SAINT LOUIS CARDINALS
Mark Lamping, President/CEO
Busch Stadium
250 Stadium Plaza
St. Louis, MO 63126
(314) 421-3060

SAN DIEGO PADRES
Larry Lucchino, President/CEO
Qualcomm Stadium
PO Box 2000
San Diego, CA 92112
(619) 881-6500

SAN FRANCISCO GIANTS
Peter Magowan, President
Candlestick Park
3COM Park at Candlestick Point
San Francisco, CA 94124
(415) 468-3700

Triple-A League Team Addresses

INTERNATIONAL LEAGUE
Randy Mobley, President
55 South High Street #202
Dublin, OH 43017
(614) 791-9300

BUFFALO BISONS
Robert E. Rich, Jr., Principal Owner
North AmeriCare Park
PO Box 450
Buffalo, NY 14205
(716) 846-2000

CHARLOTTE KNIGHTS
Don Beaver, President
The Castle
PO Box 1207
Fort Mill, SC 29716
(704) 364-6637

COLUMBUS CLIPPERS
Don Borror, Chairman
Richard Smith, President
Cooper Stadium
1155 West Mound Street
Columbus, OH 43223
(614) 462-5250

DURHAM BULLS
James F. Goodmon, President
Durham Bulls Athletic Park
PO Box 507
Durham, NC 27702
(919) 687-6500

INDIANAPOLIS INDIANS
Henry Warren, Chairman
Max B. Schumacher, President
501 West Maryland Street
Indianapolis, IN 46225
(317) 269-3545

LOUISVILLE RIVERBATS
Daniel C. Ulmer, Jr., Chairman
Gary Ulmer, President
Cardinal Stadium
PO Box 36407
Louisville, KY 40233
(502) 367-9121

NORFOLK TIDES
Ken Young, President
Harbor Park
150 Park Avenue
Norfolk, VA 23510
(757) 622-2222

OTTAWA LYNX
Howard Darwin, President
Ottawa Stadium
300 Chemin Coventry Road
Ottawa, Ontario K1K 4P5
(613) 747-5969

PAWTUCKET RED SOX
Bernard G. Mondor, Chairman
Mike Tamburro, President
McCoy Stadium
PO Box 2365
Pawtucket RI 02861
(401) 724-7300

RICHMOND BRAVES
Bruce Baldwin, General Manager
The Diamond
PO Box 6667
Richmond, VA 23230
(804) 359-4444

ROCHESTER RED WINGS
Fred Strauss, Chairman
Elliot Curwin, President
Frontier Field

One Morrie Silver Way
Rochester NY 14608
(716) 454-1001

SCRANTON/WILKES-BARRE RED BARONS
Bill Jenkins, Chairman
Lackawanna County Stadium
P.O. Box 3449
Scranton PA 18505
(717) 969-2255

SYRACUSE SKYCHIEFS
Richard Ryan, Chairman
Donald R. Waful, President
P & C Stadium
Syracuse, NY 13208
(315) 474-7833

TOLEDO MUD HENS
Edwin Bergsmark, President
Ned Skeldon Stadium
PO Box 6212
Toledo, OH 43614
(419) 893-9483

PACIFIC COAST LEAGUE
Branch B. Rickey, President
1631 Mesa Avenue
Colorado Springs, CO 80906
(719) 636-3399

ALBUQUERQUE DUKES
Robert Lozinak, Chairman
Pat McKernan, President
Albuquerque Sports Stadium
1601 Avenida Cesar Chavez SE
Albuquerque, NM 87106
(505) 243-1791

CALGARY CANNONS
Russel A. Parker, President
Burns Stadium
2255 Crowchild Trail NW
Calgary, Alberta, Canada T2M 4S7
(403) 284-1111

COLORADO SPRINGS SKY SOX
Bob Goughan, President
Sky Sox Stadium
4385 Tutt Boulevard
Colorado Springs, CO 80922
(719) 597-1449

EDMONTON TRAPPERS
Peter Pocklington, Chairman
Mel Kowalchuk, President
TELUS Field
10233 96th Avenue
Edmonton, Alberta, Canada T5K 0A5
(403) 429-2934

FRESNO GRIZZLIES
John Carbray, President/CEO
Beiden Field
1231 "N" Street
Fresno CA 93721
(209) 442-1994

IOWA CUBS
Ken Grandquist, President
Sec Taylor Stadium
350 SW First Street
Des Moines, Iowa 50309
(515) 243-6111

LAS VEGAS STARS
Harley Frankel, President
Cashman Field
850 Las Vegas Blvd. North
Las Vegas, NV 89101
(702) 386-7200

MEMPHIS REDBIRDS
Allie Prescott, President
Tim McCarver Stadium
800 Home Run Lane
Memphis, TN 38104
(901) 721-6000

NASHVILLE SOUNDS
Bill Larsen, General Manager
Herschel Greer Stadium
PO Box 23290
Nashville, TN 37202
(615) 242-4371

NEW ORLEANS ZEPHYRS
Rob Couhig, President
Zephyr Field
6000 Airline Drive
Metairie, LA 70003
(504) 734-5155

OKLAHOMA REDHAWKS
Clayton Bennett, President
Southwestern Bell Park
PO Box 75089
Oklahoma City, OK 73147
(405) 946-8989

OMAHA GOLDENT SPIKES
Joe Adams, President
Johnny Rosenblatt Stadium
PO Box 3665
Omaha, NE 68103
(402) 734-2550

SALT LAKE BUZZ
Joe Buzas, President/CEO
Franklin-Quest Field
PO Box 4108
Salt Lake City, UT 84110
(801) 485-3800

TACOMA RAINIERS
George Foster, President/CEO
Cheney Stadium
PO Box 11087
Tacoma, WA 98411
(206) 752-7707

TUCSON SIDEWINDERS
Martin Stone, President
Tucson Electric Park
PO Box 27045
Tucson, AZ 85726
(602) 325-2621

VANCOUVER CANADIANS
John McHale, President
Nat Bailey Stadium
4601 Ontario Street
Vancouver, B.C., Canada V5V 3H4
(604) 872-5232

The Handbook is composed of four sections:
1. Players in the Baseball Hall of Fame
2. Players who debuted from 1910-1997
3. Coaches with no major league playing or managerial experience who debuted from 1910 to 1997
4. Umpires who debuted from 1910 to 1997

The address portion of the listing contains the known current address of the player if the player is now living or other information as follows:

DEBUT YEAR

    DEBUT YEAR NUMBER   **PLAYER'S NAME**   **ADDRESS OR DEATH DATA**

Debut	Number	Name	Address or Death Data
1994	003	Ausanio, Joseph John	646 Delaware Avenue/Kingston NY 12401
1993	007	Ausmus, Bradley David	15 Newbridge Circle/Cheshire CT 6910
1965	003	Aust, Dennis Ray	16614 Willow Glen Drive/Odessa FL 33556
1991	006	Austin, James Parker	1410 Green Run Lane/Reston VA 22090
1970	003	Austin, Rick Gerald	Box 347/Brookfield MO 64628
1976	009	Autry, Albert	1119 Princeton/Modesto CA 95350
1924	001	Autry, Martin Gordon	D. January 26, 1950 Savannah, Ga.
1997	004	Aven, David Bruce 'Bruce'	3506 West Park Avenue/Orange TX 77630
1956	004	Averill, Earl Douglas	1806 19th Dr NE/Auburn WA 98002
1929	004	Averill, Howard Earl	D. August 16, 1983 Everett, Wash.
1990	006	Avery, Steven Thomas	Old Add: 22138 Haig Taylor MI 48180
1949	003	Avila, Roberto Francisco Gonzalez	Navegantes Fr-19 Reforma/Veracruz Veracruz Mexico
1977	005	Aviles, Ramon Antonio	Jardines Demonico,Calle 2 C19/Manati PR 701
1950	006	Avrea, James Epherium	D. June 26, 1987 Dallas, Texas
1974	003	Ayala, Benigno 'Bennie'	Box 814/Bayamon PR 619
1992	005	Ayala, Robert Joseph	Old Add: 158 Sycamore St Oxnard CA 93030

ADDRESS NOT KNOWN – An old address is given for players for whom a current address is not known. In many cases, the year the address was last valid is shown in the data. Birth information is given if no other data is available. If no information is known about a player except his name, a blank space will appear in the address portion of the listing.

DECEASED PLAYERS – The date and place of a player's death will be listed for deceased players. Incomplete death data is given for some players because complete information is not known. The abbreviation D. with no other information in the address portion of the listing indicates that a player is reportedly deceased, but that no other data is available.

PLEASE NOTE:

■ Managers who never appeared as a player in a big league game are listed with the year they first managed in the big leagues.

■ Only those coaches who never appeared as a player in a big league game are listed in the coaches section.

■ The abbreviations used for states on addresses are standard U.S. Postal Service abbreviations.

■ B. indicates born, D. indicates deceased and other abbreviations are self-explanatory as they are used in normal written communications.

As this nation is known to be a nation of transients, one can expect that the addresses of a considerable number of the ballplayers listed will become invalid over the course of the next year or two.

Baseball Hall Of Fame Members

BBHOF177	Aaron, Henry Louis	1611 Adams Drive Sw/Atlanta GA 30311
BBHOF014	Alexander, Grover Cleveland	D. November 4, 1950 Saint Paul, Neb.
BBHOF181	Alston, Walter Emmons 'Smokey'	D. October 1, 1984 Oxford, Ohio
BBHOF017	Anson, Adrian Constantine 'Cap'	D. April 14, 1922 Chicago, Ill.
BBHOF185	Aparicio, Luis Ernest	Calle 67 #26-82 Maracaibo Venezuela
BBHOF095	Appling, Lucius Benjamin 'Luke'	D. January 3, 1991 Cumming, Ga.
BBHOF220	Ashburn, Rich	D. September 9, 1997 New York, N. Y.
BBHOF147	Averill, Howard Earl 'Earl'	D. August 16, 1983 Everett, Wash.
BBHOF074	Baker, John Franklin 'Home Run'	D. June 28, 1963 Trappe, Md.
BBHOF119	Bancroft, David James	D. October 9, 1972 Superior, Wis.
BBHOF158	Banks, Ernest 'Ernie'	16161 Ventura Blvd #814/Encino CA 91436
BBHOF203	Barlick, Albert Joseph	D. December 27, 1995 Springfield, Iil.
BBHOF063	Barrow, Edward Grant	D. December 15, 1953 Port Chester, N. Y.
BBHOF120	Beckley, Jacob Peter	D. June 25, 1918 Kansas City, Mo.
BBHOF141	Bell, James 'Cool Papa'	D. March 7, 1991 St. Louis, Mo.
BBHOF201	Bench, John Lee	324 Bishopsbridge Drive/Cincinnati Oh 45255
BBHOF064	Bender, Charles Albert 'Chief'	D. May 22, 1954 Philadelphia, Pa.
BBHOF127	Berra, Lawrence Peter	19 Highland Avenue/Montclair NJ 7042
BBHOF142	Bottomley, James Leroy	D. December 11, 1959 Saint Louis, Mo.
BBHOF115	Boudreau, Louis	415 Cedar Lane/Frankfort IL 60423
BBHOF029	Bresnahan, Roger Patrick	D. December 4, 1944 Toledo, Ohio
BBHOF190	Brock, Louis Clark	PO Box 28398/Saint Louis MO 63146
BBHOF030	Brouthers, Dennis 'Dan'	D. August 3, 1932 East Orange, N. J.
BBHOF056	Brown, Mordecai Peter Centennial	D. February 14, 1948 Terre Haute, Ind.
BBHOF006	Bulkeley, Morgan G.	D. November 6, 1922 Hartford, Conn.
BBHOF224	Bunning, James Paul David	1717 Dixie Highway #180/Fort Wright KY 41011
BBHOF039	Burkett, Jesse Cail	D. May 27, 1953 Worcester, Mass.
BBHOF111	Campanella, Roy	D. June 26, 1993 Woodland Hills, Calif.
BBHOF207	Carew, Rodney Cline	5144 East Crescent Drive/Anaheim CA 92807
BBHOF085	Carey, Max George	D. May 30, 1976 Miami, Fla.
BBHOF217	Carlton, Steven Norman	PO Box 736/Durango CO 81302
BBHOF015	Cartwright, Alexander Joy	D. July 12, 1892 Honolulu, Hawaii
BBHOF016	Chadwick, Henry	D. April 20, 1908 Brooklyn, N. Y.
BBHOF040	Chance, Frank Leroy	D. September 15, 1924 Los Angeles, Cal.
BBHOF178	Chandler, Albert Benjamin 'Happy'	D. June 15, 1991 Versailles, Ky.
BBHOF152	Charleston, Oscar Mckinley	D. October 11, 1954 Philadelphia, Pa.
BBHOF041	Chesbro, John Dwight 'Jack'	D. November 6, 1931 Conway, Mass.
BBHOF031	Clarke, Fred Clifford	D. August 14, 1960 Winfield, Kan.
BBHOF091	Clarkson, John Gibson	D. February 4, 1909 Cambridge, Mass.
BBHOF135	Clemente, Roberto Walker	D. December 31, 1972 San Juan, P. R.
BBHOF001	Cobb, Tyrus Raymond 'Ty'	D. July 17, 1995 Atlanta, Ga.
BBHOF050	Cochrane, Gordon Stanley 'Mickey'	D. June 2, 1962 Lake Forest, Ill.
BBHOF018	Collins, Edward Trowbridge	D. March 25, 1951 Boston, Mass.
BBHOF032	Collins, James Joseph	D. March 6, 1943 Buffalo, N. Y.
BBHOF116	Combs, Earle Bryan	D. July 21, 1976 Richmond, Ky.
BBHOF019	Comiskey, Charles Albert	D. October 26, 1931 Eagle River, Wis.
BBHOF143	Conlan, John Bertrand 'Jocko'	D. April 16, 1989 Scottsdale, Ariz.
BBHOF065	Connolly, Thomas Henry	D. April 28, 1961 Natick, Mass.
BBHOF153	Connor, Roger	D. January 4, 1931 Waterbury, Conn.
BBHOF112	Coveleski, Stanley Anthony	D. March 20, 1984 South Bend, Ind.
BBHOF082	Crawford, Samuel Earl	D. June 15, 1968 Hollywood, Calif.
BBHOF080	Cronin, Joseph Edward	D. September 7, 1984 Osterville, Mass.
BBHOF020	Cummings, Wiilliam Arthur 'Candy'	D. May 17, 1924 Toledo, O.
BBHOF108	Cuyler, Hazen Shirley 'Kiki'	D. February 11, 1950 Ann Arbor, Mich.
BBHOF199	Dandridge, Raymond	D. February 12, 1994 Palm Bay, Fla.
BBHOF228	Davis, George Stacey	D. October 17, 1940 Philadelphia, Pa.
BBHOF221	Day, Leon	D. March 13, 1995 Baltimore, Md.
BBHOF066	Dean, Jay Hanna 'Dizzy'	D. July 17, 1974 Reno, Nev.
BBHOF033	Delahanty, Edward James	D. July 2, 1903 Fort Erie, Ont.
BBHOF071	Dickey, William Malcolm	D. November 12, 1993 Little Rock, Ark.
BBHOF159	Dihigo, Martin	D. May 22, 1971 Cienfuegos, Cuba
BBHOF075	Dimaggio, Joseph Paul	%Engleberg 3230 Sterling Road/Hollywood FL 33021
BBHOF229	Doby, Lawrence Eugene	PO Box 193/Massapequa NY 11758
BBHOF194	Doerr, Robert Pershing	94449 Territorial Road/Junction City OR 97448
BBHOF186	Drysdale, Donald Scott	D. July 3, 1993 Montreal, Quebec
BBHOF034	Duffy, Hugh	D. October 19, 1954 Boston, Mass.
BBHOF136	Evans, William George	D. January 23, 1956 Miami, Fla.
BBHOF042	Evers, John Joseph	D. March 28, 1947 Albany, N. Y.
BBHOF021	Ewing, William Buckingham 'Buck'	D. October 20, 1906 Cincinnati, O.
BBHOF096	Faber, Urban Charles 'Red'	D. September 25, 1976 Chicago, Ill.
BBHOF087	Feller, Robert William Andrew	PO Box 157/Gates Mills OH 44040
BBHOF187	Ferrell, Richard Benjamin 'Rick'	D. July 27, 1995 Bloomfield Hills, Mich.
BBHOF212	Fingers, Roland Glen 'Rollie'	4894 Eastcliff Court/San Diego CA 91230
BBHOF092	Flick, Elmer Harrison	D. January 9, 1971 Bedford, O.
BBHOF144	Ford, Edward Charles 'Whitey'	3750 Galt Ocean Drive #1411/Fort Lauderdale FL 33308

BBHOF174	Foster, Andrew 'Rube'	D. December 9, 1930 Kankakee, Ill.
BBHOF225	Foster, William Hendrick	D. September 16, 1978 Lorman, Miss.
BBHOF059	Foxx, James Emory	D. July 21, 1967 Miami, Fla.
BBHOF117	Frick, Ford Christopher	D. April 8, 1978 Bronxville, N. Y.
BBHOF051	Frisch, Frank Francis	D. March 12, 1973 Wilmington, Del.
BBHOF102	Galvin, James F. 'Pud'	D. March 7, 1902 Pittsburgh, Pa.
BBHOF022	Gehrig, Henry Louis 'Lou'	D. June 2, 1941 Riverdale, N. Y.
BBHOF057	Gehringer, Charles Leonard	D. January 21, 1993 Bloomfield Hills, Mich.
BBHOF128	Gibson, Josh	D. January 20, 1947 Pittsburgh, Pa.
BBHOF175	Gibson, Robert	215 Belleview Blvd South/Belleview NE 68005
BBHOF167	Giles, Warren Christopher	D. February 7, 1979 Cincinnati, Ohio
BBHOF129	Gomez, Vernon Louis 'Lefty'	D. February 17, 1989 Greenbrae, Calif.
BBHOF109	Goslin, Leon Allen 'Goose'	D. May 15, 1971 Bridgeton, N. J.
BBHOF081	Greenberg, Henry Benjamin 'Hank'	D. September 4, 1986 Beverly Hills, Calif.
BBHOF043	Griffith, Clark Calvin	D. October 27, 1955 Washington, D. C.
BBHOF097	Grimes, Burleigh Arland	D. December 6, 1985 Clear Lake, Wis.
BBHOF052	Grove, Robert Moses 'Lefty'	D. May 22, 1975 Norwalk, Ohio
BBHOF121	Hafey, Charles James 'Chick'	D. July 2, 1973 Calistoga, Cal.
BBHOF118	Haines, Jesse Joseph 'Pop'	D. August 5, 1978 Dayton, O.
BBHOF086	Hamilton, William Robert	D. December 16, 1940 Worcester, Mass.
BBHOF226	Hanlon, Edward Hugh 'Ned'	D. April 14, 1937 Baltimore, Md.
BBHOF130	Harridge, William	D. April 9, 1971 Evanston, Ill.
BBHOF148	Harris, Stanley Raymond 'Bucky'	D. November 8, 1977 Bethesda, Md.
BBHOF076	Hartnett, Charles Leo 'Gabby'	D. December 20, 1972 Park Ridge, Ill.
BBHOF061	Heilmann, Harry Edwin	D. July 9, 1951 Detroit, Mich.
BBHOF149	Herman, William Jennings Bryan 'Billy'	D. September 5, 1992 West Palm Beach, Fla.
BBHOF122	Hooper, Harry Bartholomew	D. December 18, 1974 Santa Cruz, Calif.
BBHOF027	Hornsby, Rogers	D. January 5, 1963 Chicago, Ill.
BBHOF113	Hoyt, Waite Charles	D. August 25, 1984 Cincinnati, O.
BBHOF154	Hubbard, Robert Cal 'Cal'	D. October 16, 1977 St. Petersburg, Fla.
BBHOF053	Hubbell, Carl Owen	D. November 21, 1988 Scottsdale, Ariz.
BBHOF098	Huggins, Miller James	D. September 25, 1929 New York, N. Y.
BBHOF222	Hulbert, William	D. February 25, 1909
BBHOF197	Hunter, James Augustus 'Catfish'	Rural Route 1 Box 895/Hertford NC 27944
BBHOF137	Irvin, Monford Merrill 'Monte'	11 Douglas Court South/Homosassa FL 32646
BBHOF216	Jackson, Reginald Martinez 'Reggie'	305 Amador Avenue/Seaside CA 93955
BBHOF179	Jackson, Travis Calvin	D. July 27, 1987 Waldo, Ark.
BBHOF208	Jenkins, Ferguson Arthur	PO Box 1202/Guthrie OK 73044
BBHOF035	Jennings, Hugh Ambrose	D. February 1, 1928 Scranton, Pa.
BBHOF007	Johnson, Byron Bancroft 'Ban'	D. March 28, 1931 Saint Louis, Mo.
BBHOF002	Johnson, Walter Perry 'Big Train'	D. December 10, 1946 Washington, D. C.
BBHOF150	Johnson, William Julius 'Judy'	D. June 14, 1989 Wilmington, Del.
BBHOF164	Joss, Adrian 'Addie'	D. April 14, 1911 Toledo, Ohio
BBHOF170	Kaline, Albert William	945 Timberlake Drive/Bloomfield Hills MI 48302
BBHOF099	Keefe, Timothy J.	D. April 23, 1933 Cambridge, Mass.
BBHOF023	Keeler, William Henry 'Wee Willie'	D. January 1, 1923 Brooklyn, N. Y.
BBHOF182	Kell, George Clyde	700 East 9th Street #13m/Little Rock AR 72202
BBHOF123	Kelley, Joseph James	D. August 14, 1943 Baltimore, Md.
BBHOF138	Kelly, George Lange	D. October 13, 1984 Burlingame, Calif.
BBHOF036	Kelly, Michael Joseph	D. November 8, 1894 Boston, Mass.
BBHOF188	Killebrew, Harmon Clayton	PO Box 14550/Scottsdale AZ 85267
BBHOF151	Kiner, Ralph Mcpherran	48 271 Silver Spur Trail/Palm Desert CA 92260
BBHOF171	Klein, Charles Herbert 'Chuck'	D. March 28, 1958 Indianapolis, Ind.
BBHOF067	Klem, William J.	D. September 16, 1951 Miami, Fla.
BBHOF131	Koufax, Sanford 'Sandy'	PO Box 8306/Vero Beach FL 32963
BBHOF008	Lajoie, Napoleon 'Nap'	D. February 7, 1959 Daytona Beach, Fla.
BBHOF028	Landis, Kenesaw Mountain	D. November 25, 1944 Chicago, Ill.
BBHOF209	Lazzeri, Anthony Michael 'Tony'	D. August 6, 1946 San Francisco, Calif.
BBHOF186	Lemon, Robert Granville	1141 Claiborne Drive/Long Beach CA 90807
BBHOF132	Leonard, Walter Fenner 'Buck'	D. November 27, 1997 Rocky Mount, N. C.
BBHOF156	Lindstrom, Fred Charles	D. October 4, 1981 Chicago, Ill.
BBHOF160	Lloyd, John Henry	D. March 19, 1964
BBHOF195	Lombardi, Ernest Natali	D. September 26, 1977 Santa Cruz, Calif.
BBHOF161	Lopez, Alfonso Ramon	3601 Beach Drive/Tampa FL 33629
BBHOF077	Lyons, Theodore Amar	D. July 25, 1986 Sulphur, La.
BBHOF009	Mack, Cornelius Alexander 'Connie'	D. February 8, 1956 Germantown, Pa.
BBHOF230	Macphail, Leland Stanford, Jr. 'Lee'	PO Box 478/Sagaponack NY 11962
BBHOF165	Macphail, Leland Stanford 'Larry'	D. October 1, 1975 Miami, Fla.
BBHOF145	Mantle, Mickey Charles	D. August 13, 1995 Dallas, Texas
BBHOF100	Manush, Henry Emmett 'Heinie'	D. May 12, 1971 Sarasota, Fla.
BBHOF072	Maranville, Walter James Vincent 'Rabbit'	D. January 5, 1954 New York, N.Y.
BBHOF183	Marichal, Juan Antonio Sanchez	9458 Nw 54 Doral Circle Lane/Miami FL 33128
BBHOF124	Marquard, Richard William 'Rube'	D. June 1, 1980 Baltimore, Md.
BBHOF166	Mathews, Edwin Lee	13744 Recuerdo Drive/Del Mar CA 92014
BBHOF003	Mathewson, Christopher 'Christy'	D. October 7, 1925 Saranac Lake, N. Y.
BBHOF168	Mays, Willie Howard	51 Mount Vernon Lane/Atherton CA 94025
BBHOF083	McCarthy, Joseph Vincent	D. January 13, 1978 Buffalo,N. Y.
BBHOF044	McCarthy, Thomas Francis Michael	D. August 5, 1922 Boston, Mass.
BBHOF196	McCovey, Willie Lee	PO Box 620342/Woodside CA 94062

BBHOF045	McGinnity, Joseph Jerome	D. November 14, 1929 Brooklyn, N. Y.
BBHOF213	McGowan, William Aloysius	D. December 9, 1954 Silver Spring, Md.
BBHOF010	McGraw, John Joseph	D. February 25, 1934 New Rochelle, N. Y.
BBHOF088	McKechnie, William Boyd	D. October 29, 1965 Bradenton, Fla.
BBHOF110	Medwick, Joseph Michael 'Ducky'	D. March 21, 1975 St. Petersburg, Fla.
BBHOF176	Mize, John Robert	D. June 2, 1993 Demorest, Ga.
BBHOF205	Morgan, Joseph Leonard	3523 Country Club Drive/Danville CA 94506
BBHOF114	Musial, Stanley Frank	85 Trent Drive/Ladue MO 63124
BBHOF214	Newhouser, Harold	D. November 10, 1998 Detroit, Mich.
BBHOF058	Nichols, Charles Augustus 'Kid'	D. April 11, 1953 Kansas City, Mo.
BBHOF037	Orourke, James Henry	D. January 8, 1919 Bridgeport, Conn.
BBHOF060	Ott, Melvin Thomas	D. November 21, 1958 New Orleans, La.
BBHOF125	Paige, Leroy 'Satchel'	D. June 8, 1982 Kansas City, Mo.
BBHOF206	Palmer, James Alvin	2432 Still Forest Road/Baltimore MD 21208
BBHOF054	Pennock, Herbert Jefferis	D. January 30, 1948 New York, N. Y.
BBHOF210	Perry, Gaylord Jackson	PO Box 1958/Kill Devil Hills NC 27948
BBHOF046	Plank, Edward Stewart	D. February 24, 1926 Gettysburg, Pa.
BBHOF024	Radbourn, Charles 'Hoss'	D. February 5, 1897 Bloomington, Ill.
BBHOF189	Reese, Harold Henry 'Peewee'	1400 Willow Avenue/Louisville KY 40204
BBHOF093	Rice, Edgar Charles 'Sam'	D. October 13, 1974 Rossmor, Md.
BBHOF105	Rickey, Wesley Branch 'Branch'	D. December 9, 1965 Columbia, Mo.
BBHOF094	Rixey, Eppa	D. February 28, 1963 Terrace Park, Ohio
BBHOF218	Rizzuto, Philip Francis	912 Westminster Avenue/Hillside NJ 7205
BBHOF157	Roberts, Robin Evan	504 Terrace Hill Drive/Temple Terrace FL 33617
BBHOF184	Robinson, Brooks Calbert	PO Box 1168/Baltimore MD 21203
BBHOF180	Robinson, Frank	15557 Aqua Verde Drive/Los Angles CA 90077
BBHOF089	Robinson, Jack Roosevelt	D. October 24, 1972 Stamford, Conn.
BBHOF038	Robinson, Wilbert	D. August 8, 1934 Atlanta, Ga.
BBHOF231	Rogan, Wilbur 'Bullet Joe'	D. March 4, 1967 Kansas City, Mo.
BBHOF090	Roush, Edd	D. March 21, 1988 Bradenton, Fla.
BBHOF106	Ruffing, Charles Herbert 'Red'	D. February 17, 1986 Mayfield Heights, Ohio
BBHOF162	Rusie, Amos Wilson	D. December 6, 1942 Seattle, Wash.
BBHOF004	Ruth, George Herman 'Babe'	D. August 16, 1948 New York, N.Y.
BBHOF078	Schalk, Raymond William 'Cracker'	D. May 19, 1970 Chicago, Ill.
BBHOF219	Schmidt, Michael Jack	373 Eagle Drive/Jupiter FL 33477
BBHOF204	Schoendienst, Albert Fred 'Red'	1105 Jo Carr Drive/Town And Country MO 63017
BBHOF215	Seaver, George Thomas 'Tom'	PO Box 4660/Avon CO 81620
BBHOF163	Sewell, Joseph Wheeler	D. March 6, 1990 Mobile, Ala.
BBHOF068	Simmons, Aloysius Harry	D. May 26, 1956 Milwaukee, Wis.
BBHOF025	Sisler, George Harold	D. March 26, 1973 Saint Louis, Mo.
BBHOF191	Slaughter, Enos Bradsher	959 Lawson Chapel Church Rd/Roxboro NC 27573
BBHOF172	Snider, Edwin Donald 'Duke'	3037 Lakemont Drive/Fallbrook CA 92028
BBHOF139	Spahn, Warren Edward	Rural Route 2/Hartshorne OK 74547
BBHOF026	Spalding, Albert Goodwill	D. September 9, 1915 San Diego, Calif.
BBHOF011	Speaker, Tristram E.	D. December 8, 1958 Lake Whitney, Texas
BBHOF200	Stargell, Wilver Dornel 'Willie'	813 Tarpon Drive/Wilmington NC 28409
BBHOF103	Stengel, Charles Dillon 'Casey'	D. September 29, 1975 Glendale, Cal.
BBHOF232	Sutton, Donald Howard	1145 Mountain Ivy Drive/Roswell GA 30075
BBHOF073	Terry, William Harold	D. January 9, 1989 Jacksonville, Fla.
BBHOF146	Thompson, Samuel L.	D. November 7, 1922 Detroit, Mich.
BBHOF047	Tinker, Joseph Bert	D. July 27, 1948 Orlando, Fla.
BBHOF055	Traynor, Harold Joseph 'Pie'	D. March 16, 1972 Pittsburgh, Pa.
BBHOF079	Vance, Clarence Arthur 'Dazzy'	D. February 16, 1961 Homosassa Springs, Fla.
BBHOF192	Vaughan, Joseph Floyd 'Arky'	D. August 30, 1952 Eagleville, Calif.
BBHOF211	Veeck, William L. 'Bill'	D. January 2, 1986 Chicago, Ill.
BBHOF048	Waddell, George Edward 'Rube'	D. April 1, 1914 San Antonio, Tex.
BBHOF005	Wagner, John Peter 'Honus'	D. December 6, 1955 Carnegie, Pa.
BBHOF069	Wallace, Rhoderick John 'Bobby'	D. November 3, 1960 Torrance, Cal.
BBHOF049	Walsh, Edward Augustin	D. May 26, 1959 Pompano Beach, Fla.
BBHOF107	Waner, Lloyd James	D. July 22, 1982 Oklahoma City, Okla.
BBHOF062	Waner, Paul Glee	D. August 29, 1965 Sarasota, Fla.
BBHOF101	Ward, John Montgomery	D. March 4, 1925 Augusta, Ga.
BBHOF227	Weaver, Earl Sidney	501 Cypress Pointe Drive West/Pembroke Pines FL 33027
BBHOF126	Weiss, George Martin	D. August 13, 1972 Greenwich, Conn.
BBHOF140	Welch, Michael Francis 'Mickey'	D. July 30, 1941 Nashua, N. H.
BBHOF084	Wheat, Zachary Davis	D. March 11, 1972 Sedalia, Mo.
BBHOF193	Wilhelm, James Hoyt 'Hoyt'	8206 Timber Lake Lane/Sarasota FL 34243
BBHOF198	Williams, Billy Leo	586 Prince Edward Road/Glen Ellyn IL 60137
BBHOF104	Williams, Theodore Samuel	2448 North Essex Avenue/Hernando FL 34442
BBHOF223	Willis, Victor Gazaway	D. August 2, 1947 Elkton, Md.
BBHOF169	Wilson, Lewis Robert 'Hack'	D. November 23, 1948 Baltimore, Md.
BBHOF012	Wright, George	D. August 31, 1937 Boston, Mass.
BBHOF070	Wright, William Henry 'Harry'	D. October 3, 1895 Atlantic City, N. J.
BBHOF133	Wynn, Early	6151 Jack Street/Venice FL 34293
BBHOF202	Yastrzemski, Carl Michael	4621 South Ocean Blvd/Highland Beach FL 33487
BBHOF173	Yawkey, Thomas Austin	D. July 9, 1976 Boston, Mass.
BBHOF013	Young, Denton True 'Cy'	D. November 4, 1955 Newcomerstown, Ohio
BBHOF134	Youngs, Ross Middlebrook	D. October 22, 1927 San Antonio, Tex.

Players Debuting From 1910 To 1997

1954-001	Aaron, Henry Louis	1611 Adams Dr SW/Atlanta GA 30311
1962-001	Aaron, Tommie Lee	D. August 16, 1984 Atlanta, Ga.
1977-001	Aase, Donald William	5055 Via Ricardo/Yorba Linda CA 92686
1989-001	Abbott, James Anthony	Old Add: 3110 Pencombe Pl #22c Flint MI 48503
1997-001	Abbott, Jeffrey William	Old Add: 736 St Charles Ave NE Atlanta GA 30306
1993-001	Abbott, Kurt Thomas	3743 45th Way North/Saint Petersburg FL 33713
1991-001	Abbott, Lawrence Kyle 'Kyle'	27912 Calle Marin/Mission Viejo CA 92692
1910-001	Abbott, Ody Cleon	D. April 13, 1933 Washington, D. C.
1990-001	Abbott, Paul David	Old Add: 701 Rodeo Rd Fullerton CA 92635
1973-001	Abbott, William Glenn	4413 Dawson/North Little Rock AR 72116
1950-001	Aber, Albert Julius	D. May 20, 1993 Garfield Heights, Ohio
1952-001	Abernathie, William Edward	35808 Avenue E/Yucaipa CA 92399
1942-001	Abernathy, Talmadge Lafayette 'Tal'	387 Efird Street/Gastonia NC 28054
1955-001	Abernathy, Theodore Wade 'Ted'	2211 Armstrong Park Road/Gastonia NC 28052
1946-001	Abernathy, Virgil Woodrow	D. December 5, 1994 Louisville, Ky.
1947-001	Aberson, Clifford Alexander	D. June 23, 1973 Vallejo, Calif.
1987-001	Abner, Shawn Wesley	539 Brighton Place/Mechanicsburg PA 17055
1949-001	Abrams, Calvin Ross	D. February 25, 1997 Fort Lauderdale, Fla.
1923-001	Abrams, George Allen	D. December 5, 1986 Clearwater, Fla.
1985-001	Abrego, Johnny Ray	PO Box 680801/San Antonio TX 78268
1996-001	Abreu, Bob Kelly	Old Add: Aragua Venezuela
1942-002	Abreu, Joseph Lawrence	D. March 17, 1993 Hayward, Calif.
1995-001	Acevedo, Juan Carlos	1412 Kings Road/Carpentersville IL 60110
1983-001	Acker, James Justin	Box AA/Freer TX 78357
1956-001	Acker, Thomas James	242 Bartron Road/Tunkhannock PA 18657
1963-001	Ackley, Florian Frederick 'Fritz'	14884 West Phipps Road/Hayward WI 54843
1913-001	Acosta, Balmadero Pedro 'Cy'	D. November 17, 1963 Miami, Fla.
1972-001	Acosta, Cecilio 'Cy'	Aug Ramirez 1420, Col Gab Leyva Culiacan Sinaloa Mexico
1970-001	Acosta, Eduardo Elixbet	22822 Boltana/Mission Viejo CA 92675
1920-001	Acosta, Jose	D. November 16, 1977 Havana, Cuba
1994-001	Acre, Mark Robert	Old Add: 25160 Connecticut Ave Corning CA 96021
1931-001	Adair, James Aubrey	D. December 9, 1982 Dallas, Texas
1958-001	Adair, Kenneth Jerry 'Jerry'	D. May 31, 1987 Tulsa, Okla.
1970-002	Adair, Marion Danne 'Bill'	4724 Wicker Way/Mobile AL 36609
1941-001	Adams, Ace Townsend	1005 Summit Drive/Albany GA 31707
1946-002	Adams, Charles Dwight 'Red'	6058 Puerto Drive/Rancho Murieta CA 95683
1914-001	Adams, Daniel Leslie	D. October 6, 1964 St. Louis, Mo.
1922-001	Adams, Earl John 'Sparky'	D. February 24, 1989 Pottville, Pa.
1939-001	Adams, Elvin Clark 'Buster'	D. September 1, 1990 Rancho Mirage, Calif.
1975-001	Adams, Glenn Charles	Rural Route 1/Sedan NM 88436
1969-001	Adams, Harold Douglas 'Doug'	1129 Harmony Cir NE/Janesville WI 53545
1948-001	Adams, Herbert Loren	903 South Williston/Wheaton IL 60187
1912-001	Adams, James Irvin 'Willie'	D. June 18, 1937 Albany, N.Y.
1910-002	Adams, John Bertram	D. June 24, 1940 Los Angeles, Calif.
1914-002	Adams, Karl Tutwiler	D. September 17, 1967 Everett, Wash.
1947-002	Adams, Richard Leroy	4650 Dulin Road #136/Fallbrook CA 92028
1982-001	Adams, Ricky Lee	Old Add: 10195 Bolton Montclair CA 91763
1931-002	Adams, Robert Andrew	D. March 6, 1970 Jacksonville, Fla.
1925-001	Adams, Robert Burdette	D. October 17, 1996 Lemoyne, Pa.
1946-003	Adams, Robert Henry	D. February 13, 1997 Gig Harbor, Wash.
1977-002	Adams, Robert Melvin	Old Add: 7653 Desoto Ave/Canoga Park CA 91304
1972-001	Adams, Robert Michael 'Mike'	12408 Walker Way Drive NE/Albuquerque NM 87111
1923-002	Adams, Spencer Dewey	D. November 25, 1970 Ft. Lauderdale, Fla.
1995-002	Adams, Terry Wayne	11315 Howell's Ferry Road/Semmes AL 36575
1996-002	Adams, William Edward 'Willie'	11903 Kibbee Avenue/Lamirada CA 90638
1996-003	Adamson, Joel Lee	17780 Luna Court/Riverside CA 92504
1967-001	Adamson, John Michael 'Mike'	4408 Sky Glen CT Moorpark CA 93021
1950-002	Adcock, Joseph Wilbur	PO Box 385/Coushatta LA 71019
1950-003	Addis, Robert Gordon	7466 Hollycroft Lane/Mentor OH 44060
1983-002	Adduci, James David	10429 South Lamon/Oak Lawn IL 60453
1939-002	Aderholt, Morris Woodrow	D. March 18, 1955 Sarasota, Fla.
1928-001	Adkins, Grady Emmett	D. March 31, 1966 Little Rock, Ark.
1942-003	Adkins, John Dewey 'Dewey'	20323 Village 20/Camarillo CA 93012
1942-004	Adkins, Richard Earl	D. September 12, 1955 Electra, Tex.
1990-002	Adkins, Steven Thomas	Old Add: 9th & Chestnut #1429 Philadelphia PA 19107
1963-002	Adlesh, David George	9770 Avenida Monterey/Cypress CA 90630
1987-002	Afenir, Michael Troy	804 Cherry Court/San Marcos CA 92069
1962-002	Agee, Tommie Lee	2904 Butler Street/Flushing NY 11369
1954-002	Agganis, Harry	D. June 27, 1955 Cambridge, Mass.
1912-002	Agler, Joseph Abram	D. April 26, 1971 Massillon, O.
1913-002	Agnew, Samuel Lester	D. July 19, 1951 Sonoma, Calif.
1981-001	Agosto, Juan Roberto	3815 6th Street East #175/Bradenton FL 34208
1980-001	Aguayo, Luis	Dorado Del Mar Lirios #C23/Dorado PR 646
1985-002	Aguilera, Richard Warren 'Rick'	PO Box 200/Rancho Santa Fe CA 92067
1955-002	Aguirre, Henry John 'Hank'	D. September 5, 1994 Bloomfield Hills, Mich.

1995-003 ....Ahearne, Patrick Howard ....3360 Paddington Court/Rochester Hills MI 48309
1977-003 ....Aikens, Willie Mays ....610 McDonough Blvd SE #10732-031 Atlanta GA 30315
1979-001 ....Ainge, Daniel Ray ....Old Add: 10 Ordway Road Wellesley MA 02181
1910-003 ....Ainsmith, Edward Wilbur ....D. September 6, 1981 Fort Lauderdale, Fla.
1911-001 ....Aitchison, Raleigh Leonidas ....D. September 26, 1958 Columbus, Kan.
1912-003 ....Aiton, George Wilson 'Bill' ....D. August 16, 1976 Van Nuys, Calif.
1964-001 ....Aker, Jack Delane ....PO Box 31832/Tucson AZ 85751
1986-001 ....Akerfelds, Darrel Wayne ....4136 South Mobile Circle #D/Aurora CO 80013
1912-004 ....Akers, Albert Earl 'Jerry' ....D. May 15, 1979 Bay Pines, Fla.
1929-001 ....Akers, Thomas Ernest 'Bill'.......................D. April 13, 1962 Chattanooga, Tenn.
1988-001 ....Alba, Gibson Roberto ....Old Add: Proy. #5,Jardines Metro Santiago Dom. Rep.
1958-002 ....Albanese, Joseph Peter ....54 Longfellow Dr/Colonia NJ 7067
1995-004 ....Alberro, Jose Edgardo ....Old Add: San Juan PR
1978-001 ....Alberts, Francis Burt Butch.......................3063 Amberlea Ln/Baldwinsville NY 13027
1910-004 ....Alberts, Frederick Joseph 'Cy' ....D. August 27, 1917 Fort Wayne, Ind.
1941-002 ....Albosta, Edward John ....5360 Fort Road/Saginaw MI 48604
1949-002 ....Albrecht, Edward Arthur ....D. December 29, 1979 Cahokia, Ill.
1947-003 ....Albright, John Harold...............................D. July 22, 1991 San Diego, Calif.
1973-002 ....Albury, Victor ....Old Add: 6205 Alcot Court Tampa FL 33624
1976-001 ....Alcala, Santo ....Ramon Mota #18 San Pedro De Macoris Dominican Rep.
1967-002 ....Alcaraz, Angel Luis 'Luis' ....Calle Chihuahua 679 Venus Gardens Rio Piedras PR 926
1914-003 ....Alcock, John Forbes 'Scotty' ....D. January 30, 1973 Wooster, O.
1943-001 ....Alderson, Dale Leonard ....D. February 12, 1982 Garden Grove, Calif.
1990-003 ....Aldred, Scott William ....2025 North M 30/Gladwin MI 48624
1986-002 ....Aldrete, Michael Peter ....1620 Via Isola,%Peter Aldrete/Monterey CA 93940
1987-003 ....Aldrich, Jay Robert ....Old Add: 168 Salisbury Road Wayne NJ 07470
1917-001 ....Aldridge, Victor Eddington ....D. April 17, 1973 Terre Haute, Ind.
1941-003 ....Aleno, Charles ....601 Marion Court/Deland FL 32720
1929-002 ....Alexander, David Dale...............................D. March 2, 1979 Greeneville, Tenn.
1971-001 ....Alexander, Doyle Lafayette ....5416 Hunter Park Court/Arlington TX 76017
1975-002 ....Alexander, Gary Wayne ....5420 Senford Avenue/Los Angeles CA 90056
1990-004 ....Alexander, Gerald Paul ....307 Woodland Drive/Donaldsonville LA 70346
1911-002 ....Alexander, Grover Cleveland ....D. November 4, 1950 St. Paul, Neb.
1937-001 ....Alexander, Hugh.....................................1311 Batten Road/Brooksville FL 34602
1992-001 ....Alexander, Manuel Dejesus ....Calle D Barrio Rest. Casa #20 San Pedro De Macoris Dominican Rep.
1973-003 ....Alexander, Matthew ....2419 Stonewall/Shreveport LA 71103
1955-003 ....Alexander, Robert Somerville ....D. April 7, 1993 Oceanside, Calif.
1912-005 ....Alexander, Walter Ernest ....D. December 29, 1978 Fort Worth, Texas
1997-002 ....Alfonseca, Antonio...................................Old Add: La Romana Dominican Rep.
1995-005 ....Alfonzo, Edgardo Antonio ....Old Add: Caracas Venezuela
1988-002 ....Alicea, Luis Rene ....17154 Gulf Pine Circle/Wellington FL 33414
1986-003 ....Allanson, Andrew Neal ....Old Add: 621 Irving Drive Burbank CA 91504
1979-002 ....Allard, Brian Marshall ....2624 West Woodside Avenue/Spokane WA 99208
1914-004 ....Allen, Artemus Ward 'Nick' ....D. October 16, 1939 Hines, Ill.
1962-003 ....Allen, Bernard Keith................................3725 Coventry Way/Carmel IN 46033
1926-001 ....Allen, Ethan Nathan ....D. September 15, 1993 Brookings, Ore.
1910-005 ....Allen, Fletcher Manson 'Slep' ....D. October 16, 1959 Lubbock, Tex.
1912-006 ....Allen, Frank Leon ....D. July 30, 1933 Gainesville, Ala.
1966-001 ....Allen, Harold Andrew 'Hank' ....15 Staton Dr/Upper Marlboro MD 20870
1919-001 ....Allen, Horace Tanner 'Pug' ....D. July 5, 1981 Canton, N. C.
1983-003 ....Allen, James Bradley 'Brad' ....Old Add: 1203 Folsom Avenue Yakima WA 98902
1914-005 ....Allen, John Marshall ....D. September 24, 1967 Hagerstown, Md.
1932-001 ....Allen, John Thomas ....D. March 29, 1959 St. Petersburg, Fla.
1980-002 ....Allen, Kim Bryant ....2705 Lapraix Street/Highland CA 92346
1969-002 ....Allen, Lloyd Cecil ....Old Add: 1678 Marguerite Ave Corona Del Mar CA 92625
1979-003 ....Allen, Neil Patrick ....6471 Beechwood Avenue #203/Sarasota FL 34231
1963-003 ....Allen, Richard Anthony 'Richie' ....8000 Fairway Trail/Boca Raton FL 33487
1919-002 ....Allen, Robert (Alvah Charles Elliott)..............D. December 18, 1975 Naperville, Ill.
1937-002 ....Allen, Robert Earl 'Earl' ....1888 West Ames Circle/Chesapeake VA 23321
1961-001 ....Allen, Robert Gray ....PO Box 667/Tatum TX 75691
1983-004 ....Allen, Roderick Bernet..............................3150 East Woodland/Phoenix AZ 85048
1972-003 ....Allen, Ronald Fredrick ....917 Winona Dr/Youngstown OH 44511
1979-004 ....Allenson, Gary Martin ....711 SE 34th Street/Cape Coral FL 33904
1996-004 ....Allensworth, Jermaine Lamont ....1824 Euclid Drive/Anderson IN 46011
1963-004 ....Alley, Leonard Eugene 'Gene'.....................10236 Steuben Drive/Glen Allen VA 23060
1954-003 ....Allie, Gair Roosevelt ....11818 Button Willow Cove/San Antonio TX 78213
1975-003 ....Allietta, Robert George ....25 Robinson Rd/Falmouth MA 2540
1991-002 ....Allison, Dana Eric ....Old Add: 820 East Sixth Front Royal VA 22630
1911-003 ....Allison, Mack Pendleton ....D. March 13, 1964 St. Joseph, Mo.
1913-003 ....Allison, Milo Henry ....D. June 18, 1957 Kenosha, Wis.
1958-003 ....Allison, William Robert 'Bob' ....D. April 9, 1995 Rio Verde, Ariz.
1989-002 ....Allred, Dale Lebeau Beau ....Rural Route 2 Box 856/Safford AZ 85546
1933-001 ....Almada, Melo Baldomero ....D. August 13, 1988 Hermosillo, Sonora Mexico
1997-003 ....Almanzar, Carlos Manuel ....Old Add: Santo Domingo Dom. Rep.
1911-004 ....Almeida, Rafael D. ....D. March 19, 1968 Havana, Cuba
1974-001 ....Almon, William Francis ....35 Sarahs Trace/East Greenwich RI 2818
1950-004 ....Aloma, Luis Barba ....D. April 7, 1997 Park Ridge, Ill.
1988-003 ....Alomar, Roberto ....Urb. Monserrate B-56, Box 367/Salinas PR 751
1964-002 ....Alomar, Santos Condes 'Sandy' ....PO Box 367/Salinas PR 751

1988-004	Alomar, Santos Jr.	Urb. Monserrate B-56, Box 367/Salinas PR 751
1958-004	Alou, Felipe Rojas	7263 Davit Circle/Lake Worth FL 33467
1963-005	Alou, Jesus Maria	Apartado Postal 5392 Lafaria Santo Domingo Dominican Rep.
1960-001	Alou, Mateo Rojas	PO Box 30063 M. Proncolo #16 Santo Domingo Dominican Rep.
1990-005	Alou, Moises Rojas	875 East 93rd Street/Brooklyn NY 11236
1996-005	Alston, Garvin James	Old Add: Mount Vernon NY 10550
1954-004	Alston, Thomas Edison	D. December 30, 1993 Winston-Salem, N. C.
1936-001	Alston, Walter Emmons 'Smokey'	D. October 1, 1984 Oxford, O.
1977-004	Alston, Wendell 'Del'	Old Add: 3 Granada Crescent #1/White Plains NY 10603
1982-002	Altamarino, Porfirio	Old Add: Caracas Venezuela
1920-002	Alten, Ernest Matthias	D. September 9, 1981 Napa, Calif.
1916-001	Altenburg, Jesse Howard	D. March 12, 1973 Lansing, Mich.
1959-001	Altman, George Lee	2818 Foxdale Drive/Jefferson City MO 65109
1955-004	Altobelli, Joseph	10 Stowell Drive #3/Rochester NY 14616
1958-005	Alusik, George Joseph	581 Garden Avenue/Woodbridge NJ 7095
1968-001	Alvarado, Luis Cesar	Box 853/Lajas PR 667
1995-006	Alvarez, Cesar Octavio 'Tavo'	Old Add: 148 E./24th St Tucson AZ 85713
1973-004	Alvarez, Jesus Orlando	Cummunidad Dolores 37/Rio Grande PR 745
1981-002	Alvarez, Jose Lino	114 Mellyn Street/Piedmont SC 29673
1958-006	Alvarez, Oswaldo Gonzales 'Ossie'	Santuario 3137,Col. Chapalita Guadalajara Jalisco Mexico
1960-002	Alvarez, Rogelio	5010 Nw 183rd St/Carol City FL 33055
1989-003	Alvarez, Wilson Eduardo	Calle 868 Con Ave. 3a #868-20 Maracaibo Venezuela
1962-004	Alvis, Roy Maxwell 'Max'	806 Hunterwood Dr/Jasper TX 75951
1965-001	Alyea, Brant Ryerson	PO Box 25/Columbus NC 28722
1954-005	Amalfitano, John Joseph	265 Bowstring Drive/Sedona AZ 86336
1991-003	Amaral, Richard Louis	3122 Country Club Drive/Costa Mesa CA 92626
1958-007	Amaro, Ruben	4098 Cinnamon Way/Weston FL 33331
1991-004	Amaro, Ruben Jr.	4098 Cinnamon Way/Weston FL 33331
1937-003	Ambler, Wayne Harper	D. January 3, 1998 Ponte Vedra Beach, Fla.
1984-001	Amelung, Edward Allen	Old Add: 17045 Royal View Dr Hacienda Heights CA 91745
1955-005	Amor, Vincente Alvarez	3905 West 8th Court/Hialeah FL 33012
1952-002	Amoros, Edmundo Isasi 'Sandy'	D. June 27, 1992 Miami, Fla.
1915-001	Ancker, Walter	D. February 13, 1954 Englewood, N.J.
1975-004	Andersen, Larry Eugene	8624 133rd Avenue NE/Redmond WA 98052
1941-004	Anderson, Alfred Walton	D. June 23, 1985 Albany, Ga.
1986-004	Anderson, Allan Lee	1491 Lancaster Kirkerville Rd/Lancaster OH 43130
1948-002	Anderson, Andy Holm	D. July 18, 1982 Seattle, Wash.
1937-004	Anderson, Arnold Revola 'Red'	D. August 7, 1972 Sioux City, Ia.
1988-005	Anderson, Brady Kevin	5092 Dorsey Hall Drive #202/Ellicott City MD 21042
1993-002	Anderson, Brian James	3571 North Meyers Road/Geneva OH 44041
1983-005	Anderson, David Carter	679 Blackhawk Court/Lake Mary FL 32746
1971-002	Anderson, Dwain Cleaven	1807 Fallbrook Drive/Alamo CA 94507
1946-004	Anderson, Ferrell Jack 'Andy'	D. March 12, 1978 Joplin, Mo.
1994-002	Anderson, Garret Joseph	23415 Kingston Place/Valencia CA 91354
1914-006	Anderson, George Andrew Jendrus	D. May 28, 1962 Cleveland, O.
1959-002	Anderson, George Lee 'Sparky'	PO Box 6415/Thousand Oaks CA 91360
1932-002	Anderson, Harold	D. May 1, 1974 St. Louis, Mo.
1957-001	Anderson, Harry Walter	D. June 11, 1998 Greenville, Del.
1978-002	Anderson, James Lea	Old Add: 3931 Calle Valle/Vista Newbury Park CA 91320
1958-008	Anderson, John Charles	Old Add: PO Box 49/Browning MT 59417
1982-003	Anderson, Karl Adam 'Bud'	240 Twin Lane/East Wanaeugh NY 11793
1989-004	Anderson, Kent McKay	925 East Twin Church Road/Timmonsville SC 29161
1974-002	Anderson, Lawrence Dennis	Old Add: 378 Castaie/Shell Beach CA 93449
1971-003	Anderson, Michael Allen	Rr One/Timmonsville SC 29161
1993-003	Anderson, Michael James	140 Clear Spring/Georgetown TX 78628
1961-002	Anderson, Norman Craig 'Craig'	1525 Willowbrook Drive/Bethlehem PA 18015
1986-005	Anderson, Richard Arlen	8865 Deep Creek Drive/West Jordan UT 84088
1979-005	Anderson, Richard Lee	D. June 23, 1989 Wilmington, Calif.
1957-002	Anderson, Robert Carl	4209 East 104th/Tulsa OK 74107
1987-004	Anderson, Scott Richard	5617 Southwood Drive/Lake Oswego OR 97035
1917-002	Anderson, Walter Carl	D. January 6, 1990 Battle Creek, Mich.
1925-002	Anderson, William Edward	D. March 13, 1983 Medford, Mass.
1910-006	Anderson, Wingo Charlie	D. December 19, 1950 Fort Worth, Tex.
1955-006	Andre, John Edward	D. November 25, 1976 Centerville, Mass.
1946-005	Andres, Ernest Henry	5714 Garden Lakes Drive/Bradenton FL 34203
1975-005	Andrew, Kim Darrell	10052 Densmore Ave/Sepulveda CA 91343
1995-007	Andrews, Darrell Shane Shane	710 Spyglass Drive/Carlsbad NM 88220
1925-003	Andrews, Elbert Devore	D. November 25, 1979 Greenwood, S. C.
1976-002	Andrews, Fred	8239 South Kingston/Chicago IL 60617
1947-004	Andrews, Herbert Carl 'Hub'	2305 2nd Street/Dodge City KS 67801
1931-003	Andrews, Ivy Paul	D. November 23, 1970 Dora, Ala.
1973-005	Andrews, John Richard	9292 Gordon Ave/Lahabra CA 90631
1966-002	Andrews, Michael Jay	375 Longwood Avenue/Boston MA 2215
1937-005	Andrews, Nathan Hardy	D. April 26, 1991 Winston-Salem, N. C.
1975-006	Andrews, Robert Patrick	1280 Mountbatten CT Concord CA 94518
1939-005	Andrews, Stanley Joseph	D. June 10, 1995 Bradenton, Fla.
1931-004	Andrus, William Morgan	D. March 12, 1982 Washington, D. C.
1976-003	Andujar, Joaquin	Ave.L.Amiama Tio #47 San Pedro De Macoris Dominican Rep.
1995-008	Andujar, Luis Sanchez	Old Add: Bani Dominican Republic

1972-004	Angelini, Norman Stanley	15063 East Chenango Place/Aurora CO 80015
1929-003	Angley, Thomas Samuel	D. October 26, 1952 Wichita, Kan.
1936-002	Ankenman, Fred Norman 'Pat'	D. January 13, 1989 Houston, Texas
1989-005	Anthony, Eric Todd	42 Fosters Glen/Sugar Land TX 77479
1944-001	Antolick, Joseph	723 2nd Street/Catasauqua PA 18032
1948-003	Antonelli, John August	PO Box 580/Pittsford NY 14534
1944-002	Antonelli, John Lawrence	D. April 18, 1990 Memphis, Tenn.
1953-001	Antonello, William James	D. March 4, 1993 Fridley, Minn.
1956-002	Aparicio, Luis Ernest	Calle 67 #26-82 Maracaibo Venezuela
1973-006	Apodaca, Robert John	PO Box 8045/Port Saint Lucie FL 34985
1980-003	Aponte, Luis Eduardo	Res Las Girasoles #17a,St Elena Barquisimeto Lara Venezuela
1989-006	Appier, Robert Kevin 'Kevin'	Old Add:/Lancaster CA 93534
1915-002	Appleton, Edward Samuel	D. January 27, 1932 Arlington, Tex.
1927-001	Appleton, Peter William	D. January 18, 1974 Trenton, N.J.
1930-001	Appling, Lucius Benjamin 'Luke'	D. January 3, 1991 Cumming, Ga.
1986-006	Aquino, Luis Antonio Colon	Old Add: 30 So 1506 Caparra Ter Rio Piedras PR 00921
1941-005	Aragon, Angel Valdes, Jr. 'Jack'	D. April 4, 1988 Clearwater, Fla.
1914-007	Aragon, Angel Valdes, Sr. 'Jack'	D. January 24, 1952 New York, N.Y.
1923-003	Archdeacon, Maurice Bruce	D. September 5, 1954 St. Louis, Mo.
1936-003	Archer, Frederick Marvin	D. October 31, 1981 Charlotte, N. C.
1961-003	Archer, James William	1414 Oleander Dr/Tarpon Springs FL 33589
1938-001	Archie, George Albert	820 Marquette Drive/Nashville TN 37205
1968-002	Arcia, Jose Raimundo	7325 Nw 3rd St/Miami FL 33125
1961-004	Ardell, Daniel Miers	554 Hazel Drive/Corona Del Mar CA 92625
1947-005	Ardizoia, Rinaldo Joseph 'Rugger'	130 Santa Rosa Avenue/San Francisco CA 94112
1948-004	Arft, Henry Irvin	109 Sunnyside Lane/Ballwin MO 63021
1992-002	Arias, Alejandro	45 Pinehurst Avenue #65/New York NY 10033
1996-006	Arias, George Albert	2751 North Malibu/Tucson AZ 85705
1959-003	Arias, Rodolfo Martinez 'Rudy'	3911 Nw 11th St/Miami FL 33126
1931-005	Arlett, Russell Loris 'Buzz'	D. May 16, 1964 Minneapolis, Minn.
1965-002	Arlich, Donald Louis	7877 South 73rd St/Cottage Grove MN 55016
1969-003	Arlin, Stephen Ralph	6338 Camino Corto/San Diego CA 92120
1976-004	Armas, Antonio Rafael	Los Mercedes #37,P.Piritu Edo. Anzoatequi Venezuela
1993-004	Armas, Marcos Rafael (Ruiz)	Calle Las Mercedes #37 Puerto Piritu Venezuela
1973-007	Armbrister, Edison Rosander	McQuay St, Box 2003 Nassau Bahamas/West Indies
1934-001	Armbrust, Orville Martin	D. October 2, 1967 Mobile, Ala.
1946-006	Armstrong, George Noble	D. July 24, 1993 Orange, N. J.
1911-005	Armstrong, Howard Elmer	D. March 8, 1926 Canisteo, N.Y.
1988-006	Armstrong, Jack William	6580 Woodlake Road/Jupiter FL 33458
1980-004	Armstrong, Michael Dennis	Old Add: PO Box 846 Halifax VA 24558
1989-007	Arndt, Larry Wayne	505 West Smith Street/Gibsonburg OH 43431
1971-004	Arnold, Christopher Paul	2219 El Capitan/Arcadia CA 91006
1988-007	Arnold, Scott Gentry	2936 Runnymeade Way/Lexington KY 40503
1986-007	Arnold, Tony Dale	2001 West Patterson Street/Eastland TX 76448
1936-004	Arnovich, Morris	D. July 20, 1959 Superior, Wis.
1986-008	Arnsberg, Bradley Jeff	706 Chaffee Court/Arlington TX 76006
1943-002	Arntzen, Orie Edgar	D. January 28, 1970 Cedar Rapids, Ia.
1993-005	Arocha, Rene	14273 SW 24th Street/Miami FL 33175
1961-005	Arrigo, Gerald William	3740 Redthorne Dr/Amelia OH 45102
1975-007	Arroyo, Fernando	4917 First Parkway/Sacramento CA 95823
1955-007	Arroyo, Luis Enrique	Box 354/Penuelas PR 724
1971-005	Arroyo, Rudolph	828 Sierra Vista/Mountain View CA 94040
1986-009	Asadoor, Randall Carl	PO Box 756/Coarsegold CA 93614
1938-002	Asbell, James Marion	D. July 6, 1967 San Mateo, Calif.
1928-002	Asbjornson, Robert Anthony	D. January 21, 1970 Williamsport, Pa.
1925-004	Ash, Kenneth Lowther	D. November 15, 1979 Clarksburg, W. Va.
1948-005	Ashburn, Rich	D. September 9, 1997 New York, N. Y.
1973-008	Ashby, Alan Dean	14711 Cantwell Bend/Cypress TX 77429
1991-005	Ashby, Andrew Jason	5701 Northwest Parkdale Circle/Kansas City MO 64152
1976-005	Ashford, Thomas Steven 'Tucker'	502 Maple St/Covington TN 38019
1992-003	Ashley, Billy Manual	4331 West Mariposa Grande/Glendale AZ 85310
1957-003	Aspromonte, Kenneth Joseph	% Coors/10400 Harwin Houston TX 77036
1956-003	Aspromonte, Robert Thomas	5110 San Felipe Street #304w/Houston TX 77056
1976-006	Asselstine, Brian Hanly	1488 Country CT Santa Ynez CA 93460
1986-010	Assenmacher, Paul Andre	413 Colonsay Court/Duluth GA 30097
1992-004	Astacio, Pedro Julio	666 Dundee Road #704/Northbrook IL 60062
1945-001	Astroth, Joseph Henry	151 South Moyer Road/Chalfont PA 18914
1983-006	Atherton, Keith Rowe	PO Box 571/Cobbs Creek VA 23035
1950-005	Atkins, James Curtis	1030 County Road 1518/Cullman AL 35055
1927-002	Atkinson, Hubert Burley 'Lefty'	D. February 12, 1961 Chicago, Ill.
1976-007	Atkinson, William Cecil Glenn	15 Argyle Crescent/Chatham Ontario N7L 4T7 Canada
1926-002	Attreau, Richard Gilbert	D. July 5, 1964 Chicago, Ill.
1952-003	Atwell, Maurice Dailey 'Toby'	PO Box 686/Purcellville VA 22132
1936-005	Atwood, William Franklin	D. September 14, 1993 Snyder, Texas
1996-007	Aucoin, Derek Alfred	Old Add: Montreal Quebec
1993-006	Aude, Richard Thomas	Old Add: 10467 Eon Avenue Chatsworth CA 91311
1971-006	Auerbach, Frederick Steven 'Rick'	Old Add: 25 Glenbar Sedona AZ 86336
1988-008	August, Donald Glenn	24442 Diamante/Mission Viejo CA 92692
1973-009	Augustine, David Ralph	Old Add: 14850 SW 280th St #25 Homestead FL 33030

1975-008	Augustine, Gerald Lee	S69/W13442/Hales Park Court/Muskego WI 53150
1933-002	Auker, Elden Leroy	15 Sailfish Road/Vero/Beach FL 32960
1947-006	Aulds, Leycester Doyle	Yancey Star Route Box 16/Hondo TX 78861
1976-008	Ault, Douglas Reagan	Old Add: PO Box 572443 Houston TX 77257
1995-009	Aurilia, Richard Santo	1164 67th Street,%Mike Aurilia/Brooklyn NY 11219
1994-003	Ausanio, Joseph John	646 Delaware Avenue/Kingston NY 12401
1993-007	Ausmus, Bradley David	15 Newbridge Circle/Cheshire CT 6910
1965-003	Aust, Dennis Ray	16614 Willow Glen Drive/Odessa FL 33556
1991-006	Austin, James Parker	1410 Green Run Lane/Reston VA 22090
1970-003	Austin, Rick Gerald	Box 347/Brookfield MO 64628
1976-009	Autry, Albert	1119 Princeton/Modesto CA 95350
1924-001	Autry, Martin Gordon	D. January 26, 1950 Savannah, Ga.
1997-004	Aven, David Bruce 'Bruce'	3506 West Park Avenue/Orange TX 77630
1956-004	Averill, Earl Douglas	1806 19th Dr NE/Auburn WA 98002
1929-004	Averill, Howard Earl	D. August 16, 1983 Everett, Wash.
1990-006	Avery, Steven Thomas	Old Add: 22138 Haig Taylor MI 48180
1949-003	Avila, Roberto Francisco Gonzalez	Navegantes Fr-19 Reforma/Veracruz Veracruz Mexico
1977-005	Aviles, Ramon Antonio	Jardines Demonico,Calle 2 C19/Manati PR 701
1950-006	Avrea, James Epherium	D. June 26, 1987 Dallas, Texas
1974-003	Ayala, Benigno 'Bennie'	Box 814/Bayamon PR 619
1992-005	Ayala, Robert Joseph	Old Add: 158 Sycamore St Oxnard CA 93030
1997-005	Aybar, Manuel Antonio	Old Add: Bani Dominican Rep.
1947-007	Ayers, William Oscar	D. September 24, 1980 Newnan, Ga.
1913-004	Ayers, Yancey Wyatt 'Doc'	D. May 26, 1968 Pulaski, Va.
1953-002	Aylward, Richard John	D. June 11, 1983 Spring Valley, Calif.
1996-008	Ayrault, Joseph Allen	Old Add: 3451 Queens Sarasota FL 34231
1992-006	Ayrault, Robert Cunningham	3012 Green Drive/Carson City NV 89701
1960-003	Azcue, Jose Joaquin	7609 West 115th St/Overland Park KS 66210
1990-007	Azocar, Oscar Gregorio	Old Add: 6650 N. Andrews Ave Ft. Lauderdale FL 33309
1979-006	Babcock, Robert Ernest	4652 Old Pittsburgh Rd/New Castle PA 16101
1952-004	Babe, Loren Rolland	D. February 14, 1984 Omaha, Neb.
1934-002	Babich, John Charles	6111 Rosalind Avenue/Richmond CA 94803
1915-003	Babington, Charles Percy	D. March 22, 1957 Providence, R.I.
1981-003	Babitt, Mack N. 'Shooty'	4912 Plaza Circle/Richmond CA 94804
1980-005	Backman, Walter Wayne	327 North Elm Street/Prineville OR 97754
1917-003	Bacon, Edgar Suter	D. October 2, 1963 Frankfort, Ky.
1975-009	Bacsik, Michael James	935 Green Ridge Dr/Duncanville TX 75137
1953-003	Baczewski, Frederick John	D. November 14, 1976 Culver City, Calif.
1912-007	Bader, Lore Verne 'King'	D. June 2, 1973 Leroy, Kan.
1929-005	Badgro, Morris Hiram 'Red'	D. July 13, 1998 Kent, Wash.
1926-003	Baecht, Edward Joseph	D. August 15, 1957 Quarry Twp., Ill.
1990-008	Baerga, Carlos Obed (Ortiz)	Old Add: Ruta Rural 142 Buzon 181g Caguas PR 00625
1977-006	Baez, Jose Antonio	40 Booraem Avenue/Jersey City NJ 7307
1990-009	Baez, Kevin Richard	2019 63rd Street/Brooklyn NY 11204
1938-003	Bagby, James Charles Jacob, Jr.	D. September 2, 1988 Marietta, Ga.
1912-008	Bagby, James Charles Jacob, Sr.	D. July 28, 1954 Marietta, Ga.
1991-007	Bagwell, Jeffrey Robert	Old Add: 3350 McCue Road #1802 Houston TX 77056
1923-004	Bagwell, William Mallory	D. October 5, 1976 Choudrant, La.
1966-003	Bahnsen, Stanley Raymond	PO Box 5414/Pompano Beach FL 33062
1946-007	Bahr, Edson Garfield	326 217th Place Sw/Bothell WA 98021
1914-008	Baichley, Grover Cleveland	D. June 30, 1956 San Jose, Calif.
1986-011	Bailes, Scott Alan	2415 East Edgewood Street/Springfield MO 65804
1919-003	Bailey, Abraham Lincoln	D. September 27, 1939 Joliet, Ill.
1917-004	Bailey, Arthur Eugene	D. November 14, 1973 Houston, Tex.
1995-010	Bailey, Charles Roger 'Roger'	9715 South Merimbula Street/Highlands Ranch CO 80126
1916-002	Bailey, Fred Middleton	D. August 16, 1972 Huntington, W. Va.
1911-006	Bailey, Harry Lewis	D. October 17, 1967 Seattle, Wash.
1981-004	Bailey, Howard L.	425 Orchard Street/Grand Haven MI 49417
1959-004	Bailey, James Hopkins	7960 Fayetteville Road/Fairburn GA 30213
1984-002	Bailey, John Mark 'Mark'	32703 Waltham Crossing/Fulshear TX 77441
1953-004	Bailey, Lonas Edgar 'Ed'	642 Broome Road/Knoxville TN 37919
1993-008	Bailey, Philip Cory 'Cory'	19752 Galatia Post Road/Marion IL 62959
1962-005	Bailey, Robert Sherwood	Old Add: 5175 East 28th/Long Beach CA 90815
1967-003	Bailey, Steven John	8335 Andersen Avenue NE/Warren OH 44484
1975-010	Bailor, Robert Michael	1950 Swan Lane/Palm Harbor FL 34683
1945-002	Bain, Herbert Loren 'Loren'	D. November 24, 1996 Chetek, Wisc.
1980-006	Baines, Harold Douglas	PO Box 10/Saint Michaels MD 21663
1976-010	Bair, Charles Douglas 'Doug'	560 Ohio Pike/Cincinnati OH 45255
1917-005	Baird, Albert Wells	D. November 27, 1976 Shreveport, La.
1915-004	Baird, Howard Douglass	D. June 13, 1967 Thomasville, Ga.
1962-006	Baird, Robert Allen	D. April 11, 1974 Chattanooga, Tenn.
1964-003	Bakenhaster, David Lee	3710 Rome Corners Road/Galena OH 43021
1938-004	Baker, Albert Jones	D. November 6, 1982 Kenedy, Texas
1978-003	Baker, Charles Joseph	3035 Mescalero Drive/Lake Havasu City AZ 86404
1982-004	Baker, David Glenn	2216 Highway S23/Lacona IA 50139
1914-009	Baker, Delmar David	D. September 11, 1973 San Antonio, Tex.
1984-003	Baker, Douglas Lee	6814 Maple Leaf Drive/Carlsbad CA 92009
1953-005	Baker, Eugene Walter	2202 East 48th Street/Davenport IA 52807
1943-003	Baker, Floyd Wilson	3033 Idlewood Avenue/Youngstown OH 44511

1969-004	Baker, Frank	Old Add: 383 Girard Avenue Somerset NJ 08873
1970-004	Baker, Frank Watts	Box 3066/Meridian MS 39301
1912-009	Baker, Howard Francis	D. January 16, 1964 Bridgeport, Conn.
1976-011	Baker, Jack Edward	5513 Hunter's Hill Road/Irondale AL 35210
1911-007	Baker, Jesse Ormand	D. September 26, 1972 Tacoma, Wash.
1968-003	Baker, Johnnie B. 'Dusty'	40 Livingston Terrace Drive/San Bruno CA 94066
1919-004	Baker, Michael Myron 'Jesse'	D. July 29, 1976 West Los Angeles, Calif.
1927-003	Baker, Neal Vernon	D. January 5, 1982 Houston, Tex.
1995-011	Baker, Scott	7424 Cypress Grove Court/Las Vegas NV 89127
1978-004	Baker, Steven Byrne	27527 Easy Acres Drive/Eugene OR 97405
1935-001	Baker, Thomas Calvin	D. January 3, 1991 Fort Worth, Texas
1963-006	Baker, Thomas Henry	D. March 9, 1980 Port Townsend, Wash.
1911-008	Baker, Tracy Lee	D. March 14, 1975 Placerville, Calif.
1940-001	Baker, William Presley	250 Manor Circle/Myrtle Beach SC 29575
1938-005	Balas, Mitchell Francis	5 Colorado Drive/Tyngsboro MA 1879
1974-004	Balaz, John Larry	3757 Udall Street #301/San Diego CA 92107
1981-005	Balboni, Stephen Charles	117 Burlington Road/Murray Hill NJ 7974
1956-005	Balcena, Robert Rudolph	D. January 4, 1990 San Pedro, Calif.
1961-006	Baldschun, Jack Edward	311 Erie Road/Green Bay WI 54311
1966-004	Baldwin, David George	Old Add: 3737 Nobel Drive #2215 San Diego CA 92122
1953-006	Baldwin, Frank Dewitt	6359 Beaver Pike/Beaver OH 45613
1927-004	Baldwin, Henry Clay	D. February 24, 1964 Philadelphia, Pa.
1924-002	Baldwin, Howard Edward 'Harry'	D. January 23, 1958 Baltimore, Md.
1995-012	Baldwin, James	Old Add: 316 Lake Ave #112c Maitland FL 32751
1990-010	Baldwin, Jeffrey Allen	Old Add: 805 12th Street Kenora WV 25530
1978-005	Baldwin, Reginald Conrad	763 Liebold/Detroit MI 48217
1975-011	Baldwin, Rick Alan	PO Box 1068/Salida CA 95368
1975-012	Baldwin, Robert Harvey 'Billy'	878 Packard Dr/Akron OH 44320
1911-009	Balenti, Michael Richard	D. August 4, 1955 Altus, Okla.
1966-005	Bales, Wesley Owen 'Lee'	Old Add: 7223 Augustine/Houston TX 77036
1987-005	Ballard, Jeffrey Scott	4828 Rimrock Road/Billings MT 59102
1928-003	Ballenger, Pelham Ashby	D. December 8, 1948 Greenville County, S. C.
1982-005	Baller, Jay Scot	Old Add: 221 12th St #308n Philadelphia PA 19107
1971-007	Ballinger, Mark Alan	%D. Ballinger 176 Dale Newbury Park CA 91320
1925-005	Ballou, Noble Winfield 'Win'	D. January 30, 1963 San Francisco, Calif.
1962-007	Balsamo, Anthony Fred	160-15 86th St/Howard Beach NY 11414
1951-001	Bamberger, George Irvin	455 North Bath Club Blvd/North Redington Beach FL 33708
1948-006	Bamberger, Harold Earl	Rural Route/1 Box 317/Birdsboro PA 19508
1915-005	Bancroft, David James	D. October 9, 1972 Superior, Wis.
1981-006	Bando, Christopher Michael	35640 Brushwood Drive/Solon OH 44139
1966-006	Bando, Salvatore Leonard	104 West Juniper Ln/Mequon WI 53092
1973-010	Bane, Edward Norman	7728 Corte Promenade/Carlsbad CA 92209
1969-005	Baney, Richard Lee	1412 Damon Ave/Anaheim CA 92802
1991-008	Banister, Jeffery Todd	Old Add: 10447 Rustic Gate Laporte TX 77571
1947-008	Bankhead, Daniel Robert	D. May 2, 1976 Houston, Tex.
1986-012	Bankhead, Michael Scott Scott	1236 Idlewood/Asheboro NC 27203
1996-009	Banks, Brian Glen	Old Add: 1345 E. University Dr Mesa AZ 85203
1953-007	Banks, Ernest 'Ernie'	16161 Ventura Blvd #814/Encino CA 91436
1962-008	Banks, George Edward	D. March 1, 1985 Spartanburg, S. C.
1991-009	Banks, Willie Anthony	Old Add: 225 N. Gilbert Road #262 Mesa AZ 85203
1915-006	Bankston, Wilborn Everett 'Bill'	D. February 26, 1970 Griffin, Ga.
1974-005	Bannister, Alan	405 48th Street Nw/Bradenton FL 34209
1977-007	Bannister, Floyd Franklin	6701 East Caballo Drive/Paradise Valley AZ 85253
1947-009	Banta, John Kay	3215 East 30th Avenue/Hutchinson KS 67502
1914-010	Barbare, Walter Lawrence	D. October 28, 1965 Greenville, S.C.
1943-004	Barbary, Donald Odell 'Red'	402 West Curtis/Simpsonville SC 29681
1926-004	Barbee, David Monroe	D. July 1, 1968 Albemarle, N. C.
1995-013	Barber, Brian Scott	7123 Yacht Basin Avenue #327/Orlando FL 32835
1960-004	Barber, Stephen David	3156 Swallow Lane/Las Vegas NV 89121
1970-005	Barber, Steven Lee	1517 Cushman Dr/Sierra Vista AZ 85635
1915-007	Barber, Tyrus Turner	D. October 20, 1968 Milan, Tenn.
1991-010	Barberie, Bret Edward	11607 Bos Street/Cerritos CA 90701
1966-007	Barbieri, James Patrick	13619 East 5th Ave/Spokane WA 99216
1957-004	Barclay, Curtis Cordell	D. March 27, 1985 Missoula, Mont.
1972-005	Bare, Raymond Douglas	D. March 29, 1994 Miami, Fla.
1981-007	Barfield, Jesse Lee	4208 Canterwood Drive/Houston TX 77068
1989-008	Barfield, John David	Old Add: 1009 South Wolfe Little Rock AR 72202
1922-002	Barfoot, Clyde Raymond	D. March 11, 1971 Highland Park, Calif.
1983-007	Bargar, Greg Robert	22319 Avis Court/Torrance CA 90505
1995-014	Bark, Brian Stuart	2755 Quarry Heights Way/Pikesville MD 21208
1976-012	Barker, Leonard Harold	6555 Old Cabin Road Nw/Atlanta GA 30328
1960-005	Barker, Raymond Harold	303 Greenbriar Road/Martinsburg WV 25401
1984-004	Barkley, Jeffrey Carver	264 Third Ave NE/Hickory NC 28601
1937-006	Barkley, John Duncan 'Red'	1200 Lawrence Drive/Waco TX 76710
1975-013	Barlow, Michael Roswell	%Sheftic 4524 Francis Road Cazenovia NY 13035
1953-008	Barmes, Bruce Raymond	509 McDonald Avenue/Charlotte NC 28203
1937-007	Barna, Herbert Paul 'Babe'	D. May 18, 1972 Charleston, W. Va.
1927-005	Barnabe, Charles Edward	D. August 16, 1977 Waco, Tex.
1990-011	Barnes, Brian Keith	1224 Carolina Street/Roanoke Rapids NC 27870

1927-006	Barnes, Emile Deering 'Red'	D. July 3, 1959 Mobile, Ala.
1923-005	Barnes, Everett Duane 'Eppie'	D. November 17, 1980 Mineola, N. Y.
1957-005	Barnes, Frank	1508 Brazil/Greenville MS 38701
1929-006	Barnes, Frank Samuel 'Lefty'	D. September 27, 1967 Houston, Tex.
1915-008	Barnes, Jesse Lawrence	D. September 9, 1961 Santa Rosa, N.Mex.
1926-005	Barnes, John Francis 'Honey'	D. June 18, 1981 Lockport, N. Y.
1934-003	Barnes, Junie Shoaf	D. December 31, 1963 Jacksonville, N. C.
1972-006	Barnes, Luther Owen	7693 Wheatland Road North/Salem OR 97303
1982-006	Barnes, Richard Monroe 'Rich'	Old Add: 1661 Creek Drive San Jose CA 95125
1924-003	Barnes, Robert Avery	D. December 8, 1993 Peoria, Ill.
1921-001	Barnes, Samuel Thomas	D. February 19, 1981 Montgomery, Ala.
1919-005	Barnes, Virgil Jennings	D. July 24, 1958 Wichita, Kan.
1983-008	Barnes, William Henry 'Skeeter'	10865 Players Drive/Indianapolis IN 46229
1915-009	Barney, Edmund J.	D. October 4, 1967 Rice Lake, Wis.
1943-005	Barney, Rex Edward	D. August 12, 1997 Baltimore, Md.
1920-003	Barnhart, Clyde Lee	D. January 21, 1980 Hagerstown, Md.
1924-004	Barnhart, Edgar Vernon	D. September 14, 1984 Columbia, Mo.
1928-004	Barnhart, Leslie Earl	D. October 7, 1971 Scottsdale, Ariz.
1944-003	Barnhart, Victor Dee	13102 Linger Road/Hagerstown MD 21741
1939-004	Barnicle, George Bernard	D. October 10, 1990 Largo, Fla.
1965-004	Barnowski, Edward Anthony	1610 Crane Street/Schenectady NY 12303
1982-007	Barojas, Salome Romero	Old Add: Mexico City Mexico
1960-006	Barone, Richard Anthony	730 Monte Carlo Drive/Hollister CA 95023
1971-008	Barr, James Leland	6335 Oak Hill Drive/Roseville CA 95661
1935-002	Barr, Robert Alexander	Barrington Mobile Homes/Barrington NH 3825
1974-006	Barr, Steven Charles	2520 14th Street Southeast/Winter Haven FL 33884
1961-007	Barragan, Facundo Anthony 'Cuno'	1824 St. Ann Court/Carmichael CA 95608
1979-007	Barranca, German Michael	Old Add: 40 Dew Drop Court York PA 17403
1937-008	Barrett, Charles Henry 'Red'	D. July 28, 1990 Wilson, N. C.
1939-005	Barrett, Francis Joseph	D. March 8, 1998 Leesburg, Fla.
1942-005	Barrett, John Joseph	D. August 17, 1974 Seabrook Beach, N. H.
1982-008	Barrett, Martin Glenn	9708 Buckhorn Drive/Las Vegas NV 89134
1923-006	Barrett, Robert Schley	D. January 18, 1982 Atlanta, Ga.
1988-009	Barrett, Thomas Loren	5941 West Venus Way/Chandler AZ 85226
1988-010	Barrett, Timothy Wayne	PO Box 138/Otwell IN 47564
1933-003	Barrett, Tracey Souter 'Dick'	D. November 7, 1966 Seattle, Wash.
1921-002	Barrett, William Joseph	D. January 26, 1951 Cambridge, Mass.
1974-007	Barrios, Francisco Xavier	D. April 9, 1982 Hermosillo Sonora Mexico
1982-009	Barrios, Jose Manuel	6484 SW 25th St/Miami FL 33155
1997-006	Barrios, Manuel Antonio	Old Add: Cabecera Panama
1996-010	Barron, Anthony Dirk 'Tony'	3045 Fremont Street #8/Las Vegas NV 89104
1929-007	Barron, David Irenus 'Red'	D. October 4, 1982 Atlanta, Ga.
1914-011	Barron, Frank John	D. September 18, 1964 Pleasants Co., W. Va.
1912-010	Barry, Hardin	D. November 5, 1969 Carson City, Nev.
1995-015	Barry, Jeffrey Finas	Old Add: 2379 Temple Dr Medford OR 97504
1969-006	Barry, Richard Donovan	Old Add: 47275 Mio Mio Loop/Kaneohe HI 96744
1996-011	Bartee, Kimera Anotchi	Old Add: Omaha NE
1927-007	Bartell, Richard William	D. August 4, 1995 Alameda, Calif.
1944-004	Barthelson, Robert Edward	40 Meadowlark Lane/Northford CT 6472
1928-005	Bartholomew, Lester Justin	D. September 19, 1972 Madison, Wis.
1952-005	Bartirome, Anthony Joseph	1104 Palma Sola Blvd/Bradenton FL 34209
1943-006	Bartley, Boy Owen	7500 Noreast Drive/Fort Worth TX 76180
1938-006	Bartling, Irving Henry	D. June 12, 1973 Westland, Mich.
1965-005	Barton, Robert Wilbur	1661 Palomar Drive/San Marcos CA 92069
1992-007	Barton, Shawn Edward	3975 River Road #3/Keizer OR 97303
1931-006	Barton, Vincent David	D. September 13, 1973 Toronto, Ont.
1945-003	Bartosch, David Robert	25212 Avenida Dorena/Newhall CA 91321
1948-007	Basgall, Romanus 'Monty'	2745 St. Andrews Drive/Sierra Vista AZ 85635
1912-011	Bashang, Albert C.	D. June 23, 1967 Cincinnati, O.
1936-006	Bashore, Walter Franklin	D. September 26, 1984 Sebring, Fla.
1944-005	Basinski, Edwin Frank	4110 SE Jackson/Milwaukie OR 97222
1911-010	Baskette, James Blaine	D. July 30, 1942 Athens, Tenn.
1982-010	Bass, Kevin Charles	3630 Maranatha/Sugar Land TX 77479
1961-008	Bass, Norman Delaney	8814 Third Ave/Inglewood CA 90305
1977-008	Bass, Randy William	Rr 3 Box 23c/Lawton OK 73501
1939-006	Bass, Richard William	D. February 3, 1989 Graceville, Fla.
1918-001	Bass, William Capers 'Doc'	D. January 12, 1970 Macon, Ga.
1913-005	Bassler, John Landis	D. June 29, 1979 Santa Monica, Calif.
1923-007	Batchelder, Joseph Edmund	D. May 5, 1989 Beverly, Mass.
1993-009	Batchelor, Richard Anthony	1004 Pineneedle Road/Hartsville SC 29550
1963-007	Bateman, John Alvin	D. December 6, 1966 Sand Springs, Okla.
1969-007	Bates, Charles Richard 'Dick'	5859 West Cielo Grande/Glendale AZ 85310
1927-008	Bates, Charles William	D. January 29, 1980 Topeka, Kans.
1970-006	Bates, Delbert Oakley	8336 133rd NE/Redmond WA 98052
1939-007	Bates, Hubert Edgar	D. April 29, 1987 Long Beach, Calif.
1995-016	Bates, Jason Charles	Old Add: 33531 Breckenridge Trail Anaheim CA 92801
1913-006	Bates, Raymond	D. August 15, 1970 Tucson, Ariz.
1989-009	Bates, William Derrick	PO Box 1133/Cedar Point TX 78010
1986-013	Bathe, William David	7821 East Sabina Crest Place/Tucson AZ 85715

1996-012	Batista, Leocadio Francisco 'Tony'	Old Add: Mao Dominican Rep.
1992-008	Batista, Miguel Jerry Descartes	30 De Marzoh #31 San Pedro De Macoris Dominican Rep.
1973-011	Batista, Rafael	Box 211 San Pedro De Macoris Dominican Rep.
1989-010	Batiste, Kevin Wade	3624 Avenue M/Galveston TX 77550
1991-011	Batiste, Kimothy Emil	16163 Aikens Road/Prairieville LA 70769
1916-003	Batsch, William McKinley	D. December 31, 1963 Canton, O.
1912-012	Batten, George Bernard	D. August 4, 1972 New Port Richey, Fla.
1955-008	Battey, Earl Jesse	2501 SW 3rd Street/Ocala FL 32674
1995-017	Battle, Allen Zelmo	Old Add: West NC Hwy 55 Mount Olive NC 28365
1995-018	Battle, Howard Dean	420 Fayard Street/Biloxi MS 39530
1927-009	Battle, James Milton	D. September 30, 1965 Chico, Calif.
1976-013	Batton, Christopher Sean	6109 West 77th St/Los Angeles CA 90045
1947-010	Batts, Matthew Daniel	1946 Woodale Blvd/Baton Rouge LA 70866
1948-008	Bauer, Henry Albert	12705 West 108th Street/Overland Park KS 66210
1918-002	Bauer, Louis Walter	D. February 4, 1979 Pomona, N. J.
1936-007	Bauers, Russell Lee	D. January 21, 1995 Hines, Ill.
1911-011	Baumann, Charles John 'Paddy'	D. November 20, 1969 Indianapolis, Ind.
1955-009	Baumann, Frank Matthew	7712 Sunray Ln/Saint Louis MO 63123
1949-004	Baumer, James Sloan	D. July 8, 1996 Paoli, Pa.
1912-013	Baumgardner, George Washington	D. December 13, 1970 Barboursville, W. Va.
1978-006	Baumgarten, Ross	1020 Bluff Rd/Glencoe IL 60022
1920-004	Baumgartner, Harry E.	D. December 3, 1930 Augusta, Ga.
1953-009	Baumgartner, John Edward	1181 County Road 37/Hayden AL 35079
1914-013	Baumgartner, Stanwood Fulton	D. October 4, 1955 Philadelphia, Pa.
1947-011	Baumholtz, Frank Conrad	D. December 14, 1997 Winter Springs, Fla.
1960-007	Bauta, Eduardo Galvez	1400 South Nova Road/Daytona Beach FL 32114
1993-010	Bautista, Daniel	Francisco Del Rosario #65 Santo Domingo Dominican Rep.
1988-011	Bautista, Jose Joaquin	380 SW 181st Way/Pembroke Pines FL 33029
1959-005	Baxes, Dimitrios Speros 'Jim'	D. November 14, 1996 Garden Grove, Calif.
1956-006	Baxes, Michael	303 Wickman Dr/Mill Valley CA 94941
1970-007	Baylor, Don Edward	56 325 Riviera/Laquinta CA 92253
1919-006	Bayne, William Lear	D. May 27, 1981 St. Louis, Mo.
1913-007	Beall, John Woolf	D. June 13, 1926 Beltsville, Md.
1975-014	Beall, Robert Brooks	513 Birchwood Rd/Hillsboro OR 97123
1924-005	Beall, Walter Esau	D. January 28, 1959 Suitland, Md.
1978-007	Beamon, Charles Alonzo Jr.	421 Oakland Ave #6/Oakland CA 94611
1956-007	Beamon, Charles "Alonzo, Sr."	1717 Woodland Ave #3/East Palo Alto CA 94303
1996-013	Beamon, Clifford 'Trey'	Old Add: Dallas TX
1930-002	Bean, Beveric Benton 'Belve'	D. June 1, 1988 Comanche, Texas
1987-006	Bean, William Daro	Old Add: 25622 Eastwind Drive Dana Point CA 92627
1984-005	Beane, William Lamar	1720 Knoll Field Way/Encinitas CA 92024
1980-007	Beard, Charles David 'Dave'	Old Add: 813 E. Bloomingdale #284 Brandon FL 33511
1948-009	Beard, Cramer Theodore 'Ted'	10517 Stelors Court/Fishers IN 46038
1974-008	Beard, Michael Richard	Old Add: 4710 Sam Peck Rd #1133 Little Rock AR 72212
1954-006	Beard, Ralph William	1367 Berkshire Dr/West Palm Beach FL 33406
1947-012	Bearden, Henry Eugene 'Gene'	PO Box 176/Helena AR 72342
1976-014	Beare, Gary Ray	12718 Shadowline Street/Poway CA 92064
1963-008	Bearnarth, Lawrence Donald	5103 Queen Palm Terrace NE/Saint Petersburg FL 33703
1990-012	Bearse, Kevin Gerard	6 Bowne Avenue/Atlantic Highlands NJ 7716
1991-012	Beasley, Christopher Charles	1139 East Palm Avenue/Orange CA 92666
1977-009	Beasley, Lewis Paige	Old Add: Rr 1 Box 65/Bowling Green VA 22427
1978-008	Beattie, James Louis	50 Belvedere Place/Westmount Quebec H3Y 1G6 Canada
1914-014	Beatty, Desmond	D. October 6, 1969 Norway, Me.
1989-011	Beatty, Gordon Blaine 'Blaine'	867 Kolodzey Road/Victoria TX 77905
1963-009	Beauchamp, James Edward	105 Paula Drive/Tyrone GA 30290
1941-006	Beazley, John Andrew	D. April 21, 1990 Nashville, Tenn.
1926-006	Beck, Clyde Eugene	D. July 15, 1988 Temple City, Calif.
1914-015	Beck, Ernest George B	D. October 29, 1973 South Bend, Ind.
1965-006	Beck, Richard Henry	8218 North Sumter Court/Spokane WA 99208
1991-013	Beck, Rodney Roy	Old Add: 4382 North 78th Street #603 Scottsdale AZ 85251
1924-006	Beck, Walter William 'Boom Boom'	D. May 7, 1987 Champaign, Ill.
1913-008	Beck, Zinn Bertram	D. March 19, 1981 West Palm Beach, Fla.
1911-012	Becker, Charles S.	D. July 30, 1928 Washington, D.C.
1943-007	Becker, Heinz Reinhard	D. November 11, 1991 Dallas, Texas
1936-008	Becker, Joseph Edward	D. January 11, 1998 Sunset Hills, Mo.
1915-010	Becker, Martin Henry	D. September 25, 1957 Cincinnati, O.
1993-011	Becker, Richard Godhard 'Rich'	1738 Roanoke/Aurora IL 60506
1965-007	Beckert, Glenn Alfred	2 Winsmill Terrace/Placida FL 33946
1996-014	Beckett, Robert Joseph 'Robbie'	Old Add: Austin TX
1927-010	Beckman, James Joseph	D. December 5, 1974 Cincinnati, O.
1939-008	Beckmann, William Aloysius	D. January 2, 1990 Florissant, Mo.
1979-008	Beckwith, Thomas Joseph Joe	2057 Country Squire Rd/Auburn AL 36830
1955-010	Becquer, Julio Vellegas	829 Vincent Ave/Minneapolis MN 55411
1962-009	Bedell, Howard William	1187 Crestwood Dr/Pottstown PA 19464
1925-006	Bedford, William Eugene	D. October 6, 1977 San Antonio, Texas
1922-003	Bedgood, Philip Burlette	D. November 8, 1927 Fort Pierce, Fla.
1912-014	Bedient, Hugh Carpenter	D. July 21, 1965 Jamestown, N.Y.
1930-003	Bednar, Andrew Jackson	D. November 26, 1937 Graham, Tex,
1981-008	Bedrosian, Stephen Wayne	3915 Gordon Road/Senoia GA 30276

1996-015	Beech, Lucas Matthew 'Matt'	Old Add: San Antonio TX
1944-006	Beeler, Joseph Sam 'Jodie'	3709 Nabholtz/Mesquite TX 75150
1968-004	Beene, Frederick Ray	Box 143/Oakhurst TX 77359
1983-009	Beene, Ramon Andrew Andy	9919 Lila/Dallas TX 75220
1948-010	Beers, Clarence Scott	2630 North Winslet Blvd/Tucson AZ 85716
1938-007	Beggs, Joseph Stanley	D. July 19, 1983 Indianapolis, Ind.
1924-007	Begley, James Lawrence	D. February 22, 1957 San Francisco, Calif.
1921-003	Behan, Charles Frederick 'Petie'	D. January 21, 1957 Bradford, Pa.
1983-010	Behenna, Richard Kipp	164 Bradford Station Drive/Sharpsburg GA 30277
1970-008	Behney, Melvin Brian	2800 Woodshire/Arlington TX 76016
1946-008	Behrman, Henry Bernard	D. January 20, 1987 New York, N. Y.
1934-004	Bejma, Aloysius Frank 'Ollie'	D. January 3, 1995 South Bend, Ind.
1965-008	Belanger, Mark Henry	D. October 6, 1998 New York, N. Y.
1950-007	Belardi, Carroll Wayne 'Wayne'	D. October 21, 1993 Santa Cruz, Calif.
1990-013	Belcher, Kevin Donnell	2829 Madison Avenue #C/Waco TX 76706
1987-007	Belcher, Timothy Wayne	Spring Street/Sparta OH 43350
1989-012	Belinda, Stanley Peter	454 Sylvan Drive/State College PA 16803
1962-010	Belinsky, Robert 'Bo'	Old Add: 1801 S. Catalina #204 Redondo Beach CA 90277
1996-016	Belk, Timothy William	10523 Norton/Houston TX 77043
1972-007	Bell, David Gus 'Buddy'	9017 Decima Street/Cincinnati OH 45242
1995-019	Bell, David Michael	9017 Decima Street/Cincinnati OH 45242
1950-008	Bell, David Russell 'Gus'	D. May 7, 1995 Cincinnati, Ohio
1991-014	Bell, Derek Nathaniel	9820 Bay Island Drive/Tampa FL 33615
1985-003	Bell, Eric Alvin	1601 Couchman Lane/Modesto CA 95355
1939-009	Bell, Fernando Jerome Lee 'Fern'	43611 Virginian Street/Palm Desert CA 92211
1958-009	Bell, Gary	% American Sports 1436 North Flores San Antonio TX 78212
1924-008	Bell, Herman S. 'Hi'	D. June 7, 1949 Glendale, Calif.
1986-014	Bell, Jay Stuart	3835 Cold Creek Drive/Valrico FL 33594
1971-009	Bell, Jerry Houston	2045 Nonaville Road/Mount Juliet TN 37122
1981-009	Bell, Jorge Antonio	L.Amiama #14,Bell Segunda Plantor San Pedro De Macoris Dom. Rep.
1989-013	Bell, Juan	Old Add: Calle T174 Bo Restauracion San Pedro De Macoris D. Rep.
1976-015	Bell, Kevin Robert	Old Add: 2341 Algonquin Pkwy Rolling Meadows IL 60008
1923-008	Bell, Lester Rowland	D. November 26, 1985 Harrisburg, Pa.
1990-014	Bell, Michael Allen	1331 Noah Avenue/Spring Hill FL 34608
1912-015	Bell, Ralph A.	D. October 18, 1959 Burlington, Ia.
1935-003	Bell, Roy Chester 'Beau'	D. September 14, 1977 College Station, Texas
1986-015	Bell, Terence William	315 Watervliet Avenue/Dayton OH 45420
1952-006	Bell, William Samuel	D. October 11, 1962 Durham, N. C.
1957-006	Bella, John Zeke	24 Taylor Drive/Cos Cob CT 6807
1989-014	Belle, Albert Jojuan	55 West Goethe Street #1226/Chicago IL 60610
1997-007	Bellhorn, Mark Christian	1544 Chipmunk Lane/Oviedo FL 32765
1982-011	Belliard, Rafael Leonidas	Domingo Castellano 17,Gurabito Santiago Dominican Rep.
1975-015	Belloir, Robert Edward	335 Mimosa Drive/Fayetteville GA 30214
1997-008	Beltran, Rigoberto	Old Add: San Diego CA 92101
1991-015	Beltre, Esteban (Valera)	15 #28 Laloma San Pedro De Macoris Dominican Rep.
1995-020	Benard, Marvin Larry	Old Add: Cudahy CA 90201
1991-016	Benavides, Alfredo	2502 Garfield/Laredo TX 78040
1967-004	Bench, John Lee	324 Bishopbridge Drive/Cincinnati OH 45255
1978-009	Benedict, Bruce Edwin	335 Quietwater Lane/Dunwoody GA 30338
1995-021	Benes, Alan Paul	1400 W. Everett,%Chas Benes/Lake Forest IL 60045
1989-015	Benes, Andrew Charles	4001 Woodcastle Road/Evansville IN 47711
1931-007	Benes, Joseph Anthony	D. March 7, 1975 Elmhurst N. Y.
1925-007	Benge, Raymond Adelphia	D. June 27, 1997 Centerville, Tex.
1923-009	Bengough, Bernard Oliver	D. December 22, 1968 Philadelphia, Pa.
1971-010	Beniquez, Juan Jose	Calle 99a Blk.87 #12/Carolina PR 630
1994-004	Benitez, Armando German	Batey El Soco Ramon Santana Dominican Rep.
1995-022	Benitez, Yamil Antonio	Calle 13 Bo. 918 Caperra Terrace/Rio Piedras PR 921
1939-010	Benjamin, Alfred Stanley 'Stan'	2100 Kings Highway #53/Port Charlotte FL 33980
1989-016	Benjamin, Michael Paul	810 North Criss Street/Chandler AZ 85226
1914-016	Benn, Homer Omer	D. June 4, 1967 Mendota, Wis.
1964-004	Bennett, David Hans	408 Fairchild St/Yreka CA 96097
1962-011	Bennett, Dennis John	630 North 5th/Klamath Falls OR 97601
1995-023	Bennett, Erik Hans	PO Box 884/Yreka CA 96097
1927-011	Bennett, Francis Allen	D. March 18, 1966 Wilmington, Del.
1995-024	Bennett, Gary David	1403 West Beach Road/Waukegan IL 60087
1923-010	Bennett, Herschell Emmett	D. September 9, 1964 Springfield, Mo.
1928-006	Bennett, James Fred	D. May 12, 1957 Atkins, Ark.
1918-003	Bennett, Joseph Harley	D. November 21, 1957 Joel, Mo.
1923-011	Bennett, Joseph Rosenblum	D. July 11, 1987 Morro Bay, Calif.
1997-009	Bennett, Shayne Anthony	Old Add: Worongary Australia
1934-005	Benson, Allen Wilbert	Hurley SD 57036
1943-008	Benson, Vernon Adair	PO Box 127/Granite Quarry NC 28072
1913-009	Bentley, John Needles	D. October 24, 1969 Olney, Md.
1978-010	Benton, Alfred Lee 'Butch'	Old Add: 895 Vil Lakes #102 Saint Petersburg FL 33701
1934-006	Benton, John Alton 'Al'	D. April 14, 1968 Lynwood, Calif.
1910-007	Benton, John Clebon 'Rube'	D. December 12, 1937 Dothan, Ala.
1923-012	Benton, Lawrence James	D. April 3, 1953 Cincinnati, O.
1922-004	Benton, Sidney Wright	D. March 8, 1977 Fayetteville, Ark.
1922-005	Benton, Stanley 'Rabbit'	D. June 7, 1984 Dallas, Texas

1911-013 ....Benz, Joseph Louis ....D. April 23, 1957 Chicago, Ill.
1987-008 ....Benzinger, Todd Eric ....3502 Behmer Road/Cincinnati OH 45245
1939-011 ....Berardino, John ....D. May 19, 1996 Los Angeles, Calif.
1954-007 ....Berberet, Louis Joseph ....2500 Keppel Sands/Las Vegas NV 89134
1997-010 ....Berblinger, Jeffrey James ....102 Swanee Street/Goddard KS 67052
1993-012 ....Bere, Jason Phillip ....11 Beeching Avenue/Wilmington MA 1887
1978-011 ....Berenguer, Juan Bautista ....17908 Inverness Curve/Eden Prairie MN 55347
1980-008 ....Berenyi, Bruce Michael ....20355 NE 34th Court #1424/Aventure FL 33180
1923-013 ....Berg, Morris 'Moe' ....D. May 29, 1972 Belleville, N. J.
1944-007 ....Bergamo, August Samuel ....D. August 19, 1974 Grosse Pointe City, Mich.
1914-017 ....Berger, Clarence Edward..............................D. June 30, 1959 Washington, D. C.
1922-006 ....Berger, John Henne ....D. May 7, 1979 Lake Charles, La.
1913-010 ....Berger, Joseph August ....D. March 5, 1956 Rock Island, Ill.
1932-003 ....Berger, Louis William 'Boze' ....D. November 3, 1992 Bethesda, Md.
1930-004 ....Berger, Walter Antone ....D. November 30, 1988 Redondo Beach, Calif.
1911-014 ....Berghammer, Martin Andrew ....D. December 21, 1957 Pittsburgh, Pa.
1916-004 ....Bergman, Alfred Henry ....D. June 21, 1961 Fort Wayne, Ind.
1975-016 ....Bergman, David Bruce ....728 Canterbury Court/Grosse Pointe Woods MI 48236
1993-013 ....Bergman, Sean Frederick ....18405 West Donahue Road/Wilmington IL 60481
1924-009 ....Berly, John Chambers ....D. June 26, 1977 Houston, Tex.
1918-004 ....Berman, Robert Leon ....D. August 2, 1988 Bridgeport, Conn.
1977-010 ....Bernal, Victor Hugo ....4632 Abner St/Los Angeles CA 90032
1978-012 ....Bernard, Dwight Vern ....Rural Route 1/Belle Rive IL 62810
1979-009 ....Bernazard, Antonio (Garcia) ....Santa Av D-25,Urb Santa Elvira/Caguas PR 625
1976-016 ....Bernhardt, Juan Ramon..................................Eduardo Brito 13 San Pedro De Macoris Dominican Rep.
1918-005 ....Bernhardt, Walter Jacob ....D. July 26, 1958 Watertown, N. Y.
1953-010 ....Bernier, Carlos Rodriguez ....D. April 6, 1989 Juana Diaz, P.R.
1948-011 ....Bero, John George ....D. May 11, 1985 Gardena, Calif.
1977-011 ....Berra, Dale Anthony ....19 Highland Avenue/Montclair NJ 7042
1946-009 ....Berra, Lawrence Peter ....19 Highland Avenue/Montclair NJ 7042
1912-016 ....Berran, Dennis Martin ....D. April 28, 1943 Boston, Mass.
1934-007 ....Berres, Raymond ....111 Hawthorne Road/Twin Lakes WI 53181
1989-017 ....Berroa, Geronimo Emiliano ....3681 Broadway #23/New York NY 10031
1962-012 ....Berry, Allen Kenneth 'Ken' ....3421 Briarwood Lane/Topeka KS 66611
1925-008 ....Berry, Charles Francis ....D. September 6, 1972 Evanston, Ill.
1948-012 ....Berry, Cornelius John 'Connie'.....................407 Inkster Avenue/Kalamazoo MI 49001
1942-006 ....Berry, Jonas Arthur ....D. September 27, 1958 Anaheim, Calif.
1921-004 ....Berry, Joseph Howard, Jr. ....D. April 29, 1976 Philadelphia, Pa.
1990-015 ....Berry, Sean Robert..Old Add: 74 Dapplegray Lane Rolling Hills Estates CA
1987-009 ....Berryhill, Damon Scott..................................8 Saint Paul/Laguna Niguel CA 92677
1964-005 ....Bertaina, Frank Louis ....2076 Mount Olive Way/Santa Rosa CA 95404
1960-008 ....Bertell, Richard George ....25332 Remesa Dr/Mission Viejo CA 92675
1953-011 ....Bertoia, Reno Peter ....705-5125 Riverside Drive East/Windsor Ontario N8S 4L8 Canada
1995-025 ....Bertotti, Michael David..................................Jupiter Road/Highland Mills NY 10930
1936-009 ....Bertrand, Roman Mathias ....1909 Mount Hood/The Dalles OR 97058
1995-026 ....Berumen, Andres ....1343 North Blanchard/Banning CA 92220
1956-008 ....Besana, Frederick Cyril ....222 Diamond Oaks Dr/Roseville CA 95678
1940-002 ....Besse, Herman ....D. August 13, 1972 Los Angeles, Calif.
1955-011 ....Bessent, Fred Donald 'Don' ....D. July 7, 1990 Jacksonville, Fla.
1983-011 ....Best, Karl John ....Old Add: 11132 NE 129th Kirkland WA 98034
1978-013 ....Beswick, James William ....6911 Buckhorn Drive/Columbus GA 31904
1910-008 ....Betcher, Franklin Lyle ....D. November 27, 1981 Wynnewood, Pa.
1964-006 ....Bethea, William Lamar ....Ath. Dept., Arkansas State PO Box 1000 Jonesboro AR 72467
1965-009 ....Bethke, James Charles ....6209 North Robinhood Lane/Kansas City MO 64151
1928-007 ....Bettencourt, Lawrence Joseph ....D. September 15, 1978 New Orleans, La.
1984-006 ....Bettendorf, Jeffrey Allen ....528 North Lupine/Lompoc CA 93446
1920-005 ....Betts, Walter Martin 'Huck' ....D. June 13, 1987 Millsboro, Del.
1914-018 ....Betzel, Christian Frederick Albert.................D. February 7, 1965 West Hollywood,Fla
1971-011 ....Bevacqua, Kurt Anthony ....2607 Pirineos Way #11/Carlsbad CA 92008
1952-007 ....Bevan, Harold Joseph ....D. October 5, 1968 New Orleans, La.
1944-008 ....Bevens, Floyd Clifford 'Bill'.........................D. October 26, 1991 Salem, Ore.
1996-017 ....Bevil, Brian Scott ....Old Add: Houston TX
1942-007 ....Bevil, Louis Eugene ....D. February 1, 1973 Dixon, Ill.
1995-027 ....Bevington, Terry Paul ....2600 Halle Pkwy/Collierville TN 38017
1917-006 ....Bezdek, Hugh Francis ....D. September 19, 1952 Atlantic City, N.J.
1982-012 ....Biancalana, Roland Americo 'Buddy'............7901 30th Avenue North/Saint Petersburg FL 33710
1975-017 ....Bianco, Thomas Anthony ....Old Add: 4 Curvewood Rd/Port Washington NY 11050
1949-005 ....Biasatti, Henry Arcado ....D. April 20, 1996 Dearborn, Mich.
1972-008 ....Bibby, James Blair ....1826 South Coolwell Road/Madison Heights VA 24572
1988-012 ....Bichette, Alphonse Dante 'Dante'.................3511 Markham Woods Road/Longwood FL 32779
1948-013 ....Bickford, Vernon Edgell.................................D. May 8, 1960 Richmond, Va.
1948-014 ....Bicknell, Charles Stephen ....6981 Fords Station Road/Germantown TN 38138
1984-007 ....Bielecki, Michael Joseph ....5907 Foxhall Manor Drive/Baltimore MD 21228
1920-006 ....Biemiller, Harry Lee ....D. May 25, 1965 Orlando, Fla.
1997-011 ....Bieser, Steven Ray ....Old Add: St Genevieve MO 63670
1916-005 ....Bigbee, Carson Lee ....D. October 17, 1964 Portland, Ore.
1920-007 ....Bigbee, Lyle Randolph..................................D. August 5, 1942 Portland, Ore.
1929-008 ....Bigelow, Elliot Allardice................................D. August 10, 1933 Tampa, Fla.
1988-013 ....Biggio, Craig Alan ....102 Passaic Avenue/Spring Lake NJ 7762

1932-004 ....Biggs, Charles Orval ....D. May 24, 1954 French Lick, Ind.
1917-007 ....Bigler, Ivan Edward ....D. April 1, 1975 Coldwater, Mich.
1970-009 ....Biittner, Larry David ....26817 520th Street/Pocahontas IA 50574
1949-006 ....Bilbrey, James Melvin ....D. December 26, 1985 Toledo, O.
1937-009 ....Bildilli, Emil ....D. September 16, 1946 Hartford City, Ind.
1949-007 ....Bilko, Stephen Thomas ....D. March 7, 1978 Wilkes-Barre, Pa.
1983-012 ....Billardello, Dann James ....1501 Menorca Court/West Palm Beach FL 33414
1968-005 ....Billingham, John Eugene ....8945 Lake Irma Point East/Orlando FL 32817
1927-012 ....Billings, Haskell Clark ....D. December 26, 1983 Greenbrae, Calif.
1913-011 ....Billings, John Augustus 'Josh' ....D. December 30, 1981 Santa Monica, Calif.
1968-006 ....Billings, Richard Arlin ....1917 Creekwood Dr/Arlington TX 76010
1944-009 ....Binks, George Eugene ....4803 Belmont Road/Downers Grove IL 60515
1944-010 ....Biras, Stephen Alexander ....D. April 21, 1965 St. Louis, Mo.
1973-012 ....Bird, James Douglas 'Doug' ....1405 SW 19th Lane/Cape Coral FL 33991
1921-005 ....Bird, James Edward 'Red' ....D. March 23, 1972 Murfreesboro, Tenn.
1986-016 ....Birkbeck, Michael Laurence ....1705 West Hill Drive/Orrville OH 44667
1933-004 ....Birkofer, Ralph Joseph ....D. March 16, 1971 Cincinnati, O.
1955-012 ....Birrer, Werner Joseph 'Babe' ....115 Ranch Trail West/Williamsville NY 14221
1985-004 ....Birtsas, Timothy Dean ....43 Robertson Court/Clarkston MI 48346
1942-008 ....Biscan, Frank Stephen ....D. May 22, 1959 St. Louis, Mo.
1925-009 ....Bischoff, John George ....D. December 28, 1981 Granite City, Ill.
1952-008 ....Bishop, Charles Tuller ....D. July 5, 1993 Lawrenceville, Ga.
1923-014 ....Bishop, James Morton ....D. September 20, 1973 Mexico, Mo.
1914-019 ....Bishop, Lloyd Clifton ....D. June 17, 1968 Wichita, Kan.
1924-010 ....Bishop, Max Frederick ....D. February 4, 1962 Waynesboro, Pa.
1983-013 ....Bishop, Michael David ....3119 Hampton Drive/Santa Maria CA 93454
1921-006 ....Bishop, William Henry ....D. February 14, 1956 St. Joseph, Mo.
1912-017 ....Bisland, Rivington Martin ....D. January 11, 1973 Salzburg, Austria
1928-008 ....Bissonette, Delphia Louis ....D. June 9, 1972 Augusta, Me.
1942-009 ....Bithorn, Hiram Gabriel ....D. January 1, 1952 El Mante, Mex.
1990-016 ....Bitker, Joseph Anthony ....6235 Odessa Court/Magalia CA 95954
1986-017 ....Bittiger, Jeffrey Scott ....695 3rd Street/Secaucus NJ 7094
1935-004 ....Bivin, James Nathaniel ....D. November 7, 1982 Pueblo, Colo.
1983-014 ....Bjorkman, George Anton ....3216 Bandolino Lane/Plano TX 75075
1914-020 ....Black, David ....D. October 27, 1936 Pittsburgh, Pa.
1943-009 ....Black, Donald Paul ....D. April 21, 1959 Cuyahoga Falls, O.
1981-010 ....Black, Harry Ralston 'Bud' ....3364 Calle Margarita/Olivenheim CA 92024
1911-015 ....Black, John Falcnor ....D. March 19, 1962 Rutherford, N. J.
1924-011 ....Black, John William 'Bill' ....D. January 14, 1968 Philadelphia, Pa.
1952-009 ....Black, Joseph ....1904 Greyhound Towers/Phoenix AZ 85077
1952-010 ....Black, William Carroll ....1233 Mount Olive Avenue/University City MO 63130
1962-013 ....Blackaby, Ethan Allen ....2308 East Orangewood/Phoenix AZ 85020
1912-018 ....Blackburn, Earl Stuart ....D. August 4, 1966 Mansfield, O.
1915-011 ....Blackburn, Foster Edwin 'Babe' ....D. March 9, 1984 Newport Richey, Fla.
1948-015 ....Blackburn, James Ray ....D. October 26, 1969 Cincinnati, O.
1958-010 ....Blackburn, Ronald Hamilton ....D. April 29, 1998 Morganton, N. C.
1910-009 ....Blackburne, Russell Aubrey 'Lena' ....D. February 29, 1968 Riverside, N. J.
1928-009 ....Blackerby, George Franklin ....D. March 30, 1987 Wichita Falls, Texas
1942-010 ....Blackwell, Ewell 'The Whip' ....D. October 29, 1996 Hendersonville, N. C.
1917-008 ....Blackwell, Fredrick William ....D. December 8, 1975 Morgantown, Ky.
1974-009 ....Blackwell, Timothy P. ....143 El Camino Pequero/El Cajon CA 92019
1922-007 ....Blades, Francis Raymond ....D. May 18, 1979 Lincoln, Ill.
1969-008 ....Bladt, Richard Alan ....12297 Meridian Road NE/Mount Angel OR 97362
1925-010 ....Blaeholder, George Franklin ....D. December 29, 1947 Garden Grove, Calif.
1941-007 ....Blaemire, Rae Bertrum ....D. December 23, 1975 Champaign, Ill.
1929-009 ....Blair, Clarence Vick ....D. July 1, 1982 Texarkana, Tex.
1974-010 ....Blair, Dennis Herman ....PO Box 850371/Richardson TX 75085
1942-011 ....Blair, Louis Nathan ....D. June 7, 1996 Monroe, La.
1964-007 ....Blair, Paul L. D. ....Old Add: Box 284 Bedford Hills NY 10507
1990-017 ....Blair, William Allen 'Willie' ....62 Elder Lane/Pikeville KY 41501
1951-002 ....Blake, Edward James ....208 Willow Creek Court/Belleville IL 62223
1920-008 ....Blake, John Frederick 'Huck' ....D. October 31, 1982 Beckley, W. Va.
1934-008 ....Blakely, Lincoln Howard ....D. September 28, 1976 Oakland, Calif.
1955-013 ....Blanchard, John Edwin ....2250 South Plymouth Road #306/Minnetonka MN 55305
1935-005 ....Blanche, Prosper Albert 'Al' ....D. April 2, 1997 Melrose, Mass.
1972-009 ....Blanco, Damaso ....Old Add: 659 Catamaran St #2/Foster City CA
1965-010 ....Blanco, Gilbert Henry ....18403 North 16th Place/Phoenix AZ 85022
1997-012 ....Blanco, Henry Ramon ....Old Add: Guarenas Venezuela
1970-010 ....Blanco, Osvaldo Carlos ....Old Add: De Lozada B1 E16 San Jose De Avila Venezuela
1910-010 ....Blanding, Fred James ....D. July 16, 1950 Salem, Va.
1922-008 ....Blankenship, Homer ....D. June 22, 1974 Longview, Tex.
1988-014 ....Blankenship, Kevin Dewayne ....4785 Third Street/Rocklin CA 95677
1988-015 ....Blankenship, Lance Robert ....2675 Meadow Glen Drive/San Ramon CA 94583
1922-009 ....Blankenship, Theodore ....D. January 14, 1945 Atoka, Okla.
1972-010 ....Blanks, Larvell ....408 Waters Avenue/Del Rio TX 78840
1934-009 ....Blanton, Darrell Elijah 'Cy' ....D. September 13, 1945 Norman, Okla.
1955-014 ....Blasingame, Donald Lee ....9040 North Longfeather/Fountain Hills AZ 85268
1963-010 ....Blasingame, Wade Allen ....5207 Riverhill Rd NE/Marietta GA 30067
1964-008 ....Blass, Stephen Robert ....1756 Quigg Drive/Pittsburgh PA 15241

1971-012 ....Blateric, Stephen Lawrence ....1015 Myrtle Avenue/Calistoga CA 94515
1948-016 ....Blatnik, John Louis ....68615 Chermont Rd PO Box 24 Lansing OH 43934
1942-012 ....Blattner, Robert Garnett 'Buddy' ....576 Highway 44/Lake Ozark MO 65049
1987-010 ....Blauser, Jeffrey Michael ....1730 North Clark Street #4301/Chicago IL 60614
1959-006 ....Blaylock, Gary Nelson ....Box 241/Malden MO 63863
1950-009 ....Blaylock, Marvin Edward ....D. October 23, 1993 Conway, Ark.
1956-009 ....Blaylock, Robert Edward ....Rural Route 2 Box 96/Muldrow OK 74948
1996-018 ....Blazier, Ronald Patrick ....610 North Ninth Street/Bellwood PA 16617
1965-011 ....Blefary Curtis Leroy ....82 Briarwood Drive/West Palm Beach FL 33415
1960-009 ....Blemker, Raymond 'Buddy'...........................D. February 15, 1994 Evansville, Ind.
1972-011 ....Blessitt, Isaiah Ike ....19712 Anglin/Detroit MI 48234
1923-015 ....Blethen, Clarence Waldo ....D. April 11, 1973 Frederick, Md.
1942-013 ....Block, Seymour 'Cy'....................................10 South Middleneck Road/Great Neck NY 11021
1985-005 ....Blocker, Terry Fennell ....745 Guide Post Lane/Stone Mountain GA 30086
1969-009 ....Blomberg, Ronald Mark ....11660 Mountain Laurel Drive/Roswell GA 30075
1995-028 ....Blomdahl, Benjamin Earl ....5370 Nottingham Road/Riverside CA 92506
1937-010 ....Bloodworth, James Henry ....PO Box 232/Apalachicola FL 32320
1963-011 ....Bloomfield, Clyde Stalcup 'Bud' ....4603 West Hope Road/Rogers AR 72756
1993-014 ....Blosser, Gregory Brent ....8351 Boleyn Drive/Sarasota FL 34240
1924-012 ....Blott, Jack Leonard ....D. June 11, 1964 Ann Arbor, Mich.
1989-018 ....Blowers, Michael Roy ....22211 42nd Avenue East/Spanaway WA 98387
1921-007 ....Blue, Luzerne Atwell ....D. July 28, 1958 Alexandria, Va.
1969-010 ....Blue, Vida ....PO Box 1449/Pleasanton CA 94556
1922-010 ....Bluege, Oswald Louis ....D. October 15, 1985 Edina, Minn.
1932-005 ....Bluege, Otto Adam ....D. June 28, 1977 Chicago, Ill.
1914-021 ....Bluejacket, James ....D. March 26, 1947 Pekin, Ill.
1918-006 ....Bluhm, Harvey Fred 'Red' ....D. May 7, 1952 Flint, Mich.
1996-019 ....Bluma, James Andrew 'Jaime' ....15219 Reeds/Overland Park KS 66223
1922-011 ....Blume, Clinton Willis ....D. June 12, 1973 Islip, N. Y.
1970-011 ....Blyleven, Rikalbert Bert 'Bert' ....2658 Shriver Drive/Fort Myers FL 33901
1953-012 ....Blyzka, Michael John ....1615 East 13th Street #1/Cheyenne WY 82001
1960-010 ....Boak, Chester Robert 'Chet' ....D. November 28, 1983 Emporium, Pa.
1913-012 ....Boardman, Charles Louis ....D. August 10, 1968 Sacramento, Calif.
1968-007 ....Bobb, Mark Randall 'Randy' ....D. June 13, 1982 Carnelian Bay, Calif.
1963-012 ....Boccabella, John Dominic...............................1035 Lea Dr/San Rafael CA 94903
1933-005 ....Bocek, Milton Frank ....2342 South 61st Court/Cicero IL 60804
1974-011 ....Bochte, Bruce Anton ....3688 Hastings Court/Lafayette CA 94549
1995-029 ....Bochtler, Douglas Eugene ....4277 Forest Lane/West Palm Beach FL 33406
1978-014 ....Bochy, Bruce Douglas..................................16144 Brittany Park Lane/San Diego CA 92064
1946-010 ....Bockman, Joseph Edward 'Eddie' ....1400 Milbrae Avenue #2/Millbrae CA 94030
1986-018 ....Bockus, Randy Walter ....1908 Higby Drive #A/Stow OH 44224
1980-009 ....Boddicker, Michael James ....11324 West 121st Street/Overland Park KS 66213
1911-016 ....Bodie, Frank Stephan 'Ping' ....D. December 12, 1961 San Francisco, Calif.
1917-009 ....Boeckel, Norman Doxie ....D. February 16, 1924 Torrey Pines, Calif.
1912-019 ....Boehler, George Henry ....D. June 23, 1958 Lawrenceburg, Ind.
1912-020 ....Boehling, John Joseph ....D. September 8, 1941 Richmond, Va.
1967-005 ....Boehmer, Leonard Joseph ....3570 Highway P/Wentzville MO 63385
1995-030 ....Boehringer, Brian Edward ....%G.Boehringer 7 Sunset Drive Festus MO 63026
1932-006 ....Boerner, Lawrence Hyer ....D. October 16, 1969 Staunton, Va.
1985-006 ....Boever, Joseph Martin..................................Old Add: 5141 Towne South Road Saint Louis MO 63128
1993-015 ....Bogar, Timothy Paul ....Old Add: 1631 North 2750 W. Road Kankakee IL 60901
1920-009 ....Bogart, John Renzie.....................................D. December 7, 1986 Clarence, N. Y.
1982-013 ....Bogener, Terry Wayne ....411 McCabe/Palmyra MO 63461
1928-010 ....Boggs, Raymond Joseph ....D. November 27, 1989 Grand Junction, Colo.
1976-017 ....Boggs, Thomas Winston ....67 Emanuel Circle/Hot Springs National AR 71909
1982-014 ....Boggs, Wade Anthony ....6006 Windham Place/Tampa FL 33647
1968-008 ....Bogle, Warren Frederick ....11605 SW 103rd Ave/Miami FL 33156
1990-018 ....Bohanon, Brian Edward ....283 Old Spring Lane/Houston TX 77015
1913-013 ....Bohen, Leo Ignatius 'Pat' ....D. April 8, 1942 Napa, Calif.
1916-006 ....Bohne, Samuel Arthur ....D. May 23, 1977 Palo Alto, Calif.
1982-015 ....Bohnet, John Kelly ....224 Panorama Dr/Benicia CA 94510
1974-012 ....Boisclair, Bruce Armand ....Old Add: 29064 W. Saddle Brook Agoura CA 91301
1978-015 ....Boitano, Danny Jon ....15400 Winchester Blvd #43/Los Gatos CA 95030
1951-003 ....Bokelmann, Richard Werner ....629 North Belmont Avenue/Arlington Heights IL 60004
1933-006 ....Boken, Robert Anthony ....D. October 6, 1988 Las Vegas, Nev.
1936-010 ....Bokina, Joseph ....D. October 25, 1991 Chattanooga, Tenn.
1915-012 ....Boland, Bernard Anthony ....D. September 12, 1973 Detroit, Mich.
1934-010 ....Boland, Edward John ....D. February 5, 1993 Clearwater, Fla.
1914-022 ....Bold, Charles Dickens ....D. July 29, 1978 Chelsea, Mass.
1919-007 ....Bolden, William Horace ....D. December 8, 1966 Jefferson City, Tenn.
1926-007 ....Bolen, Stewart O_neal ....D. August 30, 1969 Jackson, Ala.
1962-014 ....Boles, Carl Theodore ....6191 Gerdts Drive/San Jose CA 95135
1996-020 ....Boles, John Egan ....6307 Spanish Oak Drive/Orlando FL 32809
1927-013 ....Boley, John Peter 'Joe' ....D. December 30, 1962 Mahanoy City, Pa.
1950-010 ....Bolger, James Cyril ....5524 Sidney Road/Cincinnati OH 45238
1993-016 ....Bolick, Frank Charles....................................348 South Poplar/Mount Carmel PA 17851
1961-009 ....Bolin, Bobby Donald ....Box East/Six Mile SC 29682
1954-008 ....Bolling, Frank Elmore ....171 Fenwick Rd/Mobile AL 36608
1939-012 ....Bolling, John Edward 'Jack' ....D. April 13, 1998 Panama City, Fla.

1952-011	Bolling, Milton Joseph	2752 Fontainebleau Dr South/Mobile AL 36606
1965-012	Bollo, Gregory Gene	15207 Regina St/Allen Park MI 48101
1950-011	Bollweg, Donald Raymond	D. May 26, 1996 Wheaton, Ill.
1928-011	Bolton, Cecil Glenford	D. August 25, 1993 Jackson, Miss.
1993-017	Bolton, Rodney Earl	9550 E. B. Road/Chattanooga TN 37421
1987-011	Bolton, Thomas Edward	Rural Route 1, Nolensville Road/Brentwood TN 37027
1931-008	Bolton, William Clifton	D. April 21, 1979 Lexington, N. C.
1978-016	Bomback, Mark Vincent	2482 Riverside Avenue/Somerset MA 2726
1960-011	Bond, Walter Franklin	D. September 14, 1967 Houston, Tex.
1986-019	Bonds, Barry Lamar	Old Add: 9595 Wilshire #711 Beverly Hills CA 90212
1968-009	Bonds, Bobby Lee	175 Lyndhurst/San Carlos CA 94070
1991-017	Bones, Ricardo/Ricky	Villa Rosa 2 A19/Guayama PR 654
1937-011	Bonetti, Julio	D. June 17, 1952 Belmont, Calif.
1927-014	Boney, Henry Tate	736 Country Club Drive/Highlands NC 28741
1938-008	Bongiovanni, Anthony Thomas 'Nino'	416 Rosewood Avenue/San Jose CA 95117
1940-003	Bonham, Ernest Edward 'Tiny'	D. September 15, 1949 Pittsburgh, Pa.
1971-013	Bonham, William Gordon	1605 Sycamore Way/Solvang CA 93463
1962-015	Bonikowski, Joseph Peter	6701 Old Reid Rd/Charlotte NC 28210
1981-011	Bonilla, Juan Guillermo	Old Add: Rural Route 3 Box 262 Quincy FL 32351
1986-020	Bonilla, Roberto Martin Antoni O	390 Round Hill Road/Greenwich CT 6831
1913-014	Bonin, Ernest Luther	D. January 3, 1965 Sycamore, O.
1977-012	Bonnell, Robert Barry	2102 179th Court NE/Redmond WA 98052
1980-011	Bonner, Robert Averill	Kafulafata Mission,Box 90247 Luanshyn Zambia
1944-011	Bonness, William John	D. December 3, 1977 Cleveland, O.
1920-010	Bono, Adlai Wendell 'Gus'	D. December 3, 1948 Dearborn, Mich.
1934-011	Bonura, Henry John 'Zeke'	D. March 9, 1987 New Orleans, La.
1913-015	Booe, Everett Little	D. May 21, 1969 Kennedy, Tex.
1983-015	Booker, Gregory Scott	1535 Charleigh Court/Elon College NC 27244
1966-008	Booker, Richard Lee	Box 59/Brookneal VA 24528
1987-012	Booker, Roderick Stewart	526 West Altadena Drive/Altadena CA 91001
1928-012	Bool, Albert	D. September 27, 1981 Lincoln, Neb.
1997-013	Boone, Aaron John	18571 Villa Drive/Villa Park CA 92667
1992-009	Boone, Bret Robert	2137 Eastern Avenue/Cincinnati OH 45202
1981-012	Boone, Daniel Hugh	320 Minnesota/El Cajon CA 92020
1922-012	Boone, Isaac Morgan 'Ike'	D. August 1, 1958 Northport, Ala.
1919-008	Boone, James Albert 'Danny'	D. May 11, 1968 Tuscaloosa, Ala.
1913-016	Boone, Lute Joseph	D. July 29, 1982 Pittsburgh, Pa.
1948-017	Boone, Raymond Otis	15420 Olde Hwy 80 #137/El Cajon CA 92021
1972-012	Boone, Robert Raymond	18571 Villa Drive/Villa Park CA 92667
1996-021	Booty, Joshua Gibson	Old Add: 209 Plantation Club Dr Melbourne FL 32940
1962-016	Boozer, John Morgan	D. January 24, 1986 Lexington, S. C.
1992-010	Borbon, Pedro Felix	962 North Noble/Texas City TX 77591
1969-011	Borbon, Pedro Rodriguez	Old Add: Urb Las Palmas Santo Domingo Dom Rep
1934-012	Bordagaray, Stanley George 'Frenchy'	395 Crestwood Avenue/Ventura CA 93003
1988-016	Borders, Patrick Lance	1135 South Lakeshore Blvd/Lake Wales FL 33853
1980-011	Bordi, Richard Albert	979 Golf Course Drive #187/Rohnert Park CA 94928
1990-019	Bordick, Michael Todd	1401 Labelle Avenue/Ruxton MD 21204
1980-011	Bordley, William Clarke	Old Add: 3605 West Hidden Ln #321 Palos Verdes CA 90274
1972-013	Borgmann, Glenn Dennis	16 Lundy Ter/Butler NJ 7405
1982-016	Boris, Paul Stanley	28 Sunnyside Lane/Hillsborough NJ 8876
1964-009	Bork, Frank Bernard	8488 Dunsinanne Lane/Dublin OH 43017
1950-012	Borkowski, Robert Vilarian	1031 Gerhard Street/Dayton OH 45404
1960-012	Borland, Thomas Bruce	624 Cherokee Dr/Stillwater OK 74074
1994-005	Borland, Toby Shawn	806 Corn Tassle Trail/Martinsville VA 24112
1944-012	Borom, Edward Jones 'Red'	827 Highland Oaks/Dallas TX 75232
1957-007	Boros, Stephen	1400 Grasslands Blvd #57/Lakeland FL 33803
1995-031	Borowski, Joseph Thomas	120 East Curtis Street/Linden NJ 7036
1942-014	Borowy, Henry Ludwig 'Hank'	Beacon Hill #9c Maryland Avenue/Pt. Pleasant Bch NJ 8742
1912-021	Borton, William Baker 'Babe'	D. July 29, 1954 Berkeley, Calif.
1966-009	Bosch, Donald John	14446 North State Hwy 3/Fort Jones CA 96032
1976-018	Bosetti, Richard Alan	%Paul Bosetti 1233 Hill Street Anderson CA 96007
1986-021	Bosio, Christopher Louis	Old Add: PO Box 690 Shingle Springs CA 95682
1990-020	Boskie, Shawn Kealoha	Old Add: 2110 Denio Drive Reno NV 89509
1977-013	Bosley, Thaddis	950 North Michigan Avenue #3604/Chicago IL 60611
1966-010	Bosman, Richard Allan	391 Whispering Lakes Blvd/Tarpon Springs FL 34689
1928-013	Boss, Elmer Harley	D. May 15, 1964 Nashville, Tenn.
1945-004	Bosser, Melvin Edward	D. March 26, 1986 Crossville, Tenn.
1915-013	Bostick, Henry Landers	D. September 16, 1968 Denver, Colo.
1975-018	Bostock, Lyman Wesley	D. September 24, 1978 Gary, Ind.
1984-008	Boston, Daryl Lamont	1016 Valley Lane/Cincinnati OH 45229
1964-010	Boswell, David Wilson	309 Roxbury CT Joppa MD 21085
1967-006	Boswell, Kenneth George	Old Add: PO Box 161954 Austin TX 78716
1982-017	Botelho, Derek Wayne	474 Northeast 4th Street/Boca Raton FL 33432
1994-006	Bottalico, Richard Paul 'Ricky'	37 Valley View Drive/Newington CT 6111
1937-012	Bottarini, John Charles	D. October 8, 1976 Spring, N. Mex.
1992-011	Bottenfield, Kent Dennis	12168 142nd Court North/Palm Beach Gardens FL 33418
1979-010	Botting, Ralph Wayne	7 Somerset/Dove Canyon CA 92679
1922-013	Bottomley, James Leroy	D. December 11, 1959 Saint Louis, Mo.
1962-017	Botz, Robert Allen	4592 Monches Rd/Colgate WI 53017

1956-010	Bouchee, Edward Francis	1621 East Tremaine Avenue/Gilbert AZ 85234
1914-023	Boucher, Alexander Francis	D. June 23, 1974 Torrance, Calif.
1991-018	Boucher, Denis	644 36th Avenue #201/Lachine Quebec H8T 3M1 Canada
1914-024	Boucher, Medric Charles Francis	D. March 12, 1974 Martinez, Calif.
1938-009	Boudreau, Louis	415 Cedar Lane/Frankfort IL 60423
1961-010	Bouldin, Carl Edward	40 Fairway Drive/Southgate KY 41071
1996-022	Bourgeois, Steven James	PO Box 143/Paulina LA 70763
1980-013	Bourjos, Christopher	14796 North 100th Place/Scottsdale AZ 85260
1992-012	Bournigal, Rafael Antonio	613 Butternut Place/Lakeland FL 33813
1971-014	Bourque, Patrick Daniel	2013 East Harvard Dr/Tempe AZ 85283
1962-018	Bouton, James Alan	265 Cedar Lane/Teaneck NJ 7666
1997-014	Bovee, Michael Craig	Old Add: Mira Mesa CA 92196
1970-012	Bowa, Lawrence Robert	1029 Morris Avenue/Bryn Mawr PA 19010
1914-025	Bowden, David Timon	D. October 25, 1949 Emory, Ga.
1919-009	Bowen, Emmons Joseph 'Chick'	D. August 9, 1948 New Haven, Conn.
1991-019	Bowen, Ryan Eugene	Old Add:/Hanford CA 93230
1977-014	Bowen, Samuel Thomas	8 High Hill Drive/Brunswick GA 31520
1963-013	Bowens, Samuel Edward	Rural Route 4 Box 27/National Avenue Leland NC 28451
1996-023	Bowers, Brent Raymond	Old Add: Bridgeview Il
1949-008	Bowers, Grover Bill	D. September 17, 1996 Wynne, Ark.
1997-015	Bowers, Shane Patrick	Old Add: Covina CA 91722
1935-006	Bowers, Stewart Cole	1620 Ridgway Road/Havertown PA 19083
1994-007	Bowie, James R.	620 Suisun Street/Suisun CA 94585
1931-009	Bowler, Grant Tierney	D. June 25, 1968 Denver, Colo.
1943-010	Bowles, Charles James	13 20th Avenue Northeast/Hickory NC 28601
1922-014	Bowles, Emmett Jerome	D. September 3, 1959 Flagstaff, Ariz.
1967-007	Bowlin, Lois Weldon 'Hoss'	Box 1026/Livingston AL 35470
1976-019	Bowling, Stephen Shaddon	Old Add: 1784 West 63rd St Tulsa OK 74132
1914-026	Bowman, Alvah Edson	D. October 11, 1979 Longview, Texas
1920-011	Bowman, Elmer Wilhelm	D. December 17, 1985 Los Angeles, Calif.
1961-011	Bowman, Ernest Ferrell 'Buddy'	Route 17, East Shore Apt #8/Johnson City TN 37601
1932-007	Bowman, Joseph Emil	D. November 22, 1990 Kansas City, Mo.
1939-013	Bowman, Robert James	D. September 4, 1972 Bluefield, W. Va.
1955-015	Bowman, Robert Leroy	702 West Mountain Ridge Road/Lake Almanor CA 96137
1949-009	Bowman, Roger Clinton	D. July 21, 1997 Los Angeles, Calif.
1910-011	Bowser, James Harvey 'Red'	D. May 22, 1943 Moundsville, W. Va.
1958-011	Bowsfield, Edward Oliver 'Ted'	PO Box 1492/Nipomo CA 93444
1982-018	Boyd, Dennis Ray Oil Can	1611 20th Street/Meridian MS 39301
1969-012	Boyd, Gary Lee	15308 Haas/Gardena CA 90249
1910-012	Boyd, Raymond C.	D. February 11, 1920 Houtonville, Ill.
1951-004	Boyd, Robert Richard	2811 North Vassar Avenue/Wichita KS 67220
1955-016	Boyer, Cletis Leroy	2034 20th Avenue Pkwy/Indian Rock Beach FL 33785
1949-010	Boyer, Cloyd Victor	14528 Country Road 210/Jasper MO 64755
1955-017	Boyer, Kenton Lloyd	D. September 7, 1982 St. Louis, Mo.
1978-014	Boyland, Dorian Scott 'Doe'	Old Add: 1205 18th Portland OR 97205
1926-008	Boyle, James John	D. December 24, 1958 Cincinnati, O.
1912-022	Boyle, John Bellew	D. April 3, 1971 Fort Lauderdale, Fla.
1929-010	Boyle, Ralph Francis 'Buzz'	D. November 12, 1978 Cincinnati, O.
1938-010	Boyles, Harry	101 Sioux Road #1473/Pharr TX 78577
1996-024	Boze, Marshall Wayne	Old Add: Soldotna Ak
1966-011	Brabender, Eugene Mathew	D. December 27, 1996 Madison, Wisc.
1937-013	Brack, Gilbert Herman 'Gib'	D. January 20, 1960 Greenville, Tex.
1964-011	Bradey, Donald Eugene	3686 Oakleaf Road/West Bloomfield MI 48324
1966-012	Bradford, Charles William 'Buddy'	6440 Spring Park Ave/Ladera Heights CA 90056
1943-011	Bradford, Henry Victor 'Vic'	D. June 10, 1994 Paris, Ky.
1977-015	Bradford, Larry	D. September 11, 1998 Atlanta, Ga.
1956-011	Bradford, William	Box 1343/Fairfield Bay AR 72088
1948-018	Bradley, Frederick Langdon	4540 South Layman Avenue/Pico Rivera CA 90660
1946-011	Bradley, George Washington	D. October 19, 1982 Lawrenceburg, Tenn.
1927-015	Bradley, Herbert Theodore	D. October 16, 1959 Clay Center, Kan.
1910-013	Bradley, Hugh Frederick	D. January 26, 1949 Worcester, Mass.
1916-007	Bradley, John Thomas	D. March 18, 1969 Tulsa, Okla.
1981-013	Bradley, Mark Allen	Old Add: 413 Pierce Street Elizabethtown KY 42701
1983-016	Bradley, Philip Poole	PO Box 491096/Key Biscayne FL 33149
1984-009	Bradley, Scott William	112 Murphy Drive/Pennington NJ 8534
1983-017	Bradley, Steven Bert 'Bert'	Rural Route 1/Toledo IL 62468
1969-013	Bradley, Thomas William	Old Add: 2800 University Blvd N/Jacksonville FL 32211
1917-010	Bradshaw, Dallas Carl	D. December 11, 1939 Herrin, Ill.
1952-012	Bradshaw, George Thomas	D. November 4, 1994 Hendersonville, N. C.
1929-011	Bradshaw, Joe Siah	D. January 30, 1985 Tavares, Fla.
1995-032	Bradshaw, Terry Leon	Old Add: %S.Bradshaw, Hwy 635 Zuni VA 23899
1989-019	Brady, Brian Phelan	67 School Street/Malverne NY 11565
1920-012	Brady, Clifford Francis	D. September 25, 1974 Belleville, Ill.
1915-014	Brady, Cornelius Joseph 'Neal'	D. June 19, 1947 Fort Mitchell, Ky.
1956-012	Brady, James Joseph	4454 Maywood Drive/Jacksonville FL 32211
1946-012	Brady, Robert Jay	D. April 22, 1996 Manchester, Conn.
1995-033	Brady, Stephen Douglas 'Doug'	831 Glastonbury Road #4119/Nashville TN 37217
1912-023	Brady, William A.	
1940-004	Bragan, Robert Randall	1901 Indian Creek Drive/Fort Worth TX 76107

1994-008 ....Bragg, Darren William ....Old Add: 264 Lyman Road Wolcott CT 06716
1986-022 ....Braggs, Glenn Erick ....Old Add: 2876 State Street San Bernardino CA 92405
1914-027 ....Brainard, Frederick.......................................D. April 17, 1959 Galveston, Tex.
1915-015 ....Braithwood, Alfred..D. November 24, 1960 Rowlesburg, W. Va.
1928-014 ....Brame, Ervin Beckham ....D. November 22, 1949 Hopkinsville, Ky.
1935-007 ....Bramhall, Arthur Washington ....D. September 4, 1985 Madison, Wis.
1944-013 ....Branca, Ralph Theodore Joseph ....Westchester Country Club/Rye NY 10580
1939-014 ....Brancato, Albert ....108 Green Valley Road/Upper Darby PA 19082
1962-019 ....Branch, Harvey Alfred...................................4995 Jolly Dr/Memphis TN 38101
1941-008 ....Branch, Norman Downs................................D. November 21, 1971 Navasota, Tex.
1979-011 ....Branch, Roy ....Old Add: 2925 Zacatecas Dri #25 Eagle Pass TX 78852
1963-014 ....Brand, Ronald George ....969 Keith Drive/Roseville CA 95661
1995-034 ....Brandenburg, Mark Clay ....%D.Brandenburg 9801 Cantertrot Humble TX 77338
1966-013 ....Brandon, Darrell ....Old Add: White Cliff Drive Plymouth MA 02360
1928-015 ....Brandt, Edward Arthur ....D. November 1, 1944 Spokane, Wash.
1956-013 ....Brandt, John George ....611 Osage Drive/Papillion NE 68046
1941-009 ....Brandt, William George ....D. May 16, 1968 Fort Wayne, Ind.
1928-016 ....Brannan, Otis Owen ....D. June 6, 1967 Little Rock, Ark.
1927-016 ....Branom, Edgar Dudley 'Dud'........................D. February 4, 1980 Sun City, Ariz.
1992-013 ....Branson, Jeffrey Glenn ....208 S. Mulberry,%Jw Cowan/Butlr AL 36904
1996-027 ....Brant, Brown Michael ....Old Add: Porterville CA 93258
1980-014 ....Brant, Marshall Lee ....604 Scotland Drive/Santa Rosa CA 95409
1991-020 ....Brantley, Clifford ....42 Morningstar Road/Staten Island NY 10303
1988-017 ....Brantley, Jeffrey Hoke ....300 Monterey Drive/Clinton MS 39056
1986-023 ....Brantley, Michael Charles 'Mickey'............3089 Southwest Ventura Street/Port Saint Locie FL 34953
1921-008 ....Bratche, Frederick Oscar ....D. January 7, 1962 Massillon, O.
1924-013 ....Bratcher, Joseph Warlick ....D. October 13, 1977 Fort Worth, Tex.
1964-012 ....Braun, John Paul ....2835 Unicornio Street #B/Carlsbad CA 92009
1971-015 ....Braun, Stephen Russell ....PO Box 55/Titusville NJ 8560
1969-014 ....Bravo, Angel Alfonso ....Old Add: Calle Camino Nuevo #208 Aracaibo Venezuela
1921-009 ....Braxton, Edgar Garland ....D. February 25, 1966 Norflok, Va.
1941-010 ....Bray, Clarence Wilbur 'Buster' ....D. September 4, 1982 Evansville, Ind.
1921-010 ....Brazill, Frank Leo ....D. November 3, 1976 Oakland, Calif.
1943-012 ....Brazle, Alpha Eugene ....D. October 24, 1973 Grand Junction, Col.
1983-018 ....Bream, Sidney Eugene ....115 Sable Run/Zelienope PA 16063
1969-015 ....Breazeale, James Leo ....717 Bolling Lane/Houston TX 77076
1940-005 ....Brecheen, Harry David ....1134 South Highschool/Ada OK 74820
1929-012 ....Breckinridge, William Robertson ....D. August 23, 1958 Tulsa, Okla.
1996-025 ....Brede, Brent David ....660 West Second/Trenton IL 62293
1969-016 ....Breeden, Danny Richard ....111/B Avenue/Loxley AL 36551
1971-016 ....Breeden, Harold Noel ....Rr1 Box 311/Leesburg GA 31763
1960-013 ....Breeding, Marvin Eugene ....302 Quailwood Lane/Decatur AL 35603
1980-015 ....Breining, Fred Lawrence ....1218 33rd Ave/San Francisco CA 94122
1937-014 ....Bremer, Herbert Frederick ....D. November 28, 1979 Columbus, Ga.
1914-028 ....Brenegan, Olaf Selmar ....D. April 20, 1956 Galesville, Wis.
1981-014 ....Brenly, Robert Earl ....9726 East Laurel Lane/Scottsdale AZ 85260
1910-014 ....Brennan, Addison Foster ....D. January 7, 1962 Kansas City, Mo.
1933-007 ....Brennan, James Donald 'Don' ....D. April 26, 1953 Boston, Mass.
1981-015 ....Brennan, Thomas Martin ....10701 South Keating Avenue #2c/Oak Lawn IL 60453
1988-018 ....Brennan, William Raymond ....127 Huntington Place/Macon GA 31210
1965-013 ....Brenneman, James Leroy ....Old Add: 1855 East Rose #12a/Orange CA 92667
1912-024 ....Brenner, Delbert Henry ....D. April 11, 1971 St. Louis Park, Minn.
1913-017 ....Brenton, Lynn Davis ....D. October 14, 1968 Los Angeles, Calif.
1932-008 ....Brenzel, William Richard ....D. June 12, 1979 Oakland, Calif.
1914-029 ....Bressler, Raymond Bloom 'Rube' ....D. November 7, 1966 Mt. Washington, O.
1956-014 ....Bressoud, Edward Francis ....515 Marble Canyon Lane/San Ramon CA 94583
1913-018 ....Breton, John Frederick 'Jim'.......................D. May 30, 1973 Beloit, Wis.
1973-013 ....Brett, George Howard ....PO Box 419969/Kansas City MO 64141
1924-014 ....Brett, Herbert James ....D. November 25, 1974 St Petersburg, Fla.
1967-008 ....Brett, Kenneth Allen ....PO Box 138/Cayucos CA 93430
1939-015 ....Breuer, Marvin Howard ....D. January 17, 1991 Rolla, Mo.
1984-010 ....Brewer, Anthony Bruce ....2260 Brentwood Court/East Palo Alto CA 94303
1944-014 ....Brewer, Jack Herndon ....28271 West Worcester Road/Sun City CA 92586
1960-014 ....Brewer, James Thomas ....D. November 16, 1987 Tyler, Texas
1986-024 ....Brewer, Michael Quinn ....40 Armhurst/Menlo Park CA 94025
1990-021 ....Brewer, Rodney Lee ....931 N. State Rd 434 #1201-359/Altamonte Springs FL 32714
1954-009 ....Brewer, Thomas Austin ....409 State Rd/Cheraw SC 29520
1993-018 ....Brewer, William Robert Billy ....7405 Woodway Drive/Waco TX 76712
1995-035 ....Brewington, Jamie Chancellor ....300 Woodside Road/Greenville NC 27834
1943-013 ....Brewster, Charles Lawrence ....2844 Ware Street/Blackshear GA 31516
1961-012 ....Brice, Alan Healey ....7121 River Club Blvd/Bradenton FL 34202
1958-012 ....Brickell, Fritz Darrell ....D. October 15, 1965 Wichita, Kan.
1926-009 ....Brickell, George Frederick 'Fred' ....D. April 8, 1961 Wichita, Kan.
1913-019 ....Brickley, George Vincent ....D. February 23, 1947 Everett, Mass.
1952-013 ....Brickner, Ralph Harold ....D. May 9, 1994 Bridgetown, Oho
1951-005 ....Brideweser, James Ehrenfeld ....D. August 25, 1989 El Toro, Calif.
1951-006 ....Bridges, Everett Lamar 'Rocky' ....2927 Julia Street #59/Coeur D'Alene ID 83814
1959-007 ....Bridges, Marshall ....D. September 3, 1990 Jackson, Miss.
1930-005 ....Bridges, Thomas Jefferson Davis ....D. April 19, 1968 Nashville, Tenn.

1912-025	Brief, Anthony Vincent 'Bunny'	D. February 10, 1963 Milwaukee, Wis.
1975-019	Briggs, Daniel Lee	231 France St/Sonoma CA 95476
1964-013	Briggs, John Edward	99 Rutledge Avenue/East Orange NJ 7017
1956-015	Briggs, John Tift	Old Add: 8724 Sherry Drive/Orangevale CA 95662
1958-013	Bright, Harry James	2048 50th Ave/Sacramento CA 95827
1965-014	Briles, Nelson Kelley	1324 Clearview Drive/Greensburg PA 15501
1988-019	Briley, Gregory	Rural Route 5 Box 141/Greenville NC 27834
1922-015	Brillheart, James Benson	D. September 2, 1972 Radford, Va.
1992-014	Brink, Bradford Albert	3409 Wycliffe Drive/Modesto CA 95355
1912-026	Brinker, William Hutchinson	D. February 5, 1965 Arcadia, Calif.
1969-017	Brinkman, Charles Ernest	11849 Williams County Road/Bryan OH 43506
1961-013	Brinkman, Edwin Albert	PO Box 58620/Cincinnati OH 45258
1952-014	Brinkopf, Leon Clarence	D. July 2, 1998 Cape Girardeau, Mo.
1991-021	Briscoe, John Eric	3310 Jacquelyn Terrace/Duncan OK 73533
1947-013	Brissie, Leland Victor 'Lou'	1908 Whitepine Drive/North Augusta Sc/29841
1966-014	Bristol, James David 'Dave'	1748 Fairview Road/Andrews NC 28901
1992-015	Brito, Bernardo (Perez)	B #90 Sabana Palenque Dominican Rep.
1995-036	Brito, Jorge Michael	%Tomas Brito 308 Mart St SW Decatur AL 35601
1996-026	Brito, Tilson Manuel	Old Add: Santo Domingo Dom. Rep.
1937-015	Brittain, August Schuster	D. February 16, 1974 Wilmington, N. C.
1950-013	Brittin, John Albert	D. January 5, 1994 Springfield, Ill.
1967-009	Britton, James Alan	825 Forestwalk Drive/Suwanee GA 30174
1913-020	Britton, Stephen Gilbert	D. June 20, 1983 Parsons, Kan.
1979-012	Brizzolara, Anthony John	1638 Princess Cir NE/Atlanta GA 30345
1934-013	Broaca, John Joseph	D. May 16, 1985 Lawrence, Mass.
1971-017	Broberg, Peter Sven	220 Monterey Rd/Palm Beach FL 33480
1992-016	Brocail, Douglas Keith	253 West Hahns Peak Avenue/Pueblo West CO 81007
1982-019	Brock, Gregory Allen	201 South 46th Street/Milwaukee WI 53214
1917-011	Brock, John Ray	D. October 27, 1951 Clayton, Mo.
1961-014	Brock, Louis Clark	PO Box 28398/Saint Louis MO 63146
1997-016	Brock, Terrence Christopher 'Chris'	222 Adelaide Drive/Altamonte Springs FL 32701
1952-015	Brodowski, Richard Stanley	82 Clark Street/Lynn MA 1902
1959-008	Broglio, Ernest Gilbert	2838 Via Carmen/San Jose CA 95124
1992-017	Brogna, Rico Joseph	The Taft School/Watertown CT 6795
1972-014	Brohamer, John Anthony 'Jack'	39017 Narcissus Drive/Palm Desert CA 92211
1944-015	Brondell, Kenneth Leroy	7029 Decelis Place/Van Nuys CA 91406
1993-019	Bronkey, Jacob Jeffrey 'Jeff'	622 Sunny Brook Drive/Edmond OK 73034
1910-015	Bronkie, Herman Charles	D. May 27, 1968 Somers, Conn.
1959-009	Bronstad, James Warren	693 Quail Ridge Road/Aledo TX 76008
1975-020	Brookens, Edward Dwain 'Ike'	1053 Brookens Road/Fayetteville PA 17222
1979-013	Brookens, Thomas Dale	488 Black Gap Road/Fayetteville PA 17222
1980-016	Brooks, Hubert	15001 Olive Street/Hesperia CA 92345
1993-020	Brooks, Jerome Edward	4600 Onondaga Blvd #16/Syracuse NY 13219
1925-011	Brooks, Jonathan Joseph 'Mandy'	D. June 17, 1962 Kirkwood, Mo.
1969-018	Brooks, Robert	D. October 11, 1994 Harbor City, Calif.
1991-022	Brosius, Scott David	1187 SE 48th Avenue/Milwaukie OR 97222
1940-006	Broskie, Sigmund Theodore	D. May 17, 1975 Canton, O.
1954-010	Brosnan, James Patrick	7742 West Churchill Street/Morton Grove IL 60053
1991-023	Bross, Terrance Paul	Old Add: Bridgewater NJ 08807
1969-019	Brosseau, Franklin Lee	41 Island Road/Saint Paul MN 55127
1916-008	Brottem, Anton Christian 'Tony'	D. August 5, 1929 Chicago, Ill.
1980-017	Brouhard, Mark Steven	6289 Jackie Ave/Woodland Hills CA 91367
1955-018	Brovia, Joseph John	D. August 15, 1994 Santa Cruz, Calif.
1993-021	Brow, Scott John	616 NE Sundance Court/Hillsboro OR 97124
1920-013	Brower, Frank Willard	D. November 20, 1960 Baltimore, Md.
1931-010	Brower, Louis Lester	D. March 4, 1994 Tyler, Texas
1986-025	Brower, Robert Richard	123 South Dickenson Avenue/Sterling VA 20164
1997-017	Brown, Adrian Demond	Old Add: Summit MS 39666
1951-007	Brown, Alton Leo	253 Consul Avenue/Virginia Beach VA 23462
1911-017	Brown, Carroll William 'Boardwalk'	D. February 8, 1977 Burlington, N. J.
1911-018	Brown, Charles Roy 'Curly'	D. June 10, 1968 Spring Hill, Kan.
1928-017	Brown, Clinton Harold	D. December 31, 1955 Rocky River,O.
1973-014	Brown, Curtis	201 Arbor Crest Way/Sacramento CA 95838
1983-019	Brown, Curtis Steven	Old Add: 104 E. Hemingway Cir Coconut Creek FL 33063
1981-016	Brown, Darrell Wayne	Old Add: 5843 Fifth Avenue Los Angeles CA 90043
1914-030	Brown, Delos Hight	D. December 21, 1964 Carbondale, Ill.
1915-016	Brown, Donald	Old Add: 712 Ellas Street Beatrice NE 68310
1913-021	Brown, Drummond Nicol	D. January 27, 1927 Platte Co., Mo.
1920-014	Brown, Edward William	D. September 10, 1956 Vallejo, Calif.
1969-020	Brown, Edwin Randolph 'Randy'	Old Add: PO Box 940103 Maitland FL 32794
1911-019	Brown, Elmer Young	D. January 23, 1955 Indianapolis, Ind.
1997-018	Brown, Emil Quincy	Old Add: Chicago IL 60601
1951-008	Brown, Hector Harold 'Hal'	4216 Henderson Road/Greensboro NC 27410
1969-021	Brown, Isaac Ike	Lincoln CT #A-4/Lakeland FL 33805
1970-013	Brown, Jackie Gene	Rr 3 Box 50b/Holdenville OK 74848
1986-026	Brown, James Kevin 'Kevin'	R Sims Road/McIntyre GA 31054
1937-016	Brown, James Roberson	D. December 29, 1977 Bath, N. C.
1991-024	Brown, Jarvis Ardel	Old Add: 2314 Joppa Avenue #2 Zion IL 60099
1975-021	Brown, Jerald Ray 'Jake'	D. December 18, 1981 Houston, Texas

1984-011	Brown, John Christopher	5015 Brighton Ave/Los Angeles CA 90062
1937-017	Brown, John Lindsay	D. January 1, 1967 San Antonio, Tex.
1968-010	Brown, Jophery Clifford	3008 West 81st St/Inglewood CA 90305
1927-017	Brown, Joseph Henry	D. March 7, 1950 Los Angeles, Calif.
1988-020	Brown, Keith Edward	3760 Northridge Drive/Concord CA 94518
1990-022	Brown, Kevin Dewayne	Old Add: 1004 Rogers Street Broderick CA 95605
1996-028	Brown, Kevin Lee	Old Add: Winslow IN 47598
1963-015	Brown, Larry Lesley	13158 Lamirada Circle/West Palm Beach FL 33414
1976-020	Brown, Leon	7537 South Larosa/Tempe AZ 85283
1925-012	Brown, Lloyd Andrew	D. January 14, 1974 Opalocka, Fla.
1935-008	Brown, Mace Stanley	305 North Holden Road/Greensboro NC 27410
1984-012	Brown, Mark Anthony	Old Add: 59 Church Street North Walpole NH 03608
1988-021	Brown, Marty Leo	711 Southview Drive/Rolla MO 65401
1983-020	Brown, Michael Charles	Old Add: 312 Copco Lane San Jose CA 95123
1982-020	Brown, Michael Gary	8712 Pine Needles CT Vienna VA 22180
1922-016	Brown, Myrl Lincoln	D. February 23, 1981 Harrisburg, Pa.
1943-014	Brown, Norman	D. May 31, 1995 Bennettsville, S. C.
1965-015	Brown, Ollie Lee	8462 Country Club Dr/Buena Park CA 90621
1969-022	Brown, Oscar Lee	19113 Gunlock Ave/Carson CA 90746
1961-015	Brown, Paul Dwayne	Rural Route 4 Box 244/Holdenville OK 74848
1957-008	Brown, Richard Ernest	D. April 12, 1970 Baltimore, Md.
1930-006	Brown, Robert Murray	D. August 3, 1990 Pembroke, Mass.
1946-013	Brown, Robert William	4100 Clark Avenue/Fort Worth TX 76107
1979-014	Brown, Rogers Lee 'Bobby'	1460 Contillion Blvd/Mays Landing NJ 8330
1981-017	Brown, Scott Edward	1238 Alton Pierce Road/Dequincy LA 70633
1983-021	Brown, Stephen Elbert	1203 West 8th Street/Davis CA 95616
1978-018	Brown, Thomas Dale	Old Add: PO Box 230 Hagerstown MD 21741
1944-016	Brown, Thomas Michael	8119 Shady Place/Brentwood/Tn 37027
1963-016	Brown, Thomas William	27981 Nanticoke Road/Salisbury MD 21801
1925-013	Brown, Walter George 'Jumbo'	D. October 2, 1966 Freeport, N. Y.
1947-014	Brown, Walter Irving	D. February 3, 1991 Westfield, N. Y.
1947-015	Brown, Willard Jesse	D. August 8, 1996 Houston, Texas
1963-017	Brown, William James 'Gates'	17206 Santa Barbara/Detroit MI 48221
1912-027	Brown, William Verna	D. May 15, 1965 Lubbock, Tex.
1965-016	Browne, Byron Ellis	Old Add: 3421 W. Dunlap Ave #226 Phoenix AZ 85051
1935-009	Browne, Earl James	D. January 12, 1993 Whittier, Calif.
1986-027	Browne, Jerome Austin	2a Prince Street/Christiansted VI 820
1962-020	Browne, Prentice Almont 'Pidge'	D. June 3, 1997 Houston, Texas
1960-015	Browning, Calvin Duane	713 South 18th Street/Clinton OK 73601
1910-016	Browning, Frank	D. May 19, 1948 San Antonio, Tex.
1984-013	Browning, Thomas Leo	Old Add: 710 Hurstborne Ln Edgewood KY 41017
1967-010	Brubaker, Bruce Ellsworth	322 West Fourth Street/Owensboro KY 42301
1932-009	Brubaker, Wilbur Lee 'Bill'	D. April 2, 1978 Laguna Hills, Calif.
1959-010	Bruce, Robert James	16635 Huebner Road/San Antonio TX 78248
1961-016	Bruckbauer, Fred John	5589 Byrneland/Madison WI 53711
1948-019	Brucker, Earle Francis	629 Mundy Terrace/El Cajon CA 92020
1937-018	Brucker, Earle Francis, Sr.	D. May 8, 1981 San Diego, Calif.
1992-018	Bruett, Joseph Timothy 'J.T.'	Minnesota Baseball 516 15th Avenue SE Minneapolis MN 55455
1921-011	Bruggy, Frank Leo	D. April 5, 1959 Elizabeth, N. J.
1978-019	Bruhert, Michael Edwin	Athletic Dept. Fordham University Bronx NY 10458
1992-019	Brumfield, Jacob Darnell	43275 Tillman Drive/Hammond LA 70403
1987-013	Brumley, Anthony Michael	8177 South Harvard Avenue #333/Tulsa OK 74137
1994-009	Brumley, Duff Lechaun	131 Eagle Drive Nw/Cleveland TN 37312
1964-014	Brumley, Tony Mike 'Mike'	8177 South Harvard Avenue #333/Tulsa OK 74137
1981-018	Brummer, Glenn Edward	2243 Springrain Drive/Clearwater FL 34623
1993-022	Brummett, Gregory Scott	5712 Bentgrass Court/Monroe NC 28110
1981-019	Brunansky, Thomas Andrew	13411 Summit Circle/Poway CA 92064
1949-011	Bruner, Jack Raymond	1641 North 76th/Street/Lincoln NE 68505
1939-016	Bruner, Walter Roy	D. November 30, 1986 St. Matthews, Ky.
1956-016	Brunet, George Stuart	D. October 25, 1991 Poza Rica, Mexico
1976-021	Bruno, Thomas Michael	Old Add: 8887 West Yale Avenue Denver CO 80227
1966-015	Brunsberg, Arlo Adolph	883 104th Lane Nw/Coon Rapids MN 55433
1995-037	Bruske, James Scott	Old Add: Palmdale CA
1977-016	Brusstar, Warren Scott	3320 Redwood Rd/Napa CA 94558
1953-013	Bruton, William Haron	D. December 5, 1995 Wilmington, Del.
1961-017	Bryan, Billy Ronald	3001 Hickory Lane/Opelika AL 36801
1935-010	Bryant, Claiborne Henry	1046 Aloha Way/Lady Lake FL 32159
1979-015	Bryant, Derek Russell	Old Add: C-12 Cooperstown Lexington KY 40508
1966-016	Bryant, Donald Ray	1844 Swiss Oaks Street/Jacksonville FL 32259
1985-007	Bryant, Ralph Wendell	Old Add: Rural Route 4 Box 374 Leesburg GA 31763
1967-011	Bryant, Ronald Raymond	2318 Shire Lane/Davis CA 95616
1986-028	Bryden, Thomas Ray 'T. R.'	320 Chinook Avenue #B1/Enumclaw WA 98022
1970-014	Brye, Stephen Robert	621 South Spring Street #603/Los Angeles CA 90014
1922-017	Bubser, Harold Fred	D. June 22, 1959 Melrose Park, Ill.
1948-020	Bucha, John George	D. April 28, 1996 Bethlehem, Pa.
1985-008	Buchanan, Robert Gordon	2035 Bever Avenue SE/Cedar Rapids IA 52403
1961-018	Buchek, Gerald Peter	%J.P. Buchek 3950a Wilmington Saint Louis MO 63116
1934-014	Bucher, James Quinter	207 Gravel Hill Road/Palmyra PA 17078
1994-010	Buckels, Gary Scott	2529 Sandalwood Court/Anaheim CA 92806

1918-007	Buckeye, Garland Maiers	D. November 14, 1975 Stone Lake, Wis.
1916-009	Buckles, Jess Robert	D. August 2, 1975 Westminster, Calif.
1984-014	Buckley, Kevin John	34 Calvin St/Braintree MA 2184
1969-023	Buckner, William Joseph	4405 East Wild Horse Lane/Boise ID 83712
1978-020	Budaska, Mark David	2306 North Lamer Street/Burbank CA 91504
1956-017	Buddin, Donald Thomas	27 Harvest Court/Greenville SC 29601
1946-014	Budnick, Michael Joe	307 West Blaine/Seattle WA 98119
1985-009	Buechele, Steven Bernard	PO Box 3273/Wrightwood CA 92397
1913-022	Bues, Arthur Frederick	D. November 7, 1954 Whitefish Bay, Wis.
1993-023	Buford, Damon Jackson	15412 Valley Vista Blvd/Sherman Oaks CA 91403
1963-018	Buford, Donald Alvin	% Baysox PO Box 1661 Bowie MD 20717
1953-014	Buhl, Robert Ray	26 Laurel Oak Drive/Winter Haven FL 33880
1987-014	Buhner, Jay Campbell	1420 Nw Gilman Blvd #2666/Issaquah WA 98027
1987-015	Buice, Dewayne Allison	PO Box 5185/Incline Village NV 89450
1945-005	Buker, Cyril Owen	108 Central Avenue/Greenwood WI 54437
1954-011	Bullard, George Donald	7 Dyer Court/Danvers MA 1923
1991-025	Bullett, Scott Douglas	220 Vicky Bullett Street/Martinsburg WV 25401
1977-017	Bulling, Terry Charles 'Bud'	327977 North Hwy 2/Newport WA 99156
1992-020	Bullinger, James Eric	2504 Elise Avenue/Metairie LA 70003
1985-010	Bullock, Eric Jerald	9501 West Sahara #1115/Las Vegas NV 89117
1936-011	Bullock, Malton Joseph	D. June 27, 1988 Pascagoula, Miss.
1972-015	Bumbry, Alonzo Benjamin	28 Tremblant CT Lutherville MD 21093
1995-038	Bunch, Melvin Lynn	Rural Route 13/Texarkana TX 75501
1963-019	Bunker, Wallace Edward	Rural Route 1 Box 182/Lowell OH 45744
1955-019	Bunning, James Paul David	1717 Dixie Highway #180/Fort Wright KY 41011
1990-023	Burba, David Allen	4227 Carona/Springfield OH 45503
1969-024	Burbach, William David	Box 3/Dickeyville WI 53808
1955-020	Burbrink, Nelson Edward	9895 88th Way North/Seminole FL 33377
1969-025	Burchart, Larry Wayne	8308 East 109th Street/Tulsa OK 74133
1962-021	Burda, Edward Robert 'Bob'	Old Add: 6100 E. Camelback Rd #45 Scottsdale AZ 85251
1962-022	Burdette, Freddie Thomason	1200 Kingston CT #G5/Albany GA 31707
1950-014	Burdette, Selva Lewis 'Lou'	2019 Beneva Road/Sarasota FL 34232
1910-017	Burg, Joseph Peter	D. April 28, 1969 Joliet, Ill.
1949-012	Burgess, Forrest Harrill 'Smoky'	D. September 15, 1991 Asheville, N. C.
1954-012	Burgess, Thomas Roland	97 Sunray Avenue/London Ontario N6P 1C6 Canada
1968-011	Burgmeier, Thomas Henry	13118 Walmer/Overland Park KS 66209
1943-015	Burgo, William Ross	D. October 19, 1988 Morgan City, La.
1993-024	Burgos, Enrique	Old Add: Calle Quinta Vista Alegre Arrajian Panama City
1942-015	Burich, William Max	1175 Lamoree Road #62/San Marcos CA 92069
1910-018	Burk, Charles Sanford	D. October 11, 1934 Brooklyn, N.Y.
1956-018	Burk, Mack Edwin	5710 Glen Pines/Houston TX 77069
1915-017	Burkam, Chauncey Depew	D. May 9, 1964 Kalamazoo, Mich.
1936-012	Burkart, Elmer Robert	D. February 6, 1995 Baltimore, Md.
1976-022	Burke, Glenn Lawrence	D. May 30, 1995 Oakland, Calif.
1996-029	Burke, John C.	Old Add: Highlands Ranch CO 80126
1958-014	Burke, Leo Patrick	1729 Woodburn Drive/Hagerstown MD 21742
1923-016	Burke, Leslie Kingston	D. May 6, 1975 Danvers, Mass.
1924-015	Burke, Patrick Edward	D. July 7, 1965 St. Louis, Mo.
1927-018	Burke, Robert James	D. February 8, 1971 Joliet, Ill.
1977-018	Burke, Steven Michael	4656 Hibiscus Rd/Stockton CA 95205
1985-011	Burke, Timothy Philip	3691 North 150/West Columbia City, IN 46725
1910-019	Burke, William Ignatius	D. February 9, 1967 Worcester, Mass.
1987-016	Burkett, John David	104 Crandon Circle/Beaver PA 15009
1945-006	Burkhart, William Kenneth 'Ken'	3708 Splendor Drive, Rr 7/Knoxville TN 37918
1987-017	Burks, Ellis Rena	4924 South Elizabeth/Englewood/Co 80110
1974-013	Burleson, Richard Paul 'Rick'	241 East Country Hills Drive/Lahabra CA 90631
1927-019	Burnett, John Henderson	D. August 12, 1959 Tampa, Fla.
1956-019	Burnette, Wallace Harper	6112 Spring Garden Road/Blairs VA 24527
1993-025	Burnitz, Jeromy Neal	119 Brian Road/Marathon FL 33050
1923-017	Burns, Dennis	D. May 21, 1969 Tulsa, Okla.
1912-028	Burns, Edward James	D. June 1, 1942 Monterey, Calif.
1914-032	Burns, George Henry	D. January 7, 1978 Kirkland, Wash.
1911-020	Burns, George Joseph	D. August 15, 1966 Gloversville, N.Y.
1930-007	Burns, John Irving	D. April 18, 1975 Boston, Mass.
1910-020	Burns, Joseph Francis	D. July 12, 1987 Beverly, Mass.
1924-016	Burns, Joseph Francis	D. January 7, 1986 Trenton, N. J.
1943-016	Burns, Joseph James	D. June 24, 1974 Bryn Mawr, Pa.
1978-021	Burns, Robert Britt 'Britt'	5911 Bark Lane/Birmingham AL 35244
1988-022	Burns, Todd Eric	1210 West Sharon Lane/Schaumburg IL 60193
1955-021	Burnside, Peter Willits	1945 Chestnut/Wilmette IL 60091
1978-022	Burnside, Sheldon John	Old Add: 4351 Bloor St #34 Etobicke Ont. M9c 2a4 Can.
1946-015	Burpo, George Harvie	8981 East Palms Drive/Tucson AZ 85715
1914-033	Burr, Alexander Thomson	D. November 1, 1918 France
1962-023	Burright, Larry Allen	1239 East Palm Dr/Glendora CA 91740
1973-015	Burris, Bertram Ray 'Ray'	2304 Woodsong Trail/Arlington TX 76016
1948-021	Burris, Paul Robert	12816 Mayes Road/Huntersville NC 28078
1970-015	Burroughs, Jeffrey Alan	6155 Laguna CT Long Beach CA 90803
1943-017	Burrows, John	D. April 27, 1987 Coal Run, O.
1994-011	Burrows, Terry Dale	7019 Burgundy Drive/Lake Charles LA 70605

1919-010 ....Burrus, Maurice Lennon 'Dick' ....D. December 2, 1972 Elizabeth City, N. C.
1958-015 ....Burton, Ellis Narrington ....Old Add: Rural Route Ss Apple Valley CA 92307
1975-022 ....Burton, Jim Scott ....7716 England Street #B/Charlotte NC 28273
1950-015 ....Burtschy, Edward Frank ....519 Montview Court/Cincinnati OH 45238
1985-012 ....Burtt, Dennis Allen ....135 West Stadium Drive/Stockton CA 95204
1960-016 ....Burwell, Richard Matthew ....PO Box 1825/Twin Falls ID 83301
1920-015 ....Burwell, William Edwin ....D. June 11, 1973 Ormond Beach, Fla.
1950-016 ....Busby, James Franklin ....D. July 8, 1996 Augusta, Ga.
1996-030 ....Busby, Michael J. ....Old Add: Wilmington CA 90744
1941-011 ....Busby, Paul Miller ....2011 35th Avenue/Meridian MS 39301
1972-016 ....Busby, Steven Lee ....Old Add: Box 783 Blue Springs Mo
1943-018 ....Busch, Edgar John ....D. January 17, 1987 Shiloh Valley Twp,St. Clair Co,Ill.
1995-039 ....Busch, Michael Anthony ....804 8th Street Court/Donahue IA 52746
1965-017 ....Buschhorn, Donald Lee ....17804 East 26th St/Independence MO 64057
1923-018 ....Bush, Guy Terrell ....D. July 2, 1985 Shannon, Miss.
1997-019 ....Bush, Homer Giles ....Old Add: East Saint Louis IL 62201
1912-029 ....Bush, Leslie Ambrose 'Joe' ....D. November 1, 1974 Fort Lauderdale, Fla.
1982-021 ....Bush, Robert Randall 'Randy' ....Old Add: 38 Olympic Court New Orleans LA 70114
1927-020 ....Bushey, Francis Clyde ....D. March 18, 1972 Topeka, Kan.
1993-026 ....Bushing, Christopher Shawn ....1383 Vera Cruz Lane/Fort Lauderdale FL 33327
1926-010 ....Buskey, Joseph Henry ....D. April 11, 1949 Cumberland, Md.
1977-019 ....Buskey, Michael T. ....2 Blackhawk/Coto De Caza CA 92671
1973-016 ....Buskey, Thomas William ....476 Allegheny Dr/Harrisburg PA 17111
1971-018 ....Busse, Raymond Edward ....4265 Lemon Street/Cocoa FL 32926
1936-013 ....Butcher, Albert Maxwell 'Max' ....D. September 15, 1957 Logan, W. Va.
1911-021 ....Butcher, Henry Josdph ....D. December 28, 1979 Hazel Crest, Ill.
1980-018 ....Butcher, John Daniel ....820 Woodridge Drive South/Chaska MN 55318
1992-021 ....Butcher, Michael Dana ....1211 48th Avenue #36/East Moline IL 61244
1980-019 ....Butera, Salvatore Philip ....324 Tersas Court/Lake Mary FL 32746
1943-019 ....Butka, Edward Luke ....131 West College Street/Canonsburg PA 15317
1940-007 ....Butland, Wilburn Rue 'Bill' ....D. September 19, 1997 Terre Haute, Ind.
1911-022 ....Butler, Arthur Edward ....D. October 7, 1984 Fall River, Mass.
1981-020 ....Butler, Brett Morgan ....315 Longvue Court/Duluth GA 30097
1962-024 ....Butler, Cecil Dean ....5126 Hickory Gap/Dallas GA 30132
1933-008 ....Butler, Charles Thomas ....D. May 10, 1964 Brunswick, Ga.
1926-011 ....Butler, John Stephen ....D. April 29, 1967 Long Beach, Calif.
1997-020 ....Butler, Richard Dwight ....Old Add: Toronto Ontario
1993-027 ....Butler, Robert Frank John 'Rob' ....Old Add: 27 Barrington Ave Toronto Ontario M4c 4y6
1969-026 ....Butler, William Franklin ....PO Box 51/Stephens City VA 22655
1962-025 ....Butters, Thomas Arden ....46 Appleton Pl/Durham NC 27705
1938-011 ....Buxton, Ralph Stanley ....D. January 6, 1988 San Leandro, Calif.
1945-007 ....Buzas, Joseph John ....PO Box 4108/Salt Lake City UT 84110
1958-016 ....Buzhardt, John William ....37 Brinton Hite Road/Prosperity SC 29127
1943-020 ....Byerly, Eldred William 'Bud' ....8611 Sappington Road/Saint Louis MO 63126
1987-018 ....Byers, Randell Parker ....PO Box 1721/Bridgeton NJ 8302
1950-017 ....Byrd, Harry Gladwin ....D. May 14, 1985 Darlington, S. C.
1993-028 ....Byrd, James Edward ....511 Woodridge Drive/Lawton OK 73507
1977-020 ....Byrd, Jeffrey Alan ....12672 Shayann Lane/Lakeside CA 92040
1995-040 ....Byrd, Paul Gregory ....%Greg Byrd 3812 Shannon Run Tr Louisville KY 40299
1929-013 ....Byrd, Samuel Dewey ....D. May 11, 1981 Mesa, Ariz.
1929-014 ....Byrne, Gerald Wilford ....D. August 11, 1955 Lansing, Mich.
1943-021 ....Byrne, Thomas Joseph ....617 Shinetown Lane/Wake Forest NC 27587
1943-022 ....Byrnes, Milton John ....D. February 1, 1979 St. Louis, Mo.
1980-020 ....Bystrom, Martin Eugene ....PO Box 26/Geigertown PA 19523
1944-017 ....Caballero, Ralph Joseph 'Putsy' ....6773 Milne Street/New Orleans LA 70119
1972-017 ....Cabell, Enos Milton ....4103 Frost Lake Court/Missouri City TX 77459
1913-023 ....Cabrera, Alfredo ....D./Havana, Cuba
1989-020 ....Cabrera, Francisco (Paulino) ....Old Add: H.Mirabol, Villa K9 Atras "Dela Viesa Hab #128,Sto Domingo Dr'
1997-021 ....Cabrera, Jose Alberto ....Old Add: Santiago Dom. Rep.
1997-022 ....Cabrera, Orlando Luis ....Old Add: Cartagena Colombia
1977-021 ....Cacek, Craig ....909 6th Street #3/Santa Monica CA 90403
1995-041 ....Caceres, Edgar F. ....Old Add: Barquisimeto Venezuela
1987-019 ....Cadaret, Gregory James ....6408 Black Butte Road/Shingletown CA 96088
1915-018 ....Cadore, Leon Joseph ....D. March 16, 1958 Spokane, Wash.
1912-030 ....Cady, Forrest Leroy 'Hick' ....D. March 3, 1946 Cedar Rapids, Ia.
1937-019 ....Cafego, Thomas ....D. October 29, 1961 Detroit, Mich.
1956-020 ....Caffie, Joseph Clifford ....PO Box 1932/Warren OH 44482
1978-023 ....Cage, Wayne Levell ....121 Cage Road/Choudrant LA 71227
1968-012 ....Cain, Leslie ....Old Add: 3804 Ohio Avenue/Richmond CA 94804
1932-010 ....Cain, Merritt Patrick 'Sugar' ....D. April 3, 1975 Atlanta, Ga.
1949-013 ....Cain, Robert Max ....D. April 8, 1997 Cleveland, Ohio
1996-031 ....Cairo, Miguel Jesus ....Old Add: Anaco Venezuela
1934-015 ....Caithamer, George Theodore ....D. June 1, 1954 Chicago, Ill.
1984-015 ....Calderon, Ivan ....Old Add: 334 Est. 34 Buzon Loiza PR 00672
1950-018 ....Calderone, Samuel Francis ....1000 South Cooper Street/Beverly NJ 8010
1928-018 ....Caldwell, Bruce ....D. February 15, 1959 West Haven, Conn.
1925-014 ....Caldwell, Charles William ....D. November 1, 1957 Princeton, N. J.
1928-019 ....Caldwell, Earl Welton ....D. September 15, 1981 Mission, Texas
1971-019 ....Caldwell, Ralph Michael 'Mike' ....1645 Brook Run Dr/Raleigh NC 27614

1910-021 ....Caldwell, Raymond Benjamin ....D. August 17, 1967 Salamanca, N. Y.
1984-016 ....Calhoun, Jeffrey Wilton ....1212 Park St/McComb MS 39648
1913-024 ....Calhoun, William Davitte ....D. January 28, 1955 Sandersville, Ga.
1941-012 ....Caligiuri, Frederick John ....PO Box 429/Rimersburg PA 16248
1922-018 ....Callaghan, Martin Francis ....D. June 24, 1975 Norwood, Mass.
1983-022 ....Callahan, Benjamin Franklin ....1152 Ashford Green Drive/Concord NC 28027
1910-022 ....Callahan, David Joseph ....D. October 28, 1969 Ottawa, Ill.
1939-017 ....Callahan, Joseph Thomas ....D. May 24, 1949 South Boston, Mass.
1913-025 ....Callahan, Leo David ....D. May 2, 1982 Erie, Pa.
1915-019 ....Callahan, Raymond James ....D. January 23, 1973 Olympia, Wash.
1913-026 ....Callahan, Wesley Leroy ....D. September 13, 1953 Dayton,O.
1921-012 ....Callaway, Frank Burnett ....D. August 21, 1987 Knoxville, Tenn.
1958-017 ....Callison, John Wesley ....2316 Oakdale Street/Glendale PA 19038
1963-020 ....Calmus, Richard Lee ....3823 South 28th West Avenue/Tulsa OK 74107
1983-023 ....Calvert, Mark ....908 West Waco Street/Broken Arrow OK 74011
1942-016 ....Calvert, Paul Leo Emile ....2775 Dumanoir #502/Sherbrooke Quebec J1L 2E5 Canada
1913-027 ....Calvo, Jacinto 'Jack' ....D. June 15, 1965 Miami, Fla.
1980-021 ....Camacho, Ernie Carlos ....746 St. Regis/Salinas CA 93905
1970-016 ....Cambria, Frederick Dennis ....12 Iris CT Northport NY 11768
1943-023 ....Camelli, Henry Richard ....D. July 14, 1996 Wellesley, Mass.
1995-042 ....Cameron, Michael Terrance ....318 Render Street/Lagrange GA 30240
1933-009 ....Camilli, Adolf Louis 'Dolph' ....D. October 21, 1997 San Mateo, Calif.
1960-017 ....Camilli, Douglas Joseph ....872 Oriole Drive SE/Winter Haven FL 33880
1969-027 ....Camilli, Louis Steven ....8280 Bob O Link Drive/West Palm Beach FL 33412
1987-020 ....Caminiti, Kenneth Gene ....2210 Quarter Path/Richmond TX 77469
1917-012 ....Camp, Howard Lee ....D. May 8, 1950 Eastaboga, Ala.
1976-023 ....Camp, Rick Lamar ....1223 Defoors Ferry Court/Atlanta GA 30318
1948-022 ....Campanella, Roy..D. June 26, 1993 Woodland Hills, Calif.
1964-015 ....Campaneris, Dagoberto Bert ....PO Box 5096/Scottsdale AZ 85261
1943-024 ....Campanis, Alexander Sebastian ....3113 Coronado Drive/Fullerton CA 92632
1966-017 ....Campanis, James Alexander.............................17082 Cascades Ave/Yorba Linda CA 92686
1928-020 ....Campbell, Archibald Stewart ....D. December 22, 1989 Sparks, Nev.
1930-008 ....Campbell, Bruce Douglas ....D. June 17, 1995 Fort Myers Beach, Fla.
1940-008 ....Campbell, Clarence 'Soup' ....Sparta VA 22552
1977-022 ....Campbell, David Allen ....Old Add: Rr 10 Lynn Ter #2 Johnson City TN 37601
1967-012 ....Campbell, David Wilson ....1415 Ledge Rock Terrace/Colorado Springs CO 80919
1990-024 ....Campbell, James Marcus ....1671 Sixth Street/Oroville CA 95965
1962-026 ....Campbell, James Robert ....1924 Knollwood Ln/Los Altos CA 94022
1970-017 ....Campbell, James Robert ....209 West Seven Pines/Lamar SC 29069
1933-010 ....Campbell, John Millard ....D. April 24, 1995 Daytona Beach, Fla.
1967-013 ....Campbell, Joseph Earl ....2151 Scottsville Road/Bowling Green KY 42104
1991-026 ....Campbell, Kevin Wade....................................Rural Route 2 Box 143e/Des Arc AR 72040
1987-021 ....Campbell, Michael Thomas ....6412 Southwest Hinds/Seattle WA 98116
1941-013 ....Campbell, Paul McLaughlin...............................Old Add: PO Box 1724 Fairfield Glade TN 38558
1964-016 ....Campbell, Ronald Thomas ....4120 Peerle/Cleveland TN 37312
1933-011 ....Campbell, William Gilthorpe 'Gilly'......................D. February 21, 1973 Los Angeles, Calif.
1973-017 ....Campbell, William Richard ....133 South Hale Street/Palatine IL 60067
1977-023 ....Camper, Cardell ....25488 Toluca Drive/San Bernardino CA 92404
1969-028 ....Campisi, Salvatore John ....Old Add: 3303 Lakewood Drive/Holiday FL 33590
1951-009 ....Campos, Francisco Jose Lopez 'Frank'.................840 Nw 87th Avenue #306/Miami FL 33172
1988-023 ....Campusano, Silvestre ....C. Guzman #5 Casa 19,Manoguayabo Santo Domingo Dominican Rep.
1989-021 ....Canale, George Anthony ....2330 Arenham Avenue Sw/Roanoke VA 24014
1993-029 ....Canate, Emisael William 'Bill' ....Old Add: 963 Manzanita Ave Pasadena CA 91103
1918-008 ....Canavan, Hugh Edward ....D. September 4, 1967 Boston, Mass.
1986-029 ....Candaele, Casey Todd ....251 Broad Street/San Luis Obispo CA 93405
1975-023 ....Candelaria, John Robert ....606 Wingspraed/Peachtree City GA 30269
1943-025 ....Candini, Milo Cain ....D. March 17, 1998 Manteca, Calif.
1983-024 ....Candiotti, Thomas Caeser ....1775 Sharon Drive/Concord CA 94519
1977-024 ....Caneira, John Cascaes ....18 Spruce St/Naugatuck CT 6770
1985-013 ....Cangelosi, John Anthony ....3209 West 69th Street/Bradenton FL 34203
1996-032 ....Canizaro, Jason Kyle 'Jay' ....4711 Burns Circle/Orange TX 77630
1960-018 ....Cannizzaro, Christopher John ....6960 Camino Amero/San Diego CA 92111
1977-025 ....Cannon, Joseph Jerome 'J. J.' ....3017 Cedarwood Village/Pensacola FL 32514
1989-022 ....Cano, Joselito Soriano ....Old Add: Vila Dolores 2da #41 San Pedro De Macoris Dom Rep
1985-014 ....Canseco, Jose ....3025 Meadow Lane/Fort Lauderdale FL 33331
1990-025 ....Canseco, Osvaldo ....5601 Collins Avenue #Cu1/Miami FL 33140
1925-015 ....Cantrell, Dewey Guy ....D. January 31, 1961 McAlester, Okla.
1927-021 ....Cantwell, Benjamin Caldwell ....D. December 4, 1962 Salem, Mo.
1916-010 ....Cantwell, Michael Joseph ....D. January 9, 1953 Oteen, N.C.
1988-024 ....Capel, Michael Lee ....23103 Harpergate Drive/Spring TX 77373
1976-024 ....Capilla, Douglas Edmond ....3254 Kilo Avenue/San Jose CA 95124
1981-021 ....Cappuzzello, George Angelo..............................PO Box 512/Gotha FL 34734
1971-020 ....Capra, Lee William 'Buzz' ....7112 Riverside Dr/Berwyn IL 60402
1982-022 ....Capra, Nick Lee ....4001 East Willow Road/Enid OK 73701
1944-018 ....Capri, Patrick Nicholas ....D. June 14, 1989 New York, N.Y.
1912-031 ....Capron, Ralph Earl ....D. September 19, 1980 Los Angeles, Calif.
1993-030 ....Caraballo, Ramon Sanchez ....Old Add: Santo Domingo Dom Rep
1930-009 ....Caraway, Cecil Bradford Patrick 'Pat' ....D. June 9, 1974 El Paso, Tex.
1969-029 ....Carbo, Bernardo ....6740 Browder Drive/Theodore AL 36582

1946-016 ....Carden, John Bruton ....D. February 8, 1949 Mexia, Tex.
1963-021 ....Cardenal, Jose Domec ....12 Country Club #Uc/Prospect Heights IL 60070
1960-019 ....Cardenas, Leonardo Lazaro 'Chico' ....Old Add: 5369 Bahama Ter #7/Cincinnati OH 45223
1963-022 ....Cardinal, Conrad Seth 'Randy' ....3810 Verde Way/North Las Vegas NV 89030
1943-026 ....Cardoni, Armand Joseph 'Ben' ....D. April 2, 1969 Jessup, Pa.
1957-009 ....Cardwell, Donald Eugene ....PO Box 454/Clemmons NC 27012
1967-014 ....Carew, Rodney Cline ....5144 East Crescent Drive/Anaheim CA 92807
1952-016 ....Carey, Andrew Arthur ....Old Add: 1601 Dove Street #220 Newport Beach CA 92660
1910-023 ....Carey, Max George ....D. May 30, 1976 Miami, Fla.
1993-031 ....Carey, Paul Stephen ....47 Kingman Street/Weymouth MA 2188
1935-011 ....Carey, Thomas Francis Aloysius ....D. February 21, 1970 Rochester, N. Y.
1932-011 ....Carleton, James Otto 'Tex' ....D. January 11, 1977 Fort Worth, Tex.
1941-014 ....Carlin, James Arthur ....1215 33rd St Reet/Birmingham AL 35218
1967-015 ....Carlos, Francisco Manuel 'Cisco' ....6027 North 7th Street/Phoenix AZ 85014
1948-023 ....Carlsen, Donald Herbert ....3600 East Easter Avenue/Littleton CO 80122
1996-033 ....Carlson, Dan Scott ....12600 SE Alder Street #36/Portland OR 97233
1917-013 ....Carlson, Harold Gust ....D. May 28, 1930 Chicago, Ill.
1920-016 ....Carlson, Leon Alton ....D. September 15, 1961 Jamestown, N. Y.
1911-023 ....Carlstrom, Albin Oscar 'Swede' ....D. April 23, 1935 Elizabeth, N.J.
1965-018 ....Carlton, Steven Norman ....PO Box 736/Durango CO 81302
1927-022 ....Carlyle, Hiram Cleo ....D. November 12, 1967 Los Angeles, Calif.
1925-016 ....Carlyle, Roy Edward..D. November 22, 1956 Norcross, Ga.
1983-025 ....Carman, Donald Wayne ....555 Murex Drive/Naples FL 34102
1959-011 ....Carmel, Leon James 'Duke'............................10 Pheasant Valley Drive/Coram NY 11727
1995-043 ....Carmona, Rafael ....Old Add: Comerio PR 00782
1941-015 ....Carnett, Edwin Elliott ....1010 Indian Creek Drive/Lebanon MO 65536
1997-023 ....Carpenter, Christopher John............................2 Donna Lane/Raymond NH 3077
1988-025 ....Carpenter, Cris Howell ....1760 Lakeview Circle/Gainesville GA 30501
1943-027 ....Carpenter, Lewis Emmett ....D. April 25, 1979 Marietta, Ga.
1916-011 ....Carpenter, Paul Calvin ....D. March 14, 1968 Newark, O.
1940-009 ....Carpenter, Robert Louis ....9321 South Sacramento Avenue/Evergreen Park IL 60642
1965-019 ....Carpin, Frank Dominic ....% Carolyn Taylor PO Box 18235 Richmond VA 23226
1990-026 ....Carr, Charles Lee Glenn ....Old Add: 16607 Reed Street Fontana CA 92335
1995-044 ....Carrara, Giovanni Jiminez ....Santa Rosa Car. 3 Casa#1-52 Barquisimeto Venezuela
1994-012 ....Carrasco, Hector (Pacheco) ....Cle L. Valera #42 Miramar San Pedro De Macoris Dominican Rep.
1939-018 ....Carrasquel, Alejandro Alexander ....D. August 19, 1969 Caracas, Venezuela
1950-019 ....Carrasquel, Alfonso Colon 'Chico' ....4625 South Wisconsin Avenue/Forest View IL 60402
1991-027 ....Carreno, Amalio Rafael (Adrian)......................Calle La Playa,Edo Nua "Chacachacare,Esparta Venezuela/"
1959-012 ....Carreon, Camilo Garcia ....D. September 2, 1987 Tucson, Ariz.
1987-022 ....Carreon, Mark Steven ....2102 Country Club Road/McComb MS 39648
1991-028 ....Carrillo, Matias ....Colonia Las Villas #95 Guaymas Sonora/Mexico
1970-018 ....Carrithers, Donald George ....9367 Sunny Glade Court/Elk Grove CA 95624
1964-017 ....Carroll, Clay Palmer ....3410 1/2 Redding Road/Chattanooga TN 37415
1919-011 ....Carroll, Dorsey Lee 'Dixie' ....D. October 13, 1984 Jacksonville, Fla.
1929-015 ....Carroll, Edgar Fleischer ....D. October 13, 1984 Rossville, Md.
1925-017 ....Carroll, Owen Thomas ....D. June 8, 1975 Orange, N. J.
1916-012 ....Carroll, Ralph Arthur 'Doc' ....D. June 27, 1983 Worcester, Mass.
1955-022 ....Carroll, Thomas Edward ....5900 Lagorre Drive/Miami Beach FL 33140
1974-014 ....Carroll, Thomas Michael ....16063 Hamilton Station Road/Waterford VA 20197
1910-024 ....Carson, Albert James ....D. November 26, 1962 San Diego, Calif.
1934-016 ....Carson, Walter Lloyd 'Kit' ....D. June 21, 1983 Long Beach, Calif.
1953-015 ....Carswell, Frank Willis ....3517 Stanford/Houston TX 77006
1994-013 ....Carter, Andrew Godfrey ....106 Montgomery Avenue/Erdenheim PA 19118
1944-019 ....Carter, Arnold Lee ....D. April 12, 1989 Louisville, Ky.
1974-015 ....Carter, Gary Edmund ....15 Huntly Drive/Palm Beach Gardens FL 33418
1991-029 ....Carter, Jeffrey Allen ....2028 Alafia Oaks Drive/Valrico FL 33594
1926-012 ....Carter, John Howard 'Howie' ....D. July 24, 1991 New York, N. Y.
1983-026 ....Carter, Joseph Chris ....1800 Northeast 51st/Oklahoma City OK 73111
1992-022 ....Carter, Larry Gene ....651 Highway 3227/Haughton LA 71037
1925-018 ....Carter, Otis Leonard 'Blackie' ....D. September 10, 1978 Greenville, S. C.
1914-034 ....Carter, Paul Warren 'Nick' ....D. September 11, 1984 Lake Park, Ga.
1931-011 ....Carter, Solomon Mobley ....2402 Gale Place/El Dorado AR 71730
1989-023 ....Carter, Steven Jerome ....13425 Tamarack Road/Silver Spring MD 20904
1963-023 ....Carty, Ricardo Adolfo Jacabo 'Rico' ....5 Ens Enriquillo San Pedro De Macoris Dominican Rep.
1985-015 ....Cary, Charles Douglas ....Old Add: 3323 Casa Grande Dr San Ramon CA 94583
1947-016 ....Cary, Scott Russell ....926 Block Road Box 205/Bronson MI 49028
1958-018 ....Casale, Jerry Joseph ....635 Harmon Cove Towers/Secaucus NJ 7094
1965-020 ....Casanova, Ortiz Paulino 'Paul' ....Old Add: 1312 Edenville Dr District Heights MD 20028
1996-034 ....Casanova, Raul ....Old Add: Ponce PR 00731
1934-017 ....Cascarella, Joseph Thomas ....7111 Park Heights Avenue/Baltimore MD 21215
1937-020 ....Case, George Washington ....D. January 23, 1989 Trenton, N. J.
1935-012 ....Casey, Hugh Thomas ....D. July 3, 1951 Atlanta, Ga.
1997-024 ....Casey, Sean T. ....Old Add: Pittsburgh PA 15201
1969-030 ....Cash, David ....16308 Birkdale Drive/Odessa FL 33556
1958-019 ....Cash, Norman Dalton ....D. October 12, 1986 Beaver Island, Mich.
1973-018 ....Cash, Ronald Forest ....Old Add: PO Box 723270/Atlanta GA 30329
1911-024 ....Cashion, Jay Carl ....D. November 17, 1935 Lake Millicent, Wis.
1990-027 ....Casian, Lawrence Paul ....Old Add: 165 East Linda Vista Rd Grants Pass OR 97527
1973-019 ....Caskey, Craig Douglas ....836 Yvonne Pl/Anaheim CA 92801

1949-014	Cassini, Jack Dempsey	24 East Vera Lane/Tempe Az/85284
1993-032	Castellano, Pedro Orlando (Arrieta)	Parcela 63 #63-6, Cabudare Lara Venezuela
1934-018	Caster, George Jasper	D. December 18, 1955 Lakewood, Calif.
1942-017	Castiglia, James Vincent	5301 Westbard Circle #313/Bethesda MD 20816
1947-017	Castiglione, Peter Paul	1320 NE 26th Terrace/Pompano Beach FL 33062
1991-030	Castilla, Vinicio (Soria) 'Vinny'	Old Add: Oaxaca Oaxaca Mexico
1995-045	Castillo, Alberto Terrero	Old Add: Las Matas Defar Dom. Rep.
1978-024	Castillo, Anthony Beltran	Old Add: 10300 Joyce Court San Jose CA 95127
1988-026	Castillo, Antonio Jose	El Molino Via Sanare Quibor Lara Venezuela
1991-031	Castillo, Braulio Robinson Medrano	Old Add: Castellano #259,Luperon Anto Domingo Dominican Rep.
1997-025	Castillo, Carlos	Old Add: Miami FL 33101
1980-022	Castillo, Esteban Manuel 'Manny'	Costa Rica 112,Ens. Ozama Santo Domingo Dominican Rep.
1991-032	Castillo, Frank Anthony	10533 Texwood/El Paso TX 79925
1986-030	Castillo, Juan	Calle Elia Camarena 100 San Pedro De Macoris Dominican Rep.
1994-014	Castillo, Juan Francisco	Ave 4, Quinta, Santa Ana La Boyera Caracas Venezuela
1996-035	Castillo, Luis Antonio Donato	Old Add: San Pedro De Mac. Dom. Rep.
1981-022	Castillo, Martin Horace	2669 Baylor Street/Anaheim CA 92801
1982-023	Castillo, Monte Carmelo 'Carmelo'	Old Add: 189 Audubon Ave #3n New York NY 10032
1977-026	Castillo, Robert Ernie	2837 Sierra St/Los Angeles CA 90031
1979-016	Castino, John Anthony	6624 Gleason Rd/Edina MN 55435
1943-028	Castino, Vincent Charles	D. March 6, 1967 Sacramento, Calif.
1973-020	Castle, Donald Hardy	24 Country Club Drive/Senatobia MS 38668
1910-025	Castle, John Francis	D. April 13, 1929 Philadelphia, Pa.
1934-019	Castleman, Clydell	D. March 2, 1998 Nashville, Tenn.
1954-013	Castleman, Foster Ephraim	8250 Graves Road/Cincinnati OH 45243
1923-019	Castner, Paul Henry	D. March 3, 1986 St. Paul, Minn.
1995-046	Castro, Juan C.	Old Add: Los Mochis Mexico
1974-016	Castro, Williams Radhames	5231 Raven Dr/Greendale WI 53129
1997-026	Catalanatto, Frank John	Old Add: Smithtown NY 11787
1964-018	Cater, Danny Anderson	500 East Anderson Lane #176I/Austin TX 78752
1997-027	Cather, Michael Peter	Old Add: Folsom CA 95630
1912-033	Cather, Theodore P.	D. April 9, 1945 Elkton, Md.
1942-018	Cathey, Hardin	D. July 27, 1997 Nashville, Tenn.
1983-027	Cato, John Keefe	98 Maryton Road/White Plains NY 10603
1917-014	Caton, James Howard 'Buster'	D. January 8, 1948 Zanesville, O.
1979-017	Caudill, William Holland	3221 Mayfair Drive SW #A/Tumwater WA 98512
1946-017	Caulfield, John Joseph	D. December 16, 1986 San Francisco, Calif.
1918-009	Causey, Cecil Algernon 'Red'	D. November 11, 1960 Tampa, Fla.
1955-023	Causey, James Wayne	2905 Paynter Dr/Ruston LA 71270
1919-012	Cavanaugh, John J.	D. January 14, 1961 New Brunswick, N. J.
1934-020	Cavarretta, Philip Joseph	7225 Tara Drive/Villa Rica GA 30180
1922-019	Caveney, James Christopher 'Ike'	D. July 6, 1949 San Francisco, Calif.
1911-025	Cavet, Tiller 'Pug'	D. August 4, 1966 San Luis Obispo, Calif.
1955-024	Ceccarelli, Arthur Edward	63 Hall Dr/Orange CT 6477
1988-027	Cecena, Jose Isabel	Old Add: Cd. Obregon Sonora Mexico
1944-020	Cecil, Rex Holston	D. October 30, 1966 Long Beach, Calif.
1990-028	Cedeno, Andujar	Laromana Dominican Rep.
1970-019	Cedeno, Cesar Eugenio	47 Silver Falls Circle/Kissimmee FL 34743
1993-033	Cedeno, Domingo (Domastorg)	Ave. Padre Abreu #13 Laromana Dominican Rep.
1995-047	Cedeno, Roger Leonard	Old Add: Carabobo Venezuela
1942-019	Center, Marvin Earl 'Pete'	PO Box 64/Campton/Ky 41301
1958-020	Cepeda, Orlando Manuel	331 Barzelton Court/Suisun City CA 94585
1975-025	Cerone, Richard Rick	63 Eisenhower/Cresskill NJ 7626
1985-016	Cerutti, John Joseph	14 Holmes/Albany NY 12203
1951-010	Cerv, Robert Henry	3130 Williamsburg Drive/Lincoln NE 68516
1971-021	Cey, Ronald Charles	22714 Creole Rd/Woodland Hills CA 91364
1960-020	Chacon, Elio Rodriguez	D. April 24, 1992 Caracas, Venezuela
1986-031	Chadwick, Ray Charles	607 Gaddis Street/Durham NC 27702
1929-016	Chagnon, Leon Wilbur	D. July 30, 1953 Amesbury, Mass.
1951-011	Chakales, Robert Edward	206 Moreland Drive/Richmond VA 23229
1973-021	Chalk, David Lee	Old Add: 6126 Summer Creek Circle Dallas TX 75231
1910-026	Chalmers, George W.	D. August 5, 1960 Bronx, N. Y.
1979-018	Chamberlain, Craig Philip	PO Box 473/Surfside CA 90743
1990-029	Chamberlain, Wesley Polk	Old Add: Chicago IL 60607
1932-012	Chamberlain, William Vincent	D. February 6, 1994 Brockton, Mass.
1934-021	Chamberlin, Joseph Jeremiah	D. January 28, 1983 San Francisco, Calif.
1983-028	Chambers, Albert Eugene	1303 North 14th St/Harrisburg PA 17103
1948-024	Chambers, Clifford Day	10237 Prairie Road/Boise ID 83702
1937-021	Chambers, Johnnie Monroe	D. May 11, 1977 Palatka, Fla.
1910-027	Chambers, William Christopher	D. March 27, 1962 Fort Wayne, Ind.
1971-022	Chambliss, Carroll Christopher 'Chris'	107 Stephenson Terrace/Briarcliff NY 10510
1969-031	Champion, Buford Billy 'Billy'	Rural Route 3 Box 188/Wytheville VA 24382
1976-025	Champion, Robert Michael 'Mike'	Old Add: 9160 Lemon Avenue Lamesa CA 91941
1963-024	Chance, Robert	900 Arboretum Way #15/Newport News VA 23602
1961-019	Chance, Wilmer Dean 'Dean'	9505 W. Smithville Western/Wooster OH 44691
1947-018	Chandler, Edward Oliver	3553 Day Dawn Street/Las Vegas/Nv 89117
1937-022	Chandler, Spurgeon Ferdinand 'Spud'	D. January 9, 1990 St. Petersburg, Fla.
1969-032	Chaney, Darrel Lee	Old Add: 2235 St. Thomas Way Suwanee GA 30174
1913-028	Chaney, Estey Cleon	D. February 5, 1952 Cleveland, O.

1910-028	Channell, Lester Clark	D. May 7, 1954 Denver, Colo.
1975-024	Chant, Charles Joseph	7831 Sycamore Avenue/Riverside CA 92504
1991-033	Chapin, Darrin John	328 Portage Easterly/Cortland OH 44410
1920-017	Chaplin, Bert Edgar	D. August 15, 1978 Sanford, Fla.
1928-021	Chaplin, James Bailey 'Tiny'	D. March 25, 1939 National City, Calif.
1935-013	Chapman, Calvin Louis	D. April 1, 1983 Batesville, Miss.
1933-012	Chapman, Edwin Volney	Old Add: Rural Route 2 Lambert MS 38643
1939-019	Chapman, Frederick William	D. March 27, 1997 Kannapolis, N. C.
1934-022	Chapman, Glenn Justice	D. November 5, 1988 Richmond, Ind.
1912-034	Chapman, Harry E.	D. October 21, 1918 Nevada, Mo.
1924-017	Chapman, John Joseph	D. November 3, 1953 Philadelphia, Pa.
1979-019	Chapman, Kelvin Keith	9301 Laughlin Way/Redwood Valley CA 94570
1912-035	Chapman, Raymond Johnson	D. August 17, 1920 New York, N.Y.
1938-012	Chapman, Samuel Blake	11 Andrew Drive #39/Tiburon CA 94920
1930-010	Chapman, William Benjamin 'Ben'	D. July 7, 1993 Hoover, Ala.
1978-025	Chappas, Harry Perry	1440 Northwest 52nd Avenue/Lauderhill FL 33313
1913-029	Chappell, Laverne Ashford 'Larry'	D. November 8, 1918 San Francisco, Calif.
1980-023	Charboneau, Joseph	PO Box 39239/North Ridgeville OH 44039
1962-027	Charles, Edwin Douglas	57 Park Terrace East #B58/New York NY 10034
1988-028	Charlton, Norman Wood	312 Estes Drive/Rockport TX 78382
1940-010	Chartak, Michael George	D. July 25, 1967 Oakdale, la.
1964-019	Charton, Frank Lane 'Pete'	27 Vincinda Ln/Harriman TN 37748
1936-014	Chase, Kendall Fay	D. January 16, 1985 Oneonta, N. Y.
1930-011	Chatham, Charles L. 'Buster'	D. December 15, 1975 Waco, Texas
1966-018	Chavarria, Oswaldo Quijano	9061 Horner Street #201/Burnaby British Columbia V3N 4L2 Canada
1997-028	Chavez, Anthony Francisco 'Tony'	Old Add: Merced CA 95340
1967-016	Chavez, Nestor Isaias Silva	D. March 16, 1969 Maracaibo, Venez.
1996-036	Chavez, Raul Alexander	Old Add: Valencia Venezuela
1973-022	Cheadle, David Baird	3015 Little Island Road/Virginia Beach VA 23456
1997-029	Checo, Robinson Perez	Old Add: Santiago Dominican Rep.
1910-029	Cheek, Harry G.	D. June 25, 1956 Paramus, N. J.
1920-018	Cheeves, Virgil Earl 'Chief'	D. May 5, 1979 Dallas, Texas
1935-014	Chelini, Italo Vincent	D. August 25, 1972 San Francisco, Calif.
1911-026	Cheney, Laurance Russell	D. January 6, 1969 Daytona Beach, Fla.
1957-010	Cheney, Thomas Edgar	1725 West Oakridge Drive #9/Albany GA 31707
1937-023	Chervinko, Paul	D. June 3, 1976 Danville, Ill.
1948-025	Chesnes, Robert Vincent	D. May 23, 1979 Everett, Wash.
1945-008	Chetkovich, Mitchell	D. August 24, 1971 Grass Valley, Calif.
1977-027	Chevez, Antonio Silvio	Telia D Pto. Leon/Nicaragua
1990-030	Chiamparino, Scott Michael	169 Ortega Avenue/Mountain View CA 94040
1982-024	Chiffer, Floyd John	4325 Levelside Ave/Lakeside CA 90712
1930-012	Child, Harry Patrick	D. November 8, 1972 Alexandria, Va.
1985-017	Childress, Rodney Osborne Rocky	5 Meadowglen Court/Santa Rosa CA 95404
1971-023	Chiles, Richard Francis	4501 San Ramon Dr/Davis CA 95616
1935-015	Chiozza, Dino Joseph	D. April 23, 1972 Memphis, Tenn.
1934-023	Chiozza, Louis Peo	D. February 28, 1971 Memphis, Tenn.
1941-016	Chipman, Robert Howard	D. November 8, 1973 Huntington, N.Y.
1945-009	Chipple, Walter John	D. June 8, 1988 Tonawanda, N. Y.
1979-020	Chism, Thomas Raymond	532 West Brookhaven Road #F1/Brookhaven PA 19015
1950-020	Chiti, Harry	3852 Thistle Valley Lane/Memphis TN 38134
1990-031	Chitren, Stephen Vincent	Old Add: 2766 Vegas Valley Dr Las Vegas NV 89121
1958-021	Chittum, Nelson Boyd	616 Bonita Parkway/Hendersonville TN 37075
1970-020	Chlupsa, Robert Joseph	55 Willow Street/Garden City NY 11530
1960-021	Choate, Donald Lee	9506 Mary Ann Drive/Fairview Heights IL 62208
1910-030	Chouinard, Felix George	D. April 28, 1955 Hines, Ill.
1996-037	Chouinard, Robert William	Old Add: Forest Grove OR 97116
1910-031	Chouneau, William 'Chief'	D. September 17, 1948 Cloquet, Minn.
1937-024	Chozen, Harry Kenneth	D. September 16, 1994 Houston, Texas
1979-021	Chris, Michael	12437 Woodgreen St/Los Angeles CA 90066
1957-011	Chrisley, Barbra O'Neil 'Neil'	106 Shalott Court/Greenwood SC 29646
1919-013	Christenbury, Lloyd Reid	D. December 13, 1944 Birmingham, Ala.
1971-024	Christensen, Bruce Ray	Box 178/Moroni UT 84646
1984-017	Christensen, John Lawrence	20950 Via Contento/Yorba Linda CA 92686
1926-013	Christensen, Walter Niels	D. December 20, 1984 Menlo Park, Calif.
1979-022	Christenson, Gary Richard	1610 Washington Ave/New Hyde Park NY 11040
1973-023	Christenson, Larry Robert	100 Front Street #825/Conshohocken PA 19428
1968-013	Christian, Robert Charles	D. February 20, 1974 San Diego, Calif.
1984-018	Christiansen, Clay C.	Rural Route 3/Columbus KS 66725
1995-048	Christianson, Jason Samuel	15277 Spencer Street/Omaha NE 68116
1938-013	Christman, Marquette Joseph	D. October 9, 1976 St. Louis, Mo.
1983-029	Christmas, Stephen Randall	251 East Second Street/Chuluota FL 32766
1959-013	Christopher, Joseph O'Neal	PO Box 65240/Baltimore MD 21209
1945-010	Christopher, Loyd Eugene	D. September 5, 1991 Richmond, Calif.
1991-034	Christopher, Michael Wayne	24610 Cox Road/Petersburg VA 23803
1942-020	Christopher, Russell Ormand	D. December 5, 1954 Point Richmond, Calif.
1950-021	Church, Emory Nicholas 'Bubba'	3304 Afton Circle/Birmingham AL 35242
1966-019	Church, Leonard	D. April 22, 1988 Richardson, Texas
1957-012	Churn, Clarence Nottingham 'Chuck'	Box 39/Greenbush VA 23357
1924-018	Churry, John	D. February 8, 1970 Zanesville, O.

1951-012 ....Ciaffone, Lawrence Thomas ....D. December 14, 1991 Brooklyn, N. Y.
1992-023 ....Cianfrocco, Angelo Dominic ....708 West Dominick Street/Rome NY 13440
1987-023 ....Ciardi, Mark Thomas ....21 Mitchell Avenue/Piscataway NJ 8854
1983-030 ....Cias, Darryl Richard ....12330 Lithuania St/Granada Hills CA 91344
1929-017 ....Cicero, Joseph Francis ....D. March 30, 1983 Clearwater, Fla.
1957-013 ....Cicotte, Alva Warren ....D. November 29, 1982 Westland, Mich.
1944-021 ....Cieslak, Thaddeus Walter 'Ted' ....Old Add: South 79 W 17430 Alan Dr Muskego WI 53150
1945-011 ....Cihocki, Albert Joseph ....43 Cochise Circle/Medford Lakes NJ 8055
1932-013 ....Cihocki, Edward Joseph ....D. November 9, 1987 Newark, Del.
1965-021 ....Cimino, Peter William ....14 Fillmore St/Bristol PA 19007
1956-021 ....Cimoli, Gino Nicholas ....39 Mooring Drive/Daly City CA 94014
1994-015 ....Cimorelli, Frank Thomas ....5 Franklin Road/Hyde Park NY 12538
1943-029 ....Ciola, Louis Alexander ....D. October 18, 1981 Austin, Minn.
1961-020 ....Cipriani, Frank Dominick ....14 Oakhill Drive/West Seneca NY 14224
1994-016 ....Cirillo, Jeffrey Howard ....918 Northwest 132nd/Seattle WA 98177
1937-025 ....Cisar, George Joseph ....2520 South 56th Court/Cicero IL 60650
1961-021 ....Cisco, Galen Bernard ....8250 State Route 703 #46/Celina OH 45822
1928-022 ....Cissell, Chalmer William 'Bill' ....D. March 15, 1949 Chicago, Ill.
1983-031 ....Citarella, Ralph Alexander ....29 East Sherman Ave/Colonia NJ 7067
1926-014 ....Clabaugh, John William 'Moose' ....D. July 11, 1984 Tucson, Ariz.
1920-019 ....Claire, David Matthew ....D. January 7, 1956 Las Vegas, Nev.
1911-027 ....Clancy, Albert Harrison ....D. October 17, 1951 Las Cruces, N. Mex.
1977-028 ....Clancy, James ....2598 Gary Circle #102/Dunedin FL 34698
1924-019 ....Clancy, John William 'Bud' ....D. September 26, 1968 Ottumwa, Ia.
1922-020 ....Clanton, Ucal Curt ....D. February 24, 1960 Antlers, Okla.
1976-026 ....Clarey, Douglas William ....2116 Hillhurst Avenue/Los Angeles CA 90027
1947-019 ....Clark, Alfred Aloysius 'Allie' ....250 North Stevens Avenue/South Amboy NJ 8879
1995-049 ....Clark, Anthony Christopher ....1306 Petree Street #463/El Cajon CA 92020
1927-023 ....Clark, Bailey Earl ....D. January 16, 1938 Washington, D. C.
1981-023 ....Clark, Bryan Donald ....508 North Clark Street/Madera CA 93637
1922-021 ....Clark, Daniel Curran ....D. May 23, 1937 Meridian, Miss.
1986-032 ....Clark, David Earl ....106 Road 686/Tupelo MS 38801
1913-030 ....Clark, George Myron ....D. November 14, 1940 Sioux City, Ia.
1967-017 ....Clark, Glen Ester ....5605 Marblehead/Dallas TX 75232
1975-026 ....Clark, Jack Anthony ....2708 Moffett Court/Plano TX 75095
1948-026 ....Clark, James ....D. October 24, 1990 Santa Monica, Calif.
1971-025 ....Clark, James ....659 South Indian Hill Blvd #C/Claremont CA 91711
1911-028 ....Clark, James Francis ....D. March 20, 1969 Beaumont, Tex.
1988-029 ....Clark, Jerald Dwayne ....Old Add: 618 Sycamore Street Crockett TX 75838
1938-014 ....Clark, John Carroll 'Cap' ....D. February 16, 1957 Fayetteville, N. C.
1991-035 ....Clark, Mark Willard ....Old Add: PO Box 33 Bath IL 62617
1951-013 ....Clark, Melvin Earl ....PO Box 97/West Columbia/Wv/25287
1952-017 ....Clark, Michael John ....D. January 15, 1996 Camden, N. J.
1958-022 ....Clark, Philip James ....228 Pineknoll Road/Sylvester GA 31791
1992-024 ....Clark, Phillip Benjamin ....2715 Smithfield Drive/Orlando FL 32837
1967-018 ....Clark, Rickey Charles ....Old Add: 27446 Oakley St Livonia MI 48154
1979-023 ....Clark, Robert Cale ....1030 Pervisito St/Perris CA 92370
1920-020 ....Clark, Robert William ....D. May 18, 1944 Carlsbad, N. M.
1966-020 ....Clark, Ronald Bruce ....700 Starkey Rd #511/Largo FL 33541
1988-030 ....Clark, Terry Lee ....Old Add: 15234 Hartsville Lapuente CA 91744
1986-033 ....Clark, William Nuschler Will ....504 Potomac Place/Southlake TX 76092
1945-012 ....Clark, William Otis 'Otey' ....2735 East Bass Lake Road/Grand Rapids MN 55744
1924-020 ....Clark, William Watson 'Watty' ....D. March 4, 1972 Clearwater, Fla.
1921-013 ....Clarke, Alan Thomas ....D. March 11, 1975 Cheverly, Md.
1965-022 ....Clarke, Horace Meredith ....Box 891/Frederiksted VI 840
1944-022 ....Clarke, Richard Grey 'Grey' ....D. November 25, 1993 Kannapolis, N. C.
1923-020 ....Clarke, Rufus Rivers ....D. February 8, 1983 Columbia, S. C.
1983-032 ....Clarke, Stanley Marten ....5533 Sanders Drive/Toledo OH 43615
1920-021 ....Clarke, Sumpter Mills ....D. March 16, 1962 Knoxville, Tenn.
1955-025 ....Clarke, Vibert Ernesto 'Webbo' ....D. June 14, 1970 Cristobal, Canal Zone
1929-018 ....Clarke, William Stuart 'Stu' ....D. August 26, 1985 Hayward, Calif.
1952-018 ....Clarkson, James Buster 'Bus' ....D. January 18, 1989 Jeannette, Pa.
1927-024 ....Clarkson, William Henry ....D. August 27, 1971 Raleigh, N. C.
1942-021 ....Clary, Ellis ....206 West Alden Street/Valdosta GA 31603
1987-024 ....Clary, Martin Keith ....205 Yorktown Court/Easley SC 29642
1933-013 ....Claset, Gowell Sylvester ....D. March 8, 1981 St. Petersburg, Fla.
1913-031 ....Clauss, Albert Stanley ....D. September 13, 1952 New Haven, Conn.
1943-030 ....Clay, Dain Elmer ....D. August 28, 1994 Chula Vista, Calif.
1988-031 ....Clay, Danny Bruce ....Old Add: 2626 Travis Road #A Columbus OH 43209
1977-029 ....Clay, Kenneth Earl ....Old Add: 221 Longwood Ln Clarksville TN 37043
1991-036 ....Clayton, Royce Spencer ....401 West Fairview Blvd/Inglewood CA 90302
1979-024 ....Clear, Mark Alan ....3229 Armsley Drive/Chino Hills CA 91709
1945-013 ....Cleary, Joseph Christopher ....135 West 225 Street/New York NY 10463
1939-020 ....Clemens, Chester Spurgeon ....423 Crespi/San Clemente CA 92672
1914-035 ....Clemens, Clement Lambert ....D. November 18, 1967 St Petersburg, Fla.
1960-022 ....Clemens, Douglas Horace ....Old Add: Lower Mountain Rd/Lahaska PA 18931
1984-019 ....Clemens, William Roger Roger ....11535 Quail Hollow/Houston TX 77024
1939-021 ....Clemensen, William Melville ....D. February 18, 1994 Alta, Calif.
1955-026 ....Clemente, Roberto Walker ....D. December 31, 1972 San Juan, P. R.

1985-018	Clements, Patrick Brian	Old Add: 125 Parmac Rd #5 Chico CA 95926
1997-030	Clemons, Christopher Hale	109 Goliad Street/McGregor TX 76657
1971-026	Clemons, Lance Levis	4516 Golf Club Lane/Brooksville FL 34609
1914-036	Clemons, Robert Baxter	D. April 5, 1964 Los Angeles, Calif.
1916-013	Clemons, Verne James	D. May 5, 1959 Bay Pines, Fla.
1961-022	Clendenon, Donn Alvin	2709 South Sandstone Circle/Sioux Falls SD 57103
1969-033	Cleveland, Reginald Leslie	Old Add: Box 1088/St. Catherines Ontario
1954-014	Clevenger, Truman Eugene 'Tex'	74 North Carmelita/Porterville CA 93257
1980-024	Cliburn, Stanley Gene	4807 Highway 80/Jackson MS 39209
1984-020	Cliburn, Stewart Walker	727 Nimitz Drive/Jackson MS 39209
1934-024	Clift, Harlond Benton	D. April 27, 1992 Yakima, Wash.
1934-025	Clifton, Herman Earl 'Flea'	D. December 22, 1997 Cincinnati, Ohio
1960-023	Cline, Tyrone Alexander	676 Ayers/Charleston SC 29412
1970-021	Clines, Eugene Anthony	820c South May Street/Chicago IL 60607
1960-024	Clinton, Luciean Louis	D. December 6, 1997 Wichita, Kans.
1961-023	Cloninger, Tony Lee	159 Sellars Road/Kings Mountain NC 28086
1995-050	Clontz, John Bradley 'Brad'	Rural Route 2 Box 3020/Patrick Springs VA 24133
1966-021	Closter, Alan Edward	1006 Miami Street/Creighton NE 68729
1997-031	Cloude, Kenneth Brian	Old Add: Baltimore Md
1924-021	Clough, Edgar George	D. January 30, 1944 Harrisburg, Pa.
1926-015	Clowers, William Perry	D. January 13, 1978 Sweeny, Tex.
1986-034	Clutterbuck, Bryan Richard	1986 Lovell,% Mm Clutterbuck/Milford MI 48381
1997-032	Clyburn, Danny	1156 9th Street/Lancaster SC 29720
1973-024	Clyde, David Eugene	% McCauley Lumber 27210 Fm 149 Tomball TX 77375
1943-031	Clyde, Thomas Knox	14700 Marsh Lane #1014/Farmers Branch TX 75234
1990-032	Coachman, Bobby Dean 'Pete'	PO Box 44/Cottonwood AL 36320
1946-018	Coan, Gilbert Fitzgerald	PO Box 558/Brevard/Nc 28712
1956-022	Coates, James Alton	PO Box 516/Lively VA 22507
1929-019	Cobb, Herbert Edward	D. January 8, 1980 Tarboro, N. C.
1918-010	Cobb, Joseph Stanley	D. December 24, 1947 Allentown, Pa.
1939-022	Coble, David Lamar	D. October 15, 1971 Orlando, Fla.
1983-033	Cocanower, James Stanley 'Jaime'	3620 Gersham Drive/Conway AR 72032
1915-020	Cochran, Alvah Jackson	D. May 23, 1947 Atlanta, Ga.
1918-011	Cochran, George Leslie	D. May 21, 1960 Harbor City, Calif.
1986-035	Cochrane, David Carter	27 Bogey Lane/Coto De Caza CA 92679
1925-019	Cochrane, Gordon Stanley 'Mickey'	D. June 2, 1962 Lake Forest, Ill.
1996-038	Cockrell, Atlee Alan 'Alan'	Old Add: Colorado Springs CO 80901
1913-032	Cocreham, Eugene	D. December 27, 1945 Luling, Tex.
1982-025	Codiroli, Christopher Allen	2700 Hillcrest Drive/Cameron Park CA 95682
1912-036	Coffey, John Joseph Smith 'Jack'	D. December 4, 1962 New York, N. Y.
1937-026	Coffman, George David	1120 Beacon Pkwy East #612/Birmingham AL 35209
1987-025	Coffman, Kevin Reese	313 Kelly Drive/Victoria TX 77904
1927-025	Coffman, Samuel Richard 'Dick'	D. March 24, 1972 Athens, Ala.
1967-019	Coggins, Franklin	Old Add: PO Box 92 Griffin GA 30224
1972-018	Coggins, Richard Allen	Old Add: 3801 Parkview Irvine CA 92713
1931-012	Cohen, Alta Albert	333 Elmwood Avenue #D546/ Maplewood NJ 7040
1926-016	Cohen, Andrew Howard	D. October 29, 1988 El Paso, Texas
1955-027	Cohen, Hyman	737 Cedar Point Place/Westlake Village CA 91362
1934-026	Cohen, Sydney Harry	D. April 9, 1988 El Paso, Texas
1958-023	Coker, Jimmie Goodwin	D. October 29, 1991 Throckmorton,Texas
1955-028	Colavito, Rocco Domenico 'Rocky'	656 Scenic Drive/Bernville PA 19506
1978-026	Colbern, Michael Malloy	Old Add: 1059 East Fairmont Tempe AZ 85282
1992-025	Colbert, Craig Charles	16613 Glenn Lane/Pearland TX 77584
1966-022	Colbert, Nathan	Old Add: 1017 So. Boone St,%Gulls Aberdeen WA 94545
1970-022	Colbert, Vincent Norman	1417 'E' Street SE/Washington Dc 20003
1969-034	Colborn, James William	2932 Solimar Beach Drive/Ventura CA 93001
1992-026	Colbrunn, Gregory Joseph	9690 Cypress/Fontana CA 92335
1921-014	Cole, Albert George	D. May 30, 1975 San Mateo, Calif.
1990-033	Cole, Alexander	Old Add: 1071 Robmont Drive Richmond VA 23236
1950-022	Cole, David Bruce	104 Wilcox Drive/Williamsport MD 21795
1938-015	Cole, Edward William	Old Add: 6853 Larmanda Dallas TX 75231
1951-014	Cole, Richard Roy	3149 Medeira Avenue/Costa Mesa CA 92626
1991-037	Cole, Stewart Bryan	6527 Willow Gale Lane/Charlotte NC 28215
1992-027	Cole, Victor Alexander	138 Estonalie Road/Mercer TN 38392
1961-024	Coleman, Clarence 'Choo Choo'	Old Add: 726 Cornelia Court/Orlando FL 32807
1912-037	Coleman, Curtis Hancock	D. July 1, 1980 Newport, Ore.
1977-030	Coleman, David Lee	4303 Delhi Dr/Dayton OH 45432
1949-015	Coleman, Gerald Francis	1004 Havenhurst Drive/Lajolla CA 92037
1959-014	Coleman, Gordon Calvin	D. March 12, 1994 Cincinnati, Ohio
1965-023	Coleman, Joseph Howard	17851 Eagle View Lane/Cape Coral FL 33909
1942-022	Coleman, Joseph Patrick	D. April 9, 1997 Fort Myers, Fla.
1997-033	Coleman, Michael/D.	7144 Poplar Creek Trace/Nashville TN 37221
1932-014	Coleman, Parke Edward 'Ed'	D. August 5, 1964 Oregon City, Ore.
1947-020	Coleman, Raymond Leroy	PO Box 8/Hornbrook CA 96044
1913-033	Coleman, Robert Hunter	D. July 16, 1959 Boston, Mass.
1985-019	Coleman, Vincent Maurice	Old Add: 1864 Hermitage Imperial MO 63052
1955-029	Coleman, Walter Gary 'Rip'	90 Spruce Road/Wolfeboro NH 3894
1914-037	Coles, Cadwallader R.	D. June 30, 1942 Miami, Fla.
1958-024	Coles, Charles Edward	D. January 25, 1966 Myrtle Beach. S. C.

1983-034 ....Coles, Darnell ....306 Signature Terrace/Safety Harbor FL 34695
1972-019 ....Coletta, Christopher Michael............................206 SW 45th Street/Cape Coral FL 33914
1911-029 ....Collamore, Allan Edward ....D. August 8, 1980 Battle Creek, Mi.
1927-026 ....Collard, Earl Clinton 'Hap' ....D. July 14, 1968 Jamestown, N. Y.
1997-034 ....Collier, Louis Keith...Old Add: Chicago IL 60601
1931-013 ....Collier, Orlin Edward ....D. September 9, 1944 Memphis, Tenn.
1913-034 ....Collins, Cyril Wilson ....D. February 28, 1941 Knoxville, Tenn.
1975-027 ....Collins, David Scott ....3000 Beal Road/Franklin OH 45005
1977-031 ....Collins, Donald Edward ....127 Deerwood Trail/Sharpsburg GA 30277
1939-023 ....Collins, Edward Trowbridge ....53 East Jonathan Court/Kennett Square PA 19348
1920-022 ....Collins, Harry Warren 'Rip' ....D. May 27, 1968 Bryan, Tex.
1931-014 ....Collins, James Anthony 'Rip' ....D. April 16, 1970 New Haven, N. Y.
1914-038 ....Collins, John Edgar 'Zip' ....D. December 19, 1983 Manassas, Va.
1910-032 ....Collins, John Francis 'Shano' ....D. September 10, 1955 Newton, Mass.
1948-027 ....Collins, Joseph Edward ....D. August 30, 1989 Union, N.J.
1965-024 ....Collins, Kevin Michael ....97 W. Elmwood St/Clawson MI 48017
1923-021 ....Collins, Philip Eugene ....D. August 14, 1948 Chicago, Ill.
1940-011 ....Collins, Robert Joseph ....D. April 19, 1969 Pittsburgh, Pa.
1994-017 ....Collins, Terry Lee ....5162 Chevy Chase Drive/Houston TX 77056
1919-014 ....Collins, Tharon Leslie 'Pat' ....D. May 19, 1960 Kansas City, Kan.
1910-033 ....Collins, William Shirley ....D. June 26, 1961 San Bernardino, Calif.
1951-015 ....Collum, Jack Dean ....PO Box 82/Grinnell IA 50112
1942-023 ....Colman, Frank Loyd ....D. February 19, 1983 London, Ont.
1997-035 ....Colon, Bartolo ....Old Add: Puerto Plata Dom. Rep.
1992-028 ....Colon, Cristobal (Martinez) ....Casa Anna Avenue "Alamo, Laguira Venezuela/"
1970-023 ....Colpaert, Richard Charles ....47412 Eldon/Utica MI 48317
1970-024 ....Colson, Loyd Albert ....PO Box 128/Hollis OK 73550
1968-014 ....Colton, Lawrence Robert................................3558 Northeast Morris Street/Portland OR 97212
1973-025 ....Coluccio, Robert Pasquali ....Old Add: 417 Wildcat Street SE Olympia WA 98503
1980-025 ....Combe, Geoffrey Wade ....Old Add: 2384 East Avenida Otono 1000 Oaks CA 91362
1924-022 ....Combs, Earle Bryan ....D. July 21, 1976 Richmond, Ky.
1947-021 ....Combs, Merrill Russell....................................D. July 8, 1981 Riverside, Calif.
1989-024 ....Combs, Patrick Dennis ....2219 Spanish Forest Lane/Richmond TX 77469
1945-014 ....Comellas, Jorge ....13015 Southwest 50th Street/Miami FL 33165
1967-020 ....Comer, Harry Wayne 'Wayne' ....145 Marcus Street/Shenandoah VA 22849
1978-027 ....Comer, Steven Michael ....20500 Summerville Rd/Excelsior MN 55331
1954-015 ....Command, James Dalton ....3104 Plaza Drive NE #D14/Grand Rapids MI 49505
1926-017 ....Comorsky, Adam Anthony ....D. March 2, 1951 Swoyersville, Pa.
1911-030 ....Compton, Anna Sebastian 'Pete' ....D. February 3, 1978 Kansas City, Mo.
1911-031 ....Compton, Harry Leroy 'Jack' ....D. July 4, 1974 Lancaster, O.
1970-025 ....Compton, Michael Lynn ....8624 Leighton Dr/Tampa FL 33614
1972-020 ....Compton, Robert Clinton 'Clint' ....Old Add: Union Grove Road/Albertville AL 35950
1984-021 ....Comstock, Keith Martin ....9615 East Desert Trail/Scottsdale AZ 85260
1913-035 ....Comstock, Ralph Remick ....D. September 13, 1966 Toledo, O.
1948-028 ....Conatsor, Clinton Astor ....26701 Quail Creek #191/Laguna Hills CA 92653
1970-026 ....Concepcion, David Ismael................................Urb. Los Caobos Botalon 5d, 5 Piso Maracay Venezuela
1980-026 ....Concepcion, Onix (Cardona)............................Parcela 61aa-Bo.Higuillar/Dorado PR 646
1962-028 ....Conde, Ramon Luis ....Box 57/Juana Diaz PR 665
1986-036 ....Cone, David Brian ....17080 Harbour Point Drive/Fort Myers FL 33908
1915-021 ....Cone, Robert Earl ....D. May 24, 1955 Galveston, Tex.
1940-012 ....Conger, Richard ....D. February 16, 1970 Los Angeles, Calif.
1964-020 ....Conigliaro, Anthony Richard............................D. February 24, 1990 Salem, Mass.
1969-035 ....Conigliaro, William Michael ....154 Lynnway #514/Lynn MA 1902
1990-034 ....Conine, Jeffrey Guy ....17321 Lakepointe Drive/Riverside CA 92503
1920-023 ....Conkwright, Allen Howard................................D. July 30, 1991 Lamesa, Calif.
1934-027 ....Conlan, John Bertrand 'Jocko' ....D. April 16, 1989 Scottsdale, Ariz.
1952-019 ....Conley, Donald Eugene 'Gene' ....1 Farrington Road/Foxboro MA 2035
1914-039 ....Conley, James Patrick 'Snipe' ....D. January 7, 1978 Desoto, Tex.
1958-025 ....Conley, Robert Burns ....Old Add: 411 Highland Ave/Palisades Park NJ 07650
1923-022 ....Conlon, Arthur Joseph.....................................D. August 5, 1987 Falmouth, Mass.
1983-035 ....Connally, Fritzie Lee ....8080 North Central Exwy #850/Dallas TX 75206
1921-015 ....Connally, George Walter 'Sarge'.....................D. January 27, 1978 Temple, Texas
1925-020 ....Connally, Mervin Thomas ....D. June 12, 1964 Berkeley, Calif.
1931-015 ....Connatser, Broadus Milburn 'Bruce' ....D. January 27, 1971 Terre Haute, Ind.
1931-016 ....Connell, Eugene Joseph ....D. August 31, 1937 Waverly, N. Y.
1926-018 ....Connell, Joseph Bernard ....D. September 21, 1977 Trexlertown, Pa.
1920-024 ....Connelly, Thomas Martin ....D. February 18, 1941 Hines, Ill.
1945-015 ....Connelly, William Wirt ....D. November 27, 1980 Richmond, Va.
1929-020 ....Connolly, Edward Joseph ....D. November 14, 1963 Pittsfield, Mass.
1964-021 ....Connolly, Edward Joseph ....D. July 1, 1998 New Canaan, Conn.
1913-036 ....Connolly, Joseph Aloysius ....D. September 1, 1943 Springfield, R.I.
1921-016 ....Connolly, Joseph George ....D. March 30, 1960 San Francisco, Calif.
1915-022 ....Connolly, Thomas Francis ....D. May 14, 1966 Boston, Mass.
1949-016 ....Connors, Kevin Joseph 'Chuck' ....D. November 10, 1992 Los Angeles, Calif.
1937-027 ....Connors, Mervyn James ....1131 Addison Street/Berkeley CA 94702
1966-023 ....Connors, William Joseph ....507 Fayette Circle North/Safety Harbor FL 34695
1978-028 ....Conroy, Timothy James...................................3861 Newton Drive/Murrysville PA 15668
1923-023 ....Conroy, William Frederick 'Pep' ....D. January 23, 1970 Chicago, Ill.
1935-016 ....Conroy, William Gordon ....D. November 13, 1997 Bloomington, Ill.

1953-016	Consolo, William Angelo	1266 Willsbrook Court/Westlake Village CA 91360
1956-023	Constable, James Lee	Rr 14 - Box 540/Jonesboro TN 37659
1950-023	Consuegra, Sandalio Simeon	3255 Flagler Street #14/Miami FL 33125
1980-027	Contreras, Arnaldo Juan Nardie	17546 Willow Pond Drive/Lutz FL 33549
1993-034	Converse, James Daniel	8021 Stone Canyon Circle/Citrus Heights CA 95610
1911-032	Conway, Charles Connell	D. September 12, 1968 Youngstown, O.
1941-017	Conway, Jack Clements	D. June 11, 1993 Waco, Texas
1920-025	Conway, Jerome Patrick	D. April 16, 1980 Holyoke, Mass.
1915-023	Conway, Owen Sylvester	D. March 12, 1942 Philadelphia, Pa.
1918-012	Conway, Richard Daniel 'Rip'	D. December 3, 1971 St Paul, Minn.
1911-033	Conwell, Edward James	D. May 1, 1926 Norwood Park, Ill.
1950-024	Conyers, Herbert Leroy	D. September 16, 1964 Cleveland, O.
1913-037	Conzelman, Joseph Harrison	D. April 17, 1979 Mountain Brook, Ala.
1950-025	Coogan, Dale Roger	D. March 8, 1989 Mission Viejo Calif.
1993-035	Cook, Andrew Bernard	4001 McWeeny Avenue/Memphis TN 38128
1988-032	Cook, Dennis Bryan	5017 Cedar Creek/Dickinson TX 77539
1941-018	Cook, Earl Davis	D. November 21, 1996 Markham, Ontario
1985-020	Cook, Glen Patrick	34 Johnson Street/Tonawanda NY 14150
1913-038	Cook, Luther Almus 'Doc'	D. June 30, 1973 Lawrenceburg, Tenn.
1986-037	Cook, Michael Horace	618 Poinsetta Road #2/Charleston SC 29407
1959-015	Cook, Raymond Clifford 'Cliff'	605 Williamsburg Manor/Arlington TX 76014
1915-024	Cook, Rollin Edward	D. August 11, 1975 Toledo, O.
1970-027	Cook, Ronald Wayne	1916 Franklin/Longview TX 75601
1930-013	Cooke, Allen Lindsey 'Dusty'	D. November 21, 1987 Raleigh, N. C.
1992-029	Cooke, Steven Montague	19581 SW Jessica Court/Aloha OR 97006
1995-051	Cookson, Brent Adam	1232 Manzanita Drive/Santa Paula CA 93060
1989-025	Coolbaugh, Scott Richard	6214 Hickory Hollow/San Antonio TX 78239
1914-040	Coombs, Cecil Lysander	D. November 25, 1975 Fort Worth, Tex.
1963-025	Coombs, Daniel Bernard	14130 Cleobrook/Houston TX 77070
1933-014	Coombs, Raymond Frank 'Bobby'	D. October 21, 1991 Ogunquit, Maine
1995-052	Coomer, Ronald Bryan	10498 West 163rd Place/Orland Park IL 60462
1917-015	Cooney, James Edward	D. August 7, 1991 Warwick, R. I.
1921-017	Cooney, John Walter	D. July 8, 1986 Sarasota, Fla.
1931-017	Cooney, Robert Daniel	D. May 4, 1976 Glen Falls, N. Y.
1912-038	Cooper, Arley Wilbur	D. August 7, 1973 Encino, Calif.
1948-029	Cooper, Calvin Asa	D. July 4, 1994 Clinton, S. C.
1971-027	Cooper, Cecil Celester	1431 Misty Bend/Katy TX 77450
1913-039	Cooper, Claude William	D. January 21, 1974 Plainview, Tex.
1981-024	Cooper, Donald James	2122 Seward Drive/Sarasota FL 34234
1991-038	Cooper, Gary Clifton	318 West 1060 South/Orem UT 84058
1980-028	Cooper, Gary Nathaniel	4723 Augusta Road/Garden City GA 31408
1914-041	Cooper, Guy Evans	D. August 2, 1951 Santa Monica, Calif.
1938-016	Cooper, Morton Cecil	D. November 17, 1958 Little Rock, Ark.
1946-019	Cooper, Orge Patterson 'Pat'	D. March 15, 1993 Charlotte, N. C.
1990-035	Cooper, Scott Kendrick	808 Sugar Valley Court/Saint Peters MO 63376
1940-013	Cooper, William Walker 'Walker'	D. April 11, 1991 Scottsdale, Ariz.
1935-017	Copeland, Mays	D. November 29, 1982 Indio, Calif.
1996-039	Coppinger, John Thomas 'Rocky'	7208 Alto Rey Avenue/El Paso TX 79912
1935-018	Coppola, Henry Peter	D. July 10, 1990 Norfolk, Mass.
1987-026	Cora, Jose Manuel	Calle 17, F12 Villa Nueva/Caguas PR 625
1980-029	Corbett, Douglas Mitchell	223 Altamonte Commerce #1306/Altamonte Spgs FL 32714
1936-015	Corbett, Eugene Louis	510 Georgia Avenue/#J/Salisbury MD 21801
1988-033	Corbett, Sherman Stanley	3901 Cheshire Court/Bryan TX 77802
1971-028	Corbin, Alton Ray	922 Liberty St/Live Oak FL 32060
1991-039	Corbin, Archie Ray	4935 Ada Lane/Beaumont TX 77708
1945-016	Corbitt, Claude Elliott	D. May 1, 1978 Cincinnati, O.
1915-025	Corcoran, Arthur Andrew	D. July 27, 1958 Chelsea, Mass.
1910-034	Corcoran, Michael Joseph 'Mickey'	D. December 9, 1950 Buffalo, N.Y.
1977-032	Corcoran, Timothy Michael	4349 Friar Circle/Laverne CA 91750
1992-030	Cordero, Wilfredo Nieva	Res. Kennedy Edi 7 Apt. 61/Mayaguez PR 708
1996-040	Cordova, Francisco	Old Add: Veracruz Mexico
1995-053	Cordova, Martin Keevin	%N.Cordova 2816 Painted Rose Henderson NV 89014
1918-013	Corey, Edward Norman	D. September 17, 1970 Kenosha, Wis.
1979-025	Corey, Mark Mundell	PO Box 161/Evergreen CO 80439
1925-021	Corgan, Charles Howard	D. June 13, 1928 Wagoner, Okla.
1911-034	Corhan, Roy George	D. November 24, 1958 San Francisco, Calif.
1969-036	Corkins, Michael Patrick	Old Add: 6354 Duchess Drive Riverside CA 92509
1991-040	Cormier, Rheal Paul	RR 1, Robicahud Ofc (Box 135)/Cap' Pele New Bruns. E0A 2F0 Canada
1978-029	Cornejo, Neives Mardie Mardie	321 East Third Street/Wellington KS 67152
1995-054	Cornelius, Jonathan Reid 'Reid'	1013 Terrilynn Drive/Thomasville AL 36784
1984-022	Cornell, Jeffery Ray	Rural Route 2 Box 130/Odessa MO 64076
1994-018	Cornett, Brad Byron	1301 East 63rd/Odessa TX 79762
1977-033	Cornutt, Terry Stanton	179 West Hazel/Roseburg OR 97470
1995-055	Cornwell, Craig John	14917 American Eagle Court/Fort Myers FL 33912
1964-022	Corrales, Patrick	571 Big Canoe/Jasper GA 30143
1985-021	Correa, Edwin Joseph	Milagros Cabezas #Ar Carolina Alta Carolina PR 987
1993-036	Correia, Ronald Douglas 'Rod'	23 Winter Street/Rehoboth MA 2769
1972-021	Correll, Victor Crosby	119 Kentucky Downs/Perry GA 31069
1946-020	Corriden, John Michael	1010 North Lynnwood/Indianapolis In/46201

1910-035 ....Corriden, John Michael 'Red' ....D. September 28, 1959 Indianapolis, Ind.
1988-034 ....Corsi, James Bernard ....157 Hartford Street #A/Natick MA 1760
1977-034 ....Cort, Barry Lee ....12208 North Ola Avenue/Tampa FL 33612
1923-024 ....Cortazzo, John Frank 'Shine' ....D. March 4, 1963 Pittsburgh, Pa.
1951-016 ....Corwin, Elmer Nathan 'Al' ....1412 Sherwood/Geneva IL 60134
1935-019 ....Coscarart, Joseph Marvin ....D. April 5, 1993 Sequim, Wash.
1938-017 ....Coscarart, Peter Joseph ....2808 Julinda Way/Escondido CA 92029
1980-030 ....Cosey, Donald Ray ....139 Byxbee St/San Francisco CA 94132
1972-022 ....Cosgrove, Michael John ....3827 West Belmont/Phoenix AZ 85051
1966-024 ....Cosman, James Harry ....Old Add: 6195 Green Meadows Rd Memphis TN 38119
1913-040 ....Costello, Daniel Francis.................................D. March 26, 1936 Pittsburgh, Pa.
1988-035 ....Costello, John Reilly ....68 Royal Oak Court #206/Vero Beach FL 32962
1992-031 ....Costo, Timothy Roger ....22 West 486 Arbor Lane/Glen Ellyn IL 60137
1926-019 ....Cote, Warren Peter 'Pete' ....D. October 17, 1987 Middleton, Mass.
1926-020 ....Cotter, Edward Christopher...........................D. June 14, 1959 Hartford, Conn.
1922-022 ....Cotter, Harvey Louis ....D. August 6, 1955 Los Angeles, Calif.
1911-035 ....Cotter, Richard Raphael ....D. April 4, 1945 Brooklyn, N. Y.
1959-016 ....Cottier, Charles Keith....................................7129 Lake Ballinger Way/Edmonds WA 98020
1984-023 ....Cotto, Henry ....2659 Meadowood Court/Fort Lauderdale FL 33332
1911-036 ....Cottrell, Ensign Stover..................................D. February 27, 1947 Syracuse, N.Y.
1917-016 ....Couch, John Daniel ....D. December 8, 1975 Palo Alto, Calif.
1983-036 ....Couchee, Michael Eugene ....3060 North Ridgecrest #155/Mesa AZ 85207
1960-025 ....Coughtry, James Marlan 'Marlan' ....11008 NE 183rd Street/Battle Ground WA 98604
1969-037 ....Coulter, Thomas Lee 'Chip' ....718 Trenton Street/Toronto OH 43964
1914-042 ....Coumbe, Frederick Nicholas 'Fritz' ....D. March 21, 1978 Paradise, Calif.
1951-017 ....Courtney, Clinton Dawson ....D. June 16, 1985 Rochester, N. Y.
1919-015 ....Courtney, Henry Seymour ....D. December 11, 1954 Lyme, Ct.
1995-056 ....Courtright, John Charles ....2111 Altura Drive/Signal Mountain TN 37377
1923-025 ....Cousineau, Ed 'D' ....D. July 14, 1951 Watertown, Mass.
1912-039 ....Coveleski, Stanley Anthony ....D. March 20, 1984 South Bend, Ind.
1944-023 ....Covington, Chester Rogers ....D. June 11, 1976 Pembroke Park, Fla.
1913-041 ....Covington, Clarence Calvert 'Tex' ....D. January 4, 1963 Denison, Tex.
1956-024 ....Covington, John Wesley 'Wes' ....905 10145 119th Street/Edmonton Alberta T5K 1Z2 Canada
1911-037 ....Covington, William Wilkes ....D. December 10, 1931 Denison, Tex.
1963-026 ....Cowan, Billy Roland ....1539 Via Coronel/Palos Verdes Estates CA 90274
1974-017 ....Cowens, Alfred Edward ....5723 Keniston Ave/Los Angeles CA 90043
1982-026 ....Cowley, Joseph Alan ....102 Summertree Drive/Nicholasville KY 40356
1983-037 ....Cox, Danny Bradford ....306 Feagin Mill Rd/Warner Robins GA 31093
1925-022 ....Cox, Elmer Joseph 'Dick' ....D. June 1, 1966 Morro Bay, Calif.
1922-023 ....Cox, Ernest Thompson ....D. April 29, 1974 Birmingham, Ala.
1928-023 ....Cox, George Melvin ....D. December 17, 1995 Bedford, Texas
1955-030 ....Cox, Glenn Melvin ....PO Box 432/Los Molinos CA 96055
1973-026 ....Cox, James Charles ....8370 East Charter Oak Drive/Scottsdale AZ 85260
1980-031 ....Cox, Jeffrey Lindon ....2727 Vanderhoof Dr/West Covina CA 91791
1966-025 ....Cox, Joseph Casey 'Casey' ....Old Add: 630 Grand Avenue Long Beach CA 90814
1973-027 ....Cox, Larry Eugene ....D. February 17, 1990 Bellefontaine, Ohio
1926-021 ....Cox, Leslie Warren ....D. October 14, 1934 San Angelo, Tex.
1920-026 ....Cox, Plateau Rex ....D. October 15, 1984 Roanoke, Va.
1968-015 ....Cox, Robert Joseph 'Bobby' ....4491 Chattahoochee Plantation/Marietta GA 30068
1970-028 ....Cox, Terry Lee ....Old Add: 2166 Ledgewood Cir West Jordan UT 84084
1936-016 ....Cox, William Donald ....D. February 16, 1988 Charleston, Ill.
1941-019 ....Cox, William Richard ....D. March 30, 1978 Harrisburg, Pa.
1977-035 ....Cox, William Ted 'Ted' ....Old Add: 113 West Pratt Drive Midwest City OK 73110
1914-043 ....Coyne, Martin Albert 'Toots' ....D. September 18, 1939 St. Louis, Mo.
1945-017 ....Cozart, Charles Rhubin ....1975 Freedom Lane/Hudson NC 28638
1912-040 ....Crabb, James Roy ....D. March 30, 1940 Lewiston, Mont.
1910-036 ....Crable, George ....Old Add: 121 6th Avenue Brooklyn Ny
1929-021 ....Crabtree, Estel Crayton ....D. January 4, 1967 Logan, O.
1995-057 ....Crabtree, Timothy Lyle ....6347 Adams/Coloma MI 49038
1955-031 ....Craddock, Walter Anderson ....D. July 6, 1980 Parma Heights Ohio
1937-028 ....Craft, Harry Francis ....D. August 3, 1995 Conroe, Texas
1916-014 ....Craft, Maurice Montague 'Molly' ....D. October 25, 1978 Los Angeles, Calif.
1931-018 ....Craghead, Howard Oliver ....D. July 15, 1962 San Zieloe, Calif.
1964-023 ....Craig, Peter Joel ....5915 Carmel Lane/Raleigh NC 27609
1979-026 ....Craig, Rodney Paul 'Rocky' ....Old Add: 23230 Sesame St Torrance CA 90504
1955-032 ....Craig, Roger Lee ....26658 San Felipe Rd/Warner Spring CA 92086
1969-038 ....Cram, Gerald Allen ....2 Castletree/Las Flores CA 92688
1929-022 ....Cramer, Roger Maxwell ....D. September 9, 1990 Manahawkin, N. J.
1912-041 ....Cramer, William Wendell ....D. September 11, 1966 Fort Wayne, Ind.
1949-017 ....Crandall, Delmar Wesley ....25 Rock Cliff Place/Pomona CA 91766
1914-044 ....Crane, Samuel Byren ....D. November 12, 1955 Philadelphia, Pa.
1996-041 ....Crawford, Carlos Lamonte ....Old Add: Charlotte NC 28201
1937-029 ....Crawford, Charles Lowrie 'Larry' ....D. December 20, 1994 Hanover, Pa.
1929-023 ....Crawford, Clifford Rankin 'Pat' ....D. January 25, 1994 Kinston, N. C.
1945-018 ....Crawford, Glenn Martin ....D. January 2, 1972 Saginaw, Mich.
1973-028 ....Crawford, James Frederick ....Old Add: 48621 I-94 Service Dr/Belleville MI 48111
1997-036 ....Crawford, Joseph Randol ....Old Add: Hillsboro OH 45133
1915-026 ....Crawford, Kenneth Daniel ....D. November 11, 1976 Pittsburgh, Pa.
1952-020 ....Crawford, Rufus 'Jake' ....Rural Route 1 Box 134c/Clifton AR 76634

1980-032 ....Crawford, Steve Ray ....9810 East 99th Place/Tulsa OK 74133
1964-024 ....Crawford, Willie Murphy ....PO Box 491054/Los Angeles CA 90049
1943-032 ....Creeden, Cornelius Stephen ....D. November 30, 1969 Santa Ana, Calif.
1931-019 ....Creeden, Patrick Francis ....D. April 20, 1992 Brockton, Mass.
1995-058 ....Creek, Paul Douglas 'Doug' ....203 Forest Drive/Martinsburg WV 25401
1945-019 ....Creel, Jack Dalton ....7119 Oak Arbor/Houston TX 77088
1982-027 ....Creel, Steven Keith Keith........................527 Trail Ridge Drive/Duncanville TX 75116
1947-022 ....Creger, Bernard Odell ....15 Greenwell Court/Lynchburg VA 24502
1927-027 ....Cremins, Robert Anthony ....415 Manor Ridge Road/Pelham NY 10803
1938-018 ....Crespi, Frank Angelo Joseph 'Creepy' ....D. March 1, 1990 Florissant, Mo.
1996-042 ....Crespo, Felipe Javier Clauso ....Old Add: Caguas PR 00725
1948-030 ....Cress, Walker James ....D. April 21, 1996 Baton Rouge, La.
1987-027 ....Crews, Stanley Timothy Tim ....D. March 23, 1993 Orlando, Fla.
1969-039 ....Crider, Jerry Stephen ....Old Add: 821 Kensington Dr/Orlando FL 32801
1987-028 ....Crim, Charles Robert ....Hcr 6 Box 4787-362/Reeds Spring Mo 65737
1951-018 ....Crimian, John Melvin ....3012 Green Street/Claymont/De/19703
1978-030 ....Cripe, David Gordon ....1091 Joseph Drive/Hemet CA 92545
1977-036 ....Criscione, David Gerald ....87 Hamlet St/Fredonia NY 14063
1942-024 ....Criscola, Anthony Paul ....4025 Bayard/San Diego CA 92109
1910-037 ....Crisp, Joseph Shelby ....D. February 5, 1939 Kansas City, Mo.
1951-019 ....Cristante, Leo Dante ....D. August 24, 1977 Dearborn, Mich.
1924-023 ....Critz, Hugh Melville ....D. January 10, 1980 Greenwood, Miss.
1944-024 ....Crocker, Claude Arthur ....Merrie Oaks/Clinton SC 29325
1974-018 ....Cromartie, Warren Livingston ....19364 East Country Club Drive/Aventura FL 33180
1993-037 ....Cromer, Roy Bunyan 'Tripp' ....Old Add: PO Box 2064 Lexington SC 29071
1937-030 ....Crompton, Herbert Bryan ....D. August 5, 1963 Moline, Ill.
1991-041 ....Cron, Christopher John ....4408 East Mountain Sage Drive/Phoenix AZ 85044
1954-016 ....Crone, Raymond Hayes ....508 Panorama/Waxahachie TX 75165
1929-024 ....Cronin, James John ....D. June 10, 1983 Richmond, Calif.
1926-022 ....Cronin, Joseph Edward ....D. September 7, 1984 Osterville, Mass.
1928-024 ....Cronin, William Patrick ....D. October 26, 1966 Newton, Mass.
1970-029 ....Crosby, Edward Carlton ....6952 Brightwood Lane #9/Garden Grove CA 92645
1975-028 ....Crosby, Kenneth Stewart........................Box 680306/Park City UT 84068
1932-015 ....Crosetti, Frank Peter Joseph ....65 West Monterey Avenue/Stockton CA 95204
1942-025 ....Cross, Joffre James 'Jeff' ....D. July 23, 1997 Huntsville, Texas
1912-042 ....Crossin, Frank Patrick ....D. December 6, 1965 Kingsport, Pa.
1930-014 ....Crouch, Jack Albert ....D. August 25, 1972 Leesburg, Fla.
1939-024 ....Crouch, William Elmer ....D. December 26, 1980 Howell, Mich.
1910-038 ....Crouch, William Henry ....D. December 22, 1945 Highland Park, Mich.
1988-036 ....Crouch, Zachary Quinn ....3122 Tory/Sacramento CA 95827
1939-025 ....Croucher, Frank Donald ....D. May 21, 1980 Houston, Texas
1923-026 ....Crouse, Clyde Ellsworth 'Buck' ....D. October 23, 1983 Muncie, Ind.
1982-028 ....Crow, Donald Leroy ....PO Box 1742/Fort Mill SC 29716
1926-023 ....Crowder, Alvin Floyd 'Gen' ....D. April 3, 1972 Winston-Salem, N. C.
1952-021 ....Crowe, George Daniel ....311 Silas Tompkins Road/Long Eddy NY 12760
1997-037 ....Crowell, James E. ....4003 Sleighbell Lane/Valparaiso IN 46383
1915-027 ....Crowell, Minot Joy 'Cap' ....D. September 30, 1962 Central Falls, R.I.
1928-025 ....Crowley, Edgar Jewel ....D. April 14, 1970 Birmingham, Ala.
1969-040 ....Crowley, Terrence Michael ....10626 Anglohill Rd/Cockeysville MD 21030
1945-020 ....Crowson, Thomas Woodrow Wilson 'Woody'.D. August 14, 1947 Mayodan, N. C.
1914-045 ....Cruise, Walton Edwin........................D. January 9, 1975 Sylacauga Ala.
1917-017 ....Crum, Calvin Carl ....D. December 7, 1945 Tulsa, Okla.
1945-021 ....Crumling, Eugene Leon ....135 Lisa Circle/York PA 17406
1924-024 ....Crump, Arthur Elliott ....D. September 7, 1976 Raleigh, N. C.
1920-027 ....Crumpler, Ray Maxton ....D. October 6, 1969 Fayetteville, N. C.
1997-040 ....Crus, Luis Ivan 'Ivan' ....Old Add: Fajardo PR 00738
1914-046 ....Crutcher, Richard Louis ....D. June 19, 1952 Frankfort, Ky.
1913-042 ....Cruthers, Charles Preston 'Press' ....D. December 27, 1976 Kenosha, Wisc.
1973-029 ....Cruz, Cirilo 'Tommy' ....Urb. Jardines De Arroyo Calle Ee C 104 Arroyo PR 714
1997-038 ....Cruz, Deivi Garcia ....Old Add: Bani Dominican Rep.
1994-019 ....Cruz, Fausto Santiago ....Federico De Jesus Garcia #112 Villa Vasquez Dominican Rep.
1973-030 ....Cruz, Hector Luis ....Calle H-E-8/Arroyo PR 615
1975-029 ....Cruz, Henry Acosta ....06 Urb Monte Brisas/Fajardo PR 738
1996-043 ....Cruz, Jacob ....Old Add: Oxnard CA 93030
1970-030 ....Cruz, Jose Delan ....10718 Braes Forest/Houston TX 77071
1997-039 ....Cruz, Jose "L., Jr." ....10718 Braes Forest/Houston TX 77071
1977-037 ....Cruz, Julio Louis ....40 Orcas Key/Bellevue WA 98006
1997-041 ....Cruz, Nelson ....Old Add: Miami FL 33101
1978-031 ....Cruz, Todd Ruben ....16442 Jurupa Avenue/Fontana CA 92337
1978-032 ....Cruz, Victor Manuel ....Old Add: Alex Fleming #67 Santo Domingo Dom. Rep.
1974-019 ....Cubbage, Michael Lee ....3349 Carroll Creek Road/Keswick VA 22947
1935-020 ....Cuccinello, Alfred Edward........................106 Legion Place/Malverne NY 11565
1930-015 ....Cuccinello, Anthony Francis 'Tony' ....D. September 21, 1995 Tampa, Fla.
1943-033 ....Cuccurullo, Arthur Joseph 'Cookie' ....D. January 23, 1983 West Orange, N. J.
1977-038 ....Cuellar, Bobby ....705 East Sixth Street/Alice TX 78332
1950-026 ....Cuellar, Jesus Patracis 'Charlie'........................D. October 11, 1994 Tampa, Fla.
1959-017 ....Cuellar, Miguel Santana ....Old Add: 5108 Louis Drive/El Paso TX 79904
1961-025 ....Cueto, Dagoberto Concepcion ....El Corojo San Luis Pinar Del Rio/Cuba
1914-047 ....Cueto, Manuel Melo ....D. June 29, 1942 Regla, Havana Cuba

1943-034 ....Culberson, Delbert Leon 'Leon' ....D. September 17, 1989 Rome, Ga.
1962-029 ....Cullen, John Patrick................................164 Alexander Ave/Nutley NJ 7110
1966-026 ....Cullen, Timothy Leo ....159 West G Street/Benicia CA 94510
1938-019 ....Cullenbine, Roy Joseph............................D. May 28, 1991 Mount Clemens, Mich.
1936-017 ....Culler, Richard Broadus ....D. June 16, 1964 Chapel Hill, N. C.
1926-024 ....Cullop, Henry 'Nick' ....D. December 8, 1978 Westerville, O.
1913-043 ....Cullop, Norman Andrew 'Nick' ....D. April 15, 1961 Tazewell, Va.
1925-023 ....Culloton, Bernard Aloysius 'Bud' ....D. November 9, 1976 Kingston, N. Y.
1983-038 ....Culmer, Wilfred Hillard.............................Box N9762 Nassau/Bahamas
1942-026 ....Culp, Benjamin Baldy ....3827 Karen St Reet/Philadelphia PA 19114
1963-027 ....Culp, Ray Leonard ....7400 Waterline/Austin TX 78731
1910-039 ....Culp, William Edward ....D. September 3, 1969 Arnold, Pa.
1966-027 ....Culver, George Richard ....5409 Rustic Canyon Street/Bakersfield CA 93306
1968-016 ....Cumberland, John Sheldon......................PO Box 451/Odessa FL 33556
1993-038 ....Cummings, John Russell ....21 Park Paseo/Laguna Niguel CA 92677
1926-025 ....Cummings, John William ....D. October 5, 1962 West Mifflin, Pa.
1993-039 ....Cummings, Midre Almeric ....Old Add: 8900 NE 4th Ave Miami FL 33138
1989-026 ....Cummings, Steven Brent ....11010 Sagecrest/Houston TX 77089
1997-042 ....Cunnane, William Joseph 'Will' ....Old Add: Congers NY 10920
1929-025 ....Cunningham, Bruce Lee ....D. March 8, 1984 Hayward, Calif.
1916-015 ....Cunningham, George Harold ....D. March 10, 1972 Chattanooga, Tenn.
1954-017 ....Cunningham, Joseph Robert ....Rural Route 1 Box 80a/Koshkonong MO 65692
1931-020 ....Cunningham, Raymond Lee ....4801 Allendale Road #205/Houston TX 77017
1921-018 ....Cunningham, William Aloysius ....D. September 26, 1953 Colusa, Calif.
1910-040 ....Cunningham, William James.....................D. February 21, 1946 Schenectady, N. Y.
1975-030 ....Currence, Delancy Lafayette ....1238 Stanley Dr/Rock Hill SC 29730
1916-016 ....Currie, Murphy Archibald ....D. June 22, 1939 Asheboro, N.C.
1955-033 ....Currie, William Cleveland ....125 Lake Side Drive/Arlington GA 31713
1947-023 ....Currin, Perry Gilmore ....818 Amberstone Drive/San Antonio TX 78258
1960-026 ....Curry, George Anthony 'Tony' ....PO Box 7054 Nassau/Bahamas
1911-038 ....Curry, George James ....D. October 5, 1963 Stratford, Conn.
1988-037 ....Curry, Stephen Thomas ....29112 White Road/Perrysburg OH 43551
1992-032 ....Curtis, Chad David ....Old Add: 590 N. San Pedro Benson AZ 85602
1961-026 ....Curtis, Jack Patrick ....4993 Poplar View Lane/Granite Falls NC 28630
1970-031 ....Curtis, John Duffield ....Old Add: 858 Andromeda Lane Foster City CA 94404
1943-035 ....Curtis, Vernon Eugene............................D. June 24, 1992 Cairo, Ill.
1943-036 ....Curtright, Guy Paxton ....D. August 23, 1997 Sun City Center, Fla.
1951-020 ....Cusick, John Peter ....D. November 17, 1989 Englewood, N.J.
1912-043 ....Cutshaw, George William ....D. August 22, 1973 San Diego, Calif.
1921-019 ....Cuyler, Hazen Shirley 'Kiki' ....D. February 11, 1950 Ann Arbor, Mich.
1990-036 ....Cuyler, Milton ....962 Lamar Road/Macon GA 31210
1922-024 ....Cvengros, Michael John ....D. August 2, 1970 Hot Springs, Ark.
1914-048 ....Cypert, Alfred Boyd ....D. January 9, 1973 Washington, D.C.
1994-020 ....Czajkowski, James Mark ....1648 Rivergate Drive/Sevierville TN 37862
1993-040 ....Daal, Omar Jose (Cordero) ....Fun Val li,Manzana#6 Casa#24 Flor Amar Valencia Venezuela
1973-031 ....Dacquisto, John Francis ....3440 Fir St/San Diego CA 92104
1975-031 ....Dade, Lonnie Paul 'Paul' ....Old Add: 764 Santaclara Ave Alameda CA 94501
1943-037 ....Dagenhard, John Douglas ....285 Harrison Street #514/Magnolia OH 44643
1932-016 ....Daglia, Peter George ....D. March 11, 1952 Willits, Calif.
1955-034 ....Dagres, Angelo George ....PO Box 27/Rowley MA 1969
1963-028 ....Dahl, Jay Steven ....D. June 20, 1965 Salisbury, N. C.
1935-021 ....Dahlgren, Ellsworth Tenney 'Babe' ....D. September 4, 1996 Bradbury, Calif.
1956-025 ....Dahlke, Jerome Alexander ....201 Pine Lake Drive/Batesville MS 38606
1929-026 ....Dailey, Samuel Laurence ....D. December 2, 1979 Columbia, Mo.
1961-027 ....Dailey, William Garland ....Rr 1 Box M8/Dublin VA 24084
1967-021 ....Dal Canton, John Bruce...........................624 Ray Dr/Carnegie PA 15106
1911-039 ....Dale, Emmett Eugene 'Gene'.....................D. March 20, 1958 St. Louis, Mo.
1989-027 ....Dalena, Peter Martin ....4951 North Thorne/Fresno CA 93704
1994-021 ....Dalesandro, Mark Anthony ....1226 West Flourney Street/Chicago IL 60607
1955-035 ....Daley, Buddy Leo ....30 Chitten/Lander WY 82520
1912-044 ....Daley, John Francis ....D. August 31, 1988 Mansfield, Ohio
1911-040 ....Daley, Jud Lawrence ....D. January 26, 1967 Gadsden, Ala.
1955-036 ....Daley, Peter Harvey ....4019 Calle Mira Monte/Newbury Park CA 91320
1937-031 ....Dallessandro, Nicholas Dominic 'Dom' ....D. April 29, 1988 Indianapolis, Ind.
1960-027 ....Dalrymple, Clayton Errol ....8750 Shasta Avenue/Los Molinas CA 96055
1915-028 ....Dalrymple, William Dunn ....D. July 14, 1967 San Diego, Calif.
1991-042 ....Dalton, Michael Edward ....1522 Canna Court/Mountain View CA 94043
1910-041 ....Dalton, Talbot Percy 'Jack' ....Old Add: 2 Prospect Ave/Catonsville MD 21228
1913-044 ....Daly, Thomas Daniel ....D. November 7, 1946 Medford, Mass.
1963-029 ....Damaska, Jack Lloyd ....252 Blackhawk Rd/Beaver Falls PA 15010
1996-044 ....Damico, Jeffrey/Charles...........................6903 Cedar Ridge Drive/Pinellas Park FL 34665
1995-059 ....Damon, Johnny David ....12847 Lamar Avenue/Overland Park KS 66209
1915-029 ....Damrau, Harry Robert ....D. August 21, 1957 Staten Island, N. Y.
1928-026 ....Daney, Arthur Lee ....D. March 11, 1988 Scottsdale, Ariz.
1911-041 ....Danforth, David Charles ....D. September 19, 1970 Baltimore, Md.
1957-014 ....Daniel, Charles Edward ....1640 Babs Rd/Memphis TN 38116
1937-032 ....Daniel, Handley Jacob ....D. April 23, 1996 Lagrange, Ga.
1957-015 ....Daniels, Bennie ....938 West 156th Street/Compton CA 90220
1910-042 ....Daniels, Bernard Elmer 'Bert' ....D. June 6, 1958 Cedar Grove, N.J.

1945-022 ....Daniels, Frederick Clinton ....522 Salisbury Road/Statesville NC 28677
1952-022 ....Daniels, Harold Jack 'Jack' ....3715 Elmridge Drive/Evansville IN 47711
1986-038 ....Daniels, Kalvoski ....1530 Seabay Road/Fort Lauderdale FL 33326
1915-030 ....Danner, Henry Frederick 'Buck' ....D. September 21, 1949 Boston, Mass.
1933-015 ....Danning, Harry ....212 Fox Chapel Court/Valparaiso IN 46385
1928-027 ....Danning, Ike ....D. March 28, 1983 Santa Monica, Calif.
1944-025 ....Dantonio, John James ....D. May 28, 1993 New Orleans, La.
1942-027 ....Dapper, Clifford Roland ....733 Burma Road/Fallbrook CA 92028
1974-020 ....Darcy, Patrick Leonard ....515 South Columbus Blvd/Tucson AZ 85711
1914-049 ....Daringer, Clifford Clarence ....D. December 12, 1971 Sacramento, Calif.
1914-050 ....Daringer, Rolla Harrison ....D. May 23, 1974 Seymour, Ind.
1946-021 ....Dark, Alvin Ralph ....103 Cranberry Way/Easley Sc/29642
1983-039 ....Darling, Ronald Maurice ....19 Woodland Street/Millbury MA 1527
1954-018 ....Darnell, Robert Jack ....D. January 1, 1995 Fredericksburg, Texas
1977-039 ....Darr, Michael Edward ....1762 Sumac Place/Corona CA 91720
1934-028 ....Darrow, George Oliver ....D. March 24, 1983 Sun City, Ariz.
1962-030 ....Darwin, Arthur Bobby Lee ....17509 Alora Street/Cerritos CA 90701
1978-033 ....Darwin, Daniel Wayne ....13913 South Fm 372/Valley View TX 76272
1994-022 ....Darwin, Jeffrey Scott ....1010 Russell Avenue/Bonham TX 75418
1988-038 ....Dascenzo, Douglas Craig ....PO Box 7/Hiller PA 15444
1924-025 ....Dashiell, John Wallace 'Wally' ....D. May 20, 1972 Pensacola, Fla.
1913-045 ....Dashner, Lee Claire ....D. December 16, 1960 El Dorado, Kan.
1945-023 ....Dasso, Francis Joseph Nicholas ....1413 Madison/Wenatchee WA 98801
1989-028 ....Datz, Jeffrey William ....86 South Main Street/Mullica Hill NJ 8062
1915-031 ....Daubert, Harry J. ....D. January 8, 1944 Detroit, Mich.
1910-043 ....Daubert, Jacob Elsworth ....D. October 9, 1924 Cincinnati, O.
1976-027 ....Dauer, Richard Fremont ....2510 Brook Haven Lane/Hinckley OH 44233
1951-021 ....Daugherty, Harold Ray ....195 Lakeview Circle/Russell Springs/Ky 42542
1987-029 ....Daugherty, John Michael 'Jack' ....11290 Corte Playa Azteca/San Diego CA 92124
1937-033 ....Daughters, Robert Francis ....D. August 22, 1988 Southbury, Conn.
1983-040 ....Daulton, Darren Arthur ....5 Meadow Lane/Arkansas City KS 67005
1912-045 ....Dauss, George August 'Hooks' ....D. July 27, 1963 St. Louis, Mo.
1953-017 ....Davalillo, Pompeyo Romero 'Yoyo' ....Old Add: Lista De Correo, Nueva/"Granda, Caracas Venezuela"
1963-030 ....Davalillo, Victor Jose ....Calle Trujillo 7, "Mariperez,Q.V, Caracas Venezuela/"
1969-041 ....Davanon, Frank Gerald ....2727 Elmside Drive #134/Houston TX 77042
1920-028 ....Davenport, Claude Edwin ....D. June 13, 1976 Corpus Christi, Tex.
1914-051 ....Davenport, David W. ....D. October 16, 1954 El Dorado, Ark.
1958-026 ....Davenport, James Houston ....1016 Hewitt Dr/San Carlos CA 94070
1921-020 ....Davenport, Joubert Lum ....D. April 21, 1961 Dallas, Tex.
1977-040 ....Davey, Michael Gerard ....South 5118 Madelia/Spokane WA 99203
1962-031 ....Daviault, Raymond Joseph Robert........12116 Ontario East Pointes Aux Trembles Quebec Canada
1984-024 ....David, Andre Anter ....1142 SE Oriental Avenue/Port Saint Lucie FL 34952
1918-014 ....Davidson, Claude Boucher ....D. April 18, 1956 Weymouth, Mass.
1986-039 ....Davidson, John Mark ....1606 Museum Road/Statesville NC 28677
1989-029 ....Davidson, Robert Bruce ....Old Add: 496 Warmsprings Drive Fayetteville NC 28303
1965-025 ....Davidson, Thomas Eugene 'Ted' ....515 De Armond Place/Santa Maria CA 93454
1959-018 ....Davie, Gerald Lee ....22000 Haggerty Road/Belleville MI 48111
1914-052 ....Davies, Lloyd Garrison 'Chick' ....D. September 5, 1973 Middletown, Conn.
1984-025 ....Davis, Alvin, Glenn ....1221 Flemington Road/Riverside CA 92506
1965-026 ....Davis, Arthur Willard 'Bill' ....6638 Knox Ave South/Minneapolis MN 55423
1963-031 ....Davis, Bryshear Barnett 'Brock' ....2080 West Ontario Avenue/Corona CA 91720
1981-025 ....Davis, Charles Theodore 'Chili' ....10040 East Happy Valley Rd #328/Scottsdale AZ 85255
1934-029 ....Davis, Curtis Benton ....D. October 12, 1965 Covina, Calif.
1988-039 ....Davis, Douglas Raymond ....Rural Route 4 Box 145/Bloomsburg PA 17815
1984-026 ....Davis, Eric Keith ....5616 Farralone Avenue/Woodland Hills CA 91367
1912-046 ....Davis, Frank Talmadge 'Dixie'............D. February 4, 1944 Raleigh, N.C.
1912-047 ....Davis, George Allen ....D. June 4, 1961 Buffalo, N.Y.
1982-029 ....Davis, George Earl 'Storm' ....Old Add: PO Box 14025 Savannah GA 31416
1926-026 ....Davis, George Willis 'Kiddo' ....D. March 4, 1983 Bridgeport, Conn.
1983-041 ....Davis, Gerald Edward ....72 Theresa Street/Trenton NJ 8618
1984-027 ....Davis, Glenn Earle ....4882 Champions Way/Columbus GA 31909
1932-017 ....Davis, Harry Albert ....D. March 3, 1997 Shreveport, La.
1959-019 ....Davis, Herman Thomas 'Tommy' ....9767 Whirlaway/Alta Loma CA 91701
1919-016 ....Davis, Isaac Marion ....D. April 2, 1984 Tucson, Ariz.
1962-032 ....Davis, Jacke Sylvesta ....1109 West Panola Street/Carthage TX 75633
1954-019 ....Davis, James Bennett ....D. December 6, 1995 San Mateo, Calif.
1981-026 ....Davis, Jody Richard ....Old Add: Rural Route 1, Ben Hill Dr Oakwood GA 30566
1985-022 ....Davis, Joel Clark ....609 Matterhorn Road/Jacksonville FL 32216
1941-020 ....Davis, John Humphrey ....PO Box 2742/Laurel MS 39442
1987-030 ....Davis, John Kirk ....343 Mill Run/Shepherdville KY 40165
1915-032 ....Davis, John Wilbur 'Bud' ....D. May 26, 1967 Lightfoot, Va.
1940-014 ....Davis, Lawrence Columbus 'Crash' ....4767 Champion Court/Greensboro NC 27410
1991-043 ....Davis, Mark Anthony ....1672 East Mountain Street/Pasadena CA 91104
1980-033 ....Davis, Mark William ....Old Add: 8038 East Tuckey Lane Scottsdale AZ 85253
1980-034 ....Davis, Michael Dwayne ....2491 San Ramon Valley #1407/San Ramon CA 94583
1980-035 ....Davis, Odie Ernest ....1014 Montana St/San Antonio TX 78203
1946-022 ....Davis, Otis Allen ....1115 Royal Troon Court/Tarpon Springs FL 34689
1936-018 ....Davis, Ray Thomas 'Peaches'...............D. April 28, 1995 Duncan, Okla.
1977-041 ....Davis, Richard Earl......................................2415 West Alondra/Compton CA 90220

1952-023	Davis, Robert Brandon 'Brandy'	222 Cheltenham Road/Newark/De/19712
1958-027	Davis, Robert Edward	37 West 12th Street #5j/New York NY 10011
1973-032	Davis, Robert John Eugene	Box 132/Locust Grove OK 74352
1962-033	Davis, Ronald Everette	D. September 5, 1992 Houston, Texas
1978-034	Davis, Ronald Gene	Old Add: 8103 Coyton Houston TX 77061
1994-023	Davis, Russell Stuart	3351 Crescent Drive/Hueytown AL 35025
1985-023	Davis, Steven Kennon	Old Add: 3500 South Hiwassee Rd Choctaw OK 73020
1979-027	Davis, Steven Michael	Old Add: 2150 N. Meridian #1803 Wichita KS 67203
1949-018	Davis, Thomas Oscar 'Tod'	D. December 31, 1978 West Covina, Calif.
1994-024	Davis, Timothy Howard	Rural Route 1 Box 122b/Bristol FL 32321
1985-024	Davis, Trench Neal	Old Add: 916 Seagull Ave Baltimore MD 21225
1928-028	Davis, Virgil Lawrence 'Spud'	D. August 14, 1984 Birmingham, Ala.
1983-042	Davis, Wallace McArthur 'Butch'	1108 Brucemont Drive/Garner NC 27529
1960-028	Davis, William Henry 'Willie'	Old Add: 4419 Buena Vista #203/Dallas TX 75202
1938-020	Davis, Woodrow Wilson	PO Box 87/Odum GA 31555
1969-042	Davison, Michael Lynn	578 Prospect/Hutchinson MN 55350
1995-060	Davison, Scotty Ray	Old Add: Redondo Beach CA
1983-043	Dawley, William Chester	Rr 2, Kendall Road Ext/Lisbon CT 6417
1976-028	Dawson, Andre Nolan	6295 Southwest 58th Place/Miami FL 33143
1924-026	Dawson, Ralph Fenton 'Joe'	D. January 4, 1978 Longview, Tex.
1913-046	Dawson, Rexford Paul	D. October 20, 1958 Indianapolis, Ind.
1969-043	Day, Charles Frederick 'Boots'	12617 Westport Drive/Saint Louis MO 63146
1924-027	Day, Clyde Henry 'Pea Ridge'	D. March 21, 1934 Kansas City, Mo.
1983-044	Dayett, Brian Kelly	10 Hemlock Terrace Ext/Deep River CT 6417
1982-030	Dayley, Kenneth Grant	2115 East 12th Street/The Dalles OR 97058
1912-048	Deal, Charles Albert	D. September 16, 1979 Covina, Calif.
1947-024	Deal, Ellis Ferguson 'Cot'	9505 North Silver Lake Drive/Oklahoma City OK 73162
1939-026	Deal, Lindsay Fred	D. April 18, 1979 Little Rock, Ark.
1936-019	Dean, Alfred Lovill 'Chubby'	D. December 21, 1970 Riverside, N. J.
1941-021	Dean, James Harry	D. June 1, 1960 Rockmart, Ga.
1930-016	Dean, Jay Hanna 'Dizzy'	D. July 17, 1974 Reno, Nev.
1934-030	Dean, Paul Dee	D. March 17, 1981 Springdale, Ark.
1967-022	Dean, Tommy Douglas	Rr2/Iuka MS 38852
1924-028	Dean, Wayland Ogden	D. April 10, 1930 Huntington, W. Va.
1927-028	Dear, Paul Stanford	D. August 29, 1989 Radford, Va.
1977-042	Debarr, Dennis Lee	33843 Juliet Circle/Fremont CA 94555
1916-017	Deberry, John Herman 'Hank'	D. September 10, 1951 Savannah, Tenn.
1920-029	Deberry, Joseph Gaddy	D. October 9, 1944 Southern Pines, N. C.
1917-018	Debus, Adam Joseph	D. May 13, 1977 Chicago, Ill.
1962-034	Debusschere, David Albert	136 Hampton Road/Garden City NY 11530
1922-025	Decatur, Arthur Rue	D. April 25, 1966 Talladega, Ala.
1973-033	Decinces, Douglas Vernon	124 Riviera Way/Laguna Beach CA 92651
1983-045	Decker, Dee Martin 'Marty'	Old Add: 920 Gate Lane Pilot Hill CA 95664
1969-044	Decker, George Henry 'Joe'	7981 West Powell Street/Boise ID 83703
1990-037	Decker, Steven Michael	Old Add: Rock Island IL 61201
1916-018	Dede, Arthur Richard	D. September 6, 1971 Keene, N.H.
1935-022	Dedeaux, Raoul Martial 'Rod'	1430 South Eastman Avenue/Los Angeles CA 90023
1983-046	Dedmon, Jeffrey Linden	21102 South Broadwell/Torrance CA 90502
1995-061	Dedrick, James Michael	%War. Dedrick 5101 23rd Ave West Everett WA 98203
1915-033	Dee, Maurice Leo 'Shorty'	D. August 12, 1971 Jamaica Plains, Mass.
1984-028	Deer, Robert George	Old Add: 2003 East Clipper Lane Gilbert AZ 85234
1963-032	Dees, Charles Henry	1247 West 186th Street/Gardena CA 90248
1917-019	Defate, Clyde Herbert 'Tony'	D. September 3, 1963 New Orleans, La.
1978-035	Defreites, Arturo Simon	PO Box 161 San Pedro De Macoris Dominican Rep.
1961-028	Degerick, Michael Arthur	3120 Cynthia Lane/Lake Worth FL 33461
1997-043	Dehart, Richard Allen	Old Add: Topeka KS 66601
1974-021	Deidel, James Lawrence	205 Spring Drive/Louisville CO 80027
1940-015	Dejan, Mike Dan	D. February 2, 1953 West Los Angeles, Calif.
1997-044	Dejean, Michael Dwain	9430 Prince Charles Street/Denham Springs LA 70726
1974-022	Dejesus, Ivan	14608 Velleux Drive/Orlando FL 32837
1988-040	Dejesus, Jose Luis	7e6 Villa Del Carmen/Cidra PR 639
1982-031	Dejohn, Mark Stephen	Old Add: 966 Worthington Ridge Berlin CT 06037
1945-024	Dekoning, William Callahan	D. July 26, 1979 Palm Harbor, Fla.
1944-026	Delacruz, Tomas	D. September 6, 1958 Havana, Cuba
1960-029	Delahoz, Miguel Angel	1367 SW 14th Street/Miami FL 33145
1997-045	Delamaza, Roland Robert	9388 Dorrington Place/Pacoima CA 91331
1932-018	Delancey, William Pinkney	D. November 28, 1946 Phoenix, Ariz.
1924-029	Delaney, Arthur Dewey	D. May 2, 1970 Hayward, Calif.
1991-044	Delarosa, Francisco	Quisqueya Pro Jecto Kennedy San Pedro De Macoris Dominican Rep.
1975-032	Delarosa, Jesus	20 #28 Los Minos Santo Domingo Dominican Rep.
1983-047	Deleon, Jose	Old Add: 207 Patterson Perth Amboy NJ 08861
1981-027	Deleon, Luis Antonio	Old Add: San Anton #120 Ponce PR 00731
1996-045	Delgado, Alexander	Old Add: Palmerejo Venezuela
1993-041	Delgado, Carlos Juan (Hernandez)	Rpto Ramos #9,Bo. Borinquer/Aguadillo PR 605
1977-043	Delgado, Luis Felipe	PO Box 879/Hatillo PR 659
1996-046	Delgado, Wilson Duran	Old Add: San Cristobal Dom. Rep.
1952-024	Delgreco, Robert George	625 Southview Drive/Pittsburgh PA 15226
1912-049	Delhi, Lee William 'Flame'	D. May 9, 1966 Greenbrae, Calif.
1955-037	Delis, Juan Francisco	Old Add: 3a #24508,Reparto Dolores Havana Cuba

1929-027 ....Delker, Edward Albert ....D. May 14, 1997 Pottsville, Pa.
1912-050 ....Dell, William George 'Wheezer' ....D. August 24, 1966 Independence, Calif.
1997-046 ....Dellucci, David Michael ....18489 Lake Tulip Avenue/Baton Rouge LA 70817
1933-016 ....Delmas, Albert Charles ....D. December 4, 1979 Huntington Beach, Calif.
1952-025 ....Delock, Ivan Martin 'Ike'............................120 Hillside Avenue/Needham MA 2194
1988-041 ....Delossantos, Luis Manuel ....575 West 172nd Street/New York NY 10032
1974-023 ....Delossantos, Ramon ....Calle Bonaire #154,Alma Rosa Santo Domingo Dominican Rep.
1943-038 ....Delsavio, Garton Orville ....55 North Western Hwy/Blauvelt NY 10913
1948-031 ....Delsing, James Henry ....1569 Walpole Drive/Chesterfield MO 63017
1990-038 ....Delucia, Richard Anthony ....3 Muirfield Drive/Reading PA 19607
1951-022 ....Demaestri, Joseph Paul..............................50 Fairway/Novato CA 94947
1912-051 ....Demaree, Albert Wentworth ....D. May 2, 1962 Long Beach, Calif.
1932-019 ....Demaree, Joseph Franklin ....D. August 30, 1958 Los Angeles, Calif.
1948-032 ....Demars, William Lester ....770 Island Way #N305/Clearwater FL 34630
1957-016 ....Demerit, John Stephen ....550 West Walters St/Port Washington WI 53074
1974-024 ....Demery, Lawrence Calvin ....3317 West 81st Street/Englewood CA 90305
1956-026 ....Demeter, Donald Lee ....6240 South Country Club Drive/Oklahoma City OK 73159
1959-020 ....Demeter, Steven ....2805 Marincliff Dr/Parma OH 44134
1974-025 ....Demola, Donald John ....352 Village Drive/Hauppauge NY 11788
1910-044 ....Demott, Benyew Harrison ....D. July 5, 1963 Somerville, N.J.
1951-023 ....Dempsey, Cornelius Francis 'Con' ....1530 Cordilleras Road/Redwood City CA 94062
1969-045 ....Dempsey, John Rikard 'Rick' ....637 Indian Oak Lane #101/Oak Park CA 91301
1982-032 ....Dempsey, Mark Steven ....673 West Martindale/Union OH 45322
1967-023 ....Denehy, William Francis ....5096 Eastwinds Drive/Orlando FL 32812
1982-033 ....Denman, Brian John ....33 Parkhurst Boulevard/Buffalo NY 14223
1923-027 ....Dennehey, Thomas Francis 'Tod' ....D. August 8, 1977 Philadelphia, Pa.
1942-028 ....Denning, Otto George ....D. May 25, 1992 Chicago, Ill.
1965-027 ....Dennis, Donald Ray ....Rr2/Uniontown KS 66779
1974-026 ....Denny, John Allen ....13430 Eastcamina La Cebadilla/Tucson AZ 85749
1989-030 ....Denson, Andrew ....1718 Avonlea Avenue/Cincinnati OH 45237
1973-034 ....Dent, Russell Earl 'Bucky'........................8895 Indian River Run/Boynton Beach FL 33437
1947-025 ....Dente, Samuel Joseph ....19 Redman Terrace/West Caldwell Nj/7006
1943-039 ....Dephillips, Anthony Andrew ....D. May 5, 1994 Port Jefferson, N. Y.
1980-036 ....Dernier, Robert Eugene ....13153 Carter/Overland Park KS 66213
1910-045 ....Derrick, Claud Lester ....D. July 15, 1974 Clayton, Ga.
1970-032 ....Derrick, James Michael ....107 Oliver/West Columbia Cayce SC 29033
1931-021 ....Derringer, Paul ....D. November 17, 1987 Sarasota, Fla.
1956-027 ....Derrington, Charles James 'Jim' ....10509 Bryson Ave/South Gate CA 90281
1944-027 ....Derry, Alva Russell 'Russ' ....Princeton MO 64673
1980-037 ....Desa, Joseph ....D. December 20, 1986 San Juan, P. R.
1930-017 ....Desautels, Eugene Abraham ....D. November 5, 1994 Flint, Mich.
1984-029 ....Deshaies, James Joseph.............................151 North Taylor Point Drive/The Woodlands TX 77382
1990-039 ....Deshields, Delino Lamont ....100 Shady Brook Walk/Fairburn GA 30213
1932-020 ....Deshong, James Brooklyn ....D. October 16, 1993 Lower Paxson Twp., Pa.
1993-042 ....Desilva, John Reed ....32750 Airport Road/Fort Bragg CA 95437
1916-019 ....Desjardien, Paul Raymond 'Shorty' ....D. March 7, 1956 Monrovia, Calif.
1996-047 ....Dessens, Elmer ....Old Add: Hermosillo Mexico
1987-031 ....Destrade, Orestes.....................................Old Add: PO Box 3368 Pinellas Park FL 34664
1980-038 ....Detherage, Robert Wayne ....322 Turf Street/Carl Junction MO 64834
1930-018 ....Detore, George Francis ....D. February 7, 1991 Utica, N. Y.
1994-025 ....Dettmer, John Franklin ....549 Hickory View Lane/Ballwin MO 63011
1973-035 ....Dettore, Thomas Anthony ....1120 McEwen Ave/Canonsburg PA 15317
1942-029 ....Detweiler, Robert Sterling 'Ducky' ....312 Holt Street/Federalsburg MD 21632
1946-023 ....Deutsch, Melvin Elliott ....Old Add: 373a Rr 2 Caldwell TX 77836
1995-062 ....Devarez, Cesar Salvatore ....Old Add: San Francisco De Macoris Dominican Rep.
1932-021 ....Devens, Charles ....79 Milk Street, 9th Floor/Boston MA 2109
1987-032 ....Devereaux, Michael ....2236 West Doublegrove Street/West Covina CA 91790
1973-036 ....Devine, Paul Adrian 'Adrian' ....271 Timber Laurel Lane/Lawrenceville GA 30245
1918-015 ....Devine, William Patrick 'Mickey' ....D. October 1, 1957 Albany, N. Y.
1920-030 ....Deviney, John Harold 'Hal' ....D. January 4, 1933 Westwood, Mass.
1924-030 ....Deviveiros, Bernard John ....D. July 5, 1994 Oakland, Calif.
1944-028 ....Devlin, James Raymond ....130 Worman St, Espy/Bloomsburg PA 17815
1913-047 ....Devogt, Rex Eugene ....D. November 9, 1935 Alma, Mich.
1918-016 ....Devormer, Albert E. ....D. August 29, 1966 Grand Rapids, Mich.
1990-040 ....Dewey, Mark Alan.....................................9245 South 56th Avenue/Montague MI 49437
1987-033 ....Dewillis, Jeffrey Allen ....3105 Yost Road/Pearland TX 77581
1992-033 ....Diaz, Alexis ....Old Add: Calle 10-R-4 San Sebastian PR 00685
1977-044 ....Diaz, Baudilio Jose ....D. November 23, 1990 Caracas, Venezuela
1982-034 ....Diaz, Carlos Anthony ....47-709 Waiohia Street/Kaneohe HI 96744
1990-041 ....Diaz, Carlos Francisco ....3720 Derby Drive #1204/Palm Harbor FL 34684
1997-047 ....Diaz, Eddy Javier ....Old Add: Barquisimeto Venezuela
1986-040 ....Diaz, Edgar Serrano ....Old Add: Cle Diamante #32 V.Blanca Caguas PR 00625
1996-048 ....Diaz, Einar Antonio ....Old Add: Chiriqui Panama
1987-034 ....Diaz, Mario Rafael....................................Old Add: Urb. Jaime/Rodriguez Str 2 Yabucoa PR 00767
1983-048 ....Diaz, Michael Anthony ....248 Candace/Arroyo Grande CA 93420
1988-042 ....Dibble, Robert Keith ....54 Summit Farms Road/Southington CT 6489
1924-031 ....Dibut, Pedro ....D. December 4, 1979 Hialeah, Fla.
1964-025 ....Dicken, Paul Franklin ....8141 Southwest 53rd Court/Ocala FL 34476
1923-028 ....Dickerman, Leo Louis ....D. April 30, 1982 Atkins, Ark.

1917-020	Dickerson, George Clark	D. July 9, 1938 Los Angeles, Calif.
1935-023	Dickey, George Willard 'Skeets'	D. June 16, 1976 Dewitt, Ark.
1928-029	Dickey, William Malcolm	D. November 12, 1993 Little Rock, Ark.
1936-020	Dickman, George Emerson	D. April 27, 1981 New York, N. Y.
1936-021	Dickshot, John Oscar	D. November 4, 1997 Waukegan, Ill.
1963-033	Dickson, James Edward	PO Box 2514/Gearhart OR 97138
1996-049	Dickson, Jason Royce	281 North Napan Road/Chatham New Brunswick Canada E1N 3A3
1990-042	Dickson, Lance Michael	5750 Amaya Drive #42/Lamesa CA 92042
1939-027	Dickson, Murry Monroe	D. September 21, 1989 Kansas City, Kan.
1910-046	Dickson, Walter R.	D. December 9, 1918 Ardmore, Okla.
1969-046	Didier, Robert Daniel	544 SW 335th Street/Federal Way WA 98023
1942-030	Diehl, George Krause	D. August 24, 1986 Kingsport, Tenn.
1947-026	Diering, Charles Edward Allen	1 Nob Hill Drive/Saint Louis MO 63138
1964-026	Dierker, Lawrence Edwards	8318 North Tahoe/Houston TX 77040
1933-017	Dietrich, William John	D. June 20, 1978 Philadelphia, Pa.
1927-029	Dietrick, William Alexander	D. May 6, 1946 Bethesda, Md.
1940-016	Dietz, Lloyd Arthur 'Dutch'	D. October 29, 1972 Beaumont, Tex.
1966-028	Dietz, Richard Allen	PO Box 766/Pawley's Island SC 29585
1954-020	Dietzel, Leroy Louis	2331 Cartwright Pl/Charlotte NC 28208
1948-033	Difani, Clarence Joseph 'Jay'	1186 Weaver Road/Festus Mo/63028
1996-050	Difelice, Michael William	Old Add: Knoxville TN 37901
1934-031	Diggs, Reese Wilson	D. October 30, 1978 Baltimore, Md.
1969-047	Dilauro, Jack Edward	168 East Mohawk/Malvern OH 44644
1959-021	Dillard, David Donald 'Don'	Rural Route 3 Box 725/Waterloo SC 29384
1988-043	Dillard, Gordon Lee	1290 Rider Avenue/Salinas CA 93905
1975-033	Dillard, Stephen Bradley	Rural Route 2 Box 162/Saltillo MS 38866
1917-021	Dillhoefer, William Martin 'Pickles'	D. February 22, 1922 St. Louis, Mo.
1914-054	Dillinger, Harley Hugh	D. January 8, 1959 Cleveland, O.
1946-024	Dillinger, Robert Bernard	15380 Rhododendron Drive/Canyon County CA 91351
1967-024	Dillman, William Howard	1929 Summerfield Rd/Winter Park FL 32792
1963-034	Dillon, Stephen Edward	130 West 228th St/Bronx NY 10463
1974-027	Dilone, Miguel Angel	Calle El Sol #190 Santiago Dominican Rep.
1940-017	Dimaggio, Dominic Paul	6110 North Ocean Blvd #24/Ocean Ridge FL 33435
1936-022	Dimaggio, Joseph Paul	%Engleberg 3230 Sterling Road Hollywood FL 33021
1937-034	Dimaggio, Vincent Paul	D. October 3, 1986 North Hollywood, Calif.
1988-044	Dimichele, Frank Lawrence	812 Tasker Street/Philadelphia PA 19148
1977-045	Dimmel, Michael Wayne	3730 North Josey Lane #5101/Carrollton TX 75007
1975-034	Dineen, Kerry Michael	Old Add: 702 Elder Avenue/Chula Vista CA 92010
1945-025	Dinges, Vance George	D. October 4, 1990 Harrisonburg, Va.
1973-037	Diorio, Ronald Michael	2 White Oak Ln/Waterbury CT 6705
1951-024	Dipietro, Robert Louis Paul	909 Carriage Hill Drive/Yakima WA 98902
1981-028	Dipino, Frank Michael	3837 Oran Delphi Road/Manlius NY 13104
1993-043	Dipoto, Gerard Peter 'Jerry'	12952 Granada Lane/Leawood KS 66209
1989-031	Disarcina, Gary Thomas	%Gen. Disarcina 6 Patrick Avenue Billerica MA 1866
1995-063	Dishman, Gleneig Edward	1200 Brookdale Drive/Brentwood CA 94513
1969-048	Distaso, Alec John	321 East Grant Street/Macomb IL 61455
1984-030	Distefano, Benito James	Old Add: 20 Fonda Drive Stony Point NY 10980
1918-017	Distel, George Adam 'Dutch'	D. February 12, 1967 Madison, Ind.
1954-021	Ditmar, Arthur John	6687 Wisteria Drive/Myrtle Beach SC 29575
1952-026	Dittmer, John Douglas	200 North Main Street/Elkader IA 52043
1916-101	Divis, Edward G. 'Moxie'	D. December 19, 1955 Lakewood, Ohio
1953-018	Dixon, John Craig 'Sonny'	7920 Steele Creek Road/Charlotte NC 28217
1984-031	Dixon, Kenneth John	Old Add: 3043 North 37th St Milwaukee WI 53210
1925-024	Dixon, Leo Moses	D. April 11, 1984 Chicago, Ill.
1993-044	Dixon, Steven Ross	6510 Hollow Tree Road/Louisville KY 40228
1977-046	Dixon, Thomas Earl	2945 South Delaney Street/Orlando FL 32806
1912-052	Doak, William Leopold	D. November 26, 1954 Bradenton, Fla.
1924-032	Dobb, John Kenneth	D. July 31, 1991 Muskegon, Mich.
1959-022	Dobbek, Daniel John	4042 SE Yamhill/Portland OR 97214
1929-028	Dobens, Raymond Joseph	D. April 21, 1980 Stuart, Fla.
1939-028	Dobernic, Andrew Joseph 'Jess'	D. July 16, 1998 Saint Louis, Ill.
1966-029	Dobson, Charles Thomas	2104 Jarboe Street/Kansas City MO 64108
1939-029	Dobson, Joseph Gordon	D. June 23, 1994 Jacksonville, Fla.
1967-025	Dobson, Patrick Edward	1209 Varela Street/Key West FL 33040
1947-027	Doby, Lawrence Eugene	PO Box 193/Massapequa NY 11758
1945-026	Dockins, George Woodrow	D. January 22, 1997 Clyde, Kan.
1945-026	Dockins, George Woodrow	D. January 22, 1997 Clyde, Kan.
1912-053	Dodd, Oran A. 'Ona'	D. March 31, 1929 Newport, Ark.
1986-041	Dodd, Thomas Marion	3735 Northeast Shaver/Portland OR 97212
1912-054	Dodge, John Lewis	D. June 19, 1916 Mobile, Ala.
1921-021	Dodge, Samuel Edward	D. April 5, 1966 Utica, N. Y.
1986-042	Dodson, Patrick Neal	1034 Hillside Road/Grove OK 74344
1937-035	Doerr, Robert Pershing	94449 Territorial Road/Junction City OR 97448
1992-034	Doherty, John Harold	202 Alpine Place/Tuckahoe NY 10707
1974-028	Doherty, John Michael	109 Wakefield St/Reading MA 1867
1914-055	Dolan, Leon Mark 'Biddy'	D. July 15, 1950 Indianapolis, Ind.
1930-019	Doljack, Frank Joseph	D. January 23, 1948 Cleveland, O.
1935-024	Doll, Arthur James	D. April 28, 1978 Calumet City, Ill.
1923-029	Donahue, John Frederick	D. October 3, 1949 Boston, Mass.

1943-040 ....Donahue, John Stephen Micheal ....812 North Salem Lane/Carpentersville IL 60110
1938-021 ....Donald, Richard Atley 'Atley' ....D. October 19, 1992 West Monroe, La.
1912-055 ....Donalds, Edward Alexander ....D. July 3, 1950 Columbus, O.
1966-030 ....Donaldson, John David ....3331 Benard Ave/Charlotte NC 28206
1929-029 ....Dondero, Leonard Peter ....2500 Country Drive/Fremont CA 94536
1911-042 ....Donnelly, Edward ....D. November 28, 1957 Rutland, Vt.
1959-023 ....Donnelly, Edward Vincent ....D. December 25, 1992 Houston, Texas
1944-029 ....Donnelly, Sylvester Urban 'Blix' ....D. June 20, 1976 Olivia, Minn.
1991-045 ....Donnels, Chris Barton ....35 Sunningdale/Coto De Caza CA 92679
1961-029 ....Donohue, James Thomas ....16 Huntleigh Downs/Saint Louis MO 63131
1921-022 ....Donohue, Peter Joseph ....D. February 23, 1988 Fort Worth, Texas
1979-028 ....Donohue, Thomas James ....33 Rugby Road/Westbury NY 11590
1955-038 ....Donoso, Lino Galata ....D. October 13, 1990 Vera/Cruz, Mexico
1950-027 ....Donovan, Richard Edward.................................D. January 6, 1997 Weymouth, Mass.
1942-031 ....Donovan, Willard Earl 'Bill' ....D. September 25, 1997 Maywood, Ill.
1985-025 ....Dopson, John Robert ....3337 Old Gamber Road/Finksburg MD 21048
1982-035 ....Doran, William Donald ....Miami Baseball 230 Millott/Hall Oxford OH 45056
1922-026 ....Doran, William James ....D. March 9, 1978 Santa Monica, Calif.
1947-028 ....Dorish, Harry ....68 Eley Street/Kingston PA 18704
1923-030 ....Dorman, Charles William ....D. November 15, 1928 San Francisco, Calif.
1928-030 ....Dorman, Dwight Dexter ....D. December 7, 1974 Anaheim, Calif.
1987-035 ....Dorsett, Brian Richard ....4719 Springfield Drive/Terre Haute IN 47803
1940-018 ....Dorsett, Calvin Leavelle ....D. October 22, 1970 Elk City, Okla.
1980-039 ....Dorsey, James Edward ....335 Elm Street/Seekonk MA 2771
1911-043 ....Dorsey, Jeremiah ....Old Add: Gadsden AL 35901
1996-051 ....Doster, David Eric ....205 Sara Drive/New Haven IN 46774
1979-029 ....Dotson, Richard Elliott ....7 Colonel Watson/New Richmond OH 45157
1961-030 ....Dotter, Gary Richard ....1639 Hursh/Wichita Falls TX 76302
1957-017 ....Dotterer, Henry John 'Dutch' ....2706 Grant Blvd/Syracuse NY 13208
1957-017 ....Dotterer, Henry John 'Dutch' ....2706 Grant Blvd/Syracuse NY 13208
1995-064 ....Dougherty, James E. ....Old Add: 121 Wampun Drive Kitty Hawk NC 27949
1921-023 ....Douglas, Astyanax Saunders ....D. January 26, 1975 El Paso, Texas
1957-018 ....Douglas, Charles William 'Whammy' ....PO Box 70/Hubert NC 28539
1945-027 ....Douglas, John Franklin ....D. February 11, 1984 Miami, Fla.
1912-056 ....Douglas, Philips Brooks ....D. August 1, 1952 Sequatchie Valley, Tenn.
1915-034 ....Douglass, Howard Lawrence 'Larry' ....D. November 4, 1949 Jellico, Tenn.
1923-031 ....Douthit, Taylor Lee ....D. May 28, 1986 Fremont, Calif.
1910-047 ....Dowd, James Joseph 'Skip' ....D. December 20, 1960 Holyoke, Mass.
1919-017 ....Dowd, Raymond Bernard ....D. April 4, 1962 Northampton, Mass.
1987-036 ....Dowell, Kenneth Allen ....2720 Castro Way/Sacramento CA 95818
1964-027 ....Dowling, David Barclay ....5927 North Paseo Ventuso/Tucson AZ 85750
1961-031 ....Downing, Alphonso Erwin ....2800 Neilson Way #412/Santa Monica CA 90405
1973-038 ....Downing, Brian Jay ....8095 County Road 135/Celina TX 75009
1972-023 ....Downs, David Ralph ....925 East 1050 North/Bountiful UT 84010
1986-043 ....Downs, Kelly Robert ....925e 1050n, %Ralph Downs/Bountiful UT 84010
1978-036 ....Doyle, Brian Reed ....PO Box 9156/Winter Haven FL 33880
1943-041 ....Doyle, Howard James 'Danny' ....322 South Payne/Stillwater OK 74074
1910-048 ....Doyle, James Francis ....D. February 1, 1912 Syracuse, N.Y.
1983-049 ....Doyle, Jeffrey Donald ....233 NE Azalea Drive/Corvallis OR 97330
1925-025 ....Doyle, Jesse Herbert ....D. April 15, 1961 Belleville, Ill.
1969-049 ....Doyle, Paul Sinnott ....5832 Woodboro Dr/Huntington Beach CA 92649
1970-033 ....Doyle, Robert Dennis 'Denny' ....PO Box 9156/Winter Haven FL 33880
1935-025 ....Doyle, William Carl ....D. September 4, 1951 Knoxville, Tenn.
1986-044 ....Dozier, Thomas Dean ....Old Add: 3804 Don Way Richmond CA 94806
1992-035 ....Dozier, William Henry 'D.J.' ....5821 Cherokee Cluster/Virginia Beach VA 23462
1947-029 ....Dozier, William Joseph 'Buzz' ....2609 Braemer/Waco TX 76710
1986-045 ....Drabek, Douglas Dean ....15 Ivy Pond Place/The Woodlands TX 77381
1956-028 ....Drabowsky, Myron Walter 'Moe' ....4741 Oak Run Drive/Sarasota FL 34243
1969-050 ....Drago, Richard Anthony ....Old Add: PO Box 353/Sanibel Island FL 33957
1991-046 ....Drahman, Brian Stacy ....Old Add: 4050 North 15th Avenue Ft. Lauderdale FL 33334
1911-044 ....Drake, Delos Daniel ....D. October 3, 1965 Findlay, O.
1945-028 ....Drake, Larry Francis ....D. July 14, 1985 Houston, Texas
1922-027 ....Drake, Logan Gaffney ....D. June 1, 1940 Columbia, S. C.
1960-030 ....Drake, Samuel Harrison ....Old Add: 6302 Overhill Dr #2 Los Angeles CA 90034
1956-029 ....Drake, Solomon Louis ....1732 Corning St/Los Angeles CA 90035
1939-030 ....Drake, Thomas Kendall ....D. July 2, 1988 Birmingham, Ala.
1993-045 ....Draper, Michael Anthony ....18317 Manor Church Rpad/Boonsboro MD 21713
1982-036 ....Dravecky, David Francis ....19995 Chisholm Trail/Monument CO 80132
1991-047 ....Drees, Thomas Kent ....4505 Hibiscus Avenue/Edina MN 55435
1931-022 ....Dreesen, William Richard ....D. November 9, 1971 Mount Vernon, N. Y.
1994-026 ....Dreifort, Darren John ....Old Add: E. Lincoln St Wichita KS 67207
1944-030 ....Dreisewerd, Clement John ....800 Rue Rampart #201/Metairie La/70005
1944-031 ....Drescher, William Clayton ....D. May 15, 1968 Congers, N. Y.
1925-026 ....Dressen, Charles Walter ....D. August 10, 1966 Detroit, Mich.
1914-056 ....Dressen, Leo August ....D. June 30, 1931 Diller, Neb.
1991-048 ....Dressendorfer, Kirk Richard ....1403 Roy Court/Pearland TX 77581
1975-035 ....Dressler, Robert Alan ....Old Add: 3002 N. 46th St Phoenix AZ 85018
1988-045 ....Drew, Cameron Steward ....31 Highbridge Road/Yardville NJ 8620
1944-032 ....Drews, Frank John ....D. April 22, 1972 Buffalo, N. Y.

1946-025	...........Drews, Karl August	......................................D. August 15, 1963 Dania, Fla.
1993-046	...........Dreyer, Steven William	..................................1662 East 3350south/Salt Lake City UT 84106
1973-039	...........Driessen, Daniel	......................97 Stoney Creek Road/Hilton Head Island SC 29928
1970-034	...........Driscoll, James Bernard	..........................4135 North 81st Street/Scottsdale AZ 85251
1917-022	...........Driscoll, John Leo 'Paddy'	.......................D. June 28, 1968 Chicago, Ill.
1916-020	...........Driscoll, Michael Columbus	..................D. March 22, 1953 Foxboro, Mass.
1913-048	...........Drohan, Thomas F.	................................D. September 17, 1926 Kewanee, Ill.
1949-019	...........Dropo, Walter	..............................65 East India Row/Boston MA 2110
1957-019	...........Drott, Richard Fred	............................D. August 16, 1985 Glendale Heights, Ill.
1987-037	...........Drummond, Timothy Darnell	.........................Old Add: Hwy 925s Box 335e Waldorf MD 20601
1978-037	...........Drumright, Keith Alan	.......................Old Add: 422 East Downing Springfield MO 65807
1956-030	...........Drysdale, Donald Scott	..............................D. July 3, 1993 Montreal, Quebec
1944-033	...........Dubiel, Walter John 'Monk'	...................D. October 25, 1969 Hartford, Conn.
1989-032	...........Dubois, Brian Andrew	......................................159 Ridge Street/Braidwood IL 60402
1987-038	...........Ducey, Robert Thomas	.......................699 Richmond Close/Tarpon Springs FL 34689
1963-035	...........Duckworth, James Raymond	...........................PO Box 8084/Mammoth Lakes CA 93546
1929-030	...........Dudley, Elise Clise 'Clise'	....................D. January 12, 1989 Moncks Corner, S. C.
1941-022	...........Dudra, John Joseph	..............................D. October 24, 1965 Pana, Ill.
1977-047	...........Dues, Hal Joseph	......................................Drawer R/Dickinson TX 77539
1922-028	...........Duff, Cecil Elba 'Larry'	......................D. November 10, 1969 Bend, Ore.
1961-032	...........Duffalo, James Francis	...........................%Joseph Duffalo PO Box 1082 Dubois PA 15801
1967-026	...........Duffie, John Brown	......................................3453 Glen Road/Decatur GA 30032
1913-049	...........Duffy, Bernard Allen	............................D. February 9, 1962 Abilene, Tex.
1970-035	...........Duffy, Frank Thomas	......................................1740 East Silver Street/Tucson AZ 85719
1928-031	...........Dugan, Daniel Phillip	............................D. June 25, 1968 Green Brook, N. J.
1917-023	...........Dugan, Joseph Anthony	.........................D. July 7, 1982 Norwood, Mass.
1930-020	...........Dugas, Augustin Joseph 'Gus'	.............D. April 14, 1997 Colchester, Conn.
1913-050	...........Dugey, Oscar Joseph	............................D. January 1, 1966 Dallas, Tex.
1911-045	...........Duggan, James Elmer	............................D. December 5, 1951 Indianapolis, Ind.
1969-051	...........Dukes, Jan Noble	......................................959 Helena Drive/Sunnyvale CA 94087
1967-027	...........Dukes, Thomas Earl	......................................325 Monte Vista Rd/Arcadia CA 91007
1959-024	...........Duliba, Robert John	......................................327 Philadelphia Avenue/West Pittston PA 18643
1915-035	...........Dumont, George Henry	...........................D. October 13, 1956 Minneapolos, Minn.
1977-048	...........Dumoulin, Daniel Lynn	.........................Old Add: Rural Route Hh/Escondido CA 92025
1923-032	...........Dumovich, Nicholas	............................D. December 12, 1979 Laguna Hills, Calif.
1995-065	...........Dunbar, Matthew Marshall	..................2312 Brynmawr Drive/Tallahassee FL 32303
1983-050	...........Dunbar, Thomas Jerome	.......................558 South Palm Drive/Aiken SC 29801
1964-028	...........Duncan, David Edwin	......................................455 West Rapa/Tucson AZ 85704
1915-036	...........Duncan, Louis Baird 'Pat'	....................D. July 17, 1960 Columbus, O.
1985-026	...........Duncan, Mariano	......................Ingenio Angelina #137 San Pedro De Macoris Dominican Rep.
1977-049	...........Duncan, Taylor McDowell	...........................83 Hampton Street/Asheville NC 28803
1913-051	...........Duncan, Vernon Van Dyke	.....................D. June 1, 1954 Daytona Beach, Fla.
1970-036	...........Dunegan, James William	.......................1405 South 12th Street/Burlington IA 52601
1926-027	...........Dunham, Leland Huffield	.......................D. May 11, 1961 Atlanta, Ill.
1953-019	...........Dunlap, Grant Lester	......................................6401 El Pato Court/Carlsbad CA 92009
1929-031	...........Dunlap, William James	.........................D. November 29, 1980 Reading, Pa.
1913-052	...........Dunlop, George Henry	............................D. December 12, 1972 Meriden, Conn.
1952-027	...........Dunn, James William 'Bill'	...................1656 Summit Drive/Gadsden AL 35901
1974-029	...........Dunn, Ronald Ray	......................................1161 Husted Avenue/San Jose CA 95125
1994-027	...........Dunn, Steven Robert	......................................6225 Colchester Road/Fairfax VA 22030
1996-052	...........Dunn, Todd Kent	......................................Old Add: Jacksonville FL 32201
1987-039	...........Dunne, Michael Dennis	.......................5115 West Ancient Oak Drive/Peoria IL 61615
1970-037	...........Dunning, Steven John	.........................12437 Highland Drive/Tustin CA 92680
1985-027	...........Dunston, Shawon Donnell	....................Old Add: 66 Snyder Way Fremont CA 94536
1997-048	...........Dunwoody, Todd Franklin	....................Old Add: West Lafayette IN 47906
1976-029	...........Dupree, Michael Dennis	.......................5164 E. Ashlan #129/Fresno CA 93727
1981-029	...........Duran, Daniel James	......................................201 Del Norte/Sunnyvale CA 94086
1997-049	...........Duran, Roberto Alejandro	....................Old Add: Moca Dominican Republic
1996-053	...........Durant, Michael Joseph	.......................7199 Innisfree Lane/Dublin OH 43017
1954-022	...........Duren, Rinold George	.........................5674 Steeple Chase Drive/Waunkee WI 53597
1972-024	...........Durham, Donald Gary	............................2627 Pennington Bend Road/Nashville TN 37214
1929-032	...........Durham, Edward Fant	............................D. April 27, 1976 Chester, S. C.
1954-023	...........Durham, Joseph Vann	............................9715 Mendoza Rd/Randallstown MD 21133
1980-040	...........Durham, Leon	......................................3932 Dickson Ave/Cincinnati OH 45229
1995-066	...........Durham, Ray 'Sugar Ray'	....................1815 Lake Drive/Charlotte NC 28214
1957-020	...........Durnbaugh, Robert Eugene	................1638 North Central Drive/Dayton OH 45432
1925-027	...........Durning, George Dewey	.......................D. April 18, 1986 Tampa, Fla.
1917-024	...........Durning, Richard Knott	........................D. September 23, 1948 Castle Point, N. Y.
1925-028	...........Durocher, Leo Ernest	............................D. October 7, 1991 Palm Springs, Calif.
1944-034	...........Durrett, Elmer Charles 'Red'	...............D. January 17, 1992 Waxahachie, Texas
1922-029	...........Durst, Cedric Montgomery	...................D. February 16, 1971 San Diego, Calif.
1941-023	...........Dusak, Ervin Frank	............................D. November 6, 1994 Glendale Heights, Ill.
1956-031	...........Duser, Carl Robert	......................................3021 Cornwall Rd/Bethlehem PA 18017
1963-036	...........Dustal, Robert Andrew	........................1234 Reynolds Road #8/Lakeland FL 33803
1973-040	...........Dwyer, James Edward	......................................7607 West 159th Place/Tinley Park IL 60477
1937-036	...........Dwyer, Joseph Michael	.........................D. October 21, 1992 Glen Ridge, N. J.
1980-041	...........Dybzinski, Jerome Matthew	................112 Honey Locust Court/Painesville OH 44077
1951-025	...........Dyck, James Robert	......................................1704 Second Street/Cheney WA 99004
1996-054	...........Dye, Jermaine Terrell	.........................Old Add: Vacaville CA 95687

1914-057 ....Dyer, Benjamin Franklin ....D. August 7, 1959 Kenosha, Wis.
1968-017 ....Dyer, Donald Robert 'Duffy' ....742 West Las Palmaritas/Phoenix AZ 85021
1922-030 ....Dyer, Edwin Hawley ....D. April 20, 1964 Houston, Tex.
1989-033 ....Dyer, Michael Lawrence...............................22392 Manacor/Mission Viejo CA 92692
1918-018 ....Dykes, James Joseph ....D. June 15, 1976 Philadelphia, Pa.
1985-028 ....Dykstra, Lenny Kyle ....236 Chester Road/Devon PA 19333
1959-025 ....Eaddy, Donald Johnson ....5394 Effingham Drive SE/Grand Rapids MI 49508
1915-037 ....Eakle, Charles Emory......................................D. June 15, 1959 Baltimore, Md.
1984-032 ....Earl, William Scott ....Box 63/North Vernon IN 47265
1960-031 ....Earley, Arnold Carl ....4341 Captains Ln/Flint MI 48507
1938-022 ....Earley, Thomas Francis Aloysius ....D. April 5, 1988 Nantucket Island, Mass.
1986-046 ....Earley, William Albert.....................................783 Sundance Drive/Cincinnati OH 45223
1939-031 ....Early, Jacob Willard ....D. May 31, 1985 Melbourne, Fla.
1928-032 ....Earnshaw, George Livingston ....D. December 1, 1976 Little Rock, Ark.
1973-041 ....Easler, Michael Anthony ....407 Bluff Court/San Antonio TX 78216
1992-036 ....Easley, Damion Jacinto ....14125 North 65th Avenue/Glendale AZ 85306
1987-040 ....Easley, Kenneth Logan Logan ....748 Washington Street North #1/Twin Falls ID 83301
1915-038 ....East, Carlton William ....D. January 15, 1953 Whitesburg, Ky.
1941-024 ....East, Gordon Hugh ....D. November 2, 1981 Charleston, S. C.
1949-020 ....Easter, Luscious Luke ....D. March 29, 1979 Euclid, O.
1928-033 ....Easterling, Paul ....D. March 15, 1993 Reidsville, Ga.
1974-030 ....Easterly, James Morris 'Jamie' ....1306 Plantation/Crockett TX 75835
1944-035 ....Easterwood, Roy Charles ....D. August 24, 1984 Graham, Texas
1955-039 ....Easton, John David ....605 Scotch Road/Pennington NJ 8534
1974-031 ....Eastwick, Rawlins Jackson ....10 River Meadow Drive/West Newbury MA 1985
1979-030 ....Eaton, Craig ....3307 Baltusrol Ln/Lake Worth FL 33467
1944-036 ....Eaton, Zebulon Vance ....D. December 17, 1989 West Palm Beach, Fla.
1988-046 ....Eave, Gary Louis ....Old Add: 1609 King Avenue Bastrop LA 71220
1935-026 ....Eaves, Vallie Ennis ....D. April 19, 1960 Norman, Okla.
1913-053 ....Eayrs, Edwin ....D. November 30, 1969 Warwick, R.I.
1915-039 ....Eccles, Harry Josiah ....D. June 28, 1955 Jamestown, N.Y.
1996-055 ....Echevarria, Angel Santos ....Old Add: Bridgeport CT 06602
1939-032 ....Echols, John Gresham ....D. November 13, 1972 Atlanta, Ga.
1975-036 ....Eckersley, Dennis Lee ....39 Plympton Road/Sudbury MA 1776
1930-021 ....Eckert, Albert George ....D. April 20, 1974 Milwaukee, Wis.
1919-018 ....Eckert, Charles William ....D. August 22, 1986 Trevose, Pa.
1932-022 ....Eckhardt, Oscar George 'Ox' ....D. April 22, 1951 Yorktown, Tex.
1995-067 ....Eddy, Christopher Mark ....%Dan Eddy 338 Swan Ridge Duncanville TX 75137
1970-038 ....Eddy, Donald Eugene ....Box 537/Rockwell IA 50469
1979-031 ....Eddy, Steven Allen ....485 South Dobson #101/Chandler AZ 85224
1981-030 ....Edelen, Benny Joe Joe ....603 9th Street/Snyder OK 73566
1932-023 ....Edelen, Edward Joseph ....D. February 1, 1982 Laplata, Md.
1955-040 ....Edelman, John Rogers ....922 Monte Vista Drive/West Chester PA 19380
1976-030 ....Eden, Edward Michael ....11531 Forest Hills Drive/Tampa FL 33612
1995-068 ....Edenfield, Kenneth Edward.............................4407 Barbara Drive/Knoxville TN 37918
1987-041 ....Edens, Thomas Patrick ....2033 Quailridge Court/Clarkston WA 99403
1979-032 ....Edge, Claude Lee 'Butch' ....Old Add: 3728 Marconi Ave Sacramento CA 95821
1966-031 ....Edgerton, William Albert ....1725 East Jefferson Blvd/Mishawaka IN 46545
1912-057 ....Edington, Jacob Frank 'Stump' ....D. November 29, 1969 Bastrop,La.
1980-042 ....Edler, David Delmar ....1504 South 34th Ave/Yakima WA 98902
1993-047 ....Edmonds, James Patrick ....21801 Paint Brush/Diamond Bar CA 91765
1913-054 ....Edmondson, Edward Earl ....D. May 10, 1971 Leesburg, Fla.
1922-031 ....Edmondson, George Henderson ....D. July 11, 1973 Waco, Tex.
1969-052 ....Edmondson, Paul Michael ....D. February 13, 1970 Santa Barbara, Calif.
1946-026 ....Edwards, Charles Bruce ....D. April 25, 1975 Sacramento, Calif.
1978-038 ....Edwards, David Leonard ....Old Add: 15544 Prairie Avenue Riverside CA 92504
1925-029 ....Edwards, Foster Hamilton ....D. January 4, 1980 Orleans, Mass.
1941-025 ....Edwards, Henry Albert ....D. June 22, 1988 Santa Ana, Calif.
1962-035 ....Edwards, Howard Rodney 'Doc' ....2106 79th Court/Vero/Beach FL 32966
1922-032 ....Edwards, James Corbette 'Jim Joe'................D. January 19, 1965 Calhoun County, Miss.
1961-033 ....Edwards, John Alban ....10118 Springwood Forest Drive/Houston TX 77055
1981-031 ....Edwards, Marshall Lynn ....Old Add: 15544 Prairie Ave Riverside CA 92504
1977-050 ....Edwards, Michael Lewis ....Old Add: 3216 Wadsworth Ave Los Angeles CA 90011
1915-040 ....Edwards, Ralph Strunk ....D. January 5, 1949 White Plains, N. Y.
1934-032 ....Edwards, Sherman Stanley ....D. March 8, 1992 El Dorado, Ark.
1989-034 ....Edwards, Wayne Maurice ....9738 Aqueduct Avenue/Sepulveda CA 91343
1994-028 ....Eenhoorn, Robert Franciscus ....Zermilieplaats 15 3068j Rotterdam/Netherlands
1963-037 ....Egan, Richard Wallis ....1611 West Thunderhill Drive/Phoenix AZ 85045
1965-028 ....Egan, Thomas Patrick ....184 East Myrna Lane/Tempe AZ 85284
1927-030 ....Eggert, Elmer Albert.......................................D. April 9, 1971 Rochester, N. Y.
1991-049 ....Egloff, Bruce Edward ....3136 South Emporia Court/Denver CO 80231
1915-041 ....Ehmke, Howard Jonathan ....D. March 17, 1959 Philadelphia, Pa.
1924-033 ....Ehrhardt, Welton Claude 'Rube' ....D. April 27, 1980 Chicago Heights, Ill.
1912-058 ....Eibel, Henry Hack ....D. October 16, 1945 Macon, Ga.
1978-039 ....Eichelberger, Juan Tyrone ....14674 Silverset St/Poway CA 92064
1982-037 ....Eichhorn, Mark Anthony ....147 Norma Court/Aptos CA 95003
1925-030 ....Eichrodt, Frederick George ....D. July 14, 1965 Indianapolis, Ind.
1988-047 ....Eiland, David William ....30326 Fairway Drive/Wesley Chapel FL 33543
1964-029 ....Eilers, David Louis ....602 Perkins Lane/Brenham TX 77833

1994-029	Eischen, Joseph Raymond 'Joey'	1428 East Herring/West Covina CA 91791
1944-037	Eisenhart, Jacob Henry 'Hank'	D. December 20, 1987 Huntingdon, Pa.
1982-038	Eisenreich, James Michael	1205 Arrowhead Trail/Blue Springs MO 64015
1935-027	Eisenstat, Harry	3333 Warrensville Center #214/Shaker Heights OH 44122
1949-021	Elder, George Rezin	5246 West Riviera Avenue/Banning CA 92220
1913-055	Elder, Henry Knox 'Heinie'	D. November 13, 1958 Long Beach, Calif.
1991-050	Eldred, Calvin John	N108 W7045 Berkshire Street/Cedarburg WI 53012
1966-032	Elia, Lee Constantine	11613 Innfields Drive/Odessa FL 33556
1943-042	Elko, Peter	D. September 17, 1993 Wilkes-Barre, Pa.
1917-025	Eller, Horace Owen 'Hod'	D. July 18, 1961 Indianapolis, Ind.
1919-019	Ellerbe, Francis Rogers	D. July 8, 1988 Latta, S. C.
1974-032	Ellingsen, Harold Bruce	5873 Daneland/Lakewood CA 90713
1962-036	Elliot, Lawrence Lee	13211 Vinter Way/Poway CA 92064
1923-033	Elliott, Allen Clifford	D. May 6, 1979 St. Louis, Mo.
1921-024	Elliott, Carter Ward	D. May 21, 1959 Palm Springs, Calif.
1994-030	Elliott, Donald Glenn 'Donnie'	1206 Bayou Vista/Deer Park TX 77536
1911-046	Elliott, Eugene Birminghouse	D. January 5, 1976 Huntingdon, Pa.
1910-049	Elliott, Harold B. 'Rowdy'	D. February 12, 1934 San Francisco, Calif.
1929-033	Elliott, Harold William	D. April 25, 1963 Honolulu, Haw.
1953-020	Elliott, Harry Lewis	1154 Random/El Cajon CA 92020
1947-030	Elliott, Herbert Glenn	D. July 27, 1969 Portland, Ore.
1923-034	Elliott, James Thompson	D. January 7, 1970 Terre Haute, Ind.
1972-025	Elliott, Randy Lee	PO Box 834/Somis CA 93066
1939-033	Elliott, Robert Irving	D. May 4, 1966 San Diego, Calif.
1968-018	Ellis, Dock Philip	121 E. 139th St/Los Angeles CA 90061
1967-028	Ellis, James Russell	13608 Ave 224/Tulare CA 93274
1969-053	Ellis, John Charles	97 West Main Street #28/Niantic CT 6357
1996-056	Ellis, Robert Randolph	2066 75th Avenue/Baton Rouge/La 70807
1971-029	Ellis, Robert Walter	2686 Limestone Lane NE/Grand Rapids MI 49525
1962-037	Ellis, Samuel Joseph	6111 Whiteway/Temple Terrace FL 33617
1920-031	Ellison, George Russell	D. January 20, 1978 San Francisco, Calif.
1916-021	Ellison, Herbert Spencer 'Babe'	D. August 11, 1955 San Francisco, Calif.
1958-028	Ellsworth, Richard Clark	1099 West Morris/Fresno CA 93705
1988-048	Ellsworth, Steven Clark	546 West Enterprise Avenue/Clovis CA 93611
1924-034	Elmore, Verdo Wilson	D. August 5, 1969 Birmingham, Ala.
1923-035	Elsh, Eugene Roy	D. November 12, 1978 Philadelphia, Pa.
1986-047	Elster, Kevin Daniel	5801 Marshall Drive/Huntington Beach CA 92649
1953-021	Elston, Donald Ray	D. January 2, 1995 Evanston, Ill.
1990-043	Elvira, Narcisco Delgado	Dom Conocida,El Cocuite Mun Tlalix Veracruz Veracruz/Mexico
1992-037	Embree, Alan Duane	Old Add:18407 NE 192nd Ave Brush Prairie WA 98606
1941-026	Embree, Charles William 'Red'	D. September 24, 1996 Eugene, Ore.
1923-036	Embry, Charles Akin 'Slim'	D. October 10, 1947 Nashville, Tenn.
1911-047	Emerson, Chester Arthur	D. July 2, 1971 Augusta, Me.
1963-038	Emery, Calvin Wayne	25462 Esrose Court/Lake Forest CA 92630
1924-035	Emery, Herrick Smith 'Spoke'	D. June 2, 1975 Cape Canaveral, Fla.
1916-022	Emmer, Frank William	D. October 18, 1963 Homestead, Fla.
1923-037	Emmerich, Robert George	D. November 22, 1948 Bridgeport, Conn.
1945-029	Emmerich, William Peter 'Slim'	D. September 17, 1998 Allentown, Pa.
1995-069	Encarnacion, Angelo Benjamin	Old Add: Santo Domingo Dom.Rep.
1997-050	Encarnacion, Juan Dedios	Old Add: Las Matas De Faran Dom Rep
1990-044	Encarnacion, Luis Martin	Manz 9 #6 Las Caobos De Herrera/Santo Domingo Dominican Rep.
1946-027	Endicott, William Franklin	14219 Oak Knoll Road/Sonora CA 95370
1912-059	Engel, Joseph William	D. June 12, 1969 Chattanooga, Tenn.
1985-029	Engel, Steven Michael	317 Walnut Street/Cincinnati OH 45215
1925-031	Engle, Charles August	D. October 12, 1983 San Antonio, Tex.
1981-032	Engle, Ralph David 'Dave'	7603 Shady Way/Sugar Land TX 77479
1981-033	Engle, Richard Douglas 'Doug'	Old Add: 2634 Jackson Pike Batavia OH 45103
1932-024	English, Charles Dewie	717 North Story Place/Alhambra CA 91801
1927-031	English, Elwood George 'Woody'	D. September 26, 1997 Newark, Ohio
1931-023	English, Gilbert Raymond	D. August 31, 1996 Trinity, N. C.
1946-028	Ennis, Delmar	D. February 8, 1996 Huntingdon Valley, Pa.
1926-028	Ennis, Russell Elwood	D. January 29, 1949 Superior, Wis.
1976-031	Enright, George Albert	969 Bayview Road/Lake Worth FL 33463
1917-026	Enright, John Percy	D. August 18, 1975 Pompano Beach, Fla.
1912-060	Ens, Anton 'Mutz'	D. June 28, 1950 St. Louis, Mo.
1922-033	Ens, Jewel Winklemeyer	D. January 17, 1950 Syracuse, N. Y.
1974-033	Enyart, Terry Gene	Old Add: 520 Seal Avenue/Piketon OH 45661
1914-058	Enzenroth, Clarence Herman 'Jack'	D. February 21, 1944 Detroit, Mich.
1914-059	Enzmann, John	D. March 14, 1984 Riverhead, N. Y.
1987-042	Eppard, James Gerhard	1517 North Sunset/Azusa CA 91702
1938-023	Epperly, Albert Paul	2621 Iowa Street/Davenport IA 52803
1935-028	Epps, Aubrey Lee	D. November 13, 1984 Ackerman, Miss.
1938-024	Epps, Harold Franklin	4500 Cypresswood #406/Spring TX 77379
1966-033	Epstein, Michael Peter	13419 Entreken Avenue/San Diego CA 92129
1977-051	Erardi, Joseph Gregory 'Greg'	42 Westgate Road/Massapequa Park NY 11762
1947-031	Erautt, Edward Lorenz Sebastian	7252 Waite Drive/Lamesa CA 91941
1950-028	Erautt, Joseph Michael	D. October 6, 1976 Portland, Ore.
1997-051	Erdos, Todd Michael	422 Cole Drive/Meadville PA 16335
1995-070	Ericks, John Edward	17000 Oketo Avenue/Tinley Park IL 60477

1958-029 ....Erickson, Don Lee ....2717 Interlachen/Springfield IL 62704
1914-060 ....Erickson, Eric George Adolph ....D. May 19, 1965 Jamestown, N. Y.
1953-022 ....Erickson, Harold James..........333 Bayshore Drive/Osprey FL 33559
1935-029 ....Erickson, Henry Nels ....D. December 13, 1964 Louisville, Ky.
1941-027 ....Erickson, Paul Walford ....363 Boyd Street/Fond Du Lac WI 54935
1929-034 ....Erickson, Ralph Lief ....1818 West 18th Street N #A94/Wichita KS 67203
1978-040 ....Erickson, Roger Farrell ....907 Mesa Drive/Chatham IL 62629
1990-045 ....Erickson, Scott Gavin ....1183 Corral Avenue/Sunnyvale CA 94088
1947-032 ....Ermer, Calvin Coolidge ....1009 Panorama Drive/Chattanooga TN 37421
1957-021 ....Ernaga, Frank John ....50 North Roop St/Susanville CA 96130
1938-025 ....Errickson, Richard Merriwell..........2976 Douglas Lane/Vineland NJ 8360
1948-034 ....Erskine, Carl Daniel ....6214 South Madison Avenue/Anderson IN 46013
1996-057 ....Erstad, Darin Charles ....510 15th Street SE/Jamestown ND 58401
1983-051 ....Esasky, Nicholas Andrew ....1779 Starlight Drive NE/Marietta GA 30062
1954-024 ....Escalera, Saturnino Cuadrado 'Nino' ....Urb. Valle Arriba Heights Dc-20 Street 201 Carolina PR 983
1982-039 ....Escarrega, Ernesto..........Apartado Postal 48g Los Mochis/Sinaloa Mexico
1915-042 ....Eschen, James Godrich..........D. September 27, 1960 Sloatsburg, N.Y.
1942-032 ....Eschen, Lawrence Edward ....PO Box 704/Gainesville GA 30503
1988-049 ....Escobar, Angel Ruben ....Old Add: Caricuao Caracas Venezuela
1991-051 ....Escobar, Jose Elias (Sanchez) ....Lasabana, Dpto Vargascalle Als/Flores Venezuela
1997-052 ....Escobar, Kelvim Jose Bolivar..........Old Add: Laguaira Venezuela
1995-071 ....Eshelman, Vaughn Michael..........16362 Morning Mist Drive/Houston TX 77090
1911-048 ....Esmond, James J. ....D. June 26, 1948 Troy, N.Y.
1982-040 ....Espino, Juan ....Eugenio M. De Cestos #50 Bonao Dominican Rep.
1974-034 ....Espinosa, Arnulfo Acevedo 'Nino' ....D. December 25, 1987 Villa Altagracia, Dominican Rep.
1984-033 ....Espinoza, Alvaro Alberto..........Urb. Michelena C/93 #86-74 Valencia Venezuela
1952-028 ....Esposito, Samuel ....7730 Astroia Place/Raleigh NC 27612
1983-052 ....Espy, Cecil Edward ....5480 Encina Drive/San Diego CA 92114
1958-030 ....Essegian, Charles Abraham ....15639 Bronco Drive/Canyon Country CA 91351
1979-033 ....Esser, Mark Gerald ....14 Briarwood Drive/Poughkeepsie NY 12601
1973-042 ....Essian, James Sarkis ....134 Eckford/Troy MI 48098
1996-058 ....Estalella, Robert M. ....1811 Nw 114th Avenue/Hollywood FL 33026
1935-030 ....Estalella, Roberto Mendez..........D. January 6, 1991 Hialeah, Fla.
1964-030 ....Estelle, Richard Harry ....2221 Taylor Ave/Point Pleasant NJ 8742
1995-072 ....Estes, Aaron Shawn Shawn ....%Tim Estes 974 Casey Street Gardnerville NV 89410
1951-026 ....Estock, George John ....595 Ray Street/Sebastian FL 32958
1960-032 ....Estrada, Charles Leonard ....Old Add: 4680 Little Uvas Dr Morgan Hills CA 95037
1971-030 ....Estrada, Francisco (Soto) ....Manuel Doblado Pte 605-A Navajoa Sonora Mexico
1929-035 ....Estrada, Oscar ....D. January 2, 1978 Havana, Cuba
1962-038 ....Etchebarren, Andrew Auguste ....1488 Vermeer Drive/Nokomis FL 34275
1943-043 ....Etchison, Clarence Hampton 'Buck'..........D. January 24, 1980 Cambridge, Md.
1967-029 ....Etheridge, Bobby Lamar ....122 Crescent Street/Greenville MS 38701
1938-026 ....Etten, Nicholas Raymond Thomas ....D. October 18, 1990 Hinsdale, Ill.
1993-048 ....Ettles, Mark Edward ....3-10 Rose Avenue South Perth/Western Australia 6151
1922-034 ....Eubanks, Uel Melvin ....D. November 21, 1954 Dallas, Tex.
1985-030 ....Eufemia, Frank Anthony ....71 Delford Avenue/Bergenfield NJ 7621
1917-027 ....Eunick, Fernandes Bowen ....D. December 9, 1959 Baltimore, Md.
1991-052 ....Eusebio, Raul Antonio 'Tony' ....46 Carretera Mella Cruce De Boca Chica Dominican Rep.
1939-034 ....Evans, Alfred Hubert ....D. April 6, 1979 Wilson, N. C.
1978-041 ....Evans, Barry Steven..........907 Dearing Street/Forest Park GA 30297
1969-054 ....Evans, Darrell Wayne ....13262 Mission Tierra Way/Granada Hills CA 91344
1972-026 ....Evans, Dwight Michael..........Old Add: 1700 Broadway #2100 Denver CO 80290
1915-043 ....Evans, Joseph Patton ....D. August 9, 1953 Gulfport, Miss.
1936-023 ....Evans, Russell Edison 'Red' ....D. June 14, 1982 Lakeview, Ark.
1997-053 ....Evans, Thomas John ....Old Add: Kirkland WA 98033
1932-025 ....Evans, William Arthur ....D. January 8, 1952 Wichita, Kans.
1916-023 ....Evans, William James ....D. December 21, 1946 Burlington, N. C.
1949-022 ....Evans, William Lawrence ....D. November 30, 1983 Grand Junction, Colo.
1993-049 ....Everett, Carl Edward ....Old Add: 4527 17th Avenue Tampa FL 33605
1969-055 ....Everitt, Edward Leon ....Old Add: Box 1894 Marshall TX 75670
1913-056 ....Evers, Joseph Francis ....D. January 4, 1949 Albany, N.Y.
1941-028 ....Evers, Walter Arthur 'Hoot' ....D. January 25, 1991 Houston, Texas
1994-031 ....Eversgerd, Bryan David ....Old Add: 906 Maces Grove Ofallon IL 62269
1921-025 ....Ewing, Reuben ....D. October 5, 1970 West Hartford, Conn.
1973-043 ....Ewing, Samuel James ....1048 Cedarview Lane/Franklin TN 37067
1919-020 ....Ewoldt, Arthur Lee ....D. December 8, 1977 Des Moines, Ia.
1997-054 ....Eyre, Scott Alan ....PO Box 253/Minersville UT 84752
1943-044 ....Eyrich, George Lincoln ....565 South 15th Street/Reading PA 19602
1923-038 ....Ezzell, Homer Estell ....D. August 3, 1976 San Antonio, Tex.
1914-061 ....Faber, Urban Charles 'Red' ....D. September 25, 1976 Chicago, Ill.
1994-032 ....Fabregas, Jorge ....4936 Southwest 6th Street/Miami FL 33134
1916-024 ....Fabrique, Albert Laverne 'Bunny' ....D. January 10, 1960 Ann Arbor, Mich.
1953-023 ....Face, Elroy Leon ....608 Della Drive #5f/North Versailles PA 15137
1980-043 ....Faedo, Leonardo Lago Lenny ....2920 Collins St/Tampa FL 33607
1919-021 ....Faeth, Anthony Joseph ....D. December 22, 1982 St. Paul, Minn.
1943-045 ....Fagan, Everett Joseph ....D. February 16, 1983 Morristown, N.J.
1918-019 ....Fahey, Francis Raymond ....D. March 19, 1954 Boston, Mass.
1912-061 ....Fahey, Howard Simpson ....D. October 24, 1971 Clearwater, Fla.
1971-031 ....Fahey, William Roger ....5740 Mona Ln/Dallas TX 75236

1951-027 ....Fahr, Gerald Warren 'Red' ....7749 Highway 49 North/Marmaduke AR 72443
1914-062 ....Fahrer, Clarence Willie 'Pete' ....D. June 10, 1967 Fremont, Mich.
1947-033 ....Fain, Ferris Roy ....PO Box 1357/Georgetown CA 95634
1919-022 ....Faircloth, James Lamar 'Rags' ....D. October 5, 1953 Tucson, Ariz.
1968-019 ....Fairey, James Burke ....218 Strawberry St/Clemson SC 29361
1958-031 ....Fairly, Ronald Ray ....Old Add: 342 Sunstone/Westlake Village CA 91361
1991-053 ....Fajardo, Hector (Navarrete) ....Old Add: Sahuayo Michoacan Mexico
1975-037 ....Falcone, Peter Frank ....1902 Jackson Street/Alexandria LA 71301
1920-032 ....Falk, Bibb August ....D. June 8, 1989 Austin, Texas
1925-032 ....Falk, Chester Emanuel 'Chet' ....D. January 7, 1982 Austin, Texas
1931-024 ....Fallenstin, Edward Joseph ....D. November 24, 1971 Orange, N.J.
1937-037 ....Fallon, George Decatur ....D. October 25, 1994 Lake Worth, Fla.
1984-034 ....Fallon, Robert Joseph ....4200 Sheridan Street #408/Hollywood FL 33021
1914-063 ....Falsey, Peter James ....D. May 23, 1976 Los Angeles, Calif.
1997-055 ....Falteisek, Steven James ....105 Aspen Street/Floral Bank NY 11001
1993-050 ....Faneyte, Rikkert ....Old Add: Amsterdam Netherlands
1945-030 ....Fannin, Clifford Bryson ....D. December 11, 1966 Sandusky, O.
1954-025 ....Fanning, William James 'Jim' ....2303 Place Dynastie/Saint Lazare Quebec J0P 1V0 Canada
1963-039 ....Fanok, Harry Michael ....12373 Old State Road/Chardon OH 44024
1949-023 ....Fanovich, Frank Joseph ....3 Fairgreen Avenue/New Smyrna Beach FL 32168
1986-048 ....Fansler, Stanley Robert ....Rural Route 2 Box 550-1/Elkins WV 26241
1910-050 ....Fanwell, Harry Clayton ....D. July 15, 1965 Baltimore, Md.
1970-039 ....Fanzone, Carmen ....Old Add: 4147 Shadyglade Studio City CA 91604
1990-046 ....Faries, Paul Tyrell ....1229 Larch Avenue/Moraga CA 94556
1991-054 ....Fariss, Monty Ted ....Rural Route 1/Leedey OK 73654
1961-034 ....Farley, Robert Jacob ....Rr 3 Box 190/Montoursville PA 17754
1971-032 ....Farmer, Edward Joseph ....Old Add: 5378 Las Virgens Rd Calabasas CA 91302
1916-025 ....Farmer, Floyd Haskell 'Jack' ....D. May 21, 1970 Columbia, La.
1990-047 ....Farmer, Howard Earl ....1675 West 10th Place/Gary IN 46404
1996-059 ....Farmer, Michael Anthony ....Old Add: Gary IN 46401
1982-041 ....Farr, James Alfred ....3 Tyndal Court/Williamsburg VA 23188
1984-035 ....Farr, Steven Michael ....Old Add: Rural Route 1 Box 33 Port Tobacco MD 20677
1925-033 ....Farrell, Edward Stephen 'Doc' ....D. December 20, 1966 Livingston, N. J.
1987-043 ....Farrell, John Edward ....12 Highland Avenue/Monmouth Beach NJ 7750
1914-064 ....Farrell, John J. ....D. March 24, 1918 Chicago, Ill.
1943-046 ....Farrell, Major Kerby ....D. December 17, 1975 Nashville, Tenn.
1956-032 ....Farrell, Richard Joseph ....D. June 11, 1977 Great Yarmouth, England
1996-060 ....Fasano, Salvatore Frank ....Old Add: Hanover Park IL 60103
1991-055 ....Fassero, Jeffrey Joseph ....1330 Johnson Lane/Springfield IL 62702
1968-020 ....Fast, Darcy Rae ....2981 Harrison Avenue/Centralia WA 98531
1953-024 ....Faszholz, John Edward 'Jack' ....Rural Route Hh2/Belle MO 65013
1962-039 ....Faul, William Alvan ....9562 Kincaid Road/Hillsboro OH 45133
1927-032 ....Faulkner, James Leroy ....D. June 2, 1962 West Palm Beach, Fla.
1944-038 ....Fausett, Robert Shaw ....D. May 2, 1994 College Station, Tex.
1911-049 ....Faust, Charles Victor ....D. June 18, 1915 Fort Steilacoom, Wash.
1916-026 ....Fautsch, Joseph Roamon ....D. March 16, 1971 New Hope, Minn.
1962-040 ....Fazio, Ernest Joseph ....2310 Royal Oaks Drive/Alamo CA 94507
1952-029 ....Fear, Luvern Carl ....D. September 6, 1976 Spencer, Ia.
1951-028 ....Federoff, Alfred ....10150 Mortonview/Taylor MI 48180
1934-033 ....Fehring, William Paul 'Dutch' ....1735 Poppy Avenue/Menlo Park CA 94023
1938-027 ....Feinberg, Edward ....D. April 20, 1986 Hollywood, Fla.
1985-031 ....Felder, Michael Otis ....322 South 17th Street/Richmond CA 94804
1942-033 ....Felderman, Marvin Wilfred ....10633 Hyacinth Lane/Moreno Valley CA 92388
1941-029 ....Feldman, Harry ....D. March 16, 1962 Fort Smith, Ark.
1923-039 ....Felix, August Guenther ....D. May 12, 1960 Montgomery, Ala.
1989-035 ....Felix, Junior Francisco ....Dona Antonia #42, Villa Elina Guayubin Dominican Rep.
1958-032 ....Feller, Jack Leland ....3122 Timberly Lane/Lakeland FL 33810
1936-024 ....Feller, Robert William Andrew ....PO Box 157/Gates Mills OH 44040
1915-044 ....Felsch, Oscar Emil 'Happy' ....D. August 17, 1964 Milwaukee, Wis.
1968-021 ....Felske, John Fredrick ....3804 Ridge Road/Spring Grove IL 60081
1979-034 ....Felton, Terry Lane ....1253 Cordoba Drive/Zachary LA 70791
1921-026 ....Fenner, Horace Alfred 'Hod' ....D. November 20, 1954 Detroit, Mich.
1972-027 ....Fenwick, Robert Richard ....51201 Hutchinson Road/Three Rivers MI 49093
1942-034 ....Ferens, Stanley ....D. October 7, 1994 Hempfield Twp., Pa.
1918-020 ....Ferguson, James Alexander ....D. April 28, 1976 Sepulveda, Calif.
1970-040 ....Ferguson, Joseph Vance ....1095 West El Camino Real/Sunnyvale CA 94087
1944-039 ....Ferguson, Robert Lester ....PO Box 15/Wetumpka AL 36092
1987-044 ....Fermin, Felix Jose ....Calle K - Esq. Mirador, Cerro Alto Santiago Dominican Rep.
1995-073 ....Fermin, Ramon Antonio ....Pro Yecto Aguayo Cle F #4 San Francisco De Macoris Dominican Rep.
1940-019 ....Fernandes, Edward Paul ....D. November 27, 1968 Hayward, Calif.
1990-048 ....Fernandez, Alexander ....13301 Northwest 38th Court/Miami FL 33054
1983-053 ....Fernandez, Charles Sidney 'Sid' .....992 Awaawaanoa Place #C/Honolulu HI 96825
1967-030 ....Fernandez, Frank ....37 Coughlan Ave/Staten Island NY 10310
1942-035 ....Fernandez, Froilan 'Nanny' ....D. September 19, 1996 Harbor City, Calif.
1956-033 ....Fernandez, Humberto Perez 'Chico' ...8401 Nw 40th Court/Sunrise FL 33351
1968-022 ....Fernandez, Lorenzo Marto ....1310 SW 97th Ave/Miami FL 33175
1983-054 ....Fernandez, Octavio Antonio Tony .....Calle N#3,B.Restauracion San Pedro De Macoris Dominican Rep.
1996-061 ....Fernandez, Osvaldo X. ....Old Add: Santo Domingo Dom. Rep.
1963-040 ....Ferrara, Alfred John ....Old Add: 3049 Las Vegas Blvd S. #236 Las Vegas NV 89109

1955-041 ....Ferrarese, Donald Hugh..................................15290 Myalon Road/Apple Valley CA 92307
1966-034 ....Ferraro, Michael Dennis..............................479 Nw 93rd Avenue/Coral Springs FL 33071
1935-031 ....Ferrazzi, William Joseph ....D. August 10, 1993 Keystone Heights, Fla.
1985-032 ....Ferreira, Anthony Ross ....3756 Lofton Place/Riverside CA 92501
1929-036 ....Ferrell, Richard Benjamin ....D. July 27, 1995 Bloomfield Hills, Mich.
1927-033 ....Ferrell, Wesley Cheek ....D. December 9, 1976 Sarasota, Fla.
1974-035 ....Ferrer, Sergio ....Old Add: Pedro Areilage Hx/Levittown Lakes PR 00632
1941-030 ....Ferrick, Thomas Jerome ....D. October 15, 1996 Lima, Pa.
1979-035 ....Ferris, Robert Eugene ....Hc5 Box 6790b/Palmer AK 99645
1945-031 ....Ferriss, David Meadow 'Boo' ....510 Robinson Drive/Cleveland/Ms/38732
1910-051 ....Ferry, John Francis ....D. August 29, 1954 Pittsfield, Mass.
1937-038 ....Fette, Louis Henry William ....D. January 3, 1981 Warrensburg, Mo.
1989-036 ....Fetters, Michael Lee ....1207 North Crystal Shores Drive/Gilbert AZ 85234
1917-028 ....Fewster, Wilson Lloyd 'Chick'......................D. April 16, 1945 Baltimore, Md.
1981-034 ....Fiala, Neal Stephen ....Belleville Area Cc Baseball 2500 Carlyle Road Belleville IL 62221
1944-040 ....Fick, John Ralph ....D. June 9, 1958 Somers Point, N. J.
1976-032 ....Fidrych, Mark Steven ....260 West Street/Northboro MA 1532
1932-026 ....Fieber, Clarence Thomas 'Lefty' ....D. August 20, 1985 Redwood City, Calif.
1985-033 ....Fielder, Cecil Grant ....700 Pinehurst Avenue/Melbourne FL 32940
1986-049 ....Fields, Bruce Alan ....20160 Renfrew/Detroit MI 48221
1973-044 ....Fife, Danny Wayne ....5854 Misty Hill Drive/Clarkston MI 48346
1997-056 ....Figga, Michael Anthony ....Old Add: Tampa FL 33601
1992-038 ....Figueroa, Bienvenido (Deleon) ....3205 Katherine Speed Court/Tallahassee FL 32303
1974-036 ....Figueroa, Eduardo ....Calle 41 A-N15/Santa Juanita PR 619
1980-044 ....Figueroa, Jesus Maria ....Santa Cruz Villa Mella Km 8 1/2 #23 H. Mirabel Santo Domingo Dominican Rep.
1940-020 ....File, Lawrence Samuel ....550 Ocean Pines/Berlin MD 21811
1982-042 ....Filer, Thomas Carson ....425 Fox Hollow Drive/Longhorne PA 19053
1944-041 ....Filipowicz, Stephen Charles ....D. February 21, 1975 Wilkes-Barre, Pa.
1934-034 ....Filley, Marcus Lucius ....D. January 20, 1995 Yarmouth, Maine
1915-045 ....Fillingim, Dana ....D. February 3, 1961 Tuskegee, Ala.
1982-043 ....Filson, William Peter 'Pete' ....6601 Double Trace Lane/Orlando FL 32819
1983-055 ....Fimple, John Joseph ....8012 Cliftrose Street/Windsor CA 95492
1979-036 ....Finch, Joel ....68571 Oak Spring Rd/Edwardsburg MI 49112
1916-027 ....Fincher, William Allen ....D. May 7, 1946 Shreveport, La.
1947-034 ....Fine, Thomas Morgan ....1610 Westridge/Cleborne TX 76031
1968-023 ....Fingers, Roland Glen 'Rollie' ....4894 Eastcliff Court/San Diego CA 92130
1954-026 ....Finigan, James Leroy ....D. May 16, 1981 Quincy, Ill.
1935-032 ....Fink, Herman Adam ....D. August 24, 1980 Salisbury, N. C.
1986-050 ....Finley, Charles Edward ....1 Barrenger Court/Newport Beach CA 92660
1943-047 ....Finley, Robert Edward ....D. January 2, 1986 West Covina, Calif.
1989-037 ....Finley, Steven Allen ....Old Add: 6603 Buffalo Speedway Houston TX 77005
1930-022 ....Finn, Cornelius Francis 'Mickey' ....D. July 7, 1933 Altoona, Pa.
1912-062 ....Finneran, Joseph Ignatius 'Happy'............D. February 3, 1942 Orange, N.J.
1931-025 ....Finney, Harold Wilson ....D. December 20, 1991 Lafayette, Ala.
1931-026 ....Finney, Louis Klopsche ....D. April 22, 1966 Lafayette, Ala.
1994-033 ....Finnvold, Anders Gar 'Gar' ....830 Southwest 15th Street/Boca Raton FL 33432
1968-024 ....Fiore, Michael Gary Joseph........................17 Silver St/Malverne NY 11565
1981-035 ....Fireovid, Stephen John ....457 Oakwood Avenue/Bryan OH 43506
1981-036 ....Firova, Daniel Michael ....1606 Grant/Laredo TX 78040
1919-023 ....Fisburn, Samuel ....D. April 11, 1965 Bethlehem, Pa.
1930-023 ....Fischer, Charles William 'Carl' ....D. December 10, 1963 Medina, N. Y.
1962-041 ....Fischer, Henry William ....7552 Navarre Parkway #1/Navarre FL 32566
1987-045 ....Fischer, Jeffrey Thomas ....215 Worth Court North/West Palm Beach FL 33405
1941-031 ....Fischer, Reuben Walter 'Rube' ....2880 Lumber Lane/Green Bay Wi/54313
1986-051 ....Fischer, Todd Richard ....12581 McGregor Blvd/Fort Myers FL 33919
1913-057 ....Fischer, William Charles ....D. September 4, 1945 Richmond, Va.
1956-034 ....Fischer, William Charles ....139 Upland Drive/Council Bluffs IA 51501
1977-052 ....Fischlin, Michael ....1454 Jay Court/Snellville GA 30078
1988-050 ....Fishel, John Alan ....2957 Shamrock Avenue/Brea CA 92621
1911-050 ....Fisher, Augustus Harris ....D. April 8, 1972 Portland, Ore.
1985-034 ....Fisher, Brian Kevin ....3660 South Uraven Street/Aurora CO 80013
1919-024 ....Fisher, Clarence Henry ....D. November 2, 1965 Point Pleasant, W. Va.
1945-032 ....Fisher, Donald Raymond ....D. July 29, 1973 Mayfield Heights, O.
1959-026 ....Fisher, Eddie Gene ....408 Cardinal Circle South/Altus OK 73521
1964-031 ....Fisher, Frederick Brown 'Fritz' ....3703 Barcelona Drive/Toledo OH 43615
1923-040 ....Fisher, George Aloys ....D. May 15, 1994 St. Cloud, Minn.
1951-029 ....Fisher, Harry Devereaux ....D. September 20, 1981 Waterloo, Ont.
1910-052 ....Fisher, John Gus 'Red' ....D. January 1, 1940 Louisville, Ky.
1959-027 ....Fisher, John Howard 'Jack'..........................608 South Greenwood Ave #C2/Easton PA 18045
1955-042 ....Fisher, Maurice Wayne ....15920 Lucerne Rd/Fredericktown OH 43019
1910-053 ....Fisher, Raymond Lyle ....D. November 3, 1982 Ann Arbor, Mich.
1912-063 ....Fisher, Robert Taylor ....D. August 4, 1963 Jacksonville, Fla.
1967-031 ....Fisher, Thomas Gene ....5213 Nob Lane/Indianapolis IN 46226
1916-028 ....Fisher, Wilbur McCullough ....D. October 24, 1960 Welch, W. Va.
1969-056 ....Fisk, Carlton Ernest ....16612 Catawba Rd/Lockport IL 60441
1914-065 ....Fiske, Maximilian Patrick............................D. May 15, 1928 Chicago, Ill.
1914-066 ....Fittery, Paul Clarence ....D. January 28, 1974 Cartersville, Ga.
1928-034 ....Fitzberger, Charles Caspar ....D. January 25, 1965 Baltimore, Md.
1948-035 ....Fitzgerald, Edward Raymond ....431 Christopher Street/Folsom CA 95630

1922-035	Fitzgerald, Howard Chumney	D. February 26, 1959 Eagle Falls, Tex.
1958-033	Fitzgerald, John Francis	Old Add: Box 62/Middletown NY 10940
1911-051	Fitzgerald, Justin Howard 'Mike'	D. January 17, 1945 San Mateo, Calif.
1988-051	Fitzgerald, Michael Patrick	10412 Indigo Road/Savannah GA 31406
1983-056	Fitzgerald, Michael Roy	Old Add: 3741 Manor Drive Lakewood CA 90712
1931-027	Fitzgerald, Raymond Francis	D. September 6, 1977 Westfield, Mass.
1924-036	Fitzke, Paul Frederick Herman	D. June 30, 1950 Sacramento, Calif.
1966-035	Fitzmaurice, Shaun Earle	1911 Normandstone Drive/Midlothian VA 23113
1969-057	Fitzmorris, Alan James	15980 South Switzer Street/Olathe KS 66062
1915-046	Fitzpatrick, Edward Henry	D. October 23, 1965 Bethlehem, Pa.
1925-034	Fitzsimmons, Frederick Landis	D. November 18, 1979 Yucca Valley, Calif.
1919-025	Fitzsimmons, Thomas William	D. December 20, 1971 Oakland, Calif.
1914-067	Flack, Max John	D. July 31, 1975 Belleville, Ill.
1945-033	Flager, Walter Leonard	D. December 16, 1990 Keizer, Ore.
1917-029	Flagstead, Ira James	D. March 13, 1940 Olympia, Wash.
1992-039	Flaherty, John Timothy	337 Svahn Drive/Valley Cottage NY 10989
1941-032	Flair, Albert Dell	D. July 25, 1988 New Orleans, La.
1975-038	Flanagan, Michael Kendall	15010 York Road/Sparks MD 21152
1913-058	Flanigan, Charles James	D. January 8, 1930 San Francisco, Calif.
1946-029	Flanigan, Raymond Arthur	D. March 28, 1993 Baltimore, Md.
1954-027	Flanigan, Thomas Anthony	114 East 40th/Covington KY 41015
1977-053	Flannery, John Michael	9002 Scottish Pastures Drive/Austin TX 78750
1979-037	Flannery, Timothy Earl	715 Hymattus Avenue/Leucadia CA 92024
1927-034	Flaskamper, Raymond Harold	D. February 3, 1978 San Antonio, Tex.
1964-032	Flavin, John Thomas	424 Groton Drive/Burbank CA 91504
1948-036	Fleitas, Angel Felix Husta	Old Add: 689 Ebony Street Melbourne FL 32935
1991-056	Fleming, David Anthony	37 Laurel Woods Lane/Southbury CT 6488
1940-021	Fleming, Leslie Fletcherd 'Bill'	800 Redfield Pkwy Bldg 8 #83/Reno NV 89509
1939-035	Fleming, Leslie Harvey 'Les'	D. March 5, 1980 Cleveland, Texas
1993-051	Flener, Gregory Alan 'Huck'	8965 East Florida Avenue #S-204/Denver CO 80231
1989-038	Fletcher, Darrin Glen	Old Add: Rr 1 Box 408 Oakwood IL 61832
1993-052	Fletcher, Edward Paul 'Paul'	431 Harpold Street/Ravenswood WV 26164
1934-035	Fletcher, Elburt Preston	D. March 9, 1994 Milton, Mass.
1914-068	Fletcher, Oliver Frank	D. October 7, 1974 St. Petersburg, Fla.
1981-037	Fletcher, Scott Brian	300 Birkdale Drive/Fayetteville GA 30215
1962-042	Fletcher, Thomas Wayne	Rr 1 Box 408/Oakwood IL 61858
1955-043	Fletcher, Vanoide	2404 Whitaker Road/Boonville NC 27011
1943-048	Flick, Lewis Miller	D. December 7, 1990 Weber City, Va.
1917-030	Flinn, Don Raphiel	D. March 9, 1959 Waco, Tex.
1978-042	Flinn, John Richard	6221 Lake Providence Lane/Charlotte NC 28277
1942-036	Flitcraft, Hildreth Milton 'Hilly'	50 East Avenue PO Box 260 Woodstown NJ 8098
1934-036	Flohr, Moritz Herman 'Mort'	D. June 2, 1994 Hornell, N. Y.
1956-035	Flood, Curtis Charles	D. January 10, 1997 Los Angeles, Calif.
1991-057	Flora, Kevin Scot	3854 Lealma Avenue/Claremont CA 91711
1995-074	Florence, Donald Emery	65 Irving Drive/Weare NH 3281
1926-029	Florence, Paul Robert	D. May 28, 1986 Gainesville, Fla.
1977-054	Flores, Gilberto	Bda Salazar 1 #38/Ponce PR 731
1942-037	Flores, Jesse Sandoval	D. December 17, 1991 Orange, Calif.
1994-034	Florie, Bryce Bettencourt	PO Box 1744/Goose Creek SC 29445
1951-030	Flowers, Bennett	901 Tremont Road/Wilson NC 27895
1940-022	Flowers, Charles Wesley 'Wes'	D. December 31, 1988 Wynne, Ark.
1923-041	Flowers, D'Arcy/Raymond 'Jake'	D. December 27, 1962 Clearwater, Fla.
1993-053	Floyd, Cornelius Clifford 'Cliff'	3804 Edgewater Drive/Hazel Crest IL 60429
1944-042	Floyd, Leslie Roe 'Bubba'	612 Sunny Lane/Irving TX 75060
1968-025	Floyd, Robert Nathan	1757 SE Dominic Avenue/Port Saint Lucie FL 34952
1915-047	Fluhrer, John L.	D. July 17, 1946 Columbus, O.
1910-054	Flynn, John Anthony	D. March 23, 1935 Providence, R.I.
1975-039	Flynn, Robert Douglas 'Doug'	2465 Vale Drive/Lexington KY 40514
1936-025	Flythe, Stuart McGuire	D. October 18, 1963 Durham, N. C.
1958-034	Fodge, Eugene Arlen	1505 North Chicago Street/South Bend IN 46628
1953-025	Foiles, Henry Lee	4333 Silverleaf Court/Virginia Beach VA 23462
1978-043	Foley, Marvis Edwin	4058 Lancaster Drive/Sarasota FL 34241
1928-035	Foley, Raymond Kirwin	D. March 22, 1980 Vero Beach, Fla.
1983-057	Foley, Thomas Michael	5237 Karlsburg Place/Palm Harbor FL 34685
1970-041	Foli, Timothy John	105 Willow Bend Lane/Ormond Beach FL 32174
1970-042	Folkers, Richard Nevin	7100 3rd Avenue North/Saint Petersburg FL 33710
1951-031	Fondy, Dee Virgil	1326 Pine Valley Road/Banning CA 92250
1921-027	Fonseca, Lewis Albert	D. November 26, 1989 Ely, Iowa
1983-058	Fontenot, Silton Ray 'Ray'	1674 North Crestview Drive/Lake Charles LA 70605
1995-075	Fonville, Chad Everette	926 Cleveland Street #G211/Greenville SC 29601
1971-033	Foor, James Emerson	42 South Schlueter/Saint Louis MO 63135
1973-045	Foote, Barry Clifton	Old Add: 10021 Whitemark Ln/Cary NC 27511
1985-035	Ford, Curtis Glenn	229 Sweetcreek Drive#A/Ballwin MO 63021
1975-040	Ford, Darnell Glenn 'Dan'	8807 Digger Pine/Riverside CA 92508
1978-044	Ford, David Alan	Old Add: 3585 West 49th St Cleveland OH 44102
1950-029	Ford, Edward Charles 'Whitey'	3750 Galt Ocean Drive Drive #1411/Fort Lauderdale FL 33308
1936-026	Ford, Eugene Matthew	D. September 7, 1970 Emmetsburg, Ia.
1919-026	Ford, Horace Hills 'Hod'	D. January 29, 1977 Winchester, Mass.
1973-046	Ford, Percival Edmund Wentworth	D. July 8, 1980 Nassau Bahamas

1970-043 ....Ford, Theodore Henry ....430 North 4th Street/Vineland NJ 8360
1997-057 ....Fordham, Thomas James ....14559 Miguel Lane/El Cajon CA 92021
1995-076 ....Fordyce, Brook Alexander...................%Tr Fordyce 7 Hillwood Rd West Old Lyme CT 6371
1924-037 ....Foreman, August ....D. February 13, 1953 New York, N. Y.
1952-030 ....Fornieles, Jose Miguel 'Mike' ....D. February 11, 1998 St. Petersburg, Fla.
1970-044 ....Forsch, Kenneth Roth ....794 South Ridgeview Road/Anaheim CA 92807
1974-037 ....Forsch, Robert Herbert ....1532 Highland Valley Circle/Chesterfield MO 63005
1971-034 ....Forster, Terry Jay ....Old Add: 3504 Mt. Lawrence/San Diego CA 92117
1915-048 ....Forsyth, Edward James ....D. June 22, 1956 Hoboken, N. J.
1992-040 ....Fortugno, Timothy Shawn ....9171 Mediterranean Drive/Huntington Beach CA 92646
1916-029 ....Fortune, Garrett Reese ....D. September 23, 1955 Washington, D. C.
1964-033 ....Fosnow, Gerald Eugene ....369 Caddie/Debary FL 32713
1921-028 ....Foss, George Dueward ....D. November 10, 1969 Miami, Fla.
1961-035 ....Foss, Lawrence Curtis ....4303 East English Street/Wichita KS 67218
1988-052 ....Fossas, Emilio Anthony 'Tony' ....Old Add: 12 St. Peters Street Boston MA 02130
1967-032 ....Fosse, Raymond Earl ....2230 Knightsbridge Place/Oxnard CA 93030
1967-033 ....Foster, Alan Benton ....10330 Grandview Drive/Lamesa CA 91941
1910-055 ....Foster, Edward Cunningham ....D. January 15, 1937 Washington, D.C.
1969-058 ....Foster, George Arthur ....4 Knollwood Drive East/Greenwich CT 6831
1913-059 ....Foster, George 'Rube' ....D. March 1, 1976 Bokoshe, Okla.
1993-054 ....Foster, Kevin Christopher ....Old Add: 1802 Monroe Street Evanston IL 60202
1963-041 ....Foster, Larry Lynn ....205 West Obell Street/Whitehall MI 49461
1971-035 ....Foster, Leonard Norris.....................699 Glensprings Drive/Cincinnati OH 45246
1970-045 ....Foster, Roy ....Old Add: Box 936/Grove OK 74344
1991-058 ....Foster, Stephen Eugene ....1201 Hillview/Waxahachie TX 75165
1922-036 ....Fothergill, Robert Roy 'Fatty' ....D. March 20, 1938 Detroit, Mich.
1973-047 ....Foucault, Steven Raymond ....PO Box 410501/Melbourne FL 32941
1997-058 ....Foulke, Keith Charles........................3506 Dryburgh Court/Huffman TX 77336
1912-064 ....Fournier, John Frank ....D. September 5, 1973 Tacoma, Wash.
1924-038 ....Fowler, Jesse 'Pete' ....D. September 23, 1973 Columbia, S. C.
1954-028 ....Fowler, John Arthur 'Art'.................3046 East Main Extension/Spartanburg SC 29301
1923-042 ....Fowler, Joseph Chester 'Chet' ....D. October 8, 1988 Dallas, Texas
1941-033 ....Fowler, Richard John ....D. May 22, 1972 Oneonta, N. Y.
1982-044 ....Fowlkes, Alan Kim ....3065 Westminster Road/Lumberton NC 28358
1996-062 ....Fox, Andrew Junipero ....3548 Imperial Way/Sacramento CA 95826
1997-059 ....Fox, Chad Douglas...........................17809 Mossforest Drive/Houston TX 77090
1942-038 ....Fox, Charles Francis ....50 Mounds Road #612/San Mateo CA 94402
1992-041 ....Fox, Eric Hollis ....Old Add: Creston Star Route Paso Robles CA 93446
1933-018 ....Fox, Ervin 'Pete' ....D. July 5, 1966 Detroit, Mich.
1944-043 ....Fox, Howard Francis ....D. October 9, 1955 San Antonio, Tex.
1947-035 ....Fox, Jacob Nelson 'Nellie' ....D. December 1, 1975 Baltimore, Md.
1960-033 ....Fox, Terrence Edward ....2317 Sugar Mill Road/New Iberia LA 70560
1925-035 ....Foxx, James Emory ....D. July 21, 1967 Miami, Fla.
1966-036 ....Foy, Joseph......................................D. October 12, 1989 Bronx, N.Y.
1953-026 ....Foytack, Paul Eugene ....5590 Tadworth Place/West Bloomfield MI 48322
1972-028 ....Frailing, Kenneth Douglas ....13060 North Branch Road/Sarasota FL 34240
1960-034 ....Francis, Earl Coleman ....28 Quail Hill Rd/Pittsburgh PA 15214
1922-037 ....Francis, Ray James ....D. July 14, 1932 Atlanta, Ga.
1984-036 ....Franco, John Anthony ....111 Cliffwood Avenue/Staten Island NY 10304
1982-045 ....Franco, Julio Cesar ....Old Add: 1269 Cedarland Plaza Dr Arlington TX 76011
1995-077 ....Franco, Matthew Neil ....Old Add: Thousand Oaks CA 91359
1956-036 ....Francona, John Patsy 'Tito' ....1109 Penn Avenue/New Brighton PA 15066
1981-038 ....Francona, Terry Jon ....958 Hunt Drive/Yardley PA 19067
1927-035 ....Frankhouse, Frederick Meloy ....D. August 17, 1989 Port Royal, Pa.
1944-044 ....Franklin, James Wilford 'Jack' ....D. November 15, 1991 Panama City, Fla.
1971-036 ....Franklin, John William 'Jay' ....Old Add: 2305 Stryker Ave/Vienna Va
1997-060 ....Franklin, Micah Ishanti ....Old Add: San Francisco CA 94101
1941-034 ....Franklin, Murray Asher ....D. March 16, 1978 Harbor City, Calif.
1939-036 ....Franks, Herman Louis ....2745 Comanche Drive/Salt Lake City UT 84108
1994-035 ....Frascatore, John Vincent ....73 Anchor Avenue/Oceanside NY 11572
1986-052 ....Fraser, William Patrick 'Willie' ....3908 Plantation Blvd/Leesburg FL 34748
1931-028 ....Frasier, Victor Patrick ....D. January 10, 1977 Jacksonville, Tex.
1993-055 ....Frazier, Arthur Louis 'Lou' ....8550 McDowell/Scottsdale AZ 85257
1978-045 ....Frazier, George Allen ....Rural Route 1 Box 229/Wagoner OK 74463
1947-036 ....Frazier, Joseph Filmore ....519 Fairway Drive/Broken Arrow Ok/74012
1929-037 ....Frederick, John Henry ....D. June 18, 1977 Tigard, Ore.
1993-056 ....Fredrickson, Scott Eric ....12637 King Oaks/San Antonio TX 78233
1942-039 ....Freed, Edwin Charles ....840 McDow Drive/Rock Hill Sc/29730
1970-046 ....Freed, Roger Vernon ....D. January 9, 1996 Chino, Calif.
1961-036 ....Freehan, William Ashley ....%U Of Michigan 1000 South State Street Ann Arbor MI 48109
1921-029 ....Freeman, Alexander Vernon 'Buck' ....D. February 21, 1953 Fort Sam Houston, Texas
1921-030 ....Freeman, Harvey Bayard ....D. January 10, 1970 Kalamazoo, Mich.
1952-031 ....Freeman, Hershell Baskin ....5437 San Marino Place/Orlando FL 32807
1972-029 ....Freeman, Jimmy Lee ....Old Add: 2164 South Urbana/Tulsa OK 74114
1927-036 ....Freeman, John Edward ....D. April 14, 1958 Washington, D. C.
1989-039 ....Freeman, Lavel Maurice ....2501 Gardenale Road/Sacramento CA 95822
1959-028 ....Freeman, Mark Price ....2552 East Alameda Avenue #41/Denver CO 80209
1986-053 ....Freeman, Marvin ....20135 Mohawk Trail/Olympia Fields IL 60461
1955-044 ....Freese, Eugene Lewis ....6504 Glendale/Metairie LA 70003

1953-027	Freese, George Walter	3341 SW Marigold Street/Portland OR 97219
1925-036	Freeze, Carl Alexander 'Jake'	D. April 9, 1983 San Angelo, Tex.
1961-037	Fregosi, James Louis	1092 Copeland CT Tarpon Springs FL 34689
1941-035	Freiburger, Vernon Donald	D. February 27, 1990 Palm Springs, Calif.
1922-038	Freigau, Howard Earl	D. July 18, 1932 Chattanooga, Tenn.
1974-038	Freisleben, David James	2119 Peach Ln/Pasadena TX 77502
1932-027	Freitas, Antonio	D. March 13, 1994 Orangevale, Calif.
1917-031	French, Frank Alexander 'Pat'	D. July 13, 1969 Bath, Me.
1929-038	French, Lawrence Robert	D. February 9, 1987 San Diego, Calif.
1920-033	French, Raymond Edward	D. April 3, 1978 Alameda, Calif.
1965-029	French, Richard James 'Jim'	1060 West North Shore Drive/Chicago IL 60626
1923-043	French, Walter Edward	D. May 13, 1984 Mountain Home, Ark.
1929-039	Frey, Benjamin Rudolph	D. November 1, 1937 Jackson, Mich.
1980-045	Frey, James Gottfried	119a Versailles Cicle/Towson MD 21204
1933-019	Frey, Linus Reinhard 'Lonny'	995 West Woodlawn Drive/Hayden ID 83835
1989-040	Frey, Steven Francis	1414 Second Street Pike/Southampton PA 18966
1997-061	Frias, Hanley Acevedo	Old Add: Villa Altagracia Dom. Rep.
1973-048	Frias, Jesus Maria 'Pepe'	Old Add: Cle 4 Casa 9 Ing Consuelo San Pedro De Mac Dom Rep
1919-027	Friberg, Gustaf Bernhard	D. December 8, 1958 Lynn, Mass.
1952-032	Fricano, Marion John	D. May 18, 1976 Tijuana, Mex.
1923-044	Friday, Grier William 'Skipper'	D. August 25, 1962 Gastonia, N. C.
1952-033	Fridley, James Riley	540 Jasmine Nw Avenue/Port Charlotte FL 33952
1920-034	Fried, Arthur Edwin 'Cy'	D. October 10, 1970 San Antonio, Tex.
1932-028	Friedrichs, Robert George	D. April 15, 1997 Jasper, Ind.
1949-024	Friend, Owen Lacey	2055 Porter Street #103/Wichita KS 67203
1951-032	Friend, Robert Bartmess	4 Salem Circle/Fox Chapel PA 15238
1941-036	Frierson, Robert Lawrence 'Buck'	D. June 26, 1996 Paris, Texas
1910-056	Frill, John Edmund	D. September 28, 1918 Westerly, R. I.
1934-037	Frink, Frederick Ferdinand	D. May 19, 1995 Miami Springs, Fla.
1919-028	Frisch, Frank Francis	D. March 12, 1973 Wilmington, Del.
1967-034	Frisella, Daniel Vincent	D. January 1, 1977 Phoenix, Ariz.
1913-060	Fritz, Harry Koch	D. November 4, 1974 Columbus, O.
1975-041	Fritz, Laurence Joseph	2632 Schrage Ave/Whiting IN 46394
1955-045	Froats, William John	D. February 9, 1998 Minneapolis, Minn.
1982-046	Frobel, Douglas Stephen	63 Glenridge Road/Ottawa Ontario K2G 2Z8 Canada
1987-046	Frohwirth, Todd Gerard	6608 West Chambers Street/Milwaukee WI 53210
1977-055	Frost, Carl David 'Dave'	2206 Ocana Dr/Long Beach CA 90815
1978-046	Fry, Jerry Ray	3300 Stanton Street/Springfield IL 62703
1923-045	Fry, Johnson	D. April 7, 1959 Carmi, Ill.
1940-023	Frye, Charles Andrew	D. May 25, 1945 Hickory, N. C.
1992-042	Frye, Jeffrey Dustin	608 Chaffee Drive/Arlington TX 76006
1990-049	Fryman, David Travis Travis	3201 Windmill Circle/Cantonment FL 32533
1966-037	Fryman, Woodrow Thompson	Rr 1 Box 21/Ewing KY 41039
1942-040	Fuchs, Charles Rudolph	D. June 10, 1969 Weehawken, N. J.
1929-040	Fuchs, Emil Edwin	D. December 5, 1961 Boston, Mass.
1983-059	Fuentes, Michael Jay	6001 Cellini Street/Coral Gables FL 33146
1969-059	Fuentes, Miguel	D. January 29, 1970 Loiza Aldea, P. R.
1965-030	Fuentes, Rogoberto Peat 'Tito'	61 South Maddux Drive/Reno NV 89512
1921-031	Fuhr, Oscar Lawrence	D. March 27, 1975 Dallas, Tex.
1922-039	Fuhrman, Alfred George 'Ollie'	D. January 11, 1969 Peoria, Ill.
1921-032	Fulghum, James Lavoisier 'Dot'	D. November 11, 1947 Miami, Fla.
1979-038	Fulghum, John Thomas	Old Add: 802 Sunnybrook Drive Edmond OK 73034
1915-049	Fuller, Frank Edward	D. October 29, 1965 Warren, Mich.
1973-049	Fuller, James	4215 Haiti Lane/Pasadena TX 77505
1974-039	Fuller, John Edward	Old Add: 33022 Christina/Dana Point CA 92629
1964-034	Fuller, Vern Gordon	% Registry 7901 24th Avenue South Minneapolis MN 55420
1921-033	Fullerton, Curtis Hooper	D. January 2, 1975 Winthrop, Mass.
1928-036	Fullis, Charles Philip 'Chick'	D. March 28, 1946 Ashland, Pa.
1997-062	Fullmer, Bradley Ryan	Old Add: Chatsworth CA 91311
1987-047	Fulton, William David	Old Add: 217 Dorothy Drive Pittsburgh PA 15235
1981-039	Funderburk, Mark Clifford	6924 Old Providence Road/Charlotte NC 28226
1929-041	Funk, Elias Calvin 'Liz'	D. January 17, 1968 Oklahoma City, Okla.
1960-035	Funk, Franklin Ray	64 East Greentree Drive/Tempe AZ 85284
1986-054	Funk, Thomas James	2905 NE 56th Terrace/Kansas City MO 64119
1946-030	Furillo, Carl Anthony	D. January 21, 1989 Stony Creek Mills, Pa.
1922-040	Fussell, Frederick Morris	D. October 23, 1966 Syracuse, N. Y.
1952-034	Fusselman, Lester Leroy	D. May 21, 1970 Cleveland, O.
1996-063	Fyhrie, Michael Edwin	Old Add: Westminster CA 92683
1935-033	Gabler, Frank Harold	D. November 1, 1967 Long Beach, Calif.
1959-029	Gabler, John Richard	8606 West 81st St/Overland Park KS 66204
1958-035	Gabler, William Louis	714 East Carrie Avenue/Saint Louis MO 63147
1945-034	Gables, Kenneth Harlin	D. January 2, 1960 Walnut Grove, Mo.
1960-036	Gabrielson, Leonard Gary	24230 Hillview Road/Los Altos Hills CA 94024
1939-037	Gabrielson, Leonard Hilbourne	1387 Glen Drive/San Leandro CA 94577
1938-028	Gaddy, John Wilson	D. May 3, 1966 Albemarle, N. C.
1951-033	Gaedel, Edward Carl	D. June 19, 1961 Chicago, Ill.
1981-040	Gaetti, Gary Joseph	7612 Rainwater Road/Raleigh NC 27615
1982-047	Gaff, Brent Allen	5925 South State Road #9/Albion IN 46701
1936-027	Gaffke, Fabian Sebastian 'Fabe'	D. February 8, 1992 Milwaukee, Wisc.

1963-042 ....Gagliano, Philip Joseph ....730 Oakhall Lane/Manchester MO 63021
1965-031 ....Gagliano, Ralph Michael ....1756 Overton Park Avenue/Memphis TN 38112
1983-060 ....Gagne, Gregory Carpenter ....746 Whetstone Hill Road/Somerset MA 2726
1914-069 ....Gagnier, Edward J. ....D. September 13, 1946 Detroit, Mich.
1922-041 ....Gagnon, Harold Dennis 'Chick'....................D. April 30, 1970 Wilmington, Del.
1997-063 ....Gaillard, Julian Edward 'Eddie'.....................830 Windermere Way/West Palm Beach FL 33418
1993-057 ....Gainer, Jonathan Keith 'Jay' ....1015 Kurze Avenue/Panama City FL 32401
1960-037 ....Gaines, Arnesta Joe ....77 Anair Way/Oakland CA 94605
1921-034 ....Gaines, Willard Roland 'Nemo' ....D. January 26, 1979 Warrenton, Va.
1985-036 ....Gainey, Telmanch 'Ty' ....Old Add: 127 Jericho Street Cheraw SC 29520
1991-059 ....Gakeler, Daniel Michael ....3622 Two Oaks Drive/Greensboro NC 27410
1934-038 ....Galan, August John ....D. December 28, 1993 Fairfield, Calif.
1985-037 ....Galarraga, Andres Jose Padovani ....Barrio Nuevo Chapellin Clejon Soledad #5 Caracas Venezuela
1977-056 ....Galasso, Robert Jose.....................................1705 Loblolly Lane/Cumming GA 30131
1933-020 ....Galatzer, Milton ....D. January 29, 1976 San Francisco, Calif.
1978-047 ....Gale, Richard Blackwell ....3 York Drive/Durham NH 3824
1934-039 ....Galehouse, Dennis Ward ....D. October 12, 1998 Doylestown, Ohio
1970-047 ....Gallagher, Alan Mitchell Edward...................Old Add: 1852 Beverly Avenue/Clovis CA 93612
1987-048 ....Gallagher, David Thomas ....% Stridell 177 Applegate Drive Trenton NJ 8690
1962-043 ....Gallagher, Douglas Eugene............................1690 Maple Ln/Fremont OH 43420
1932-029 ....Gallagher, Edward Michael ....D. December 22, 1981 Hyannis Port, Mass.
1915-050 ....Gallagher, John Carroll ....D. March 30, 1952 Norfolk, Va.
1923-046 ....Gallagher, John Laurence ....D. September 10, 1984 Gladwyn, Pa.
1939-038 ....Gallagher, Joseph Emmett ....D. February 25, 1998 Houston, Texas
1922-042 ....Gallagher, Lawrence Kirby 'Gil' ....D. January 6, 1957 Washington, D. C.
1972-030 ....Gallagher, Robert Collins ....315 Fair Ave/Santa Cruz CA 95060
1942-041 ....Galle, Stanley Joseph ....7 North Reed Avenue/Mobile/AL 36604
1985-038 ....Gallego, Michael Anthony ....10800 East Cactus Road #17/Scottsdale AZ 85259
1912-065 ....Gallia, Melvin Allys 'Bert'..............................D. March 19, 1976 Devine, Tex.
1931-029 ....Gallivan, Philip Joseph ....D. November 24, 1969 St. Paul, Minn.
1919-029 ....Galloway, Clarence Edward 'Chick' ....D. November 7, 1969 Clinton, S. C.
1912-066 ....Galloway, James Cato 'Bad News' ....D. May 3, 1950 Fort Worth, Tex.
1986-055 ....Galvez, Balvino ....Batey Labomba Div Porv'lr San Pedro De Macoris Dominican Rep.
1930-024 ....Galvin, James Joseph ....D. September 30, 1969 Marietta, Ga.
1972-031 ....Gamble, John Robert ....369 Caliente Street/Reno NV 89509
1935-034 ....Gamble, Lee Jesse ....D. October 5, 1994 Punxsutawney, Pa.
1969-060 ....Gamble, Oscar Charles ....2926 Susan Drive/Montgomery AL 36116
1910-057 ....Gandil, Charles Arnold 'Chick' ....D. December 12, 1970 Calistoga, Calif.
1916-030 ....Gandy, Robert Brinkley ....D. June 19, 1945 Jacksonville, Fla.
1987-049 ....Gant, Ronald Edwin ....2005 Kings Cross Road/Alpharetta GA 30022
1939-039 ....Gantenbein, Joseph Stephen ....D. August 2, 1993 San Francisco, Calif.
1976-033 ....Gantner, James Elmer ....Box 156/Eden WI 53019
1927-037 ....Ganzel, Foster Pirie 'Babe' ....D. February 6, 1978 Jacksonville/Fla.
1946-031 ....Garagiola, Joseph Henry ....7433 East Tuckey Lane/Scottsdale Az/85250
1994-036 ....Garagozzo, Keith John ....4045 West McNab Road #6209/Pompano Beach FL 33069
1944-045 ....Garbark, Nathaniel Michael 'Mike' ....D. August 31, 1994 Charlotte, N.C.
1934-040 ....Garbark, Robert Michael ....D. August 15, 1990 Meadville, Pa.
1969-061 ....Garber, Henry Eugene 'Gene' ....771 Stonemill Drive/Elizabethtown PA 17022
1956-021 ....Garber, Robert Mitchell ....101 Acacia Ln/Redwood City CA 94062
1984-037 ....Garbey, Barbaro Garbey ....Old Add: 181-10 Nw 56th St Miami FL 33178
1952-035 ....Garbowski, Alexander ....110 Elliott Street/Yonkers NY 10705
1990-050 ....Garces, Richard Aron ....Sector 2, Calle 2 No. 2 Maracay Aragua Venezuela
1976-034 ....Garcia, Alfonso Rafae 'Kiko' ....Old Add: 526a North Civic Drive/Walnut Creek CA 94596
1990-051 ....Garcia, Carlos Jesus ....Old Add: Bolivar Venezuela
1978-048 ....Garcia, Damaso Domingo ....Sanchez No. 104 Moca Dominican Rep.
1981-041 ....Garcia, Daniel Raphael ....250 Fairhaven #D5/Jericho NY 11753
1977-057 ....Garcia, David ....15420 Olde Hwy 80 #129/El Cajon CA 92021
1948-037 ....Garcia, Edward Miguel 'Mike' ....D. January 13, 1986 Fairview Park, O.
1995-078 ....Garcia, Freddy Adrian ....Quisquella Gta Etapa M22 #52 La Ramona Dominican Rep.
1995-079 ....Garcia, Gustavo Karim 'Karim' ....Moreles #725 Ote Ciudad/Obregon/Sonora 8500 Mexico
1987-050 ....Garcia, Leonardo Antonio ....Juan Saltitopa #28 E.Bolival Santiago Dominican Rep.
1987-051 ....Garcia, Miguel Angel ....Carlos Delgado Chalbaud Blq6 Letra C #6 Caracas Venezuela
1973-050 ....Garcia, Pedro Modesto ....Parque Del Condado L-4,B.Park/Caguas PR 725
1972-032 ....Garcia, Ralph ....7441 Brian Lane/Lapalma CA 90623
1991-060 ....Garcia, Ramon Antonio ....Bo. Colombia N. Callejon 2 Gaunare Edo.Portyguesa Venezuela
1948-038 ....Garcia, Ramon Garcia ....Hatuey 259/E. Oriente Y Camaguey Arroyo Havana Cuba
1996-064 ....Garciaparra, Anthony Nomar 'Nomar' ....Old Add: Las Vegas NV 89101
1945-035 ....Gardella, Alfred Steve ....3761 Nw 35th Street/Coconut Creek FL 33066
1944-046 ....Gardella, Daniel Lewis ....16 Morsemere Place/Yonkers NY 10701
1981-042 ....Gardenhire, Ronald Clyde ....668 County Road B2/Little Canada MN 55117
1923-047 ....Gardiner, Arthur Cecil ....D. October 21, 1954 Copiague, N. Y.
1990-052 ....Gardiner, Michael James ....Old Add: Terre Haute IN 47808
1975-042 ....Gardner, Arthur Junior ....Rr 2 Box 41/Walnut Grove MS 39189
1991-061 ....Gardner, Christopher John ....Old Add: 2151 Big Buck Lane Paso Robles CA 93446
1945-036 ....Gardner, Glenn Mileso ....D. July 7, 1964 Rochester, N. Y.
1911-052 ....Gardner, Harry Ray ....D. August 2, 1961 Canby, Ore.
1991-062 ....Gardner, Jeffrey Scott ....1906 Port Weybridge Place/Newport Beach CA 92660
1989-041 ....Gardner, Mark Allan ....489 Burgan Street/Clovis CA 93612
1929-042 ....Gardner, Raymond Vincent ....D. May 3, 1968 Frederick, Md.

1965-032	Gardner, Richard Frank 'Rob'	7 West End Avenue/Binghamton NY 13905
1984-038	Gardner, Wesley Brian	2 Rivercrest Drive NE/Benton AR 72015
1954-030	Gardner, William Frederick	35 Dayton Rd/Waterford CT 6385
1936-028	Garibaldi, Arthur Edward	D. October 20, 1967 Sacramento, Calif.
1962-044	Garibaldi, Bob Roy	2143 Oregon Avenue/Stockton CA 95204
1931-030	Garland, Louis Lyman	D. August 30, 1990 Idaho Falls, Id.
1973-051	Garland, Marcus Wayne 'Wayne'	1026 Ridgegreen Loop North/Lakeland FL 33809
1969-062	Garman, Michael Douglas	15144 Kings Row Road/Caldwell ID 83605
1932-030	Garms, Debs C.	D. December 16, 1984 Glen Rose, Texas
1973-052	Garner, Philip Mason	2451 Lake Village Drive/Kingwood TX 77339
1968-026	Garr, Ralph Allan	7819 Chaseway Dr/Missouri City TX 77459
1982-048	Garrelts, Scott William	206 East Elm/Buckley IL 60918
1915-051	Garrett, Clarence Raymond	D. February 11, 1977 Moundsville, W. Va.
1970-048	Garrett, Gregory	Old Add: 14963 Sandra/San Fernando CA 91340
1966-038	Garrett, Henry Adrian 'Ade'	Box 201/Manchaca TX 78652
1969-063	Garrett, Ronald Wayne 'Wayne'	4331 Linwood Street/Sarasota FL 34232
1964-035	Garrido, Gil Gonzalo	PO Box 527948/Miami FL 33152
1946-032	Garriott, Cecil Virgil	D. February 20, 1990 Lake Elsinore, Calif.
1928-037	Garrison, Clifford William	D. August 25, 1994 Woodland, Calif.
1943-049	Garrison, Robert Ford 'Ford'	5075 65th Avenue North/Pinellas Park FL 34665
1996-065	Garrison, Webster Leotis	Old Add: New Orleans LA 70101
1931-031	Garrity, Francis Joseph 'Hank'	D. September 3, 1962 Boston, Mass.
1948-039	Garver, Ned Franklin	PO Box 114/Ney OH 43549
1969-064	Garvey, Steven Patrick	Old Add: 11822 Kearsarge Street Los Angeles CA 90049
1977-058	Garvin, Theodore Jarde 'Jerry'	Old Add: 75 Zaca Lane #100/San Luis Obispo CA 93401
1969-065	Gaspar, Rodney Earl	28771 Peach Blossom/Mission Viejo CA 92692
1944-047	Gassaway, Charles Cason	D. January 15, 1992 Miami, Fla.
1955-046	Gastall, Thomas Everett	D. September 20, 1956 Chesapeake Bay, Md.
1920-035	Gaston, Alexander Nathaniel	D. February 8, 1979 Santa Monica, Calif.
1967-035	Gaston, Clarence Edwin	2 Blythdale Road/Toronto Ontario M4N 3M2 Canada
1924-039	Gaston, Nathaniel Milton	D. April 26, 1996 Hyannis, Mass.
1993-058	Gates, Brent Robert	6131 Regal Drive Southwest/Grandville MI 49418
1978-049	Gates, Joseph Daniel	1517 East Nineteenth Ave/Gary IN 46407
1981-043	Gates, Michael Grant	Hc 075 Box 45c/Kooskia ID 83539
1963-043	Gatewood, Aubrey Lee	5 Pine Tree Loop/North Little Rock AR 72116
1978-050	Gaudet, James Jennings	182 Riley Avenue #D/Macon GA 31204
1925-037	Gautreau, Walter Paul 'Doc'	D. August 23, 1970 Salt Lake City, Utah
1936-029	Gautreaux, Sidney Allen	D. April 19, 1980 Morgan City, La.
1920-036	Gaw, George Joseph 'Chippy'	D. May 26, 1968 Boston, Mass.
1923-048	Gazella, Michael	D. September 11, 1978 Odessa, Tex.
1947-037	Gearhart, Lloyd William	16 Clifton Road/Xenia OH 45385
1923-049	Gearin, Dennis John 'Dinty'	D. March 11, 1959 Providence, R. I.
1942-042	Geary, Eugene Francis Joseph 'Huck'	D. January 27, 1981 Cuba, N. Y.
1918-021	Geary, Robert Norton	D. January 31, 1980 Cincinnati, O.
1971-037	Gebhard, Robert Henry	1700 Broadway #2100/Denver CO 80290
1947-038	Gebrian, Peter	811 SW Southwest Drive #207/Stuart FL 34997
1972-033	Geddes, James Lee	Old Add: 1644 Clark Avenue/Columbus Oh
1939-040	Gedeon, Elmer John	D. April 20, 1944 Saint Pol, France
1913-061	Gedeon, Elmer Joseph	D. May 19, 1941 San Francisco, Calif.
1980-046	Gedman, Richard Leo	10 Parmenter Road/Framingham MA 1701
1939-041	Gee, John Alexander	D. January 23, 1988 Cortland, N. Y.
1923-050	Gehrig, Henry Louis 'Lou'	D. June 2, 1941 Riverdale, N. Y.
1924-040	Gehringer, Charles Leonard	D. January 21, 1993 Bloomfield Hills, Mich.
1937-039	Gehrman, Paul Arthur	D. October 23, 1986 Bend, Ore.
1958-036	Geiger, Gary Merle	D. April 24, 1996 Murphysboro, Ill.
1978-051	Geisel, John David 'Dave'	608 North Middletown Road/Media PA 19063
1969-066	Geishert, Vernon William	PO Box 471/Spring Green WI 53588
1929-043	Gelbert, Charles Magnus	D. January 13, 1967 Easton, Pa.
1964-036	Gelnar, John Richard	Rural Route 1 Box 252/Granite OK 73547
1922-043	Genewich, Joseph Edward	D. December 21, 1985 Lockport, N. Y.
1950-030	Genovese, George Michael	11474 Erwin Street/Hollywood CA 91606
1957-022	Gentile, James Edward	1016 Neptune/Edmond OK 73034
1943-050	Gentile, Samuel Christopher	D. May 4, 1998 Everett, Mass.
1969-067	Gentry, Gary Edward	6219 North 9th Place/Phoenix AZ 85014
1954-031	Gentry, Harvey William	109 Eaton Ln/Bristol TN 37620
1943-051	Gentry, James Ruffus 'Rufe'	D. July 3, 1997 Winston-Salem, N. C.
1955-047	George, Alex Thomas	8432 Linden Drive/Prairie Village KS 66207
1935-035	George, Charles Peter 'Greek'	PO Box 2960/Covington LA 70434
1991-063	George, Christopher Sean	428 Kathy Lynn Drive/Pittsburgh PA 15239
1911-053	George, Thomas Edward 'Lefty'	D. May 13, 1955 York, Pa.
1938-029	Georgy, Oscar John	PO Box 464/Marion LA 71260
1936-030	Geraghty, Benjamin Raymond	D. June 18, 1963 Jacksonville, Fla.
1962-045	Gerard, David Frederick	318 Doone Pl/Fairless Hills PA 19030
1985-039	Gerber, Craig Stuart	4297 Pershing Avenue/San Bernardino CA 92407
1914-070	Gerber, Walter	D. June 19, 1951 Columbus, O.
1962-046	Gerberman, George Alois	1501 Michael/El Campo TX 77437
1988-053	Geren, Robert Peter	14290 Hickory Links #1912/Fort Myers FL 33912
1974-040	Gerhardt, Allen Russell 'Rusty'	PO Box 426/New London TX 75682
1986-056	Gerhart, Harold Kenneth 'Ken'	1111 Campbell Court/Murfreesboro TN 37130

1943-052	Gerheauser, Albert	D. May 28, 1972 Springfield, Mo.
1927-038	Gerken, George Herbert	D. October 23, 1977 Arcaida, Calif.
1945-037	Gerkin, Stephen Paul	D. November 8, 1978 Bay Pines, Fla.
1938-030	Gerlach, John Glenn	5721 Dogwood Place/Madison WI 53705
1919-030	Gerner, Edwin Frederick	D. May 15, 1970 Philadelphia, Pa.
1952-036	Gernert, Richard Edward	1420 Rose Virginia Road/Reading PA 19615
1969-068	Geronimo, Cesar Francisco	120 West 97th #9e/New York NY 10025
1913-062	Gervais, Luciean Edward 'Lefty'	D. October 19, 1950 Los Angeles, Calif.
1945-038	Gettel, Allen James	5620 Parliament Drive/Virginia Beach VA 23462
1910-058	Geyer, Jacob Bowman 'Rube'	D. October 12, 1962 Wahkon, Minn.
1924-041	Geygan, James Edward 'Chappie'	D. March 16, 1966 Columbus, O.
1916-031	Gharrity, Edward Patrick 'Patsy'	D. October 10, 1966 Beloit, Wis.
1983-061	Ghelfi, Anthony Paul	3414 Geneva Lane/Lacrosse WI 54601
1958-037	Giallombardo, Robert Paul	145 Wellington Court #1d/Staten Island NY 10314
1995-080	Giambi, Jason Gilbert	216 North Delay Avenue/Covina CA 91723
1991-064	Giannelli, Raymond John	56 East Saltaire Road/Lindenhurst NY 11757
1911-054	Giannini, Joseph Francis	D. September 26, 1942 San Francisco, Calif.
1925-038	Giard, Joseph Oscar	D. July 10, 1956 Worcester, Mass.
1960-038	Gibbon, Joseph Charles	Rural Route 2 Garlandsville Newton MS 39345
1984-039	Gibbons, John Michael	105 Metz Drive/Ruidoso NM 88345
1962-047	Gibbs, Jerry Dean 'Jake'	225 St. Andrews Circle/Oxford MS 38655
1995-081	Gibraltor, Stephen Benson	1618 Nob Hill/Duncanville TX 75137
1924-042	Gibson, Charles Griffin	D. December 18, 1990 Lagrange, Ga.
1913-063	Gibson, Frank Gilbert	D. April 27, 1961 Austin, Tex.
1967-036	Gibson, John Russell 'Russ'	495 Gardners Neck Road/Swansea MA 2777
1979-039	Gibson, Kirk Harold	17108 Mack Avenue/Grosse Pointe MI 48230
1988-054	Gibson, Paul Marshall	PO Box 354/Center Moriches NY 11934
1959-030	Gibson, Robert	215 Belleview Blvd South/Belleview NE 68005
1983-062	Gibson, Robert Louis	751 West Rolling Road/Springfield PA 19064
1926-030	Gibson, Samuel Braxton	D. January 31, 1983 High Point, N. C.
1937-040	Gick, George Edward	3 Brady Court/Lafayette IN 47905
1987-052	Gideon, Byron Brett	PO Box 822/Georgetown TX 78627
1975-043	Gideon, James Leslie	5623 Braesvalley/Houston TX 77035
1913-064	Giebel, Joseph Henry	D. March 17, 1981 Silver Spring, Md.
1939-042	Giebell, Floyd George	607 Laurelwood Drive/Wilkesboro NC 28697
1954-032	Giel, Paul Robert	13400 McGinty Road East/Minneapolis MN 55343
1959-031	Giggie, Robert Thomas	89 McAndrew Rd/Braintree MA 2184
1967-037	Gigon, Norman Phillip	205 Paxinosa Rd East/Easton PA 18042
1993-059	Gil, Romar Benjamin 'Benji'	6532 Parkside Avenue/San Diego CA 92139
1967-038	Gil, Tomas Gustavo 'Gus'	Urb. Urdaveta,Vereda 15#1 Caracas Venezuela
1997-064	Gilbert, Albert Shawn 'Shawn'	2192 East Rush/Fresno CA 93720
1942-043	Gilbert, Andrew	D. August 29, 1992 Davis, Calif.
1940-024	Gilbert, Charles Mader	D. August 13, 1983 New Orleans, La.
1959-032	Gilbert, Drew Edward 'Buddy'	1913 Belcaro Dr/Knoxville TN 37918
1950-031	Gilbert, Harold Joseph 'Tookie'	D. June 23, 1967 New Orleans, La.
1972-034	Gilbert, Joe Dennis	1952 North Bowie St/Jasper TX 75951
1914-071	Gilbert, Lawrence William	D. February 17, 1965 New Orleans, La.
1985-040	Gilbert, Mark David	Old Add: 3151 North Course Ln #201 Pompano Beach FL
1928-038	Gilbert, Walter John	D. September 8, 1959 Duluth, Minn.
1972-035	Gilbreath, Rodney Joe	1438 Ridgeland Way/Lilburn GA 30247
1971-038	Gilbreth, William Freeman	Old Add: 690 East North 16th St/Abilene TX 79601
1959-033	Gile, Donald Loren	570 Seahorse Lane/Redwood City CA 94065
1981-044	Giles, Brian Jeffrey	8607 Glenhaven Street/San Diego CA 92123
1995-082	Giles, Brian Stephen	Old Add: %B.Giles,444 Graves Ave El Cajon CA 92020
1920-037	Gilham, George Lewis	D. April 25, 1937 Lansdowne, Pa.
1911-055	Gilhooley, Frank Patrick	D. July 11, 1959 Toledo, O.
1990-053	Gilkey, Otis Bernard 'Bernard'	Old Add: 7895 Trenton University City MO 63130
1919-031	Gill, Edward James	D. October 10, 1995 Brockton, Mass.
1937-041	Gill, George Lloyd	PO Box 211/Raymond MS 39154
1923-051	Gill, Harold Edward	D. August 1, 1932 Brockton, Mass.
1927-039	Gill, John Wesley	D. December 26, 1984 Nashville, Tenn.
1940-025	Gillenwater, Carden Edison	45 Country Club Drive/Largo FL 33543
1923-052	Gillenwater, Claral Lewis	D. February 26, 1978 Pensacola, Fla.
1990-054	Gilles, Thomas Bradford	2409 North Sheridan Road/Peoria IL 61604
1922-044	Gillespie, John Patrick	D. February 15, 1954 Vallejo, Calif.
1942-044	Gillespie, Paul Allen	D. August 11, 1970 Anniston, Ala.
1944-048	Gillespie, Robert William	123 Carol Road/Winston-Salem NC 27106
1953-028	Gilliam, James William 'Junior'	D. October 8, 1978 Inglewood, Calif.
1967-039	Gilliford, Paul Gant	7 Woodland Dr/Malvern PA 19355
1927-040	Gillis, Grant	D. February 4, 1981 Thomasville, Ala.
1914-072	Gilmore, Ernest Grover	D. November 25, 1919 Sioux City, Ia.
1944-049	Gilmore, Leonard Preston	Rural Route 2 Box 213c/Jones OK 73049
1968-027	Gilson, Harold	Old Add: 1509 Julie St #B/Berkeley CA 94703
1915-052	Gingras, Joseph Elzead John	D. September 6, 1947 Jersey City, N.J.
1914-073	Ginn, Tinsley Rucker	D. August 30, 1931 Atlanta, Ga.
1948-040	Ginsberg, Myron Nathan 'Joe'	12635 SW Kingsway Circle #D1/Lake Suzy FL 33821
1944-050	Gionfriddo, Albert Francis	2629 Quail Valley Road/Solvang CA 93463
1953-029	Giordano, Thomas Arthur	176 Riverside Avenue/Amityville NY 11701
1995-083	Giovanala, Edward Thomas	1741 Nomark Court/San Jose CA 95125

1910-059	Girard, Charles August	D. August 6, 1936 Brooklyn, N. Y.
1989-042	Girardi, Joseph Elliott	5513 Avenue Du Soleil/Lutz FL 33549
1936-031	Giuliani, Angelo John	1985 Norfolk Avenue/Saint Paul MN 55116
1962-048	Giusti, David John	524 Clair Dr/Pittsburgh PA 15241
1995-084	Givens, Brian	Old Add: 1634 Biscay Circle Aurora CO 80011
1946-033	Gladd, James Walter	D. November 8, 1977 Long Beach, Calif.
1983-063	Gladden, Clifton Daniel Dan	888 Brook Grove Ln/Cupertino CA 95014
1961-038	Gladding, Fred Earl	4721 Macmont Cir/Powell TN 37819
1944-051	Gladu, Roland Edwin	D. July 26, 1994 Montreal, Que.
1920-038	Glaiser, John Burke	D. March 7, 1959 Houston, Tex.
1996-066	Glanville, Douglas Matunwa	Old Add: Teaneck NJ 07666
1925-039	Glass, Thomas Joseph	D. December 15, 1981 Greensboro, N. C.
1913-065	Glavenich, Luke Frank	D. May 22, 1935 Stockton, Calif.
1949-025	Glaviano, Thomas Giatano	23905 Hitching Post Road/Sonora CA 95370
1987-053	Glavine, Thomas Michael	3050 Compton Court/Alpharetta GA 30302
1920-039	Glazner, Charles Franklin 'Whitey'	D. June 6, 1989 Orlando, Fla.
1920-040	Gleason, Joseph Paul	D. September 8, 1990 Phelps, N. Y.
1963-044	Gleason, Roy William	Old Add:1115 Wilcox Ave Monterey Park CA 91754
1916-032	Gleason, William Patrick	D. January 9, 1957 Holyoke, Mass.
1979-040	Gleaton, Jerry Don	3008 Avenue K/Brownwood TX 76801
1936-032	Gleeson, James Joseph	D. May 1, 1996 Kansas City, Mo.
1919-032	Gleich, Frank Elmer	D. March 27, 1949 Columbus, O.
1920-041	Glenn, Burdette 'Bob'	D. June 3, 1977 Richmond, Calif.
1915-053	Glenn, Harry Melville	D. October 12, 1918 St. Paul, Minn.
1960-039	Glenn, John	502 Fifth Avenue Nw/Moultrie GA 31768
1932-031	Glenn, Joseph Charles	D. May 6, 1985 Tunkhannock, Pa.
1930-025	Gliatto, Salvador Michael	D. November 2, 1995 Tyler, Texas
1994-037	Glinatsis, George	467 Gardenwood Drive/Youngstown OH 44512
1914-074	Glockson, Norman Stanley	D. August 5, 1955 Maywood, Ill.
1939-043	Glossop, Alban	D. July 2, 1991 Walnut Creek, Calif.
1975-044	Glynn, Edward Paul	157 San Carlos Street/Toms River NJ 8757
1949-026	Glynn, William Vincent	6916 51st/San Diego CA 92120
1974-041	Godby, Danny Ray	Rural Route 2 Box 17a/Chapmanville WV 25508
1972-036	Goddard, Joseph Harold	303 Ridgepark Drive/Beckley WV 25801
1922-045	Goebel, Edwin	D. August 12, 1959 Brooklyn, N. Y.
1960-040	Goetz, John Hardy	3253 Myddleton/Troy MI 48084
1990-055	Goff, Jerry Lee	15 Stevens Place/San Rafael CA 94901
1972-037	Goggin, Charles Francis	1206 Davidson Road/Nashville TN 37205
1970-049	Gogolewski, William Joseph	1522 Graham Ave/Oshkosh WI 54901
1993-060	Gohr, Gregory James	589 Lincoln Street #8/Santa Clara CA 95050
1960-041	Golden, James Edward	8630 SW 10th/Topeka KS 66606
1910-060	Golden, Roy Kramer	D. October 4, 1961 Norwood, O.
1928-039	Goldman, Jonah John	D. August 17, 1980 Palm Beach, Fla.
1949-027	Goldsberry, Gordon Frederick	D. February 23, 1996 Lake Forest, Ill.
1926-031	Goldsmith, Harold Eugene	D. October 20, 1985 Riverhead, N. Y.
1932-032	Goldstein, Isadore	D. September 24, 1993 Delray Beach, Fla.
1943-053	Goldstein, Leslie Elmer 'Lonnie'	6516 Sabrosa Court West/Fort Worth TX 76133
1962-049	Goldy, Purnal William	1318 Cherryville Rd/Littleton CO 80120
1941-037	Goletz, Stanley	6006 Big Horn Drive/Granbury TX 76048
1949-028	Goliat, Mike Mitchel	2650 Green Lawn Drive/Seven Hills OH 44131
1972-038	Goltz, David Allan	Rr 6 Box 230/Fergus Falls MN 56537
1922-046	Golvin, Walter George	D. June 11, 1973 Gardena, Calif.
1997-065	Gomes, Wayne Maurice	5 Boykin Lane/Hampton VA 23663
1993-061	Gomez, Chris Cory	3416 Camino Largo/Carlsbad CA 92009
1935-036	Gomez, Jose Luis Rodriguez	D. December 1, 1992 Nuevo Laredo, Mexico
1990-056	Gomez, Leonardo	PO Box 1630-542/Canovanos PR 729
1974-042	Gomez, Luis Jose	676 Chesterfield Drive/Lawrenceville GA 30245
1993-062	Gomez, Patrick Alexander	7217 Oakberry Way/Citrus Heights CA 95621
1944-052	Gomez, Preston Martinez	23 Belcourt Drive South/Newport Beach CA 92660
1984-040	Gomez, Randall Scott 'Rocky'	Old Add: 1200 East Hillsdale #44b Foster City CA 94404
1953-030	Gomez, Ruben Colon	N43 Calle Luisa East/Toa Baja PR 949
1930-026	Gomez, Vernon Louis 'Lefty'	D. February 17, 1989 Greenbrae, Calif.
1960-042	Gonder, Jesse Lemar	1976 Galbreath Road/Pinole CA 94564
1979-041	Gonzales, Daniel David	Old Add: 12319 Cullman Ave Whittier CA 90604
1918-022	Gonzales, Eusebio Miguel	D. February 14, 1976 Havana, Cuba
1937-042	Gonzales, Joe Madrid	D. November 16, 1996 Torrance, Calif.
1977-059	Gonzales, Julio C.	Old Add: Bo. Rio Canas, Box 86 Caguas PR 00625
1949-029	Gonzales, Julio Enrique	D. February 15, 1991 Banes, Cuba
1993-063	Gonzales, Lawrence Christopher 'Larry'	Old Add: West Covina CA
1984-041	Gonzales, Rene Adrian	755 Orangewood/Covina CA 91723
1955-048	Gonzales, Wenceslao O'Reilly 'Vince'	D. March 11, 1981 Ciudad Del Carmen,Camp. Mexico
1994-038	Gonzalez, Alexander Scott	8620 Southwest 102nd Avenue/Miami FL 33173
1960-043	Gonzalez, Andres Antonio 'Tony'	8011 SW 196th Ter/Miami FL 33189
1984-042	Gonzalez, Denio Mariano	Calle San Luis #131, Gualey Santo Domingo Dominican Rep.
1997-066	Gonzalez, Geremis Segundo 'Jeremi'	Old Add: Maracaibo Venezuela
1988-055	Gonzalez, German Jose	Old Add: Rio Caribe Venezuela
1972-039	Gonzalez, Jose Fernando 'Fernando'	Old Add: Bo Hato Viejo Box 611 Arecibo PR 00612
1985-041	Gonzalez, Jose Rafael	Calle Antera Mota #35 Puerto Plata Dominican Rep.
1989-043	Gonzalez, Juan Alberto	Ext. Catoni A-9/Vega Baja PR 763

1990-057	Gonzalez, Luis Emilio	7410 Greatwood Lake Drive/Sugarland TX 77479
1912-067	Gonzalez, Miguel Angel Cordero 'Mike'	D. February 19, 1977 Havana, Cuba
1976-035	Gonzalez, Orlando Eugene	Old Add: 1890 West 56th Street Hialeah FL 33012
1963-045	Gonzalez, Pedro	104 Gen Cabral San Pedro De Macoris Dominican Rep.
1929-044	Gooch, Charles Furman	D. May 30, 1982 Lanham, Md.
1921-035	Gooch, John Beverley	D. May 15, 1975 Nashville, Tenn.
1915-054	Gooch, Lee Currin	D. May 18, 1966 Raleigh, N.C.
1910-061	Good, Ralph Nelson	D. November 24, 1965 Waterville, Me.
1928-040	Goodell, John Henry William 'Bill'	D. September 21, 1993 Mesquite, Texas
1984-043	Gooden, Dwight Eugene	6755 30th Street South/St Petersburg FL 33712
1935-037	Goodman, Ival Richard	D. November 25, 1984 Cincinnati, O.
1947-039	Goodman, William Dale	D. October 1, 1984 Sarasota, Fla.
1970-050	Goodson, James Edward 'Ed'	2330 Cold Spring Lane/Galax VA 24333
1914-075	Goodwin, Claire Vernon 'Pep'	D. February 15, 1972 Oakland, Calif.
1995-085	Goodwin, Curtis Lamar	3264 Sweetwater Drive/San Leandro CA 94578
1975-045	Goodwin, Danny Kay	PO Box 4064/Atlanta GA 30302
1948-041	Goodwin, James Patrick	11533 Francetta Lane/Saint Louis Mo/63138
1916-033	Goodwin, Marvin Mardo	D. October 21, 1925 Houston, Tes.
1991-065	Goodwin, Thomas John	1034 East Manhattan Avenue/Fresno CA 93720
1946-034	Goolsby, Raymond Daniel	548 Lake Doe Blvd/Apopka FL 32703
1965-033	Goossen, Gregory Bryant	12321 Blix St/North Hollywood CA 91607
1955-049	Gorbous, Glen Edward	D. June 12, 1990 Calgary, Alberta
1986-057	Gordon, Donald Thomas	8622 98th Street/Woodhaven NY 11421
1938-031	Gordon, Joseph Lowell	D. April 14, 1978 Sacramento, Calif.
1993-064	Gordon, Keith Bradley	4601 Thornhurst Drive/Olney MD 20832
1977-060	Gordon, Michael William	35 Longview Road/Brockton MA 2401
1941-038	Gordon, Sidney	D. June 17, 1975 New York, N.Y.
1988-056	Gordon, Thomas	115 East State Street/Avon Park FL 33825
1921-036	Gordonier, Raymond Charles	D. November 15, 1960 Rochester, N. Y.
1997-067	Gorecki, Richard John 'Rick'	Old Add: 4848 153rd Street Oak Forest IL 60452
1954-033	Gorin, Charles Perry	2617 Fiset Dr/Austin TX 78731
1977-061	Gorinski, Robert John	Box 133/Calumet PA 15621
1952-037	Gorman, Herbert Allen	D. April 5, 1953 San Diego, Calif.
1937-043	Gorman, Howard Paul	D. April 29, 1984 Harrisburg, Pa.
1952-038	Gorman, Thomas Aloysius	D. December 26, 1992 Valley Stream, Ny.
1939-044	Gorman, Thomas David	D. August 11, 1986 Closter, N. J.
1981-045	Gorman, Thomas Patrick	2523 North Boones Ferry Rd/Woodburn OR 97071
1941-039	Gornicki, Henry Frank	D. February 16, 1996 Riviera Beach, Fla.
1940-026	Gorsica, John Joseph Perry	PO Box 1518/Beckley/Wv 25801
1957-023	Goryl, John Albert	107 North Central/Apopka FL 32703
1963-046	Gosger, James Charles	1823 7th Street/Port Huron MI 48060
1921-037	Goslin, Leon Allen 'Goose'	D. May 15, 1971 Bridgeton, N. J.
1962-050	Goss, Howard Wayne	D. July 31, 1996 Reno, Nev.
1972-040	Gossage, Richard Michael 'Goose'	35 Marland Drive/Colorado Springs CO 80906
1913-066	Gossett, John Star 'Dick'	D. October 6, 1962 Massillon, O.
1960-044	Gotay, Julio Enrique	Old Add: Cartagena St L34/Ponce PR 00731
1982-049	Gott, James William	1260 East Mendocino Street/Altadena CA 91001
1912-068	Goulait, Theodore Lee	D. July 15, 1936 St. Clair, Mich.
1916-034	Gould, Albert Frank	D. August 8, 1982 San Jose, Calif.
1944-053	Goulish, Nicholas Edward	D. May 15, 1984 Youngstown, O.
1910-062	Gowdy, Harry 'Hank'	D. August 1, 1966 Columbus, O.
1972-041	Gowell, Lawrence Clyde	3401 Cotton Mill Drive #205/Raleigh NC 27612
1989-044	Gozzo, Mauro Paul	825 Crystal Spring Drive/Roseville TN 38066
1969-069	Grabarkewitz, Billy Cordell	2205 Copper Ridge Road/Arlington TX 76006
1958-038	Graber, Rodney Blaine	4674 Mount Armet Dr/San Diego CA 92117
1929-045	Grabowski, Alfons Francis	D. October 29, 1966 Memphis, N. Y.
1924-043	Grabowski, John Patrick	D. May 23, 1946 Albany, N. Y.
1932-033	Grabowski, Reginald John	D. April 2, 1955 Syracuse, N. Y.
1938-032	Grace, Joseph Laverne	D. September 18, 1969 Murphysboro, Ill.
1988-057	Grace, Mark Eugene	Old Add: 14882 Foxcraft Tustin CA 92680
1995-086	Grace, Michael James	1156 Buell Avenue/Joliet IL 60435
1978-052	Grace, Michael Lee	12791 Big Lake Road/Davisburg MI 48019
1929-046	Grace, Robert Earl	D. December 22, 1980 Phoenix, Ariz.
1913-067	Graf, Frederick Gottlieb	D. October 4, 1979 Chattanooga, Tenn.
1957-024	Graff, Milton Edward	3602 Tanglewood Drive/Bryan TX 77802
1996-067	Graffanino, Anthony Joseph	535 Connetqout Avenue/Islip Terrace NY 11752
1934-041	Graham, Arthur William 'Skinny'	D. July 10, 1967 Arlington, Mass.
1910-063	Graham, Bert	D. June 17, 1971 Cottonwood, Ariz.
1979-042	Graham, Daniel Jay	33 Madrid Plaza/Mesa AZ 85201
1914-076	Graham, Dawson Frank 'Tiny'	D. December 29, 1962 Nashville, Tenn.
1946-035	Graham, John Bernard	1521 Interlachen #258k/Seal Beach CA 90740
1924-044	Graham, Kyle	D. December 1, 1973 Oak Grove, Ala.
1983-064	Graham, Lee William	Old Add: PO Box 1012 Belleview FL 32620
1922-047	Graham, Roy Vincent	D. April 26, 1933 Manilla, Phillipines
1963-047	Graham, Wayne Leon	Rice Univ. Baseball 6100 South Main Houston TX 77005
1966-039	Graham, William Albert	Rr 2 Box 275/Flemingsburg KY 41041
1990-058	Grahe, Joseph Milton	2317 North Wallen Drive/Lake Park FL 33410
1968-028	Gramly, Bert Thomas 'Tom'	16485 Redwood Circle Rural Route 1 McKinney TX 75069
1954-034	Grammas, Alexander Peter	3432 Oakdale Dr/Birmingham AL 35223

1927-041 ....Grampp, Henry Erchardt ....D. March 24, 1986 New York, N. Y.
1993-065 ....Granger, Jeffrey Adam...2905 Glasgow Drive/Arlington TX 76015
1968-029 ....Granger, Wayne Allen ....Box 134, Aldrich Ave/Huntington MA 1050
1923-053 ....Grant, George Addison ....D. March 25, 1986 Montgomery, Ala.
1942-045 ....Grant, James Charles ....D. July 8, 1970 Rochester, Minn.
1923-054 ....Grant, James Ronald ....D. November 30, 1985 Des Moines, Iowa
1958-039 ....Grant, James Timothy 'Mudcat' ....1020 South Dunsmuir/Los Angeles CA 90019
1984-044 ....Grant, Mark Andrew ....123 Fairlane Dr/Joliet IL 60435
1983-065 ....Grant, Thomas Raymond ....36 Millville Road/Mendon MA 1756
1922-048 ....Grantham, George Farley ....D. March 16, 1954 Kingman, Ariz.
1983-066 ....Grapenthin, Richard Ray ....Rural Route 1/Linn Grove IA 51033
1948-042 ....Grasmick, Louis Junior ....6715 Quad Avenue/Baltimore MD 21237
1946-036 ....Grasso, Newton Michael 'Mickey' ....D. October 15, 1975 Miami Fla.
1945-039 ....Grate, Donald ....1245 Nw 203rd Street/Miami FL 33169
1991-066 ....Grater, Mark Anthony ....1136 Indiana Avenue/Monaca PA 15061
1996-068 ....Graves, Daniel Peter ....Old Add: 4028 Highlands Dr Valrico FL 33594
1926-032 ....Graves, Joseph Ebenezer ....D. December 22, 1980 Salem, Mass.
1927-042 ....Graves, Samuel Sidney 'Sid'....................................D. December 26, 1983 Biddeford, Me.
1964-037 ....Gray, David Alexander ....3140 West 3rd Avenue #A/Durango CO 81301
1977-062 ....Gray, Gary George ....Box 98/Laplace LA 70068
1988-058 ....Gray, Jeffrey Edward ....5013 Londonderry Drive/Tampa FL 33647
1954-035 ....Gray, John Leonard ....500 NE 14th Avenue #4/Fort Lauderdale FL 33301
1982-050 ....Gray, Lorenzo ....Old Add: 3263 Palm Avenue #A Lynwood CA 90262
1937-044 ....Gray, Milton Marshall..D. June 30, 1969 Quincy, Fla.
1945-040 ....Gray, Peter ....203 Phillips Street/Nanticoke PA 18634
1958-040 ....Gray, Richard Benjamin..503 South Hampton/Anaheim CA 92804
1924-045 ....Gray, Samuel David ....D. April 16, 1953 McKinney, Tex.
1912-069 ....Gray, Stanley Oscar ....D. October 11, 1964 Snyder, Tex.
1946-037 ....Gray, Theodore Glenn ....2917 South Ocean Blvd #1005/Highland Beach FL 33487
1959-034 ....Grba, Eli ....20842 Harris Loop/Elmont AL 35620
1954-036 ....Greason, William Henry ....PO Box 7972/Birmingham AL 35228
1990-059 ....Grebeck, Craig Allen ....29522 Michelis Street/Laguna Niguel CA 92677
1997-068 ....Green, Bertrum Scarborough 'Scarborough' ..Old Add: Ballwin MO 63011
1984-045 ....Green, Christopher Dewayne ....Old Add: 3740 59th Avenue West Bradenton FL 33507
1981-046 ....Green, David Alejandro ....Colinia Managua Grupo H#47 Managua/Nicaragua
1959-035 ....Green, Elijah Jerry 'Pumpsie' ....Berkeley H.S./2246 Milva Berkeley CA 94704
1959-036 ....Green, Fred Allen ....D. December 22, 1996 Titusville, N. J.
1986-058 ....Green, Gary Allen ....939 Kennebec Street/Pittsburgh PA 15217
1957-025 ....Green, Gene Leroy ....D. May 23, 1981 St. Louis, Mo.
1960-045 ....Green, George Dallas 'Dallas' ....548 South Guernsey Road/West Grove PA 19390
1935-038 ....Green, Harvey George ....D. July 24, 1970 Franklin, La.
1924-046 ....Green, Joseph Henry ....D. February 4, 1972 Bryn Mawr, Pa.
1928-041 ....Green, Julius Foust 'June' ....D. March 19, 1974 Glendora, Calif.
1957-026 ....Green, Leonard Charles ....18693 Sunset St/Detroit MI 48234
1963-048 ....Green, Richard Larry ....3924 Ridgemoor Drive/Rapid City SD 57702
1993-066 ....Green, Shawn David ....Old Add: 1831 Overview Circle Santa Ana CA 92705
1993-067 ....Green, Tyler Scott ....Old Add: 5558 South Lansing CT Englewood CO 80111
1930-027 ....Greenberg, Henry Benjamin ....D. September 4, 1986 Beverly Hills, Calif.
1979-043 ....Greene, Altar Alphonse ....18294 Marlowe/Detroit MI 48235
1996-069 ....Greene, Charles Patrick ....10760 Kendale South Blvd/Miami FL 33176
1989-045 ....Greene, Ira Thomas 'Tommy' ....6001 Dalecross Way/Glen Allen VA 23060
1924-047 ....Greene, Nelson George ....D. April 6, 1983 Lebanon, Pa.
1996-070 ....Greene, Todd Anthony ....Old Add: Evans GA 30809
1992-043 ....Greene, William Louis Willie ....Rural Route 1 Box 440/Haddock GA 31033
1924-048 ....Greenfield, Kent ....D. March 14, 1978 Guthrie, Ky.
1952-039 ....Greengrass, James Raymond ....232 Talking Rock Creek Pkwy Dr/Chatsworth GA 30705
1985-042 ....Greenwell, Michael Lewis ....12250 North River Raod/Alva FL 33920
1954-037 ....Greenwood, Robert Chandler ....D. September 1, 1994 Hayward, Calif.
1977-063 ....Greer, Brian ....Old Add: Aliso Viejo CA 92656
1993-068 ....Greer, Kenneth William ....64 Hillside Drive/Portsmouth NH 3801
1994-039 ....Greer, Thurman Clyde 'Rusty' ....607 Fairmont Street/Albertville AL 35950
1913-068 ....Gregg, David Charles ....D. November 12, 1965 Clarkston, Wash.
1943-054 ....Gregg, Harold Dana ....D. May 13, 1991 Bishop, Calif.
1911-056 ....Gregg, Sylveanus Augustus 'Vean' ....D. July 29, 1964 Aberdeen, Wash.
1987-054 ....Gregg, William Thomas Tommy ....300 Winding Forest Drive/Winston Salem NC 27104
1912-070 ....Gregory, Frank Ernst ....D. November 5, 1955 Beloit, Wis.
1964-038 ....Gregory, Grover Leroy 'Lee' ....6456 North Teilman/Fresno CA 93705
1911-057 ....Gregory, Howard Watterson ....D. May 30, 1970 Tulsa, Okla.
1932-034 ....Gregory, Paul Edwin ....PO Box 1535/Tunica MS 38676
1971-039 ....Greif, William Briley ....807 East 31st/Austin TX 78705
1940-027 ....Gremp, Louis Edward ....D. January 30, 1995 Manteca, Calif.
1919-033 ....Grevell, William ....D. June 21, 1923 Philadelphia, Pa.
1970-051 ....Grich, Robert Anthony ....31 Madison Lane/Coto De Gaza CA 92679
1920-042 ....Griesenbeck, Carlos Philippe Timothy............D. March 25, 1953 San Antonio, Tex.
1997-069 ....Grieve, Benjamin ....Old Add: 3206 Heritage CT Arlington TX 76016
1970-052 ....Grieve, Thomas Alan ....4107 Carnation Drive/Arlington TX 76016
1946-038 ....Griffeth, Leon Clifford ....PO Box 51641/Durham NC 27717
1989-046 ....Griffey, George Kenneth Junior ....1420 Nw Gilman Blvd #2717/Issaquah WA 98027
1973-053 ....Griffey, George Kenneth 'Ken' ....8216 Princeton Glendale Rd#103/West Chester OH 45069

1976-036	Griffin, Alfredo Claudino	Luis A. Tio #45 San Pedro De Macoris Dominican Rep.
1970-053	Griffin, Douglas Lee	43 Highland View/Irvine CA 92715
1917-032	Griffin, Francis Arthur 'Pug'	D. October 12, 1951 Colorado Springs Colo.
1919-034	Griffin, Ivy Moore	D. August 25, 1957 Gainesville, Fla.
1911-058	Griffin, James Linton 'Hank'	D. February 11, 1950 Terrell, Tex.
1928-042	Griffin, Martin John	D. November 19, 1951 Los Angeles, Calif.
1979-044	Griffin, Michael Leroy	1620 Grove Avenue/Woodland CA 95695
1914-077	Griffin, Patrick Richard	D. June 7, 1927 Yoingstown, O.
1969-070	Griffin, Thomas James	13147 Avenida La Velencia/Poway CA 92064
1922-049	Griffith, Bartholomew Joseph	D. May 5, 1973 Bishop, Calif.
1963-049	Griffith, Robert Derrell 'Derrell'	201 East Central/Anadarko OK 73005
1913-069	Griffith, Thomas Herman	D. April 13, 1967 Cincinnati, O.
1956-038	Griggs, Harold Lloyd	1217 West Wabash/Tucson AZ 85705
1923-055	Grigsby, Denver Clarence	D. November 10, 1973 Sapulpa, Okla.
1966-040	Grilli, Guido John	250 Sloan Lane/Locust Grove AR 72550
1975-046	Grilli, Stephen Joseph	8637 Briar Patch/Baldwinsville NY 13027
1954-038	Grim, Robert Anton	D. October 23, 1996 Shawnee, Kan.
1916-035	Grimes, Burleigh Arland	D. December 6, 1985 Clear Lake, Wis.
1931-032	Grimes, Edward Adelbert	D. October 4, 1974 Chicago, Ill.
1938-033	Grimes, Oscar Ray, Jr.	D. May 19, 1993 Westlake,/O.
1920-043	Grimes, Oscar Ray, Sr.	D. May 25, 1953 Minerva, O.
1920-044	Grimes, Roy Austin	D. September 13, 1954 Hanoverton, O.
1916-036	Grimm, Charles John	D. November 15, 1983 Scottsdale, Ariz.
1989-047	Grimsley, Jason Alan	Old Add: Rr 6 Box 195 Cleveland TX 77327
1951-034	Grimsley, Ross Albert	D. February 6, 1994 Memphis, Tenn.
1971-040	Grimsley, Ross Albert	53 Wandworth Bridge Way/Timonium MD 21093
1912-071	Griner, Donald Dexter 'Dan'	D. June 3, 1950 Bishopville, S.C.
1934-042	Grissom, Leo Theo	1851 Colussa Street/Corning CA 96021
1989-048	Grissom, Marquis Dean	175 Cherokee Rose Lane/Fairburn GA 30213
1946-039	Grissom, Marvin Edward	13975 Noble Way/Red Bluff CA 96080
1952-040	Groat, Richard Morrow	%Champion Lakes Rural Route 1 Box 288 Bolivar PA 15923
1956-039	Grob, Conrad George	D. September 28, 1997 Madison, Wisc.
1941-040	Grodzicki, John	D. September 1, 1998
1912-072	Groh, Henry Knight 'Heinie'	D. August 22, 1968 Cincinnati,O.
1919-035	Groh, Lewis Carl	D. October 20, 1960 Rochester, N. Y.
1941-041	Gromek, Stephen Joseph	2229 Juniper Court/Shelby Township MI 48316
1992-044	Groom, Wedsel Gary Buddy	PO Box 10/Red Oak TX 75154
1955-050	Gross, Donald John	Old Add: 9007 Lighthouse Dr Lake MI 48632
1925-040	Gross, Ewell 'Turkey'	D. January 22, 1936 Dallas, Tex.
1973-054	Gross, Gregory Eugene	16 Rabbit Run Road/Malvern PA 19355
1983-067	Gross, Kevin Frank	Old Add: 402 4th Street Fillmore CA 93015
1990-060	Gross, Kip Lee	28489 Championship Drive/Moreno Valley CA 92555
1976-037	Gross, Wayne Dale	45 Leonard Court/Danville CA 94526
1930-028	Grossklos, Howard Hoffman 'Howdie'	310 Llwyd's Lane/Vero Beach FL 32960
1952-041	Grossman, Harley Joseph	5606 Harmony Woods Lane/Evansville IN 47720
1963-050	Grote, Gerald Wayne 'Jerry'	3201 Cherry Ridge Street #C315/San Antonio TX 78230
1992-045	Grotewold, Jeffrey Scott	23919 Lake Drive/Crestline CA 92325
1947-040	Groth, Ernest William	Blackhawk-Negly Road/Beaver Falls PA 15010
1946-040	Groth, John Thomas	177 Queens Lane/Palm Beach FL 33480
1995-087	Grott, Matthew Alan	4714 Rolling Green Drive/Ooltewah/Tn 37363
1940-028	Grove, Orval Leroy	D. April 20, 1992 Carmichael, Calif.
1925-041	Grove, Robert Moses 'Lefty'	D. May 22, 1975 Norwalk, O.
1913-070	Grover, Charles Bert	D. May 24, 1971 Emmett Twp., Calhoun Co.,Mich
1916-037	Grover, Roy Arthur	D. February 7, 1978 Milwaukie. Ore.
1912-073	Grubb, Harvey Harrison	D. January 25, 1970 Corpus Christi, Tex.
1972-042	Grubb, John Raymond	10700 Gadwell Court/Chesterfield VA 23831
1920-045	Grubbs, Thomas Dillard	D. January 28, 1986 Lexington, Ky.
1931-033	Grube, Franklin Thomas	D. July 2, 1945 New York, N. Y.
1984-046	Gruber, Kelly Wayne	3300 Bee Cave Road #650-227/Austin TX 78746
1995-088	Grudzielanek, Mark James	%Tom Grudzielanek 550 E. Mona Drive Oak Creek WI 53154
1996-071	Grundt, Kenneth Allan	4814 West Parker Avenue/Chicago IL 60639
1955-051	Grunwald, Alfred Henry	21001 Plummer Street/Chatsworth CA 91311
1938-034	Gryska, Sigmund Stanley	D. August 27, 1994 Hines, Ill.
1961-039	Grzenda, Joseph Charles	Gouldsboro PA 18424
1982-051	Guante, Cecilio (Magallane)	Jalisco 67 Simon Bolivar Santo Domingo Dominican Rep.
1993-069	Guardado, Edward Adrian	9810 Pioneer Avenue/Las Vegas NV 89117
1984-047	Gubicza, Mark Steven	Old Add: 593 Monastery Avenue Philadelphia PA 19128
1929-047	Gudat, Marvin John	D. March 2, 1954 Los Angeles, Calif.
1937-045	Guerra, Fermin Romero 'Mickey'	D. October 9, 1992 Miami Beach, Fla.
1992-046	Guerrero, Juan Antonio	Las Palmas 22,/Bo.Gringo Haina Dominican Rep.
1973-055	Guerrero, Mario Miguel	Calle Duarte #450 Santo Domingo Dominican Rep.
1978-053	Guerrero, Pedro	4004 St. Andrews Drive/Rio Rancho NM 87124
1996-072	Guerrero, Vladimir	Old Add: Nizao Bani Dominican Rep.
1996-073	Guerrero, Wilton	Old Add: Nizao Bani Dominican Rep.
1984-048	Guetterman, Arthur Lee 'Lee'	23407 140th Avenue SE/Kent WA 98042
1997-070	Guevara, Giomar Antonio	Old Add: Miranda Venezuela
1975-047	Guidry, Ronald Ames	PO Box 666/Scott LA 70583
1997-071	Guillen, Jose Manuel	Old Add: San Cristobal Dom. Rep.
1985-043	Guillen, Oswaldo Jose	Cle San Jose #52,/El Rodeo Del Tuy Miranda Venezuela

1964-039	Guindon, Robert Joseph	Old Add: Thornhill Inn Jackson NH 03846
1968-030	Guinn, Drannon Eugene 'Skip'	Rural Route 3 Box 790/Stilwell OK 74960
1946-041	Guintini, Benjamin John	151 Rimma Way/Roseville CA 95661
1940-029	Guise, Witt Orison	D. August 13, 1968 North Little Rock, Ark.
1916-038	Guisto, Louis Joseph	D. October 15, 1989 Napa, Calif.
1997-072	Gulan, Michael Watts	151 Hollywood Blvd/Steubenville OH 43952
1978-054	Gulden, Bradley Lee	1136 Fox Run Road/Waconia MN 55387
1970-054	Gullett, Donald Edward	Rural Route 1 Box 615n/South Shore KY 41175
1923-056	Gulley, Thomas Jefferson	D. November 24, 1966 St. Charles, Ark.
1930-029	Gullic, Tedd Joseph	PO Box 703/West Plains MO 65775
1979-045	Gullickson, William Lee	300 Brentvale Lane/Brentwood TN 37027
1982-052	Gulliver, Glenn James	8123 Cortland/Allen Park MI 48101
1935-039	Gumbert, Harry Edward	D. January 4, 1995 Wimberley, Texas
1982-053	Gumpert, David Lawrence	921 Chambers St/South Haven MI 49090
1936-033	Gumpert, Randall Pennington	49 School Street/Douglassville PA 19518
1990-061	Gunderson, Eric Andrew	Old Add: 7817 NE 69th St Vancouver WA 98662
1916-039	Gunkel, Woodrow William 'Red'	D. April 19, 1954 North Chicago, Ill.
1911-059	Gunning, Hyland	D. March 28, 1975 Togus, Me.
1970-055	Gura, Larry Cyril	PO Box 94/Litchfield Park AZ 85340
1911-060	Gust, Ernest Herman Frank	D. October 26, 1945 Maupin, Ore.
1939-045	Gustine, Frank William	D. April 1, 1991 Davenport, Iowa
1972-043	Guth, Charles Henry 'Bucky'	202 Morris Dr/Salisbury MD 21801
1989-049	Guthrie, Mark Andrew	PO Box 394/Venice FL 34284
1967-040	Gutierrez, Cesar Dario	Pinto A Miseria #100 Caracas Venezuela
1983-068	Gutierrez, Joaquin Fernando	Old Add: Amb. 3er Callejon #29-35 Cartagena Colombia
1993-070	Gutierrez, Ricardo	17131 Nw 49th Avenue/Miami FL 33055
1936-034	Gutteridge, Donald Joseph	804 Lakeview Drive/Pittsburg KS 66762
1991-067	Guzman, Dionini Ramon	Hatillo Palma #215 Montecristi Dominican Rep.
1985-044	Guzman, Jose Alberto	Old Add: 990 N. Lake Shore Dr #5c Chicago IL 60611
1991-068	Guzman, Juan Andres	5100 Northwest 106th Avenue/Miami FL 33178
1969-071	Guzman, Santiago Donovan	Ens Restaurosin M4ta #12 San Pedro De Macoris Dominican Rep.
1981-047	Gwosdz, Douglas Wayne	2822 Monticello/Houston TX 77045
1982-054	Gwynn, Anthony Keith	15643 Boulder Ridge Lane/Poway CA 92064
1987-055	Gwynn, Christopher Karlton	3524 Delta Avenue/Long Beach CA 90810
1933-021	Gyselman, Richard Reynald	D. September 20, 1990 Seattle, Wash.
1937-046	Haas, Berthold John	4604 Kensington Avenue/Tampa FL 33629
1915-055	Haas, Bruno Philip	D. June 5, 1952 Sarasota, Fla.
1976-038	Haas, Bryan Edmond 'Moose'	Old Add: 9393 N. 90th St #102-266 Scottsdale AZ 85258
1957-027	Haas, George Edwin 'Eddie'	4025 Old Us Highway45 South/Paducah KY 42003
1925-042	Haas, George William 'Mule'	D. June 30, 1974 New Orleans, La.
1991-069	Haas, Robert David 'Dave'	10405 Davison Road/Davison MI 48423
1951-035	Habenicht, Robert Julius	D. December 24, 1980 Richmond, Va.
1985-045	Habyan, John Gabriel	4 Dorfer Lane/Nesconset NY 11767
1932-035	Hack, Stanley Camfield	D. December 15, 1979 Dixon, Ill.
1971-041	Hacker, Richard Warren	2900 18th Fairway/Belleville IL 62221
1948-043	Hacker, Warren Louis	PO Box 41/Lenzburg IL 62255
1952-042	Haddix, Harvey	D. January 8, 1994 Springfield, O.
1926-033	Hadley, Irving Darius 'Bump'	D. February 15, 1963 Lynn, Mass.
1958-041	Hadley, Kent William	5025 Mohawk Street/Pocatello ID 83204
1915-056	Haeffner, William Bernhard	D. January 27, 1982 Delaware Co., Pa.
1943-055	Haefner, Milton Arnold 'Mickey'	D. January 3, 1995 New Athens, Ill.
1924-049	Hafey, Charles James 'Chick'	D. July 2, 1973 Calistoga, Calif.
1935-040	Hafey, Daniel Albert 'Bud'	D. July 27, 1986 Sacramento, Calif.
1939-046	Hafey, Thomas Francis	D. October 2, 1996 El Cerrito, Calif.
1911-061	Hageman, Kurt Moritz 'Casey'	D. April 1, 1964 New Bedford, Pa.
1983-069	Hagen, Kevin Eugene	24826 Southeast 164th Avenue/Kent WA 98042
1968-031	Hague, Joe Clarence	D. November 5, 1994 San Antonio, Texas
1969-072	Hahn, Donald Antone	1046 Boise Dr/Campbell CA 95008
1952-043	Hahn, Frederick Aloys	D. August 16, 1984 Valhalla, N.Y.
1940-030	Hahn, Richard Frederick	D. November 5, 1992 Orlando, Fla.
1919-036	Haid, Harold Augustine	D. August 13, 1952 Los Angeles, Calif.
1923-057	Haines, Henry Luther 'Hinkey'	D. January 9, 1979 Sharon Hill, Pa.
1918-023	Haines, Jesse Joseph 'Pop'	D. August 5, 1978 Dayton, O.
1973-056	Hairston, Jerry Wayne	3770 First Street West/Birmingham AL 35207
1969-073	Hairston, John Louis	3612 4th St West/Birmingham AL 35207
1951-036	Hairston, Samuel Harding	D. October 31, 1997 Birmingham, Ala.
1913-071	Haislip, James Clifton	D. January 22, 1970 Dallas, Tex.
1941-042	Hajduk, Chester	6838 Concord Lane/Niles IL 60648
1995-089	Hajek, David Vincent	5190 Bitterweed Lane/Colorado Springs CO 80917
1919-037	Halas, George Stanley	D. October 31, 1983 Chicago, Ill.
1931-034	Hale, Arvel Odell	D. June 9, 1980 El Dorado, Ark.
1914-078	Hale, George Wagner	D. November 1, 1945 Wichita, Kan.
1974-043	Hale, John Steven	2200 Pine Street/Bakersfield CA 93301
1955-052	Hale, Robert Houston	616 Overhill Avenue/Park Ridge IL 60068
1920-046	Hale, Samuel Douglas	D. September 6, 1974 Wheeler, Tex.
1989-050	Hale, Walter William Chip	190 Driftwood Court/Aptos CA 95003
1915-057	Haley, Raymond Timothy	D. October 8, 1973 Bradenton, Fla.
1974-044	Halicki, Edward Louis	19605 Paddle Wheel Lane/Reno NV 89511
1981-048	Hall, Albert	1628 Spaulding Rd/Birmingham AL 35211

1986-059 ....Hall, Andrew Clark 'Drew' ....177 Fighting Fork/Grayson KY 41143
1911-062 ....Hall, Herbert Ernest ....D. July 18, 1948 Seattle, Wash.
1918-024 ....Hall, Herbert Silas ....D. July 1, 1970 Fresno, Calif.
1943-056 ....Hall, Irvin Gladstone.....................................1153 Deanwood Road/Baltimore MD 21234
1963-051 ....Hall, Jimmie Randolph...................................2510 Marybeth Court #A/Wilson NC 27896
1948-044 ....Hall, John Sylvester ....D. January 17, 1995 Midwest City, Okla.
1994-040 ....Hall, Joseph Geroy ....1034 Dundale Road/Paducah KY 42003
1910-064 ....Hall, Marcus ....D. February 24, 1915 Joplin, Mo.
1981-049 ....Hall, Melvin ....Old Add: Rural Route 1 Route 90 Cayaga NY 13034
1994-041 ....Hall, Michael Darren 'Darren' ....3028 Monet Court/Flower Mound TX 75028
1952-044 ....Hall, Richard Wallace ....403 Plumbridge Court #202/Timonium MD 21093
1949-030 ....Hall, Robert Lewis ....D. March 12, 1983 St. Petersburg, Fla.
1968-032 ....Hall, Thomas Edward ....3592 Lillian Avenue/Riverside CA 92504
1913-072 ....Hall, William Bernard ....D. August 15, 1947 Newport, Ky.
1954-039 ....Hall, William Lee ....D. January 1, 1986 Moultrie, Ga.
1925-043 ....Hallahan, William Anthony ....D. July 8, 1981 Binghamton, N. Y.
1961-040 ....Haller, Thomas Frank.....................................75315 Montecito Drive/Indian Wells CA 92210
1940-031 ....Hallett, Jack Price ....D. June 11, 1982 Toledo, O.
1916-040 ....Halliday, Newton Reese ....D. April 6, 1918 Great Lakes, Ill.
1911-063 ....Hallinan, Edward ....D. August 24, 1940 San Francisco, Calif.
1914-079 ....Halt, Alva William ....D. January 22, 1973 Sandusky, O.
1997-073 ....Halter, Shane David ....Old Add: Papillion NE 68046
1922-050 ....Hamann, Elmer Joseph 'Doc' ....D. January 11, 1973 Milwaukee, Wis.
1971-042 ....Hambright, Roger Dee ....8709 NE 37th Avenue/Vancouver WA 98665
1926-034 ....Hamby, James Sanford 'Sandy' ....D. October 21, 1991 Springfield, Ill.
1993-071 ....Hamelin, Robert James ....13702 Solitaire Way/Irvine CA 92720
1988-059 ....Hamilton, Darryl Quinn ....4721 Southwind Drive/Baton Rouge LA 70816
1972-044 ....Hamilton, David Edward ....9464 Cherry Hills Ln/San Ramon CA 94583
1911-064 ....Hamilton, Earl Andrew ....D. November 17, 1968 Anaheim, Calif.
1962-051 ....Hamilton, Jack Edwin ....109 Rocky Road/Ridgedale MO 65739
1986-060 ....Hamilton, Jeffrey Robert ....945 North Pasadena Street #149/Mesa AZ 85201
1994-042 ....Hamilton, Johns Joseph 'Joey'...........................234 Allenwood Drive/Statesboro GA 30458
1961-041 ....Hamilton, Steve Absher ....D. December 2, 1997 Morehead, Ky.
1952-045 ....Hamilton, Thomas Ball ....D. November 29, 1973 Tyler, Tex.
1957-028 ....Hamlin, Kenneth Lee ....Rural Route 3 Box 2298a/McMillan MI 49853
1933-022 ....Hamlin, Luke Daniel 'Hot Potato' ....D. February 18, 1978 Clare, Mich.
1970-056 ....Hamm, Peter Whitfield ....525 Lockhart Bulch Road/Santa Cruz CA 95060
1981-050 ....Hammaker, Charlton Atlee ....2739 Stubb Bluff Rd/Knoxville TN 37932
1990-062 ....Hammond, Christopher Andrew ....1003 NE 26th Avenue/Hallandale FL 33009
1982-055 ....Hammond, Steven Ben ....11130 Winston Willow Court/Windermere FL 34786
1915-058 ....Hammond, Walter Charles 'Jack' ....D. March 4, 1942 Kenosha, Wis.
1993-072 ....Hammonds, Jeffrey Bryan ....Old Add: Scotch Plains NJ 07076
1944-054 ....Hamner, Granville Wilbur 'Granny'.....................D. September 12, 1993 Philadelphia, Pa.
1946-042 ....Hamner, Ralph Conant ....PO Box 752/Bradley AR 71826
1945-041 ....Hamner, Wesley Garvin 'Gar' ....Rural Route 2 Box 91/Mechanicsville Va/23111
1974-045 ....Hampton, Isaac Bernard 'Ike' ....1604 Lee St/Camden SC 29020
1993-073 ....Hampton, Michael William ....3815 North Ringdove Point/Crystal River FL 34428
1955-053 ....Hamric, Odbert Herman 'Bert' ....D. August 8, 1984 Springboro, O.
1943-057 ....Hamrick, Raymond Bernard ....349 St. Andrews Drive/Franklin/Tn 37069
1940-032 ....Hancken, Morris Medlock 'Buddy' ....3110 Oakmont Drive/Orange TX 77630
1949-031 ....Hancock, Fred James ....D. March 12, 1986 Clearwater, Fla.
1995-090 ....Hancock, Leland David ....Old Add: Saratoga CA 95070
1978-055 ....Hancock, Ronald Garry ....2217 Green Hills Dr/Valrico FL 33594
1996-074 ....Hancock, Ryan Lee 'Lee' ....637 East 12860 South/Draper UT 84020
1970-057 ....Hand, Richard Allen ....752 Bellechase Road/Granbury TX 76048
1911-065 ....Handiboe, Aloysius James 'Mike'.........................D. January 31, 1953 Savannah, Ga.
1946-043 ....Handley, Eugene Louis ....8656 Fresno Drive #506a/Huntington Beach CA 92646
1936-035 ....Handley, Lee Elmer ....D. April 8, 1970 Pittsburgh, Pa.
1964-040 ....Handrahan, James Vernon 'Vern' ....36 Newland Crescent/Charlottetown PEI C1A 4H5 Canada
1965-034 ....Hands, William Alfred ....PO Box 334/Orient NY 11957
1953-031 ....Hanebrink, Harry Aloysius ....D. September 9, 1996 Bridgeton, Mo.
1991-070 ....Haney, Christopher Deane ....PO Box 97/Barboursville VA 22923
1922-051 ....Haney, Fred Girard ....D. November 9, 1977 Beverly Hills, Calif.
1992-047 ....Haney, Todd Michael ....3000 Inverness/Waco TX 76710
1966-041 ....Haney, Wallace Larry 'Larry' ....PO Box 157/Barboursville VA 22923
1914-080 ....Hanford, Charles Joseph ....D. July 19, 1963 Trenton, N.J.
1927-043 ....Hankins, Donald Wayne ....D. May 16, 1963 Winston-Salem, N. C.
1961-042 ....Hankins, Jay Nelson ....26509 East 150 Hwy/Greenwood MO 64034
1913-073 ....Hanley, Joseph Patrick ....D. May 1, 1961 Elmhurst, N. Y.
1975-048 ....Hanna, Preston Lee ....5555 Mayfair Dr/Pensacola FL 32506
1918-025 ....Hannah, James Harrison 'Truck' ....D. April 27, 1982 Fountain Valley, Calif.
1976-039 ....Hannahs, Gerald Ellis ....1411 Andover Ridge/Little Rock AR 72227
1962-052 ....Hannan, James John ....3907 Cherry Hill Way/Annandale VA 22003
1939-047 ....Hanning, Loy Vernon ....D. July 8, 1986 Anaconda, Mo.
1995-091 ....Hansell, Gregory Michael ....Old Add: 4404 Foxglove Dr Nw Lapalma CA 90623
1944-055 ....Hansen, Andrew Viggo ....252 Orange Tree Drive/Lake Worth FL 33462
1990-063 ....Hansen, David Andrew ....2362 Agostino/Rowland Heights CA 91748
1951-037 ....Hansen, Douglas William..................................155 South 1200 West #27/Orem UT 84058
1997-074 ....Hansen, Jed Ramon ....820 4th Avenue West/Olympia WA 98502

1974-046 ....Hansen, Robert Joseph ....19 North Kelsey Ave/Evansville IN 47711
1958-042 ....Hansen, Ronald Lavern ....13602 Alliston Drive/Baldwin MD 21013
1930-030 ....Hansen, Roy Emil Frederick 'Snipe'..............D. September 11, 1978 Chicago, Ill.
1918-026 ....Hansen, Roy Inglof...D. February 9, 1977 Beloit, Wis.
1943-058 ....Hanski, Donald Thomas...................................D. September 2, 1957 Worth, Ill.
1921-038 ....Hanson, Earl Sylvester 'Ollie' ....D. August 19, 1951 Clifton, N.J.
1988-060 ....Hanson, Erik Brian ....735 Ridge Road/Kinnelon NJ 7405
1913-074 ....Hanson, Harry Francis ....D. October 5, 1966 Savannah, Ga.
1942-046 ....Hanyzewski, Edward Michael ....D. October 8, 1991 Fargo, N. Dak.
1923-058 ....Happenny, John Clifford ....D. December 29, 1988 Coral Springs, Fla.
1928-043 ....Harder, Melvin Leroy ....130 Center Street #6a/Chardon OH 44024
1918-027 ....Hardgrove, William Henry 'Pat' ....D. January 26, 1973 Jackson, Miss.
1967-041 ....Hardin, James Warren ....D. March 9, 1991 Key West, Fla.
1952-046 ....Hardin, William Edgar 'Bud' ....D. July 28, 1997 Rancho Santa Fe, Calif.
1913-075 ....Harding, Charles Harold ....D. October 30, 1971 Bold Springs, Tenn.
1996-075 ....Hardtke, Jason Robert ....Old Add: San Jose CA 95101
1958-043 ....Hardy, Carroll William ....27875 East Whiteword Drive/Steamboat Springs CO 80477
1951-038 ....Hardy, Francis Joseph 'Red'.........................2233 East Behrend Drive #208/Phoenix AZ 85024
1974-047 ....Hardy, Howard Lawrence 'Larry' ....2402 Drawbridge/Arlington TX 76012
1989-051 ....Hardy, John Graydon ....8440 SW 39th Court/Davie FL 33328
1991-071 ....Hare, Shawn Robert ....1975 Deer Path Trail/Oxford MI 48371
1965-035 ....Hargan, Steven Lowell ....2502 Morango Trail/Palm Springs CA 92264
1980-047 ....Hargesheimer, Alan Herbert ....107 North Evanston/Arlington Heights IL 60004
1979-046 ....Hargis, Gary Lynn ....157 Gemini Ave/Lompoc CA 93436
1913-076 ....Hargrave, Eugene Franklin 'Bubbles'..............D. February 23, 1969 Cincinnati, O.
1923-059 ....Hargrave, William McKinley 'Pinky' ....D. October 3, 1942 Ft. Wayne, Ind.
1923-060 ....Hargreaves, Charles Russell ....D. May 9, 1979 Neptune, N. J.
1974-048 ....Hargrove, Dudley Michael 'Mike' ....3925 Ramblewood Road/Richfield OH 44286
1995-092 ....Harikkala, Timothy Alan................................%A.Harikkala 1721 Crestwood Blvd Lake Worth FL 33460
1988-061 ....Harkey, Michael Anthony ....23930 Strange Creek Drive/Diamond Bar CA 91765
1910-065 ....Harkness, Frederick Harvey 'Specs' ....D. May 18, 1952 Compton, Calif.
1961-043 ....Harkness, Thomas William 'Tim' ....29 Englewood Place/Whitby Ontario L1M 8Z9 Canada
1975-049 ....Harlow, Larry Duane ....Old Add: 1002 Townsend Ave Aztec NM 87410
1941-043 ....Harman, William Bell ....9 Guyenne Road/Wilmington/De 19807
1954-040 ....Harmon, Charles Byron ....6035a Ridgeacre Dr/Cincinnati OH 45237
1967-042 ....Harmon, Terry Walter ....Oakwood Dr/Medford NJ 8055
1988-062 ....Harnisch, Peter Thomas ....2 Cornfield Lane/Commack NY 11725
1979-047 ....Harper, Brian David ....10115 East Corrine Drive/Scottsdale AZ 85260
1916-041 ....Harper, George Washington ....D. August 18, 1978 Magnolia, Ark.
1913-077 ....Harper, Harry Clayton ....D. April 23, 1963 Layton, N.J.
1915-059 ....Harper, John Wesley ....D. June 18, 1927 Halstead, Kan.
1980-048 ....Harper, Terry Joe ....4225 Jailette Road/College Park GA 30349
1962-053 ....Harper, Thomas ....5 Cow Hill Road/Sharon MA 2067
1911-066 ....Harper, William Homer...................................D. June 17, 1951 Somerville, Tenn.
1969-074 ....Harrah, Colbert Dale 'Toby' ....316 Leewood Circle/Azle TX 76020
1969-075 ....Harrell, John Robert ....756 Erie Cir/Milpitas CA 95035
1912-074 ....Harrell, Oscar Martin 'Slim' ....D. April 30, 1971 Hillsboro, Tex.
1935-041 ....Harrell, Raymond James ....D. January 28, 1984 Alexandrias, La.
1955-054 ....Harrell, William ....253 Mount Hope Drive/Albany NY 12202
1965-036 ....Harrelson, Derrel McKinley 'Bud' ....25 Falcon Dr/Hauppauge NY 11787
1963-052 ....Harrelson, Kenneth Smith 'Hawk'................150 Crossways Park West/Woodbury NY 11797
1968-033 ....Harrelson, William Charles ....Old Add: 8201 Camino Media #223 Bakersfield CA 93311
1913-078 ....Harrington, Andrew Francis ....D. November 12, 1938 Malden, Mass.
1925-044 ....Harrington, Andrew Matthew ....D. January 26, 1979 Boise, Idaho
1963-053 ....Harrington, Charles Michael 'Mike'............135 Scenic Drive/Hattiesburg MS 39401
1953-032 ....Harrington, William Womble ....72 Cleveland School Road/Garner NC 27529
1967-043 ....Harris, Alonzo ....6652 7th Avenue/Los Angeles CA 90043
1925-046 ....Harris, Anthony Spencer ....D. July 3, 1982 Minneapolis, Minn.
1914-081 ....Harris, Benjamin Franklin ....D. April 29, 1927 St. Louis, Mo.
1955-055 ....Harris, Boyd Gail ....9008 Weir Street/Manassas VA 22110
1941-044 ....Harris, Chalmer Luman 'Lum' ....D. November 11, 1996 Pell City, Ala.
1948-045 ....Harris, Charles 'Bubba' ....PO Box 159/Nobleton FL 34263
1925-045 ....Harris, David Stanley ....D. September 18, 1973 Atlanta, Ga.
1991-072 ....Harris, Donald ....916 Hubert/Waco TX 76704
1981-051 ....Harris, Greg Allen ....91 Bumps River Road/Osterville MA 2655
1988-063 ....Harris, Gregory Wade ....180 2nd Avenue SE/Saint Petersburg FL 33701
1936-036 ....Harris, Herbert Benjamin ....D. January 18, 1991 Crystal Lake, Ill.
1996-076 ....Harris, Hernando Petrocelli 'Pep' ....995 Ten Oaks Drive/Lancaster SC 29720
1968-034 ....Harris, James William ....114 West Brandywine Circle/Wilmington NC 28403
1979-048 ....Harris, John Thomas ....7064 Chelsea/Amarillo TX 79109
1914-082 ....Harris, Joseph ....D. December 10, 1959 Renton, Pa.
1988-064 ....Harris, Leonard Anthony ....3210 Nw Tenth Avenue/Miami FL 33127
1940-033 ....Harris, Maurice Charles 'Mickey' ....D. April 15, 1971 Farmington, Mich.
1990-064 ....Harris, Reginald Allen ....55 Ashleigh Drive #8/Waynesboro VA 22980
1938-035 ....Harris, Robert Arthur ....D. August 8, 1989 North Platte, Neb.
1941-045 ....Harris, Robert Ned ....D. December 18, 1976 West Palm Beach, Fla.
1919-038 ....Harris, Stanley Raymond 'Bucky' ....D. November 8, 1977 Bethesda, Md.
1989-052 ....Harris, Tyrone Eugene Gene ....1267 NE 16th Avenue/Okeechobee FL 33472
1972-045 ....Harris, Victor Lanier ....5420 Garth Avenue/Los Angeles CA 90056

1970-058	Harris, Walter Francis 'Buddy'	2305 Carol Lane/Norristown PA 19401
1923-061	Harris, William Milton	D. August 21, 1965 Indian Trail, N. C.
1957-029	Harris, William Thomas	322 South Reed/Kennewick WA 99336
1965-037	Harrison, Charles William	Old Add: 3411 Duckview Court Arlington TX 76016
1955-056	Harrison, Robert Lee	Old Add: 253 Brierley Way Indianapolis IN 46032
1972-046	Harrison, Roric Edward	602 Del Dios/San Clemente CA 92672
1965-038	Harrison, Thomas James	Old Add: 4221 E. 60th St #H/Huntington Park CA 90255
1920-047	Harriss, William Jennings Bryan 'Slim'	D. September 19, 1963 Temple, Texas
1945-042	Harrist, Earl	D. September 1, 1998 Simsboro, La.
1937-047	Harshaney, Samuel	419 Thelma Drive/San Antonio TX 78212
1948-046	Harshman, John Elvin 'Jack'	2227 Commonwealth/San Diego CA 92104
1915-060	Harstad, Oscar Theander	D. November 14, 1985 Corvallis, Ore.
1980-049	Hart, James Michael 'Mike'	409 Larkspur/Portage MI 49081
1963-054	Hart, James Ray 'Jim Ray'	Old Add: 6769 Cedar Blvd/Newark CA 94560
1989-053	Hart, John Henry	1570 Adelaide Court/Cleveland OH 44145
1984-049	Hart, Michael Lawrence	16552 West Crescent Dr/New Berlin WI 53151
1943-059	Hart, William Woodrow	D. July 29, 1968 Lykins,Pa.
1965-039	Hartenstein, Charles Oscar	10735 Cassia Drive/Austin TX 78759
1912-075	Harter, Franklin Pierce	D. April 14, 1959 Breese, Ill.
1914-083	Hartford, Bruce Daniel	D. May 25, 1975 Los Angeles, Calif.
1995-093	Hartgraves, Dean Charles	%Brian Hartgraves 515 Kings Ctourt Central Point OR 97502
1939-048	Hartje, Christian Henry	D. June 26, 1946 Seattle, Wash.
1911-067	Hartley, Grover Allen	D. October 19, 1964 Daytona Beach, Fla.
1989-054	Hartley, Michael Edward	1415 Cascade Place/El Cajon CA 92021
1962-054	Hartman, J. C.	3425 Rosedale St/Houston TX 77004
1959-037	Hartman, Robert Louis	2580 18th Street/Kenosha WI 53140
1922-052	Hartnett, Charles Leo 'Gabby'	D. December 20, 1972 Park Ridge, Ill.
1913-079	Hartranft, Raymond Charles	D. February 10, 1955 Chester Co., Pa.
1973-057	Harts, Gregory Rudolph	205-10 Hiogh Court Place #10I/Decatur GA 30032
1950-032	Hartsfield, Roy Thomas	PO Box 236/East Ellijay GA 30539
1992-048	Hartsock, Jeffrey Roger	1720 Swannano Drive/Greensboro NC 27410
1947-041	Hartung, Clinton 'Hondo'	1018 East Fulton/Sinton TX 78387
1976-040	Hartzell, Paul Franklin	Old Add: 1140 Summers Lane Novato CA 94947
1928-044	Harvel, Luther Raymond	D. April 10, 1986 Kansas City, Mo.
1987-056	Harvey, Bryan Stanley	6397 Hudson Chapel Road/Catawba NC 28609
1916-042	Hasbrook, Robert Lyndon 'Ziggy'	D. February 9, 1976 Garland, Tex.
1997-075	Hasegawa, Shigetoshi	Old Add: Kobe Japan
1990-065	Haselman, William Joseph	Old Add: 13631 Beaumont Ave Saratoga CA 95070
1945-043	Hasenmayer, Donald Irvin	721 Golf Drive/Warrington PA 18976
1940-034	Hash, Herbert Howard	7246 Sperryville Pike/Boston VA 22713
1933-023	Haslin, Michael Joseph 'Mickey'	171 George Avenue/Plains PA 18705
1936-037	Hassett, John Aloysius 'Buddy'	D. August 23, 1997 Westwood, N. J.
1978-056	Hassey, Ronald William	6460 North Thimble Pass/Tucson AZ 85715
1971-043	Hassler, Andrew Earl	Old Add: Box 17101 Tucson Az
1928-045	Hassler, Joseph Frederick	D. September 4, 1971 Duncan, Okla.
1937-048	Hasson, Charles Eugene 'Gene'	535 East Bonita/San Dimas CA 91773
1919-039	Hasty, Robert Keller	D. May 28, 1972 Dallas, Ga.
1979-049	Hatcher, Michael Vaughn 'Mickey'	4202 East Crescent Avenue/Mesa AZ 85206
1984-050	Hatcher, William Augustus	1227 Darlington Oak Circle NE/Saint Petersburg FL 33703
1950-033	Hatfield, Fred James	D. May 22, 1998 Tallahassee, Fla.
1992-049	Hathaway, Hillary Houston	2672 Forest Blvd/Jacksonville FL 32216
1945-044	Hathaway, Ray Wilson	25 Leisure Mount Road/Asheville NC 28804
1995-094	Hatteberg, Scott Allen	4375 Silverton Road NE/Salem OR 97305
1946-044	Hatten, Joseph Hilarian	D. December 16, 1988 Redding, Calif.
1935-042	Hatter, Clyde Melno	D. October 16, 1937 Yosemite, Ky.
1946-045	Hatton, Grady Edgebert	PO Box 97/Warren TX 77664
1912-076	Hauger, John Arthur	D. August 2, 1944 Redwood City, Calif.
1943-060	Haughey, Christopher Francis	4141 Stevenson Blvd #202/Fremont CA 94538
1997-076	Haught, Gary Allen	16067 NE 23rd Street/Choctaw OK 73020
1947-042	Haugstad, Philip Donald	D. October 21, 1998 Black River Falls, Wisc.
1910-066	Hauser, Arnold George	D. May 22, 1956 Aurora, Ill.
1922-053	Hauser, Joseph John	D. July 11, 1997 Sheboygan, Wis.
1975-050	Hausman, Thomas Matthew	3165 Westfield Cir/Las Vegas NV 89121
1944-056	Hausmann, Clemens Raymond	D. August 29, 1972 Baytown, Tex.
1944-057	Hausmann, George John	218 Fawn Valley/Boerne TX 78006
1981-052	Havens, Bradley David	2341 North Main Street/Royal Oak MI 48073
1996-077	Hawblitzel, Ryan Wade	7972 South Four Oaks Point/Floral City FL 34436
1951-039	Hawes, Roy Lee	1231 Hackett Mill Road #809/Ringgold GA 30736
1911-068	Hawk, Edward	D. March 26, 1936 Neosho, Mo.
1995-095	Hawkins, Latroy	5017 West 11th Avenue/Gary IN 46404
1982-056	Hawkins, Melton Andrew Andy	PO Box 8812/Waco TX 76714
1960-046	Hawkins, Wynn Firth	5326 Cottage Ln/Cortland OH 44410
1921-039	Hawks, Nelson Louis 'Chick'	D. May 26, 1973 San Rafael, Calif.
1915-061	Haworth, Homer Howard	D. January 28, 1953 Troutdale, Ore.
1970-059	Haydel, John Harold 'Hal'	304 Lynwood Dr/Houma LA 70360
1958-044	Hayden, Eugene Franklin	1597 Alamo Dr #188/Vacaville CA 95688
1982-057	Hayes, Ben Joseph	3501 10th St NE/St Petersburg FL 33704
1988-065	Hayes, Charles Dewayne	22503 Holly Creek Trail/Tomball TX 77375
1933-024	Hayes, Franklin Witman	D. June 22, 1955 Point Pleasant, N. J.

1935-043	Hayes, James Millard	D. November 26, 1993 Lithonia, Ga.
1927-044	Hayes, Minter Carney 'Jackie'	D. February 9, 1983 Birmingham, Ala.
1981-053	Hayes, Von Frank	970 Monte Cristo Blvd/Tierra Verde FL 33715
1980-050	Hayes, William Ernest	4602 East Earll Drive/Phoenix AZ 85018
1994-043	Haynes, Heath Burnett	245 Springdale Road/Wheeling WV 26003
1995-096	Haynes, Jimmy Wayne	%Ernest Haynes 160 Pine Circle Lagrange GA 30240
1939-049	Haynes, Joseph Walter	D. January 6, 1967 Hopkins, Minn.
1986-061	Hayward, Raymond Alton	11404 Bluff Creek Drive/Oklahoma City OK 73160
1968-035	Haywood, William Kiernan	212 Glenwood Road/Americus GA 31709
1944-058	Hayworth, Myron Claude 'Red'	507 Oak View Road/High Point NC 27265
1926-035	Hayworth, Raymond Hall	230 Shuler Circle/Thomasville NC 27360
1980-051	Hazewood, Drungo Larue	Old Add: 5130 Del Norte Blvd Sacramento CA 95820
1955-057	Hazle, Robert Sidney	D. April 25, 1992 Columbia, S. C.
1940-035	Head, Edward Marvin	D. January 31, 1980 Bastrop, La.
1923-062	Head, Ralph	D. October 8, 1962 Muscadine, Ala.
1969-076	Healy, Francis Xavier	1 Primrose Ln/Holyoke MA 1040
1930-031	Healy, Francis Xavier Paul	71 Penacook Street/Springfield MA 1104
1915-062	Healy, Thomas Fitzgerald	D. January 15, 1974 Cleveland, O.
1954-041	Heard, Jehosie	17 Third Avenue South/Birmingham AL 35205
1910-067	Hearn, Bunn 'Bunny'	D. October 11, 1959 Wilson, N.C.
1910-068	Hearn, Edmund	D. September 8, 1952 Sawtelle, Calif.
1986-062	Hearn, Edward John	9138 Allman/Lenexa KS 66219
1926-036	Hearn, Elmer Lafayette 'Bunny'	D. March 31, 1974 Venice, Fla.
1947-043	Hearn, James Tolbert	D. June 10, 1998 Boca Grande, Fla.
1985-046	Hearron, Jeffrey Vernon	2748 Suwanee Way SE/Marietta GA 30067
1936-038	Heath, John Geoffrey 'Jeff'	D. December 9, 1975 Seattle, Wash.
1982-058	Heath, Kelly Mark	2566 Gary Circle Circle #9a/Dunedin FL 34698
1978-057	Heath, Michael Thomas	5203 Troon Place/Valrico FL 33594
1931-035	Heath, Minor Wilson 'Mickey'	D. July 30, 1986 Dallas, Texas
1920-048	Heath, Spencer Paul	D. January 25, 1930 Chicago, Ill.
1935-044	Heath, Thomas George	D. February 26, 1967 Los Gatos, Calif.
1965-040	Heath, William Chris	2111 Plantation Dr/Richmond TX 77469
1983-070	Heathcock, Ronald Jeffrey 'Jeff'	Old Add: 12861 Aspenwood Lane Garden Grove CA 92640
1918-028	Heathcote, Clifton Earl	D. January 19, 1939 York, Pa.
1982-059	Heaton, Neal	3 Nursery Court/East Patchogue NY 11772
1975-051	Heaverlo, David Wallace	3720 West Lakeshore Drive/Moses Lake WA 98837
1931-036	Hebert, Wallace Andrew	3408 Westwood Road/West Lake LA 70665
1968-036	Hebner, Richard Joseph 'Richie'	6 Therault Street/Walpole MA 2081
1912-077	Hechinger, Michael Vincent	D. August 13, 1967 Chicago, Ill.
1913-080	Hedgepeth, Harry Malcolm	D. July 30, 1966 Richmond, Va.
1965-041	Hedlund, Michael David	2412 Klinger Rd/Arlington TX 76016
1979-050	Heep, Daniel William	327 Teakwood Ln/San Antonio TX 78216
1992-050	Heffernan, Bertram Alexander	322 Oxhead Road/Stony Brook NY 11790
1934-043	Heffner, Donald Henry	D. August 1, 1989 Pasadena, Calif.
1963-055	Heffner, Robert Frederick	910 North Twelfth/Allentown PA 18102
1996-078	Heflin, Bronson Wade	302 Hunting Drive/Gallatin TN 37066
1945-045	Heflin, Randolph Rutherford	935 34th Street Sw/Hickory NC 28602
1941-046	Hegan, James Edward	D. June 17, 1984 Swampscott, Mass.
1964-041	Hegan, James Michael 'Mike'	7 Wild Turkey Run/Hilton Head Island SC 29926
1985-047	Hegman, Robert Hilmer	1609 NE Ball Drive/Lees Summit MO 64063
1918-029	Hehl, Herman Jacob 'Jake'	D. July 4, 1961 Brooklyn, N. Y.
1969-077	Heidemann, Jack Seale	1255 West Baseline #108/Mesa AZ 85202
1914-084	Heilmann, Harry Edwin	D. July 9, 1951 Southfield, Mich.
1942-047	Heim, Val Raymond	PO Box 423/Superior/Ne 68978
1920-049	Heimach, Fred Amos	D. June 1, 1973 Fort Myers, Fla.
1983-071	Heimueller, Gorman John	2148 West 12405 South/Riverton UT 84065
1921-040	Heine, William Henry 'Bud'	D. September 2, 1976 Fort Lauderdale, Fla.
1988-066	Heinkel, Donald Elliott	1160 Santa Maria Court/Mobile AL 36693
1937-049	Heintzelman, Kenneth Alphonse	406 South Church/Saint Peters MO 63376
1973-058	Heintzelman, Thomas Kenneth	406 South Church/St Peters MO 63376
1934-044	Heise, Clarence Edward 'Lefty'	2425 Albion Avenue/Orlando FL 32833
1957-030	Heise, James Edward	2425 Albion Avenue/Orlando FL 32833
1967-044	Heise, Robert Lowell	361 Innocent Way/Copperopolis CA 95228
1961-044	Heiser, Leroy Barton	1038 Grove Hill Rd/Baltimore MD 21227
1960-047	Heist, Alfred Michael	PO Box 70/Cookson OK 74427
1918-030	Heitmann, Henry Anton	D. December 15, 1958 Brooklyn, N. Y.
1956-040	Held, Melvin Nicholas	103 Hogan Lane/Bryan OH 43506
1954-042	Held, Woodson George	Big Diamond Ranch/Dubois WY 82513
1938-036	Helf, Henry Hartz	D. October 27, 1984 Austin, Texas
1993-074	Helfand, Eric James	8679 Circle R Valley Lane/Escondido CA 92026
1915-063	Helfrich, Emory Wilbur 'Ty'	D. March 18, 1955 Pleasantville, N.J.
1994-044	Helling, Ricky Allen	2706 Henry/Irving TX 75062
1964-042	Helms, Tommy Vann	5427 Blue Sky Dr/Cincinnati OH 45247
1997-077	Helton, Todd Lynn	9005 Cloverleaf Lane/Knoxville TN 37922
1943-061	Heltzel, William Wade 'Heinie'	Rural Route 2/York PA 17403
1961-045	Heman, Russell Frederick	5555 Canyon Crest Drive #30/Riverside CA 92507
1914-085	Hemingway, Edson Marshall	D. July 5, 1969 East Grand Rapids, Mich
1989-055	Hemond, Scott Mathew	263 Florida Ave,%J. Hemond/Dunedin FL 33928
1928-046	Hemsley, Ralston Burdett 'Rollie'	D. July 31, 1972 Washington, D. C.

1949-032 ....Hemus, Solomon Joseph 'Solly' ....6565 West Loop South #555/Bellaire TX 77401
1921-041 ....Henderson, Bernard ....D. June 4, 1966 Linden, Texas
1981-054 ....Henderson, David Lee ....6004 142nd Court SE/Bellevue WA 98006
1914-086 ....Henderson, Edward J. ....D. January 15, 1964 New York, N. Y.
1974-049 ....Henderson, Joseph Lee ....Old Add:125 Inquero Ln #38/El Paso Tx
1965-042 ....Henderson, Kenneth Joseph ....Old Add: 14865 Andrew Court Saratoga CA 95070
1979-051 ....Henderson, Rickey Henley ....10561 Englewood Dr/Oakland CA 94621
1994-045 ....Henderson, Rodney Wood....................537 Pleasant Pointe Court/Lexington KY 40517
1977-064 ....Henderson, Stephen Curtis ....3010 St. Conrad Street/Tampa FL 33607
1930-032 ....Henderson, William Maxwell ....D. October 6, 1966 Pensacola, Fla.
1961-046 ....Hendley, Charles Robert 'Bob' ....645 Wimbish/Macon GA 31204
1971-044 ....Hendrick, George Andrew ....2016 Nightrider Drive/Las Vegas NV 89134
1923-063 ....Hendrick, Harvey Lee ....D. October 29, 1941 Covington, Tenn.
1910-069 ....Hendricks, Edward ....D. November 28, 1930 Jackson, Mich.
1968-037 ....Hendricks, Elrod Jerome ....4113 Holbrook Road/Randallstown MD 21133
1945-046 ....Hendrickson, Donald William ....D. January 19, 1977 Norfolk, Va.
1911-069 ....Hendrix, Claude Raymond ....D. March 22, 1944 Allentown, Pa.
1911-070 ....Hendryx, Timothy Green ....D. August 14, 1957 Corpus Christi, Tex.
1986-063 ....Hengel, David Lee ....1501 Quintana Way/Fremont CA 94538
1919-040 ....Henion, Lafayette Marion ....D. July 22, 1955 San Luis Obispo, Calif.
1982-060 ....Henke, Thomas Anthony ....Rr Six/Jefferson City MO 65101
1954-043 ....Henley, Gail Curtice ....7338 Alta Vista/Laverne CA 91750
1921-042 ....Henline, Walter John 'Butch'....................D. October 9, 1957 Sarasota, Fla.
1987-057 ....Henneman, Michael Alan ....7002 Oxford Court/McKinney TX 75070
1937-050 ....Hennessey, George ....D. January 15, 1988 Princeton, N. J.
1913-081 ....Hennessy, Lester Baker ....D. November 20, 1976 New York, N. Y.
1969-078 ....Hennigan, Phillip Winston ....PO Box 1212/Center TX 75935
1914-087 ....Henning, Ernest Herman 'Pete'....................D. November 9, 1939 Dyer, Ind.
1973-059 ....Henninger, Richard Lee ....PO Box 941323/Plano TX 75094
1990-066 ....Hennis, Randall Philip ....Old Add: 8980 Ferguson San Diego CA 92119
1924-050 ....Henrich, Frank Wilde 'Fritz' ....D. May 1, 1959 Philadelphia, Pa.
1957-031 ....Henrich, Robert Edward ....1531 Via Los Coyotes/Lahabra CA 90631
1937-051 ....Henrich, Thomas David ....1985 Shadow Valley Drive/Prescott AZ 86305
1911-071 ....Henriksen, Olaf ....D. October 17, 1962 Norwood, Mass.
1997-078 ....Henriquez, Oscar Eduardo ....Old Add: Laguaira Venezuela
1984-051 ....Henry, Dwayne Allen ....502 Hampstead Road/Middletown DE 19709
1944-059 ....Henry, Earl Clifford ....PO Box 43/White Cottage OH 43791
1992-051 ....Henry, Floyd Buford Butch ....10144 Suez/El Paso TX 79925
1921-043 ....Henry, Frank John 'Dutch'....................D. August 23, 1968 East Cleveland, O.
1922-054 ....Henry, Frederick Marshall ....D. October 12, 1987 Wendell, N.C.
1936-039 ....Henry, James Francis ....D. August 15, 1976 Memphis, Tenn.
1910-070 ....Henry, John Park ....D. November 24, 1941 Fort Huachuca, Ariz.
1991-073 ....Henry, Richard Douglas 'Doug' ....Old Add: 2216 Dracena Street Hayward CA 94545
1961-047 ....Henry, Ronald Baxter ....987 South Evanston Circle/Aurora CO 80012
1966-042 ....Henry, William Francis ....190 Boulevard/Kenilworth NJ 7033
1952-047 ....Henry, William Rodman ....302 Christine/Houston TX 77017
1933-025 ....Henshaw, Roy Knikelbine ....D. June 8, 1993 Lagrange, Ill.
1935-045 ....Hensiek, Philip Frank ....D. February 21, 1972 St. Louis, Mo.
1986-064 ....Hensley, Charles Floyd ....3220 Peninsula Road #261/Oxnard CA 93035
1991-074 ....Hentgen, Patrick George ....14451 Knightsbridge Drive/Shelby Twp. MI 48315
1966-043 ....Hepler, William Lewis ....10271 Blossom Lake Drive/Seminole FL 33542
1963-056 ....Herbel, Ronald Samuel ....2084 Palisade Blvd/Dupont WA 98327
1913-082 ....Herbert, Ernie Albert ....D. January 13, 1968 Dallas, Tex.
1915-064 ....Herbert, Frederick ....D. May 29, 1963 Tice, Fla.
1950-034 ....Herbert, Raymond Ernest ....9360 Taylors Turn/Stanwood MI 49346
1996-079 ....Heredia, Felix Perez ....Old Add: Barahona Dominican Rep.
1991-075 ....Heredia, Gilbert....................4710 West Calle Don Manuel/Tucson AZ 85746
1987-058 ....Heredia, Ubaldo Jose ....Ave. Fuerzas Amados San Francisco Piso Apt 21 Caracas Venezuela
1995-097 ....Heredia, Wilson ....Ens. La Hos No. 47 Altos La Romana Dominican Rep.
1926-037 ....Herman, Floyd Caves 'Babe' ....D. November 27, 1987 Glendale, Calif.
1931-037 ....Herman, William Jennings Bryan ....D. September 5, 1992 West Palm Beach, Fla.
1923-064 ....Hermann, Albert Bartel ....D. August 20, 1980 Lewes, Del.
1943-062 ....Hermanski, Eugene Victor ....1 Fairwoods Court/Homosassa FL 34446
1995-098 ....Hermanson, Dustin Michael ....20621 North 17th Street/Phoenix AZ 85024
1967-045 ....Hermoso, Angel Remigio ....Res.Doradotorre De Piso 6,#63d Caracas Venezuela
1974-050 ....Hernaiz, Jesus Rafael ....24 Street Block 76 #47 Villa/Carolina PR 630
1990-067 ....Hernandez, Carlos Alberto ....Alfinger Manzana 16 #5 San Felix Bolivar Venezuela
1992-052 ....Hernandez, Cesar Dario (Prez) ....16 #19 Ensanche Capitillo Santo Domingo Dominican/Rep.
1996-080 ....Hernandez, Eisler Livan 'Livan' ....Old Add: Miami FL 33101
1971-045 ....Hernandez, Enzo Octavio ....Vereda North 5e-4, Guantra Puerta Lacruz Anz Venezuela
1997-079 ....Hernandez, Fernando ....Old Add: Santiago Dom. Rep.
1989-056 ....Hernandez, Francis Xavier Xavier....................3549 Lay Avenue/Groves TX 77619
1956-041 ....Hernandez, Gregorio Evelio ....3004 SW 113th Ave/Miami FL 33165
1977-065 ....Hernandez, Guillermo Willie ....Bo Espina, Calle C Buzon 125/Aguada PR 602
1965-043 ....Hernandez, Jacinto Zulueta 'Jackie'....................13390 NE Seventh Avenue #103/North Miami FL 33181
1991-076 ....Hernandez, Jeremy Stuart ....Old Add: 9069 Nagle Avenue Arleta CA 91331
1991-077 ....Hernandez, Jose Antonio (Figueroa) ....Calle Sur #22/Vega Alta PR 762
1974-051 ....Hernandez, Keith ....255 East 49th #28d/New York NY 10017
1982-061 ....Hernandez, Leonardo Jesus ....Urb. El Milagro,Calle Sucre 38 Edo Miranda Venezuela

1986-065	Hernandez, Manuel Antonio	Eugenio A. Alfionada #35 Laromana Dominican Rep.
1979-052	Hernandez, Pedro Julio	Old Add: 87-14 162nd St #1 Jamaica NY 11432
1967-046	Hernandez, Ramon Gonzalez	Reparto, Rosamaria Calle 5f-19/Carolina PR 630
1991-078	Hernandez, Roberto Manuel	Calle 5, #32 Puerto Real/Cabo Roja PR 623
1972-047	Hernandez, Rodolfo	2470 'C' Street #3/San Diego CA 92103
1960-048	Hernandez, Rudolph Albert	8 Calle Rodriguez Serra/Condado PR 907
1942-048	Hernandez, Salvador Jose Ramos	D. January 3, 1986 Havana, Cuba
1984-052	Hernandez, Tobias Rafael	Ira Calle Guamachito #47-49 "Calabozo, Guarico Venezuela/"
1974-052	Herndon, Larry Darnell	6149 Brunswick Road/Arlington TN 38002
1979-053	Herr, Thomas Mitchell	1077 Olde Forge Crossing/Lancaster PA 17601
1911-072	Herrell, Walter William	D. January 23, 1949 Front Royal, Va.
1967-047	Herrera, Jose Concepcion	Maraven Adri 12 Cen.Com. Lagunillas E. Zulia Venezuela
1995-099	Herrera, Jose Ramon Catalino	Old Add: Santo Domingo Dom. Rep.
1958-045	Herrera, Juan Francisco 'Frank'	PO Box 420683/Miami FL 33242
1951-040	Herrera, Procopio Rodriguez 'Tito'	Apdo Postal 257/Ciudad Satelite Edo Mexico
1925-047	Herrera, Ramon 'Mike'	D. February 3, 1978 Havana, Cuba
1956-042	Herriage, William Troy	900 Old Stockton Road #126/Oakville CA 95361
1954-044	Herrin, Thomas Edward	5020 Laurel Drive/Concord CA 94521
1929-048	Herring, Arthur L.	D. December 2, 1995 Marion, Ind.
1912-078	Herring, Herbert Lee	D. April 22, 1964 Tucson, Ariz.
1915-065	Herring, William Francis	D. September 10, 1962 Honesdale, Pa.
1967-048	Herrmann, Edward Martin	13153 Tobiasson Road/Poway CA 92064
1932-036	Herrmann, Leroy George	D. July 3, 1972 Livermore, Calif.
1918-031	Herrmann, Martin John	D. September 11, 1956 Cincinnati, O.
1962-055	Herrnstein, John Ellett	603 Seminole Rd/Chillicothe OH 45602
1962-056	Herrscher, Richard Franklin 'Rick'	313 Maple Avenue #4f/Dallas TX 75201
1956-043	Hersh, Earl Walter	3201 Murkle Rd/Westminster MD 21157
1961-048	Hershberger, Norman Michael ' Mike'	2887 Carrie Hill Circle Nw/Massillon OH 44646
1938-037	Hershberger, Willard McKee	D. August 3, 1940 Boston, Mass.
1983-072	Hershiser, Orel Leonard Quinton	5277 Isleworth Country Club Dr/Windermere FL 34786
1952-048	Hertweck, Neal Charles	111 Leesburg Lane/Troutman NC 28166
1964-043	Hertz, Stephen Allan	10211 SW 96th Terrace/Miami FL 33156
1956-044	Herzog, Dorrel Norman Elvert 'Whitey'	9426 Sappington Estates Drive/Saint Louis MO 63127
1984-053	Hesketh, Joseph Thomas	1476 Briargrove Way/Oldsmar FL 34677
1916-043	Hesselbacher, George Edward	D. February 18, 1980 Rydal, Pa.
1945-047	Hetki, John Edward	4004 Stary Drive/Parma OH 44134
1989-057	Hetzel, Eric Paul	2271 Hetzel Road/Crowley LA 70526
1935-046	Heusser, Edward Burleton	D. March 1, 1956 Aurora, Colo.
1920-050	Heving, John Aloysius	D. December 24, 1968 Salisbury, N. C.
1930-033	Heving, Joseph William	D. April 11, 1970 Covington, Ky.
1973-060	Heydeman, Gregory George	1175 Barbara Court/Seaside CA 93955
1964-044	Hiatt, Jack E.	170 Arrow Drive/Sedona AZ 86336
1993-075	Hiatt, Philip Farrell	4597 Monpellier Drive/Pensacola FL 32505
1989-058	Hibbard, James Gregory Greg	3540 Davieshire Drive/Memphis TN 38133
1967-049	Hibbs, James Kerr	4659 Foothill Road/Ventura CA 93003
1991-079	Hickerson, Bryan David	2490 East Stephens Place/Chandler AZ 85225
1942-049	Hickey, James Robert	D. September 20, 1997 Manchester, Conn.
1981-055	Hickey, Kevin John	5715 South Mason/Chicago IL 60638
1915-066	Hickman, David James	D. December 30, 1958 Brooklyn, N. Y.
1962-057	Hickman, James Lucius	PO Box 455/Henning TN 38041
1965-044	Hickman, Jesse Owens	208 South Summerlin Avenue/Orlando FL 32801
1956-045	Hicks, Clarence Walter 'Buddy'	2830 Okeechobee Drive/Lake Havasu City AZ 86406
1964-045	Hicks, James Edward	Old Add: 3717 Euclid Avenue East Chicago IN 46312
1959-038	Hicks, William Joseph 'Joe'	2707 Brookmere Rd/Charlottesville VA 22901
1997-080	Hidalgo, Richard Jose	Old Add: Guarenas Venezuela
1937-052	Higbe, Walter Kirby	D. May 6, 1985 Columbia, S. C.
1922-055	Higbee, Mahlon Jesse	D. April 7, 1968 Depauw, Ind.
1949-033	Higdon, William Travis	D. August 30, 1986 Pascagoula, Miss.
1966-044	Higgins, Dennis Dean	2204 Anderson Dr/Jefferson City MO 65101
1993-076	Higgins, Kevin Wayne	4928 Thor Way/Carmichael CA 95608
1989-059	Higgins, Mark Douglas	Old Add: 3700 Carlyle Close #940 Mobile AL 33609
1930-034	Higgins, Michael Franklin 'Pinky'	D. March 21, 1969 Dallas, Tex.
1995-100	Higginson, Robert Leigh	Old Add: 626 E. Cheltenham Philadelphia PA 19120
1922-056	High, Andrew Aird	D. February 22, 1981 Toledo, O.
1919-041	High, Charles Edwin	D. September 11, 1960 Portland, Ore.
1913-083	High, Hugh Jenken	D. November 16, 1962 St. Louis Co., Mo.
1985-048	Higuera, Teodoro Valenzuela	Old Add: Cardenas 50 Ote. Ciudad De Juarez Mexico
1931-038	Hilcher, Walter Frank	D. November 21, 1962 Minneapolis, Minn.
1931-039	Hildebrand, Oral Clyde	D. September 8, 1977 Southport, Ind.
1913-084	Hildebrand, Palmer Marion	D. January 25, 1960 North Canton, O.
1969-079	Hilgendorf, Thomas Eugene	PO Box 124/Camanche IA 52730
1915-067	Hill, Carmen Proctor 'Bunker'	D. January 1, 1990 Indianapolis, Ind.
1917-033	Hill, Clifford Joseph 'Red'	D. August 11, 1938 El Paso, Tex.
1957-032	Hill David, Burnham	4 Chinquapin Drive/Arden NC 28704
1983-073	Hill, Donald Earl	26161 Paseo Marbella/San Juan Capistrano CA 92675
1969-080	Hill, Garry Alton	PO Box 8/Newell NC 28126
1989-060	Hill, Glenallen	Old Add: 111 McPherson Street Santa Cruz CA 95060
1915-068	Hill, Herbert Lee	D. September 2, 1970 Farmers Branch, Tex.
1969-081	Hill, Herman Alexander	D. December 14, 1970 Magallanes, Ven.

1935-047	Hill, Jesse Terrill	D. August 31, 1993 Pasadena, Calif.
1939-050	Hill, John Clinton	D. September 20, 1970 Decatur, Ga.
1988-067	Hill, Kenneth Wade	4262 Northlake Blvd/Palm Beach Gardens FL 33410
1973-061	Hill, Marc Kevin	203 Maple Street/Elsberry MO 63343
1991-080	Hill, Milton Giles	PO Box 3198/Cumming GA 30128
1987-059	Hillegas, Shawn Patrick	870 Rockville Road/South Fork PA 15956
1961-049	Hiller, Charles Joseph	411 55th Avenue/Saint Petersburg FL 33706
1946-046	Hiller, Frank Walter	D. January 8, 1987 West Chester, Pa.
1920-051	Hiller, Harvey Max 'Hob'	D. December 27, 1956 Lehighton, Pa.
1965-045	Hiller, John Frederick	1104 Fair Banks/Iron Mountain MI 49801
1924-051	Hillis, Malcolm David 'Mack'	D. June 16, 1961 Cambridge, Mass.
1955-058	Hillman, Darius Dutton 'Dave'	849 Mimosa Dr/Kingsport TN 37660
1992-053	Hillman, John Eric	6349 Creekbed Lane/Citrus Heights CA 95621
1914-088	Hilly, William Edward	D. July 25, 1953 Eureka, Mo.
1990-068	Hilton, Howard James	3139 South 'N' Street/Oxnard CA 93030
1972-048	Hilton, John David 'Dave'	7432 East Sunnyside Drive/Scottsdale AZ 85280
1961-050	Himsl, Avitus Bernard 'Vedie'	5127 West Hutchinson/Chicago IL 60641
1977-066	Hinds, Samuel Russell	Old Add: 6394 Townsend Fresno CA 93727
1934-045	Hinkle, Daniel Gordon 'Gordie'	D. March 19, 1972 Houston, Tex.
1951-041	Hinrichs, Paul Edwin	1982 Brett Drive/Madisonville KY 42431
1910-071	Hinrichs, William Louis	D. August 18, 1972 Selma, Calif.
1982-062	Hinshaw, George Addison	Old Add: 543 Evergreen Street Inglewood CA 90302
1964-046	Hinsley, Jerry Dean	4255 Holiday Lane/Las Cruces NM 88005
1928-047	Hinson, James Paul	D. September 23, 1960 Muskogee, Okla.
1961-051	Hinton, Charles Edward	6330 16th St Nw/Washington Dc 20011
1971-046	Hinton, Richard Michael	Old Add: 730 Agave Place Tucson AZ 85718
1987-060	Hinzo, Thomas Lee	185 Jamul Avenue/Chula Vista CA 91911
1966-045	Hippauf, Herbert August	D. July 17, 1995 Santa Clara, Calif.
1971-047	Hiser, Gene Taylor	1450 Caldwell Lane/Hoffman Estates IL 60194
1968-038	Hisle, Larry Eugene	312 Saddleworth Court West/Mequon WI 53092
1951-042	Hisner, Harley Parnell	14322 Monroeville Road/Monroeville IN 46773
1992-054	Hitchcock, Sterling Alex	1085 Shipwatch Circle Tampa, FL 33602
1992-054	Hitchcock, Sterling Alex	11101 Us 92 East/Seffner FL 33584
1942-050	Hitchcock, William Clyde	1117 West Collinwood Circle/Opelika/Al 36801
1917-034	Hitt, Bruce Smith	D. November 10, 1973 Portland, Ore.
1949-034	Hittle, Lloyd Eldon	2031 West Elm/Street/Lodi CA 95242
1931-040	Hoag, Myril Oliver	D. July 28, 1971 High Springs, Fla.
1954-045	Hoak, Donald Albert	D. October 9, 1969 Pittsburgh, Pa.
1961-052	Hobaugh, Edward Russell	527 5th Ave/Ford City PA 16226
1957-033	Hobbie, Glen Frederick	Rural Route 2 Box 234a/Ramsey IL 62080
1981-056	Hobbs, John Douglas	3 Wade Dr/Cherry Hill NJ 8034
1913-085	Hobbs, William Lee	D. January 5, 1945 Hamilton, O.
1975-052	Hobson, Clell Lavern 'Butch'	3705 Dearing Downs Drive/Tuscaloosa AL 35405
1920-052	Hock, Edward Francis	D. November 21, 1963 Portsmouth, O.
1975-053	Hockenbery, Charles Marion	701 Parkridge Place/Onalaska WI 54650
1938-039	Hockett, Oris Leon	D. March 23, 1969 Hawthorne, Calif.
1934-046	Hockette, George Edward	D. January 20, 1974 Plantation, Fla.
1993-077	Hocking, Dennis Lee	21618 Ellinwood Drive/Torrance CA 90503
1925-048	Hodapp, Urban John	D. June 14, 1980 Cincinnati, O.
1951-043	Hoderlein, Melvin Anthony	535 Cinti Batavia Pike/Cincinnati OH 45244
1920-053	Hodge, Clarence Clemet 'Shovel'	D. December 31, 1967 Fort Walton Beach, Fla.
1984-054	Hodge, Ed Oliver	Old Add: Rr 2, Williams Rd #2 Seymour TN 37865
1942-051	Hodge, Edward Burton 'Bert'	Rural Route 19/Knoxville TN 37920
1971-048	Hodge, Harold Morris 'Gomer'	119 Marys Lane/Rutherfordton NC 28139
1943-063	Hodges, Gilbert Raymond	D. April 2, 1972 West Palm Beach, Fla.
1973-062	Hodges, Ronald Wray	3498 Old Forge Road/Rocky Mount VA 24151
1939-051	Hodgin, Elmer Ralph 'Ralph'	3203 Farmington Drive/Greensboro/Nc 27407
1980-052	Hodgson, Paul Joseph Denis	5 McGloin Street/Fredericton New Bruns. E3A 4J9 Canada
1946-047	Hodkey, Aloysius Joseph 'Eli'	5163 Broadway/Lorain OH 44052
1952-049	Hoeft, William Frederick	9965 Lost Canyon Drive/Stanwood MI 49346
1963-057	Hoerner, Joseph Walter	D. October 4, 1996 Hermann, Mo.
1940-036	Hoerst, Frank Joseph	31 Village Lane/Mount Laurel/Nj 8054
1911-073	Hoff, Chester Cornelius	D. September 17, 1998 Daytona Beach, Fla.
1944-060	Hofferth, Stewart Edward	D. March 7, 1994 Valparaiso, Ind.
1929-049	Hoffman, Clarence Casper 'Dutch'	D. December 6, 1962 Belleville, Ill.
1915-069	Hoffman, Edward Adolph 'Tex'	D. May 19, 1947 New Orleans, La.
1980-053	Hoffman, Glenn Edward	201 Old Bridge Road/Anaheim Hills CA 92807
1979-054	Hoffman, Guy Alan	411 Phoenix Avenue/Bloomington IL 61701
1964-047	Hoffman, John Edward	2315 Nw 85th/Seattle WA 98117
1942-052	Hoffman, Raymond Lamont	3509 Silver Lace Lane #53/Boynton Beach FL 33436
1993-078	Hoffman, Trevor William	640 South Westford Street/Anaheim CA 92807
1939-052	Hoffman, William Joseph	425 Hermitage Street/Philadelphia PA 19128
1949-035	Hofman, Robert George	D. April 5, 1994 Chesterfield, Mo.
1919-042	Hofmann, Fred	D. November 19, 1964 St. Helena, Calif.
1914-089	Hogan, George A.	D. February 28, 1922 Bartlesville, Okla.
1925-049	Hogan, James Francis 'Shanty'	D. April 7, 1967 Boston, Mass.
1921-044	Hogan, Kenneth Sylvester	D. January 2, 1980 Cleveland, O.
1911-074	Hogan, William Henry 'Happy'	D. September 28, 1974 San Jose, Calif.
1911-075	Hogg, Carter Bradley	D. April 2, 1935 Buena Vista, Ga.

1934-047	Hogg, Wilbert George 'Bert'	D. November 5, 1973 Detroit, Mich.
1929-050	Hogsett, Elon Chester 'Chief'	1307 Truman Street/Great Bend KS 67530
1952-050	Hogue, Calvin Grey	1050 Berkshire Road/Dayton OH 45419
1948-047	Hogue, Robert Clinton	D. December 22, 1987 Miami, Fla.
1927-045	Hohman, William Henry	D. October 29, 1968 Baltimore, Md.
1910-072	Hohnhurst, Edward Henry	D. March 26, 1916 Covington, Ky.
1989-061	Hoiles, Christopher Allen	8688 Jerry City Road/Wayne OH 43466
1996-081	Holbert, Aaron Keith	Old Add: Long Beach CA 90801
1994-046	Holbert, Ray Arthur	20450 North 40th Drive/Glendale AZ 85308
1944-061	Holborow, Walter Albert	D. July 14, 1986 Fort Lauderdale, Fla.
1935-048	Holbrook, James Marbury 'Sammy'	D. April 10, 1991 Jackson, Miss.
1945-048	Holcombe, Kenneth Edward	32 Botany Drive/Asheville/Nc 28805
1934-048	Holden, Joseph Francis	D. May 10, 1996 Saint Clair, Pa.
1913-086	Holden, William Paul	D. September 14, 1971 Pensacola, Fla.
1972-049	Holdsworth, Fredrick William	47300 West Main St/Northville MI 48167
1914-090	Holke, Walter Henry	D. October 12, 1954 St Louis, Mo.
1920-054	Hollahan, William James	D. November 27, 1965 New York, New York
1977-067	Holland, Alfred Willis	Old Add: 28 Acorn Hill Dr Voorhees NJ 08043
1926-038	Holland, Howard Arthur 'Mul'	D. February 16, 1969 Westchester, Va.
1932-037	Holland, Robert Clyde 'Dutch'	D. June 16, 1967 Lumberton, N.C.
1939-053	Holland, William David	504 Cashwell Place/Goldsboro NC 27534
1995-101	Hollandsworth, Todd Mathew	5049 Athens Drive/San Roman CA 94583
1979-055	Holle, Gary Charles	820 Fifth Ave/Watervliet NY 12189
1928-048	Holley, Edward Edgar	D. October 26, 1986 Paducah, Ky.
1921-045	Holling, Carl	D. July 28, 1962 Sonoma, Calif.
1935-049	Hollingsworth, Albert Wayne 'Boots'	D. April 28, 1996 Austin, Texas
1922-057	Hollingsworth, John Burnett 'Bonnie'	D. January 4, 1990 Shannondale, Tenn.
1990-069	Hollins, David Michael	245 Angle Road/West Seneca NY 14224
1992-055	Hollins, Jessie Edward	PO Box 92/Apple Springs TX 75926
1949-036	Hollmig, Stanley Ernest	D. December 4, 1981 San Antonio, Texas
1918-032	Hollocher, Charles Jacob	D. August 14, 1940 Stratman, Mo.
1953-033	Holloman, Alva Lee 'Bobo'	D. May 1, 1987 Athens, Ga.
1929-051	Holloway, James Madison	D. April 15, 1997 Baton Rouge, La.
1922-058	Holloway, Kenneth Eugene	D. September 25, 1968 Thomasville, Ga.
1977-068	Holly, Jeffrey Owen	Old Add: 2601 Alvord St Redondo Beach CA 90278
1924-052	Holm, Roscoe Albert 'Wattie'	D. May 19, 1950 Everly, Ia.
1943-064	Holm, William Fred	D. July 27, 1977 East Chicago, Ind.
1993-079	Holman, Bradley Thomas	1625 Park Place/Wichita KS 67203
1988-068	Holman, Brian Scott	Old Add: 22877 SE Cole Creek Rd Atlanta KS 67008
1968-039	Holman, Gary Richard	PO Box 1621/Wrightwood CA 92397
1980-054	Holman, Randy Scott	Old Add: 750 Mobile Ave #48 Camarillo CA 93010
1989-062	Holman, Shawn Leroy	Route 3, Edgewood Road/Sewickley PA 15143
1990-070	Holmes, Darren Lee	PO Box 764/Fletcher NC 28732
1918-033	Holmes, Elwood Marter	D. April 15, 1954 Camden, N. J.
1942-053	Holmes, Thomas Francis	1 Pine Drive/Woodbury NY 11797
1930-035	Holshouser, Herman Alexander	D. July 26, 1994 Concord, N. C.
1996-082	Holt, Christopher Michael	4877 Fallon Place/Dallas TX 75227
1925-050	Holt, James Emmett Madison 'Red'	D. February 2, 1961 Birmingham, Ala.
1968-040	Holt, James William	924 Monroe Hold Road/Graham NC 27253
1980-055	Holt, Roger Boyd	Old Add: 1615 Sailfish Ave Fruitland Park FL 32731
1965-046	Holtgrave, Lavern George 'Vern'	389 North 8th St/Breese IL 62230
1985-049	Holton, Brian John	831 Stanislaus Circle/Claremont CA 91711
1996-083	Holtz, Michael James	Rural Route 4/Ebensburg PA 15931
1965-047	Holtzman, Kenneth Dale	115 Valley Trail Drive #A/Ballwin MO 63011
1993-080	Holzemer, Mark Harold	10044 South Macalister Trail/Highlands Ranch CO 80126
1977-069	Honeycutt, Frederick Wayne 'Rick'	207 Forrest Road/Fort Oglethorpe GA 30742
1925-051	Hood, Albie Larrison	D. October 14, 1988 Chesapeake, Va.
1973-063	Hood, Donald Harris	708 Firestone Dr/Florence SC 29501
1949-037	Hood, Wallace James	966 Eilinita Avenue/Glendale CA 91208
1920-055	Hood, Wallace James, Sr.	D. May 2, 1965 Hollywood, Calif.
1995-102	Hook, Christopher Wayne	9775 North 93rd Way #260/Scottsdale AZ 85258
1957-034	Hook, James Wesley 'Jay'	PO Box 90/Maple City MI 49664
1935-050	Hooks, Alexander Marcus	D. June 19, 1993 Edgewood, Texas
1950-035	Hooper, Robert Nelson	D. March 17, 1980 New Brunswick, N. J.
1974-053	Hooten, Michael Leon	461 North 11th St/Coos Bay OR 97420
1971-049	Hooton, Burt Carlton	3619 Granby Court/San Antonio TX 78217
1990-071	Hoover, John Nicklaus	1615 West Fountain/Fresno CA 93705
1952-051	Hoover, Richard Lloyd	D. April 12, 1981 Lake Placid, Fla.
1943-065	Hoover, Robert Joe	D. September 2, 1965 Los Angeles, Calif.
1993-081	Hope, John Alan	1701 27th Street East/Bradenton FL 34208
1975-054	Hopkins, Donald	Old Add: 8041 Village Drive Cincinnati OH 45242
1968-041	Hopkins, Gail Eason	118 South County Line Road/Hinsdale IL 60521
1934-049	Hopkins, Meredith Hilliard 'Marty'	D. November 20, 1963 Dallas, Tex.
1927-046	Hopkins, Paul Henry	131 Main Street/Deep River CT 6417
1939-054	Hopp, John Leonard	1914 Avenue N/Scottsbluff NE 69361
1946-048	Hopper, James McDaniel	D. January 23, 1982 Charlotte, N. C.
1913-087	Hopper, William Booth	D. January 14, 1965 Allen Park, Mich.
1924-053	Horan, Joseph Patrick 'Shags'	D. February 13, 1969 Los Angeles, Calif.
1961-053	Horlen, Joel Edward	3718 Chartwell Drive/San Antonio TX 78230

1987-061	Horn, Samuel Lee	7686 Skyline Drive/San Diego CA 92114
1929-052	Horne, Berlyn Dale 'Trader'	D. February 3, 1983 Franklin, O.
1978-058	Horner, James Robert Bob	209 Steeplechase Drive/Irving TX 75062
1915-070	Hornsby, Rogers	D. January 5, 1963 Chicago, Ill.
1912-079	Horsey, Hanson	D. December 1, 1949 Millington, Md.
1991-081	Horsman, Vincent Stanley Joseph	Old Add: 25a Kennedy Drive Dartmouth Nova Scotia
1917-035	Horstman, Oscar Theodore	D. May 11, 1977 Salina, Kan.
1964-048	Horton, Anthony Darrin	17001 Livorno Dr/Pacific Palisades CA 90272
1984-055	Horton, Ricky Neal	16026 Aston Court/Chesterfield MO 63005
1963-058	Horton, William Wattersn	%Reid 15124 Warwick Detroit MI 48223
1995-103	Hosey, Dwayne Samuel	7914 Ruby Court/Highland CA 92346
1992-056	Hosey, Steven Bernard	Old Add: 532 West Olive Street #20 Inglewood CA 90301
1953-034	Hoskins, David Taylor	D. April 2, 1970 Flint, Mich.
1970-060	Hosley, Timothy Kenneth	401 West Henry St/Spartanburg SC 29301
1956-046	Host, Eugene Earl	1415 Fulton St/Nashville TN 37206
1944-062	Hostetler, Charles Cloyd	D. February 18, 1971 Fort Collins, Colo.
1981-057	Hostetler, David Alan	5068 Santorini Way/Oceanside CA 92056
1971-050	Hottman, Kenneth	Old Add: 8559 Banff Vista/Elk Grove CA 95624
1912-080	Houck, Byron Simon	D. June 17, 1969 Santa Cruz, Calif.
1970-061	Hough, Charles Oliver	2266 Shade Tree Cir/Brea CA 92621
1947-044	Houk, Ralph George	3000 Plantation Road/Winter Haven FL 33884
1950-036	House, Henry Franklin 'Frank'	875 Calellmium Way/Birmingham AL 35242
1967-050	House, Patrick Lory	2554 West Penick Point Court/Meridian ID 83642
1971-051	House, Thomas Ross	12794 Via Felino/Del Mar CA 92014
1913-088	House, Willard Edwin	D. November 16, 1923 Kansas City, Mo.
1980-056	Householder, Paul Wesley	Old Add: Rural Route Box 1815e North Monmouth Me 04265
1910-073	Houser, Benjamin Franklin	D. January 15, 1952 Augusta, Me.
1914-091	Houser, Joseph William	D. January 3, 1953 Orlando, Fla.
1991-082	Housie, Wayne Tyrone	5180 Tyler Street #23/Riverside CA 92503
1996-084	Houston, Tyler Sam	Old Add: Las Vegas NV 89101
1945-049	Houtteman, Arthur Joseph	1755 West Buell Road/Oakland MI 48363
1969-082	Hovley, Stephen Eugene	205 1/2 South Lomita Avenue/Ojai CA 93023
1918-034	Hovlik, Edward C.	D. March 20, 1955 Painesville, O.
1963-059	Howard, Bruce Ernest	8705 Misty Creek Drive/Sarasota FL 34241
1993-082	Howard, Christian	32 Maple Avenue/Nahant MA 1908
1991-083	Howard, Christopher Hugh	15905 Lakeview/Houston TX 77040
1912-081	Howard, David Austin	D. January 26, 1956 Dallas, Tex.
1991-084	Howard, David Wayne	5618 Pinnacle Heights Cir #202/Tampa FL 33624
1972-050	Howard, Douglas Lynn	8038 Deer Creek Road/Salt Lake City UT 84121
1918-035	Howard, Earl Nycum	D. April 4, 1937 Everett, Pa.
1955-059	Howard, Elston Gene	D. December 14, 1980 New York, N. Y.
1958-046	Howard, Frank Oliver	6574 Palisades Avenue/Centreville VA 22020
1979-056	Howard, Fred Irving	88 Scamman St/South Portland Me 4106
1914-092	Howard, Ivan Chester	D. March 30, 1967 Medford, Ore.
1970-062	Howard, Larry Rayford	Old Add: 1171 School Avenue Patrick Afb FL 32925
1946-049	Howard, Lee Vincent	27821 Via Madrina/San Juan Capistrano CA 92675
1996-085	Howard, Matthew Christopher	11859 Ramsdell Court/San Diego CA 92131
1981-058	Howard, Michael Fredric	Old Add: 4981 46th St Sacramento CA 95820
1990-072	Howard, Steven Bernard	4712 Shetland Avenue/Oakland CA 94605
1990-073	Howard, Thomas Sylvester	822 8th Avenue/Middletown OH 45044
1973-064	Howard, Wilbur Leon	Old Add: 12500 Dunlap #423/Houston TX 77031
1971-052	Howarth, James Eugene	Old Add: 108 Via Nicola Watsonville CA 95076
1974-054	Howe, Arthur Henry	711 Kahldon Court/Houston TX 77079
1952-052	Howe, Calvin Earl	3352 Waverly Pointe/Holland MI 49424
1923-065	Howe, Lester Curtis	D. July 16, 1976 Woodmere, N. Y.
1980-057	Howe, Steven Roy	PO Box 1355/Warsaw IN 46581
1947-045	Howell, Homer Elliott 'Dixie'	D. October 5, 1990 Binghamton, N. Y.
1985-050	Howell, Jack Robert	822 South Lehigh Drive/Tucson AZ 85710
1980-058	Howell, Jay Canfield	6330 Sunbriar Drive/Cumming GA 30130
1984-056	Howell, Kenneth	22090 Buckingham Drive/Farmington MI 48335
1940-037	Howell, Millard Fillmore 'Dixie'	D. March 18, 1960 Hollywood, Fla.
1941-047	Howell, Murray Donald 'Red'	D. October 1, 1950 Greenville, S. C.
1992-057	Howell, Patrick O_neal	4513 Connie Avenue/Eight Mile AL 36613
1912-082	Howell, Roland Boatner	D. May 31, 1973 Baton Rouge, La.
1974-055	Howell, Roy Lee	1201 East Cypress/Lompoc CA 93436
1949-038	Howerton, William Ray	%Bill Howerton Jr. 516 3rd Street Dunmore PA 18512
1989-063	Howitt, Dann Paul John	63 Allison/Battle Creek WI 49017
1913-089	Howley, Daniel Philip	D. March 10, 1944 East Weymouth, Mass.
1961-054	Howser, Richard Dalton	D. June 17, 1987 Kansas City, Mo.
1992-058	Hoy, Peter Alexander	770 Lambert Street/Cardinal Ontario K0E 1E0 Canada
1952-053	Hoyle, Roland Edison	D. July 4, 1994 Carbondale, Pa.
1979-057	Hoyt, Dewey Lamarr 'Lamarr'	513 Killington Court/Columbia SC 29212
1918-036	Hoyt, Waite Charles	D. August 25, 1984 Cincinnati, O.
1970-063	Hrabosky, Alan Thomas	% Kplr 4935 Lindell Blvd Saint Louis MO 63108
1981-059	Hrbek, Kent Alan	2611 West 112th Street/Bloomington MN 55431
1968-042	Hriniak, Walter John	18 Stacy Drive/North Andover MA 1845
1978-059	Hubbard, Glenn Dee	1515 King's Crossing/Stone Mountain GA 30087
1995-104	Hubbard, Michael Wayne	227 Lakeview Drive/Madison Heights VA 24572
1994-047	Hubbard, Trenidad Aviel 'Trent'	2654 East 77th Street/Chicago IL 60649

1928-049	Hubbell, Carl Owen	D. November 21, 1988 Scottsdale, Ariz.
1919-043	Hubbell, Wilbert William 'Bill'	D. August 3, 1980 Lakewood, Co.
1961-055	Hubbs, Kenneth Douglass	D. February 15, 1964 Utah Lake, Utah
1920-056	Huber, Clarence Bill	D. February 22, 1965 Laredo, Tex.
1939-055	Huber, Otto	D. April 9, 1989 Passaic, N.J.
1935-051	Huckleberry, Earl Eugene	Bowlegs OK 74830
1994-048	Hudek, John Raymond	7603 Shady Way Drive/Sugar Land TX 77479
1983-074	Hudgens, David Mark	PO Box 8734/Scottsdale AZ 85252
1923-066	Hudgens, James Price	D. August 26, 1955 St. Louis, Mo.
1984-057	Hudler, Rex Allen	Old Add: 503 East Menlo Fresno CA 93710
1926-039	Hudlin, George Willis 'Willis'	14 Betsey Lane/Little Rock AR 72205
1972-051	Hudson, Charles	Rural Route 5 Box 570/Coalgate OK 74538
1983-075	Hudson, Charles Lynn	2112 Matagorda Drive/Dallas TX 75232
1952-054	Hudson, Hal Campbell	17133 Denver/Detroit MI 48224
1969-083	Hudson, Jessie James	% James/Hudson 1013 Eloise Street Mansfield LA 70114
1936-040	Hudson, John Wilson	D. November 7, 1970 Bryan, Tex.
1995-105	Hudson, Joseph Paul	% Anita Hudson 86 Tallowood Drive Medford NJ 8055
1974-056	Hudson, Rex Haughton	4704 Spring Mows/Midland TX 79705
1940-038	Hudson, Sidney Charles	1309 Westwood Drive/Waco TX 76710
1914-093	Huenke, Albert A.	D. September 20, 1974 Saint Marys, O.
1989-064	Huff, Michael Kale	1630 Chicago Avenue #2006/Evanston IL 60201
1937-053	Huffman, Benjamin Franklin	2 Cedar Lane/Luray VA 22835
1979-058	Huffman, Phillip Lee	Old Add: 334 Caladium St Lake Jackson TX 77566
1974-057	Hughes, James Michael	7526 El Manor Avenue/Los Angeles CA 90045
1952-055	Hughes, James Robert	5006 Circle Court/Crestwood IL 60445
1987-062	Hughes, Keith Wills	1263 Rose Lane/Berwyn PA 19312
1966-046	Hughes, Richard Henry	Box 598/Stephens AR 71764
1935-052	Hughes, Roy John	D. March 5, 1995 Asheville, N. C.
1970-064	Hughes, Terry Wayne	532 Pierpont Avenue Ext./Spartanburg SC 29303
1959-039	Hughes, Thomas Edward	610 Kimswick Court/Deer Park TX 77536
1930-036	Hughes, Thomas Franklin	D. August 10, 1989 Beaumont, Texas
1941-048	Hughes, Thomas Owen	D. November 28, 1990 Wilkes-Barre, Pa.
1914-094	Hughes, Vernon Alexander	D. September 26, 1961 Sewickley, Pa.
1921-046	Hughes, William Nesbert	D. February 25, 1963 Birmingham, Ala.
1941-049	Hughson, Cecil Carlton 'Tex'	D. August 6, 1993 Austin, Texas
1915-071	Huhn, Emil Hugo	D. September 5, 1925 Camden, S.C.
1983-076	Huisman, Mark Lawrence	1407 Woodcreek Circle/Blue Springs MO 64015
1995-106	Huisman, Richard Allen 'Rick'	17w25 Oak Lane/Bensenville IL 60106
1983-077	Hulett, Timothy Craig	Rr 5/Springfield IL 62707
1922-059	Hulihan, Harry Joseph	D. September 11, 1980 Rutland, Vt.
1992-059	Hulse, David Lindsey	1301 Kenwood Drive/San Angelo TX 76903
1923-067	Hulvey, James Hensel 'Hank'	D. April 9, 1982 Mount Sidney, Va.
1977-070	Hume, Thomas Hubert	1802 24th Avenue West/Palmetto FL 34221
1911-076	Humphrey, Albert	D. May 13, 1961 Ashtabula, O.
1938-040	Humphrey, Byron William	D. February 13, 1992 Springfield, Mo.
1971-053	Humphrey, Terryal Gene	Old Add: 21 Ensueno West/Irvine CA 92701
1991-085	Humphreys, Michael Butler	Old Add: PO Box 152689 Dallas TX 75315
1962-058	Humphreys, Robert William	121 Poplar Hill Drive/Farmville VA 23901
1910-074	Humphries, Albert	D. September 21, 1945 Orlando, Fla.
1938-041	Humphries, John William	D. June 24, 1965 New Orleans, La.
1964-049	Hundley, Cecil Randolph 'Randy'	122 East Forest Ln/Palatine IL 60067
1990-074	Hundley, Todd Randolph	122 East Forest Lane/Palatine IL 60067
1922-060	Hungling, Bernard Herman	D. March 30, 1968 Dayton, O.
1926-040	Hunnefield, William Fenton	D. August 28, 1976 Nantucket, Mass.
1910-075	Hunt, Benjamin Franklin	D. September 27, 1927 Greybull, Wyo.
1985-051	Hunt, James Randall Randy	117 Destin St/Montgomery AL 36110
1959-040	Hunt, Kenneth Lawrence	D. June 8, 1997 Gardena, Calif.
1961-056	Hunt, Kenneth Raymond	268 East 300 North/Morgan UT 84050
1931-041	Hunt, Oliver Joel	D. July 24, 1978 Teague, Texas
1963-060	Hunt, Ronald Kenneth	2806 Jackson Rd/Wentzville MO 63385
1994-049	Hunter, Brian Lee	1300 SE 181st Avenue/Vancouver WA 98683
1991-086	Hunter, Brian Raynold	12141 Centralia #219/Lakewood CA 90715
1933-026	Hunter, Edison Franklin	D. March 14, 1967 Colerain Twp., O.
1911-077	Hunter, Frederick Creighton 'Newt'	D. October 24, 1963 Columbus, O.
1953-035	Hunter, Gordon William 'Billy'	104 East Seminary Avenue/Lutherville MD 21093
1971-054	Hunter, Harold James	14616 Fir Circle/Plattsmouth NE 68048
1916-044	Hunter, Herbert Harrison	D. July 26, 1970 Orlando, Fla.
1965-048	Hunter, James Augustus 'Catfish'	Rr One Box 895/Hertford NC 27944
1991-087	Hunter, James Macgregor	108 Tindall Road/Middletown NJ 7748
1996-086	Hunter, Richard Thomas 'Rich'	Old Add: Temecula CA 92591
1997-081	Hunter, Torii Kedar	2408 Belmoor Drive/Pine Bluff AR 71601
1962-059	Hunter, Willard Mitchell	2562 Poppleton Ave/Omaha NE 68105
1912-083	Hunter, William Ellsworth	D. April 10, 1934 Buffalo, N.Y.
1967-051	Huntz, Stephen Michael	22495 Haber/Cleveland OH 44126
1923-068	Huntzinger, Walter Henry	D. August 11, 1981 Upper Darby, Pa.
1983-078	Huppert, David Blaine	5735 Rick Drive/Zephyrhills FL 33541
1954-046	Hurd, Thomas Carr	D. September 5, 1982 Waterloo, Iowa
1977-071	Hurdle, Clinton Merrick	3568 SW Sunset Trace Circle/Palm City FL 34990
1980-059	Hurst, Bruce Vee	Old Add: 46 Pleasant Street Wellesley MA 02181

1928-050 ....Hurst, Frank O 'Donnell 'Don' ....D. December 6, 1952 Los Angeles, Calif.
1994-050 ....Hurst, James Lavon ....1413 Van Pelt Road/Sebring FL 33870
1997-082 ....Hurst, Jimmy Oneal ....Old Add: Tuscaloosa AL 35660
1992-060 ....Hurst, Jonathan ....308 Woodburn Creek Road/Spartanburg SC 29302
1996-087 ....Hurst, William Hansel......................................Old Add: Miami FL 33101
1995-107 ....Hurtado, Edwin Amilgar...................................Old Add: 221 N. Lasalle St Chicago IL 60601
1993-083 ....Huskey, Robert Leon ....4801 Nw Meadowbrook Drive/Lawton OK 73505
1988-069 ....Huson, Jeffrey Kent ....10349 Rowluck Way/Parker CO 80134
1925-052 ....Husta, Carl Lawrence ....D. November 6, 1951 Kingston, N. Y.
1937-054 ....Huston, Warren Llewellyn ....12 Robinwood Road Rural Route 3 Buzzard Bay MA 2532
1933-027 ....Hutcheson, Joseph Johnson ....D. February 23, 1993 Tyler, Texas
1940-039 ....Hutchings, John Richard Joseph ....D. April 27, 1963 Indianapolis, Ind.
1939-056 ....Hutchinson, Frederick Charles ....D. November 12, 1964 Bradenton, Fla.
1933-028 ....Hutchinson, Ira Kendall ....D. August 21, 1973 Chicago, Ill.
1974-058 ....Hutson, George Herbert 'Herb' ....7203 West Sugartree Court/Savannah GA 31410
1925-053 ....Hutson, Roy Lee ....D. May 20, 1957 Lamesa, Calif.
1970-065 ....Hutto, James Neamon ....1317 John Carroll Drive/Pensacola FL 32504
1993-084 ....Hutton, Mark Steven ....6 Corfu Court, Westlakes Adelaide/Australia 5021
1966-047 ....Hutton, Thomas George ....18 Huntly Drive/Palm Beach Gardens FL 33410
1955-060 ....Hyde, Richard Elde ....204 Dorchester Drive/Mahomet IL 61853
1994-051 ....Hyers, Timothy James ....241 Ridge Road/Covington CA 30209
1996-088 ....Ibanez, Raul Javier ....Old Add: Miami FL 33101
1973-065 ....Ignasiak, Gary Raymond ....3084 Angelos Drive/Waterford MI 48329
1991-088 ....Ignasiak, Michael James ....533 Old Creek Court/Saline MI 48176
1994-052 ....Ilsley, Blaise Francis ....Old Add: 1274 Long Rapids Rd Alpena MI 49707
1913-090 ....Imlay, Harry Miller 'Doc'..................................D. October 7, 1948 Bordentown, N.J.
1986-066 ....Incaviglia, Peter Joseph ....PO Box 526/Pebble Beach CA 93953
1987-063 ....Infante, Fermin Alexis ....Urb. Colinas De La Rosaleda Calle 4 Casa #20 Barquisimeto Venezuela
1914-095 ....Ingersoll, Robert Randolph ....D. January 13, 1927 Minneapolis, Minn.
1911-078 ....Ingerton, William John 'Scotty'......................D. June 15, 1956 Cleveland, O.
1994-053 ....Ingram, Garey Lamar ....6060 Harvest Drive/Columbus GA 31907
1929-053 ....Ingram, Melvin David ....D. October 28, 1979 Medford, Ore.
1994-054 ....Ingram, Riccardo Benay ....1226 Turner Street/Douglas GA 31533
1987-064 ....Innis, Jeffrey David ....4920 Woodlong Lane/Cumming GA 30130
1977-072 ....Iorg, Dane Charles ....1271 Fort Drive/Pleasant Grove UT 84062
1978-060 ....Iorg, Garth Ray ....1446 Js Davis Lane/Knoxville TN 37932
1941-050 ....Iott, Clarence Eugene 'Hooks'........................D. August 17, 1980 St. Petersburg, Fla.
1997-083 ....Irabu, Hideki ....Old Add: Chiba Japan
1914-096 ....Irelan, Harold ....D. July 16, 1944 Carmel, Ind.
1981-060 ....Ireland, Timothy Neal ....20932 Times Ave/Hayward CA 94541
1949-039 ....Irvin, Monford Merrill 'Monte' ....11 Douglas Court South/Homosassa FL 32646
1912-084 ....Irvin, William Edward ....D. February 18, 1916 Philadelphia, Pa.
1990-075 ....Irvine, Daryl Keith ....Rural Route 14 Box 102/Harrisonburg VA 22801
1938-042 ....Irwin, Thomas Andrew ....D. April 25, 1996 Altoona, Pa.
1921-047 ....Irwin, Walter Kingsley ....D. August 18, 1976 Spring Lake, Mich.
1980-060 ....Isales, Orlando ....Old Add: 16s 1171 Cabarra Ter Rio Piedras PR 00921
1995-108 ....Isringhausen, Jason Derik..............................207 East Center Street/Brighton IL 62012
1971-055 ....Ivie, Michael Wilson ....534 Midland Park Dr/Stone Mountain GA 30083
1967-052 ....Izquierdo, Enrique Roberto 'Hank' ....6011 SW 97th Ave/Miami FL 33173
1953-036 ....Jablonski, Raymond Leo ....D. November 25, 1985 Chicago, Ill.
1959-041 ....Jackson, Alvin Neil ....3321 SE Morningside Blvd/Port Saint Lucie FL 34952
1915-072 ....Jackson, Charles Herbert ....D. May 27, 1968 Ratford, Va.
1987-065 ....Jackson, Charles Leo ....5727 37th Avenue South/Seattle WA 98118
1996-089 ....Jackson, Damian Jacques ....Old Add: Concord CA 94520
1983-079 ....Jackson, Danny Lynn ....Old Add: 17050 Imperial Valley #104 Houston TX 77060
1978-061 ....Jackson, Darrell Preston ....PO Box 4424/Downey CA 90241
1985-052 ....Jackson, Darrin Jay ....1500 North Sunview Pkwy #82/Gilbert AZ 85234
1911-079 ....Jackson, George Christopher ....D. November 25, 1972 Cleburne, Tex.
1965-049 ....Jackson, Grant Dwight ....212 Mesa Circle/Upper Saint Clair PA 15241
1933-029 ....Jackson, John Lewis ....D. October 24, 1956 Somers Point, N. J.
1987-066 ....Jackson, Kenneth Bernard ....PO Box 613/Waskom TX 75692
1955-061 ....Jackson, Lawrence Curtis ....D. August 28, 1990 Boise, Idaho
1958-047 ....Jackson, Louis Clarence ....D. May 27, 1969 Tokyo, Japan
1986-067 ....Jackson, Michael Ray ....Old Add: 7234 Wiley St Houston TX 77016
1970-066 ....Jackson, Michael Warren ....288 East 19th Street/Paterson NJ 7524
1950-037 ....Jackson, Ransom Joseph 'Randy' ....250 Hunnicut Drive/Athens GA 30601
1967-053 ....Jackson, Reginald Martinez 'Reggie' ....305 Amador Avenue/Seaside CA 93955
1963-061 ....Jackson, Roland Thomas 'Sonny' ....3576c Wildwood Forrest Court/Palm Beach Gdns FL 33403
1954-047 ....Jackson, Ronald Allen ....210 Raintree Circle/Kalamazoo MI 49007
1975-055 ....Jackson, Ronnie ....Old Add: 1940 W. Orangewood #110 Orange CA 92668
1977-073 ....Jackson, Roy Lee ....8269 County Road 54/Auburn AL 36830
1922-061 ....Jackson, Travis Calvin ....D. July 27, 1987 Waldo, Ark.
1986-068 ....Jackson, Vincent Edward Bo ....100 Oak Ridge Drive/Burr Ridge IL 60521
1914-097 ....Jackson, William Riley ....D. September 26, 1958 Peoria, Ill.
1948-048 ....Jacobs, Anthony Robert ....D. December 21, 1980 Nashville, Tenn.
1939-057 ....Jacobs, Arthur Evan ....D. June 8, 1967 Inglewood, Calif.
1954-048 ....Jacobs, Forrest Vandergrift 'Spook' ....Box 66/Milford DE 19963
1960-049 ....Jacobs, Lamar Gary 'Jake' ....103 St. Johns Way East/Apollo Beach FL 33572
1937-055 ....Jacobs, Newton Smith ....D. June 15, 1990 Richmond, Va.

1918-037	Jacobs, Otto Albert	D. November 19, 1955 Chicago, Ill.
1928-051	Jacobs, Raymond F.	D. April 5, 1952 Los Angeles, Calif.
1914-098	Jacobs, William Elmer	D. February 10, 1958 Salem, Mo.
1915-073	Jacobson, Merwin John William	D. January 13, 1978 Baltimore, Md.
1915-074	Jacobson, William Chester 'Baby Doll'	D. January 16, 1977 Orion, Ill.
1918-038	Jacobus, Stuart Louis 'Larry'	D. August 19, 1965 North College Hill, Ohio
1981-061	Jacoby, Brook Wallace	9646 East Laurel Lane/Scottsdale AZ 85260
1994-055	Jacome, Jason James	5115 North Camino Esplendora/Tucson AZ 85718
1971-056	Jacquez, Patrick Thomas	4430 Annadale Drive/Stockton CA 95219
1964-050	Jaeckel, Paul Henry	328 West 7th Street/Claremont CA 91711
1920-057	Jaeger, Joseph Peter	D. December 13, 1963 Hampton, Ia.
1992-061	Jaha, John Emile	2506 Nw 24th Circle/Camas WA 98607
1925-054	Jahn, Arthur Charles	D. January 9, 1948 Little Rock, Ark.
1936-041	Jakucki, Sigmund	D. May 28, 1979 Galveston, Texas
1924-054	Jamerson, Charley Dewey	D. August 4, 1980 Mocksville, N. C.
1975-056	James, Arthur	4531 Garland Ave/Detroit MI 48214
1960-050	James, Charles Wesley	104 Collier St/Fulton MO 65221
1968-043	James, Cleo Joel	6020 Kittyhawk Dr/Riverside CA 92504
1983-080	James, Dion	804 Ninth Avenue/Sacramento CA 95818
1986-069	James, Donald Christopher Chris	Rural Route 2 Box 231/Alto TX 75925
1968-044	James, Jeffrey Lynn	Old Add: 39095 Mountain Home Dr Lebanon OR 97355
1958-048	James, John Phillip	6037 East Larkspur/Scottsdale AZ 85254
1995-109	James, Michael Elmo	115 Austin Court/Mary Esther FL 32569
1977-074	James, Philip Robert 'Skip'	7716 W. 72nd Ter/Overland Park KS 66204
1967-054	James, Richard Lee	2860 Tupelo Drive/Panama City FL 32407
1929-054	James, Robert Byrne 'Bernie'	D. August 1, 1994 San Antonio, Texas
1978-062	James, Robert Harvey	15844 Cindy Court/Canyon Country CA 91351
1912-085	James, William A. 'Lefty'	D. May 3, 1933 Portsmouth, O.
1911-080	James, William Henry	D. May 24, 1942 Venice, Calif.
1913-091	James, William Lawrence	D. March 10, 1971 Oroville, Calof.
1915-075	Jamieson, Charles Devine	D. October 27, 1969 Paterson, N.J.
1970-067	Janeski, Gerald Joseph 'Jerry'	28901 Via Buena Vis/San Juan Capistrano CA 92675
1953-037	Janowicz, Victor Felix	D. February 27, 1996 Columbus, O.
1947-046	Jansen, Lawrence Joseph 'Larry'	3207 SW Highway 47/Forest Grove OR 97116
1910-076	Jansen, Raymond William	D. March 19, 1934 St. Louis, Mo.
1912-086	Jantzen, Walter C. 'Heinie'	D. April 1, 1948 Hines, Ill.
1911-081	Janvrin, Harold Chandler	D. March 1, 1962 Boston, Mass.
1996-090	Janzen, Martin Thomas	Old Add: Gainesville FL 32602
1994-056	Jarvis, Kevin Thomas	3220 Darlington Circle/Lexington KY 40509
1944-063	Jarvis, Leroy Gilbert	D. January 13, 1990 Oklahoma City, Okla.
1969-084	Jarvis, Raymond Arnold	PO Box 9452/Providence RI 2940
1966-048	Jarvis, Robert Patrick 'Pat'	4425 East Kingspoints Circle/Dunwoody GA 30338
1914-099	Jasper, Harry W. 'Hi'	D. May 22, 1937 St. Louis, Mo.
1965-050	Jaster, Larry Edward	12926 Meadowbend Drive/West Palm Beach FL 33414
1972-052	Jata, Paul	12780 Hutton Drive/Walton KY 41094
1940-040	Javery, Alva William	D. September 13, 1977 Woodstock, Conn.
1976-041	Javier, Ignacio Alfredo	Barrio Libre #96 Ingcon San Pedro De Macoris Dominican Rep.
1960-051	Javier, Manuel Julian 'Julian'	Old Add: B#12 Urb Pina/San Francisco De Macoris Dom Rep
1953-038	Jay, Joseph Richard 'Joey'	7209 Battenwood Court/Tampa FL 33615
1993-085	Jean, Domingo	Calle E Pueblo Nuevo #12 San Pedro De Macoris Dominican Rep.
1921-048	Jeanes, Ernest Lee 'Tex'	D. April 5, 1973 Longview, Tex.
1936-042	Jeffcoat, George Edward	D. October 13, 1978 Leesville, S. C.
1948-049	Jeffcoat, Harold Bentley 'Hal'	4016 Wisconsin Avenue/Tampa FL 33616
1983-081	Jeffcoat, James Michael 'Mike'	Old Add: Rr 1 Box 289 Pine Bluff AR 71603
1987-067	Jefferies, Gregory Scott	Old Add: 70 Dumont CT Millbrae CA 94030
1973-066	Jefferson, Jesse Harrison	1421 Railroad Ave/Midlothian VA 23113
1991-089	Jefferson, Reginald Jirod	2693 Miccosukee Road/Tallahassee FL 32308
1986-070	Jefferson, Stanley	2420-3e Hunter Avenue/Bronx NY 10475
1930-037	Jeffries, Irvine Franklin	D. June 8, 1982 Louisville, Ky.
1990-076	Jelic, Christopher John	1106 Hawthorne Circle/Oakdale PA 15071
1941-051	Jelincich, Frank Anthony	D. June 27, 1992 Rochester, Minn.
1987-068	Jelks, Gregory Dion	615 Bay Springs Road/Centre AL 35960
1983-082	Jeltz, Larry Steven Steve	615 West 28th Place/Lawrence KS 66044
1965-051	Jenkins, Ferguson Arthur	PO Box 1202/Guthrie OK 73044
1922-062	Jenkins, John Robert	D. August 3, 1968 Columbia, Mo.
1914-100	Jenkins, Joseph Daniel	D. June 21, 1974 Fresno, Calif.
1925-055	Jenkins, Thomas Griffin	D. May 3, 1979 Weymouth, Mass.
1962-060	Jenkins, Warren Washington 'Jack'	3810 Obispo/Tampa FL 33609
1988-070	Jennings, James Douglas 'Doug'	4455 Nw 24th Avenue/Boca Raton FL 33431
1996-091	Jennings, Robin Christopher	Old Add: Annandale VA 22003
1951-044	Jennings, William Lee	7065 Foxcrofort Drive/Affton MO 63123
1931-042	Jensen, Forrest Ducenus 'Woody'	3021 Benjamin Street/Wichita KS 67204
1950-038	Jensen, Jack Eugene	D. July 14, 1982 Charlottesville, Va.
1996-092	Jensen, Marcus C.	Old Add: Oakland CA 94601
1912-087	Jensen, William Christian	D. March 27, 1917 Philadelphia, Pa.
1929-055	Jessee, Daniel Edward	D. April 30, 1970 Venice, Ca.
1969-085	Jestadt, Garry Arthur	9875 East Larkspur Drive/Scottsdale AZ 85260
1952-056	Jester, Virgil Milton	8130 Raleigh Place/Westminster CO 80030
1995-110	Jeter, Derek Sanderson	%Dorothy Jeter 2415 Cumberland Street Kalamzoo MI 49001

1969-086	Jeter, John	1590 Metrpolitan Ave #2f/Bronx NY 10462
1992-062	Jeter, Shawn Darrell	4287 Walford Street/Columbus OH 43224
1950-039	Jethroe, Samuel	2312 German Street/Erie PA 16503
1983-083	Jimenez, Alfonso 'Houston'	Old Add: Navojoa Sonora Mexico
1964-051	Jimenez, Felix Elvio 'Elvio'	Manzana A, Ed. 19 #1b "Cansino Segundo, Santo Domingo Dominican Rep."
1962-061	Jimenez, Manuel Emilio	24 Simon Bolivar San Pedro De Macoris Dominican Rep.
1988-071	Jiminez, German	Calle Justo Sierra #118 "Santiago, Ixcuintia/Mexico/"
1974-059	Jiminez, Juan Antonio	Calle 9,Casa 1n El Ensueno Santiago Dominican Rep.
1993-086	Jiminez, Miguel Anthony	128 Post Avenue/New York NY 10034
1963-062	John, Thomas Edward	6202 Seton House Lane/Charlotte NC 28277
1926-041	Johns, Augustus Francis	D. September 12, 1975 San Antonio, Tex.
1995-111	Johns, Douglas Alan	1131 Southwest 72nd Avenue/Plantation FL 33317
1915-076	Johns, William R. 'Pete'	D. August 9, 1964 Cleveland, O.
1941-052	Johnson, Adam Rankin 'Rank'	1308 1/2 Warren Avenue/Williamsport PA 17701
1914-101	Johnson, Adam Rankin, Sr.	D. July 2, 1972 Williamsport, Pa.
1964-052	Johnson, Alexander	7650 Grand River/Detroit MI 48206
1981-062	Johnson, Anthony Clair	Old Add: 4446 Janssen Dr Memphis TN 38128
1927-047	Johnson, Arthur Gilbert	D. June 7, 1982 Sarasota, Fla.
1940-041	Johnson, Arthur Henry	23 Hemlock Drive/Holden MA 1520
1959-042	Johnson, Benjamin Franklin	112 Locksley Dr/Greenwood SC 29646
1981-063	Johnson, Bobby Earl	Old Add: 3432 South Loop 12 Dallas TX 75224
1994-057	Johnson, Brian David	63 Castle Park Way/Oakland CA 94611
1994-058	Johnson, Charles Edward	16341 Northwest 17th Street/Pembroke Pines FL 33028
1946-050	Johnson, Chester Lillis	D. April 10, 1983 Seattle, Wash.
1969-087	Johnson, Clair Barth 'Bart'	904 Indian Boundary Drive/Westmont IL 60559
1972-053	Johnson, Clifford	Rural Route 1 Box 226j/Converse TX 78109
1953-039	Johnson, Clifford 'Connie'	1900 East 54th Street/Kansas City MO 64130
1994-059	Johnson, Dane Edward	Old Add: Miami FL
1952-057	Johnson, Darrell Dean	65 Willotta Drive/Suisun CA 94585
1965-052	Johnson, David Allen	1064 Howell Road/Winter Park FL 32789
1974-060	Johnson, David Charles	3202 Woodhollow Circle/Abilene TX 79606
1987-069	Johnson, David Wayne	7101 Mount Vista Road/Kingsville MD 21087
1960-052	Johnson, Deron Roger	D. April 23, 1992 Poway, Calif.
1947-047	Johnson, Donald Roy	1925 NE 19th Avenue #5a/Portland OR 97212
1943-066	Johnson, Donald Spore	580 Brooks/Laguna Beach CA 92651
1940-042	Johnson, Earl Douglas	D. December 3, 1994 Seattle, Wash.
1920-058	Johnson, Edwin Cyril	D. July 3, 1975 Morganfield, Ky.
1912-088	Johnson, Ellis Watt	D. January 14, 1965 Minneapolis, Minn.
1914-102	Johnson, Elmer Ellsworth	D. October 31, 1966 Hollywood, Fla.
1993-087	Johnson, Erik Anthony	PO Box 2989/San Ramon CA 94583
1912-089	Johnson, Ernest Rudolph	D. May 1, 1952 Monrovia, Calif.
1950-040	Johnson, Ernest Thorwald	500 Dorris Road/Alpharetta GA 30201
1966-049	Johnson, Frank Herbert	568 North Center St/Mesa AZ 85201
1922-063	Johnson, Frederick Edward	D. June 14, 1973 Kerrville, Tex.
1913-092	Johnson, George Howard 'Chief'	D. June 12, 1922 Des Moines, Ia.
1925-056	Johnson, Henry Ward	D. August 20, 1982 Bradenton, Fla.
1982-063	Johnson, Howard Michael 'Hojo'	PO Box 413/Lake Arrowhead CA 92352
1970-068	Johnson, James Brian	Old Add: Rr 3 Box 436e South Haven MI 49090
1997-084	Johnson, Jason Michael	3063 Featherstone Drive/Burlington KY 41005
1968-045	Johnson, Jerry Michael	Old Add: 7858 Cowles Mtn CT San Diego CA 92119
1944-064	Johnson, John Clifford	D. June 26, 1991 Iron Mountain, Mich.
1978-063	Johnson, John Henry	Old Add: 7578 Young Circle Reno NV 89511
1985-053	Johnson, Joseph Richard	14 Evergreen Road/Plainville MA 2762
1987-070	Johnson, Kenneth Lance 'Lance'	Old Add: 6004 Buford Drive Mobile AL 36608
1958-049	Johnson, Kenneth Travis	121 Myrtlewood Dr/Pineville LA 71360
1947-048	Johnson, Kenneth Wandersee	326 Brookfield/Wichita KS 67206
1974-061	Johnson, Lamar	4105 Sangre Trail/Arlington TX 76016
1972-054	Johnson, Larry Doby	Old Add: 3115 East 98th Street Cleveland OH 44104
1934-050	Johnson, Lloyd William	D. October 8, 1980 Stockton, Calif.
1960-053	Johnson, Louis Brown	7100 Latijera Blvd #I202/Los Angeles CA 90045
1995-112	Johnson, Mark Patrick	22 Sagamore Road #6a/Bronxville NY 10708
1997-085	Johnson, Michael Keith	Old Add: Edmonton Alberta
1974-062	Johnson, Michael Norton	Old Add: Rr 1/Faribault MN 55021
1911-082	Johnson, Otis L.	D. November 9, 1915 Johnson City, N. Y.
1920-136	Johnson, Paul Oscar	D. February 14, 1973 McAllen, Tex.
1988-072	Johnson, Randall David	6947 Coal Creek Pkwy SE#358/Newcastle WA 98059
1982-064	Johnson, Randall Glenn	2207 Sawgrass Glen/Escondido CA 92026
1980-061	Johnson, Randall Scott	Old Add: 40 West 64th Street Hialeah FL 33012
1958-050	Johnson, Richard Allan	808-B North Beeline/Payson AZ 85541
1969-088	Johnson, Robert Dale	120 Ashland Avenue/Medford OR 97504
1933-030	Johnson, Robert Lee	D. July 6, 1982 Tacoma, Wash.
1960-054	Johnson, Robert Wallace	1474 Barclay St/Saint Paul MN 55106
1982-065	Johnson, Ronald David	Old Add: 11371 Kathy Lane Garden Grove CA 92640
1986-071	Johnson, Rondin Allen	3620 Southwest 102 Nd/Seattle WA 98146
1929-056	Johnson, Roy Cleveland	D. September 10, 1973 Tacoma, Wash.
1982-066	Johnson, Roy Edward	Old Add: 902 North St. Louis Chicago IL 60651
1918-040	Johnson, Roy J. 'Hardrock'	D. January 10, 1986 Scottsdale, Ariz.
1916-045	Johnson, Russell Conwell 'Jing'	D. December 6, 1950 Pottstown, Pa.
1928-052	Johnson, Silas Kenneth	D. May 12, 1994 Sheridan, Ill.

1960-055	Johnson, Stanley Lucius	56 Morningside Dr/Daly City CA 94015
1922-064	Johnson, Sylvester	D. February 20, 1985 Portland, Ore.
1974-063	Johnson, Thomas Raymond	2200 Midland Grove #109/Saint Paul MN 55113
1973-067	Johnson, Timothy Evald	603 Crawford Street/Clay Center KS 67432
1944-065	Johnson, Victor Oscar	1515 Drury Avenue/Eau Claire WI 54701
1981-064	Johnson, Wallace Darnell	PO Box M618/Gary IN 46401
1983-084	Johnson, William Charles	Old Add: 1701 North Lincoln St Wilmington DE 19806
1991-090	Johnson, William Jeffrey 'Jeff'	424 North Hardee Street/Durham NC 27703
1916-046	Johnson, William Lawrence	D. November 5, 1950 Los Angeles, Calif.
1943-067	Johnson, William Russel	2903 Lake Forest Drive/Augusta GA 30909
1997-086	Johnson, William Russell 'Russ'	Old Add: Denham Springs LA 70726
1979-059	Johnston, Gregory Bernard	Old Add: 1406 Prospect Dr Pomona CA 91766
1911-083	Johnston, James Harle	D. February 14, 1967 Chattanooga, Tenn.
1991-091	Johnston, Joel Raymond	824 Sugarmans Court/West Chester PA 19382
1913-093	Johnston, John Thomas	D. March 7, 1940 San Diego, Calif.
1964-053	Johnston, Rex David	6712 Country Circle/Huntington Beach CA 92648
1924-055	Johnston, Wilfred Ivey 'Fred'	D. July 14, 1959 Tyler, Tex.
1993-088	Johnstone, John William	65 Bayberry Circle/Liverpool NY 13090
1966-050	Johnstone, John William 'Jay'	853 Chaperal/Pasadena CA 91107
1934-051	Joiner, Roy Merrill 'Pop'	D. December 26, 1989 Red Bluff, Calif.
1954-049	Jok, Stanley Edward	D. March 6, 1972 Buffalo, N. Y.
1930-038	Jolley, Smead Powell	D. November 17, 1991 Alameda, Calif.
1953-040	Jolly, David	D. May 27, 1963 Durham, N. C.
1983-085	Jones, Alfornia	19 E Street/Charleston MS 38921
1996-093	Jones, Andruw Rudolf	Old Add: Willemstad Curacao
1932-038	Jones, Arthur Lenox	D. November 25, 1980 Columbia, S. C.
1986-072	Jones, Barry Louis	411 South Morton Avenue/Centerville IN 47330
1991-092	Jones, Calvin Douglas	1212 San Eduardo Avenue/Henderson NV 89015
1916-047	Jones, Carroll Elmer 'Deacon'	D. December 28, 1952 Pittsburg, Kan.
1991-093	Jones, Christopher Carlos	Old Add: 12 Juniper Lane Liverpool NY 13088
1985-054	Jones, Christopher Dale	1821 Westward Ho Cir/El Cajon CA 92021
1967-055	Jones, Clarence Woodrow	140 Amherst Place Nw/Atlanta GA 30327
1963-063	Jones, Cleon Joseph	751 Edward St/Mobile AL 36610
1928-053	Jones, Coburn Dyas	D. June 3, 1969 Denver, Colo.
1941-053	Jones, Dale Eldon	D. November 8, 1980 Orlando, Fla.
1979-060	Jones, Darryl Lee	State Farm Ins., Box 5132/Conneaut Lake PA 16316
1996-094	Jones, Dax Xenos	600 Willow Court/Waukegan IL 60085
1926-042	Jones, Dectaur Poindexter 'Dick'	D. August 2, 1994 Burlingame, Calif.
1982-067	Jones, Douglas Reid	129 Navilla/Covina CA 91723
1945-050	Jones, Earl Leslie	D. January 14, 1989 Fresno, Calif.
1970-069	Jones, Gary Howell	475 S. Westridge Cir/Anaheim Hills CA 92807
1954-050	Jones, Gordon Bassett	D. April 25, 1994 Lodi, Calif.
1962-062	Jones, Grover William 'Deacon'	1015 Goldfinch/Sugarland TX 77478
1961-057	Jones, Harold Marion	4125 Palmyra Rd/Los Angeles CA 90008
1921-049	Jones, Howard	D. July 15, 1972 Jeannette, Pa.
1986-073	Jones, James Condia	3054 Newcastle Drive/Dallas TX 75220
1964-054	Jones, James Dalton 'Dalton'	13546 Kintyre Court/Mathews NC 28105
1941-054	Jones, James Murrell 'Jake'	PO Box 156/Epps/La 71237
1983-086	Jones, Jeffery Raymond	311 White Horse Pl/Haddon Heights NJ 8035
1980-062	Jones, Jeffrey Allen	51 Emmons Court/Wynadotte MI 48192
1923-069	Jones, Jesse F. 'Broadway'	D. September 7, 1977 Lewes, Del.
1924-056	Jones, John Joseph 'Binky'	D. May 13, 1961 St. Louis, Mo.
1919-044	Jones, John Paul	D. June 5, 1980 Ruston, La.
1923-070	Jones, John William	D. November 3, 1956 Baltimore, Md.
1991-094	Jones, Joseph Stacy 'Stacy'	Old Add: Rr 2 Box 349a Attalla AL 35954
1924-057	Jones, Kenneth Frederick	D. May 15, 1991 Hartford, Conn.
1993-089	Jones, Larry Wayne 'Chipper'	1001 Tullamore Place/Alpharetta GA 30022
1979-061	Jones, Lynn Morris	Rural Route 2 Box 161/Conneautville PA 16406
1961-058	Jones, Mack	184 Nathan Rd/Atlanta GA 30331
1980-063	Jones, Michael Carl	Old Add: 6182 Hillview Court Jacksonville FL 32210
1940-043	Jones, Morris E. 'Red'	D. June 30, 1975 Lincoln, Calif.
1975-057	Jones, Odell	17800 Lysander Dr/Carson CA 90746
1920-059	Jones, Percy Lee	D. March 18, 1979 Dallas, Texas
1973-068	Jones, Randall Leo	2638 Cranston Drive/Escondido CA 92025
1986-074	Jones, Ricky Miron	Old Add: 4071 Greenstone Court Decatur GA 30035
1993-090	Jones, Robert Joseph	PO Box 472/Kerman CA 93630
1997-087	Jones, Robert Mitchell	32 Elm Street/Rutherford NJ 7070
1974-064	Jones, Robert Oliver	413 South Zurich/Tulsa OK 74112
1917-036	Jones, Robert Walter	D. August 30, 1964 San Diego, Calif.
1988-073	Jones, Ronald Glen	2316 Chapman/Seguin TX 78155
1984-059	Jones, Ross A.	Old Add: 5371 West 12th Avenue Hialeah FL 33012
1976-042	Jones, Ruppert Sanderson	Old Add: 13647 Orchard Court Rd Poway CA 92064
1951-045	Jones, Samuel	D. November 5, 1971 Morgantown, W. Va.
1914-103	Jones, Samuel Pond 'Sad Sam'	D. July 6, 1966 Barnesville, O.
1946-051	Jones, Sheldon Leslie 'Available'	D. April 18, 1991 Greenville, N. C.
1960-056	Jones, Sherman Jarvis	3736 Weaver Drive/Kansas City KS 66104
1967-056	Jones, Steven Howell	8116 Kingsdale Dr/Knoxville TN 37919
1996-095	Jones, Terry Lee	Old Add: Birmingham AL 35201
1976-043	Jones, Thomas Frederick	Old Add: 4835 Manville Cir Jacksonville FL 32210

1977-075 ....Jones, Timothy Byron ....6204 Greeneyes Way/Orangevale CA 95662
1993-091 ....Jones, Todd Barton Givin ....4205 Mays Bend Drive/Pell City AL 35125
1986-075 ....Jones, Tracy Donald ....7050 Overton Way/Maineville OH 45039
1946-052 ....Jones, Vernal Leroy 'Nippy' ....D. October 3, 1995 Sacramento, Calif.
1911-084 ....Jones, William Dennis ....D. October 10, 1946 Boston, Mass.
1911-085 ....Jones, William Roderick 'Tex'..........................D. February 26, 1938 Wichita, Kan.
1988-074 ....Jones, William Timothy 'Tim' ....3530 Autumn Glen Drive/Valrico FL 33594
1947-049 ....Jones, Willie Edward ....D. October 18, 1983 Cincinnati, O.
1920-060 ....Jonnard, Clarence James 'Bubber' ....D. August 23, 1977 New York, N. Y.
1921-050 ....Jonnard, Claude Alfred ....D. August 27, 1959 Nashville, Tenn.
1936-043 ....Joost, Edwin David ....303 Belhaven Circle/Santa Rosa CA 95409
1927-048 ....Jordan, Baxter Byerly 'Buck' ....D. March 18, 1993 Salisbury, N. C.
1992-063 ....Jordan, Brian O'Neal ....1050 Bedford Gardens Drive/Alpharetta GA 30022
1933-031 ....Jordan, James William....................................D. December 4, 1957 Gastonia, N. C.
1995-113 ....Jordan, Kevin Wayne ....1018 Bowdoin Street/San Francisco CA 94124
1953-041 ....Jordan, Milton Mignot ....D. May 13, 1993 Ithaca, N. Y.
1951-046 ....Jordan, Niles Chapman ....1114 Metcalf/Sedro-Woolley WA 98284
1988-075 ....Jordan, Paul Scott Ricky ....11548 Sutters Mill Circle/Gold River CA 95670
1912-090 ....Jordan, Raymond Willis 'Rip' ....D. June 5, 1960 Meriden, Conn.
1995-114 ....Jordan, Ricardo ....Old Add: Delray Beach FL 33444
1988-076 ....Jordan, Scott Allan ....Old Add: 351 Hamilton Station Columbus GA 31909
1944-066 ....Jordan, Thomas Jefferson ....2909 South Wyoming/Roswell NM 88201
1929-057 ....Jorgens, Arndt Ludwig 'Art' ....D. March 1, 1980 Wilmette, Ill.
1935-053 ....Jorgens, Orville Edward ....D. January 11, 1992 Colorado Springs, Colo.
1937-056 ....Jorgensen, Carl ....119 Minnie Street/Santa Cruz CA 95062
1947-050 ....Jorgensen, John Donald 'Spider' ....8267 Kirkwood Court/Cucamonga CA 91730
1968-046 ....Jorgensen, Michael ....1820 Harbor Mill Drive/Fenton MO 63026
1989-065 ....Jorgensen, Terry Allen ....Old Add: 3364 Nautical Avenue Green Bay WI 54311
1988-077 ....Jose, Domingo Felix ....Calle 30 De Mayo #7a Ing. Ozama San Luis Dominican Rep.
1964-055 ....Joseph, Ricardo Emelindo ....D. September 8, 1979 Santiago, Dom .Rep.
1965-053 ....Josephson, Duane Charles ....D. January 30, 1997 New Hampton, Iowa
1969-089 ....Joshua, Von Everett ....1055 West 42nd Street/San Bernardino CA 92407
1916-048 ....Jourdan, Theodore Charles.............................D. September 23, 1961 New Orleans, La.
1962-063 ....Joyce, Michael Lewis ....1609 Whitman Ln/Wheaton IL 60187
1965-054 ....Joyce, Richard Edward ....101 Paragon Drive/Montvale NJ 7645
1939-058 ....Joyce, Robert Emmett ....D. December 10, 1981 San Francisco, Calif.
1986-076 ....Joyner, Wallace Keith ....Old Add: 25606 Timber Meadows CT Lees Summit MO 64063
1997-088 ....Judd, Michael Galen ....9805 Shadow Road/Lamesa CA 91941
1927-049 ....Judd, Ralph Wesley ....D. May 6, 1957 Lapeer, Mich.
1941-055 ....Judd, Thomas William Oscar 'Oscar' ....D. December 27, 1995 Ingersoll, Ontario
1991-095 ....Juden, Jeffrey Daniel ....85 Proctor Street/Salem MA 1970
1915-077 ....Judge, Joseph Ignatius ....D. March 11, 1963 Washington, D.C.
1940-044 ....Judnich, Walter Franklin ....D. July 12, 1971 Glendale, Calif.
1948-050 ....Judson, Howard Kolls ....239 Fairway Circle NE/Winter Haven FL 33881
1935-054 ....Judy, Lyle Leroy ....D. January 15, 1991 Ormond Beach, Fla.
1939-059 ....Juelich, John Walter ....D. December 25, 1970 St. Louis, Mo.
1940-045 ....Jumonville, George Benedict ....D. December 12, 1996 Mobile, Ala.
1937-057 ....Jungels, Kenneth Peter ....D. September 9, 1975 West Bend, Wis.
1982-068 ....Jurak, Edward James ....3650 South Walker Ave/San Pedro CA 90731
1965-055 ....Jurewicz, Michael Allen ....13804 Evregreen Court/Apple Valley MN 55124
1931-043 ....Jurges, William Frederick ....D. March 3, 1997 Clearwater, Fla.
1944-067 ....Jurisich, Alvin Joseph ....D. November 3, 1981 New Orleans, La.
1944-068 ....Just, Joseph Erwin..7708 West Kangaroo Lake Road/Baileys Harbor Wi/54202
1989-066 ....Justice, David Christopher ....Old Add: PO Box 56647 Atlanta GA 31156
1972-055 ....Jutze, Alfred Henry 'Skip' ....3395 Zephyr CT Wheat Ridge CO 80033
1914-104 ....Juul, Earl Herbert ....D. January 4, 1942 Chicago, Ill.
1911-086 ....Juul, Herbert Victor ....D. November 14, 1928 Chicago, Ill.
1959-043 ....Kaat, James Lee ....3212 SE Fairway West/Stuart FL 34997
1910-077 ....Kading, John Frederick ....D. June 2, 1964 Chicago, Ill.
1913-094 ....Kafora, Frank Jacob 'Jake' ....D. March 23, 1928 Chicago, Ill.
1922-065 ....Kahdot, Isaac Leonard 'Ike'.............................2218 Northwest 42nd/Oklahoma City OK 73112
1938-043 ....Kahle, Robert Wayne ....D. December 16, 1988 Inglewood, Calif.
1910-078 ....Kahler, George Rannels....................................D. February 14, 1924 Battle Creek, Mich.
1930-039 ....Kahn, Owen Earle 'Jack' ....D. January 17, 1981 Richmond, Va.
1980-064 ....Kainer, Donald Wayne ....1923 Sieber/Houston TX 77017
1911-087 ....Kaiser, Alfred Edward ....D. April 11, 1969 Cincinnati, O.
1955-062 ....Kaiser, Clyde Donald 'Don' ....2901 East 12th/Ada OK 74820
1985-055 ....Kaiser, Jeffrey Patrick ....21001 Sylvan Drive/Flat Rock MI 48134
1971-057 ....Kaiser, Robert Thomas 'Tom' ....Old Add: 1774 Terraza/Oceanside CA 92054
1914-105 ....Kaiserling, George ....D. March 2, 1918 Steubenville, O.
1937-058 ....Kalfass, William Philip ....D. September 8, 1968 Brooklyn, N. Y.
1940-046 ....Kalin, Frank Bruno ....D. January 12, 1975 Weirton, W. Va.
1953-042 ....Kaline, Albert William......................................945 Timberlake Drive/Bloomfield Hills MI 48302
1918-041 ....Kallio, Rudolph ....D. April 6, 1979 Newport, Ore.
1991-096 ....Kamieniecki, Scott Andrew ....1240 Woodnoll Drive/Flint MI 48507
1923-071 ....Kamm, William Edward 'Willie' ....D. December 21, 1988 Belmont, Calif.
1978-064 ....Kammeyer, Robert Lynn ....4711 Del Rio Rd/Sacramento CA 95822
1924-058 ....Kamp, Alphonse Francis ....D. February 25, 1955 Boston, Mass.
1934-052 ....Kampouris, Alexis William ....D. May 29, 1993 Sacramento, Calif.

1915-078	Kane, Francis Thomas	D. December 2, 1962 Brockton, Mass.
1925-057	Kane, John Francis	D. July 25, 1956 Chicago, Ill.
1938-044	Kane, Thomas Joseph	D. November 26, 1973 Chicago, Ill.
1962-064	Kanehl, Roderick Edwin	1550 Brockton #8/Los Angeles CA 90025
1914-106	Kantlehner, Ervine Lester	D. February 3, 1990 Santa Barbara, Calif.
1995-115	Karchner, Matthew Dean	% Marl.Karchner 211 Duval Street Berwick PA 18603
1936-044	Kardow, Paul Otto	D. April 27, 1968 San Antonio, Texas
1986-077	Karkovice, Ronald Joseph	2510 Oak Island Pointe Road/Orlando FL 32809
1943-068	Karl, Anton Andrew	D. April 8, 1989 Lajolla, Calif.
1995-116	Karl, Randall Scott 'Scott'	%John Karl 4503 Salisbury Drive Carlsbad CA 92008
1930-040	Karlon, William John 'Jack'	D. December 7, 1964 Ware, Mass.
1927-050	Karow, Martin Gregory	D. April 27, 1986 Bryan, Texas
1995-117	Karp, Ryan Jason	Old Add: Beverly Hills CA 90210
1946-053	Karpel, Herbert	D. January 24, 1995 San Diego, Calif.
1920-061	Karr, Benjamin Joyce	D. December 8, 1968 Memphis, Tenn.
1991-097	Karros, Eric Peter	6212 Madra Avenue/San Diego CA 92120
1993-092	Karsay, Stefan Andrew	12042 East Mission Lane Circle/Scottsdale AZ 85259
1915-079	Karst, John Gottlieb	D. May 21, 1976 Cape May Court House, N. J.
1997-089	Kashiwada, Takashi	Old Add: Tokyo Japan
1957-035	Kasko, Edward Michael	317 Burnwick Rd/Richmond VA 23227
1952-058	Katt, Raymond Frederick	711 Rudeloff Road/Seguin TX 78155
1944-069	Katz, Robert Clyde	D. December 14, 1962 St. Joseph, Mich.
1912-091	Kauff, Benjamin Michael	D. November 17, 1961 Columbus,O.
1914-107	Kauffman, Howard Richard 'Dick'	D. April 17, 1948 Lewisburg, Pa.
1921-051	Kaufman, Anthony Charles	D. June 4, 1982 Elgin, Ill.
1982-069	Kaufman, Curt Gerrard	24417 Brothers Avenue/Glenwood IA 51534
1914-108	Kavanagh, Charles Hugh	D. September 6, 1973 Reedsburg, Wis.
1914-109	Kavanagh, Leo Daniel	D. August 10, 1950 Chicago, Ill.
1914-110	Kavanagh, Martin Joseph	D. July 28, 1960 Taylor, Mich.
1948-051	Kazak, Edward Terrance	802 Newman Drive/Austin TX 78703
1953-043	Kazanski, Theodore Stanley	850 Stephenson Hwy #400/Troy MI 48083
1996-096	Keagle, Gregory Charles	Old Add: Horseheads NY 14845
1968-047	Kealey, Steven William	1080 1700 Avenue/Abilene KS 67410
1961-059	Keane, John Joseph	D. January 6, 1967 Houston, Tex.
1979-062	Kearney, Robert Henry	11611 Piccadilly Circle/San Antonio TX 78251
1920-064	Kearns, Edward Joseph	D. December 21, 1949 Trenton, N. J.
1942-054	Kearse, Edward Paul	D. July 15, 1968 Eureka, Calif.
1912-092	Keating, Raymond Herbert	D. December 28, 1963 Sacramento, Calif.
1913-095	Keating, Walter Francis 'Chick'	D. July 13, 1959 Philadelphia, Pa.
1981-065	Keatley, Gregory Steven	140 Rocky Ridge Court/Lexington SC 29022
1922-066	Keck, Frank Joseph 'Cactus'	D. February 6, 1981 St. Louis, Mo.
1985-056	Keedy, Charles Patrick 'Pat'	2429 Joseph Circle/Gardendale AL 35071
1917-037	Keefe, David Edwin	D. February 4, 1978 Kansas City, Mo.
1959-044	Keegan, Edward Charles	PO Box 764/Malaga NJ 8328
1953-044	Keegan, Robert Charles	101 Sandstone Drive/Rochester NY 14616
1944-070	Keely, Robert William	17117 Gulf Blvd #231/North Redington Beach FL 33708
1918-042	Keen, Howard Victor	D. December 10, 1976 Salisbury, Md.
1911-088	Keen, William Brown	D. July 16, 1947 South Point, O.
1920-062	Keenan, James William	D. June 5, 1980 Seminole, Fla.
1982-070	Keener, Jeffrey Bruce	114 Greenview Drive/Mount Carmel IL 62863
1976-044	Keener, Joseph Donald	44404 National Trails Hwy/Newberry Springs CA 92365
1925-058	Keesey, James Ward	D. September 5, 1951 Boise, Ida.
1980-065	Keeton, Rickey	3433 Stathem Avenue/Cincinnati OH 45211
1942-055	Kehn, Chester Laurence	D. April 5, 1984 San Diego, Calif.
1914-111	Keifer, Sherman Carl	D. February 19, 1927 Outwood, Ky.
1965-056	Kekich, Michael Dennis	5314 Canada Vista Place Nw/Albuquerque NM 87120
1911-089	Keliher, Maurice Michael	D. September 7, 1930 Washington, D.C.
1952-059	Kell, Everett Lee 'Skeeter'	3285 College Avenue/Conway AR 72033
1943-069	Kell, George Clyde	700 East 9th Street #13m/Little Rock AR 72202
1916-049	Kelleher, Albert Aloysius 'Duke'	D. September 28, 1947 Staten Island, N. Y.
1942-056	Kelleher, Francis Eugene	D. April 13, 1979 Stockton, Calif.
1935-055	Kelleher, Harold Joseph	D. August 27, 1989 Cape May Court House, N. J.
1912-093	Kelleher, John Patrick	D. August 21, 1960 Brighton, Mass.
1972-056	Kelleher, Michael Dennis 'Mick'	1451 Alamo Pintado Road/Solvang CA 93463
1939-060	Keller, Charles Ernest	D. May 23, 1990 Frederick, Md.
1949-040	Keller, Harold Kefauver	2018 245th Avenue SE/Issaquah WA 98027
1966-051	Keller, Ronald Lee	169 Surfsong Road/Johns Island SC 29455
1953-045	Kellert, Frank William	D. November 19, 1976 Oklahoma City, Okla.
1923-072	Kellett, Alfred Henry	D. July 14, 1960 New York, N. Y.
1934-053	Kellett, Donald Stafford 'Red'	D. November 5, 1970 Ft. Lauderdale, Ala.
1925-059	Kelley, Harry Leroy	D. March 23, 1958 Parkin, Ark.
1964-056	Kelley, Richard Anthony	D. December 12, 1991 Northridge, Calif.
1964-057	Kelley, Thomas Henry	Old Add: 7036 Northway Dr Nw Roanoke VA 24019
1919-045	Kelliher, Francis Mortimer	D. March 4, 1956 Somerville, Mass.
1948-052	Kellner, Alexander Raymond	D. May 3, 1996 Tucson, Ariz.
1952-060	Kellner, Walter Joseph	3737 North Tucson Blvd/Tucson AZ 85716
1914-112	Kellogg, William Dearstyne	D. December 12, 1971 Baltimore, Md.
1910-079	Kelly, Albert Michael 'Red'	D. January 29, 1961 Zephyrhills, Fla.
1986-078	Kelly, Bryan Keith	8012 Rose Avenue/Orlando FL 32810

1980-066	Kelly, Dale Patrick Pat	5176 San Simeon Dr/Santa Barbara CA 93111
1914-113	Kelly, Edward Leo	D. November 4, 1928 Red Lodge, Mont.
1915-080	Kelly, George Lange	D. October 13, 1984 Burlingame, Calif.
1967-057	Kelly, Harold Patrick 'Pat'	6748 Friendship Drive/Sarasota FL 34241
1914-114	Kelly, Herbert Barrett	D. May 18, 1973 Torrance, Calif.
1914-115	Kelly, James Robert	D. April 10, 1961 Kingsport, Tenn.
1975-058	Kelly, Jay Thomas 'Tom'	1643 Carrie Street/Maplewood MN 55119
1914-116	Kelly, Joseph Henry	D. August 16, 1977 St. Joseph, Mo.
1926-043	Kelly, Joseph James	D. November 24, 1967 Lynbrook, N. Y.
1926-044	Kelly, Michael J.	Old Add: 5853 Von Vessen Avenue Saint Louis Mo
1994-060	Kelly, Michael Raymond	9951 Kyle Street/Los Alamitos CA 90720
1991-098	Kelly, Patrick Franklin	1131 Howertown Road/Catasauqua PA 18032
1923-073	Kelly, Reynolds Joseph 'Ren'	D. August 24, 1963 Millbrae, Calif.
1987-071	Kelly, Robert Conrado	4 Ciudad Radial Juana Diaz/Panama
1951-047	Kelly, Robert Edward	9 Mohawk Drive/Nientic CT 6359
1969-090	Kelly, Van Howard	11 Beauregard Dr/Spencer NC 28159
1920-063	Kelly, William Henry	D. April 8, 1990 Syracuse, N. Y.
1910-080	Kelly, William Joseph	D. June 3, 1940 Detroit, Mich.
1964-058	Kelso, William Eugene	917 Monterrey Street/Bedford TX 76022
1937-059	Keltner, Kenneth Frederick	D. December 12, 1991 New Berlin, Wisc.
1954-051	Kemmerer, Russell Paul	6335 Colebrook Drive/Indianapolis IN 46220
1929-058	Kemner, Herman John 'Dutch'	D. January 16, 1988 Quincy, Ill.
1977-076	Kemp, Steve F.	Old Add: 12979 Claymont Court San Diego CA 92130
1969-091	Kendall, Fred Lynn	20304 Wayne Avenue/Torrance CA 90503
1996-097	Kendall, Jason Daniel	20304 Wayne Avenue/Torrance CA 90503
1961-060	Kenders, Albert Daniel George	8744 Matilija Ave/Van Nuys CA 91402
1928-054	Kenna, Edward Aloysius	D. August 21, 1972 San Francisco, Calif.
1970-070	Kennedy, James Earl	17035 Nw Brugger Road/Portland OR 97229
1962-065	Kennedy, John Edward	2 Rodney Road/West Peabody MA 1960
1957-036	Kennedy, John Irvin	D. April 27, 1998 Jacksonville, Fla.
1974-065	Kennedy, Junior Raymond	Old Add: 6001 Eucalyptus Bakersfield CA 93306
1993-093	Kennedy, Kevin Curtis	Old Add: 375 E. Los Colinas Blvd #278 Irving TX 75039
1934-054	Kennedy, Lloyd Vernon 'Vern'	D. January 28, 1993 Mendon, Mo.
1946-054	Kennedy, Montia Calvin	D. March 1, 1997 Midlothian, Va.
1916-050	Kennedy, Raymond Lincoln	D. January 18, 1969 Casselberry, Fla.
1939-061	Kennedy, Robert Daniel	5505 East McLellan Road #103/Mesa AZ 85205
1978-065	Kennedy, Terrence Edward	PO Box 30460/Mesa AZ 85275
1948-053	Kennedy, William Aulton	D. April 8, 1983 Seattle, Wash.
1942-057	Kennedy, William Gorman	D. August 20, 1995 Alexandria, Va.
1938-045	Kenney, Arthur Joseph	3 Timber Lane/North Reading MA 1864
1967-058	Kenney, Gerald	1980 Harrison/Beloit WI 53511
1992-064	Kent, Jeffrey Franklin	Old Add: 8872 Midbury Drive Huntington Beach CA 92646
1912-094	Kent, Maurice Allen	D. April 19, 1966 Iowa City, Ia.
1962-066	Kenworthy, Richard Lee	5119 Norway Drive/Indianapolis IN 46219
1912-095	Kenworthy, William Jennings 'Duke'	D. September 21, 1950 Eureka, Calif.
1968-048	Keough, Joseph William	Old Add: 2958 Liberty Dr Pleasanton CA 94566
1977-077	Keough, Matthew Lon	6281 Front South Road/Livermore CA 94550
1956-047	Keough, Richard Martin 'Marty'	32764 North 69th Street/Scottsdale AZ 85262
1984-060	Kepshire, Kurt David	141 Folino Drive/Bridgeport CT 6606
1985-057	Kerfeld, Charles Patrick	5225 Braeburn/Bellaire TX 77401
1950-041	Keriazakos, Constantine Nicholas 'Gus'	D. May 4, 1996 Hilton Head, S. C.
1939-062	Kerksieck, Wayman William 'Bill'	D. March 11, 1970 Little Rock, Ark.
1915-081	Kerlin, Orie Milton	D. October 29, 1974 Shreveport, La.
1974-066	Kern, James Lester	6009 Amberwood CT Arlington TX 76016
1962-067	Kern, William George	625 Green St/Allentown PA 18102
1965-057	Kernek, George Boyd	7 Timberlake Drive/Purcell OK 73080
1945-051	Kerns, Russell Eldon	22000 Lawrence Road/Fiddletown CA 95629
1923-074	Kerr, John Francis	D. October 19, 1993 Long Beach, Calif.
1914-117	Kerr, John Jonas 'Doc'	D. June 9, 1937 Baltimore, Md.
1943-070	Kerr, John Joseph 'Buddy'	341 Grove Street/Oradell NJ 7649
1925-060	Kerr, John Melville 'Mel'	D. August 9, 1980 Vero Beach, Fla.
1919-046	Kerr, Richard Henry	D. May 4, 1963 Houston, Tex.
1976-045	Kerrigan, Joseph Thomas	1503 Liberty Court/North Wales PA 19454
1964-059	Kessinger, Donald Eulon	3705 Lyles Drive/Oxford MS 38655
1993-094	Kessinger, Robert Keith 'Keith'	3705 Lyles Drive/Oxford MS 38655
1968-049	Kester, Richard Lee	Box 623/Gardnerville NV 89410
1922-067	Ketchum, August Franklin 'Gus'	D. September 10, 1980 Oklahoma City, Okla.
1912-096	Ketter, Philip	D. April 9, 1965 St. Louis, Mo.
1914-118	Keupper, Henry J.	D. August 14, 1960 Marion, Ill.
1984-061	Key, James Edward	2217 Chapel Valley Lane/Timonium MD 21093
1995-118	Keyser, Brian Lee	Old Add: 250 Park Lake Cir Walnut Creek CA 94596
1985-058	Khalifa, Sam	8825 East Second Place/Tucson AZ 85710
1925-061	Kibbie, Horace Kent 'Hod'	D. October 19, 1975 Fort Worth, Tex.
1912-097	Kibble, John Westly	D. December 13, 1969 Roundup, Mont.
1990-077	Kiecker, Dana Ervin	4104 Prairie Ridge Road/Saint Paul MN 55123
1920-065	Kiefer, Joseph William	D. July 5, 1975 Utica, N. Y.
1993-095	Kiefer, Mark Andrew	11822 Old Fashion/Garden Grove CA 92640
1984-062	Kiefer, Steven George	11822 Old Fashion/Garden Grove CA 92640
1991-099	Kiely, John Francis	84 Brown Street/Brockton MA 2401

1951-048 ....Kiely, Leo Patrick ....D. January 18, 1984 Glen Ridge, N. J.
1996-098 ....Kieschnick, Michael Brooks 'Brooks' ....Old Add: Caldwell TX 77836
1917-038 ....Kilduff, Peter John ....D. February 14, 1930 Pittsburg, Kan.
1991-100 ....Kile, Darryl Andrew ....3302 Oakland Drive/Sugar Land TX 77479
1987-072 ....Kilgus, Paul Nelson ....2102 Smallhouse Road/Bowling Green KY 42101
1914-119 ....Kilhullen, Joseph Isadore 'Pat' ....D. November 2, 1922 Oakland, Calif.
1969-092 ....Kilkenny, Michael David ....274 Holland Street/West Bradford Ontario Canada
1954-052 ....Killebrew, Harmon Clayton ....PO Box 14550/Scottsdale AZ 85267
1959-045 ....Killeen, Evans Henry ....123 Main St/Westhampton NY 11978
1911-090 ....Killilay, John William ....D. October 21, 1968 Tulsa, Okla.
1937-060 ....Kimball, Newell W. 'Newt' ....1425 Griffith Avenue/Las Vegas NV 89104
1936-045 ....Kimberlin, Harry Lydle ....1100 Davis Street #102/Poplar Bluff MO 63901
1945-052 ....Kimble, Richard Louis ....3733 Larchmont Parkway/Toledo OH 43613
1920-066 ....Kime, Harold Lee ....D. May 16, 1939 Columbus, O.
1976-046 ....Kimm, Bruce Edward ....3168 121st Street/Amana IA 52203
1919-047 ....Kimmick, Walter Lyons ....D. July 14, 1989 Boswell, Pa.
1929-059 ....Kimsey, Clyde Elias 'Chad' ....D. December 3, 1942 Pryor, Okla.
1956-048 ....Kindall, Gerald Donald ....Athletic Dept. Univ Of Arizona Tucson AZ 85721
1946-055 ....Kinder, Ellis Raymond ....D. October 16, 1968 Jackson, Tenn.
1946-056 ....Kiner, Ralph McPherran ....48 271 Silver Spur Trail/Palm Desert CA 92260
1954-053 ....King, Charles Gilbert 'Chick' ....Rural Route 1 Box 68b/Paris TN 38242
1944-071 ....King, Clyde Edward ....103 Stratford Road/Goldsboro/Nc 27530
1997-090 ....King, Curtis Albert ....1 Brooks Lane/Plymouth Meeting PA 19462
1916-051 ....King, Edward Lee ....D. September 16, 1967 Shinnstown, W. Va.
1916-052 ....King, Edward Lee ....D. September 7, 1938 Chelsea, Mass.
1986-079 ....King, Eric Steven ....1063 Stanford Drive/Simi Valley CA 93065
1967-059 ....King, Harold ....7231 Jonquil Road/Orlando FL 32818
1955-063 ....King, James Hubert ....720 Stokenbury Road/Elkins AR 72727
1989-067 ....King, Jeffrey Wayne ....391 Skyline Drive/Hamilton MT 59840
1993-096 ....King, Kevin Ray ....Rural Route 1 Box 107/Braggs OK 74423
1935-056 ....King, Lynn Paul ....D. May 11, 1972 Atlantic, Ia.
1954-054 ....King, Nelson Joseph ....126 James Pl/Pittsburgh PA 15228
1932-039 ....Kingdon, Wescott William ....D. April 19, 1975 Capistrano, Calif.
1986-080 ....Kingery, Michael Scott ....PO Box 358/Atwater MN 56209
1979-063 ....Kingman, Brian Paul ....Old Add: 11tokeneke Trail Darien CT 06820
1971-058 ....Kingman, David Arthur ....PO Box 11771/Zephyr Cove NV 89448
1914-120 ....Kingman, Henry Lees ....D. December 27, 1982 Oakland, Calif.
1996-099 ....Kingsale, Eugene Humphrey..........................Old Add: Aruba Netherland Antilles
1978-066 ....Kinney, Dennis Paul ....PO Box 304/Schnecksville PA 18078
1918-043 ....Kinney, Walter William ....D. July 1, 1971 Escondido, Calif.
1980-067 ....Kinnunen, Michael John ....5818 McKinley Place North/Seattle WA 98103
1919-048 ....Kinsella, Robert Francis ....D. December 30, 1951 Los Angeles, Calif.
1989-068 ....Kinzer, Matthew Roy ....Old Add: 5879 North 400 West Uniondale IN 46791
1934-055 ....Kinzy, Henry Hensel 'Harry' ....3721 Arroyo Road/Fort Worth TX 76109
1957-037 ....Kipp, Fred Leo ....%Klc 6613 West 126th Terrace Overland Park KS 66209
1985-059 ....Kipper, Robert Wayne ....117 Tuscany Way/Greer SC 29650
1953-046 ....Kipper, Thornton John..................................8780 East McKellops #340/Scottsdale AZ 85257
1914-121 ....Kippert, Edward August ....D. June 3, 1960 Detroit, Mich.
1969-093 ....Kirby, Clayton Laws ....D. October 11, 1991 Arlington, Va.
1949-041 ....Kirby, James Herschel ....729 Dover Road/Nashville TN 37211
1912-098 ....Kirby, Larue ....D. June 10, 1961 Lansing, Mich.
1991-101 ....Kirby, Wayne Leonard ....113 Kirby Lane/Yorktown VA 23693
1919-049 ....Kircher, Michael Andrew ....D. June 26, 1972 Rochester, N. Y.
1947-051 ....Kirk, Thomas Daniel ....D. August 1, 1974 Philadelphia, Pa.
1961-061 ....Kirk, William Parthemore ....2255 North Point Drive/York PA 17402
1910-081 ....Kirke, Judson Fabian 'Jay' ....D. August 31, 1968 New Orleans, La.
1958-051 ....Kirkland, Willie Charles ....Old Add: 17155 Santa Rosa/Detroit MI 48221
1962-068 ....Kirkpatrick, Edgar Leon ....24791 Via Larga/Laguna Niguel CA 92677
1912-099 ....Kirkpatrick, Enos Claire ....D. April 14, 1964 Pittsburgh, Pa.
1974-067 ....Kirkwood, Donald Paul ....455 West Elmwood/Clawson MI 48017
1950-042 ....Kirrene, Joseph John..................................2557 Kilpatrick Court/San Ramon CA 94583
1910-082 ....Kirsch, Harry Louis ....D. December 25, 1925 Pittsburgh, Pa.
1991-102 ....Kiser, Garland Routhard ....267 Carr Drive/Blountville TN 37617
1945-053 ....Kish, Ernest Alexander ....D. December 21, 1993 Kirtland, Ohio
1971-059 ....Kison, Bruce Eugene ....1403 Riverview Circle/Bradenton FL 33529
1954-055 ....Kitsos, Christopher Anestos ....1219 Anchor Drive/Mobile AL 36693
1982-071 ....Kittle, Ronald Dale ....728 North Old Suman Road/Valparaiso IN 46383
1934-056 ....Klaerner, Hugo Emil ....D. January 3, 1982 Fredericksburg, Texas
1966-052 ....Klages, Fred Anthony ....Old Add: 261 Berry Street Baden PA 15005
1964-060 ....Klaus, Robert Francis ....10661 Gabacho Dr/San Diego CA 92124
1952-061 ....Klaus, William Joseph ....PO Box 662/Valle Crucis NC 28691
1985-060 ....Klawitter, Thomas Carl ....3220 Dover Court/Janesville WI 53546
1925-062 ....Klee, Ollie Chester ....D. February 9, 1977 Toledo, O.
1928-055 ....Klein, Charles Herbert ....D. March 28, 1958 Indianapolis, Ind.
1944-072 ....Klein, Harold John ....D. December 10, 1957 St. Louis, Mo.
1943-071 ....Klein, Louis Frank ....D. June 20, 1976 Metairie, La.
1934-057 ....Kleinhans, Theodore Otto ....D. July 24, 1985 Redington Beach, Fla.
1935-057 ....Kleinke, Norbert George ....D. March 16, 1950 Marin, Calif.
1911-091 ....Klepfer, Edward Lloyd ....D. August 9, 1950 Tulsa, Okla.

1992-065 ....Klesko, Ryan Anthony ....9219 Nickels Blvd/Boynton Beach FL 33436
1976-047 ....Kleven, Jay Allen ....118 Via Bolsa/San Lorenzo CA 94580
1943-072 ....Klieman, Edward Frederick ....D. November 15, 1979 Homos Assa, Fla.
1958-052 ....Klimchock, Louis Stephen ....8876 South Myrtle Avenue/Tempe AZ 85284
1969-094 ....Klimkowski, Ronald Bernardo ....791 Edgewood Dr/Westbury NY 11590
1955-064 ....Kline, John Robert 'Bobby' ....6656 31st Way/Saint Petersburg FL 33712
1930-041 ....Kline, Robert George ....D. March 16, 1987 Westerville, O.
1952-062 ....Kline, Ronald Lee ....Main Street/Po/Box 155/Callery PA 16024
1970-071 ....Kline, Steven Jack ....Box 429/Chelan WA 98816
1997-091 ....Kline, Steven James ....Old Add: Winfield PA 17889
1994-061 ....Klingenbeck, Scott Edward ....6230 Kingora Court/Cincinnati OH 45233
1927-051 ....Klinger, Joseph John ....D. July 31, 1960 Little Rock, Ark.
1938-046 ....Klinger, Robert Harold ....D. August 19, 1977 Villa Ridge, Mo.
1987-073 ....Klink, Joseph Charles ....652 Pelican Bay Drive/Daytona Beach FL 32119
1950-043 ....Klippstein, John Calvin ....1176 Aberdeen Road/Palatine IL 60067
1944-073 ....Klopp, Stanley Harold ....D. March 11, 1980 Robesonia, Pa.
1931-044 ....Kloza, John Clarence 'Nap' ....D. June 11, 1962 Milwaukee, Wis.
1921-052 ....Klugmann, Josie ....D. July 18, 1951 Moberly, Mo.
1934-058 ....Klumpp, Elmer Edward ....D. October 18, 1996 Menomonee Falls, Wisc.
1947-052 ....Kluszewski, Theodore Bernard ....D. March 29, 1988 Cincinnati, O.
1976-048 ....Klutts, Gene Ellis 'Mickey' ....2575 East 19th Street #115/Signal Hill CA 90806
1942-058 ....Kluttz, Clyde Franklin ....D. May 12, 1979 Salisbury, N. C.
1993-097 ....Kmak, Joseph Robert ....1021 Hatteras/Foster City CA 94404
1990-078 ....Knackert, Brent Bradley ....16802 Leafwood Circle/Huntington Beach CA 92647
1975-059 ....Knapp, Robert Christian 'Chris' ....1415 Castle CT St Joseph MI 49085
1910-083 ....Knaupp, Henry Antone 'Cotton' ....D. July 6, 1967 New Orleans, La.
1926-045 ....Kneisch, Rudolph Frank ....D. April 6, 1965 Baltimore, Md.
1976-049 ....Knepper, Robert Wesley ....627 Forest View Way/Monument CO 80132
1945-054 ....Knerr, Wallace Luther 'Lou'. ....D. March 23, 1980 Lancaster, P. A.
1979-064 ....Knicely, Alan Lee ....Box 433/Dayton VA 22821
1947-053 ....Knickerbocker, Austin Jay ....D. February 18, 1997 Clinton Corners, N. Y.
1933-032 ....Knickerbocker, William Hart ....D. September 8, 1963 Sebastopol, Calif.
1974-068 ....Knight, Charles Ray 'Ray' ....2308 Tara Drive/Albany GA 31707
1922-068 ....Knight, Elma Russell 'Jack'. ....D. July 30, 1976 San Antonio, Tex.
1912-100 ....Knisely, Peter C. ....D. July 1, 1948 Brownsville,Pa.
1991-103 ....Knoblauch, Edward Charles Chuck ....101 Westcott #1105/Houston TX 77007
1920-067 ....Knode, Kenneth Thomson 'Mike' ....D. December 20, 1980 South Bend, Ind.
1923-075 ....Knode, Robert Troxell 'Ray' ....D. April 13, 1982 Battle Creek, Mich.
1964-061 ....Knoop, Robert Frank ....2543 East Mountain Sky Avenue/Phoenix AZ 85044
1991-104 ....Knorr, Randy Duane ....4902 Fortim/Baldwin Park CA 91706
1932-040 ....Knothe, George Bertram ....D. July 3, 1981 Dover, N. J.
1932-041 ....Knothe, Wilfred Edgar 'Fritz' ....D. March 22, 1963 Passaic, N. J.
1933-033 ....Knott, John Henry ....D. October 13, 1981 Brownwood, Texas
1965-058 ....Knowles, Darold Duane ....2322 Dora Drive/Clearwater FL 33765
1915-082 ....Knowlson, Thomas Herbert....................................D. April 11, 1943 Miami Shores, Fla.
1920-068 ....Knowlton, William Young ....D. February 25, 1944 Philadelphia, Pa.
1924-060 ....Knox, Clifford Hiram 'Bud' ....D. September 24, 1965 Oskaloosa, Ia.
1972-057 ....Knox, John Clinton ....Old Add: 34 Pell Mell Drive/Bethel CT 06850
1992-066 ....Knudsen, Kurt David ....5155 Patti Jo Drive/Carmichael CA 95608
1985-061 ....Knudson, Mark Richard ....881 West 100th Ave/Northglenn CO 80221
1953-047 ....Koback, Nicholas Nicholia ....71 Hopmeadow Street #9a1/Simsbury CT 6070
1973-069 ....Kobel, Kevin Richard ....Eddy Rd/Colden NY 14033
1963-064 ....Koch, Alan Goodman ....1517 Ridgeland Road East/Mobile AL 36695
1944-074 ....Koch, Barnett ....D. June 6, 1987 Tacoma, Wash.
1912-101 ....Kocher, Bradley Wilson ....D. January 13, 1965 White Haven, Pa.
1946-057 ....Koecher, Richard Finley ....11101 Quail Village Way #104/Naples FL 34119
1970-072 ....Koegel, Peter John ....33 Barclay Street #9/Saugerties NY 12477
1925-063 ....Koehler, Horace Levering 'Pop' ....D. December 8, 1986 Tacoma, Wash.
1993-098 ....Koelling, Brian Wayne ....522 Laurel Wood Drive/Cleves OH 45002
1932-042 ....Koenecke, Leonard George....................................D. September 17, 1935 Toronto, Ont.
1925-064 ....Koenig, Mark Anthony ....D. April 22, 1993 Willows, Calif.
1919-050 ....Koenigsmark, Willis Thomas ....D. July 1, 1972 Waterloo, Ill.
1910-084 ....Koestner, Elmer Joseph ....D. October 27, 1959 Fairbury, Ill.
1937-061 ....Kohlman, Joseph James ....D. March 16, 1974 Philadelphia, Pa.
1948-054 ....Kokos, Richard Jerome ....D. April 9, 1986 Chicago, Ill.
1960-057 ....Kolb, Gary Alan ....Old Add: 164 Circle Drive Cross Lane WV 25356
1940-047 ....Kolloway, Donald Martin ....D. June 30, 1994 Blue Island, Ill.
1921-053 ....Kolp, Raymond Carl ....D. July 29, 1967 New Orleans, La.
1915-083 ....Kolseth, Karl Dickey ....D. May 3, 1956 Cumberland, Md.
1962-069 ....Kolstad, Harold Everette ....15149 Bel Escou Dr/San Jose CA 95124
1913-096 ....Kommers, Fred Raymond ....D. June 14, 1943 Chicago, Ill.
1983-087 ....Komminsk, Brad Lynn ....688 Fallside Lane/Westerville OH 43081
1997-092 ....Konerko, Paul Henry ....12 Leading Street/Johnston RI 2919
1973-070 ....Konieczny, Douglas James ....9503 Dundalk/Spring TX 77379
1948-055 ....Konikowski, Alexander James ....D. September 28, 1997 Seymour, Conn.
1942-059 ....Konopka, Bruce Bruno ....D. September 27, 1996 Denver, Colo.
1944-075 ....Konstanty, Casimir James 'Jim' ....D. June 11, 1976 Oneonta, N. Y.
1995-119 ....Konuszewski, Dennis John ....3054 Yorkshire Drive/Bay City MI 48706
1915-084 ....Koob, Ernest Gerald...D. November 12, 1941 Lemay, Mo.

1962-070 ....**Koonce, Calvin Lee** ....D. October 28, 1993 Winston-Salem, N. C.
1967-060 ....**Koosman, Jerry Martin** ....4101 Pelicans Nest Drive/Bonita Springs FL 33923
1966-053 ....**Kopacz, George Felix**.................................14150 Somerset Court/Orland Park IL 60462
1921-054 ....**Kopf, Walter Henry**.....................................D. April 30, 1979 Cincinnati, O.
1913-097 ....**Kopf, William Lorenz 'Larry'** ....D. October 15, 1986 Anderson Twp., Hamilton Co., Ohio
1961-062 ....**Koplitz, Howard Dean** ....623 Boyd St/Oshkosh WI 54901
1915-085 ....**Kopp, Merlin Henry** ....D. May 7, 1960 Sacramento, Calif.
1958-053 ....**Koppe, Joseph** ....7887 Beatrice St/Westland MI 48185
1923-076 ....**Kopshaw, George Karl** ....D. December 26, 1934 Lynchburg, Va.
1954-056 ....**Korcheck, Stephen Joseph** ....6424 Fox Hunt Lane/Bradenton FL 34202
1915-086 ....**Kores, Arthur Emil** ....D. March 26, 1974 Milwaukee, Wis.
1966-054 ....**Korince, George Eugene** ....Old Add: 83 Shoreline Dr St. Catherines Ont. L2n 5n7
1965-059 ....**Kosco, Andrew John** ....9329 New Springfield Road/Poland OH 44514
1952-063 ....**Koshorek, Clement John** ....D. September 8, 1991 Royal Oak, Mich.
1951-049 ....**Koski, William John** ....1120 Valencia Drive/Modesto CA 95350
1941-056 ....**Koslo, George Bernard 'Dave'** ....D. December 1, 1975 Menasha, Wis.
1992-067 ....**Koslofski, Kevin Craig** ....521 East Washington/Maroa IL 61756
1944-076 ....**Kosman, Michael Thomas** ....2110 South 6th/Lafayette IN 47904
1931-045 ....**Koster, Frederick Charles** ....D. April 24, 1979 Saint Matthews, Ky.
1962-071 ....**Kostro, Frank Jerry** ....36 Steele Street #20/Denver CO 80206
1997-093 ....**Kotsay, Mark Steven** ....Old Add: Pembroke Pines FL 33084
1955-065 ....**Koufax, Sanford Sandy** ....PO Box 8306/Vero Beach FL 32963
1925-065 ....**Koupal, Louis Laddie** ....D. December 8, 1961 San Gabriel, Calif.
1932-043 ....**Kowalik, Fabian Lorenz** ....D. August 14, 1954 Karnes City, Tex.
1995-120 ....**Kowitz, Brian Mark** ....% J. P./Kowitz 13224 Longnecker Road Glyndon MD 21071
1938-047 ....**Koy, Ernest Anyz** ....1047 South Oak/Bellville TX 77418
1948-056 ....**Kozar, Albert Kenneth** ....169 Atlantis Blvd #302/Lake Worth FL 33462
1939-063 ....**Kracher, Joseph Peter** ....D. December 25, 1981 San Angelo, Texas
1989-069 ....**Kraemer, Joseph Wayne** ....3212 NE 401st Circle/La Center WA 98629
1914-122 ....**Kraft, Clarence Otto** ....D. March 26, 1958 Fort Worth, Tex.
1937-062 ....**Krakauskas, Joseph Victor Lawrence** ....D. December 8, 1960 Hamilton, Ont.
1959-046 ....**Kralick, John Francis** ....Old Add: 378 West Beluga Ave/Soldotna AK 99669
1953-048 ....**Kraly, Steven Charles** ....12 Davis Avenue/Johnson City NY 13790
1939-064 ....**Kramer, John Henry 'Jack'** ....D. May 18, 1995 Metairie, La.
1988-078 ....**Kramer, Randall John** ....Old Add: 239 Castillon Way San Jose CA 95119
1991-105 ....**Kramer, Thomas Joseph** ....10665 Hamilton Avenue/Cincinnati OH 45231
1962-072 ....**Kranepool, Edward Emil** ....% Monica Kranepool 177 High Pond Drive Jericho NY 11753
1911-092 ....**Krapp, Eugene H.** ....D. April 13, 1923 Detroit, Mich.
1943-073 ....**Kraus, John William 'Tex'** ....D. January 2, 1976 San Antonio, Tex.
1961-063 ....**Krausse, Lewis Bernard** ....12811 NE 186th/Holt MO 64048
1931-046 ....**Krausse, Lewis Bernard, Sr.** ....D. September 6, 1988 Sarasota, Fla.
1975-060 ....**Kravec, Kenneth Peter** ....6752 Taeda Drive/Sarasota FL 34241
1956-049 ....**Kravitz, Daniel** ....Rural Route 1 Box 1119/Dushore PA 18614
1984-063 ....**Krawczyk, Raymond Allen** ....21906 Raintree Lane/Lake Forest CA 92630
1931-047 ....**Kreevich, Michael Andreas** ....D. April 25, 1994 Pana, Ill.
1943-074 ....**Kreitner, Albert Joseph 'Mickey'** ....6666 Brookmont Terrace #1209/Nashville TN 37205
1911-093 ....**Kreitz, Ralph Wesley** ....D. July 20, 1941 Portland, Ore.
1924-061 ....**Kremer, Remy Peter 'Ray'** ....D. February 8, 1965 Pinole, Calif.
1990-079 ....**Kremers, James Edward** ....9525 South 95th East Avenue/Tulsa OK 74133
1973-071 ....**Kremmel, James Louis** ....W524 18th Avenue/Spokane WA 99203
1979-065 ....**Krenchicki, Wayne Richard** ....2524 Hawthorne Drive/Beloit WI 53511
1947-054 ....**Kress, Charles Steven** ....3102 Duncan/Saint Joseph MO 64507
1927-052 ....**Kress, Ralph 'Red'** ....D. November 29, 1962 Los Angeles, Calif.
1946-058 ....**Kretlow, Louis Henry** ....3302 Goldfinch/Enid OK 73701
1975-061 ....**Kreuger, Richard Allen** ....Old Add: 1143 Powers Nw Grand Rapids MI 49504
1988-079 ....**Kreuter, Chad Michael** ....Old Add: 32106 Harbor View Westlake Village CA 91361
1962-073 ....**Kreutzer, Franklin James** ....921 Windwhisper Lane/Annapolis MD 21403
1911-094 ....**Krichell, Paul Bernard** ....D. June 4, 1957 New York, N.Y.
1949-042 ....**Krieger, Kurt Ferdinand** ....D. August 16, 1970 St. Louis, Mo.
1937-063 ....**Krist, Howard Wilbur** ....D. April 23, 1989 Delavan, N.Y.
1995-121 ....**Krivda, Rick Michael** ....112 Dolores Drive/Irwin PA 15642
1978-067 ....**Krol, John Thomas Jack** ....D. May 30, 1994 Winston-Salem, N. C.
1964-062 ....**Kroll, Gary Melvin** ....9038 East 40th St/Tulsa OK 74145
1935-058 ....**Kroner, John Harold**...................................D. August 26, 1968 St. Louis, Mo.
1995-122 ....**Kroon, Marc Jason** ....Old Add: Phoenix Az
1960-058 ....**Krsnich, Michael** ....2453 Stonegate Drive/West Palm Beach FL 33414
1949-043 ....**Krsnich, Rocco Peter** ....5701 West 92nd Street/Overland Park KS 66207
1913-098 ....**Krueger, Ernest George** ....D. April 22, 1976 Waukegan, Ill.
1983-088 ....**Krueger, William Culp** ....1255 Michelbrook Lane/McMinnville OR 97128
1965-060 ....**Krug, Everett Ben 'Chris'** ....PO Box 1350/Wildomar CA 92595
1981-066 ....**Krug, Gary Eugene** ....1327 Baylor Dr/Colorado Springs CO 80909
1912-102 ....**Krug, Martin John** ....D. June 27, 1966 Glendale, Calif.
1986-081 ....**Kruk, John Martin** ....Rural Route 4 Box 31/Keyser WV 26726
1976-050 ....**Krukow, Michael Edward** ....6094 Madbury Court/San Luis Obispo CA 93401
1949-044 ....**Kryhoski, Richard David** ....18855 Warwick Road/Beverly Hills MI 48025
1957-038 ....**Kubek, Anthony Christopher**.......................N8323 North Shore Road/Menasha WI 54952
1967-061 ....**Kubiak, Theodore Roger** ....16443 Mount Shadow Lane/Ramona CA 92065
1997-094 ....**Kubinski, Timothy Mark**.............................Old Add: San Luis Obispo CA 93401
1961-064 ....**Kubiszyn, Jack Joseph** ....2306 University Blvd/Tuscaloosa AL 35401

1980-068 ....Kubski, Gilbert Thomas ....4542 Scenario Drive/Huntington Beach CA 92649
1950-044 ....Kucab, John Albert ....D. May 26, 1977 Youngstown, O.
1974-069 ....Kucek, John Andrew Charles ....1219 Warren Rd/Newton Falls OH 44444
1955-066 ....Kucks, John Charles ....15 Oakland St/Hillsdale NJ 7642
1949-045 ....Kuczek, Stanislaw Leo 'Steve' ....769 Sacandaga Road/Scotia NY 12302
1943-075 ....Kuczynski, Bernard Carl 'Barney'..............D. January 19, 1997 Allentown, Pa.
1976-051 ....Kuehl, Karl Otto ....PO Box 17017/Fountain Hill AZ 85269
1952-064 ....Kuenn, Harvey Edward ....D. February 18, 1988 Peoria, Ariz.
1977-078 ....Kuhaulua, Fred Mahele ....89-203 Nalakahiki Pl/Nanakuli HI 96792
1930-042 ....Kuhel, Joseph Anthony ....D. February 26, 1984 Kansas City, Kan.
1924-062 ....Kuhn, Bernard Daniel 'Bub'........................D. November 20, 1956 Lansing, Mich.
1955-067 ....Kuhn, Kenneth Harold ....69 Skyline Terrace/Mill Valley CA 94941
1912-103 ....Kuhn, Walter Charles ....D. June 14, 1935 Fresno, Calif.
1974-070 ....Kuiper, Duane Eugene ....13216 Washington Avenue/Sturtevant WI 53050
1955-068 ....Kume, John Mike ....Rr2 Woodard Rd/Andover OH 44003
1984-064 ....Kunkel, Jeffrey William ....Old Add: 1 Nautilus Dr Leonardo NJ 07737
1961-065 ....Kunkel, William Gustave James ....D. May 4, 1985 Red Bank, N. J.
1979-066 ....Kuntz, Russell Jay 'Rusty'..........................402 Berwick Way/Melbourne FL 32940
1923-077 ....Kunz, Earl Dewey ....D. April 14, 1963 Sacramento, Calif.
1975-062 ....Kurosaki, Ryan Yoshitomo ....1324 High View Pl/Honolulu HI 96816
1941-057 ....Kurowski, George John 'Whitey' ....310 Springside Drive/Shillington PA 19607
1968-050 ....Kurtz, Harold James.....................................103 Green Street/Centerville MD 21617
1941-058 ....Kush, Emil Benedict......................................D. November 26, 1969 River Grove, Ill.
1973-072 ....Kusick, Craig Robert ....14228 Garrett Avenue/Apple Valley MN 55124
1970-073 ....Kusnyer, Arthur William ....6598 Taeda Drive/Sarasota FL 34241
1986-082 ....Kutcher, Randy Scott ....35918 42nd Street East/Palmdale CA 93550
1911-095 ....Kutina, Joseph Peter ....D. April 13, 1945 Chicago, Ill.
1959-047 ....Kutyna, Marion John 'Marty' ....2255 Nw 14th Street/Delray Beach FL 33445
1990-080 ....Kutzler, Jerry Scott ....38703 Sheridan Road #164/Zion IL 60099
1946-059 ....Kuzava, Robert Leroy ....1118 Vinewood Avenue/Wyandotte MI 48192
1942-060 ....Kvasnak, Alexander ....3265 Hempstead Avenue/Arcadia CA 91006
1912-104 ....Kyle, Andrew Ewing ....D. September 6, 1971 Toronto, Ont.
1937-064 ....Laabs, Chester Peter ....D. January 26, 1983 Warren, Mich.
1950-045 ....Labine, Clement Walter ....311 North Grove Isle Circle/Vero Beach FL 32962
1969-095 ....Laboy, Jose Alberto 'Coco' ....19th Street B20/#24 Sabana Gardens Carolina PR 630
1977-079 ....Lacey, Robert Joseph ....2816 South Pennington/Mesa AZ 85202
1969-096 ....Lachemann, Marcel Ernest ....PO Box 587/Penryn CA 95663
1965-061 ....Lachemann, Rene George ....7500 East Boulders Pkwy #66/Scottsdale AZ 85262
1983-089 ....Lachowicz, Allen Robert ....310 Roosevelt Ave/McKees Rock PA 15136
1914-128 ....Laclaire, George Lewis ....D. October 10, 1918 Farnham, Que.
1972-058 ....Lacock, Ralph Pierre 'Pete' ....9725 Riggs/Overland Park KS 66212
1975-063 ....Lacorte, Frank Joseph ....1667 El Dorado Dr/Gilroy CA 95020
1978-068 ....Lacoss, Michael James ....PO Box 44033/Lemon Cove CA 93244
1996-100 ....Lacy, Kerry Ardeen ....Old Add: Higdon AL 35479
1972-059 ....Lacy, Leondaus Lee ....4424 Webster Street/Oakland CA 94609
1926-046 ....Lacy, Osceola Guy ....D. November 19, 1953 Cleveland, Tenn.
1979-067 ....Ladd, Peter Linwood ....3100 West Lynne Place/Tucson AZ 85741
1946-060 ....Lade, Doyle Marion ....445 North 12th Street/Geneva NE 68361
1947-055 ....Lafata, Joseph Joseph....................................29321 Brittany Court West/Roseville MI 48066
1945-055 ....Laforest, Byron Joseph 'Ty' ....D. May 5, 1947 Arlington, Mass.
1982-072 ....Lafrancois, Roger Victor ....64 Aspinook St/Jewett City CT 6351
1982-073 ....Laga, Michael Russell ....Rural Route 2 Box 2459/Shohola PA 18458
1934-059 ....Lagger, Edwin Joseph ....D. November 10, 1981 Joliet, Ill.
1970-074 ....Lagrow, Lerrin Harris ....12271 East Turquoise/Scottsdale AZ 85259
1968-051 ....Lahoud, Joseph Michael ....Hut Hill Road, Box 165/Bridgewater CT 6752
1982-074 ....Lahti, Jeffrey Allen ....4632 Tyler Drive/Hood River OR 97031
1946-061 ....Lajeskie, Richard Edward ....D. August 15, 1976 Ramsey, N. J.
1939-065 ....Lake, Edward Erving ....D. June 7, 1995 Castro Valley, Calif.
1983-090 ....Lake, Stephen Michael ....Old Add: 11101 West Sieno Place Phoenix AZ 85039
1942-061 ....Lakeman, Albert Wesley ....D. May 25, 1976 Spartanburg, S.C .
1992-068 ....Laker, Timothy John ....Old Add: 2442 North Alden Simi CA 93063
1962-074 ....Lamabe, John Alexander ....16224 Antietam Ave/Baton Rouge LA 70816
1943-076 ....Lamacchia, Alfred Anthony ....13515 Vista Bonita/San Antonio TX 78216
1940-048 ....Lamanna, Frank ....D. September 1, 1980 Syracuse, N. Y.
1941-059 ....Lamanno, Raymond Simon ....D. February 9, 1994 Berkeley, Calif.
1935-059 ....Lamanske, Frank James ....D. August 4, 1971 Olney,Ill.
1917-039 ....Lamar, William Harmong ....D. May 24, 1970 Rockport, Mass.
1937-065 ....Lamaster, Noble Wayne 'Wayne' ....D. August 4, 1989 New Albany, Ind.
1970-075 ....Lamb, John Andrew ....Sharon Valley Rd/Sharon CT 6069
1920-069 ....Lamb, Layman Raymond ....D. October 5, 1955 Fayetteville, Ark.
1969-097 ....Lamb, Raymond Richard ....1741 Tustin Ave #17c/Costa Mesa CA 92627
1946-062 ....Lambert, Clayton Patrick ....D. April 3, 1981 Ogden, Utah
1941-060 ....Lambert, Eugene Marion ....8400 Trinity Road/Cordova TN 38018
1916-053 ....Lambeth, Otis Samuel ....D. June 5, 1976 Moran, Kan.
1912-105 ....Lamline, Frederick Arthur ....D. September 20, 1970 Port Huron, Mich.
1970-076 ....Lamont, Gene William ....5293 Ashley Pkwy/Sarasota FL 34241
1920-070 ....Lamotte, Robert Eugene ....D. November 2, 1970 Chatham, Ga.
1977-080 ....Lamp, Dennis Patrick.....................................Old Add: 10 Beach/Cohasset MA 02025
1969-098 ....Lampard, Christopher Keith ....842 NE 74th Ave/Portland OR 97213

1988-080 ....Lampkin, Thomas Michael..............................3810 SE 153rd Court/Vancouver WA 98683
1935-060 ....Lanahan, Richard Anthony ....D. March 12, 1975 Rochester, Minn.
1987-074 ....Lancaster, Lester Wayne ....119 North 4th Street/Midlothian TX 76065
1977-081 ....Lance, Gary Dean ....PO Box 1415/Caguas PR 726
1982-075 ....Lancellotti, Richard Anthony Rick ....5190 Thompson Road/Clarence NY 14031
1929-060 ....Land, William Gilbert 'Doc' ....D. April 14, 1986 Livingston, Ala.
1952-065 ....Landenberger, Kenneth Henry ....D. July 28, 1960 Cleveland, O.
1977-082 ....Landestoy, Rafael Sivialdo Camilo ....3121 Southwest 140th Avenue/Miami FL 33175
1957-039 ....Landis, James Henry ....305 Deer Hollow Drive/Napa CA 94558
1963-065 ....Landis, William Henry ....525 Sycamore/Hanford CA 93230
1977-083 ....Landreaux, Kenneth Francis ....608 North Leonard Street/Montebello CA 90640
1976-052 ....Landreth, Larry Robert ....116 St. Vincents Street South/Stratford Ontario N5A 2W8 Canada
1950-046 ....Landrith, Hobert Neal 'Hobie' ....1462 Nome Court/Sunnyvale CA 94087
1991-106 ....Landrum, Cedric Bernard ....Rural Route 1 Box 92/Sweetwater AL 36782
1957-040 ....Landrum, Donald Leroy ....19 Barrie Court/Pittsburg CA 94565
1938-048 ....Landrum, Jesse Glenn ....D. June 27, 1983 Beaumont, Tex.
1950-047 ....Landrum, Joseph Butler ....715 Sharpe Road/Columbia SC 29203
1980-069 ....Landrum, Terry Lee Tito ....1121 Kentucky SE/Albuquerque NM 87108
1986-083 ....Landrum, Thomas William Bill ....715 Sharpe Road/Columbia SC 29203
1924-063 ....Lane, James Hunter 'Hunter'......................D. September 12, 1994 Memphis, Tenn.
1953-049 ....Lane, Jerald Hal ....D. July 24, 1988 Chattanooga, Tenn.
1971-060 ....Lane, Marvin ....17191 Ardmore/Detroit MI 48235
1949-046 ....Lane, Richard Harrison ....Old Add: 26609 Academy Dr Palos Verdes Peninsula CA 90274
1941-061 ....Lanfranconi, Walter Oswald ....D. August 18, 1986 Barre, Vt.
1938-049 ....Lang, Donald Charles ....5700 Kirkside Drive #F/Bakersfield CA 93309
1930-043 ....Lang, Martin John ....D. January 13, 1968 Lakewood, Colo.
1975-064 ....Lang, Robert David ....985 Homer Ave/Pittsburgh PA 15237
1914-123 ....Lange, Erwin Henry ....D. April 24, 1971 Maywood, Ill.
1910-085 ....Lange, Frank Herman ....D. December 26, 1945 Madison, Wis.
1972-060 ....Lange, Richard Otto ....3387 Brooks Rd, Rr 2/Freeland MI 48623
1926-047 ....Langford, Elton 'Sam' ....D. July 31, 1993 Plainview, Texas
1976-053 ....Langford, James Rick 'Rick' ....8330 9th Avenue Terrace Nw/Bradenton FL 34209
1984-065 ....Langston, Mark Edward ....4801 Copa De Oro/Anaheim CA 92807
1964-063 ....Lanier, Harold Clifton ....19380 SW 90th Lane Road/Dunellon FL 32640
1938-050 ....Lanier, Hubert Max 'Max' ....11250 SW 186th Circle/Dunnellon FL 34432
1971-061 ....Lanier, Lorenzo.......................................4515 East Frontenac Drive/Cleveland OH 44128
1990-081 ....Lankford, Raymond Lewis........................2048 Cherokee Road/Stockton CA 95205
1936-046 ....Lanning, John Young ....D. November 8, 1989
1916-054 ....Lanning, Lester Alfred ....D. June 13, 1962 Bristol, Conn.
1938-051 ....Lanning, Thomas Newton ....D. November 4, 1967 Marietta, Ga.
1978-069 ....Lansford, Carney Ray ....42690 Pocahontas Road/Baker OR 97814
1982-076 ....Lansford, Joseph Dale 'Jody' ....5730 San Lorenzo Drive/San Jose CA 95123
1922-069 ....Lansing, Eugene Hewett ....D. January 18, 1945 Rensselaer, N. Y.
1993-099 ....Lansing, Michael Thomas ....2935 Ridgecrest Drive/Casper WY 82604
1951-050 ....Lapalme, Paul Edmore ....167 Smith Street/Leominster MA 1453
1922-070 ....Lapan, Peter Nelson ....D. January 5, 1953 Norwalk, Calif.
1942-062 ....Lapihuska, Andrew...................................D. February 17, 1996 Millville, R. I.
1980-070 ....Lapoint, David Jeffrey ....Old Add: 1336 Village Lane Placerville CA 95667
1947-056 ....Lapointe, Ralph John ....D. September 13, 1967 Burlington, Vt.
1958-054 ....Larker, Norman Howard ....4701 Village Rd/Long Beach CA 90808
1996-101 ....Larkin, Andrew Dane ....Old Add: Medford OR 97501
1986-084 ....Larkin, Barry Louis ....9178 Solon Drive/Cincinnati OH 45242
1987-075 ....Larkin, Eugene Thomas............................916 Bellmore Road/North Bellmore NY 11710
1983-091 ....Larkin, Patrick Cliburn ....Old Add: 3901 Parkview Lane #2b Irvine CA 92715
1934-060 ....Larkin, Stephen Patrick ....D. May 2, 1969 Norristown, Pa.
1918-044 ....Larmore, Robert McCahan ....D. January 15, 1964 St. Louis, Mo.
1970-077 ....Laroche, David Eugene ....702 South Crawford/Fort Scott KS 66701
1978-070 ....Larose, Henry John 'John' ....99 Roland/Cumberland RI 2864
1968-052 ....Larose, Victor Raymond ....2908 East Sylvia St/Phoenix AZ 85028
1914-124 ....Laross, Harry Raymond............................D. March 22, 1954 Hines, Ill.
1953-050 ....Larsen, Don James ....PO Box 2863/Hayden Lake ID 83835
1936-047 ....Larsen, Erling Adeli ....2801 South Palm Springs Dr/Tucson AZ 85730
1976-054 ....Larson, Daniel James ....925 Oriole Way/Paso Robles CA 93446
1963-066 ....Larussa, Anthony ....4349 Dunmore Avenue #3/Tampa FL 33611
1954-057 ....Lary, Alfred Allen ....12115 Frank Lary Road/Northport AL 35476
1954-058 ....Lary, Frank Strong ....11813 Baseball Drive/Northport AL 35476
1929-061 ....Lary, Lynford Hobart ....D. January 9, 1973 Downey, Calif.
1963-067 ....Lasher, Frederick Walter ....Highway East/Merrillan WI 54754
1982-077 ....Laskey, William Alan ....311 East Weber St/Toledo OH 43608
1924-064 ....Lasley, Willard Almond ....D. August 21, 1990 Seattle, Wash.
1954-059 ....Lasorda, Thomas Charles ....1473 West Maxzim/Fullerton CA 92633
1957-041 ....Lassetter, Donald Oneal ....406 Gordy Street/Perry GA 31069
1997-095 ....Latham, Christopher Joseph......................Old Add: Las Vegas NV 89101
1985-062 ....Latham, William Carol ....211 Magnolia/Trussville AL 35173
1910-086 ....Lathers, Charles Ten Eyck 'Chick' ....D. July 26, 1971 Petoskey, Mich.
1913-099 ....Lathrop, William George ....D. November 20, 1958 Janesville, Wis.
1957-042 ....Latman, Arnold Barry 'Barry' ....629 S. Rancho Santa Fe Rd #397/San Marcos CA 92069
1956-050 ....Lau, Charles Richard ....D. March 18, 1984 Key Colony Beach, Fla.
1981-067 ....Laudner, Timothy Jon ....Old Add: 7412 Coventry Way Minneapolis MN 55439

1967-062	Lauzerique, George	601 Oleaster Ave/West Palm Beach FL 33414
1934-061	Lavagetto, Harry Arthur 'Cookie'	D. August 10, 1990 Orinda, Calif.
1984-066	Lavalliere, Michael Eugene	12 Scott Ave/Hocksett NH 3106
1913-100	Lavan, John Leonard 'Doc'	D. May 29, 1952 Detroit, Mich.
1974-071	Lavelle, Gary Robert	1100 Worthington Circle/Virginia Beach VA 23464
1912-106	Lavender, James Sanford	D. January 12, 1960 Cartersville, Ga.
1914-125	Lavigne, Arthur David	D. July 18, 1950 Worcester, Mass.
1969-099	Law, Ronald David	Old Add: 9000 Yucca Way/Thornton Co
1978-071	Law, Rudy Karl	Old Add: 3330 West 147th St #221 Hawthorne CA 90250
1980-071	Law, Vance Aaron	1682 North 1950 West/Provo UT 84604
1950-048	Law, Vernon Sanders	1718 North 1050 West/Provo UT 84604
1946-063	Lawing, Garland Frederick	D. September 27, 1996 Murrells Inlet, S. C.
1982-078	Lawless, Thomas James 'Tim'	1238 Laura Street/Casselberry FL 32707
1954-060	Lawrence, Brooks Ulysses	457 Dewdrop Circle #C/Cincinnati OH 45240
1963-068	Lawrence, James Ross	225 Haddington Street/Caledonia Ontario N3W 1G1 Canada
1924-065	Lawrence, Robert Andrew	D. November 6, 1983 Jamaica, N. Y.
1932-044	Lawrence, William Henry	D. June 15, 1997 Redwood City, Calif.
1916-055	Lawry, Otis Carroll	D. October 23, 1965 China, Me.
1930-044	Lawson, Alfred Voyle 'Roxie'	D. April 9, 1977 Stockport, Ia.
1972-061	Lawson, Steven George	3013 Live Oak CT Danville CA 94526
1989-070	Lawton, Marcus Dwayne	Old Add: 1700 Adams St #B Gulfport MS 39501
1995-123	Lawton, Matthew	%Pearl Lawton 27264 Hwy 67 Saucier MS 39574
1970-078	Laxton, William Harry	261 Mansion Ave/Audubon NJ 8106
1990-082	Layana, Timothy Joseph	11012 Rhoda Way/Culver City CA 90230
1915-087	Layden, Eugene Francis	D. December 12, 1984 Pittsburgh, Pa.
1948-057	Layden, Peter John	D. July 18, 1982 Edna, Texas
1927-053	Layne, Herman	D. August 27, 1973 Gallipolis, O.
1941-062	Layne, Ivoria Hillis 'Hilly'	101 Woodcliff Circle/Signal Mountain TN 37377
1948-058	Layton, Lester Lee	8780 East McKellips Road #27/Scottsdale AZ 85257
1968-053	Lazar, John Dan	8444 Oakwood Ave/Munster IN 46321
1943-077	Lazor, John Paul	8054 South 116th Street/Seattle WA 98178
1984-067	Lazorko, Jack Thomas	1360 Meandering Way/Rockwall TX 75087
1926-048	Lazzeri, Anthony Michael	D. August 6, 1946 San Francisco, Calif.
1980-072	Lea, Charles William	910 Briamat Cove/Collierville TN 38017
1923-078	Leach, Frederick	D. December 10, 1981 Hagerman, Id.
1981-068	Leach, Richard Max Rick	593 Layman Creek Circle/Grand Blanc MI 48439
1981-069	Leach, Terry Hester	203 Palm Drive/Largo FL 33770
1980-073	Leal, Luis Enrique	Calle 28 #30-60 Barquisimeto Lara Venezuela
1914-126	Lear, Charles Bernard 'King'	D. October 31, 1976 Waynesboro, Pa.
1915-088	Lear, Frederick Francis	D. October 13, 1955 East Orange, N.J.
1917-040	Leard, William Wallace	D. January 15, 1970 San Francisco, Calif.
1914-127	Leary, John Louis	D. August 18, 1961 Waltham, Mass.
1981-070	Leary, Timothy James	16948 Liverno Drive/Pacific Palisades CA 90272
1920-071	Leathers, Harold Langford	D. April 12, 1977 Modesto, Calif.
1919-051	Lebourveau, Dewitt Wiley 'Bevo'	D. December 19, 1947 Nevada City, Calif.
1915-089	Ledbetter, Ralph Overton 'Razor'	D. February 1, 1969 West Palm Beach, Fla.
1995-124	Ledesma, Aaron David	Old Add: 383 Montecarlo Union City CA 94587
1919-052	Lee, Clifford Walker	D. August 25, 1980 Denver, Colo.
1993-100	Lee, Derek Gerald	11710 Ayreshire Road/Oakton VA 22124
1997-096	Lee, Derrek Leon	Old Add: Sacramento CA 95801
1957-043	Lee, Donald Edward	9101 Palm Tree Dr/Tucson AZ 85710
1920-072	Lee, Ernest Dudley 'Dud'	D. January 7, 1971 Denver, Colo.
1930-045	Lee, Harold Burnham	D. September 4, 1989 Pascagoula, Miss.
1969-100	Lee, Leron	Old Add: 111 South Avenue Sacramento CA 95838
1985-063	Lee, Manuel Lora	Old Add: 321 Nw 31st Street Miami FL 33127
1978-072	Lee, Mark Linden	Old Add: Rt Vigo Box 89 Tulia TX 79088
1988-081	Lee, Mark Owen	Old Add: 1821 East Second Casper WY 82601
1960-059	Lee, Michael Randall	Old Add: 2511 Buena Flores Fallbrook CA 92028
1964-064	Lee, Robert Dean	2633 Glengarry Drive/Lake Havasu City AZ 86404
1945-056	Lee, Roy Edwin	D. November 11, 1985 St. Louis, Mo.
1990-083	Lee, Terry James	Old Add: 2110 W. 23rd Ave Eugene OR 97405
1933-034	Lee, Thornton Starr	D. June 9, 1997 Tucson, Ariz.
1934-062	Lee, William Crutcher	D. June 15, 1977 Plaquemine, La.
1969-101	Lee, William Francis	Rural Route 1 Box 145/Craftsburg VT 5826
1915-090	Lee, William Joseph	D. January 6, 1984 West Hazelton, Pa.
1959-048	Leek, Eugene Harold	109 Vashti Way/Medford OR 97501
1984-068	Leeper, David Dale	7730 Briarglen Loop #D/Stanton CA 90680
1921-055	Lees, George Edward	D. January 2, 1980 Mechanicsburg, Pa.
1965-062	Lefebvre, James Kenneth	9120 North 106th Place/Scottsdale AZ 85258
1980-074	Lefebvre, Joseph Henry	10 Shoreview Drive/Bow NH 3304
1938-052	Lefebvre, Wilfrid Henry 'Bill'	7349 Ulmerton Road #1379/Largo FL 34641
1920-073	Lefevre, Alfredo Modesto	D. January 21, 1982 Glen Cove, N. Y.
1983-092	Lefferts, Craig Lindsay	PO Box 547/Poway CA 92074
1924-066	Lefler, Wade Hampton	D. March 6, 1981 Hickory, N. C.
1974-072	Leflore, Ronald	Old Add: 12760 Indian Rock Rd/Largo FL 34644
1993-101	Leftwich, Phillip Dale	209 Rainbow Forest Drive/Lynchburg VA 24502
1929-062	Legett, Louis Alfred 'Doc'	D. March 6, 1988 New Orleans, La.
1986-085	Legg, Gregory Lynn	209 Kingsley Blvd/Peckville PA 18452
1932-045	Leheny, Regis Francis	D. November 2, 1976 Pittsburgh, Pa.

1961-066	Lehew, James Anthony	PO Box 552/Clendenin WV 25045
1952-066	Lehman, Kenneth Karl	447 Cain Lake Road/Sedro-Woolley WA 98294
1946-064	Lehner, Paul Eugene	D. December 27, 1967 Birmingham, Ala.
1911-096	Lehr, Clarence Emanuel	D. January 31, 1948 Detroit, Mich.
1926-049	Lehr, Norman Carl Michael	D. July 17, 1968 Conesus Lake, N. Y.
1933-035	Leiber, Henry Edward	D. November 8, 1993 Tucson, Ariz.
1913-101	Leibold, Harry Loran 'Nemo'	D. February 4, 1977 Detroit, Mich.
1979-068	Leibrandt, Charles Louis	4075 Deverell Street/Alpharetta GA 30202
1921-056	Leifer, Elmer Edwin	D. September 26, 1948 Everett, Wash.
1912-107	Leinhauser, William Charles	D. April 14, 1978 Elkins Park, Pa.
1939-066	Leip, Edgar Ellsworth	D. November 24, 1983 Zephyrhills, Fla.
1984-069	Leiper, David Paul	15115 North Airport Drive/Scottsdale AZ 85260
1987-076	Leister, John William	618 West End Street/Alma MI 48801
1987-077	Leiter, Alois Terry	10800 Nw Tenth Street/Plantation FL 33322
1990-084	Leiter, Mark Edward	Old Add: 37 Brown Avenue Pine Beach NJ 08741
1990-085	Leius, Scott Thomas	16048 Baywood Lane/Eden Prairie MN 55346
1954-061	Leja, Frank John	D. May 3, 1991 Boston, Mass.
1911-097	Lejeune, Sheldon Aldenbert 'Larry'	D. April 21, 1952 Chattanooga, Tenn.
1965-063	Lejohn, Donald Everett	154 Edwards St/Brownsville PA 15417
1973-073	Lemanczyk, David Lawrence	24 Lehigh CT Rockville Centre NY 11570
1962-075	Lemaster, Denver Clayton	4833 Carlene Way SE/Lilburn GA 30247
1975-065	Lemaster, Johnnie Lee	Pikeville Baseball 214 Sycamore Street Pikeville KY 41501
1961-067	Lemay, Richard Paul	4821 South Florence Avenue/Tulsa OK 74105
1950-049	Lembo, Stephen Neal	D. December 4, 1989 Flushing, N.Y.
1988-082	Lemke, Mark Alan	3 Olena Drive/Whitesboro NY 13492
1975-066	Lemon, Chester Earl	PO Box 951436/Lake Mary FL 32795
1950-050	Lemon, James Robert	4062 Fairway Lake Drive/Myrtle Beach SC 29577
1941-063	Lemon, Robert Granville	1141 Claiborne Drive/Long Beach CA 90807
1969-102	Lemonds, David Lee	5029 Jackson Drive/Charlotte NC 28213
1976-055	Lemongello, Mark	Old Add: 251 Atlantic St #30a Keyport NJ 07735
1950-051	Lenhardt, Donald Eugene	13317 Woodlake Village CT Saint Louis MO 63141
1928-056	Lennon, Edward Francis	D. September 13, 1947 Philadelphia, Pa.
1991-107	Lennon, Patrick Orlando	Rural Route 6 Box 1-52/Whiteville NC 28472
1954-062	Lennon, Robert Albert	8 Dudley Lane/Dix Hills NY 11746
1978-073	Lentine, James Matthew	1066 Calle Del Cerro #1411/San Clemente CA 92672
1992-069	Leon, Danilo Enrique	Calle 8 Casa 33-63 Maracaibo Venez
1968-054	Leon, Eduardo Antonio	Old Add: North Calle De La Reina/Tucson AZ 85718
1945-057	Leon, Isidore Juan	Old Add: Calle O #260 Apt 5 Vedaro Havana Cuba
1973-074	Leon, Maximino (Medina)	Cerrada De San Fernando 3era Seccin #68 Hermosillo Mexico
1974-073	Leonard, Dennis Patrick	4102 Evergreen Ln/Blue Springs MO 64015
1911-098	Leonard, Elmer Ellsworth 'Tiny'	D. May 27, 1981 Napa, Calif.
1933-036	Leonard, Emil John 'Dutch'	D. April 17, 1983 Springfield, Ill.
1913-102	Leonard, Hubert Benjamin 'Dutch'	D. July 11, 1952 Fresno, Calif.
1977-084	Leonard, Jeffrey	535 Calmwater Lane/Alpharetta GA 30202
1914-129	Leonard, Joseph Howard	D. May 1, 1920 Washington, D.C.
1990-086	Leonard, Mark David	22042 Hibiscus Drive/Cupertino CA 95014
1967-063	Leonhard, David Paul	87 Corning St/Beverly MA 1915
1928-057	Leopold, Rudolph Matas	D. September 3, 1965 Baton Rouge, La.
1941-064	Leovich, John Joseph	3531 North Reef Dr Ive/Lincoln City OR 97367
1952-067	Lepcio, Thaddeus Stanley 'Ted'	263 Greenlodge Street/Dedham MA 2026
1955-069	Leppert, Don Eugene	1630 Epping Forest Drive/Southaven MS 38671
1961-068	Leppert, Donald George	4206 SE 20th Place #105/Cape Coral FL 33904
1975-067	Lerch, Randy Louis	Old Add: PO Box 73 Kelsey CA 95643
1910-087	Lerchen, Bertram Roe	D. January 7, 1962 Detroit, Mich.
1952-068	Lerchen, George Edward	354 East Rose/Garden City MI 48135
1928-058	Lerian, Walter Irvin	D. October 22, 1929 Baltimore, Md.
1997-007	Leroy, John Michael	Old Add: West Palm Beach FL 33401
1969-103	Lersch, Barry Lee	Old Add: 1617 1/2 Palmer St/Pueblo CO 81004
1996-102	Lesher, Brian Herbert	Old Add: Newark DE 19711
1972-062	Leshnock, Donald Lee	% R. Leshnock 344 East Midlothian Youngstown OH 44507
1993-102	Leskanic, Curtis John	3717 Main Street/Munhall PA 15120
1982-079	Lesley, Bradley Jay	2535 Oxford/Turlock CA 95380
1917-041	Leslie, Roy Reid	D. April 9, 1972 Sherman, Tex.
1929-063	Leslie, Samuel Andrew	D. January 21, 1979 Pascagoula, Miss.
1939-067	Letchas, Charlie	D. March 14, 1995 Tampa, Fla.
1947-057	Levan, Jesse Roy	1802 Tulpehocken Road #280/Reading PA 19610
1913-103	Leverenz, Walter Fred	D. March 19, 1973 Atascadero, Calif.
1922-071	Leverett, Gorham Vance 'Dixie'	D. February 20, 1957 Beaverton, Ore.
1920-074	Leverette, Horace Wilbur 'Hod'	D. April 10, 1958 St. Petersburg, Fla.
1930-046	Levey, James Julius	D. March 14, 1970 Dallas, Tex.
1996-103	Levine, Alan Brian	Old Add: Belleville IL 62220
1992-070	Levis, Jesse	Old Add: 460 W. Lagoon Lane Milwaukee WI 53201
1923-079	Levsen, Emil Henry 'Dutch'	D. March 12, 1972 Minneapolis, Minn.
1940-049	Levy, Edward Clarence	2471 Southwest 82nd Avenue/Davie FL 33324
1975-068	Lewallyn, Dennis Dale	2900 Breckenridge Dr/Pensacola FL 32506
1951-051	Lewandowski, Daniel William	D. July 19, 1996 Hamilton, Ontario
1967-064	Lewis, Allan Sydney	Urb. La Florida R-15 David Chiriqui Panama
1990-087	Lewis, Darren Joel	33787 Sinsbury Way/Union City CA 94587
1910-088	Lewis, George Edward 'Duffy'	D. June 17, 1979 Salem, N. H.

1979-069 ....Lewis, James Martin ....Old Add: 16049 NE 8th Ave North Miami Beach FL 33162
1991-108 ....Lewis, James Steven ....Old Add: 5119 North Old Ranch Rd Laverne CA 91750
1911-099 ....Lewis, John David ....D. February 25, 1956 Steubenville, O.
1935-061 ....Lewis, John Kelly 'Buddy' ....PO Box 788/Gastonia NC 28053
1964-065 ....Lewis, Johnny Joe ....810 Tara/Cantonment FL 32533
1991-109 ....Lewis, Mark David ....1753 Cleveland Avenue/Hamilton OH 45313
1992-071 ....Lewis, Richie Todd ....13209 County Road East #7005/Losantville IN 47354
1990-088 ....Lewis, Scott Allen....................................Old Add: Medford OR 97501
1924-067 ....Lewis, William Burton ....D. March 24, 1950 Tonawanda, N. Y.
1933-037 ....Lewis, William Henry 'Buddy' ....D. October 24, 1977 Memphis, Tenn.
1971-062 ....Ley, Terrence Richard ....32270 Stone Road/Warren OR 97053
1986-086 ....Leyland, James Richard ....30 Midway Road/Pittsburgh PA 15216
1990-089 ....Leyritz, James Joseph ....495 Vinegarten Drive/Cincinnati OH 45255
1989-071 ....Leyva, Nicholas Tomas ....1098 Tilghman Road/Wayne PA 19087
1980-075 ....Lezcano, Carlos Manuel ....811 West Mesquite/Chandler AZ 85224
1974-074 ....Lezcano, Sixto Joaquin ....Old Add: Betances 73 #412 Bayamon PR 00959
1945-058 ....Libke, Albert Walter ....1117 South Appeland Drive/Wenatchee WA 98801
1969-104 ....Libran, Francisco ....Old Add: Calle Dr. Escade #202 Mayaguez PR 00708
1981-071 ....Lickert, John Wilbur..................................38 Hopkins Avenue/Johnston RI 2919
1990-090 ....Liddell, David Alexander ....Old Add: 4518 Prairie View Drive Riverside CA 92509
1953-051 ....Liddle, Donald Eugene ....1022 North Cherry Street/Mount Carmel IL 62863
1997-098 ....Lidle, Cory Fulton....................................2111 East Thackery Street/West Covina CA 91791
1935-062 ....Lieber, Charles Edwin 'Dutch'..................D. December 31, 1961 Los Angeles, Calif.
1994-062 ....Lieber, Jonathan Ray ....310 Main Street/Springville AL 35146
1994-063 ....Lieberthal, Michael Scott ....1740 Larkfield Avenue/Thousand Oaks CA 91362
1930-047 ....Liebhardt, Glenn Ignatius ....D. March 14, 1992 Winston-Salem, N. C.
1910-089 ....Liese, Frederick Richard ....D. June 30, 1967 Los Angeles, Calif.
1997-099 ....Ligtenberg, Kerry Dale ....8349 77th Street Court/Cottage Grove MN 55016
1936-048 ....Lillard, Robert Eugene 'Gene' ....D. April 12, 1991 Goleta, Calif.
1939-068 ....Lillard, William Beverly ....340 Old Mill Road #47/Santa Barbara CA 93110
1989-072 ....Lilliquist, Derek Jansen ....426 33rd Avenue Sw/Vero Beach FL 32968
1958-055 ....Lillis, Robert Perry ....5107 Cherry Tree Lane/Orlando FL 32819
1994-064 ....Lima, Jose Desiderio Rodriguez..............Carr. Janico Km 12 1/2 #61 Santiago Dominican Rep.
1951-052 ....Limmer, Louis ....231 Medford Court #A/Manalapan NJ 7726
1981-072 ....Linares, Rufino Delacruz ....D. May 16, 1998 San Pedro De Macoris, Dom. Rep.
1927-054 ....Lind, Henry Carl ....D. August 2, 1946 New York, N. Y.
1974-075 ....Lind, Jackson Hugh ....6351 East Redmont Drive/Mesa AZ 85215
1987-078 ....Lind, Jose ....Villa Caito #18/Dorado PR 646
1960-060 ....Lindbeck, Emerit Desmond ....210 Hillcrest Drive/Kewanee IL 61443
1965-064 ....Lindblad, Paul Anton ....2310 Garden Ln/Arlington TX 76015
1947-058 ....Linde, Lyman Gilbert ....D. October 14, 1995 Beaver Dam, Wisc.
1941-065 ....Lindell, John Harlan ....D. August 27, 1985 Newport Beach, Calif.
1986-087 ....Lindeman, James William ....2278 Scott Street/Des Plaines IL 60018
1950-052 ....Linden, Walter Charles ....4432 Harvey Avenue/Western Springs IL 60558
1943-078 ....Lindquist, Carl Emil ....Rural Route 1 Box 185a/Emporium PA 15834
1911-100 ....Lindsay, William Gibbons ....D. July 14, 1963 Greensboro, N.C.
1922-072 ....Lindsey, James Kendrick ....D. October 25, 1963 Jackson, La.
1991-110 ....Lindsey, Michael Douglas ....Old Add: 2104 Long Harbor Ln Nashville TN 37217
1987-079 ....Lindsey, William Donald ....9323 South Hampton Place/Boca Raton FL 33434
1916-056 ....Lindstrom, Axel Olaf ....D. June 25, 1940 Asheville, N. C.
1958-056 ....Lindstrom, Charles William ....28 Tam O'Shanter/Lincoln IL 62656
1924-068 ....Lindstrom, Fred Charles ....D. October 4, 1981 Chicago, Ill.
1966-055 ....Lines, Richard George ....1057 Forest Lakes Drive/Naples FL 33942
1952-069 ....Linhart, Carl James ....2647 Delmar Avenue/Granite City IL 62040
1910-090 ....Link, Frederick Theodore ....D. May 22, 1939 Houston, Texas
1933-038 ....Linke, Edward Karl ....D. June 21, 1988 Chicago, Ill.
1954-063 ....Lint, Royce James ....6814 SE Jack Rd/Milwaukie OR 97222
1929-064 ....Linton, Claud Clarence 'Bob' ....D. April 3, 1980 Destin, Fla.
1992-072 ....Linton, Douglas Warren ....Old Add: 1029 Kensington Court Kingsport TN 37664
1973-075 ....Lintz, Larry ....PO Box 98113/West Sacramento CA 95798
1962-076 ....Linz, Philip Francis..................................20 Rocky Rapids Road/Stamford CT 6903
1963-069 ....Linzy, Frank Alfred ....Rr 2 Box 395/Coweta OK 74429
1956-051 ....Lipetri, Michael Angelo 'Angelo' ....150 Yoakum Avenue/Farmingdale NY 11735
1942-063 ....Lipon, John Joseph ....D. August 17, 1998 Houston, Texas
1937-066 ....Lipscomb, Gerard 'Nig' ....D. February 27, 1978 Huntersville, N. C.
1963-070 ....Lipski, Robert Peter ....1 Snook St/Scranton PA 18505
1995-125 ....Lira, Antonio Felipe 'Felipe' ....Old Add: 1641 Nw 115th Avenue Pembroke Pines FL 33026
1987-080 ....Liriano, Nelson Arturo ....Martires 19 De Nov.#7,Ens Luperon Puerto Plata Dominican Rep.
1970-079 ....Lis, Joseph Anthony ....4055 Secretariat Drive/Newburgh IN 47630
1927-055 ....Lisenbee, Horace Milton 'Hod' ....D. November 14, 1987 Clarksville, Tenn.
1981-073 ....Lisi, Riccardo Patrick Emilio ....Old Add: 32 Riverview W. Apts#2 Pittsfield MA 01201
1929-065 ....Liska, Adolph James 'Ad' ....3831 Northwest Wasco/Portland OR 97232
1992-073 ....Listach, Patrick Alan ....401 Carver Avenue/Natchitoches LA 71457
1973-076 ....Littell, Mark Alan ....Old Add: 435 West 9th Street North Wichita KS 67203
1989-073 ....Little, Dennis Scott 'Scott' ....1321 Rosebud Lane/Jackson MO 63755
1980-076 ....Little, Donald Jeffrey Jeff ....5711 C. R. 169/Genoa OH 43430
1982-080 ....Little, Richard Bryan 'Bryan' ....4766 Tiffany Park Circle/Bryan TX 77802
1912-108 ....Little, William Arthur 'Jack' ....D. July 27, 1961 Dallas, Tex.
1980-077 ....Littlefield, John Andrew................................1214 N. Alameda St/Azusa CA 91702

1950-053	Littlefield, Richard Bernard	D. November 20, 1997 Detroit, Mich.
1927-056	Littlejohn, Charles Carlisle	D. October 27, 1977 Kansas City, Mo.
1978-074	Littlejohn, Dennis Gerald	5600 Stockdale Hwy/Bakersfield CA 93309
1981-074	Littleton, Larry Marvin	107 Avery Drive NE/Atlanta GA 30309
1989-074	Litton, Jon Gregory 'Greg'	2828 Villager Circle/Pensacola FL 32504
1952-070	Littrell, Jack Napier	7510 Floydsburg Road/Crestwood KY 40014
1940-050	Litwhiler, Daniel Webster	1411 Stroud Court/Newport Richey FL 34655
1947-059	Lively, Everett Adrian 'Bud'	8605 Esslinger Court/Huntsville AL 35802
1911-101	Lively, Henry Everett 'Jack'	D. December 5, 1967 Arab, Ala.
1939-069	Livengood, Wesley Amos	D. September 2, 1996 Winston-Salem, N. C.
1938-053	Livingston, Thompson Orville 'Mickey'	D. April 3, 1983 Houston, Texas
1991-111	Livingstone, Scott Louis	1303 Pecos Drive/Southlake TX 76092
1968-055	Llenas, Winston Enriquillo	Apartado #92 Santiago Dominican Rep.
1922-073	Llewellyn, Clement Manley	D. November 27, 1969 Charlotte, N. C.
1993-103	Lloyd, Graeme John	1695 Barrabool Road Rmb Gnarwarre Victoria Australia 3221
1995-126	Loaiza, Esteban Antonio	1229 Grove Avenue/Imperial Beach CA 91932
1912-109	Loan, William Joseph 'Mike'	D. November 12, 1966 Springfield, Pa.
1939-070	Loane, Robert Kenneth	1140 Monarch Lane #112/Pacific Grove CA 93950
1914-130	Lobert, Frank John	D. May 29, 1932 Pittsburgh, Pa.
1962-077	Lock, Donald Wilson	1330 North Walnut/Kingman KS 67068
1955-070	Locke, Charles Edward	1560 Haven Hills Road/Poplar Bluff MO 63901
1959-049	Locke, Lawrence Donald 'Bobby'	Rr 1 Box 400/Dunbar PA 15431
1964-066	Locke, Ronald Thomas	PO Box 229/Kenyon RI 2836
1965-065	Locker, Robert Awtry	3648 Happy Valley/Lafayette CA 94549
1994-065	Lockhart, Keith Virgil	Old Add: 1231 North Aldenville Covina CA 91722
1973-077	Locklear, Gene	Rr1 Box 213/Pembroke NC 28382
1955-071	Locklin, Stuart Carlton	1823 South Bouten/Appleton WI 54911
1945-059	Lockman, Carroll Walter 'Whitey'	8234 North 75th Street/Scottsdale AZ 85253
1965-066	Lockwood, Claude Edward 'Skip'	%New Directions 66 Long Wharf Boston MA 2110
1938-054	Lodigiani, Dario Anthony	745 Lathrop Street/Napa CA 94558
1928-059	Loepp, George Herbert	D. September 4, 1967 Los Angeles, Calif.
1950-054	Loes, William 'Billy'	33-08 84th Street/Jackson Heights NY 11372
1991-112	Lofton, Kenneth	PO Box 68473/Tucson AZ 85737
1926-050	Loftus, Francis Patrick	D. October 27, 1980 Belchertown, Mass.
1924-069	Loftus, Richard Joseph	D. January 21, 1972 Concord, Mass.
1951-053	Logan, John	6115 West Cleveland Avenue/Milwaukee WI 53219
1935-063	Logan, Robert Dean 'Lefty'	D. May 20, 1978 Indianapolis, Ind.
1914-131	Lohr, Howard Sylvester	D. June 9, 1977 Philadelphia, Pa.
1947-060	Lohrke, Jack Wayne 'Lucky'	2817 Lucena Drive/San Jose CA 95132
1934-063	Lohrman, William Leroy	250 Route 208/New Paltz NY 12561
1978-075	Lois, Alberto	Ingenio Consuelo Calle 5 San Pedro De Macoris Dominican Rep.
1996-104	Loiselle, Richard Frank	1621 Carmel Circle East/Upland CA 91784
1963-071	Lolich, Michael Stephen 'Mickey'	6252 Robinhill/Washington MI 48094
1971-063	Lolich, Ronald John	50 Northview Court/Lake Oswego OR 97035
1946-065	Lollar, John Sherman 'Sherm'	D. September 24, 1977 Springfield, Mo.
1980-078	Lollar, William Timothy 'Tim'	16626 West Bayard Drive/Golden CO 80401
1984-070	Loman, Douglas Edward	25 Lincoln Street/Bakersfield CA 93305
1931-048	Lombardi, Ernest Natali	D. September 26, 1977 Santa Cruz, Calif.
1986-088	Lombardi, Philip Arden	12444 Carol Place/Granada Hills CA 91344
1945-060	Lombardi, Victor Alvin	D. December 3, 1997 Fresno, Calif.
1948-059	Lombardo, Louis	141 Cedar Hollow South/Fort Mill SC 29715
1985-064	Lombardozzi, Stephen Paul	4915 Sunset Beach Road/Auburn NY 13021
1995-127	Lomon, Kevin Dale	Rural Route 1 Box 920/Cameron OK 74932
1965-067	Lonborg, James Reynold	498 First Parish Rd/Scituate MA 2066
1911-102	Lonergan, Walter E.	D. January 23, 1958 Lexington, Mass.
1922-074	Long, James Albert	D. September 14, 1970 Fort Dodge, Ia.
1963-072	Long, Jeoffrey Keith	11 Flower CT Lakeside Park KY 41017
1997-100	Long, Joey J.	Old Add: Conover OH 45317
1911-103	Long, Lester 'Lep'	D. October 21, 1958 Birmingham, Ala.
1951-054	Long, Richard Dale 'Dale'	D. January 27, 1991 Palm Coast, Fla.
1981-075	Long, Robert Earl	Old Add: 3560 Nohave Drive Grandville MI 49418
1997-101	Long, Ryan Marcus	Old Add: Houston TX 77001
1911-104	Long, Thomas Augustus	D. June 15, 1972 Mobile, Ala.
1924-070	Long, Thomas Francis	D. September 16, 1973 Louisville, Ky.
1985-065	Long, William Douglas	7699 Dimmick Road/Cincinnati OH 45241
1993-104	Longmire, Anthony Eugene	Old Add: 1737 Vermont Street Fairfield CT 06410
1956-052	Lonnett, Joseph Paul	126 Duncan Cir/Beaver PA 15009
1968-056	Look, Bruce Michael	4225 Oak Pointe Court/Okemos MI 48864
1961-069	Look, Dean Zachary	4708 Okemos Road/Okemos MI 48864
1993-105	Looney, Brian James	351 Country Club Road/Cheshire CT 6410
1944-077	Lopat, Edmund Walter	D. June 15, 1992 Darien, Conn.
1948-060	Lopata, Stanley Edward	Leisure World Manor #2239/Mesa AZ 85206
1945-061	Lopatka, Arthur Joseph	815 Leicester Road/Elk Grove Village IL 60007
1972-063	Lopes, David Earl	17762 Vineyard Lane/Poway CA 92064
1993-106	Lopez, Albert Anthony	431 North Brimhall/Mesa AZ 85203
1928-060	Lopez, Alfonso Ramon	3601 Beach Drive/Tampa FL 33629
1965-068	Lopez, Arturo	279 Clerk Street #A13/Hackensack NJ 7601
1974-076	Lopez, Aurelio Rios	D. September 22, 1992 Matehuala, Mexico
1976-056	Lopez, Carlos Antonio	Mexici #33a, Pointe Mazatlan/Sinaloa/Mexico

1955-072	Lopez, Hector Headley	11415 Faldo Court/Hudson FL 34667
1992-074	Lopez, Javier (Torres) 'Javy'	Old Add: Ponce PR
1966-056	Lopez, Jose Ramon	D. September 4, 1962 Miami, Fla.
1990-091	Lopez, Luis Antonio	636 40th Street/Brooklyn NY 11232
1993-107	Lopez, Luis Santos	Old Add: Cidra PR 00639
1963-073	Lopez, Marcelino Pons	18662 56th Avenue/Miami FL 33055
1923-080	Lord, William Carlton 'Carl'	D. August 15, 1947 Chester, Pa.
1913-104	Lorenzen, Adolph Andreas 'Lefty'	D. March 5, 1963 Davenport, Ia.
1995-128	Loretta, Mark David	2 Wildflower/Laguna Niguel CA 92677
1994-066	Lorraine, Andrew Jason	24015 Mill Valley Road/Valencia CA 91355
1916-057	Lotz, Joseph Peter	D. January 1, 1971 Hayward, Calif.
1980-079	Loucks, Scott Gregory	1801 Viola Dr/Sierra Vista AZ 85635
1910-091	Loudell, Arthur	D. February 19, 1961 Kansas City, Mo.
1967-065	Loughlin, Lawrence John	10512 Spring Lake Drive/Clermont FL 34711
1964-067	Loun, Donald Nelson	9095 Wexford Dr/Vienna VA 22180
1913-105	Love, Edward Haughton 'Slim'	D. November 30, 1942 Memphis, Tenn.
1922-075	Lovelace, Thomas Rivers	D. July 12, 1979 Dallas, Tex.
1988-083	Lovelace, Vance Odell	5608 Twelfth Avenue/Tampa FL 33610
1955-073	Lovenguth, Lynn Richard	7600 SW 149th Avenue/Beaverton OR 97007
1933-039	Lovett, Merritt Marwood 'Mem'	D. September 19, 1995 Downers Grove, Ill.
1980-080	Loviglio, John Paul 'Jay'	23 Third Avenue/East Islip NY 11730
1972-064	Lovitto, Joseph	3803 Shady Creek North/Arlington TX 76013
1963-074	Lovrich, Peter	19626 Beechnut Dr/Mokena IL 60448
1988-084	Lovullo, Salvatore Anthony	16825 Bajio Road/Encino CA 91436
1915-091	Low, Fletcher	D. June 6, 1973 Hanover, N.H.
1911-105	Lowdermilk, Louis Bailey	D. December 27, 1975 Centralia, Ill.
1997-102	Lowe, Derek Christopher	Old Add: Dearborn MI 48120
1920-075	Lowe, George Wesley	D. September 2, 1981 Somers Point, N. J.
1997-103	Lowe, Jonathan Sean 'Sean'	924 Creekview Drive/Mesquite TX 75181
1970-080	Lowenstein, John Lee	7700 Wisconsin Avenue/Bethesda MD 20814
1997-104	Lowery, Quenton Terrell 'Terrell'	Old Add: Oakland CA 94601
1951-055	Lown, Omar Joseph 'Turk'	1106 Van Buren/Pueblo CO 81004
1942-064	Lowrey, Harry Lee 'Peanuts'	D. July 2, 1986 Inglewood, Calif.
1984-071	Lowry, Dwight	D. July 10, 1997 Jamestown, N. Y.
1942-065	Lowry, Samuel Joseph	D. December 1, 1992 Philadelphia, Pa.
1986-089	Loynd, Michael Wallace	19 Randall Drive/Short Hills NJ 7078
1984-072	Lozado, William 'Willie'	Old Add: 551 Euclid Avenue Brooklyn NY 11208
1981-076	Lubratich, Steven George	606 Joya Court/Danville CA 94506
1936-049	Luby, Hugh Max	D. May 4, 1986 Eugene, Ore.
1938-055	Lucadello, John	103 Oakwood Drive/San Antonio TX 78228
1923-081	Lucas, Charles Frederick 'Red'	D. July 9, 1986 Nashville, Tenn.
1935-064	Lucas, Frederick Warrington	D. March 11, 1987 Cambridge, Md.
1980-081	Lucas, Gary Paul	1305 Lakeshore Drive/Rice Lake WI 54868
1931-049	Lucas, John Charles	D. October 31, 1970 Maryville, Ill.
1929-066	Lucas, Ray Wesley	D. October 9, 1969 Harrison, Mich.
1970-081	Lucchesi, Frank Joseph	4703 Mill Creek Drive/Colleyville TX 76034
1923-082	Luce, Frank Edward	D. February 3, 1942 Milwaukee, Wis.
1920-076	Lucey, Joseph Earl	D. July 30, 1980 Holyoke, Mass.
1943-079	Lucier, Louis Joseph	579 Highland Street/Northbridge MA 1534
1924-071	Ludolph, William Francis	D. April 8, 1952 Oakland, Calif.
1996-105	Ludwick, Eric Davis	Old Add: Las Vegas NV 89101
1925-066	Luebbe, Roy John	D. August 21, 1985 Papillion, Neb.
1971-064	Luebber, Stephen Lee	3302 Moorehead Dr/Joplin MO 64804
1993-108	Luebbers, Larry Christopher	PO Box 4673/Frankfort KY 40604
1962-078	Luebke, Richard Raymond	D. December 4, 1974 San Diego, Calif.
1989-075	Luecken, Richard Fred	2902 Fontana Drive/Houston TX 77043
1985-066	Lugo, Urbano Rafael	Rooevelt Res. Tiuna Ent Bph 44 Rosales Caracas Venezuela
1913-106	Luhrsen, William Ferdinand	D. August 15, 1973 North Little Rock, Ark.
1996-106	Lukachyk, Robert James	14706 Beacon Hill Court/Midlothian VA 23112
1996-107	Luke, Matthew Clifford	Old Add: Brea CA 92821
1941-066	Lukon, Edward Paul	D. November 7, 1996 Canonsburg, Pa.
1967-066	Lum, Michael Ken-Wai	3476 Cochise Drive Nw/Atlanta GA 30339
1957-044	Lumenti, Raphael Anthony 'Ralph'	9 Tomasso/Milford MA 1757
1956-053	Lumpe, Jerry Dean	732 Pearson Drive/Springfield MO 65804
1954-064	Luna, Guillermo Romero 'Memo'	Cardenas 50 Oriente Los Mochis Sinaloa/Mexico
1945-062	Lund, Donald Andrew	1000 South State Street/Ann Arbor MI 48109
1967-067	Lund, Gordon T.	1542 North Monitor/Chicago IL 60651
1924-072	Lundgren, Ebin Delmar 'Del'	D. October 19, 1984 Lindsborg, Kan.
1973-078	Lundstedt, Thomas Robert	PO Box 409/Ephraim WI 54211
1919-053	Lunte, Harry August	D. July 27, 1965 St. Louis, Mo.
1940-051	Lupien, Ulysses John 'Tony'	PO Box 351/Norwich VT 5055
1961-070	Luplow, Alvin David	2450 Starlite Dr/Saginaw MI 48603
1914-132	Luque, Adolfo Domingo De Guzman	D. July 3, 1957 Havana, Cuba
1987-081	Lusader, Scott Edward	4169 Bad Meadows/Oakland Township MI 48306
1910-092	Lush, Ernest Benjamin	D. February 26, 1937 Detroit, Mich.
1956-054	Luttrell, Lyle Kenneth	D. July 11, 1984 Chattanooga, Tenn.
1922-076	Lutz, Louis William	D. February 22, 1944 Cincinnati, O.
1951-056	Lutz, Rollin Joseph 'Joe'	1411 Quail Drive/Sarasota FL 33581
1923-083	Lutzke, Walter John 'Rube'	D. March 6, 1938 Milwaukee, Wis.

1970-082 ....Luzinski, Gregory Michael ....25199 Ridge Oak Drive/Bonita Springs FL 34134
1993-109 ....Lyden, Mitchell Scott ....227 Shore Court/Fort Lauderdale FL 33308
1993-110 ....Lydy, Donald Scott..3971 West Chicago Street/Chandler AZ 85226
1967-068 ....Lyle, Albert Walter 'Sparky' ....17 Signal Hill Dr/Voorhees NJ 8043
1925-067 ....Lyle, James Charles...D. October 10, 1977 Williamsport, Pa.
1920-077 ....Lynch, Adrian Ryan ....D. March 16, 1934 Davenport, Ia.
1980-082 ....Lynch, Edward Francis ....5940 SW 120th St/Miami FL 33156
1954-065 ....Lynch, Gerald Thomas......................................120 Davis Mill Court/Lawrenceville GA 30245
1948-061 ....Lynch, Matt Danny 'Dummy' ....D. June 30, 1978 Plano, Texas
1922-077 ....Lynch, Walter Edward ....D. December 21, 1976 Daytona Beach, Calif.
1916-058 ....Lynn, Byrd ....D. February 5, 1940 Napa, Calif.
1974-077 ....Lynn, Fredric Michael ....7336 El Fuerte Street/Carlsbad CA 92009
1939-071 ....Lynn, Japhet Monroe 'Red' ....D. October 27, 1977 Bellville, Tex.
1937-067 ....Lynn, Jerome Edward ....D. September 25, 1972 Scranton, Pa.
1944-078 ....Lyon, Russell Mayo ....D. December 24, 1975 Calhoun Falls, S. C.
1944-079 ....Lyons, Albert Harold ....D. December 20, 1965 Inglewood, Calif.
1986-090 ....Lyons, Barry Stephen ....1425 Cedar Way Lane/Nashville TN 37211
1996-108 ....Lyons, Curt Russell ....Old Add: 213 Keystone Dr Richmond KY 40475
1947-061 ....Lyons, Edward Hoyt..1466 Ebert Street/Winston-Salem NC 27103
1920-078 ....Lyons, George Tony ....D. August 12, 1981 Nevada, Mo.
1941-067 ....Lyons, Herschel ....7900 Dunbarton Avenue/Los Angeles CA 90045
1985-067 ....Lyons, Stephen John...Old Add: 19670 SW Madeline St Beaverton OR 97007
1929-067 ....Lyons, Terence Hilbert......................................D. September 9, 1959 Dayton, O.
1923-084 ....Lyons, Theodore Amar ....D. July 25, 1986 Sulphur, La.
1983-093 ....Lyons, Williams Allen ....Old Add: 2621 Grandview Avenue Alton IL 62002
1980-083 ....Lysander, Richard Eugene ....17446 Caminito Baya/San Diego CA 92127
1969-105 ....Lyttle, James Lawrence ....751 Camino Lake Cir/Boca Raton FL 33432
1955-074 ....Maas, Duane Fredrick 'Duke' ....D. December 7, 1976 Mount Clemens, Mich.
1990-092 ....Maas, Kevin Christian ....928 Dana Highlands Court/Lafayette CA 94549
1958-057 ....Mabe, Robert Lee ....1032 Twin Arch Drive/Danville VA 24540
1994-067 ....Mabry, John Steven ....715 Bellerive Manor Drive/Saint Louis MO 63141
1976-057 ....Maccormack, Frank Louis ....2 Schmidt Place/Secaucus NJ 7094
1928-061 ....Macdonald, Harvey Forsyth ....D. October 4, 1965 Manoa, Pa.
1990-093 ....Macdonald, Robert Joseph ....Old Add: Toms River NJ 08753
1950-055 ....Macdonald, William Paul ....D. May 4, 1991 Shasta Lake, Calif.
1987-082 ....Macfarlane, Michael Andrew ....7421 Woodside Avenue/Stockton CA 95207
1926-051 ....Macfayden, Daniel Knowles ....D. August 26, 1972 Brunswick, Me.
1974-078 ....Macha, Kenneth Edward ....6934 Berkshire Drive/Export PA 15632
1979-070 ....Macha, Michael William ....105 Neu Road/Victoria TX 77904
1989-076 ....Machado, Julio S. ....Av 2 Con C/19 #17-95,P Del Sur/"L'Canada,Maracaibo Venezuela/"
1996-109 ....Machado, Robert Alexis......................................Old Add: Caracas Venezuela
1971-065 ....Machemehl, Charles Walter................................2005 Machemehl Road/Brenham TX 77833
1978-076 ....Machemer, David Ritchie....................................1359 St. Joseph Cir/St. Joseph MI 49085
1910-093 ....Mack, Earle Thaddeus ....D. February 4, 1967 Upper Darby, Pa.
1922-078 ....Mack, Frank George ....D. July 2, 1971 Clearwater, Fla.
1945-063 ....Mack, Joseph John ....5049 159th Street #21/Oak Forest IL 60452
1994-068 ....Mack, Quinn David ....Old Add: 5631 Lockhaven Dr Buena Park 90621
1938-056 ....Mack, Raymond James ....D. May 7, 1969 Bucyrus, O.
1987-083 ....Mack, Shane Lee ....PO Box 371330/Las Vegas NV 89137
1985-068 ....Mack, Tony Lynn ....Old Add: 3304 Monta Vesta #E32 Lexington KY 40502
1973-079 ....Mackanin, Peter ....4029 Bee Ridge Road #5017/Sarasota FL 34233
1955-075 ....Mackenzie, Eric Hugh ....2002 James East/Brights Grove Ontario Canada N0N 1C0
1961-071 ....Mackenzie, Henry Gordon 'Gordy' ....36535 Micro Racetrack Road/Fruitland Park FL 32817
1960-061 ....Mackenzie, Kenneth Purvis ....15 Fair Street/Guilford CT 6437
1941-068 ....Mackiewicz, Felix Thaddeus ....D. December 20, 1993 Olivette, Mo.
1953-052 ....Mackinson, John Joseph.....................................D. October 17, 1989 Reseda, Calif.
1979-071 ....Macko, Steven Joseph ....D. November 15, 1981 Arlington, Tex.
1962-079 ....Macleod, William Daniel ....14 Heritage Way/Marblehead MA 1945
1993-111 ....Maclin, Lonnie Lee ....9635 Meeks/Saint Louis MO 63132
1938-057 ....Macon, Max Cullen ....D. August 5, 1989 Jupiter, Fla.
1922-079 ....Macphee, Walter Scott 'Waddy' ....D. January 20, 1980 Charlotte, N. C.
1944-080 ....Macpherson, Harry William ....10 Onset Road #411/Bennington NH 3442
1980-084 ....Macwhorter, Keith ....9 Manning Drive/Providence RI 2915
1916-059 ....Madden, Eugene ....D. April 6, 1949 Utica, N. Y.
1914-133 ....Madden, Francis A. ....D. April 30, 1952 Pittsburgh, Pa.
1912-110 ....Madden, Leonard Joseph ....D. September 9, 1949 Toledo, O.
1983-094 ....Madden, Michael Anthony ....4733 Frankfort Way/Denver CO 80239
1987-084 ....Madden, Morris Dewayne ....105 Jennings/Laurens SC 29360
1946-066 ....Maddern, Clarence James ....D. August 9, 1986 Tucson, Ariz.
1970-083 ....Maddox, Elliott ....Old Add: 109 Hilton Ave/Vauxhall NJ 07088
1972-065 ....Maddox, Garry Lee ....% Img 1360 East 9th Street #1300 Cleveland OH 44114
1978-077 ....Maddox, Jerry Glenn ....3141 Driftwood Street/Orange CA 92665
1986-091 ....Maddux, Gregory Alan ....3010 Compton Court/Alpharetta GA 30302
1986-092 ....Maddux, Michael Ausley ....Old Add: 4241 Rawhide Las Vegas NV 89120
1985-069 ....Madison, Charles Scott 'Scotty' ....5397 Thornapple Lane Nw/Acworth GA 30101
1950-0561 ....Madison, David Pledger ....D. December 9, 1985 Macon, Miss.
1932-046 ....Madjeski, Edward William ....D. November 11, 1994 Montgomery, Ohio
1973-080 ....Madlock, Bill ....Old Add: 18 Meeting House Ln/Shelton CT 06484
1987-085 ....Madrid, Alexander ....PO Box 814/Red River NM 87558

1947-062 ....Madrid, Salvador..............................D. February 24, 1977 Fort Wayne, Ind.
1996-110 ....Maduro, Calvin Gregory.....................Old Add: Santa Cruz Aruba
1960-062 ....Maestri, Hector Anibal ....581 SW 89th Court/Miami FL 33174
1986-093 ....Magadan, David Joseph ....4505 North A Street/Tampa FL 33609
1991-113 ....Magallanes, Everardo.......................8024 Bergman Lane/Downey CA 90242
1911-106 ....Magee, Leo Christopher ....D. March 14, 1966 Columbus, O.
1996-111 ....Magee, Wendell Errol ....Old Add: Hattiesburg MS 39401
1938-058 ....Maggert, Harl Warren ....D. July 10, 1986 Citrus Heights, Calif.
1945-064 ....Maglie, Salvatore Anthony ....D. December 28, 1992 Niagara Falls, N. Y.
1991-114 ....Magnante, Michael Anthony ....919 Bethany Road/Burbank CA 91504
1911-107 ....Magner, Edmund Burke 'Stubby' ....D. September 9, 1956 Chillicothe, O.
1970-084 ....Magnuson, James Robert ....D. May 30, 1991 Green Bay, Wisc.
1987-086 ....Magrane, Joseph David ....705 Guisando De Avila/Tampa FL 33613
1989-077 ....Magrann, Thomas Joseph ....910 North 31st Court/Hollywood FL 33021
1966-057 ....Magrini, Peter Alexander ....2402 Rancho Cabeza Drive/Santa Rosa CA 95404
1922-080 ....Maguire, Fred Edward ....D. November 3, 1961 Boston, Mass.
1950-057 ....Maguire, Jack ....4427 Gleneagles Drive/Boynton Beach FL 33436
1921-057 ....Mahady, James Bernard ....D. August 9, 1936 Cortland, N. Y.
1960-063 ....Mahaffey, Arthur ....PO Box 404/Newtown Square PA 19073
1926-052 ....Mahaffey, Lee Roy ....D. July 23, 1969 Anderson, S. C.
1940-052 ....Mahan, Arthur Leo ....1002 Kenwyn St/Philadelphia PA 19124
1912-111 ....Maharg, William Joseph ....D. November 20, 1953 Philadelphia, Pa.
1995-129 ....Mahay, Ronald Matthew.....................Old Add: %T.Mahay,10333 Mason Ave Oak Lawn IL 60453
1978-078 ....Mahlberg, Gregory John ....360 Fishburne Street/Charleston SC 29403
1977-085 ....Mahler, Michael James 'Mickey' ....7911 Quirt/San Antonio TX 78227
1979-072 ....Mahler, Richard Keith 'Rick' ....7911 Quirt Dr/San Antonio TX 78227
1992-075 ....Mahomes, Patrick Lavon ....PO Box 1025/Lindale TX 75771
1930-048 ....Mahon, Alfred Gwinn ....D. December 26, 1977 New Haven, Conn.
1910-094 ....Mahoney, Christopher John ....D. July 15, 1954 Visalia, Calif.
1911-108 ....Mahoney, Daniel Joseph ....D. September 28, 1960 Utica, N.Y.
1959-050 ....Mahoney, James Thomas ....Old Add: 150 Sycamore Ter/Glen Rock NJ 07452
1951-057 ....Mahoney, Robert Paul ....6901 Lynn/Lincoln NE 68505
1945-065 ....Maier, Robert Philip ....D. August 4, 1993 South Plainfield, N. J.
1936-050 ....Mailho, Emil Pierre ....566 Scott Street/Fremont CA 94538
1915-092 ....Mails, John Walter 'Duster' ....D. July 5, 1974 San Francisco, Calif.
1948-062 ....Main, Forrest Harry 'Woody' ....D. June 27, 1992 Whittier, Calif.
1914-134 ....Main, Miles Grant 'Alex' ....D. December 29, 1965 Royal Oak, Mich.
1943-080 ....Mains, James Royal ....D. March 17, 1969 Bridgton, Me.
1915-105 ....Maisel, Charles Louis ....D. August 25, 1953 Baltimore, Md.
1913-107 ....Maisel, Frederick Charles 'Fritz' ......D. April 22, 1967 Baltimore, Md.
1913-108 ....Maisel, George John ....D. November 20, 1968 Baltimore, Md.
1939-072 ....Majeski, Harry ....D. August 9, 1991 Staten Island, N. Y.
1937-068 ....Makosky, Frank................................D. January 10, 1987 Stroudsburg, Pa.
1975-069 ....Makowski, Thomas Anthony ....E6686 Omphis Road #2/Colden NY 14033
1992-076 ....Maksudian, Michael Bryant ....1028 Glen Grattan #F/Montgomery AL 36111
1996-112 ....Malave, Jose Francisco ....Old Add: Cumana Venezuela
1933-040 ....Malay, Joseph Charles......................D. March 19, 1989 Bridgeport, Conn.
1981-077 ....Maldonado, Candido/Candy ....Hco2 Box 16800/Arecibo PR 612
1990-094 ....Maldonado, Carlos Cesar ....Casa #1835 Chepo/Panama
1981-078 ....Maler, James Michael........................2163 NE 122nd Street/Miami FL 33181
1937-069 ....Malinosky, Anthony Joseph 'Tony' ...5540 West Fifth Street #60/Oxnard CA 93030
1934-064 ....Malis, Cyrus Sol ....D. January 12, 1971 North Hollywood, Fla.
1957-045 ....Malkmus, Robert Edward ....400 Wallingford Ter/Union NJ 7083
1959-051 ....Mallett, Gerald Gordon......................7610 Forest Park Dr/Beaumont TX 77707
1950-058 ....Mallette, Malcolm Francis ....2419 Silver Fox Lane/Reston VA 22091
1987-087 ....Mallicoat, Robbin Dale ....10406 Great Plains/Houston TX 77064
1931-050 ....Mallon, Leslie Clyde 'Clyde' ....D. April 17, 1991 Granbury, Texas
1921-058 ....Mallonee, Howard Bennett 'Ben'........D. February 19, 1978 Baltimore, Md.
1925-068 ....Mallonee, Julius Norris ....D. December 26, 1934 Charlotte, N. C.
1940-053 ....Mallory, James Baugh ....1905 Forest Hills Dr/Greenville NC 27834
1977-086 ....Mallory, Sheldon ....18640 Becker Terrace/Country Club Hills IL 60478
1910-095 ....Malloy, Archibald Alexander ....D. March 1, 1961 Ferris, Tex.
1943-081 ....Malloy, Robert Paul ....3850 Kirkup Avenue/Cincinnati OH 45213
1987-088 ....Malloy, Robert William ....Old Add: Dallas TX
1955-076 ....Malmberg, Harry William ....D. October 29, 1976 San Francisco, Calif.
1990-095 ....Malone, Charles Ray ....614 Saint Francis/Marked Tree AR 72365
1949-047 ....Malone, Edward Russell ....224 Avenida Majorca #A/Laguna Hills CA 92653
1915-093 ....Malone, Lewis Aloysius ....D. February 17, 1972 Brooklyn, N.Y.
1928-062 ....Malone, Perce Leigh 'Pat' ....D. May 13, 1943 Altoona, Pa.
1960-064 ....Maloney, James William ....7027 North Teilman Ave #102/Fresno CA 93711
1912-112 ....Maloney, Patrick William ....D. June 27, 1979 Pawtucket, R. I.
1997-105 ....Maloney, Sean Patrick ....Old Add: North Kingstown RI 02852
1913-109 ....Maloy, Paul Augustus ....D. March 18, 1976 Sandusky, O.
1943-082 ....Maltzberger, Gordon Ralph ....D. December 11, 1974 Rialto, Calif.
1955-077 ....Malzone, Frank James ....16 Aletha Rd/Needham MA 2192
1913-110 ....Mamaux, Albert Leon ....D. January 2, 1963 Santa Monica, Calif.
1928-063 ....Mancuso, August Rodney 'Gus' ....D. October 26, 1984 Houston, Texas
1944-081 ....Mancuso, Frank Octavius ....5126 Cripple Creek/Houston TX 77017
1914-135 ....Manda, Carl Alan ....D. March 9, 1983 Artesia, N. Mex.

1941-069 ....Manders, Harold Carl ....PO Box 149/Dallas Center/Ia 50063
1952-071 ....Mangan, James Daniel...............................6878 Trinidad/San Jose CA 95120
1969-106 ....Mangual, Angel Luis ....Las Delicias R10 Road Del Valle Ponce PR 731
1972-066 ....Mangual, Jose Manuel 'Pepe' ....2325 Calle Tabonuco/Ponce PR 731
1924-073 ....Mangum, Leon Allen ....D. July 9, 1974 Lima, O.
1912-113 ....Mangus, George Graham ....D. August 10, 1933 Rutland, Mass.
1920-079 ....Manion, Clyde Jennings ....D. September 4, 1967 Detroit, Mich.
1976-058 ....Mankowski, Philip Anthony ....204 Rosewood Terrace/Cheektowaga NY 14225
1944-082 ....Mann, Ben Garth 'Garth' ....D. September 11, 1980 Italy, Texas
1928-064 ....Mann, John Leo ....D. March 31, 1977 Terre Haute, Ind.
1989-078 ....Mann, Kelly John ....Old Add: 13950 Nw Passage #239 Marina Del Rey CA 90292
1913-111 ....Mann, Leslie ....D. January 14, 1962 Pasadena, Calif.
1914-136 ....Manning, Ernest Devon ....D. April 28, 1973 Pensacola, Fla.
1962-080 ....Manning, James Benjamin ....1049 Newstock Road/Weaverville NC 28789
1975-070 ....Manning, Richard Eugene ....12151 New Market/Chesterland OH 44026
1940-054 ....Manno, Donald ....D. March 11, 1995 Williamsport, Pa.
1990-096 ....Manon, Ramon (Reyes) ....Calle 18 #113 Sabana Perdida Santo Domingo Dominican Rep.
1981-079 ....Manrique, Fred Eloi ....Urb. Pedregal Calle Guradatinaja Casa L/1 Barquisimeto Venezuela
1995-130 ....Mantei, Matthew Bruce ....%Ted Mantei 13086 Three Oaks Rd Sawyer MI 49125
1956-055 ....Mantilla, Felix ....6973 North Tacoma St/Milwaukee WI 53224
1951-058 ....Mantle, Mickey Charles ....D. August 13, 1995 Dallas, Texas
1990-097 ....Manto, Jeffrey Paul ....802 Third Avenue/Bristol PA 19007
1991-115 ....Manuel, Barry Paul ....805 Oak Street/Mamou LA 70554
1969-107 ....Manuel, Charles Fuqua ....2931 Plantation Road/Winter Haven FL 33884
1975-071 ....Manuel, Jerry ....11111 Fawn Creek Lane/Orland Park IL 60467
1923-085 ....Manush, Henry Emmett 'Heinie' ....D. May 12, 1971 Sarasota, Fla.
1950-059 ....Manville, Richard Wesley ....1436 Lake Francis Drive/Apopka FL 32712
1987-089 ....Manwaring, Kurt Dean ....10938 North 123rd Street/Scottsdale AZ 85259
1991-116 ....Manzanillo, Josias ....12 Jasper/Lane/Randolph MA 2368
1988-085 ....Manzanillo, Ravelo ....Ulises Espaillat #7 San Pedro De Macoris Dominican Rep.
1919-054 ....Mapel, Rolla Mamilton ....D. April 6, 1966 San Diego, Calif.
1948-063 ....Mapes, Clifford Franklin ....D. December 5, 1996 Claremore, Okla.
1932-047 ....Maple, Howard Albert ....D. November 9, 1970 Portland, Ore.
1990-098 ....Marak, Paul Patrick ....1211 Comanche Trail/Alamogordo NM 88310
1960-065 ....Maranda, Georges Henri ....25 Louis-Brulot Street/Levis Quebec G6V 6X4 Canada
1912-114 ....Maranville, Walter James Vincent...................D. January 5, 1954 New York, N.Y.
1923-086 ....Marberry, Fredrick 'Firpo' ....D. June 30, 1976 Mexia, Tex.
1913-112 ....Marbet, Walter William ....D. September 24, 1956 Hohenwald, Tenn.
1940-055 ....Marchildon, Philip Joseph ....D. January 10, 1997 Toronto, Ontario
1933-041 ....Marcum, John Alfred ....D. September 10, 1984 Louisville, Ky.
1965-069 ....Marentette, Leo John ....33606 Beechwood Street/Westland MI 48185
1956-056 ....Margoneri, Joseph Emanuel ....341 Turkeytown Road/West Newton PA 15089
1960-066 ....Marichal, Juan Antonio Sanchez ....9458 Nw 54 Doral Circle Lane/Miami FL 33128
1914-137 ....Marion, Donald G. 'Dan' ....D. January 18, 1933 Milwaukee, Wis.
1935-065 ....Marion, John Wyeth 'Red' ....D. March 13, 1975 San Jose, Calif.
1940-056 ....Marion, Martin Whiteford 'Slats' ....8 Forcee Lane/Saint Louis MO 63124
1957-046 ....Maris, Roger Eugene ....D. December 14, 1985 Houston, Tex.
1951-059 ....Markell, Harry Duquesne 'Duke' ....D. June 14, 1984 Fort Lauderdale, Fla.
1950-060 ....Markland, Cleneth Eugene 'Gene' ....613 East Oleander Circle/Barefoot Bay FL 32976
1915-094 ....Markle, Clifford Monroe ....D. May 24, 1974 Temple City, Calif.
1951-060 ....Marlowe, Richard Burton ....D. December 30, 1968 Toledo, O.
1940-057 ....Marnie, Harry Sylvester 'Hal' ....2715 South Smetley/Philadelphia PA 19145
1953-053 ....Marolewski, Fred Daniel ....298 Bensley Avenue/Calumet City IL 60409
1969-108 ....Marone, Louis Stephen ....10651 Carbet Place/San Diego CA 92124
1931-051 ....Marquardt, Albert Ludwig 'Ollie' ....D. February 7, 1968 Port Clinton, O.
1972-067 ....Marquez, Gonzalo ....D. December 20, 1984 Valencia, Venezuela
1995-131 ....Marquez, Isidro Espinoza ....Old Add: Navajoa Sonora Mexico
1951-061 ....Marquez, Luis Angel ....D. March 1, 1988 Aguadilla, P. R.
1925-069 ....Marquis, James Milburn ....D. August 5, 1992 Jackson, Calif.
1953-054 ....Marquis, Robert Rudolph ....2075 Longfellow Drive/Beaumont TX 77706
1955-078 ....Marquis, Roger ....5 Lindbergh Ave/Holyoke MA 1040
1950-061 ....Marrero, Conrado Eugenio Ramos ....Old Add: Avontamiento #205 Apt 1 Havana Cuba
1997-106 ....Marrero, Elieser 'Eli' ....4040 SW 70th Court/Miami FL 33165
1993-112 ....Marrero, Oreste Vilato (Vazquez) ....Old Add: Urquay St T703, Forest Hill Bayamon PR 00618
1917-042 ....Marriott, William Earl ....D. August 11, 1969 Berkeley, Calif.
1932-048 ....Marrow, Charles Kennon 'Buck' ....D. November 21, 1982 Newport News, Va.
1911-109 ....Marsans, Armando ....D. September 3, 1960 Havana, Cuba
1949-048 ....Marsh, Fred Francis ....Rural Route 4/Corry PA 16407
1992-077 ....Marsh, Thomas Owen ....Old Add: 347 O'Connell St Toledo OH 43608
1941-070 ....Marshall, Charles Andrew ....1 Radcliff Court/Wilmington/De 19804
1946-067 ....Marshall, Clarence Westly ....27642-I Susan Beth Way/Saugus CA 91350
1967-069 ....Marshall, David Lewis ....4802 East Centralia Street/Long Beach CA 90808
1929-068 ....Marshall, Edward Harbert 'Doc' ....1840 Fairway Circle/San Marcos CA 92069
1958-058 ....Marshall, Jim Rufe ....5761 N. Casa Blanca/Scottsdale AZ 85253
1973-081 ....Marshall, Keith Alan ....Rural Route 1/Woodhull NY 14898
1981-080 ....Marshall, Michael Allen ....2305 Barton Creek Blvd #8/Austin TX 78735
1967-070 ....Marshall, Michael Grant ....4436 Plum Street/Zephyrhills FL 34248
1942-066 ....Marshall, Milo Max 'Max' ....D. September 6, 1993 Salem, Ore.
1912-115 ....Marshall, Roy Deverne 'Rube' ....D. June 11, 1980 Dover, O.

ALL-STAR AUTOGRAPHS

R. ALOMAR
S. ALOMAR
B. ANDERSON
J. BAGWELL
A. BELLE
D. BICHETTE
C. BIGGIO
W. BOGGS
B. BONDS
R. BOTTALICO
K. BROWN
J. BUHNER
E. BURKS
K. CAMINITI
J. CARTER
B. COX
C. FINLEY
T. FRYMAN
T. GLAVINE
K. GRIFFEY JR.
M. GRUDZIELANEK
T. GWYNN
M. HARGROVE
R. HERNANDEZ
T. HUNDLEY
L. JOHNSON
C. JONES
J. KENDALL
C. KNOBLAUCH
B. LARKIN

ALL-STAR AUTOGRAPHS

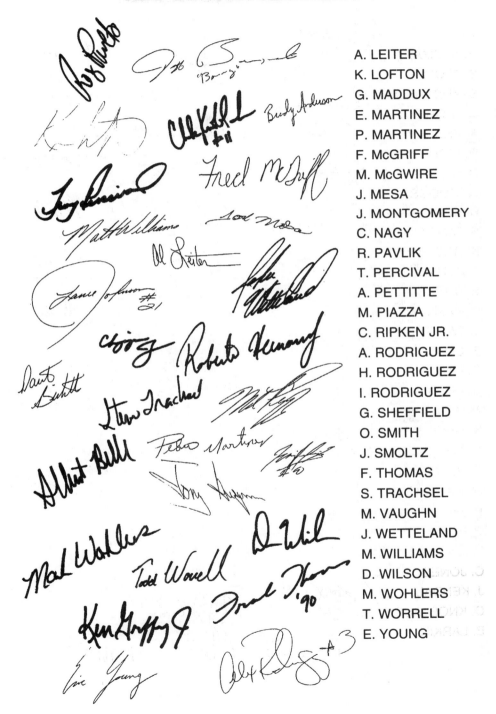

A. LEITER
K. LOFTON
G. MADDUX
E. MARTINEZ
P. MARTINEZ
F. McGRIFF
M. McGWIRE
J. MESA
J. MONTGOMERY
C. NAGY
R. PAVLIK
T. PERCIVAL
A. PETTITTE
M. PIAZZA
C. RIPKEN JR.
A. RODRIGUEZ
H. RODRIGUEZ
I. RODRIGUEZ
G. SHEFFIELD
O. SMITH
J. SMOLTZ
F. THOMAS
S. TRACHSEL
M. VAUGHN
J. WETTELAND
M. WILLIAMS
D. WILSON
M. WOHLERS
T. WORRELL
E. YOUNG

1942-067	Marshall, Willard Warren	7 Rockleigh Road/Rockleigh NJ 7647
1931-052	Marshall, William Henry	D. May 5, 1977 Sacramento, Calif.
1992-078	Martin, Albert Scales	Old Add: 2149 Aroma Drive West Covina CA 91719
1950-062	Martin, Alfred Manuel 'Billy'	D. December 25, 1989 Johnson City, N. Y.
1953-055	Martin, Barney Robert	D. October 30, 1997 Columbia, S. C.
1944-083	Martin, Boris Michael 'Babe'	14443 Bantry Lane #20/Chesterfield MO 63017
1979-073	Martin, Donald Renie Renie	PO Box 1109/Dover DE 19903
1917-043	Martin, Elwood Good 'Speed'	D. June 14, 1983 Lemon Grove, Calif.
1946-068	Martin, Fred Turner	D. June 11, 1979 Chicago, Ill.
1937-070	Martin, Hershel Ray	D. November 17, 1980 Cuba, Mo.
1974-079	Martin, Jerry Lindsey	109 Chelton Court/Columbia SC 29212
1912-116	Martin, John Christopher	D. July 4, 1980 Bronx, N. Y.
1928-065	Martin, John Leonard Roosevelt 'Pepper'	D. March 5, 1965 McAlester, Okla.
1980-085	Martin, John Robert	PO Box 1361/Palm City FL 34991
1959-052	Martin, Joseph Clifton 'J. C.'	112 Oakmont Court/Advance NC 27006
1986-094	Martin, Joseph Michael Mike	7904 Waterfalls Avenue/Las Vegas NV 89128
1949-049	Martin, Morris Webster	244 Pottery Road/Washington MO 63090
1993-113	Martin, Norberto Edonal 'Paco'	General Duberge 109 San Pedro De Macoris Dominican Rep.
1919-055	Martin, Patrick Francis	D. February 4, 1949 Brooklyn, N. Y.
1955-079	Martin, Paul Charles 'Jake'	1529 33rd Street/San Diego CA 92102
1943-083	Martin, Raymond Joseph	107 Pellana Road/Norwood MA 2062
1936-051	Martin, Stuart McGuire	D. January 11, 1997 Severn, N. C.
1997-107	Martin, Thomas Edgar	2406 East Baldwin Road/Panama City FL 32405
1968-057	Martin, Thomas Eugene 'Gene'	133 Winchester Drive/Leesburg GA 31763
1914-138	Martin, William Gloyd	D. September 15, 1949 Washington, D.C.
1936-052	Martin, William Joseph 'Joe'	D. September 28, 1960 Buffalo, N. Y.
1924-074	Martina, Joseph John	D. March 22, 1962 New Orleans, La.
1980-086	Martinez, Alfredo	2346 Thomas/Los Angeles CA 90031
1995-132	Martinez, Angel Sandy	Hermana Mirabel #166,Santa Cruz Santo Domingo Dominican Rep.
1988-086	Martinez, Carlos Alberto Escobar	Prol.,10 Marzo Blq 5 Let #706 "Laguaira,Dpo Vargas Venezuela/"
1983-095	Martinez, Carmelo	Brisas De Plata #32/Dorado PR 646
1990-099	Martinez, Constantino 'Tino'	230 Eagle Street/Tenafly NJ 7670
1986-095	Martinez, David	3266 Enterprise Road East/Safety Harbor FL 34695
1992-079	Martinez, Domingo Emilio	La Isabela,Los Alcarrizzo#35,Rd Santo Domingo Dominican Rep.
1987-090	Martinez, Edgar	Old Add: 9717 NE Juanita Drive Kirkland WA 98033
1974-080	Martinez, Felix Anthony 'Tippy'	1524 Dellsway Rd/Towson MD 21204
1997-108	Martinez, Felix Mata	Old Add: Nagua Dominican Rep.
1963-075	Martinez, Gabriel Antonio 'Tony'	D. August 24, 1991 Miami, Fla.
1969-109	Martinez, John Albert 'Buck'	6213 Vista Ave/Sacramento CA 95824
1969-110	Martinez, Jose Azcuiz	18809 Nw 79th Way/Hialeah FL 33015
1976-059	Martinez, Jose Dennis 'Dennis'	Old Add: 9795 SW 62nd Street Miami FL 33173
1994-069	Martinez, Jose Miguel (Martinez)	7971 Park Drive/Fair Oaks CA 95628
1996-113	Martinez, Manuel Dejesus	Old Add: San Pedro De Macoris D. R.
1962-082	Martinez, Orlando Olivo 'Marty'	748 North 23rd West Avenue/Tulsa OK 74127
1996-114	Martinez, Pablo Valera	Old Add: Tampa FL 33601
1993-114	Martinez, Pedro Aquino	Villa Mela El Vonito #121 Santo Domingo Dominican Rep.
1992-080	Martinez, Pedro Jaime	Principal #9,Manoguayabo,D.N. Santo Domingo Dominican Rep.
1988-087	Martinez, Ramon Jaime	Bo. San Miguel #9,Managuayaba Santo Domingo Dominican Rep.
1991-117	Martinez, Reyenaldo Igancio 'Chito'	Old Add: 1109 Mercury Avenue Metairie LA 70003
1962-081	Martinez, Rodolfo Hector	Old Add: Marianoa Havana Cuba
1950-063	Martinez, Rogelio Ulloa	Old Add: 9118 5th Avenue Brooklyn NY 11209
1977-087	Martinez, Silvio Ramon	Old Add: Carlos De Lora 25 Santiago Dominican Rep.
1970-085	Martinez, Teodoro Noel	J. Contreras #194,Ens. Lapaz Santo Domingo Dominican Rep.
1935-066	Martini, Guido Joe 'Wedo'	D. October 28, 1970 Philadelphia, Pa.
1937-071	Marty, Joseph Anton	D. October 4, 1984 Sacramento, Calif.
1957-047	Martyn, Robert Gordon	3365 SW 123rd/Beaverton OR 97005
1975-072	Martz, Gary Martz	525 Sage Hill Drive/Wenatchee WA 98801
1980-087	Martz, Randy Carl	211 HI Pointe Plaza/East Alton IL 62024
1987-091	Marzano, John Robert	1224 South 11th Street/Philadelphia PA 19147
1969-111	Mashore, Clyde Wayne	PO Box 5353/Concord CA 94524
1996-115	Mashore, Damon Wayne	1519 Heather Drive/Concord CA 94521
1939-073	Masi, Philip Samuel	D. March 29, 1990 Mount Prospect, Ill.
1966-058	Mason, Donald Stetson	8 Fawn Road/South Yarmouth MA 2664
1958-059	Mason, Henry	5523 Paseo Blvd/Kansas City MO 64110
1971-066	Mason, James Percy	Old Add: Rr 1 Box 308/Theodore AL 36582
1982-081	Mason, Michael Paul	18699 Clearview Terrace/Minnetonka MN 55345
1984-073	Mason, Roger Leroy	7510 Meadow Lane/Bellaire MI 49615
1957-048	Massa, Gordon Richard	5905 Kimberly Ave/Cincinnati OH 45213
1918-045	Massey, Roy Hardee	D. June 23, 1954 Atlanta, Ga.
1917-044	Massey, William Herbert 'Mike'	D. October 17, 1971 Shreveport, La.
1995-133	Masteller, Dan Patrick	159111 Alderside Drive/Shaker Heights OH 44120
1931-053	Masters, Walter Thomas	D. July 10, 1992 Ottawa, Ontario
1940-058	Masterson, Paul Nickalis	D. November 27, 1997 Chicago, Ill.
1939-074	Masterson, Walter Edward	4515 Carteret Drive/New Bern NC 28562
1984-074	Mata, Victor Jose	Juan Pablo Pina, #16 Alto Santo Domingo Dominican Rep.
1952-072	Matarazzo, Leonard	2715 Carlisle Street/New Castle PA 16105
1967-071	Matchick, John Thomas 'Tom'	5523 Brentwood Drive/Toledo OH 43615
1994-070	Matheny, Michael Scott	5360 Tower Hill Court/Saint Charles MO 63304
1912-117	Mathes, Joseph John	D. December 21, 1978 St. Louis, Mo.

1952-073	Mathews, Edwin Lee	13744 Recuerdo Drive/Del Mar CA 92014
1986-096	Mathews, Gregory Inman	Old Add: 5682 Tahoe Circle Buena Park CA 90621
1960-067	Mathews, Nelson Elmer	211 Crestview/Columbia IL 62236
1991-118	Mathews, Terry Alan	1132 Belgard Bend/Boyce LA 71409
1995-134	Mathews, Timothy Jay 'T. J.'	211 Crestview Drive/Columbia IL 62236
1960-068	Mathias, Carl Lynwood	Rr 2/Oley PA 19567
1985-070	Mathis, Ronald Vance	Old Add: 10326 Bon Oak Dr Saint Louis MO 63136
1970-086	Matias, John Roy	98-1616 Hoolauae St/Aiea HI 96701
1971-067	Matlack, Jonathan Trumpbour	936 Country Road 34/Norwich NY 13815
1994-071	Matos, Francisco Aguirre (Mancebo)	% Duarte #14 Estebania Anza Dominican Rep.
1914-139	Matteson, Henry Edson	D. August 31, 1943 Brocton, N.Y.
1972-068	Matthews, Gary Nathaniel	175 North Harbor #4306/Chicago IL 60601
1922-081	Matthews, John Joseph	D. February 8, 1968 Hagerstown, Md.
1923-087	Matthews, Wid Curry	D. October 5, 1965 Hollywood, Calif.
1943-084	Matthewson, Dale Wesley	D. February 20, 1984 Blairsville, Ga.
1938-059	Mattick, Robert James	20073 North Clear Canyon Drive/Surprise AZ 85374
1912-118	Mattick, Walter Joseph	D. November 5, 1968 Los Altos, Calif.
1982-082	Mattingly, Donald Arthur	12641 Browning Road/Evansville IN 47711
1931-054	Mattingly, Laurence Earl	D. September 8, 1993 Brookville, Md.
1914-140	Mattis, Ralph L.	D. September 13, 1960 Williamsport, Pa.
1929-069	Mattox, Cloy Mitchell	D. August 3, 1985 Danville, Va.
1922-082	Mattox, James Powell	D. October 12, 1973 Myrtle Beach, S. C.
1979-074	Matula, Richard Carlton	1817 Chapel Heights Dr/Wharton TX 77488
1981-081	Matuszek, Leonard James	4208 North Avenue/Cincinnati OH 45236
1934-065	Matuzak, Harry George	D. November 26, 1978 Hope, Ala.
1944-084	Mauch, Eugene William	71 Princeton/Rancho Mirage CA 92270
1934-066	Mauldin, Marshall Reese	D. September 2, 1990 Union City, Ga.
1924-075	Maun, Ernest Gerald	D. January 1, 1987 Corpus Christi, Texas
1945-066	Mauney, Richard	D. February 6, 1970 Albemarle, N. C.
1991-119	Maurer, Robert John	2315 East Powell Avenue/Evansville IN 47714
1958-060	Mauriello, Ralph	23644 Del Cer Cir/Canoga Park CA 91304
1948-064	Mauro, Carmen Louis	5757 Cypress Avenue/Carmichael CA 95608
1991-120	Mauser, Timothy Edward	1321 Saxony Road/Fort Worth TX 76116
1949-050	Mavis, Robert Henry	300 Markwood Drive/Little Rock AR 72205
1995-135	Maxcy, David Brian 'Brian'	8 Azalea Lane/Amory MS 38821
1969-112	Maxie, Larry Hans	PO Box 1930/Upland CA 91786
1962-083	Maxvill, Charles Dallan 'Dal'	1115 Eagle Creek Road/Chesterfield MO 63005
1950-064	Maxwell, Charles Richard	730 Mapleview Avenue/Paw Paw MI 49079
1968-058	May, Carlos	Old Add: 14557 Avers Ave Midlothian IL 60445
1995-136	May, Darrell Kevin	747 Menthorne/Rogue River OR 97537
1967-072	May, David Lafrance	151 Auckland Drive/Newark DE 19702
1990-100	May, Derrick Brant	Old Add: 19 Madison Drive Newark DE 19711
1917-045	May, Frank Spruiell 'Jakie'	D. June 3, 1970 Wendell, N. C.
1964-068	May, Jerry Lee	D. June 30, 1996 Swoope, Va.
1965-070	May, Lee Andrew	5593 Hill & Dale/Cincinnati OH 45211
1939-075	May, Merrill Glend 'Pinky'	51 Cruse Loop SE/Corydon IN 47112
1970-087	May, Milton Scott	6116 Shore Acres Drive/Bradenton FL 34209
1965-071	May, Rudolph	8090 North Augusta Street/Fresno CA 93720
1988-088	May, Scott Francis	4523 West Lake Shore Drive/Wonder Lake IL 60097
1924-076	May, William Herbert 'Buckshot'	D. March 15, 1984 Bakersfield, Calif.
1968-059	Mayberry, John Claiborn	11115 West 121st Terrace/Overland Park KS 66213
1959-053	Maye, Arthur Lee 'Lee'	151 Digby Court/Riverside CA 92506
1957-049	Mayer, Edwin David	440 Oakdale Ave/Corte Madera CA 94925
1912-119	Mayer, Erskine John	D. March 10, 1957 Los Angeles, Calif.
1915-095	Mayer, Samuel Frankel	D. July 1, 1962 Atlanta, Ga.
1911-110	Mayer, Walter A.	D. November 18, 1951 Minneapolis, Minn.
1911-111	Mayes, Adair Bushyhead 'Paddy'	D. May 28, 1962 Fayetteville, Ark.
1940-059	Maynard, James Walter	D. September 7, 1977 Durham, N. C.
1922-083	Maynard, Leroy Evans 'Chick'	D. January 31, 1957 Bangor, Me.
1990-101	Mayne, Brent Danem	291 Flower Street #B/Costa Mesa CA 92627
1936-053	Mayo, Edward Joseph	823 South Riviera Avenue/Banning CA 92220
1948-065	Mayo, John Lewis 'Jackie'	719 Mapleridge Drive/Youngstown OH 44512
1915-096	Mays, Carl William	D. April 4, 1971 El Cajon, Calif.
1951-062	Mays, Willie Howard	51 Mount Vernon Lane/Atherton CA 94025
1992-081	Maysey, Matthew Samuel	Old Add: 2430 India Palm Edgewater FL 32032
1956-057	Mazeroski, William Stanley	Rr6 Box 130/Greensburg PA 15601
1935-067	Mazzera, Melvin Leonard	D. December 19, 1997 Stockton, Calif.
1976-060	Mazzilli, Lee Louis	12 Carpenters Drk Rd/Greenwich CT 6830
1911-112	McAdams, George D. 'Jack'	D. May 21, 1937 San Francisco, Calif.
1930-049	McAfee, William Fort	D. July 8, 1958 Culpepper, Va.
1913-113	McAllester, William Lusk	D. March 3, 1970 Chattanooga, Tenn.
1971-068	McAnally, Ernest Lee	PO Box 942/Mount Pleasant TX 75456
1958-061	McAnany, James	11066 Rhoda Way/Culver City CA 90230
1995-137	McAndrew, James Brian	Old Add: %Ej McAndrew,16007 David Fort Myers FL 33908
1968-060	McAndrew, James Clement	1215 Moorland Woods Court/Creve Coeur MO 63146
1914-141	McArthur, Oland Alexander 'Dixie'	D. May 31, 1986 Columbus, Miss.
1914-142	McAuley, James Earl 'Ike'	D. April 6, 1928 Des Moines, Ia.
1960-069	McAuliffe, Richard John	9 Crossroads Lane/Avon CT 6001
1914-143	McAvoy, George	Old Add:/Ardmore OK 73401

1913-114 ....McAvoy, James Eugene 'Wickey' ....D. July 5, 1973 Rochester, N. Y.
1959-054 ....McAvoy, Thomas John ....Clinton Court/Stillwater NY 12118
1961-072 ....Mcbean, Alvin Oneal ....Box 4475/St Thomas VI 801
1926-053 ....Mcbee, Pryor Edward ....D. April 19, 1963 Roseville, Calif.
1973-082 ....Mcbride, Arnold Ray 'Bake'..........................Old Add: 3314 Cross Keys Dr #1 Florissant MI 63033
1959-055 ....Mcbride, Kenneth Faye ....Old Add: 3118 W. 118th Street Cleveland OH 44111
1943-085 ....Mcbride, Thomas Raymond ....3219 Carol Ann/Wichita Falls TX 76309
1964-069 ....McCabe, Joe Robert ....3003 Gulf Shore Blvd N. #904/Naples FL 34103
1946-069 ....McCabe, Ralph Herbert ....D. May 4, 1974 Windsor, Ont.
1918-046 ....McCabe, Richard James ....D. April 11, 1950 Buffalo, N. Y.
1915-097 ....McCabe, Timothy ....D. April 12, 1977 Ironton, Mo.
1918-047 ....McCabe, William Francis ....D. September 2, 1966 Chicago, Ill.
1946-070 ....McCahan, William Glenn ....D. July 3, 1986 Fort Worth, Texas
1962-084 ....McCall, Brian Allen ....105 Union St/Alexandria VA 22314
1948-066 ....McCall, John William ....9552 East Ozark Street/Tucson AZ 85748
1977-088 ....McCall, Larry Stephen ....Rr 5 Box 354/Candler NC 28715
1948-067 ....McCall, Robert Leonard ....D. January 7, 1996 Little Rock, Ark.
1927-057 ....McCallister, John ....D. October 18, 1946 Columbus, O.
1989-079 ....McCament, Larry Randall Randy ....15601 North 60th Ave/Glendale AZ 85306
1914-144 ....McCandless, Scott Cook 'John' ....D. August 17, 1961 Pittsburgh, Pa.
1920-080 ....McCann, Robert Emmett ....D. April 15, 1937 Philadelphia, Pa.
1959-056 ....McCardell, Roger Morton..............................D. November 13, 1996 Perry Point, Md.
1923-088 ....McCarren, William Joseph ....D. September 11, 1983 Denver, Colo.
1910-096 ....McCarthy, Alexander George ....D. March 12, 1978 Salisbury, Md.
1996-116 ....McCarthy, Gregory Oneil ....Old Add: Shelton CT 06484
1948-068 ....McCarthy, Jerome Francis ....D. October 3, 1965 Oceanside, N. Y.
1934-067 ....McCarthy, John Joseph.................................D. September 13, 1973 Mundelein, Ill.
1926-054 ....McCarthy, Joseph Vincent ....D. January 13, 1978 Buffalo,N. Y.
1985-071 ....McCarthy, Thomas Michael ....10 Carolyn Drive/Plymouth MA 2360
1993-115 ....McCarty, David Andrew ....2119 Shadow Park Drive/Katy TX 77494
1913-115 ....McCarty, George Lewis ....D. June 9, 1930 Reading, Pa.
1959-057 ....McCarver, James Timothy 'Tim' ....1518 Youngford Rd/Gladwynne PA 19035
1985-072 ....McCaskill, Kirk Edward ....PO Box 451/Rancho Santa Fe CA 92067
1977-089 ....McCatty, Steven Earl ....6566 Coolidge Hwy/Troy MI 48094
1961-073 ....McClain, Joe Fred...Rr 8 Box 109/Johnson City TN 37601
1931-055 ....McClanahan, Robert Hugh 'Pete' ....D. October 28, 1987 Mont Belvieu, Texas
1919-056 ....McClellan, Hervey McDowell ....D. November 6, 1925 Cynthiana, Ky.
1990-102 ....McClellan, Paul William ....1193 Cleveland Street/Redwood City CA 94061
1987-092 ....McClendon, Lloyd Glenn ....2055 West 64th Plaza/Gary IN 46410
1913-116 ....McCleskey, Jefferson Lamar..........................D. May 11, 1971 Americus, Ga.
1936-054 ....McCloskey, James Ellwood............................D. August 18, 1971 Jersey City, N. J.
1910-097 ....McClure, Lawrence Ledwith ....D. August 31, 1948 Huntington, W. Va.
1975-073 ....McClure, Robert Craig ....Old Add: 9492 Harbor Drive #18d Spirit Lake IA 51360
1915-098 ....McCluskey, Harry Robert ....D. June 7, 1962 Toledo, O.
1933-042 ....McColl, Alexander Boyd ....D. February 6, 1991 Kingsville, Ohio
1914-145 ....McConnaughey, Ralph J................................D. June 4, 1966 Detroit, Mich.
1915-099 ....McConnell, Samuel Faulkner ....D. June 27, 1981 Phoenixville, Pa.
1964-070 ....McCool, William John ....Old Add: 1560 Frontier Court Spring Valley OH 45370
1980-088 ....McCormack, Donald Ross ....Old Add: 2331 Azalea Dr Palm Harbor FL 34683
1934-068 ....McCormick, Frank Andrew ....D. November 21, 1982 Manhasset, N. Y.
1956-058 ....McCormick, Michael Francis ....532 Crawford Drive/Sunnyvale CA 94087
1940-060 ....McCormick, Myron Winthrop 'Mike' ....D. April 14, 1976 Los Angeles, Calif.
1939-076 ....McCosky, William Barney 'Barney'..................D. September 6, 1996 Venice, Fla.
1959-058 ....McCovey, Willie Lee ....PO Box 620342/Woodside CA 94062
1938-060 ....McCoy, Benjamin Jenison ....3932 East Omaha Drive Sw/Grandville MI 49418
1939-077 ....McCrabb, Lester William ....44 Cedar Acres Drive/Lancaster PA 17602
1995-138 ....McCracken, Quintin Antoine ....%Arch McCracken 803 Clarendon Southport NC 28461
1963-076 ....McCraw, Tommy Lee ....3142 Monte Vista Court/Port Saint Lucie FL 34952
1990-103 ....McCray, Rodney Duncan ....20273 Faust Avenue/Detroit MI 48219
1925-070 ....McCrea, Francis William ....D. February 25, 1981 Dover, N. J.
1914-146 ....McCreery, Esley Porterfield...........................D. October 19, 1960 Sacramento, Calif.
1922-084 ....McCue, Frank Aloysius ....D. July 5, 1953 Evergreen Park, Ill.
1985-073 ....McCullers, Lance Graye ....4309 Round Lake Court/Tampa FL 33624
1940-061 ....McCullough, Clyde Edward ....D. September 18, 1982 San Francisco, Calif.
1929-070 ....McCullough, Paul Willard ....D. November 7, 1970 Newcastle, Pa.
1942-068 ....McCullough, Philip Lamar ....25 Exeter Road/Avondale Estates GA 30002
1922-085 ....McCurdy, Harry Henry ....D. July 21, 1972 Houston, Tex.
1995-139 ....McCurry, Jeffrey Dee ....5454 Newcastle Drive/Houston TX 77081
1955-080 ....McDaniel, Lyndall Dale ....Rural Route 2 Box 353a/Hollis OK 73550
1957-050 ....McDaniel, Max Von 'Von' ....D. August 20, 1995 Lawton, Okla.
1991-121 ....McDaniel, Terrence Keith ....537 Nw 55th Terrace/Kansas City MO 64118
1994-072 ....McDavid, Ray Darnell ....3819 Hemlock/San Diego CA 92113
1912-120 ....McDermott, Frank A. 'Red' ....D. September 11, 1964 Philadelphia, Pa.
1948-069 ....McDermott, Maurice Joseph 'Mickey' ....3725 East Rockwood Drive/Phoenix AZ 85024
1972-069 ....McDermott, Terrence Michael ....7205 Sunlight Peak Drive NE/Rio Rancho NM 87124
1957-051 ....McDevitt, Daniel Eugene ....2991 Salem Rd SE/Conyers GA 30207
1997-109 ....McDill, Allen Gabriel.....................................Old Add: Hot Springs AR 71901
1912-121 ....McDonald, Charles E. 'Tex' ....D. March 31, 1943 Houston, Tex.
1969-113 ....McDonald, David Bruce ....2545 SE Third Street/Pompano Beach FL 33062

1911-113	McDonald, Edward C.	D. March 11, 1946 Albany, N.Y.
1931-056	McDonald, Henry Monroe	D. October 17, 1982 Hemet, Calif.
1997-110	McDonald, Jason Adam	Old Add: Elk Grove CA 95624
1950-065	McDonald, Jimmie Leroy	3767 Stirrup Drive/Kingman AZ 86401
1989-080	McDonald, Larry Benard 'Ben'	Old Add: Denham Springs LA 70726
1910-098	McDonald, Malcolm Joseph	D. May 30, 1963 Baytown, Texas
1943-086	McDonnell, James Joseph	D. April 24, 1993 Detroit, Mich.
1951-063	McDougald, Gilbert James	10 Warren Avenue/Spring Lake NJ 7762
1987-093	McDowell, Jack Burns	1949 North Seminary/Chicago IL 60614
1985-074	McDowell, Oddibe	5240 SW 18th Street/Hollywood FL 33023
1985-075	McDowell, Roger Alan	4793 Crestwood Rdive/Jackson MS 39211
1961-074	McDowell, Samuel Edward	7479 McClure Avenue/Pittsburgh PA 15218
1989-081	McElroy, Charles Dwayne	1049 Nederland Avenue/Port Arthur TX 77640
1916-060	McElwee, Leland Stanford	D. February 8, 1957 Union, Me.
1942-069	McElyea, Frank	D. April 19, 1987 Evansville, Ind.
1974-081	McEnaney, William Henry	1055 SW Third Street/Boca Raton FL 33486
1930-050	McEvoy, Louis Anthony	D. December 16, 1953 Webster Grove, Mo.
1968-061	McFadden, Leon	8617 10th Avenue/Inglewood CA 90305
1945-067	McFarland, Howard Alexander	D. April 7, 1993 Wichita, Kans.
1962-085	McFarlane, Orlando De Jesus	Old Add: 33 Taft Ave Asheville NC 28803
1981-082	McGaffigan, Andrew Joseph	6243 Forestwood Drive East/Lakeland FL 33811
1917-046	McGaffigan, Mark Andrew 'Patsy'	D. December 22, 1940 Carlyle, Ill.
1946-071	McGah, Edward Joseph	PO Box 1056/Alamo CA 94507
1962-086	McGaha, Fred Melvin 'Mel'	PO Box 273/Disney OK 74340
1912-122	McGarr, James Vincent	D. July 21, 1981 Miami, Fla.
1912-123	McGarvey, Daniel Francis	D. March 7, 1947 Philadelphia, Pa.
1934-069	McGee, Daniel Aloysius	D. December 4, 1991 Lakehurst, N. J.
1925-071	McGee, Francis D. 'Tubby'	D. January 30, 1934 Columbus, O.
1935-068	McGee, William Henry	D. February 11, 1987 St. Louis, Mo.
1982-083	McGee, Willie Dean	668 Turquoise Drive/Hercules CA 94547
1911-114	McGeehan, Daniel Desales	D. July 12, 1955 Hazelton, Pa.
1993-116	McGehee, George Kevin	18 Melmoore Drive/Pineville LA 71360
1912-124	McGehee, Patrick Henry	D. December 30, 1946 Paducah, Ky.
1950-066	McGhee, Warren Edward 'Ed'	D. February 13, 1986 Memphis, Tenn.
1944-085	McGhee, William Mac	D. March 10, 1984 Decatur, Ga.
1977-090	McGilberry, Randall Kent	1107 Fribourg Street/Mobile AL 36608
1944-086	McGillen, John Joseph	D. August 11, 1987 Upland, Pa.
1968-062	McGinn, Daniel Michael	1340 South 163rd St/Omaha NE 68120
1992-082	McGinnis, Russell Brent	15437 South 23rd Place/Phoenix AZ 85048
1972-070	McGlothen, Lynn Everett	D. August 14, 1984 Dubach, La.
1949-051	McGlothin, Ezra Mac 'Pat'	2317 Corefield Road/Knoxville TN 37919
1965-072	McGlothlin, James Milton	D. December 23, 1975 Union, Ky.
1922-086	McGowan, Frank Bernard 'Beauty'	D. May 6, 1982 Hamden, Conn.
1948-070	McGowan, Tullis Earl 'Mickey'	618 Spratt Street/Waycross GA 31501
1912-125	McGraner, Howard	D. October 22, 1952 Zaleski, O.
1965-073	McGraw, Frank Edwin 'Tug'	6 Rose Hill Road/Media PA 19063
1917-047	McGraw, Robert Emmett	D. June 2, 1978 Boise, Id.
1914-147	McGraw, (Roy Elmer Hoar)	D. April 27, 1967 Torrance, Calif.
1997-111	McGraw, Thomas Virgil	Old Add: Battleground WA 98604
1976-061	McGregor, Scott Houston	Old Add: 32 Chatham Court Dover DE 19901
1922-087	McGrew, Walter Howard 'Slim'	D. August 21, 1967 Port Arthur, Tex.
1986-097	McGriff, Frederick Stanley	PO Box 17257/Tampa FL 33672
1987-094	McGriff, Terence Roy	2905 Langston Drive/Fort Pierce FL 33450
1962-087	McGuire, M. C. Adolfus 'Mickey'	4236 Dorset Drive/Dayton OH 45405
1997-112	McGuire, Ryan Byron	Old Add: Woodland Hills CA 91367
1914-148	McGuire, Thomas Patrick	D. December 8, 1959 Phoenix, Az.
1988-089	McGuire, William Patrick	5705 South 135th Street/Omaha NE 68137
1986-098	McGwire, Mark David	Old Add: 6615 East Pch #260 Long Beach CA 90803
1943-087	McHale, John Joseph	2014 Royal Fern Court/Palm City FL 34990
1910-099	McHale, Martin Joseph	D. May 7, 1979 Hempstead, N. Y.
1918-048	McHenry, Austin Bush	D. November 27, 1922 Mt. Oreb, O.
1981-083	McHenry, Vance Loren	2396 Brown St-/Durham CA 95938
1921-059	McIlree, Vance Elmer	D. May 6, 1959 Kansas City, Mo.
1957-052	McIlwain, William Stover 'Stover'	D. January 15, 1966 Buffalo, N. Y.
1974-082	McIntosh, Joseph Anthony	1011 Western Avenue #803/Seattle WA 98104
1990-104	McIntosh, Timothy Alan	Old Add: 2044 Louisiana Avenue Saint Louis Park MN 55426
1911-115	McIver, Edward Otto	D. May 4, 1954 Dallas, Tex.
1937-072	McKain, Archie Richard	D. May 21, 1985 Salina, Kan.
1927-058	McKain, Harold Leroy	D. January 24, 1970 Sacramento, Calif.
1975-074	McKay, David Lawrence	9702 East La Posada Circle/Scottsdale AZ 85255
1915-100	McKay, Reeve Stewart	D. January 18, 1946 Dallas, Tex.
1972-071	McKee, James Marion	Old Add: 31 S. Hamilton/Columbus OH 43213
1913-117	McKee, Ray 'Red'	D. August 5, 1972 Saginaw, Mich.
1943-088	McKee, Rogers Hornsby	409 Forest Hill Drive/Shelby NC 28150
1996-117	McKeel, Walter Thomas	Rural Route 2 Box 105b/Stantonsburg NC 27883
1932-049	McKeithan, Emmett James 'Tim'	D. August 20, 1969 Forest City, N. C.
1915-101	McKenry, Frank Gordon 'Limb'	D. November 1, 1956 Fresno, Calif.
1986-099	McKeon, Joel Jacob	1901 Pierce Street/Hollywood FL 33020
1973-083	McKeon, John Aloysius 'Jack'	1529 Charleigh Court/Elon College NC 27244

1970-088	McKinney, Charles Richard 'Rich'	2393 East Peterson/Troy OH 45373
1960-070	McKnight, James Arthur	D. February 24, 1994 Van Buren County, Ark.
1989-082	McKnight, Jefferson Alan	PO Box 394/Charleston AR 72933
1963-077	McLain, Dennis Dale	11994 Hyne Road/Brighton MI 48116
1932-050	McLarney, Arthur James	D. December 20, 1984 Seattle, Wash.
1912-126	McLarry, Howard Zell 'Polly'	D. November 4, 1971 Bonham, Tex.
1977-091	McLaughlin, Byron Scott	Old Add: 3464 Sweetwater Mesa/Malibu CA 92154
1914-149	McLaughlin, James Anson 'Kid'	D. November 13, 1934 Allegany, N.Y.
1932-051	McLaughlin, James Robert	D. December 18, 1968 Mount Vernon, Ill.
1977-092	McLaughlin, Joey Richard	1611 South Troost/Tulsa OK 74120
1931-057	McLaughlin, Justin Theodore 'Jud'	D. September 27, 1964 Cambridge, Mass.
1976-062	McLaughlin, Michael Duane 'Bo'	536 North Grand/Mesa AZ 85201
1937-073	McLaughlin, Patrick Elmer	1535 Chantilly Lane/Houston TX 77018
1935-069	McLean, Albert Eldon 'Eldon'	D. September 29, 1990 Asheboro, N. C.
1951-064	McLeland, Wayne Gaffney	6622 Beldart/Houston TX 77017
1986-100	McLemore, Mark Tremell	312 Sheffield Drive/Southlake TX 76092
1938-061	McLeod, Ralph Alton	30 Acton Street/Wollaston MA 2170
1930-051	McLeod, Soule James 'Jim'	D. August 3, 1981 Little Rock, Ark.
1944-087	McLish, Calvin Coolidge	700 Timber Ridge Road/Edmond OK 73034
1956-059	McMahan, Jack Wally	152 Mimosa Point #C3/Hot Springs AR 71913
1957-053	McMahon, Donald John	D. July 22, 1987 Los Angeles, Calif.
1960-071	McManus, James Michael	Old Add: 1238 Boylston Street/Chestnut Hill MA 02167
1913-118	McManus, Joab Logan	D. December 23, 1955 Skelton, W. Va.
1920-081	McManus, Martin Joseph	D. February 18, 1966 St. Louis, Mo.
1968-063	McMath, Jimmy Lee	4837 Virginia Circle/Tuscaloosa AL 35401
1993-117	McMichael, Gregory Winston	305 Laurel Green Way/Alpharetta GA 30202
1922-088	McMillan, Norman Alexis	D. September 28, 1969 Latta, S. C.
1951-065	McMillan, Roy David	D. November 2, 1997 Bonham, Texas
1977-093	McMillan, Thomas Erwin	3810 West Cooper Lake Drive/Smyrna GA 30080
1996-118	McMillion, William Edward	Old Add: Sumter SC 29150
1925-072	McMullen, Hugh Raphael	D. May 23, 1986 Whittier, Calif.
1962-088	McMullen, Kenneth Lee	10 Estaban/Camarillo CA 93010
1914-150	McMullin, Frederick William	D. November 21, 1952 Los Angeles, Calif.
1983-096	McMurtry, Joe Craig 'Craig'	2835 Bottoms East Road/Troy TX 76579
1945-068	McNabb, Carl Mac	PO Box 203/Jasper/Tn 37347
1929-071	McNair, Donald Eric	D. March 11, 1949 Meridian, Miss.
1962-089	McNally, David Arthur	3305 Ramada Dr/Billings MT 59102
1915-102	McNally, Michael Joseph	D. May 29, 1965 Bethlehem, Pa.
1922-089	McNamara, George Francis	D. June 12, 1990 Hinsdale, Ill.
1992-083	McNamara, James Patrick	2526 West Meredith Drive/Vienna VA 22180
1969-114	McNamara, John Francis	1206 Beech Hill/Brentwood TN 37027
1927-059	McNamara, John Raymond	D. December 20, 1963 Arlington, Texas
1939-078	McNamara, Robert Maxey	23810 Barona Mesa Road/Ramona CA 92065
1922-090	McNamara, Thomas Henry	D. May 5, 1974 Danvers, Mass.
1922-091	McNamara, Timothy Augustine	D. November 5, 1994 North Smithfield, R. I.
1932-052	McNaughton, Gordon Joseph	D. August 6, 1942 Chicago, Ill.
1983-097	McNealy, Robert Lee	3301 Bozeman Street/Sacramento CA 95838
1924-077	McNeely, George Earl	D. July 16, 1971 Sacramento, Calif.
1993-118	McNeely, Jeffrey Laverne	405 Everette Street/Monroe NC 28110
1919-057	McNeil, Norman Francis	D. April 11, 1942 Buffalo, N. Y.
1964-071	McNertney, Gerald Edward 'Jerry'	584 193rd Street/Ames IA 50010
1922-092	McNulty, Patrick Howard	D. May 4, 1963 Hollywood, Calif.
1969-115	McNulty, William Francis	25606 99ty Avenue East/Graham WA 98338
1923-089	McQuaid, Herbert George	D. April 5, 1966 Richmond, Calif.
1934-070	McQuaig, Gerald Joseph	110 School Drive/Buford GA 30518
1969-116	McQueen, Michael Robert	3206 Cameo Dr/Houston TX 77055
1918-049	McQuillan, Hugh A.	D. August 26, 1947 New York, N. Y.
1938-062	McQuillen, Glenn Richard	D. June 8, 1989 Gardenville, Md.
1936-055	McQuinn, George Hartley	D. December 24, 1978 Alexandria, Va.
1990-105	McRae, Brian Wesley	2431 Landings Circle/Bradenton FL 34209
1968-064	McRae, Harold Abraham	2431 Landing Circle/Bradenton FL 33529
1969-117	McRae, Norman	Old Add: 1009 Laura St/Elizabeth NJ 07206
1983-098	McReynolds, Walter Kevin 'Kevin'	Old Add: 20 Hillside Ave Newport Beach CA 92060
1911-116	Mctigue, William Patrick	D. May 11, 1920 Nashville, Tenn.
1921-060	McWeeny, Douglas Lawrence	D. January 1, 1953 Melrose Park, Ill.
1978-079	McWilliams, Larry Dean	4102 Beckley Court/Colleyville TX 76034
1931-058	McWilliams, William Henry	D. January 21, 1997 Garland, Texas
1983-099	Meacham, Robert Andrew	5530 East Briarwood Circle/Littleton CO 80122
1991-122	Meacham, Russell Loren 'Rusty'	Old Add: Stuart FL
1943-089	Mead, Charles Richard	7482 Svl Box/Victorville CA 92392
1920-082	Meador, John Davis	D. April 11, 1970 Winston-Salem, N. C.
1915-103	Meadows, Henry Lee	D. January 29, 1963 Daytona Beach, Fla.
1986-101	Meadows, Michael Ray	Old Add: 20 Hadley Collins Rd Maysville NC 28555
1926-055	Meadows, Rufus Rivers	D. May 10, 1970 Wichita, Kan.
1987-095	Meads, David Donald 'Don'	Box 70 Federal Road Englishtown NJ 7726
1912-127	Meaney, Patrick	D. October 20, 1922 Philadelphia,Pa.
1914-151	Meara, Charles Edward	D. February 8, 1962 Kingsbridge, N. Y.
1993-119	Meares, Patrick James	2335 Wesley/Salina KS 67401
1995-140	Mecir, James Mason	15350 Amberly Drive #4111/Tampa FL 33647

1945-069 ....Medeiros, Ray Anton ....313 San Miguel Way/San Mateo CA 94403
1972-072 ....Medich, George Francis 'Doc' ....2206 Ridgeview Avenue/Aliquippa PA 15001
1988-090 ....Medina, Luis Main ....16015 South First Street/Phoenix AZ 85048
1949-052 ....Medlinger, Irving John ....D. September 3, 1975 Wheeling, Ill.
1988-091 ....Medvin, Scott Howard ....4712 Michael Avenue/North Olmsted OH 44070
1932-053 ....Medwick, Joseph Michael ....D. March 21, 1975 St. Petersburg, Fla.
1910-100 ....Mee, Thomas William ....D. May 16, 1981 Chicago, Ill.
1915-104 ....Meehan, William Thomas..................................D. October 8, 1982 Douglas, Wyo.
1923-090 ....Meeker, Charles Roy ....D. March 25, 1929 Orlando, Fla.
1948-071 ....Meeks, Samuel Mack ....4963 Helene/Memphis TN 38117
1972-073 ....Meeler, Charles Philip 'Phil' ....5701 Windlestraw Drive #18/Durham NC 27713
1941-071 ....Meers, Russell Harlan ....D. November 16, 1994 Lancaster, Pa.
1984-075 ....Meier, David Keith ....523 West Stuart/Fresno CA 93704
1922-093 ....Meine, Henry William 'Heinie' ....D. March 18, 1968 St. Louis, Mo.
1913-119 ....Meinert, Walter Henry ....D. November 9, 1958 Decatur, Ill.
1910-101 ....Meinke, Robert Bernard...................................D. December 29, 1952 Chicago, Ill.
1913-120 ....Meister, Karl Daniel ....D. August 15, 1967 Marietta, O.
1912-128 ....Meixell, Merton Merrill 'Moxie' ....D. August 17, 1982 Los Angeles, Calif.
1996-119 ....Mejia, Miguel ....Old Add: San Pedro De Macoris D. R.
1993-120 ....Mejia, Roberto Antonio (Diaz) ....30 Demayo #20 Hato Mayor Dominican Rep.
1955-081 ....Mejias, Roman George......................................3242 West 59th St/Los Angeles CA 90043
1976-063 ....Mejias, Samuel Ellis ....Calle Harvey #73,Los Caicazgos Santo Domingo Dominican Rep.
1937-074 ....Mele, Albert Ernest 'Dutch' ....D. February 12, 1975 Hollywood, Fla.
1947-063 ....Mele, Sabath Anthony 'Sam' ....340 Adams Street/Quincy MA 2169
1984-076 ....Melendez, Francisco ....Old Add: Rural Route 3 Box 590 Rio Piedras PR 00928
1990-106 ....Melendez, Jose Luis...Old Add: Bo. Daguao Naguabo #264 Baguabo PR 00718
1970-089 ....Melendez, Luis Antonio ....Ext. San Jose D-2/Aibonito PR 609
1926-056 ....Melillo, Oscar Donald......................................D. November 14, 1963 Chicago, Ill.
1927-060 ....Mellana, Joseph Peter ....D. November 1, 1969 San Rafael, Calif.
1910-102 ....Meloan, Paul ....D. February 11, 1950 Taft, Calif.
1937-075 ....Melton, Clifford George ....D. July 28, 1986 Baltimore, Md.
1956-060 ....Melton, David Olin ....10253 Richwood Dr/Cupertino CA 95014
1941-072 ....Melton, Reuben Franklin ....D. September 11, 1971 Greer, S. C.
1968-065 ....Melton, William Edwin ....Old Add: 212 Calle Marina San Clemente CA 92672
1985-076 ....Melvin, Robert Paul ....350 Linfield Dr/Menlo Park CA 94025
1997-113 ....Mendoza, Carlos Ramon ....Old Add: Bolivar Venezuela
1970-090 ....Mendoza, Cristobal Rigoberto 'Minnie' .....2070 Southwest 57th Court/Miami FL 33155
1974-083 ....Mendoza, Mario ....No. Re-Elecion Y Rosales #501 Navajoa Sonora/Mexico
1979-075 ....Mendoza, Michael Joseph ....Old Add: 12812 Elmfield Ln Poway CA 92064
1996-120 ....Mendoza, Ramiro ....Old Add: Los Santos Panama
1992-084 ....Menendez, Antonio Gustavo ....18730 Nw 48th Court/Carol City FL 33055
1995-141 ....Menhart, Paul Gerard ....4721 Thornwood Court/Covington GA 30209
1962-090 ....Menke, Denis John ....1246 Berkshire Lane/Tarpon Springs FL 34689
1914-152 ....Menosky, Michael William ....D. April 11, 1983 Detroit, Mich.
1912-129 ....Mensor, Edward ....D. April 20, 1970 Salem, Ore.
1918-050 ....Menze, Theodore Charles ....D. December 23, 1969 St. Louis, Mo.
1933-043 ....Meola, Emile Michael 'Mike' ....D. September 1, 1976 Fair Lawn, N. J.
1971-069 ....Meoli, Rudolph Bartholomew ....1647 North Mountain View Place/Fullerton CA 92831
1982-084 ....Mercado, Orlando (Rodriguez) ....Box 6145/Arecibo PR 613
1990-107 ....Merced, Orlando Luis (Villanueva) ....Old Add: Acacia 0-27 Park Gdns Rio Piedras PR 00926
1992-085 ....Mercedes, Henry Felipe (Perez) ....Old Add: Ed. Hache 3er, Jfk Santo Domingo Dom. Rep.
1994-073 ....Mercedes, Jose Miguel ....Seccion Anama Del Seybo Las Palmillas Dominican Rep.
1991-123 ....Mercedes, Luis Roberto...................................Old Add: San Pedrode Macoris Dominican Republic
1910-103 ....Mercer, Harry Vernon ....D. June 25, 1945 Dayton, Ohio
1912-224 ....Mercer, John Locke ....D. December 22, 1982 Shreveport, La, 71106
1981-084 ....Mercer, Mark Kenneth ....6835 11th Avenue South/Minneapolis MN 55423
1975-075 ....Merchant, James Anderson ....Bates Lake Road/Malcolm AL 36556
1989-083 ....Mercker, Kent Franklin...................................Old Add: 8228 Lone Tree Dr Dublin OH 43017
1934-071 ....Merena, John Joseph ....D. March 9, 1977 Bridgeport, Conn.
1922-094 ....Merewether, Arthur Francis............................D. February 2, 1997 Bayside, N. Y.
1984-077 ....Meridith, Ronald Knox ....Old Add: 501 Sydnor Ridgecrest CA 93555
1990-108 ....Merrill, Carl Harrison 'Stump' ....18 Merrymeeting Road/Topsham Me 4086
1993-121 ....Merriman, Brent Alan ....1429 West Bentrup Street/Chandler AZ 85224
1949-053 ....Merriman, Lloyd Archer ....6691 North Dewolf/Clovis CA 93611
1921-061 ....Merritt, Herman G. ....D. May 26, 1927 Kansas City, Mo.
1965-074 ....Merritt, James Joseph ....Old Add: 8629 Oakmont Blvd Desert Hot Springs CA 92240
1913-121 ....Merritt, John Howard ....D. November 3, 1955 Tupelo, Miss.
1957-054 ....Merritt, Lloyd Wesley ....112 Lee Ann Drive/Shelbyville TN 37160
1951-066 ....Merson, John Warren ....6264 Old Washington Road/Elk Ridge MD 21075
1943-090 ....Mertz, James Verlin ....5116 Emory Circle/Jacksonville FL 32207
1941-073 ....Merullo, Leonard Richard ....159 Summer Avenue/Reading MA 1867
1989-084 ....Merullo, Matthew Bates ....8 Fox Run Road/Madison CT 6443
1987-096 ....Mesa, Jose Roman ....4819 Prestwick Cross/Westlake OH 44145
1938-063 ....Mesner, Stephen Mathias ....D. April 6, 1981 San Diego, Calif.
1924-078 ....Messenger, Andrew Warren 'Bud' ....D. November 4, 1971 Lansing, Mich.
1968-066 ....Messersmith, John Alexander 'Andy' ....200 Lagunita Rd/Soquel CA 95073
1963-078 ....Metcalf, Thomas John ....1390 Wisconsin River Drive/Port Edwards WI 54469
1940-062 ....Metha, Frank Joseph 'Scat' ....D. March 2, 1975 Fountain Valley, Calif.
1943-091 ....Metheny, Arthur Beaureagrd 'Bud'............2757 Livingston Loop/Virginia Beach VA 23456

1922-095	Metivier, George Dewey	D. March 2, 1947 Cambridge, Mass.
1943-092	Metkovich, George Michael 'Catfish'	D. May 17, 1995 Costa Mesa, Calif.
1943-093	Metro, Charles	7890 Indiana Street/Arvada/Co 80007
1923-091	Metz, Leonard Raymond	D. February 24, 1953 Denver, Colo.
1974-084	Metzger, Clarence Edward 'Butch'	6573 Park Riviera Way/Sacramento CA 95834
1970-091	Metzger, Roger Henry	Old Add: 202 Westmoreland San Antonio Tx
1944-088	Metzig, William Andrew	2129 57th Street/Lubbock TX 79412
1925-073	Metzler, Alexander	D. November 30, 1973 Fresno, Calif.
1989-085	Meulens, Hensley Filemon	Kaya Cupido 7 Curacao/Netherlands Antilles
1914-154	Meusel, Emil Frederick 'Irish'	D. March 1, 1963 Long Beach, Calif.
1920-083	Meusel, Robert William	D. November 28, 1977 Downey, Calif.
1913-122	Meyer, Benjamin	D. February 6, 1974 Festus, Mo.
1988-092	Meyer, Brian Scott	33 Basnk/Medford NJ 8051
1974-085	Meyer, Daniel Thomas	Old Add: 222 Remington Loop Danville CA 94526
1938-064	Meyer, George Francis	D. January 3, 1992 Hoffman Estates, Ill.
1955-082	Meyer, John Robert 'Jack'	D. March 9, 1967 Philadelphia, Pa.
1937-076	Meyer, Lambert Dalton 'Dutch'	1606 Texas Street #401/Fort Worth TX 76102
1964-072	Meyer, Robert Bernard	PO Box 3024/Mission Viejo CA 92690
1946-072	Meyer, Russell Charles	D. November 16, 1997 Oglesby, Ill.
1978-080	Meyer, Scott William	Old Add: 15243 South Hamlin Ave Midlothian IL 60445
1988-093	Meyer, Tanner Joe	392 Kaimake Loop/Kailua HI 96734
1913-123	Meyer, William Adam	D. March 31, 1957 Knoxville, Tenn.
1993-122	Miceli, Daniel	8037 Hook Circle/Orlando FL 32819
1954-066	Micelotta, Robert Peter	7334 Ashley Shores Circle/Lake Worth FL 33467
1966-059	Michael, Eugene Richard	49 Union Avenue/Upper Saddle River NJ 7458
1943-094	Michaels, Casimir Eugene	D. November 12, 1982 Grosse Pointe, Mich.
1932-054	Michaels, John Joseph	D. November 18, 1996 Sebring, Fla.
1924-079	Michaels, Ralph Joseph	D. August 5, 1988 Monroeville, Pa.
1921-062	Michaelson, John August	D. April 16, 1968 Woodruff, Wis.
1950-067	Mickelson, Edward Allen	1532 Charlemont Drive/Chesterfield MO 63017
1953-056	Mickens, Glenn Roger	5920 Kini Place/Kapaa HI 96746
1917-048	Middleton, James Blaine	D. January 12, 1974 Argos, Ind.
1922-096	Middleton, John Wayne	D. November 3, 1986 Amarillo, Texas
1912-223	Midkiff, Ezra Millington	D. March 21, 1957 Huntington, W. Va.
1938-065	Midkiff, Richard James	D. October 30, 1956 Temple, Tex.
1987-097	Mielke, Gary Roger	1718 Orchid Drive South/North Mankato MN 56003
1945-070	Mierkowicz, Edward Frank	7530 Macomb #1-A/Grosse Ile MI 48138
1993-123	Mieske, Matthew Todd	6509 East Sierra Morena/Mesa AZ 85215
1948-072	Miggins, Lawrence Edward 'Larry'	2405 Kingston Drive/Houston TX 77019
1935-070	Mihalic, John Michael	D. April 24, 1987 Fort Oglethorpe, Ga.
1964-073	Mikkelsen, Peter James	141501 West North River Road/Prosser WA 99350
1944-089	Miklos, John Joseph	1730 South Broad Street #A/Griffith IN 46319
1944-090	Miksis, Edward Thomas	3906 Whitman Road/Huntingdon Valley PA 19006
1988-094	Milacki, Robert	Old Add: PO Box 1471 Lake Havasu AZ 86403
1915-106	Milan, Horace Robert	D. June 29, 1955 Texarkana, Tex.
1974-086	Milbourne, Lawrence William	9020 Hillcrest Avenue/Pittsburgh PA 15237
1996-121	Milchin, Michael Wayne	Old Add: Vero Beach FL 32960
1940-063	Miles, Carl Thomas	2855 Gulf To Bay Blvd/Clearwater FL 34619
1958-062	Miles, Donald Ray	2757 Hendricks Avenue/Jacksonville FL 32207
1968-067	Miles, James Charlie	164 Gwen Road/Senatoba MS 38668
1935-071	Miles, Wilson Daniel 'Dee'	D. November 2, 1976 Birmingham, Ala.
1975-076	Miley, Michael Wilfred	D. January 6, 1977 Baton Rouge, La
1992-086	Militello, Sam Salvatore	7901 30th Avenue North/Saint Petersburg FL 33710
1915-107	Miljus, John Kenneth	D. February 11, 1976 Fort Harrison, Mont.
1966-060	Millan, Felix Bernardo	3 Snowy Egret Court/Savannah GA 31419
1973-084	Miller, Charles Bruce	2126 Parkland Dr/Fort Wayne IN 46825
1912-130	Miller, Charles Elmer	D. April 23, 1972 Warrensburg, Mo.
1915-108	Miller, Charles Hess	D. January 13, 1951 Millersville, Pa.
1913-124	Miller, Charles Marion	D. June 16, 1961 Houston, Tex.
1984-078	Miller, Darrell Keith	21159 Via Alisa/Yorba Linda CA 92686
1975-077	Miller, Dyar K.	11343 Fonthill Drive/Indianapolis IN 46236
1921-063	Miller, Edmund John 'Bing'	D. May 7, 1966 Philadelphia, Pa.
1977-094	Miller, Edward Lee	5014 Hartnett/Richmond CA 94804
1936-056	Miller, Edward Robert	D. July 31, 1997 Lake Worth, Fla.
1912-131	Miller, Edwin	D. April 17, 1980 Lebanon, Pa.
1912-132	Miller, Elmer	D. November 28, 1944 Beloit, Wis.
1929-072	Miller, Elmer Joseph	D. January 8, 1987 Mira Loma, Calif.
1913-125	Miller, Frank Lee	D. February 19, 1974 Allegan, Mich.
1910-104	Miller, Frederick Holman	D. May 2, 1953 Brookville, Ind.
1911-117	Miller, Hugh Stanley	D. December 24, 1945 Jefferson Barracks, Mo.
1922-097	Miller, Jacob George	D. August 24, 1974 Towson, Md.
1924-080	Miller, Jacob Walter 'Jake'	D. August 20, 1975 Venice, Fla.
1944-091	Miller, James Eldridge 'Hack'	D. November 21, 1966 Dallas, Tex
1966-061	Miller, John Allen	20 Swift Court/Newport Beach CA 92663
1943-095	Miller, John Anthony 'Ox'	Hcr 3 Box 122/George West TX 78022
1962-091	Miller, John Ernest	1216 Redcliffe Rd/Baltimore MD 21228
1987-098	Miller, Keith Alan	1161 St. Andrews/Highland MI 48357
1944-092	Miller, Kenneth Albert	D. April 3, 1991 St. Louis, Mo.
1994-074	Miller, Kurt Everett	804 Dos Rios Court/Bakersfield CA 93309

1964-074 ....Miller, Larry Don ....10045 North 36th Street/Phoenix AZ 85028
1916-061 ....Miller, Lawrence H. 'Hack' ....D. September 17, 1971 Oakland, Calif.
1984-079 ....Miller, Lemmie Earl..................................16606 South 12th Place/Phoenix AZ 85048
1923-092 ....Miller, Leo Alphonso 'Red' ....D. October 20, 1973 Orlando, Fl.
1910-105 ....Miller, Lowell Otto ....D. March 29, 1962 Brooklyn, N.Y.
1988-095 ....Miller, Neal Keith ....6171 Raymond Road/Kaufman TX 75142
1965-075 ....Miller, Norman Calvin..............................Old Add: 3006 Broadmoor Sugarland TX 77478
1994-075 ....Miller, Orlando Salmon (Dixon)......................Aptdo 6-2638 Estafeta El Dorado/Panama
1927-061 ....Miller, Otis Louis 'Otto' ....D. July 26, 1959 Belleville, Ill.
1991-124 ....Miller, Paul Robert ....187 Ingalton Avenue/West Chicago IL 60185
1921-064 ....Miller, Ralph Henry ....D. February 18, 1967 White Bear Lake, Minn.
1920-084 ....Miller, Ralph Joseph.................................D. March 18, 1939 Fort Wayne, Ind.
1977-095 ....Miller, Randall Scott................................Old Add: 22506 Wetherburn Ln Katy TX 77449
1917-049 ....Miller, Raymond Peter ....D. April 7, 1927 Pittsburgh, Pa.
1985-077 ....Miller, Raymond Roger ....PO Box 41/New Athens OH 43981
1971-070 ....Miller, Richard Alan 'Rick'....................PO Box 32/Elkins NH 3233
1953-057 ....Miller, Robert Gerald ....1702 Keim Trail/Saint Charles IL 60174
1949-054 ....Miller, Robert John...................................17397 Glenmore/Detroit MI 48240
1957-055 ....Miller, Robert Lane ....D. August 6, 1993 Rancho Bernardo, Calif.
1957-056 ....Miller, Rodney Carter ....40 Mogul Mountain Drive/Reno NV 89523
1974-087 ....Miller, Roger Wesley ....D. April 26, 1993 Mill Run, Pa.
1941-074 ....Miller, Rolland Arthur 'Ronnie' ....7511 Lila Drive/Hazelwood MO 63042
1910-106 ....Miller, Roy Oscar 'Doc' ....D. July 31, 1938 Jersey City, N. J.
1929-073 ....Miller, Rudel Charles................................D. January 22, 1994 Kalamazoo, Mich.
1927-062 ....Miller, Russell Lewis ....D. August 30, 1962 Bucyrus, O.
1952-074 ....Miller, Stuart Leonard ....3701 Ocaso Court/Cameron Park CA 95682
1918-051 ....Miller, Thomas Royall ....D. August 13, 1980 Richmond, Va.
1996-122 ....Miller, Travis Eugene ....Old Add: West Manchester OH 45383
1996-123 ....Miller, Trever Douglas ....Old Add: 958 Mallard Creek Rd Louisville KY 40207
1911-118 ....Miller, Walter W. ....D. March 1, 1956 Marion, Ind.
1937-077 ....Miller, William Francis ....D. February 26, 1982 Hannibal, Mo.
1952-075 ....Miller, William Paul ....Old Add: 501 Exton Road Hatboro PA 19040
1992-087 ....Millette, Joseph Anthony ....759 Solana Drive/Lafayette CA 94549
1996-124 ....Milliard, Ralph Gregory ....Old Add: Soest Netherlands
1934-072 ....Millies, Walter Louis ....D. February 28, 1995 Oak Lawn, Ill.
1928-066 ....Milligan, John Alexandr ....D. May 15, 1972 Fort Pierce, Fla.
1987-099 ....Milligan, Randy Andre ....7164 Central Avenue/Lemon Grove CA 91945
1953-058 ....Milliken, Robert Fogle ....1875 Southwood Lane/Clearwater FL 34624
1911-119 ....Mills, Abbott Paige 'Jack' ....D. June 3, 1973 Washington, D.C.
1990-109 ....Mills, Alan Bernard ....1811 Bellgrove Street/Lakeland FL 33805
1927-063 ....Mills, Arthur Grant ....D. July 23, 1975 Utica, N. Y.
1934-073 ....Mills, Colonel Buster 'Buster' ....D. December 1, 1991 Arlington, Texas
1914-155 ....Mills, Frank Lemoyne ....D. August 31, 1983 Youngstown, O.
1934-074 ....Mills, Howard Robinson 'Lefty' ....D. September 23, 1982 Riverside, Calif.
1980-089 ....Mills, James Bradley 'Brad' ....3025 East Birch Avenue/Visalia CA 93292
1970-092 ....Mills, Richard Alan ....Old Add: 44 Wood Ave/Scituate MA 02060
1915-109 ....Mills, Rupert Frank ....D. July 20, 1929 Lake Hopatcong, N. J.
1944-093 ....Mills, William Henry ....4344 Commercial Street/Port Charlotte FL 33953
1997-115 ....Millwood, Kevin Austin ....108 West Georgia Avenue/Bessemer City NC 28016
1936-057 ....Milnar, Albert Joseph ....19520 Shawnee Avenue/Cleveland OH 44119
1948-073 ....Milne, William James 'Pete'....................1905 West Beau Terra Drive/Mobile AL 36618
1978-081 ....Milner, Brian Tate ....1401 Cairn Circle/Fort Worth TX 76134
1980-090 ....Milner, Eddie James ....491 Stambaugh/Columbus OH 43207
1971-071 ....Milner, John David ....1351 Holcomb Ave/East Point GA 30344
1944-094 ....Milosevich, Michael ....D. February 3, 1966 East Chicago, Ind.
1924-081 ....Milstead, George Earl................................D. August 9, 1977 Cleburne, Tex.
1995-142 ....Mimbs, Michael Randall ....581 Ormond Terrace/Macon GA 31206
1955-083 ....Minarcin, Rudy Anthony ....37 North First St/North Vandergrift PA 15690
1960-072 ....Mincher, Donald Ray ....PO Box 573/Meridianville AL 35759
1993-124 ....Minchey, Nathan Derek ....1212 Ramble Creek Drive/Pflugerville TX 78660
1921-065 ....Miner, Raymond Theadore ....D. September 15, 1963 Glenridge San., N. Y.
1978-082 ....Minetto, Craig Stephen ....1809 Lakeshore Drive/Lodi CA 95240
1970-093 ....Mingori, Stephen Bernard ....7703 West 114th Terrace/Overland Park KS 66210
1946-073 ....Minner, Paul Edison ....549 South Third Street/Lemoyne PA 17043
1957-057 ....Minnick, Donald Athey ....Franklin Hgts/Rocky Mount VA 24151
1992-088 ....Minor, Blas ....7139 North Dean Street/Winton CA 95388
1949-055 ....Minoso, Saturnino Orestes 'Minnie' ....4250 Marin Drive/Chicago IL 60613
1974-088 ....Minshall, James Edward ....Old Add: 4207 3rd Avenue NE/Bradenton FL 33508
1975-078 ....Minton, Gregory Brian ....5728 North Harding Drive/Paradise Valley AZ 85253
1995-143 ....Mintz, Stephen Wayne ....128 Forest Hills Drive/Leland NC 28451
1990-110 ....Minutelli, Gino Michael ....3723 Lynda Place/National City CA 91950
1978-083 ....Mirabella, Paul Thomas ....550 Knoll Rd/Boonton Manor NJ 7005
1996-125 ....Mirabelli, Douglas Anthony ....9600 North 96th Street #273/Scottsdale AZ 85258
1993-125 ....Miranda, Angel Luis ....Calle B Buzon 50 Factor 1/Arecibo PR 612
1951-067 ....Miranda, Guillermo Perez 'Willie' ....D. September 8, 1996 Baltimore, Md.
1914-156 ....Misse, John Beverly ....D. March 18, 1970 St. Joseph, Mo.
1997-116 ....Misuraca, Michael William ....Old Add: Covina CA 91722
1910-107 ....Mitchell, Albert Roy ....D. September 8, 1959 Temple, Tex.
1984-080 ....Mitchell, Charles Ross ....5017 Hasty Dr/Nashville TN 37211

1911-120	Mitchell, Clarence Elmer	D. November 6, 1963 Grand Island, Neb.
1975-079	Mitchell, Craig Seton	Box 174/Elk CA 95432
1921-066	Mitchell, John Franklin	D. November 4, 1965 Oakland Co., Mich.
1986-102	Mitchell, John Kyle	5017 Hasty Dr/Nashville TN 37211
1991-125	Mitchell, Keith Alexander	731 South 42nd Street/San Diego CA 92113
1984-081	Mitchell, Kevin Darnell	Old Add: 3867 Ocean View Blvd San Diego CA 92113
1996-126	Mitchell, Larry Paul	1040 Preston Avenue/Charlottesville VA 22903
1946-074	Mitchell, Loren Dale	D. January 5, 1987 Tulsa, Okla.
1923-093	Mitchell, Monroe Barr	D. September 4, 1976 Valdosta, Ga.
1975-080	Mitchell, Paul Michael	112 Bassett Avenue/Virginia Beach VA 23452
1980-091	Mitchell, Robert Van	11462 North Poema Place #201/Chatsworth CA 91311
1970-094	Mitchell, Robert Vance	Old Add: 4011 West College Ave Milwaukee WI 53221
1916-062	Mitterling, Ralph	D. January 22, 1956 Pittsburgh, Pa.
1966-062	Mitterwald, George Eugene	1721 Murdock Blvd/Orlando FL 32807
1936-058	Mize, John Robert	D. June 2, 1993 Demorest, Ga.
1952-076	Mizell, Wilmer David 'Vinegar Bend'	4270 Ocean Drive/Corpus Christi TX 78411
1983-100	Mizerock, John Joseph	PO Box 580/Punxsutawney PA 15767
1923-094	Mizeur, William Francis	D. August 27, 1976 Danville, Ill.
1992-089	Mlicki, David John	154 Riverside Drive/Galloway OH 43119
1989-086	Mmahat, Kevin Paul	3268 Castle Drive/Kenner LA 70065
1974-089	Moates, David Allan	7924 24th Avenue West/Bradenton FL 34209
1945-071	Modak, Michael Joseph Aloysius	D. December 12, 1995 Lakeland, Fla.
1996-127	Moehler, Brian Merritt	311 Curtis Drive/Rockingham NC 28379
1992-090	Moeller, Dennis Michael	17112 Simonds Street/Granada Hills CA 91344
1962-092	Moeller, Joseph Douglas	2600 Grandview/Manhattan Beach CA 90266
1956-061	Moeller, Ronald Ralph	3560 Gailynn Dr/Cincinnati OH 45211
1972-074	Moffitt, Randall James	110 Lakeover Drive/Athens GA 30606
1955-084	Moford, Herbert	PO Box 12/Minerva KY 41062
1911-121	Mogridge, George Anthony	D. March 4, 1962 Rochester, N.Y.
1922-098	Mohardt, John Henry	D. November 24, 1961 San Diego, Calif.
1920-085	Mohart, George Benjamin	D. October 2, 1970 Silver Creek, N.Y.
1993-126	Mohler, Michael Ross	1627 South Shirley/Gonzales LA 70737
1986-103	Mohorcic, Dale Robert	15501 Rockside Road/Maple Heights OH 44137
1953-059	Moisan, William Joseph	Box 41/Newton NH 3858
1921-067	Mokan, John Lee	D. February 10, 1985 Buffalo, N. Y.
1949-056	Mole, Fenton Leroy	738 Glen Eagle Court/Danville CA 94526
1996-128	Molina, Islay 'Izzy'	9979 Nw 25th Street/Miami FL 33157
1975-081	Molinaro, Robert Joseph	1 Harbourside Drive #2312/Delray Beach FL 33483
1978-084	Molitor, Paul Leo	Old Add: 16 Tudor Gate Toronto Ontario M2l 1n4
1914-157	Mollenkamp, Frederick Henry	D. November 1, 1948 Cincinnati, O.
1913-126	Mollwitz, Frederick August 'Fritz'	D. October 3, 1967 Bradenton, Fla.
1970-095	Moloney, Richard Henry	125 Mallard Way/Waltham MA 2154
1917-050	Molyneaux, Vincent Leo	D. May 4, 1950 Stamford, Conn.
1937-078	Monaco, Blas	410 Frost Drive/San Antonio TX 78201
1953-060	Monahan, Edward Francis	165 83rd St/Brooklyn NY 11209
1958-063	Monbouquette, William Charles	Pheasant Run Apts Bld #2/Voorheesville NY 12186
1928-067	Moncewicz, Fred Alfred	D. April 23, 1969 Brockton, Mass.
1940-064	Monchak, Alex	7414 8th Avenue West/Bradenton FL 34209
1966-063	Monday, Robert James 'Rick'	10915 Portobelo Drive/San Diego CA 92124
1993-127	Mondesi, Raul Ramon	Maria Trinidad Sanchez Kmz San Cristobal Dominican Rep.
1968-068	Money, Donald Wayne	282 Old Forest Road/Vineland NJ 8360
1975-082	Monge, Isidro Pedroza 'Sid'	716 5th Avenue/Chula Vista CA 91910
1917-051	Monroe, Edward Oliver	D. April 29, 1969 Louisville, Ky.
1921-068	Monroe, John Allen	D. June 19, 1956 Conroe, Tex.
1976-064	Monroe, Lawrence James	2247 Seaver Lane/Hoffman Esates IL 60194
1958-064	Monroe, Zachary Charles	1 Sandalwood Ln/Bartonville IL 61607
1928-068	Montague, Edward Francis	D. June 17, 1988 Daly City, Calif.
1973-085	Montague, John Evans	6001 Vineyard Lane/Montgomery AL 36117
1986-104	Montalvo, Rafael Edgardo	Los Colobos Park #206,%Caoba/Carolina PR 985
1966-064	Montanez, Guillermo Naranjo 'Willie'	Hc-05 Box 52020/Caguas PR 725
1963-079	Monteagudo, Aurelio Fauntini	D. November 10, 1990 Saltillo, Mexico
1938-066	Monteagudo, Rene Miranda	D. September 14, 1973 Hialeah, Fla.
1974-090	Montefusco, John Joseph	Old Add: 24 Downing Hill Lane Colt Neck NJ 07722
1961-075	Montejo, Manuel	Calle 28 #4415,Municipio Playa Havana/Cuba
1987-100	Monteleone, Richard	2515 West Fern Street/Tampa FL 33614
1953-061	Montemayor, Felipe Angel	Torreon #308, Mitras Centro Monterrey Nuevo Laredo Mexico
1941-075	Montgomery, Alvin Atlas	D. April 26, 1942 Waverly, Va.
1987-101	Montgomery, Jeffrey Thomas	2713 West 116th Street/Leawood KS 66211
1971-072	Montgomery, Monty Bryson	807 Corn Tassel Trail/Martinsville VA 24112
1996-129	Montgomery, Raymond James	Old Add: 125 Ocean Avenue #5e Brooklyn NY 11225
1970-096	Montgomery, Robert Edward	2 Parkway Dr/Saugus MA 1906
1996-130	Montgomery, Steven Lewis	Old Add: Cornoa Del Mar CA 92625
1993-128	Montoyo, Jose Carlos 'Charlie'	1600 SE Green Acres Circle #V103/Port Saint Lucie FL 34952
1972-075	Montreuil, Allan Arthur	2016 Laurel St/Gretna LA 70053
1954-067	Monzant, Ramon Segundo	Calle 87 Nro 2a-33 Maracaibo Edo Zulia Venezuela
1972-076	Monzon, Daniel Francisco	D. January 21, 1996 Santo Domingo, Dominican Republic
1967-073	Moock, Joseph Geoffrey	12432 Pecos Ave/Greenwell LA 70739
1997-117	Moody, Eric Lane	Old Add: Williamston SC 29697
1932-055	Moon, Leo	D. August 25, 1970 New Orleans, La.

1954-068 ....Moon, Wallace Wade ....1415 Angelina Circle/College Station TX 77840
1931-059 ....Mooney, James Irving ....D. April 27, 1979 Johnson City, Tenn.
1986-105 ....Mooneyham, William Craig ....9470 West Olive Avenue/Winton CA 95388
1925-074 ....Moore, Albert James ....D. November 29, 1974 Atlantic Ocean
1976-065 ....Moore, Alvin Earl 'Junior' ....3728 Wall Avenue/Richmond CA 94804
1946-075 ....Moore, Ansel Winn ....D. October 29, 1993 Pearl, Miss.
1964-075 ....Moore, Archie Francis ....Old Add: 3256 Agefly Road Dover NJ 07801
1970-097 ....Moore, Balor Lilbon ....901 West Viejo Drive/Friendswood TX 77546
1988-096 ....Moore, Bradley Alan............................522 Wapola Court/Loveland CO 80537
1930-052 ....Moore, Carlos Whitman ....D. July 2, 1958 New Orleans, La.
1912-133 ....Moore, Charles Wesley ....D. July 29, 1970 Portland, Ore.
1973-086 ....Moore, Charles William ....2567 Melinda Circle/Birmingham AL 35214
1936-059 ....Moore, D C 'Dee'................................D. July 2, 1997 Williston, N. D.
1975-083 ....Moore, Donnie Ray ....D. July 18, 1989 Anaheim, Calif.
1934-075 ....Moore, Euel Walton ....D. February 12, 1989 Tishomingo, Okla.
1931-060 ....Moore, Eugene, Jr. ....D. March 12, 1978 Jackson, Miss.
1914-158 ....Moore, Ferdinand Depage ....D. May 6, 1947 Atlantic City, N.J.
1970-098 ....Moore, Gary Douglas ....Old Add: 5018 Airline/Dallas TX 75205
1923-095 ....Moore, Graham Edward 'Eddie' ....D. February 10, 1976 Fort Myers, Fla.
1965-076 ....Moore, Jackie Spencer ....2721 Laurel Valley Lane/Arlington TX 76006
1928-069 ....Moore, James Stanford ....D. May 19, 1973 Seattle, Wash.
1930-053 ....Moore, James William ....D. May 7, 1986 Memphis, Tenn.
1928-070 ....Moore, John Francis ....D. April 4, 1991 Bradenton, Fla.
1930-054 ....Moore, Joseph Gregg ....PO Box 65/Gause TX 77857
1981-085 ....Moore, Kelvin Orlando ....Rr 1 Box 132/Leroy AL 36548
1996-131 ....Moore, Kerwin Lamar ....Old Add: Detroit MI 48201
1936-060 ....Moore, Lloyd Albert 'Whitey'...............D. December 10, 1987 Canton, O.
1993-129 ....Moore, Marcus Raymond ....Old Add: 1044 83rd Avenue Oakland CA 94621
1982-085 ....Moore, Michael Wayne ....1472 East Calle De Caballos/Tempe AZ 85284
1927-064 ....Moore, Randolph Edward ....D. June 12, 1992 Mount Pleasant, Texas
1952-077 ....Moore, Raymond Leroy ....D. March 2, 1995 Clinton, Md.
1965-077 ....Moore, Robert Barry 'Barry' ....Old Add: Rr 1 Box 174 Cleveland NC 27013
1985-078 ....Moore, Robert Devell ....2500 Wellington Road/Los Angeles CA 90016
1991-126 ....Moore, Robert Vincent ....3703 Hyde Park Avenue/Cincinnati OH 45209
1920-086 ....Moore, Roy Daniel ....D. April 5, 1951 Seattle, Wash.
1935-072 ....Moore, Terrence Bluford ....D. March 29, 1995 Collinsville, Ill.
1972-077 ....Moore, Tommy Joe ....Old Add: Rr 1 Dekalb TX 75559
1917-052 ....Moore, William Allen 'Scrappy' ....D. October 13, 1964 Little Rock, Ark.
1929-074 ....Moore, William Austin 'Cy' ....D. March 28, 1972 Augusta, Ga.
1925-075 ....Moore, William Christopher ....D. January 24, 1984 Corning, N. Y.
1926-057 ....Moore, William Henry ....D. May 24, 1972 Kansas City, Mo.
1986-106 ....Moore, William Ross ....419 North Astell Avenue/West Covina CA 91790
1927-065 ....Moore, William Wilcy ....D. March 29, 1963 Hollis, Okla.
1962-093 ....Moorhead, Charles Robert 'Bob' ....D. December 3, 1986 Lemoyne, Pa.
1967-074 ....Moose, Robert Ralph ....D. October 9, 1976 Martins Ferry, O.
1936-061 ....Mooty, J. T. 'Jake'............................D. April 20, 1970 Fort Worth, Tex.
1976-066 ....Mora, Andres ....Marcial Ordonez #172 Ote. Los Mochis Sinaloa/Mexico
1973-087 ....Morales, Jose Manuel ....17411 Fosgate Road/Montverde FL 34756
1969-118 ....Morales, Julio Ruben 'Jerry' ....Old Add: Villa Nueva Calle #16 Value Caguas PR 00625
1967-075 ....Morales, Richard Angelo ....Western Michigan Baseball Oakland Gymnasium Kalamazoo MI 49008
1938-067 ....Moran, Albert Thomas 'Hiker' ....D. January 7, 1998 Saratoga Springs, N. Y.
1974-091 ....Moran, Carl William 'Bill' ....200 Shore Drive/Portsmouth VA 23701
1912-134 ....Moran, Harry Edwin ....D. November 28, 1962 Beckley, West Va
1963-080 ....Moran, Richard Alan 'Al' ....34134 Banbury/Farmington Hills MI 48331
1912-135 ....Moran, Roy Ellis ....D. July 18, 1966 Atlanta, Ga.
1958-065 ....Moran, William Nelson ....205 Kristie Lane/Tyrone GA 30290
1990-111 ....Morandini, Michael Robert Mickey ....4210 Oak Grove Drive/Valparaiso IN 46383
1994-076 ....Mordecai, Michael Howard ....2702 Winsley Drive Sw/Marietta GA 30064
1924-082 ....Morehart, Raymond Anderson ....D. January 13, 1989 Dallas, Texas
1963-081 ....Morehead, David Michael ....1342 Tiki Cir/Tustin CA 92680
1957-058 ....Morehead, Seth Marvin ....8675 Grover Place/Shreveport LA 71115
1958-066 ....Morejon, Daniel Torres ....4041 Southwest 117th Avenue/Miami FL 33165
1995-144 ....Morel, Ramon Rafael ....Cle Duarte #29,Palm.V.Gonzales Santiago Dominican/Rep.
1978-085 ....Moreland, Bobby Keith Keith ....PO Box 2347/Round Rock TX 78680
1981-086 ....Moreno, Angel.....................................Gomez Fariaz #604 Aguascalientes Aguas. Mexico
1980-092 ....Moreno, Jose De Los Santos ....Correa Y Cidron 9 Santo Domingo Dominican/Rep.
1950-068 ....Moreno, Julio Gonzales ....D. January 2, 1987 Miami, Fla.
1975-084 ....Moreno, Omar ....Old Add: Apartado #5 Balboa, Ncon Panama City Panama
1970-099 ....Moret, Rogelio Roger ....Rr 1 #6742/Guayama PR 654
1913-127 ....Morey, David Beale ....D. January 4, 1986 Oak Bluff, Mass.
1935-073 ....Morgan, Chester Collins ....D. September 20, 1991 Pasadena, Texas
1921-069 ....Morgan, Cyril Arlon ....D. September 11, 1946 Lakeville, Mass.
1928-071 ....Morgan, Edward Carre ....D. April 9, 1980 New Orleans, La.
1936-062 ....Morgan, Edwin Willis ....D. June 27, 1982 Lakewood, O.
1963-082 ....Morgan, Joseph Leonard ....3523 Country Club Place/Danville CA 94506
1959-059 ....Morgan, Joseph Michael ....15 Oak Hill Drive/Walpole MA 2081
1997-118 ....Morgan, Kevin Lee ....Old Add: Duson LA 70529
1978-086 ....Morgan, Michael Thomas ....Old Add: 2008 Jansen St Las Vegas NV 89101
1911-122 ....Morgan, Raymond Caryll ....D. February 15, 1940 Baltimore, Md.

1950-069	Morgan, Robert Morris 'Bobby'	3004 Stoneybrook Road/Oklahoma City OK 73120
1951-068	Morgan, Tom Stephen	D. January 13, 1987 Anaheim, Calif.
1954-069	Morgan, Vernon Thomas	D. November 8, 1975 Minneapolis, Minn.
1961-076	Morhardt, Meredith Goodwin 'Moe'	PO Box 563/Winsted CT 6098
1935-074	Moriarty, Edward Jerome	D. September 29, 1991 Holyoke, Mass.
1973-088	Morlan, John Glen	2348 Salem Ave/Grove City OH 43123
1913-128	Morley, (William Morley Jennings	D. May 14, 1985 Lubbock, Texas
1996-132	Morman, Alvin	Old Add: Rockingham NC 28379
1986-107	Morman, Russell Lee	Old Add: 1200 Stone Creek Dr Independence MO 64056
1983-101	Morogiello, Daniel Joseph	99 Distillery Road/White Horse Station NJ 8889
1984-082	Moronko, Jeffrey Robert	2711 Grants Lake Blvd #23/Sugar Land TX 77479
1926-058	Morrell, Willard Blackmer	D. August 5, 1975 Birmingham, Ala.
1968-069	Morris, Danny Walke	Old Add: 216 Wilson Street Greenville KY 42345
1937-079	Morris, Doyt Theodore	D. July 4, 1984 Gastonia, N. C.
1986-108	Morris, John Daniel	2645 Elm Drive/North Bellmore NY 11710
1977-096	Morris, John Scott 'Jack'	527 Prairie Nest Road/Great Falls MT 59405
1966-065	Morris, John Wallace	5538 E. Paradise Ln/Scottsdale AZ 85254
1997-119	Morris, Matthew Christian	55 Heritage Lane/Montgomery NY 12549
1922-100	Morris, Walter Edward	D. March 3, 1932 Century, Fla.
1988-097	Morris, William Harold Hal	1111 Macarthur Blvd/Munster IN 46321
1915-110	Morrisette, William Lee	D. March 25, 1966 Virginia Beach, Va.
1977-097	Morrison, James Forest	500 Tamiami Trail/Charlotte Harbor FL 33980
1920-087	Morrison, John Dewey	D. March 20, 1966 Lexington, Ky.
1921-070	Morrison, Philip Melvin	D. January 18, 1955 Lexington, Ky.
1927-066	Morrison, Walter Guy	D. August 14, 1934 Grand Rapids, Mich.
1932-056	Morrissey, Joseph Anselm 'Jo-Jo'	D. May 2, 1950 Worcester, Mass.
1929-075	Morse, Newell Obediah 'Bud'	D. April 6, 1987 Sparks, Nev.
1911-123	Morse, Peter Raymond 'Hap'	D. June 19, 1974 St. Paul, Minn.
1969-119	Morton, Carl Wendle	D. April 12, 1983 Tulsa, Okla.
1914-159	Morton, Guy, Sr.	D. October 18, 1934 Sheffield, Ala.
1991-127	Morton, Kevin Joseph	26 Fullin Court/Norwalk CT 6851
1961-077	Morton, Wycliffe Nathan 'Bubba'	13716 Shelburne Street/Centreville VA 22020
1954-071	Moryn, Walter Joseph	D. July 21, 1996 Winfield, Ill.
1954-070	Moryon, Guy	567 Ferndale Avenue/Vermilion OH 44089
1965-078	Moschitto, Rosairo Allen 'Ross'	4 Oak Avenue/Tuckahoe NY 10707
1980-093	Moseby, Lloyd Anthony	9140 Los Lagos Circle South/Loomis CA 95650
1913-129	Moseley, Earl Victor	D. July 1, 1963 Alliance, O.
1937-080	Moser, Arnold Robert	1815 Enclave Pkwy #5205a/Houston TX 77077
1965-079	Moses, Gerald Braheen 'Jerry'	36 Highwood Lane/Ipswich MA 1938
1982-086	Moses, John William	18169 Nw Varese Court/Issaquah WA 98027
1935-075	Moses, Wallace	D. October 10, 1990 Valdosta, Ga.
1977-098	Moskau, Paul Richard	5041 North Apache Hills Trail/Tucson AZ 85750
1910-108	Moskiman, William Bankhead 'Doc'	D. January 11, 1953 San Leandro, Calif.
1929-076	Mosolf, James Frederick	D. December 28, 1979 Dallas, Ore.
1996-133	Mosquera, Julio Alberto	Old Add: Panama City Panama
1934-076	Moss, Charles Crosby	D. October 9, 1991 Meridian, Miss.
1930-055	Moss, Charles Malcolm 'Mal'	D. February 5, 1983 Savannah, Ga.
1942-070	Moss, Howard Glenn	D. May 7, 1989 Baltimore, Md.
1946-076	Moss, John Lester 'Les'	420 Tullis Avenue/Longwood FL 32750
1926-059	Moss, Raymond Earl	D. August 9, 1998 Chattanooga, Tenn.
1954-072	Mossi, Donald Louis	1340 Sanford Ranch Road/Ukiah CA 95482
1951-069	Mossor, Earl Dalton	D. December 29, 1988 Batavia, Ohio
1918-052	Mostil, John Anthony	D. December 10, 1970 Midlothian, Ill.
1991-128	Mota, Andres Alberto	2506 Canada Blvd #3/Glendale CA 91208
1991-129	Mota, Jose Manuel (Matos)	2506 Canada Blvd #3/Glendale CA 91208
1962-094	Mota, Manuel Rafael	2506 Canada Blvd #3/Glendale CA 91208
1981-087	Motley, Darryl Dewayne	1324 Russit Street/Portland OR 97217
1945-072	Mott, Elisha Matthew 'Bitsy'	PO Box 294/Blue Ridge GA 30513
1996-134	Mottola, Charles Edward 'Chad'	350 Somerset Way/Fort Lauderdale FL 33326
1967-076	Motton, Curtell Howard	3107 Persimmon Tree Court/Woodstock ND 21163
1946-077	Moulder, Glen Hubert	D. November 27, 1994 Decatur, Ga.
1911-124	Moulton, Albert Theodore 'Ollie'	D. July 10, 1968 Peabody, Mass.
1994-077	Mouton, James Raleigh	Old Add: 3202 N. Country Club Rd Tucson AZ 85716
1995-145	Mouton, Lyle Joseph	2704 Saddlewood Lane/Palm Harbor FL 34685
1913-130	Mowe, Raymond Benjamin	D. August 14, 1968 Sarasota, Fla.
1933-044	Mowry, Joseph Aloysius	D. February 9, 1994 St.Louis, Mo.
1910-109	Moyer, Charles Edward	D. November 18, 1962 Jacksonville, Fla.
1986-109	Moyer, Jamie	409 North Fourth Street/Souderton PA 18964
1954-073	Mrozinski, Ronald Frank	Wash. Arms Bldg 100 #D2/Washington NJ 7882
1963-083	Mudrock, Philip Ray	2548 East 6600 South/Salt Lake City UT 84121
1920-088	Mueller, Clarence Francis 'Heinie'	D. January 23, 1975 Desoto, Mo.
1948-074	Mueller, Donald Frederick	11224 Mueller Lane/Maryland Heights MO 63043
1938-068	Mueller, Emmett Jerome 'Heinie'	D. October 3, 1986 Orlando, Fla.
1950-070	Mueller, Joseph Gordon 'Gordy'	1404 Chesapeake Avenue/Middle River MD 21220
1941-076	Mueller, Leslie Clyde	PO Box 294/Millstadt IL 62260
1935-076	Mueller, Ray Coleman	D. June 29, 1994 Lower Paxton Twp., Pa.
1922-101	Mueller, Walter John	D. August 16, 1971 St. Louis, Mo.
1978-087	Mueller, Willard Lawrence 'Willie'	2320 Tolbert Lane/West Bend WI 53090
1942-071	Mueller, William Lawrence	1401 Braeborn/Wheeling IL 60090

1996-135 ....Mueller, William Richard ....11868 Charlemagne Drive/Maryland Heights MO 63043
1957-059 ....Muffett, Billy Arnold ....1145 Finks Hideaway Road/Monroe LA 71203
1924-083 ....Muich, Ignatius Andrew ....D. July 2, 1993 St. Louis, Mo.
1951-070 ....Muir, Joseph Allen ....D. June 25, 1980 Baltimore, Md.
1935-077 ....Mulcahy, Hugh Noyes ....175 Wayne Street/Beaver PA 15009
1986-110 ....Mulholland, Terence John ....339 Derrick Avenue/Uniontown PA 15401
1930-056 ....Mulleavy, Gregory Thomas ....D. February 1, 1980 Arcadia, Calif.
1910-110 ....Mullen, Charles George ....D. June 6, 1963 Seattle, Wash.
1944-095 ....Mullen, Ford Parker ....1841 Trosper Road SW #8/Tumwater WA 98512
1920-089 ....Mullen, William John ....D. May 4, 1971 St. Louis, Mo.
1933-045 ....Muller, Frederick William ....D. October 20, 1976 Davis, Calif.
1915-111 ....Mulligan, Edward Joseph ....D. March 15, 1982 San Rafael, Calif.
1934-077 ....Mulligan, Joseph Ignatius ....D. June 5, 1986 West Roxbury, Mass.
1941-077 ....Mulligan, Richard Charles ....D. December 15, 1992 Victoria, Texas
1996-136 ....Mulligan, Sean Patrick ....Old Add: Diamond Bar CA 91765
1940-065 ....Mullin, Patrick Joseph ....320 Church Street/Brownsville PA 15417
1977-099 ....Mulliniks, Steven Rance 'Rance' ....542 Meadow Willow/El Paso TX 79922
1980-094 ....Mullins, Francis Joseph ....7744 South Poplar Way/Englewood CO 80112
1921-071 ....Mulrenan, Dominick Joseph ....D. July 27, 1964 Melrose, Mass.
1930-057 ....Mulroney, Francis Joseph ....D. November 11, 1985 Aberdeen, Wash.
1974-092 ....Mumphrey, Jerry Wayne ....7709 Fm 850/Tyler TX 75705
1918-053 ....Munch, Jacob Ferdinand ....D. June 8, 1966 Lansdowne, Pa.
1937-081 ....Muncrief, Robert Cleveland ....D. February 6, 1996 Duncanville, Texas
1913-131 ....Mundy, William Edward ....D. September 23, 1958 Kalamazoo, Mich.
1943-096 ....Munger, George David 'Red' ....D. July 23, 1996 Houston, Texas
1931-061 ....Mungo, Van Lingle ....D. February 12, 1985 Pageland, S. C.
1971-073 ....Muniz, Manuel ....PO Box 6301/Caguas PR 625
1980-095 ....Munninghoff, Scott Andrew................................866 Laverty Lane/Cincinnati OH 45230
1934-078 ....Munns, Leslie Ernest ....D. February 28, 1997 Cedar Rapids, Iowa
1996-137 ....Munoz, Jose Luis ....Old Add: Yabucoa PR 00767
1995-146 ....Munoz, Juan Oscar 'Oscar' ....Old Add: 3235 W. 14th Street Hialeah FL 33012
1989-087 ....Munoz, Michael Anthony ....2606 Parker Court/Southlake TX 76092
1995-147 ....Munoz, Noe ....Old Add: Los Mochis Sinoloa Mexico
1990-112 ....Munoz, Pedro Javier ....Riocana Street 10-1-5/Ponce PR 731
1993-130 ....Munoz, Roberto ....659 West 80th Street/Hialeah FL 33014
1925-076 ....Munson, Joseph Martin Napoleon ....D. February 24, 1991 Drexel Hill, Pa.
1969-120 ....Munson, Thurman Lee ....D. August 2, 1979 Akron-Canton Airport, O.
1978-088 ....Mura, Stephen Andrew ....31892 Old Oak Road/Trabuco Canyon CA 92679
1964-076 ....Murakami, Masanori ....1-4-15-1506,Nisho Ohi Shinagawa-Ku Tokyo 140-0015 Japan
1965-080 ....Murcer, Bobby Ray ....Old Add: 401 E. 34th Street #532c New York NY 10016
1917-053 ....Murchison, Thomas Malcom 'Tim' ....D. October 20, 1962 Liberty, N. C.
1956-062 ....Murff, John Robert 'Red' ....1005 Lawndale/Brenham TX 77833
1976-067 ....Murphy, Dale Brian ....127 Peachtree Street NE #806/Atlanta GA 30302
1960-073 ....Murphy, Daniel Francis ....5030 Champion Blvd #6226/Boca Raton FL 33496
1989-088 ....Murphy, Daniel Lee ....18547 Eucalyptus Street/Hesperia CA 92435
1978-089 ....Murphy, Dwayne Keith ....6937 East Paradise Lane/Scottsdale AZ 85254
1942-072 ....Murphy, Edward Jerome ....D. December 10, 1991 Joliet, Ill.
1914-160 ....Murphy, Herbert Courtland 'Dummy' ....D. August 10, 1962 Tallahassee, Fla.
1912-136 ....Murphy, John Edward ....D. February 20, 1969 Dunmore, Pa.
1932-057 ....Murphy, John Joseph ....D. January 14, 1970 New York, N. Y.
1915-112 ....Murphy, Leo Joseph ....D. August 12, 1960 Racine, Wis.
1912-137 ....Murphy, Michael Jerome ....D. October 26, 1952 Johnson City, N.Y.
1954-074 ....Murphy, Richard Lee ....3740 Kentucky Avenue/Indianapolis IN 46221
1985-079 ....Murphy, Robert Albert ....PO Box 1600/Miami FL 33143
1918-054 ....Murphy, Robert R. 'Buzz' ....D. May 11, 1938 Denver, Colo.
1968-070 ....Murphy, Thomas Andrew ....26566 Calle Lorenzo/San Juan Capistrano CA 92675
1931-062 ....Murphy, Walter Joseph ....D. March 23, 1976 Houston, Texas
1966-066 ....Murphy, William Eugene ....3416 65th Avenue West/Tacoma WA 98466
1923-096 ....Murray, Anthony John ....D. March 19, 1974 Chicago, Ill.
1974-093 ....Murray, Dale Albert ....Rr 2 Box 1850/Yorktown TX 78164
1977-100 ....Murray, Eddie Clarence ....26911 Triumph Avenue/Canyon Country CA 91351
1917-054 ....Murray, Edward Francis.....................................D. November 8, 1970 Cheyenne, Wyo.
1922-102 ....Murray, George King ....D. October 18, 1955 Memphis, Tenn.
1996-138 ....Murray, Glenn Everett ....Old Add: Manning SC 29101
1997-120 ....Murray, Heath Robertson ....1212 Stonyridge Avenue/Troy OH 45373
1922-103 ....Murray, James Francis ....D. July 15, 1973 New York, N. Y.
1950-071 ....Murray, Joseph Ambrose ....2719 Via Santa Tomas/San Clememte CA 92672
1936-063 ....Murray, Joseph Ambrose 'Amby' ....D. February 6, 1997 Port Salerno, Fla.
1974-094 ....Murray, Larry ....Old Add: 3544 South Calumet Ave/Chicago IL 60653
1995-148 ....Murray, Matthew Michael...................................109 Greenwood Avenue/Swampscott MA 1907
1919-058 ....Murray, Patrick Joseph ....D. November 5, 1983 Rochester, N.Y.
1948-075 ....Murray, Raymond Lee ....1375 Gilman Road/Fort Worth TX 76140
1980-096 ....Murray, Richard Dale ....435 East 108th St/Los Angeles CA 90061
1923-097 ....Murray, Robert Hayes ....D. January 4, 1979 Nashua, N. H.
1917-055 ....Murray, William Allenwood ....D. September 14, 1943 Boston, Mass.
1963-084 ....Murrell, Ivan Auguste ....Old Add: 3215 S. Lakeview Circle #206 Fort Pierce FL 34949
1941-078 ....Murtaugh, Daniel Edward ....D. December 2, 1976 Chester Pa.
1969-121 ....Muser, Anthony Joseph ....11222 Martha Ann Dr/Los Alamitos CA 90720
1965-081 ....Musgraves, Dennis Eugene................................Rr Four/Centralia MO 65240

113

1941-079	Musial, Stanley Frank	85 Trent Drive/Ladue MO 63124
1986-111	Musselman, Jeffrey Joseph	Old Add: 105 Brick Avenue Lanoka Harbor NJ 08734
1982-087	Musselman, Ralph Richard	5313 Autumn Dr/Wilmington NC 28401
1912-138	Musser, Paul	D. July 7. 1973 State College, Pa.
1932-058	Musser, William Daniel 'Danny'	5136 Davidson Road/Marietta GA 30068
1944-096	Mussill, Bernard James 'Barney'	912 Moorland Drive/Grosse Pointe Woods MI 48236
1991-130	Mussina, Michael Cole	1302 Spruce Street/Montoursville PA 17754
1940-066	Mustaikis, Alexander Dominick	D. January 17, 1970 Scranton, Pa.
1991-131	Mutis, Jeffrey Thomas	630 East Wyoming Street/Allentown PA 18103
1938-069	Myatt, George Edward	1623 Canton Avenue/Orlando FL 32803
1920-090	Myatt, Glenn Calvin	D. August 9, 1969 Houston, Tex.
1925-077	Myer, Charles Solomon 'Buddy'	D. October 31, 1974 Baton Rouge, La.
1915-113	Myers, Elmer Glenn	D. July 29, 1976 Collingswood, N. J.
1987-102	Myers, Gregory Richard	2815 Shenandoah Road/Riverside CA 92506
1996-139	Myers, James Xavier	7857 Sandywood Lane/Memphis TN 38133
1938-070	Myers, Linnwood Lincoln	1111 Yverdon Drive #C1/Camp Hill PA 17011
1995-149	Myers, Michael Stanley	PO Box 3099/Milwaukee WI 53201
1910-111	Myers, Ralph Edward 'Hap'	D. June 30, 1967 San Francisco, Calif.
1985-080	Myers, Randall Kirk	6601 E. Mill Plain Blvd #A190/Vancouver WA 98661
1956-063	Myers, Richard	5400 Sampson Blvd/Sacramento CA 95820
1996-140	Myers, Rodney Demond	1816 South Third/Conroe TX 77301
1996-141	Myers, Rodney Luther	5850 Strathmoor Drive #2/Rockford IL 61107
1935-078	Myers, William Harrison	D. April 10, 1995 Carlisle, Pa.
1976-068	Myrick, Robert Howard	1923 Adeline Street/Hattiesburg MS 39401
1990-113	Nabholz, Christopher William	2030 West Market Street/Pottsville PA 17901
1915-114	Nabors, Herman John 'Jack'	D. October 29, 1923 Wilton, Ala.
1990-114	Naehring, Timothy James	7300 Pinehurst Drive/Cincinnati OH 45244
1939-079	Nagel, William Taylor	D. October 8, 1981 Freehold, N. J.
1912-139	Nagelson, Louis Marcellus	D. October 22, 1965 Fort Wayne, Ind.
1968-071	Nagelson, Russell Charles 'Rusty'	4 Carriage Court/Little Rock AR 72211
1911-125	Nagle, Walter Harold 'Judge'	D. May 27, 1971 Santa Rosa, Calif.
1990-115	Nagy, Charles Harrison	150 Old Route 9w #22/New Windsor NY 12553
1969-122	Nagy, Michael Timothy	8 Indian Trail/Bronx NY 10465
1947-064	Nagy, Stephen	2205 NE Ridgewood Drive/Poulsboro WA 98370
1938-071	Nahem, Samuel Ralph	624 Vincente/Berkeley CA 94704
1976-069	Nahorodny, William Gerard	204 South Comet Avenue/Clearwater FL 34625
1936-064	Naktenis, Peter Ernest	5200 North Ocean Drive #19d/Singer Island FL 33404
1924-084	Naleway, Frank	D. January 28, 1949 Chicago, Ill.
1912-140	Napier, Skelton Leroy 'Buddy'	D. March 29, 1968 Dallas, Tex.
1949-057	Naples, Aloysius Francis	99 Nickerson Road/Orleans MA 2653
1965-082	Napoleon, Daniel	Old Add: 28 North Stockton St Trenton NJ 08608
1951-071	Naragon, Harold Richard	1521 Hagey Drive/Barberton OH 44203
1956-064	Naranjo, Lazaro Ramon Gonzalo	Old Add: D #270 10y11 "Lawton, Havana Cuba"
1954-075	Narleski, Raymond Edmond	1183 Chews Landing Road/Laurel Springs NJ 8021
1929-077	Narleski, William Edward	D. July 22, 1964 Laurel Springs, N. J.
1979-076	Narron, Jerry Austin	113 Marie Avenue/Goldsboro NC 27530
1935-079	Narron, Samuel	D. December 31, 1996 Middlesex, N. C.
1963-085	Narum, Leslie Ferdinand 'Buster'	324 South Glenwood Avenue/Clearwater FL 33515
1967-077	Nash, Charles Francis 'Cotton'	600 Summershade Cir/Lexington KY 40502
1966-067	Nash, James Edwin	37 Regina Dr NE/Marietta GA 30067
1912-141	Nash, Kenneth Leland	D. February 16, 1977 Epsom, N. H.
1978-090	Nastu, Philip	119 Austin St/Bridgeport CT 6604
1992-091	Natal, Robert Marcel	Old Add: Chula Vista CA
1953-062	Naton, Peter Alphonsus	4136 Split Rock Rd/Camillus NY 13031
1996-142	Naulty, Daniel Donovan	Old Add: Huntington Beach CA 92647
1989-089	Navarro, Jaime	West 1797 Golden Beach Way/Mukwonago WI 53149
1962-095	Navarro, Julio Ventura	Calle 3, Bloque 10, #32 " ""Santa Rosa, Bayamon"" PR 619"
1993-131	Navarro, Norberto Rodriguez 'Tito'	Old Add: 525 North Peacock Blvd Port St. Lucie FL 34986
1942-073	Naylor, Earl Eugene	D. January 16, 1990 Winter Haven. Fla.
1917-056	Naylor, Roleine Cecil	D. June 18, 1966 Fort Worth, Tex.
1939-080	Naymick, Michael John	8334 Berwick Way/Stockton CA 95210
1991-132	Neagle, Dennis Edward	945 Waugh Chapel Road/Gambrills MD 21054
1956-065	Neal, Charles Lenard	D. November 10, 1996 Dallas, Texas
1916-064	Neale, Alfred Earle 'Greasy'	D. November 2, 1973 Lake Worth, Fl.
1952-078	Necciai, Ronald Andrew	201 Rosewood Drive/Monongahela PA 15063
1992-092	Neel, Troy Lee	PO Box 1582/El Campo TX 77437
1957-060	Neeman, Calvin Amandus	93 Champagne/Lake Saint Louis MO 63367
1914-161	Neff, Douglas William	D. May 23, 1932 Cape Charles, Va.
1952-079	Negray, Ronald Alvin	587 West Nimisila Road/Akron OH 44319
1912-142	Neher, James Gilmore	D. November 11, 1951 Buffalo, N.Y.
1915-115	Nehf, Arthur Neukom	D. December 18, 1960 Phoenix, Ariz.
1969-123	Neibauer, Gary Wayne	146 Delta Avenue/Bismarck ND 58504
1990-116	Neidlinger, James Llewellyn	74 Borestone Lane/Burlington VT 5401
1960-074	Neiger, Alvin Edward	213 Pinehurst Rd/Wilminton DE 19803
1939-081	Neighbors, Robert Otis	D. August 8, 1952 North Korea
1946-078	Neill, Thomas White	D. September 22, 1980 Houston, Texas
1920-091	Neis, Bernard Edmund	D. November 29, 1972 Inverness, Fla.
1929-078	Nekola, Francis Joseph 'Bots'	D. March 11, 1987 Rockville Centre, N. Y.
1910-112	Nelson, Albert Francis 'Red'	D. October 26, 1956 St Petersburg, Fla.

1968-072 .... Nelson, David Earl .... 29 Buck Circle/Haines City FL 33844
1935-080 .... Nelson, George Emmett .... D. August 25, 1967 Sioux Falls, S. D.
1949-058 .... Nelson, Glenn Richard 'Rocky' .... PO Box 35/Portsmouth OH 45662
1970-100 .... Nelson, James Lorin .... 5732 Lonsdale Drive/Sacramento CA 95822
1983-102 .... Nelson, James Victor .... Old Add: 16901 Sims Huntington Beach CA 92649
1992-093 .... Nelson, Jeffrey Allan .... 39 North Prospect Avenue/Catonsville MD 21228
1919-059 .... Nelson, Luther Martin .... D. November 14, 1985 Moline, Ill.
1930-058 .... Nelson, Lynn Bernard .... D. February 15, 1955 Kansas City, Mo.
1960-075 .... Nelson, Melvin Frederick .... 27420 Fisher St/Highland CA 92346
1983-103 .... Nelson, Ricky Lee .... 7250 South 46th St/Phoenix AZ 85040
1986-112 .... Nelson, Robert Augustus .... 312 Alta Vista Avenue/South Pasadena CA 91030
1955-085 .... Nelson, Robert Sidney .... 10830 Wallbrook/Dallas TX 75238
1967-078 .... Nelson, Roger Eugene .... %Ups 14650 Santa Fe Trail Lenexa KS 66118
1945-073 .... Nelson, Tom Cousineau .... D. September 24, 1973 San Diego, Calif.
1981-088 .... Nelson, Wayland Eugene 'Gene' .... PO Box 1197/San Antonio FL 33576
1963-086 .... Nen, Richard Leroy .... 6152 Killarney Avenue/Garden Grove CA 92845
1993-132 .... Nen, Robert Allen .... 48 Via Barcaza/Coto De Caza CA 92679
1911-126 .... Ness, John Charles .... D. December 3, 1957 Deland, Fla.
1967-079 .... Nettles, Graig .... 11217 Carmel Creek Road #2/San Diego CA 92130
1970-101 .... Nettles, James William .... 4632 Darien Dr/Tacoma WA 98407
1974-095 .... Nettles, Morris .... 551 1/2 San Juan/Venice CA 90291
1917-058 .... Neu, Otto Adam .... D. September 19, 1932 Kenton, O.
1925-078 .... Neubauer, Harold Charles .... D. September 9, 1949 Providence, R. I.
1972-078 .... Neumeier, Daniel George .... N2635 City Highway U/Lodi WI 53555
1925-079 .... Neun, John Henry .... D. March 28, 1990 Baltimore, Md.
1950-072 .... Nevel, Ernie Wyre .... D. July 10, 1988 Springfield, Mo.
1926-060 .... Nevers, Ernest Alonzo .... D. May 3, 1976 San Rafael, Calif.
1995-150 .... Nevin, Phil Joseph .... 8228 East Blackwillow Circle #102/Anaheim CA 92808
1949-059 .... Newcombe, Donald .... 7077 Alvern Street #A206/Los Angeles CA 90045
1987-103 .... Newell, Thomas Dean .... Old Add:1401 Leonard Gardnerville NV 89410
1993-133 .... Newfield, Marc Alexander .... 5591 Selkirk Drive/Huntington Beach CA 92649
1972-079 .... Newhauser, Donald Louis .... 321 Sheryl Dr/Deltona FL 32738
1939-082 .... Newhouser, Harold .... D. November 10, 1998 Detroit, Mich.
1934-079 .... Newkirk, Floyd Elmo .... D. April 15, 1976 Clayton, Mo.
1919-060 .... Newkirk, Joel Ivan .... D. January 22, 1966 Eldorado, Ill.
1940-067 .... Newlin, Maurice Milton .... D. August 14, 1978 Houston, Texas
1985-081 .... Newman, Albert Dwayne .... 1044 Laroda/Ontario CA 91761
1962-096 .... Newman, Frederick William .... D. June 24, 1987 Framingham, Mass.
1976-070 .... Newman, Jeffrey Lynn .... 537 Quivira CT Danville CA 94526
1971-074 .... Newman, Raymond Francis .... 1260 Malibu Lane/Myrtle Beach SC 29577
1910-113 .... Newnam, Patrick Henry .... D. June 20, 1938 San Antonio, Tex.
1929-079 .... Newsom, Norman Louis 'Bobo' .... D. December 7, 1962 Orlando, Fla.
1941-080 .... Newsome, Heber Hampton 'Dick' .... D. December 15, 1965 Ahoskie, N. C.
1935-081 .... Newsome, Lamar Ashby 'Skeeter' .... D. August 31, 1989 Columbus, Ga.
1991-133 .... Newson, Warren Dale .... 62 Wallace Gray Road/Newnan GA 30263
1946-079 .... Niarhos, Constantine Gregory 'Gus' .... 1034 Misty Court/Harrisonburg VA 22801
1952-080 .... Nicholas, Donald Leigh .... 12311 Chase/Garden Grove CA 92645
1986-113 .... Nichols, Carl Edward .... 2603 Billings Street/Compton CA 90220
1951-072 .... Nichols, Chester Raymond .... D. March 27, 1995 Lincoln, R. I.
1926-061 .... Nichols, Chester Raymond, Sr. .... D. July 11, 1982 Pawtucket, R. I.
1958-067 .... Nichols, Dolan Levon .... D. November 20, 1969 Tupelo, Miss.
1988-098 .... Nichols, Rodney Lea .... Old Add: 7612 Trail Ridge Rd NE Albuquerque NM 87109
1944-097 .... Nichols, Roy .... 104 Arias Way/Hot Springs Village AR 71901
1980-097 .... Nichols, Thomas Reid Reid .... PO Box 90111/Arlington TX 76004
1960-076 .... Nicholson, David Lawrence .... 527 Springingsguth/Roselle IL 60172
1912-143 .... Nicholson, Frank Collins .... D. November 11, 1972 Jersey Shore, Pa.
1917-057 .... Nicholson, Frederick .... D. January 23, 1972 Kilgore, Texas
1912-144 .... Nicholson, Ovid Edward .... D. March 24, 1968 Salem, Ind.
1936-065f .... Nicholson, William Beck .... D. March 8, 1996 Chestertown, Md.
1995-151 .... Nichting, Christopher Thomas .... 300 University Lane #116/Batavia OH 45103
1978-091 .... Nicosia, Steven Richard .... 8520 Hw Fifth Street/Pembroke Pines FL 33024
1921-073 .... Niebergall, Charles Arthur 'Nig' .... D. August 29, 1982 Holiday, Fla.
1992-094 .... Nied, David Glen .... PO Box 836/Grand Prairie TX 75050
1981-089 .... Niedenfuer, Thomas Edward .... 3933 Losillias Drive/Sarasota FL 34238
1925-080 .... Niehaus, Albert Bernard .... D. October 14, 1931 Cincinnati, O.
1913-132 .... Niehaus, Richard J. .... D. March 12, 1957 Atlanta, Ga.
1913-133 .... Niehoff, John Albert .... D. December 8, 1974 Inglewood, Calif.
1967-080 .... Niekro, Joseph Franklin .... 2707 Fairway Drive South/Plant City FL 33567
1964-077 .... Niekro, Philip Henry .... 6382 Nichols Road/Flowery Branch GA 30542
1992-095 .... Nielsen, Gerald Arthur .... 4631 Kewanee Street/Fair Oaks CA 95628
1986-114 .... Nielsen, Jeffrey Scott .... 2898 Valley View Avenue/Salt Lake City UT 84117
1949-060 .... Nielson, Milton Robert .... 1611 South Third Street/Saint Peter MN 56082
1943-097 .... Nieman, Elmer Leroy 'Butch' .... D. November 2, 1993 Topeka, Kan.
1951-073 .... Nieman, Robert Charles .... D. March 10, 1985 Corona, Calif.
1979-077 .... Niemann, Randal Harold .... 3317 SE West Snow Road/Port Saint Lucie FL 34984
1943-098 .... Niemes, Jacob Leland/ 'Jack' .... D. March 4, 1966 Hamilton, O.
1934-080 .... Niemiec, Alfred Joseph .... D. October 29, 1995 Kirkland, Wash.
1964-078 .... Nieson, Charles Bassett .... 6192 Dufferin Drive/Savage MN 55378
1984-083 .... Nieto, Thomas Andrew .... 2297 Canberra Drive/Rock Hill SC 29732

1915-117 ....Obrien, George Joseph ....D. March 24, 1966 Columbus, O.
1953-064 ....Obrien, John Thomas ....19504 92nd Avenue NE/Bothell WA 98011
1982-090 ....Obrien, Peter Michael................................Box 1037/Pebble Beach CA 93953
1916-065 ....Obrien, Raymond Joseph ....D. March 31, 1942 St. Louis, Mo.
1971-076 ....Obrien, Robert Allen ....3628 North Shirley/Fresno CA 93727
1969-126 ....Obrien, Sydney Lloyd ....9646 Bloomfield/Cypress CA 90630
1943-099 ....Obrien, Thomas Edward ....D. November 5, 1978 Anniston, Ala.
1911-128 ....Obrien, Thomas Joseph 'Buck'..................D. July 25, 1959 Boston, Mass.
1995-156 ....Ochoa, Alex..17490 SW 22nd Street/Miramar FL 33029
1935-082 ....Ock, Harold David 'Whitey' ....D. March 18, 1975 Mount Kisco, N. Y.
1944-099 ....Ockey, Walter Andrew ....D. December 4, 1971 Staten Island, N.Y.
1950-075 ....Oconnell, Daniel Francis ....D. October 2, 1969 Clifton, N. J.
1923-099 ....Oconnell, James Joseph ....D. November 11, 1976 Bakersfield, Calif.
1928-072 ....Oconnell, John Charles ....D. October 17, 1992 Canton, Ohio
1981-090 ....Oconnor, Jack William ....Box 430/Yucca Valley CA 92284
1916-066 ....Oconnor, John Charles ....D. May 30, 1982 Bonner Springs, Kan.
1935-083 ....Odea, James Kenneth 'Ken' ....D. December 17, 1985 Lima, N. Y.
1944-100 ....Odea, Paul ....D. December 11, 1978 Cleveland, O.
1954-076 ....Odell, William Oliver..................................225 O'Dell Road/Newberry SC 29108
1921-074 ....Odenwald, Theodore Joseph ....D. October 23, 1965 Shakopee, Minn.
1943-100 ....Odom, David Everett ....D. November 19, 1987 Myrtle Beach, S. C.
1925-081 ....Odom, Herman Boyd 'Heinie' ....D. August 31, 1970 Rusk, Texas
1964-081 ....Odom, John Lee 'Blue Moon' ....10343 Slater #204/Fountain Valley CA 92708
1954-077 ....Odonnell, George Dana ....121 High Street/Winchester IL 62694
1927-067 ....Odonnell, Harry Herman ....D. January 31, 1958 Philadelphia, Pa.
1963-087 ....Odonoghue, John Eugene ....5246 Far Oak Circle/Sarasota FL 34238
1993-135 ....Odonoghue, John Preston ....5246 Far Oak Circle/Sarasota FL 34238
1919-062 ....Odoul, Francis Joseph 'Lefty' ....D. December 7, 1969 San Francisco, Calif.
1912-145 ....Odowd, John Leo Dowd ....D. January 31, 1981 Fort Lauderdale, Fla.
1983-106 ....Oelkers, Bryan Alois ....3404 Taylor Avenue/Bridgeton MO 63044
1958-068 ....Oertel, Charles Frank ....Naubin Way/Naubin Way MI 49762
1914-162 ....Oeschger, Joseph Carl ....D. July 28, 1986 Rohnert Park, Calif.
1978-095 ....Oester, Ronald John ....3780 Ninemile Road/Cincinnati OH 45255
1915-118 ....Ofarrell, Robert Arthur ....D. February 20, 1988 Waukegan, Ill.
1990-118 ....Offerman, Jose Antonio (Dono).................Ed.B1 Urb Anacaono Moscoso San Pedro De Macoris Dominican Rep.
1972-082 ....Office, Rowland Johnnie ....Old Add: 3212 Harbor View CT Decatur GA 30034
1918-056 ....Ogden, John Mahlon ....D. November 9, 1977 Philadelphia, Pa.
1922-104 ....Ogden, Warren Harvey 'Curly' ....D. August 6, 1964 Chester, Pa.
1994-078 ....Ogea, Chad Wayne..................................418 Bonabridge Drive/Baton Rouge LA 70808
1936-067 ....Oglesby, James Dorn ....D. September 1, 1955 Tulsa, Okla.
1971-077 ....Oglivie, Benjamin Ambrosio ....2019 East Myrna Lane/Tempe AZ 85284
1936-068 ....Ogrodowski, Ambrose Francis 'Brusie' ....D. March 5, 1956 San Francisco, Calif.
1925-082 ....Ogrodowski, John Anthony ....D. June 24, 1959 Elmira, N. Y.
1994-079 ....Ohalloran, Gregory Joseph ....1021 Hedge Drive/Mississauga Ontario L4Y 1G3 Canada
1997-123 ....Ojala, Kirt Stanley....................................1155 Paradise Lake Drive SE/Grand Rapids MI 49546
1980-098 ....Ojeda, Robert Michael ....Old Add: 14884 Road 312 Visalia CA 93277
1920-092 ....Okrie, Frank Anthony ....D. October 16, 1959 Detroit, Mich.
1948-076 ....Okrie, Leonard Joseph ....2636 Burke Lane/Fayetteville NC 28301
1991-134 ....Olander, James Bentley...........................Old Add: 9402 East Magdalena Tucson AZ 85710
1914-163 ....Oldham, John Cyrus 'Red' ....D. January 28, 1961 Costa Mesa, Calif.
1956-066 ....Oldham, John Hardin ....1845 Anne Way/San Jose CA 95124
1953-065 ....Oldis, Robert Carl ....306 Virginia Drive/Iowa City IA 52246
1993-136 ....Oleary, Troy Franklin ....1060 Norwood Street/Rialto CA 92376
1989-091 ....Olerud, John Garrett ....1310 180th Avenue NE/Bellevue WA 98008
1989-092 ....Olin, Stephen Robert ....D. March 22, 1993 Little Lake Nellie, Fla.
1994-080 ....Oliva, Jose (Galvez) ....D. December 22, 1997 San Cristobal, Dominican Rep.
1962-099 ....Oliva, Pedro Tony ....212 Spring Valley Dr/Bloomington MN 55420
1960-078 ....Olivares, Edward Balzac ....Hc02 Box 12887/San German PR 753
1990-119 ....Olivares, Omar (Palqu).............................Hc 02 Box 12887 Carr. 330 K/-2/San German PR 753
1968-074 ....Oliver, Albert ....PO Box 1466/Portsmouth OH 45662
1993-137 ....Oliver, Darren Christopher ....1716 G Street/Rio Linda CA 95673
1977-105 ....Oliver, David Jacob ....3604 Newton Rd/Stockton CA 95205
1959-061 ....Oliver, Eugene George ....2805 35th St/Rock Island IL 61201
1989-093 ....Oliver, Joseph Melton ....4540 Foreland Place/Orlando FL 32806
1963-088 ....Oliver, Nathaniel ....4403 Oakhill Rd/Oakland CA 94605
1965-083 ....Oliver, Robert Lee ....1716 G Street/Rio Linda CA 95673
1930-059 ....Oliver, Thomas Noble ....D. February 16, 1988 Montgomery, Ala.
1989-094 ....Oliveras, Francisco Javier ....Old Add: Bajo K1h3 Buzon 1476 Rio Piedras PR 00928
1960-079 ....Olivo, Diomedes Antonio ....D. February 15, 1977 Santo Domingo, Dom. Rep.
1961-079 ....Olivo, Federico Emilio 'Chi-Chi' ....D. February 3, 1977 Guayubin, Dom. Rep.
1966-069 ....Ollom, James Donald ....8601 Ninth Avenue/Everett WA 98204
1943-101 ....Olmo, Luis Francisco Rodriguez ....620 Figueroa Street/Santurce PR 907
1980-099 ....Olmsted, Alan Ray ....1008 Pinecone Trail/Florissant MO 63031
1922-105 ....Olsen, Arthur 'Ole' ....D. September 12, 1980 Norwalk, Conn.
1941-082 ....Olsen, Bernard Charles ....D. March 30, 1977 Everett, Mass.
1939-083 ....Olsen, Vern Jarl ....D. July 13, 1989 Maywood, Ill.
1988-099 ....Olson, Greggory William ....Old Add: Omaha NE
1989-095 ....Olson, Gregory William ....18592 St. Mellion Place/Eden Prairie MN 55347
1911-129 ....Olson, Ivan Massie 'Ivy' ....D. September 1, 1965 Inglewood, Calif.

1951-075	Olson, Karl Arthur	PO Box 1897/Zephyr Cove NV 89448
1931-064	Olson, Marvin Clement	D. February 5, 1998 Tyndall, S. D.
1936-069	Olson, Theodore Otto	D. December 9, 1980 Weymouth, Mass.
1986-116	Olwine, Edward R.	PO Box 99/Greenville OH 45331
1982-091	Omalley, Thomas Patrick	10 Carriage Square/Montoursville PA 17754
1912-146	Omara, Oliver Edward	D. October 24, 1989 Reno, Nev.
1925-083	Oneal, Oran Herbert 'Skinny'	D. June 2, 1981 Springfield, Mo.
1984-085	Oneal, Randall Jeffrey	524 E. Rambling Dr/West Palm Beach FL 33411
1919-063	Oneil, George Michael 'Mickey'	D. April 8, 1964 St. Louis, Mo.
1946-080	Oneil, John Francis	126 Merlin Avenue #W E/Jamestown NY 14701
1939-084	Oneill, Harry Mink	D. March 8, 1945 Iwo Jima, Marianas Is.
1920-093	Oneill, James Leo	D. September 5, 1976 Chambersburg, Pa.
1922-106	Oneill, Joseph Henry 'Harry'	D. September 5, 1969 Ridgetown, Ont.
1985-084	Oneill, Paul Andrew	54 Doral Greens Drive West/Rye Brook NY 10573
1943-103	Oneill, Robert Emmett 'Emmett'	D. October 11, 1993 Sparks Nv
1911-130	Oneill, Stephen Francis	D. January 26, 1962 Cleveland, O.
1935-084	Onis, Manuel Dominguez	D. January 4, 1995 Tampa, Fla.
1912-147	Onslow, Edward Joseph	D. May 8, 1981 Dennison, O.
1912-148	Onslow, John James	D. December 22, 1960 West Acton, Mass.
1985-085	Ontiveros, Steven	Old Add: 9970 E. Charter Oak Rd Scottsdale AZ 85260
1973-089	Ontiveros, Steven Rogers	Old Add: 20 Ligget/Bakersfield CA 93307
1983-107	Oquendo, Jose Manuel	250 Stadium Plaza/Saint Louis MO 63102
1993-138	Oquist, Michael Lee	1910 Raton/Lajunta CO 81050
1955-086	Oravetz, Ernest Eugene	4417 Paul Ave/Tampa FL 33611
1997-124	Ordaz, Luis Javier	Old Add: Maracaibo Venezuela
1943-104	Ordenana, Antonio Rodriguez	D. September 29, 1988 Miami, Fla.
1997-125	Ordonez, Magglio	Old Add: Coro Falcon Venezuela
1996-145	Ordonez, Reynaldo	Old Add: Miami FL 33101
1939-085	Orengo, Joseph Charles	D. July 24, 1988 San Francisco, Calif.
1997-126	Orie, Kevin Leonard	Old Add: Pittsburgh PA 15201
1969-127	Oriley, Donald Lee	D. May 2, 1997 Kansas City, Mo.
1920-094	Orme, George William	D. March 16, 1962 Indianapolis, Ind.
1979-080	Orosco, Jesse Russell	1359 Tomol Drive/Carpinteria CA 93013
1912-149	Orourke, James Francis	D. May 14, 1986 Chatham, N. J.
1959-062	Orourke, James Patrick	N 15612 Little Spokane Drive/Spokane WA 99208
1929-080	Orourke, Joseph Leo	D. June 27, 1990 Philadelphia, Pa.
1913-136	Orr, William John	D. March 10, 1967 St. Helena, Calif.
1943-105	Orrell, Forrest Gordon	D. January 12, 1993 Chula Vista, Calif.
1927-068	Orsatti, Ernest Ralph	D. September 4, 1968 Canoga Park, Calif.
1961-080	Orsino, John Joseph	11501 Indian Spring Trail/Boynton Beach FL 33437
1983-108	Orsulak, Joseph Michael	29 Keansburg Rd/Parsippany NJ 7054
1972-083	Orta, Jorge	1201 Heather Hill Crescent/Flossmoor IL 60422
1960-080	Ortega, Filomeno Coronado 'Phil'	Old Add: 521 Market St #47/San Diego CA 92101
1973-090	Ortenzio, Frank Joseph	723 West Gettysburg/Fresno CA 93705
1982-092	Ortiz, Adalberto	Old Add: Delaro Arriba Buzon 590 Humacao PR 00661
1997-127	Ortiz, David Americo	Old Add: Haina Dominican Republic
1990-120	Ortiz, Javier Victor	Old Add: 13731 SW 38th Street Miami FL 33175
1969-128	Ortiz, Jose Luis	Calle 14 Hh-57 Villa Del Carmen Playa Ponce PR 731
1993-139	Ortiz, Louis Alberto Jochy	905 Chawan Avenue/Lynchburg VA 24502
1944-101	Ortiz, Olivrio Nunez 'Baby'	D. March 27, 1984 Central Senado, Camaguey, Cuba
1941-083	Ortiz, Roberto Gonzalo Nunez	D. September 15, 1971 Miami, Fla.
1989-096	Orton, John Andrew	100 North Rodeo Gulch Rd #5/Soquel CA 95073
1928-073	Orwoll, Oswald Christian	D. May 8, 1967 Decorah, Ia.
1975-086	Osborn, Danny Leon	7620 Knox CT Westminster CO 80030
1925-084	Osborn, Robert	D. April 19, 1960 Paris, Ark.
1992-098	Osborne, Donovan Alan	Old Add: 4440 Oakhollow Drive #186 Sacramento CA 95842
1922-107	Osborne, Ernest Preston 'Tiny'	D. January 5, 1969 Atlanta, Ga.
1957-062	Osborne, Lawrence Sidney	3309 Rough Creek Drive/Woodstock GA 31089
1935-085	Osborne, Wayne Harold	D. March 13, 1987 Vancouver, Wash.
1974-098	Osburn, Larry Pat 'Pat'	Old Add: Rr 2 Box 308 Bradenton FL 33508
1944-102	Osgood, Charles Benjamin	3 South Meadow Vlg #22/Carver MA 2330
1996-146	Osik, Keith Richard	Old Add: Shoreham NY 11786
1962-100	Osinski, Daniel	9723 West Amber Trail Drive/Sun City AZ 85351
1957-063	Osteen, Claude Wilson	6419 Saddle Ridge Road/Arlington TX 76016
1965-084	Osteen, Milton Darrell 'Darrell'	Old Add:1213 Las Posas San Clemente CA 92672
1914-164	Ostendorf, Frederick	D. March 9, 1965 Hampton, Va.
1954-078	Oster, William Charles	56 Little Reck Road/Centerport NY 11721
1921-075	Ostergard, Roy Lund 'Red'	D. January 13, 1977 Hemet, Calif.
1934-082	Ostermueller, Frederick Raymond	D. December 17, 1957 Quincy, Ill.
1973-091	Ostrosser, Brian Leonard	27 Chelsea Crescent/Stoney Creek Ontario Canada L8E 5R7
1943-106	Ostrowski, John Thaddeus	D. November 13, 1992 Chicago, Ill.
1948-077	Ostrowski, Joseph Paul	441 Tripp Street/West Wyoming PA 18644
1990-121	Osuna, Alfonso	Old Add: 401 W. Orangewood #B203 Anaheim CA 92802
1995-157	Osuna, Pedro Antonio 'Antonio'	Calle 11 Ave Mexico #436 Juan Jose Rios Sinaloa/Mexico
1945-075	Otero, Regino Jose Gomez	D. October 21, 1988 Hialeah, Fla.
1995-158	Otero, Ricardo Figueroa	33 Eleventh Avenue/Huntington Station NY 11746
1967-083	Otis, Amos Joseph	PO Box 723011/San Diego CA 92172
1912-150	Otis, Paul Franklin	D. December 15, 1990 Duluth, Minn.
1969-129	Otoole, Dennis Joseph	3453 Ridgewood Dr/Erlanger KY 41018

1958-069 ....Otoole, James Jerome ....1010 Lanette Dr/Cincinnati OH 45230
1926-062 ....Ott, Melvin Thomas ....D. November 21, 1958 New Orleans, La.
1974-099 ....Ott, Nathan Edward 'Ed' ....1511 West Hamilton Street/Allentown PA 18102
1962-101 ....Ott, William Joseph ....%County Lock 132 West Nyack Way West Nyack NY 10994
1974-100 ....Otten, James Edward ....2036 East Encanto/Mesa AZ 85203
1987-108 ....Otto, David Alan ....251 Bridlewood Court/Schaumburg IL 60173
1986-117 ....Ouellette, Philip Roland ....4771 Jones Road SE/Salem OR 97302
1933-047 ....Oulliber, John Andrew ....D. December 26, 1980 New Orleans, La.
1933-048 ....Outen, William Austin 'Chick' ....D. September 11, 1961 Durham, N. C.
1937-082 ....Outlaw, James Paulus ....118 James Street/Jackson AL 36545
1943-107 ....Overmire, Frank 'Stubby' ....D. March 3, 1977 Lakeland, Fla.
1976-072 ....Overy, Harry Michael ....101 Fairview Pl/Clinton IL 61727
1911-131 ....Ovitz, Ernest Gayhart ....D. September 11, 1980 Green Bay, Wisc.
1976-073 ....Owchinko, Robert Dennis ....4919 East Ludlow Drive/Scottsdale AZ 85254
1937-083 ....Owen, Arnold Malcolm 'Mickey' ....604 West Division/Mount Vernon MO 65712
1983-109 ....Owen, Dave ....5611 Louis Way/Arlington TX 76017
1981-091 ....Owen, Lawrence Thomas ....804 White Pine St/New Carlisle OH 45344
1931-065 ....Owen, Marvin James ....D. June 22, 1991 Mountain View, Calif.
1983-110 ....Owen, Spike Dee ....PO Box 33280 #286/Austin TX 78764
1993-140 ....Owens, Claude Jayhawk Jayhawk ....2085 Kay Road/Sardinia OH 45171
1995-159 ....Owens, Eric Blake ....PO Box 141/Rocky Mount VA 24151
1935-086 ....Owens, Furman Lee 'Jack' ....D. November 14, 1958 Greenville, S. C.
1955-087 ....Owens, James Philip ....1761 Croton Dr/Venice FL 33595
1972-084 ....Owens, Paul Francis ....Rr 2 Box 689/Mullica Hill NJ 8062
1982-093 ....Ownbey, Richard Wayne ....23785 Dolphin Cove/Laguna Niguel CA 92677
1965-085 ....Oyler, Raymond Francis ....D. January 26, 1981 Redmond, Wash.
1973-092 ....Ozark, Daniel Leonard ....Box 6666/Vero Beach FL 32960
1923-100 ....Ozmer, Horace Robert 'Doc' ....D. December 28, 1970 Atlanta, Ga.
1977-106 ....Pacella, John Lewis ....9602 Coran Drive/Westerville OH 43081
1996-147 ....Pachecho, Alexander Melchor ....Old Add: Caracas Venezuela
1987-109 ....Pacillo, Patrick Michael ....8 Rocky Glen Way/Lebanon NJ 8833
1987-110 ....Paciorek, James Joseph ....Old Add: 13432 Moenart Detroit MI 48212
1963-089 ....Paciorek, John Francis ....8400 Huntington Dr/San Gabriel CA 91775
1970-103 ....Paciorek, Thomas Marian ....2389 Broad Creek Drive/Stone Mountain GA 30087
1949-062 ....Pack, Frankie ....PO Box 1623/Hendersonville NC 28739
1912-151 ....Packard, Eugene Milo ....D. May 19, 1959 Riverside, Calif.
1975-087 ....Pactwa, Joseph Martin ....Old Add: 2045 South Haster #C2 Anaheim CA 92802
1932-059 ....Padden, Thomas Francis......................................D. June 11, 1973 Manchester, N. H.
1912-152 ....Paddock, Delmar Harold ....D. February 6, 1952 Remer, Minn.
1937-084 ....Padgett, Don Wilson ....D. December 9, 1980 High Point, N. C.
1923-101 ....Padgett, Ernest Kitchen ....D. April 15, 1957 East Orange, N. J.
1969-130 ....Paepke, Dennis Rae ....4560 Trieste Drive/Carlsbad CA 92008
1943-108 ....Pafko, Andrew ....1420 Blackhawk Drive/Mount Prospect IL 60056
1973-093 ....Pagan, David Percy ....Box 1819/Nipawin Saskatchewan S0E 1E0 Canada
1959-063 ....Pagan, Jose Antonio ....Calle Jaspe #15/Caguas PR 625
1944-103 ....Page, Joseph Francis ....D. April 21, 1980 Latrobe, Pa.
1968-075 ....Page, Michael Randy ....599 Briarcliff Drive/Woodruff SC 29388
1977-107 ....Page, Mitchell Otis ....484 Lake Park Avenue #162/Oakland CA 94610
1928-074 ....Page, Philippe Rausac ....D. June 27, 1958 Springfield, Mass.
1939-086 ....Page, Samuel Walter ....133 Plantation Drive/Woodruff SC 29388
1938-073 ....Page, Vance Linwood ....D. July 14, 1951 Wilson, N. C.
1978-096 ....Pagel, Karl Douglas ....2698 North Ellis Street/Chandler AZ 85224
1955-088 ....Pagliaroni, James Vincent...................................10388 Partridge Dr/Grass Valley CA 95945
1984-086 ....Pagliarulo, Michael Timothy ....11 Fieldstone Drive/Winchester MA 1890
1987-111 ....Pagnozzi, Thomas Alan ....1710 West Park Avenue/Chandler AZ 85224
1911-132 ....Paige, George Lynn 'Pat' ....D. June 8, 1939 Berlin, Wis.
1948-078 ....Paige, Leroy 'Satchel' ....D. June 8, 1982 Kansas City, Mo.
1951-076 ....Paine, Phillips Steere ....D. February 19, 1978 Lebanon, Pa.
1993-141 ....Painter, Lance Telford ....8028 North Santa Monica/Milwaukee WI 53217
1988-100 ....Palacios, Robert Rey ....359 Van Brunt Street/Brooklyn NY 11321
1987-112 ....Palacios, Vicente ....Domicilio Conocido Mataloma Veracruz Mexicio
1939-087 ....Palagyi, Michael Raymond ....167 14th St Reet/Conneaut OH 44030
1945-076 ....Palica, Ervin Martin ....D. May 29, 1982 Huntington Beach, Calif.
1988-101 ....Pall, Donn Steven ....154 Wellington Avenue/Bloomingdale IL 60108
1948-079 ....Palm, Richard Paul ....21 Riverview Place/Scituate MA 2066
1995-160 ....Palmeiro, Orlando ....Old Add: Miami FL
1986-118 ....Palmeiro, Rafael Corrales ....5216 Reims Court/Colleyville TX 76034
1978-097 ....Palmer, David William ....61 Sherman Avenue/Glens Falls NY 12801
1989-097 ....Palmer, Dean William ....2214 Genevieve Court/Tallahassee FL 32312
1917-059 ....Palmer, Edwin Henry ....D. January 9, 1983 Marlow, Okla.
1965-086 ....Palmer, James Alvin ....2432 Still Forest Road/Baltimore MD 21208
1969-131 ....Palmer, Lowell Raymond ....Po0 Box 5253/El Dorado Hills CA 95762
1915-119 ....Palmero, Emilio Antonio ....D. July 15, 1970 Toledo, O.
1931-066 ....Palmisano, Joseph ....D. November 5, 1971 Albuquerque, N. M.
1960-081 ....Palmquist, Edwin Lee ....1921 16th Street/Kingsburg CA 93631
1953-066 ....Palys, Stanley Francis ....Rr One/Moscow PA 18444
1996-148 ....Paniagua, Jose Luis Sanchez ....Old Add: Santo Domingo Dom. Rep.
1984-087 ....Pankovits, James Franklin ....9419 Bonnie Dale Road/Richmond VA 23229
1971-078 ....Panther, James Edward ....1125 Shari Ln/Libertyville IL 60048

1961-081	Papa, John Paul	29 Phillips Dr/Shelton CT 6484
1948-080	Papai, Alfred Thomas	D. September 7, 1995 Springfield, Ill.
1976-074	Pape, Kenneth Wayne	2617 Green Creek Street/San Antonio TX 78232
1974-101	Papi, Stanley Gerard	1111 West Sierra Madre/Fresno CA 93705
1945-077	Papish, Frank Richard	D. August 30, 1965 Pueblo, Colo.
1991-135	Pappas, Erik Daniel	Old Add: Chicago II
1957-064	Pappas, Milton Stephen	502 Highlington Court/Beecher IL 60401
1993-142	Paquette, Craig Harold	Old Add: 9542 Orangewood Avenue Garden Grove CA 92641
1985-086	Pardo, Alberto Judas	908 Hillary Circle/Lutz FL 33549
1988-102	Paredes, Johnny Alfonso	Old Add: Maracaibo Venezuela
1986-119	Parent, Mark Alan	PO Box 591/Cottonwood CA 96022
1982-094	Paris, Kelly Jay	1515 Redwood Circle/Thousand Oaks CA 91360
1943-109	Parisse, Louis Peter	D. June 2, 1956 Philadelphia, Pa.
1994-081	Park, Chan Ho	Old Add: 452 W. California Ave Glendale CA 91203
1915-120	Park, James	D. December 17, 1970 Lexington, Ky.
1937-085	Parker, Clarence McKay 'Ace'	210 Snead's Fairway/Portsmouth VA 23701
1915-121	Parker, Clarence Perkins 'Pat'	D. March 21, 1967 Claremont, N.H.
1973-094	Parker, David Gene	4036 Oak Tree Court/Loveland OH 45140
1923-102	Parker, Douglas Woolley 'Dixie'	D. May 15, 1972 Green Pond, Ala.
1936-070	Parker, Francis James 'Salty'	D. July 27, 1992 Houston, Texas
1970-104	Parker, Harry William	3324 South Ash Place/Broken Arrow OK 74012
1987-113	Parker, James Clayton Clay	1112 Charwood Lane/Hixson TN 37343
1964-082	Parker, Maurice Wesley 'Wes'	Old Add: 2140 Colorado Avenue/Santa Monica CA 90404
1990-122	Parker, Richard Alan	2641 NE 74th Street/Gladstone MO 64119
1919-064	Parker, Roy William	D. May 17, 1954 Tulsa, Okla.
1971-079	Parker, William David	Old Add: 1975 El Parque Drive Tempe AZ 85282
1921-076	Parkinson, Frank Joseph	D. July 4, 1960 Trenton, N.J.
1937-086	Parks, Artie William	D. December 6, 1989 Little Rock, Ark.
1992-099	Parks, Derek Gavin	Old Add: 859 N. Mountain Ave Upland CA 91786
1921-077	Parks, Vernon Henry 'Slicker'	D. February 21, 1978 Royal Oak, Mich.
1929-081	Parmelee, Leroy Earl	D. August 31, 1981 Monroe, Mich.
1947-065	Parnell, Melvin Lloyd	700 Turquoise Street/New Orleans LA 70124
1916-067	Parnham, James Arthur 'Rube'	D. November 25, 1963 McKeesport, Pa.
1995-161	Parra, Jose Miguel	Old Add: Santiago Dominican Rep.
1986-120	Parrett, Jeffrey Dale	722 Seattle Drive/Lexington KY 40503
1970-105	Parrilla, Samuel	D. February 9, 1994 Brooklyn, N. Y.
1995-162	Parris, Steven Michael	%Dean Parris 2307 Orchard Ln Joliet IL 60435
1977-108	Parrish, Lance Michael	5141 Via Samuel/Yorba Linda CA 92686
1974-102	Parrish, Larry Alton	407 Winter Ridge Blvd/Winter Haven FL 33881
1977-109	Parrott, Michael Everett Arch	2034 Sumac Street/Longmont CO 80501
1910-115	Parson, William Edwin 'Jiggs'	D. May 19, 1967 Inglewood, Calif.
1981-092	Parsons, Casey Robert	3712 South Woodruff Road/Spokane WA 99206
1939-088	Parsons, Edward Dixon 'Dixie'	D. October 31, 1991 Longview, Texas
1963-090	Parsons, Thomas Anthony	6556 Twickenham Street Nw/Canton OH 44708
1971-080	Parsons, William Raymond	2725 South Azalea/Tempe AZ 85281
1943-110	Partee, Roy Robert	Drawer 730/Trinidad CA 95570
1913-137	Partenheimer, Harold Philip 'Steve'	D. June 16, 1971 Mansfield, O.
1944-104	Partenheimer, Stanwood Wendell	D. January 28, 1989 Wilson, N. C.
1927-069	Partridge, James Bugg 'Jay'	D. January 4, 1974 Nashville, Tenn.
1915-122	Paschal, Benjamin Edwin	D. November 10, 1974 Charlotte, N. C.
1978-098	Paschall, William Herbert	Old Add: 5307 North Oaks Drive Greensboro NC 27405
1954-079	Pascual, Camilo Alberto	7741 SW 32nd St/Miami FL 33155
1950-076	Pascual, Carlos Alberto	2540 SW 92nd Court/Miami FL 33165
1933-049	Pasek, John Paul	D. March 13, 1976 Niagara Falls, N. Y.
1982-095	Pashnick, Larry John	506 Highland/Wynadotte MI 48192
1974-103	Pasley, Kevin Patrick	2701 Lancaster Drive/Sun City Center FL 33570
1985-087	Pasqua, Daniel Anthony	140 Circle Ridge/Burr Ridge IL 60480
1919-065	Pasquella, Michael John	D. April 5, 1965 Bridgeport, Conn.
1935-087	Passeau, Claude William	137 London Street/Lucedale MS 39452
1979-081	Pastore, Frank Enrico	1542 North Framis Way/Upland CA 91786
1983-111	Pastornicky, Clifford Scot	1616 Alton Road/Venice FL 34293
1926-063	Pate, Joseph William	D. December 26, 1948 Fort Worth, Tex.
1980-100	Pate, Robert Wayne	4858 Vineland Avenue/North Hollywood CA 91661
1968-076	Patek, Frederick Joseph	227 Willow Street/Sealy TX 77474
1941-084	Patrick, Robert Lee	Old Add: 107 North 18th Fort Smith AR 72901
1996-149	Patterson, Danny Shane	Old Add: Rosemead CA
1968-077	Patterson, Daryl Alan	20145 Tollhouse Rd/Clovis CA 93612
1979-082	Patterson, David Glenn	8425 Evanston Avenue/Raytown MO 64138
1977-110	Patterson, Gilbert Thomas	848 Nw 76th Terrace/Plantation FL 33324
1932-060	Patterson, Henry Joseph	D. September 30, 1970 Panorama City, Calif.
1995-163	Patterson, Jeffrey Simmons	Old Add: Anaheim CA 92801
1992-100	Patterson, John Allen	2647 North Miller Road #13/Scottsdale AZ 85257
1988-103	Patterson, Kenneth Brian	Rural Route 4 Box 129/Grand Saline TX 75140
1981-093	Patterson, Michael Lee	2419 Ridgeley Dr #9/Los Angeles CA 90016
1981-094	Patterson, Reginald Allen	7213 Naples Avenue South/Birmingham AL 35206
1985-088	Patterson, Robert Charles	3725 Alpine Court NE/Hickory NC 28601
1921-078	Patterson, William Jennings Bryan	D. October 1, 1977 St. Louis, Mo.
1968-078	Pattin, Martin William	2011 East 795th Road/Lecompton KS 66050
1929-082	Pattison, James Wells	D. February 22, 1991 Melbourne, Fla.

1944-105 ....Patton, Gene Tunney ....60 South 17th Avenue/Coatesville PA 19320
1935-088 ....Patton, George William ....D. March 15, 1986 Philadelphia, Pa.
1910-116 ....Patton, Harry Claude ....D. June 9, 1930 St. Louis, Mo.
1957-065 ....Patton, Thomas Allen ....807 Reservoir/Honey Brook PA 19344
1968-079 ....Paul, Michael George ....5121 Circulo Sobrio/Tucson AZ 85718
1954-080 ....Paula, Carlos (Connill) ....D. April 25, 1983 Miami, Fla.
1911-133 ....Paulette, Eugene Edward ....D. February 8, 1966 Little Rock, Ark.
1925-085 ....Paulson, Guilford Paul Hans 'Paul' ....D. April 20, 1994 Harlan, Iowa
1990-123 ....Pavlas, David Lee ....PO Box 1224/Shiner TX 77984
1957-066 ....Pavletich, Donald Stephen ....13645 Adelaide Lane/Brookfield WI 53005
1992-101 ....Pavlik, Roger Allen ....622 Beaver Bend/Houston TX 77037
1946-081 ....Pawelek, Theodore John ....D. February 12, 1964 Chicago Heights, Ill.
1955-089 ....Pawloski, Stanley Walter ....1013 Gorman St/Philadelphia PA 19116
1987-114 ....Pawlowski, John ....9 Linda Drive/Binghamton NY 13905
1977-111 ....Paxton, Michael Dewayne ....Old Add: 345 Lincoln #10 Boston MA 02111
1920-095 ....Payne, George Washington ....D. January 24, 1959 Bellflower, Calif.
1984-088 ....Payne, Michael Earl ....Box 712/Williston FL 32696
1975-088 ....Pazik, Michael Joseph ....8413 Comanche Court/Bethesda MD 20817
1937-087 ....Peacock, John Gaston ....D. October 17, 1981 Wilson, N. C.
1933-050 ....Pearce, Franklin Thomas ....D. September 3, 1950 Van Buren, N. Y.
1912-153 ....Pearce, George Thomas ....D. October 11, 1935 Joliet, Ill.
1917-060 ....Pearce, Harry James ....D. January 8, 1942 Philadelphia, Pa.
1949-063 ....Pearce, James Madison ....224 Clyde Pearce Road/Zebulon NC 27597
1958-070 ....Pearson, Albert Gregory ....Old Add: 54-552 Shoal Creek Laquinta CA 92253
1939-089 ....Pearson, Issac Overton ....D. March 17, 1985 Sarasota, Fla.
1932-061 ....Pearson, Montgomery Marcellus ....D. January 27, 1978 Fresno, Calif.
1910-117 ....Peasley, Marvin Warren ....D. December 27, 1948 San Francisco, Calif.
1915-123 ....Pechous, Charles Edward ....D. September 13, 1980 Kenosha, Wis.
1943-111 ....Peck, Harold Arthur 'Hal' ....D. April 13, 1995 Milwaukee, Wisc.
1910-118 ....Peckinpaugh, Roger Thorpe ....D. November 17, 1977 Cleveland, O.
1986-121 ....Pecota, William Joseph ....Old Add: 471 Liquid Amber Way Sunnyvale CA 94086
1953-067 ....Peden, Leslie Earl ....17437 Elsinore Drive/Jacksonville FL 32226
1985-089 ....Pederson, Stuart Russell ....200 Cle Marguerita,%S.Pederson/Los Gatos CA 95030
1991-136 ....Pedre, Jorge Enrique ....7894 Bellflower Road/Buena Park CA 90620
1987-115 ....Pedrique, Alfredo Jose ....1409 South Oak Park Drive/Tucson AZ 85710
1941-085 ....Peek, Stephen George ....D. September 20, 1991 Syracuse, N. Y.
1927-070 ....Peel, Homer Hefner ....D. April 8, 1997 Shreveport, La.
1935-089 ....Peerson, Jack Chiles ....D. October 23, 1966 Ft. Walton Beach, Fla.
1927-071 ....Peery, George A. 'Red' ....D. May 6, 1985 Salt Lake City, Utah
1956-067 ....Peete, Charles ....D. November 27, 1956 Caracas, Venez.
1992-102 ....Peguero, Julio Cesar (Santana) ....El Tio #25, San Isidro Santo Domingo Dominican Rep.
1994-082 ....Pegues, Steven Antone ....362 President Drive/Pontotoc MS 38863
1946-082 ....Pellagrini, Edward Charles ....103 Webb Street/Weymouth MA 2188
1992-103 ....Peltier, Daniel Edwar ....239 Lapp Road/Clifton Park NY 12065
1974-104 ....Pemberton, Brock ....5763 South 80th East Avenue/Tulsa OK 74145
1995-164 ....Pemberton, Rudy Hector Perez ....Old Add: San Pedro De Macoris Dominican Rep.
1981-095 ....Pena, Adalberto ....Sta. Elvira, Sta. Rosa K35/Caguas PR 625
1981-096 ....Pena, Alejandro ....PO Box 2176/Roswell GA 30075
1980-101 ....Pena, Antonio Francisco ....Comp Hab 30 Demarzo,Man #1 Ed 14 Santiago Dominican Rep.
1990-124 ....Pena, Geronimo ....Km 17 #7 Pista Duarte "Los Alcarrizzos,D.N. Dominican Rep./"
1986-122 ....Pena, Hipolito ....Old Add: 40 Seminole Avenue Albany NY 12203
1992-104 ....Pena, James Patrick ....6438 East Lewis Avenue/Scottsdale AZ 85257
1969-132 ....Pena, Jose ....A.Flores #1116 Nte C.Jiquilpan Los Mochis Sinaloa Mexico
1958-071 ....Pena, Orlando ....1750 West 46th Street #416/Hialeah FL 33012
1989-098 ....Pena, Ramon Arturo ....Calle H Esquin J, Cerro Alto Santiago Dominican Rep.
1965-087 ....Pena, Robert Cesar ....D. July 23, 1982 Santiago, Dominican Rep.
1922-108 ....Pence, Elmer Clair ....D. September 17, 1968 San Francisco, Calif.
1921-079 ....Pence, Russell William ....D. August 11, 1971 Hot Springs, Ark.
1953-068 ....Pendleton, James Edward ....D. March 20, 1996 Houston, Texas
1984-089 ....Pendleton, Terry Lee ....Old Add: 1831 Bally Bunion Dr Duluth GA 30136
1995-165 ....Penn, Shannon Dion ....1841 Hewitt Avenue/Cinncinnati OH 45207
1916-068 ....Penner, Kenneth William ....D. May 28, 1959 Sacramento, Calif.
1993-143 ....Pennington, Brad Lee ....7220 East State Road 160/Salem IN 47167
1917-061 ....Pennington, George Louis 'Kewpie' ....D. May 5, 1953 Newark, N. J.
1912-154 ....Pennock, Herbert Jefferis ....D. January 30, 1948 New York, N.Y.
1992-105 ....Pennyfeather, William Nathaniel ....621 Chamberlain Avenue/Perth Amboy NJ 8861
1954-081 ....Penson, Paul Eugene ....711 Lake Of The Forest/Bonner Springs KS 66012
1975-089 ....Pentz, Eugene David ....207 Rainbow Drive/Johnstown PA 15904
1962-102 ....Pepitone, Joseph Anthony ....32 Lois Lane/Farmingdale NY 11735
1929-083 ....Peploski, Henry Stephen ....D. January 28, 1982 Dover, N. J.
1913-139 ....Peploski, Joseph Aloysius ....D. July 13, 1971 New York, N. Y.
1966-070 ....Pepper, Donald Hoyte ....7 Breckenham Lane/Greenville SC 29609
1954-082 ....Pepper, Hugh McLaurin 'Laurin' ....8932 Davis Street/Ocean Springs MS 39564
1932-062 ....Pepper, Raymond Watson ....D. March 24, 1996 Huntsville, Ala.
1915-124 ....Pepper, Robert Ernest ....D. April 8, 1968 Ford Cliff, Pa.
1969-133 ....Peraza, Luis ....Calle 6 C.F. 13 Res. Bairoa/Caguas PR 625
1988-104 ....Peraza, Oswaldo Jose ....Old Add: Barbual #19-36, Puerto "Cabello,Carabobo Venezuela"
1995-166 ....Percival, Troy Eugene ....28920 Grelck Drive/Moreno Valley CA 92555
1980-102 ....Perconte, John Patrick ....6197 Hinterlong Court/Lisle IL 60532

1911-134 ....Perdue, Herbert Rodney 'Hub' ....D. October 31, 1968 Gallatin, Tenn.
1964-083 ....Perez, Atanasio Rigal 'Tony' ....1717 North Bayshore Drive #1551/Miami FL 33132
1995-167 ....Perez, Carlos Gross ....Carre Tara Sanchez K-M21 Nigua San Cristobal Dominican/Rep.
1996-150 ....Perez, Daniel ....Old Add: El Paso TX 79901
1995-168 ....Perez, Eduardo ....Las Flores #113/Santurce PR 911
1993-144 ....Perez, Eduardo Atanacio ....1717 North Bay Shore Drive #1551/Miami FL 33132
1958-072 ....Perez, George Thomas ....Old Add: 39646 87th Street West/Leona Valley CA 93550
1969-134 ....Perez, Martin Roman ....30 Willowick Dr/Decatur GA 30034
1987-116 ....Perez, Melido Turpen ....Nigua Km 21 1/2 Santo Domingo Dominican Rep.
1990-125 ....Perez, Michael Irvin ....Old Add: Rural Route 2 Box 165-A Yauco PR 00768
1996-151 ....Perez, Neifi Neftali Diaz ....Old Add: Santo Domingo Dom. Rep.
1980-103 ....Perez, Pascual (Gross) ....Salvador, Cucurulo #105 Santiago Dominican Rep.
1994-083 ....Perez, Robert Alexander (Jimenez) ....Vista El Sol Casado #62 Edo Bolivar Venezuela
1995-169 ....Perez, Tomas Orlando ...............................U.L.Cyepusculo Blq 17 #0102 Barquisimeto Venezuela
1991-137 ....Perez, Yorkis Miguel ....Respardo Sanchez #7 Bajos De Haina/Domincan Rep.
1988-105 ....Perezchica, Antonio Llamas ....33760 Via Echo/Palm Springs CA 92264
1997-128 ....Perisho, Matthew Alan ....Old Add: Tempe AZ 85282
1978-099 ....Perkins, Broderick Phillip ....165 Linda Vista Avenue/Pittsburg CA 94565
1967-084 ....Perkins, Cecil Boyce ....Rural Route 5 Box 163b/Martinsburg WV 25401
1930-060 ....Perkins, Charles Sullivan ....D. May 25, 1988 Salem, Ore.
1915-125 ....Perkins, Ralph Foster 'Cy' ....D. October 2, 1963 Philadelphia, Pa.
1950-077 ....Perkovich, John Joseph ....16 Athena Court/Little Rock AR 72207
1947-066 ....Perkowski, Harold Walter 211 McGinnis/Beckley/Wv/25801
1985-090 ....Perlman, Jonathan Samuel ....1019 Forrest Lane/Carthage TX 75633
1977-112 ....Perlozzo, Samuel Benedict ....14308 Old Lake Drive/Cumberland MD 21502
1942-075 ....Perme, Leonard Joseph ....3350 D Street/Hayward CA 94541
1910-119 ....Pernoll, Henry Hubbard ....D. February 18, 1944 Grants Pass, Ore.
1961-082 ....Perranoski, Ronald Peter...........................3805 Indian River Drive/Vero Beach FL 32963
1921-080 ....Perrin, John Stephenson ....D. June 24, 1969 Detroit, Mich.
1934-083 ....Perrin, William Joseph ....D. June 30, 1974 New Orleans, La.
1912-155 ....Perritt, William Dayton 'Pol' ....D. October 15, 1947 Shreveport, La.
1941-086 ....Perry, Boyd Glenn ....D. June 29, 1990 Burlington, N. C.
1962-103 ....Perry, Gaylord Jackson ....PO Box 1958/Kill Devil Hills NC 27948
1983-112 ....Perry, Gerald June ....1348 Waterford Green Close/Marietta GA 30068
1994-084 ....Perry, Herbert Edward ....Rural Route 3 Box 148/Mayo FL 32066
1915-126 ....Perry, Herbert Scott ....D. October 27, 1959 Kansas City, Mo.
1959-064 ....Perry, James Evan ....2608 Ridgeview Way/Sioux Falls SD 57105
1963-091 ....Perry, Melvin Gay 'Bob' ....621 Fox Chase Village/New Bern NC 28560
1912-156 ....Perry, William Henry 'Hank'.......................D. July 18, 1956 Pontiac, Mich.
1985-091 ....Perry, William Patrick Pat ....1115 West Franklin/Taylorville IL 62568
1915-127 ....Perryman, Emmett Key 'Parson' ....D. September 12, 1966 Starke, Fla.
1995-170 ....Person, Robert Alan ....25 Bellerive Acres/Saint Louis MO 63121
1918-057 ....Pertica, William Andrew ....D. December 28, 1967 Los Angeles, Calif.
1971-081 ....Perzanowski, Stanley ....PO Box 607/Syracuse IN 46567
1942-076 ....Pesky, John Michael ....25 Parsons Drive/Swampscott MA 1907
1994-085 ....Petagine, Roberto Antonio (Guerra)..............Ave Bolivar, Qta Dubaris #31-86 Nueva Esparta Venezuela
1989-099 ....Peterek, Jeffrey Allen ....PO Box 5/Harbert MI 49115
1942-077 ....Peterman, William David ....9823 Wisteria Street/Philadelphia PA 19115
1996-152 ....Peters, Christopher Michael ....Old Add: McMurray PA 15317
1959-065 ....Peters, Gary Charles ....7121 North Sevenda Drive/Sarasota FL 34241
1915-128 ....Peters, John William ....D. February 21, 1932 Kansas City, Mo.
1912-157 ....Peters, Otto Casper ....D. February 7, 1965 Pequannock, N. J.
1970-106 ....Peters, Raymond James ....Old Add: 154 Coldiron Court Cheektowaga NY 14225
1979-083 ....Peters, Richard Devin Ricky ....12601 South Halo Drive/Compton CA 90221
1936-071 ....Peters, Russell Dixon 'Rusty' ....261 Emerald Drive/Harrisonburg VA 22801
1987-117 ....Peters, Steven Bradley ....Old Add: Rr 11 Box 531a Oklahoma City OK 73170
1987-118 ....Peterson, Adam Charles ....5208 NE 88th Street/Vancouver WA 98665
1955-090 ....Peterson, Carl Francis 'Buddy' ....8665 Florin Rd #101/Sacramento CA 95828
1962-104 ....Peterson, Charles Andrew 'Cap' ....D. May 16, 1980 Tacoma, Wash.
1966-071 ....Peterson, Fred Ingels 'Fritz' ....Old Add:2525 Old Tavern Rd #17/Lisle IL 60532
1955-091 ....Peterson, Harding William 'Pete' ....15 Waterside Close/Tuckahoe NY 10707
1931-067 ....Peterson, James Niels ....D. April 8, 1975 Palm Beach, Fla.
1944-106 ....Peterson, Kent Franklin ....D. April 27, 1995 Highland, Utah
1943-112 ....Peterson, Sidney Herbert ....4604 University Avenue/Wichita Falls TX 76308
1991-138 ....Petkovsek, Mark Joesph ....5575 Duff/Beaumont TX 77706
1934-084 ....Petoskey, Frederick Lee ....D. November 30, 1996 Elgin, S. C.
1982-096 ....Petralli, Eugene James ....2605 Laurel Valley Lane/Arlington TX 76006
1963-092 ....Petrocelli, Americo Peter 'Rico' ....37 Green Heron Lane/Nashua NH 3062
1979-084 ....Petry, Daniel Joseph ....1808 Cartlen Drive/Placentia CA 92870
1983-113 ....Pettibone, Harry Jonathan 'Jam' ....Old Add: 1261 West Catalpa Anaheim CA 92801
1914-165 ....Pettigrew, Jim Ned ....D. August 20, 1952 Duncan, Okla.
1980-104 ....Pettini, Joseph Paul ....112 Logan Court/Bethany WV 26032
1982-097 ....Pettis, Gary George ....218 El Sendero/Vallejo CA 94589
1951-077 ....Pettit, George William Paul 'Paul'.............928 Sarazen Street/Hemet CA 92543
1935-090 ....Pettit, Leon Arthur ....D. November 21, 1974 Columbia, Tenn.
1995-171 ....Pettite, Andrew Eugene ....1714 North Park Side/Deer Park TX 77536
1921-081 ....Petty, Jesse Lee ....D. October 23, 1971 St. Paul, Minn.
1989-100 ....Pevey, Marty Ashley ....111 Runner Road/Savannah GA 31410
1914-166 ....Pezold, Lorenz Johannes 'Larry' ....D. October 22, 1957 Baton Rouge, La.

1935-091	Pezzullo, John 'Pretzles'	D. May 16, 1990 Dallas, Texas
1911-135	Pfeffer, Edward Joseph 'Jeff'	D. August 15, 1972 Chicago, Ill.
1913-138	Pfeffer, Monte	D. September 27, 1941 New York, N. Y.
1969-135	Pfeil, Robert Raymond	2922 Snowbrook Court/Stockton CA 95219
1961-083	Pfister, Daniel Albin	1436 Nw 9th Street/Dania FL 33004
1941-087	Pfister, George Edward	D. August 14, 1997 Somerset, N. J.
1945-078	Pfund, Leroy Herbert 'Lee'	1421 Princeton Court #A/Wheaton IL 60187
1936-072	Phebus, Raymond William 'Bill'	D. October 11, 1989 Bartow, Fla.
1910-120	Phelan, Arthur Thomas	D. December 27, 1964 Fort Worth, Tex.
1931-068	Phelps, Ernest Gordon 'Babe'.	D. December 10, 1992 Odenton, Md.
1980-105	Phelps, Kenneth Allen	Old Add: 7531 E. Turquoise Ave Scottsdale AZ 85258
1930-061	Phelps, Raymond Clifford	D. July 7, 1971 Ft. Pierce, Fla.
1941-088	Philley, David Earl	1336 East Polk Street/Paris TX 75460
1964-084	Phillips, Adolfo Emilio Lopez	Old Add: Apartado 6109 Cherilla Panama
1930-062	Phillips, Albert Abernathy 'Buzz'	D. November 6, 1964 Baltimore, Md.
1993-145	Phillips, Clarence Gene 'J.R.'	Old Add: 12022 Rio Vista Drive Sun City AZ 85351
1934-085	Phillips, Clarence Lemuel 'Red'	D. February 1, 1988 Wichita, Kansas
1942-078	Phillips, Damon Russell 'Dee'	PO Box 701/Joinerville TX 75658
1924-085	Phillips, Edward David	D. January 26, 1968 Buffalo, N.Y.
1969-136	Phillips, Harold Ross 'Lefty	D. June 12, 1972 Fullerton, Calif.
1953-069	Phillips, Howard Edward 'Ed'	West Ely/Hannibal MO 63401
1947-067	Phillips, Jack Dorn	721 May Road #2/Potsdam NY 13676
1945-079	Phillips, John	D. June 16, 1958 St. Louis, Mo.
1955-092	Phillips, John Melvin 'Bubba'	D. June 22, 1993 Hattiesburg, Miss.
1982-098	Phillips, Keith Anthony Tony	10181 East Aster Drive/Scottsdale AZ 85260
1973-095	Phillips, Micael Dwaine	3322 Ridgefield/Irving TX 75062
1970-107	Phillips, Norman Edwin 'Eddie'	Old Add: 2207 Edgehill Rd/Louisville KY 40205
1962-105	Phillips, Richard Eugene	D. March 29, 1998 Burnaby, Bristish Col.
1915-129	Phillips, Thomas Gerald	D. April 12, 1929 Philipsburg, Pa.
1956-068	Phillips, William Taylor 'Taylor'	594 Mein Mitchell Road/Hiram GA 30141
1966-072	Phoebus, Thomas Harold	2822 SW Lakemont Place/Palm City FL 34990
1994-086	Phoenix, Steven Robert	11212 Horizon Hills Drive/El Cajon CA 92020
1991-139	Piatt, Douglas William	2128 Concord Street/New Brighton PA 15066
1992-106	Piazza, Michael Joseph	PO Box 864, Oakwood Lane/Valley Forge PA 19481
1977-113	Picciolo, Robert Michael	11773 Invierno Drive/San Diego CA 92124
1945-080	Picciuto, Nicholas Thomas	D. January 10, 1997 Winchester, Va.
1992-107	Pichardo, Hipolito Antonio	Jicome, Esperanza Esperanza Dominican Rep.
1960-082	Piche, Ronald Jacques	100 Rue De Gaspe #128/Verdun Quebec H3E 1E5 Canada
1916-069	Picinich, Valentine John	D. December 5, 1942 Nobleboro, Me.
1914-167	Pick, Charles Thomas	D. June 26, 1954 Lynchburg, Va.
1923-103	Pick, Edgar Everett	D. May 13, 1967 West Los Angeles, Calif.
1931-069	Pickering, Urbane Henry 'Dick'	D. May 13, 1970 Modesto, Calif.
1910-121	Pickett, Charles Albert	D. May 20, 1969 Springfield, O.
1933-051	Pickrel, Clarence Douglas	D. November 4, 1983 Rocky Mount, Va.
1918-058	Pickup, Clarence William 'Ty'	D. August 2, 1974 Philadelphia, Pa.
1988-106	Pico, Jeffrey Mark	613 Texas Street/Antioch CA 94509
1947-068	Picone, Mario Peter	8876 Bay 16/Brooklyn NY 11214
1940-068	Piechota, Aloysius Edward	D. June 13, 1996 Chicago, Ill.
1913-140	Pieh, Edwin John 'Cy'	D. September 12, 1945 Jacksonville, Fla.
1992-108	Pierce, Edward John	Old Add: 21851 Newland #275 Huntington Beach CA 92626
1995-172	Pierce, Jeffrey Charles	% Ralph Herrmann 79 Hidden Brook Estates Hyde Park NY 12531
1973-096	Pierce, Lavern Jack 'Jack'	1002 Cortez Street/Laredo TX 78040
1924-086	Pierce, Raymond Lester	D. May 4, 1963 Denver, Colo.
1967-085	Pierce, Tony Michael	6119 Brittany Court/Columbus GA 31909
1945-081	Pierce, Walter William 'Billy'	1321 Baileys Crossing Drive/Lemont IL 60439
1917-062	Piercy, William Benton	D. August 28, 1951 Long Beach, Calif.
1945-082	Pieretti, Marino Paul	D. January 30, 1981 San Francisco, Calif.
1920-096	Pierotti, Albert Felix	D. February 12, 1964 Everett, Mass.
1950-078	Pierro, William Leonard	1751 74th Street/Brooklyn NY 11204
1950-079	Piersall, James Anthony	1105 Oakview Drive/Wheaton IL 60187
1918-059	Pierson, William Morris	D. February 20, 1959 Atlantic City, N. J.
1931-070	Piet, Anthony Francis	D. December 1, 1981 Hinsdale, Ill.
1914-168	Piez, Charles William 'Sandy'	D. December 29, 1930 Atlantic City, N.J.
1957-067	Pignatano, Joseph Benjamin	150 78th St/Brooklyn NY 11209
1946-083	Pike, James Willard	D. March 28, 1984 San Diego, Calif.
1956-069	Piktuzis, George Richard	D. November 28, 1993 Long Beach, Calif.
1956-070	Pilarcik, Alfred James	Box 185/St John IN 46373
1949-064	Pillette, Duane Xavier	404 Lily Ann Way/San Jose CA 95123
1917-063	Pillette, Herman Polycarp	D. April 30, 1960 Sacramento, Calif.
1915-130	Pillion, Cecil Randolph 'Squiz'	D. September 30, 1962 Pittsburgh, Pa.
1936-073	Pilney, Andrew James	D. September 15, 1996 New Orleans, La.
1968-080	Pina, Horacio Garcia	Old Add: Venustiana Carranza 207 Oahuila Mex
1918-060	Pinelli, Ralph Arthur 'Babe'	D. October 22, 1984 Daly City, Calif.
1964-085	Piniella, Louis Victor	Old Add: 57 Sheri Allendale NJ 07401
1958-073	Pinson, Vada Edward	D. October 21, 1995 Oakland, Calif.
1922-109	Pint0, William Lerton	D. May 13, 1983 Oxnard, Calif.
1932-063	Pipgras, Edward John	D. April 13, 1964 Currie, Minn.
1923-104	Pipgras, George William	D. October 19, 1986 Gainesville, Fla.
1913-141	Pipp, Walter Charles	D. January 11, 1965 Grand Rapids, Mich.

1936-074 ....Pippen, Henry Harold 'Cotton' ....D. February 15, 1981 Williams, Calif.
1993-146 ....Pirkl, Gregory Daniel ....11196 Saratoga Drive/Los Alamitos CA 90720
1978-100 ....Pirtle, Gerald Eugene ....4420 Prescott Court/Flower Mound TX 75028
1997-129 ....Pisciotta, Marc George ....5064 Hampton Lake Drive/Marietta GA 30068
1953-070 ....Pisoni, James Pete ....5500 Promise Land Drive/Frisco TX 75034
1938-074 ....Pitko, Alexander ....655 79th Way/Mesa AZ 85208
1917-064 ....Pitler, Jacob Albert ....D. February 3, 1968 Binghamton, N. Y.
1970-108 ....Pitlock, Lee Edward 'Skip' ....%C .Pitlock 215 Prospect Street Seguin TX 78155
1985-092 ....Pittaro, Christopher Francis ....42 Pintinalli Drive/Trenton NJ 8619
1921-082 ....Pittenger, Clarke Alonzo 'Pinky' ....D. November 4, 1977 Fort Lauderdale, Fla.
1981-097 ....Pittman, Joseph Wayne ....809 McKinnon Dr/Columbus GA 31907
1974-105 ....Pitts, Gaylen Richard ....214 Rocky Bluff Lane/Mountain Home AR 72653
1995-173 ....Pittsley, James Michael ....South Old Woods Road/Dubois PA 15801
1957-068 ....Pitula, Stanley ....D. August 16, 1965 Hackensack, N. J.
1957-069 ....Pizarro, Juan Cordova ....2262 Borinquen Avenue/Santurce PR 912
1979-085 ....Pladson, Gordon Cecil ....19087 87 A Avenue/Surrey British Columbia Canada V4N 3C5
1931-071 ....Planeta, Emil Joseph ....D. February 2, 1963 Rocky Hill, Conn.
1978-101 ....Plank, Edward Arthur ....North 6122 Okanagan Street/Spokane WA 99208
1993-147 ....Plantenberg, Erik John ....1420 Nw Gilman Blvd #2615/Issaquah WA 98027
1990-126 ....Plantier, Phillip Alan ....13140 Glen Circle Road/Poway CA 92064
1955-093 ....Plarski, Donald Joseph ....D. December 29, 1981 St. Louis, Mo.
1962-106 ....Plaskett, Elmo Alexander ....D. November 2, 1998 Frederiksted, V. I.
1942-079 ....Platt, Mizell George 'Whitey' ....D. July 27, 1970 West Palm Beach, Fla.
1913-142 ....Platte, Alfred Frederick Joseph ....D. August 29, 1976 Grand Rapids, Mich.
1961-084 ....Pleis, William ....3835 Little Country Road/Parrish FL 34219
1986-123 ....Plesac, Daniel Thomas ....245 East Whitehorne Lane/Valparaiso IN 46383
1956-071 ....Pless, Rance ....5528 Asheville Hwy/Greeneville TN 37743
1956-072 ....Plews, Herbert Eugene ....1460 Northwestern Rd/Longmont CO 80501
1918-061 ....Plitt, Norman William ....D. February 1, 1954 New York, N. Y.
1972-085 ....Plodinec, Timothy Alfred ....23251 Gilmore Street/West Hills CA 91307
1968-081 ....Plummer, William Francis ....Old Add: 4601 E. Piedmont Rd Phoenix AZ 85044
1986-124 ....Plunk, Eric Vaughn ....PO Box 70027/Riverside CA 92513
1991-140 ....Plympton, Jeffrey Hunter ....8 Robin Street/Plainville MA 2762
1942-080 ....Poat, Raymond Willis ....D. April 29, 1990 Oak Lawn, Ill.
1975-090 ....Pocoroba, Biff Benedict ....7002 Deshon Ridge Drive/Lithonia GA 30058
1949-065 ....Podbielan, Clarence Anthony 'Bud' ....D. October 26, 1982 Syracuse, N. Y.
1940-069 ....Podgajny, John Sigmund ....D. March 2, 1971 Chester, Pa.
1953-071 ....Podres, John Joseph ....1 Colonial Court/Glens Falls NY 12801
1975-091 ....Poepping, Michael Harold ....620 Park Avenue SE/Pierz MN 56364
1926-064 ....Poetz, Joseph Frank ....D. February 7, 1942 St. Louis, Mo.
1940-070 ....Pofahl, James Willard ....D. September 14, 1984 Owatonna, Minn.
1979-086 ....Poff, John William ....Old Add: 1464 Dexter Broomfield CO 80020
1937-088 ....Poffenberger, Cletus Elwood 'Boots' ....13 1/2 North Conococheague/Williamsport MD 21795
1950-080 ....Poholsky, Thomas George ....177 Horseshoe Drive/Kirkwood MO 63122
1936-075 ....Poindexter, Chester Jennings 'Jinks' ....D. March 3, 1983 Norman, Okla.
1963-093 ....Pointer, Aaron Elton ....612 Morgan Street/Moulton AL 35650
1943-113 ....Poland, Hugh Reid ....D. March 30, 1984 Guthrie, Ky.
1997-130 ....Polcovich, Kevin Michael ....Old Add: Auburn NY 13021
1973-097 ....Pole, Richard Henry ....21012 Whitlock Drive/Dearborn Heights MI 48127
1985-093 ....Polidor, Gustavo Adolfo ....D. April 28, 1995 Caracas, Venez.
1947-069 ....Polivka, Kenneth Lyle ....D. July 23, 1988 Aurora, Ill.
1941-089 ....Pollet, Howard Joseph ....D. August 8, 1974 Houston, Tex.
1996-153 ....Polley, Ezra Dale 'Dale' ....107 Redding Road/Georgetown KY 40324
1932-064 ....Polli, Louis Americo ....PO Box 45/Graniteville VT 5654
1937-089 ....Polly, Nicholas Joseph ....D. January 17, 1993 Chicago, Ill.
1977-114 ....Poloni, John Paul ....1714 Polo Club Drive/Tarpon Springs FL 34689
1987-119 ....Polonia, Luis Andrew ....Old Add: Tur. Sa Edcio Hach. Piso Lado Este Dominican Rep
1934-086 ....Pomorski, John Leon ....D. December 6, 1977 Brampton, Ontario
1985-094 ....Ponce, Carlos Antonio ....590 Kingsbury Court/Wellington FL 33414
1910-122 ....Pond, Ralph Benjamin ....D. September 8, 1947 Cleveland, O.
1917-065 ....Ponder, Charles Elmer ....D. April 20, 1974 Albuquerque, N. M.
1934-087 ....Pool, Harlin Welty ....D. February 15, 1963 Rodeo, Calif.
1925-086 ....Poole, James Ralph ....D. January 2, 1975 Hickory, N. C.
1990-127 ....Poole, James Richard ....320 Catalina Blvd/San Rafael CA 94901
1941-090 ....Poole, Raymond Herman ....1495 Beagle Club Road/Salisbury NC 28146
1952-081 ....Pope, David ....9020 Parmelee Avenue/Cleveland OH 44108
1964-086 ....Popovich, Paul Edward ....2604 Woodlawn/Northbrook IL 60062
1969-137 ....Popowski, Edward Joseph ....167 Washington Road/Sayreville NJ 8872
1973-098 ....Poquette, Thomas Arthur ....Rural Route 1 Box 1270/Springbrook WI 54875
1914-169 ....Porray, Edmund Joseph ....D. July 13, 1954 Lackawaxen, Pa.
1981-098 ....Porter, Charles William ....9321 Snyder Ln/Perry Hall MD 21128
1951-078 ....Porter, Daniel Edward ....7360 Cowles MT Blvd/San Diego CA 92119
1971-082 ....Porter, Darrell Ray ....1108 NE Moss Point Road/Lees Summit MO 64064
1914-170 ....Porter, Irving Marble ....D. February 20, 1971 Lynn, Mass.
1952-082 ....Porter, J. W. 'Jay' ....9677 Heather Circle West/Palm Bch Gardens FL 33410
1926-065 ....Porter, Ned Swindell ....D. June 30, 1968 Gainesville, Fla.
1929-084 ....Porter, Richard Twilley ....D. September 24, 1974 Philadelphia, Pa.
1981-099 ....Porter, Robert Lee ....2301 Buena Street/Napa CA 94558
1948-081 ....Porterfield, Erwin Coolidge 'Bob' ....D. April 28, 1980 Charlotte, N. C.

1948-082 ....Porto, Alfred ....40943 13th Street West/Palmdale CA 93550
1954-083 ....Portocarrero, Arnold Mario ....D. June 21, 1986 Kansas City, Kan.
1985-095 ....Portugal, Mark Steven ....Old Add: 11843 Orange #A Norwalk CA 90650
1995-174 ....Posada, Jorge Rafael ....Rodando 1505 El Paraiso/Rio Piedras PR 926
1960-083 ....Posada, Leopoldo Jesus ....8200 Grand Canal Drive/Miami FL 33144
1993-148 ....Pose, Scott Vernon ....4309 Dakota Drive/West Des Moines IA 50265
1938-075 ....Posedel, William John ....D. November 28, 1989 Livermore, Calif.
1932-065 ....Poser, John Falk 'Bob'...................................551 West School/Columbus WI 53925
1946-084 ....Possehl, Louis Thomas ....D. October 7, 1997 Sarasota, Fla.
1922-110 ....Post, Samuel Gilbert ....D. March 31, 1971 Portsmouth, Va.
1949-066 ....Post, Walter Charles ....D. January 6, 1982 Saint Henry, O.
1922-111 ....Pott, Nelson Adolph ....D. December 3, 1963 Mack,O.
1938-076 ....Potter, Maryland Dykes 'Dykes' ....3024 West Muddy Branch Road/Ashland KY 41101
1976-075 ....Potter, Michael Gary.....................................21582 Archer Cir/Huntington Beach CA 92646
1936-076 ....Potter, Nelson Thomas ....D. September 30, 1990 Mount Morris, Ill.
1923-105 ....Potter, Squire ....D. January 27, 1983 Ashland, Ky.
1914-171 ....Potts, John Frederick......................................D. September 5, 1962 Cleveland, O.
1996-154 ....Potts, Michael Larry ....Old Add: Lithonia GA 30058
1967-086 ....Poulsen, Ken Sterling ....Old Add: 684 East Weaver Simi Valley CA 93065
1987-120 ....Powell, Alonzo Sidney ....620 Garfield Street/San Francisco CA 94132
1930-063 ....Powell, Alvin Jacob 'Jake'............................D. November 4, 1948 Washington. D. C.
1985-096 ....Powell, Dennis Clay ....PO Box 133/Norman Park GA 31771
1963-094 ....Powell, Grover David ....D. May 21, 1985 Raleigh, N. C.
1978-102 ....Powell, Hosken ....1289 Tamara Street/Pensacola FL 32503
1995-175 ....Powell, James Willard 'Jay'..........................Martin/Collinsville MS 39325
1961-085 ....Powell, John Wesley 'Boog' ....333 West Camden Street/Baltimore MD 21201
1997-131 ....Powell, Lejon Dante 'Dante' ....6235 Riviera Circle/Long Beach CA 90815
1971-083 ....Powell, Paul Ray..1500 North Sun View Pkwy #70/Gilbert AZ 85234
1913-143 ....Powell, Raymond Reath..................................D. October 16, 1962 Chillicothe, O .
1913-144 ....Powell, Reginald Bertrand 'Jack' ....D. March 12, 1930 Memphis, Tenn.
1955-094 ....Powell, Robert Leroy ....4424 Crimson Leaf Drive/Las Vegas NV 89130
1993-149 ....Powell, Ross John ....3844 South Ivy Court/Chandler AZ 85248
1981-100 ....Power, Ted Henry ....9070 Ridgeway Close/Cincinnati OH 45236
1954-084 ....Power, Victor Pellot ....Condomineo Torre,Molinos 703/Guaynabo PR 657
1932-066 ....Powers, Ellis Foree 'Mike' ....D. December 2, 1983 Louisville, Ky.
1955-095 ....Powers, John Calvin ....221 14th Court Nw/Birmingham AL 35215
1927-072 ....Powers, John Lloyd 'Ike' ....D. December 22, 1968 Hancock, Md.
1938-077 ....Powers, Leslie Edwin ....D. November 13, 1978 Santa Monica, Calif.
1957-070 ....Powis, Carl Edgar ....Old Add: 8502 Easton Commons #104 Houston TX 77095
1995-176 ....Pozo, Arquimedez Ortiz ....Calle Versalles #25 Jardines Santo Domingo Dominican Rep.
1975-092 ....Prall, Wilfred Anthony 'Willie' ....88 Miller Road/Kinnelon NJ 7405
1949-067 ....Pramesa, John Steven ....D. September 9, 1996 Simi Valley, Calif.
1912-158 ....Pratt, Derrill Burnham 'Del' ....D. September 30, 1977 Texas City, Tex.
1921-083 ....Pratt, Francis Bruce ....D. April 8, 1974 Centreville, Ala.
1914-172 ....Pratt, Lester John 'Larry'.............................D. January 8, 1969 Peoria, Ill.
1992-109 ....Pratt, Todd Alan ....Old Add: 435 Montclair Street Chula Vista CA 92011
1963-095 ....Pregenzer, John Arthur ....6314 104th St East/Puyallup WA 98373
1940-071 ....Preibisch, Melvin Adolphus ....D. April 12, 1980 Sealy, Texas
1948-083 ....Prendergast, James Bartholomoew ....D. August 23, 1994 Amherst, N. Y.
1914-173 ....Prendergast, Michael Thomas ....D. November 18, 1967 Omaha, Neb.
1961-086 ....Prescott, George Bertrand 'Bobby' ....Old Add: Estafeta Parque Lefevre/Panama City Panama
1951-079 ....Presko, Joseph Edward ....1612 NE 77th Terrace/Kansas City MO 64118
1984-090 ....Presley, James Arthur ....2449 Bonanza Drive/Cantonment FL 32533
1938-078 ....Pressnell, Forest Charles 'Tot' ....329 East Lima Street/Findlay OH 45840
1967-087 ....Price, Jimmie William ....57152 Willow Way/Washington MI 48094
1946-085 ....Price, John Thomas Reid 'Jackie' ....D. October 2, 1967 San Francisco, Calif.
1928-075 ....Price, Joseph Preston ....D. January 15, 1961 Washington. D. C.
1980-106 ....Price, Joseph Walter ....27820 Aleutia Way/Yorba Linda CA 92687
1939-090 ....Prichard, Robert Alexander ....D. September 25, 1991 Abilene, Texas
1941-091 ....Priddy, Gerald Edward ....D. March 3, 1980 North Hollywood, Calif.
1962-107 ....Priddy, Robert Simpson ....Old Add: 519 N. Cascade Ter Sunnyvale CA 94087
1993-150 ....Pride, Curtis John ....1709 Woodwell Road/Silver Spring MD 20906
1911-136 ....Priest, John Gooding ....D. November 4, 1979 Washington, D. C.
1995-177 ....Prieto, Ariel ....1078 Nw 132nd Court/Miami FL 33182
1933-052 ....Prim, Raymond Lee ....D. April 29, 1995 Monte Rio, Calif.
1962-108 ....Prince, Donald Mark ....5006 Randall Drive/Wilmington NC 28403
1987-121 ....Prince, Thomas Albert ....6816 10th Avenue Nw/Bradenton FL 34209
1957-071 ....Pritchard, Harold William 'Buddy' ....507 East Sunny Hill Road/Fullerton CA 92635
1996-155 ....Pritchett, Christopher Davis ....Old Add: Modesto CA 95356
1959-066 ....Proctor, James Arthur ....Old Add: 609 Count Fleet CT Naperville IL 60540
1923-106 ....Proctor, Noah Richard 'Red' ....D. December 17, 1954 Richmond, Va.
1976-076 ....Proly, Michael James ....2585 Frisco Dr/Clearwater FL 33519
1923-107 ....Propst, William Jacob 'Jake'.........................D. February 24, 1967 Columbus, Miss.
1920-097 ....Prothro, James Thompson 'Doc' ....D. October 14, 1971 Memphis, Tenn.
1912-160 ....Prough, Herschel Clinton 'Bill' ....D. November 29, 1936 Richmond, Ind.
1929-085 ....Prudhomme, John Olgus...................................D. October 4, 1992 Shreveport, La.
1920-098 ....Pruess, Earl Henry 'Gibby' ....D. August 28, 1979 Branson, Mo.
1922-112 ....Pruett, Hubert Shelby ....D. January 28, 1982 Ladue, Mo.
1944-107 ....Pruett, James Calvin ....430 Kimberley Drive #41/Waukesha WI 53188

1975-093 ....Pruitt, Ronald Ralph ....910 Guilford Blvd/Medina OH 44256
1976-077 ....Pryor, Gregory Russell ....9726 West 115th Terrace/Overland Park KS 66210
1930-064 ....Puccinelli, George Lawrence ....D. April 16, 1956 San Francisco, Calif.
1984-091 ....Puckett, Kirby ....6625 West Trail/Minneapolis MN 55439
1911-137 ....Puckett, Troy Levi ....D. April 13, 1971 Winchester, Ind.
1970-109 ....Puente, Miguel Antonio ....Cobre 106,Col Morales San Luis Potosi Slp Mexico
1992-110 ....Pugh, Timothy Dean ....1806 SE Madison/Bartlesville OK 74006
1977-115 ....Puhl, Terrance Stephen ....Old Add: Box 8/Melville Saskatchewan
1974-106 ....Puig, Richard Gerald ....189 Harbourside Circle/Jupiter FL 33477
1977-116 ....Pujols, Luis Bienvenido ....3867 Jonathans Way/Lake Worth FL 33462
1981-101 ....Puleo, Charles Michael ....PO Box 1032/Louisville TN 37777
1983-114 ....Pulido, Alfonso ....H.Ricardo Mercado,Casillas 26-27 Tierra Blanca Veracruz Mexico
1994-087 ....Pulido, Juan Carlos 'Carlos' ....Ingedigi CA Ave Edif, Piso 546 Elrosal Caracas Venezuela
1991-141 ....Pulliam, Harvey Jerome ....1532 Sunnydale Avenue/San Francisco CA 94134
1995-178 ....Pulsipher, William Thomas ....6303 Clear Springs Court/Clifton VA 22024
1925-087 ....Pumpelly, Spencer Armstrong ....D. December 5, 1973 Sayre, Pa.
1964-087 ....Purdin, John Nolan ....PO Box 35/Eldred NY 12732
1926-066 ....Purdy, Everett Virgil 'Pid' ....D. January 16, 1951 Beatrice, Neb.
1954-085 ....Purkey, Robert Thomas ....5767 King School Rd/Bethel Park PA 15102
1976-078 ....Putman, Eddy William ....257 North Forestdale Avenue/Covina CA 91723
1977-117 ....Putnam, Patrick Edward ....2311 Carrell Road/Fort Myers FL 33901
1955-096 ....Pyburn, James Edward ....Longview Drive/Jasper AL 35501
1994-088 ....Pye, Robert Edward 'Eddie' ....307 Polk Street/Columbia TN 38401
1954-086 ....Pyecha, John Nicholas ....107 Nottingham Drive/Chapel Hill NC 27514
1939-091 ....Pyle, Ewald ....538 Halliday Avenue/Duquoin IL 62832
1928-076 ....Pyle, Harlan Albert ....D. January 13, 1993 Beatrice, Neb.
1932-067 ....Pytlak, Frank Anthony ....D. May 8, 1977 Buffalo, N. Y.
1986-125 ....Pyznarski, Timothy Matthew ....10716 South Austin/Chicago Ridge IL 60415
1969-138 ....Qualls, James Robert ....410 North County Road 950/Sutter IL 62373
1953-072 ....Qualters, Thomas Francis ....236 Lake Road/Somerset PA 15501
1992-111 ....Quantrill, Paul John ....Rural Route 4/Cobourg Ontario K9A 4J7 Canada
1964-088 ....Queen, Melvin Douglas ....430 Quintana #116/Morro Bay CA 93442
1942-081 ....Queen, Melvin Joseph ....D. April 4, 1982 Fort Smith, Ark.
1954-087 ....Queen, William Eddleman ....1616 East Perry Street/Gastonia NC 28052
1931-072 ....Quellich, George William ....D. August 31, 1958 Johnsville, Calif.
1939-092 ....Quick, James Harold ....D. March 9, 1974 Swansea, Ill.
1965-088 ....Quilici, Frank Ralph ....3101 Country Wood Drive/Burnsville MN 55337
1913-145 ....Quinlan, Thomas Aloysius 'Finners' ....D. February 17, 1966 Scranton, Pa.
1990-128 ....Quinlan, Thomas Raymond ....1061 South Sterling Avenue/Maplewood MN 55119
1949-068 ....Quinn, Frank William ....D. January 11, 1993 Boynton Beach, Fla.
1911-138 ....Quinn, John Edward Pick ....D. April 9, 1956 Marlboro, Mass.
1941-092 ....Quinn, Wellington Hunt 'Wimpy' ....D. September 1, 1954 Los Angeles, Calif.
1983-115 ....Quinones, Luis Raul ....Urb Sta Teresita Calle 1 Ae11/Ponce PR 731
1986-126 ....Quinones, Rey Francisco ....Cle Ronda 216 Villa Anadalucia/Rio Piedras PR 926
1988-107 ....Quintana, Carlos Narcis ....558 River Street "Mamporal,Miranda Venezuela"
1974-107 ....Quintana, Luis Joaquin ....Cascrio Catoni Ed. 11 #70/Vega Baja PR 763
1996-156 ....Quirico, Rafael Octavio Dottin ....Old Add: Santo Domingo Dom. Rep.
1962-109 ....Quirk, Arthur Leonard ....90 South Mill Drive/South Glastonbury CT 6073
1975-094 ....Quirk, James Patrick ....14114 Grandview Street/Overland Park KS 66221
1979-087 ....Quisenberry, Daniel Raymond ....D. September 30, 1998 Leawood, Kan.
1995-179 ....Raabe, Brian Charles ....38760 Kost Trail/North Branch MN 55056
1982-099 ....Rabb, John Andrew ....Old Add: 1321 West 106th St Los Angeles CA 90044
1922-113 ....Rabbitt, Joseph Patrick ....D. December 5, 1969 Norwalk, Conn.
1957-072 ....Rabe, Charles Henry ....6059 E. Sierra Blanca Street/Mesa AZ 85215
1940-072 ....Rachunok, Stephen Stepanovich ....2660 West Ball Road #3/Anaheim CA 92804
1947-070 ....Rackley, Marvin Eugene ....512 South Bibb Street/Westminster SC 29693
1992-112 ....Raczka, Michael ....72 Foley Drive/Southington CT 6489
1962-110 ....Radatz, Richard Raymond ....% Atlantic Container PO Box 348 Braintree MA 2184
1934-088 ....Radcliff, Raymond Allen 'Rip' ....D. May 23, 1962 Enid, Okla.
1911-139 ....Radebaugh, Roy ....D. January 17, 1945 Cedar Rapids, Ia.
1971-084 ....Rader, David Martin ....2114 Oakwood Dr/Bakersfield CA 93304
1913-146 ....Rader, Donald Russell ....D. June 26, 1983 Walla Walla, Wash.
1967-088 ....Rader, Douglas Lee ....112-7 Cedar Point/Stuart FL 33494
1921-084 ....Rader, Drew Leon ....D. June 5, 1975 Catskill, N. Y.
1990-129 ....Radinsky, Scott David ....4059 Yuma Street/Simi Valley CA 93063
1995-180 ....Radke, Brad William ....%Richard Radke 3107 Emerson Tampa FL 33611
1936-077 ....Radtke, Jack William ....1828 Bridgeview Blvd #116/Twin Falls ID 83301
1954-088 ....Raether, Harold Herman ....415 Lake Street North/Prescott WI 54021
1939-093 ....Raffensberger, Kenneth David ....418 Clover Drive, Rr 7/York PA 17402
1969-139 ....Raffo, Albert Martin ....Box 866/Jasper TN 37347
1997-132 ....Raggio, Brady John ....Old Add: 311 West Linda Mesa Ave Danville CA 94526
1932-068 ....Ragland, Frank Roland ....D. July 28, 1959 Paris, Miss.
1971-085 ....Ragland, Thomas ....20201 Greenlawn St/Detroit MI 48224
1975-095 ....Raich, Eric James ....3963 Edward Drive/Brunswick OH 44212
1957-073 ....Raines, Lawrence Glenn Hope ....D. January 28, 1978 Lansing, Mich.
1979-088 ....Raines, Timothy ....Old Add: 462 Deaton Court Heathrow FL 32746
1979-089 ....Rainey, Charles David ....1445 Woodfield Drive/Jackson MS 39211
1978-103 ....Rajsich, David Christopher ....1605 North Main Street/Flagstaff AZ 86004
1982-100 ....Rajsich, Gary Louis ....17421 Upper Cherry Lane/Lake Oswego OR 97034

1960-084 ....Rakow, Edward Charles..PO Box 14802/North Palm Beach FL 33408
1910-123 ....Ralston, Samuel Beryl 'Doc' ....D. August 29, 1950 Lancaster, Pa.
1946-086 ....Ramazotti, Robert Louis ....1111 South 26th Street/Altoona PA 16602
1939-094 ....Rambert, Elmer Donald 'Pep' ....D. November 16, 1974 West Palm Beach, Fla.
1926-067 ....Rambo, Warren Dawson 'Pete' ....D. June 19, 1991 Camden, N. J.
1983-116 ....Ramirez, Daniel Allan 'Allan' ....311 Teakwood Drive/Victoria TX 77901
1993-151 ....Ramirez, Manuel Aristides.................................Old Add: 320a Wil O Wisp Kinston NC 28501
1980-107 ....Ramirez, Mario ....Hc03 Box 14107/Yauco PR 698
1970-110 ....Ramirez, Milton ....7 Tulio Larrinaga St/Mayaguez PR 708
1974-108 ....Ramirez, Orlando ....Torices Paso Abadio #1325 Cartagena/Colombia
1980-108 ....Ramirez, Rafael Emilio.......................................Old Add: M.Perez #8 San Pedro De Macoris Dom. Rep
1978-104 ....Ramos, Domingo Antonio...................................Carr Duarte Km 8 1/2,Licey AL Medio Santiago Dominican Rep.
1997-133 ....Ramos, Edgar Jose Malave ....Old Add: Cuinana Venezuela
1944-108 ....Ramos, Jesus Manuel Garcia 'Chuco' ....D. September 2, 1977 Caracas, Venezuela
1991-142 ....Ramos, John Joseph ....3225 South Macdill Avenue #208/Tampa FL 33629
1997-134 ....Ramos, Kenneth Cecil ....2129 East 5th Street/Pueblo CO 81001
1955-097 ....Ramos, Pedro ....Old Add: 9367 Fontainebleau #G119 Miami FL 33172
1978-105 ....Ramos, Roberto 'Bobby' ....7901 30th Avenue North/Saint Petersburg FL 33710
1947-071 ....Ramsdell, James Willard 'Willie'........................D. October 8, 1969 Wichita, Kan.
1992-113 ....Ramsey, Fernando David ....4061 Nw Barlow Court/Camas WA 98607
1987-122 ....Ramsey, Michael James ....PO Box 262/Harlem GA 30814
1978-106 ....Ramsey, Michael Jeffrey ....11564 92nd Way North/Largo FL 34643
1945-083 ....Ramsey, William Thrace ....1846 Cour De Conti Street/Memphis TN 38138
1953-073 ....Rand, Richard Hilton ....D. January 22, 1996 Moreno Valley, Calif.
1995-181 ....Randa, Joseph Gregory ....%Greg Randa 1150 Archery Drive Waukesha WI 53188
1988-108 ....Randall, James Odell Sap ....711 Crane Avenue/Whistler AL 36612
1976-079 ....Randall, Robert Lee ....Univ. Of Kansas 220 Allen Fieldhouse Lawrence KS 66045
1971-086 ....Randle, Leonard Shenoff ....3332 Grand Avenue #116/Chino Hills CA 91710
1975-096 ....Randolph, Willie Larry ....648 Juniper Place/Franklin Lakes NJ 7417
1962-111 ....Ranew, Merritt Thomas ....PO Box 5004/Sun City Center FL 33571
1949-069 ....Raney, Frank Robert Donald 'Ribs' ....11242 Charles Drive/Warren MI 48093
1981-102 ....Ransom, Jeffery Dean ....2131 Curtis St/Berkeley CA 94702
1949-070 ....Rapp, Earl Wellington ....D. February 13, 1992 Swedesboro, N. J.
1921-085 ....Rapp, Joseph Aloysius 'Goldie' ....D. July 1, 1966 Lamesa, Calif.
1992-114 ....Rapp, Patrick Leland ....305 West Parish Road/Sulphur LA 70663
1977-118 ....Rapp, Vernon Fred ....14800 North Lowell Blvd/Broomfield CO 80020
1946-087 ....Raschi, Victor John Angelo...............................D. October 14, 1988 Groveland, N. J.
1983-117 ....Rasmussen, Dennis Lee ....3522 Swans Landing/Land O'Lakes FL 34639
1975-097 ....Rasmussen, Eric Ralph ....237 SW 45th Street/Cape Coral FL 33914
1915-131 ....Rasmussen, Henry Florian ....D. January 1, 1949 Chicago, Ill.
1968-082 ....Rath, Fred Helsher ....7308 Pelican Island Drive/Tampa FL 33614
1965-089 ....Ratliff, Kelly Eugene 'Gene'.............................3403 Millerfield Rd/Macon GA 31201
1963-096 ....Ratliff, Paul Hawthorne ....Old Add: 549 Stanford Avenue Palo Alto CA 94306
1980-109 ....Ratzer, Steven Wayne ....1218 Deleon Court/Palm Harbor FL 34683
1972-086 ....Rau, Douglas James ....1615 Treasure Oaks Drive/Katy TX 77450
1972-087 ....Rauch, Robert John ....Old Add: 1149 Olive Rd/Virginia Beach VA 23462
1966-073 ....Raudman, Robert Joyce 'Shorty' ....Old Add:17529 Chatsworth/Granada Hills CA 91344
1977-119 ....Rautzhan, Clarence George 'Lance' ....231 Parkway/Schuylkill Haven PA 17972
1978-107 ....Rawley, Shane William ....4587 Cherry Bark Court/Sarasota FL 34241
1914-174 ....Rawlings, John William ....D. October 16, 1972 Inglewood, Calif.
1915-132 ....Ray, Carl Grady ....D. April 3, 1970 Walnut Cove, N.C.
1965-090 ....Ray, James Francis ....Old Add: 7530 Prompton/Houston TX 77025
1981-103 ....Ray, John Cornelius...Rural Route 1 Box 64/Chouteau OK 74337
1982-101 ....Ray, Larry Doyle ....Old Add: Rural Route 3 Vevay IN 47043
1910-124 ....Ray, Robert Henry 'Doc' ....D. March 11, 1963 Electra, Tex.
1958-074 ....Raydon, Curtis Lowell ....1210 East Grove Street/Bloomington IL 61701
1980-110 ....Rayford, Floyd Kinnard ....14624 Woonsocket Drive/Silver Spring MD 20905
1959-067 ....Raymond, Joseph Claude ....3 De La Citiere, B.P. 911/Saint Luc Quebec J0J 2A0 Canada
1919-066 ....Raymond, Louis Anthony ....D. May 2, 1979 Rochester, N. Y.
1973-099 ....Raziano, Barry John..1315 4th St/Kenner LA 70062
1983-118 ....Ready, Randy Max ....15835 El Camino Entrada/Poway CA 92064
1969-140 ....Reams, Leroy ....6140 East 17th Street/Oakland CA 94621
1979-090 ....Reardon, Jeffrey James ....5 Marlwood Ln/Palm Beach Gardens FL 33410
1938-079 ....Rebel, Arthur Anthony ....1726 West Fore Drive/Tampa FL 33610
1968-083 ....Reberger, Frank Beall ....17304 Palatine North/Seattle WA 98133
1992-115 ....Reboulet, Jeffrey Alan ....2905 Hillview Avenue/Kettering OH 45419
1912-161 ....Redding, Philip Hayden ....D. March 30, 1929 Greenwood, Miss.
1932-069 ....Reder, John Anthony ....D. April 12, 1990 Fall River, Mass.
1928-077 ....Redfern, George Howard 'Buck' ....D. September 8, 1964 Asheville, N. C.
1976-080 ....Redfern, Peter Irvine ....12516 Haddon Avenue/Sylmar CA 91342
1988-109 ....Redfield, Joseph Randall...................................508 Mountain Lake Drive/Waco TX 76712
1974-109 ....Redmon, Glenn Vincent ....8509 Dee Circle/Riverview FL 33569
1965-091 ....Redmond, Howard Wayne 'Wayne' ....Old Add: 16557 Heyden/Detroit MI 48235
1935-092 ....Redmond, Jackson McKittrick ....D. July 28, 1968 Garland, Tex.
1982-102 ....Redus, Gary Eugene ....2202 Mallard Lane SE/Decatur AL 35601
1978-108 ....Reece, Robert Scott ....1654 Bonita/Folsom CA 95630
1990-130 ....Reed, Darren Douglas ....8101 Santa Ana Road/Ventura CA 93001
1958-075 ....Reed, Howard Dean ....D. December 7, 1984 Corpus Christi, Tex.
1984-092 ....Reed, Jeff Scott ....Rr 7 Box 3570/Elizabethton TN 37643

1981-104	Reed, Jerry Maxwell	505 Enka Lake Road/Candler NC 28715
1987-123	Reed, Jody Eric	18035 Wayne Road/Odessa FL 33556
1961-087	Reed, John Burwell 'Jack'	PO Box 97/Silver Ciy MS 39204
1911-140	Reed, Milton D.	D. July 27, 1938 Atlanta, Ga.
1915-133	Reed, Ralph Edwin 'Ted'	D. February 16, 1959 Beaver, Pa.
1988-110	Reed, Richard Allen	2205 Jefferson Avenue/Huntington WV 25704
1969-141	Reed, Robert Edward	Old Add: 108 Essex Drive Longwood FL 32750
1966-074	Reed, Ronald Lee	2613 Cliffview Dr/Lilburn GA 30247
1992-116	Reed, Steven Vincent	Old Add: Lewiston Id
1952-083	Reed, William Joseph	11807 Marrs/Houston TX 77065
1949-071	Reeder, William Edgar	Old Add: 309 Helm Lane #502 Sulphur Springs TX 75482
1918-062	Rees, Stanley Milton	D. August 29, 1937 Lexington, Ky.
1927-073	Reese, Andrew Jackson	D. January 10, 1966 Tupelo, Miss.
1997-135	Reese, Calvin 'Pokey'	Old Add: 2050 S. Beltline Blvd Columbia SC 29201
1940-073	Reese, Harold Henry 'Peewee'	1400 Willow Avenue/Louisville KY 40204
1930-065	Reese, James Hymie	D. July 13, 1994 Santa Ana, Calif.
1964-089	Reese, Richard Benjamin	1709 Shawnee Terrace/Northbrook IL 60062
1926-068	Reeves, Robert Edwin	D. June 4, 1993 Chattanooga, Tenn.
1954-089	Regalado, Rudolph Valentino	PO Box 91484/San Diego CA 92169
1917-066	Regan, Michael John	D. May 23, 1961 Albany, N. Y.
1960-085	Regan, Philip Raymond	1375 108th St/Byron Center MI 49315
1926-069	Regan, William Wright	D. June 11, 1968 Pittsburgh, Pa.
1924-087	Rego, Antone	D. January 6, 1978 Tulsa, Okla.
1912-162	Rehg, Walter Phillip	D. August 5, 1946 Burbank, Calif.
1933-053	Reiber, Frank Bernard	PO Box 6284/Sarasota FL 33578
1949-072	Reich, Herman Charles	PO Box 1292/Bonsall CA 92003
1964-090	Reichardt, Frederic Carl	4509 NW 23rd Avenue #14/Gainesville FL 32606
1922-114	Reichle, Richard Wendell	D. June 13, 1967 St. Louis, Mo.
1946-088	Reid, Earl Percy	D. May 11, 1984 Cullman, Ala.
1987-124	Reid, Jessie Thomas	2641 Carey Station Road/Greensboro GA 30642
1987-124	Reid, Jessie Thomas	3614 Cedar Avenue/Lynwood CA 90262
1969-142	Reid, Scott Donald	3611 East Nambe Court/Phoenix AZ 85044
1917-067	Reilly, Archer Edwin	D. November 29, 1963 Columbus, O.
1919-067	Reilly, Harold John	D. December 24, 1957 Chicago, Ill.
1988-111	Reimer, Kevin Michael	1206 West Salmon Arm Rd/Enderby British Col. V0E 1V0 Canada
1974-110	Reinbach, Michael Wayne	Old Add: 9459 Slope St %Cramer/Santee CA 92071
1919-068	Reinhart, Arthur Conrad	D. November 11, 1946 Houston, Tex.
1928-078	Reinholz, Arthur August	D. December 29, 1980 Newport Richey, Fla.
1915-134	Reinicker, Walter Joseph	D. April 18, 1957 Pittsburgh, Pa.
1911-141	Reis, Harrie Crane 'Jack'	D. July 20, 1939 Cincinnati, O.
1931-073	Reis, Robert Joseph Thomas	D. May 1, 1973 St. Paul, Minn.
1938-080	Reis, Thomas Edward	41 Holly Lane/Fort Thomas KY 41075
1940-074	Reiser, Harold Patrick 'Pete'	D. October 25, 1981 Palm Springs, Calif.
1911-142	Reisigl, Jacob 'Buggs'	D. February 24, 1957 Amsterdam, N.Y.
1932-070	Reiss, Albert Allen	D. May 13, 1989 Red Bank, N.J.
1972-088	Reitz, Kenneth John	Old Add: 7541 Warner Saint Louis MO 63117
1995-182	Rekar, Bryan Robert	%Robt Rekar 14325 Clearview Drive Orland Park IL 60462
1996-157	Relaford, Desmond Lamont 'Desi'	929 Jorick Court West/Jacksonville FL 32225
1991-143	Remlinger, Michael John	8 Davenport Road/Plymouth MA 2360
1979-091	Remmerswaal, Wilhelmus Abraham	Doktor Van Praag St 16 Wassenaar/Holland
1912-163	Remneas, Alexander Norman	D. August 27, 1975 Phoenix, Ariz.
1975-098	Remy, Gerald Peter	33 Viles Street/Weston MA 2193
1913-147	Renfer, Erwin Arthur	D. October 26, 1957 Sycamore, Ill.
1991-144	Renfroe, Cohen Williams 'Laddie'	236 Hickory Lane/Batesville MS 38606
1959-068	Renfroe, Marshall Dalton	D. December 10, 1970 Pensacola, Fla.
1968-084	Renick, Warren Richard 'Rick'	7320 Hawkins Road/Sarasota FL 34241
1961-088	Reniff, Harold Eugene	648 East 6th Street/Ontario CA 91764
1938-081	Reninger, James David	D. August 23, 1993 North Fort Myers, Fla.
1969-143	Renko, Steven	3408 West 129th/Leawood KS 66209
1953-074	Renna, William Benditto	1476 Lesher CT San Jose CA 95125
1930-066	Rensa, George Anthony 'Tony'	D. January 4, 1987 Wilkes-Barre, Pa.
1996-158	Renteria, Edgar Enrique	12926 Nw 20th Street/Pembroke Pines FL 33028
1986-127	Renteria, Richard Avina	26489 Ynez Road C161/Temecula CA 92591
1939-095	Repass, Robert Willis	169 Brimfield Road/Wethersfield CT 6109
1978-109	Replogle, Andrew David	16690 Bobcat Drive/Fort Myers FL 33908
1964-091	Repoz, Roger Allen	930 Whitewater Drive/Fullerton CA 92833
1953-075	Repulski, Eldon John 'Rip'	D. February 10, 1993 Waite Park, Minn.
1943-114	Rescigno, Xavier Frederick	163e Falmouth Court/Ridge NY 11961
1949-073	Restelli, Dino Paul	1860 San Carlos Avenue/San Carlos CA 94070
1968-085	Rettenmund, Mervin Weldon	9697 Hazard Center Drive/San Diego CA 92108
1922-115	Rettig, Adolph John 'Otto'	D. June 16, 1977 Stuart, Fla.
1961-089	Retzer, Kenneth Leon	746 Harvard Drive/Edwardsville IL 62025
1975-099	Reuschel, Paul Richard	Golden IL 62339
1972-089	Reuschel, Ricky Eugene 'Rick'	Old Add: 1403 Picadilly Circle Mount Prospect Il
1969-144	Reuss, Jerry	9428 Churchill Downs Drive/Las Vegas NV 89117
1992-117	Revenig, Todd Michael	4401 Circle Pines Road North/Baxter MN 56425
1978-110	Revering, David Alvin	Old Add: 3404 Meder Road Shingle Springs CA 95632
1994-089	Reyes, Carlos Alberto	7205 North Cortez Avenue/Tampa FL 33614
1997-136	Reyes, Dennis Velarde	Old Add: Higuera De Zaragova Mex.

1983-119 ....Reyes, Gilberto Rolando ....Calle 2da. #7 Los Mameyes Santo Domingo Dominican Rep.
1943-115 ....Reyes, Napoleon Aguilera ....D. September 15, 1995 Miami, Fla.
1995-183 ....Reyes, Rafael Alberto 'Al' ....S. Perdida Cle 1a Victoria 115 Santo Domingo Dominican Rep.
1942-082 ....Reynolds, Allie Pierce ....D. December 26, 1994 Oklahoma City, Okla.
1968-086 ....Reynolds, Archie Edward ....1828 Pinecrest Drive/Tyler TX 75701
1927-074 ....Reynolds, Carl Nettles ....D. May 29, 1978 Houston, Tex.
1945-084 ....Reynolds, Daniel Vance ....PO Box 55/Scotts/Nc 28699
1978-111 ....Reynolds, Donald Edward ....6035 NE 35th Place/Portland OR 97211
1975-100 ....Reynolds, Gordon Craig 'Craig' ....19 Inverness Park Way/Houston TX 77055
1983-120 ....Reynolds, Harold Craig ....2890 Nw Angelica Drive/Corvallis OR 97330
1970-111 ....Reynolds, Kenneth Lee ....182 Greenwood/Marlborough MA 1752
1992-118 ....Reynolds, Richard Shane Shane ....7422 Timberlake Drive/Sugarland TX 77479
1969-145 ....Reynolds, Robert Allen ....35416 25th Avenue SW #7-301/Federal Way WA 98023
1983-121 ....Reynolds, Robert James ....7076 El Soreno Cir/Sacramento CA 95831
1982-103 ....Reynolds, Ronn Dwayne ....1 Casa Verde Street/Austin TX 78734
1914-175 ....Reynolds, Ross Ernest ....D. June 23, 1970 Ada, Okla.
1963-097 ....Reynolds, Thomas ....1577 San Altos/Lemon Grove CA 92045
1913-148 ....Reynolds, William Dee ....D. June 5, 1924 Carnegie, Okla.
1991-145 ....Reynoso, Armando Martin (Gutierrez) ....Old Add: San Luis Potosi Mexico
1947-072 ....Rhawn, Robert John ....D. June 9, 1984 Danville, Pa.
1914-176 ....Rheam, Kenneth Johnston 'Cy' ....D. October 23, 1947 Pittsburgh, Pa.
1924-088 ....Rhem, Charles Flint ....D. July 30, 1969 Columbia, S. C.
1929-086 ....Rhiel, William Joseph ....D. August 16, 1946 Youngstown, O.
1974-111 ....Rhoden, Richard Alan 'Rick' ....PO Box 546/Crescent City FL 33118
1991-146 ....Rhodes, Arthur Lee ....Old Add: 4013 Crockers Lane #1311 Sarasota FL 34238
1952-084 ....Rhodes, James Lamar 'Dusty' ....249 Datura Street/Henderson NV 89014
1929-087 ....Rhodes, John Gordon ....D. March 22, 1960 Long Beach, Calif.
1990-131 ....Rhodes, Karl Derrick Dusty ....234 Forest Avenue/Cincinnati OH 45229
1982-104 ....Rhomberg, Kevin Jay ....5875 Sequoia Court/Mentor OH 44060
1926-070 ....Rhyne, Harold J. ....D. January 7, 1971 Orangevale, Calif.
1964-092 ....Ribant, Dennis Joseph ....18201 Von Karman Ave #900/Irvine CA 92715
1976-081 ....Riccelli, Frank Joseph ....6109 Ridgecrest Drive/North Syracuse NY 13212
1995-184 ....Ricci, Charles Mark ....%Chris Ricci 262 Old Line Avenue Laurel MD 20724
1945-085 ....Rice, Delbert ....D. January 26, 1983 Buena Park, Calif.
1915-135 ....Rice, Edgar Charles 'Sam' ....D. October 13, 1974 Rossmor, Md.
1948-084 ....Rice, Harold Houston 'Hal' ....D. December 22, 1997 Saint Petersburg, Fla.
1923-108 ....Rice, Harry Francis 'Sam' ....D. January 1, 1971 Portland, Ore.
1974-112 ....Rice, James Edward ....96 Castlemere Place/North Andover MA 1845
1944-109 ....Rice, Leonard Oliver ....D. June 13, 1992 Sonora, Calif.
1991-147 ....Rice, Patrick Edward ....1235 Berglind Road/Colorado Springs CO 80918
1926-071 ....Rice, Robert Turnbull ....D. February 20, 1986 Elizabethton, Pa.
1939-096 ....Rich, Woodrow Earl ....D. April 18, 1983 Morganton, N.C.
1971-087 ....Richard, James Rodney 'J. R.' ....Rural Route 2 Box 296/Ruston LA 71270
1971-088 ....Richard, Lee Edward 'Bee Bee' ....1621 East 14th St/Port Arthur TX 77640
1960-086 ....Richards, Duane Lee ....Box 54/Palestine OH 45352
1977-120 ....Richards, Eugene ....4360 Panorama Drive/Lamesa CA 92041
1951-080 ....Richards, Fred Charles ....1760 Dodge Northwest/Warren OH 44485
1932-071 ....Richards, Paul Rapier ....D. May 5, 1986 Waxahachie, Texas
1989-101 ....Richards, Russell Earl 'Rusty' ....Old Add: 10014 Villa Lea Houston TX 77071
1929-088 ....Richardson, Clifford Nolen ....D. September 25, 1951 Athens, Ga.
1964-093 ....Richardson, Gordon Clark ....23 St. Paul Church Road/Colquitt GA 31737
1989-102 ....Richardson, Jeffrey Scott ....1113 South Greenwich/Grand Island NE 68801
1990-132 ....Richardson, Jeffrey Scott ....% Doug Richardson 4525 North Hillcrest Wichita KS 67220
1915-136 ....Richardson, John William ....D. January 18, 1970 Marion, Ill.
1942-083 ....Richardson, Kenneth Franklin ....D. December 7, 1987 Woodland Hills, Calif.
1955-098 ....Richardson, Robert Clinton ....47 Adams/Sumter SC 29150
1917-068 ....Richardson, Thomas Mitchell ....D. November 15, 1939 Onawa, Ia.
1980-111 ....Richardt, Michael Anthony ....5054 West Donner Avenue/Fresno CA 93722
1921-086 ....Richbourg, Lance Clayton ....D. September 10, 1975 Crestview, Fla.
1962-112 ....Richert, Peter Gerard ....80 La Cerra Drive/Rancho Mirage CA 92270
1989-103 ....Richie, Robert Eugene ....Old Add: 2175 Edgemar Circle Reno NV 89512
1933-054 ....Richmond, Beryl Justice ....D. April 24, 1980 Cameron, W. Va.
1941-093 ....Richmond, Donald Lester ....D. May 24, 1981 Elmira, N. Y.
1920-099 ....Richmond, Raymond Sinclair ....D. October 21, 1969 Desoto, Mo.
1951-081 ....Richter, Allen Gordon ....PO Box 41/Virginia Beach VA 23458
1911-143 ....Richter, Emil Henry 'Reggie' ....D. August 3, 1934 Chicago, Ill.
1942-084 ....Rickert, Marvin August ....D. June 3, 1978 Oakville, Wash.
1963-098 ....Ricketts, David William ....12860 Polo Parc Drive/Saint Louis MO 63146
1959-069 ....Ricketts, Richard James ....D. March 6, 1988 Rochester, N.Y.
1969-146 ....Rico, Alfredo Cruz ....7720 Ensign Street/Sun Valley CA 91353
1916-070 ....Rico, Arthur Raymond ....D. January 3, 1919 Boston, Mass.
1923-109 ....Riconda, Harry Paul ....D. November 15, 1958 Mahopac, N. Y.
1939-097 ....Riddle, Elmer Ray ....D. May 14, 1984 Columbus, Ga.
1930-067 ....Riddle, John Ludy ....4021 Monaco Drive #D/Indianapolis IN 46220
1970-112 ....Riddleberger, Dennis Michael ....910 Westmoreland Avenue/Portsmouth VA 23707
1990-133 ....Riddoch, Gregory Lee ....5279 Isla Key Blvd #114/Saint Petersburg FL 33715
1914-177 ....Ridgway, Jacob A. 'John' ....D. February 23, 1928 Philadelphia, Pa.
1950-081 ....Ridzik, Stephen George ....3958 75th Street West #818/Bradenton FL 34209
1942-085 ....Riebe, Harvey Donald 'Hank' ....28031 Lake Shore Blvd/Euclid OH 44132

1910-125 ....Rieger, Elmer Jay ....D. October 21, 1959 Los Angeles, Calif.
1991-148 ....Riesgo, Damon Nikco Nikco ....1867 Butternut Street/Corona CA 91720
1997-137 ....Rigby, Bradley Kenneth..............................676 Mossy Branch Court/Longwood FL 32750
1911-144 ....Riggert, Joseph Aloysius ....D. December 10, 1973 Kansas City, Mo.
1992-119 ....Riggleman, James David ....14950 Gulf Blvd #1003/Madeira Beach FL 33708
1997-138 ....Riggs, Adam David ....1 Spring Lane/Stanhope NJ 7874
1934-089 ....Riggs, Lewis Sidney ....D. August 12, 1975 Durham, N. C.
1979-092 ....Righetti, David Allan ....552 Magdalena Avenue/Los Altos CA 94024
1995-185 ....Rightnowar, Ronald Gene ....8926 Stonybrook Blvd/Sylvania OH 43560
1922-116 ....Rigney, Emory Elmo 'Topper' ....D. June 6, 1972 San Antonio, Tex.
1937-090 ....Rigney, John Dungan ....D. October 21, 1984 Lombard, Ill.
1946-089 ....Rigney, William Joseph ....3136 Round Hill Road/Alamo CA 94507
1984-093 ....Rijo, Jose Antonio ....Central Cabral #66 San Cristobal Dominican Rep.
1941-094 ....Rikard, Culley ....50 Hwy 304/Olive Branch Ms/38654
1985-097 ....Riles, Ernest ....4262 Millwood Lane/Tallahassee FL 32312
1979-093 ....Riley, George Michael ....842 Locust Street/Reading PA 19604
1910-126 ....Riley, James Joseph ....D. March 25, 1949 Buffalo, N.Y.
1921-087 ....Riley, James Norman ....D. May 25, 1969 Sequin, Texas
1944-110 ....Riley, Leon Francis ....D. September 13, 1970 Schenectady, N. Y.
1980-112 ....Rincon, Andrew ....5425 Los Toros,%J.Rincon/Pico Rivera CA 90660
1997-139 ....Rincon, Ricardo ....Old Add: Veracruz Mexico
1979-094 ....Rineer, Jeffrey Alan ....176 Center Street/Troy PA 16947
1917-069 ....Ring, James Joseph ....D. July 2, 1965 New York, N.Y.
1950-082 ....Rinker, Robert John ....10 North Madison/McAdoo PA 18237
1997-140 ....Rios, Daniel ....5795 East 5th Avenue/Hialeah FL 33013
1969-147 ....Rios, Juan Onofre Velez ....D. August 28, 1995 Mayaguez, P. R.
1981-105 ....Ripken, Calvin "Edwin, Jr." ....19 Chris Eliot Court/Cockeysville MD 21030
1985-098 ....Ripken, Calvin "Edwin, Sr." ....Old Add: 410 Clover St Aberdeen MD 21001
1987-125 ....Ripken, William Oliver ....900 Mount Soma Court/Fallston MD 21047
1978-112 ....Ripley, Allen Stevens ....Old Add: Box 349, %A.Cooper North Attleboro MA 02760
1935-093 ....Ripley, Walter Franklin ....D. October 7, 1990 Attleboro, Mass.
1962-113 ....Rippelmeyer, Raymond Roy ....104 Eagle Court/Waterloo IL 62298
1944-111 ....Ripple, Charles Dawson ....D. May 6, 1979 Wilmington, N. C.
1936-078 ....Ripple, James Albert ....D. July 16, 1959 Greensburg, Pa.
1917-070 ....Risberg, Charles August 'Swede' ......D. October 13, 1975 Red Bluff, Calif.
1992-120 ....Risley, William Charles ....2312 East 11th Street/Farmington NM 87401
1964-094 ....Ritchie, Jay Seay ....330 Yachtsman Drive/Salisbury NC 28146
1997-141 ....Ritchie, Todd Everett ....645 Parkwood Circle/Duncanville TX 75116
1987-126 ....Ritchie, Wallace Reid ....341 Wonderview Drive/Glendale CA 91202
1986-128 ....Ritter, Reggie Blake ....Rural Route 1 Box 685/Donaldson AR 71941
1912-164 ....Ritter, William Herbert 'Hank' ....D. September 3, 1964 Akron, O.
1970-113 ....Rittwage, James Michael ....23931 Columbus Rd/Bedford Heights OH 44146
1989-104 ....Ritz, Kevin D. ....Rural Route 9/Bloomfield IA 52537
1992-121 ....Rivera, Bienvenido ....Cle Club De Leames #11 San Pedro De Macoris Dominican Rep.
1983-122 ....Rivera, German ....Old Add: Vialeticia #4e4,V.Fontana Carolina PR 00630
1975-101 ....Rivera, Jesus Bombo ....G#2 Amalia Maria/Ponce PR 732
1986-129 ....Rivera, Luis Antonio ....Lazaro Ramos #16/Cidra PR 639
1952-085 ....Rivera, Manuel Joseph 'Jim' ....6707 West Canal Pointe Lane/Fort Wayne IN 46801
1995-186 ....Rivera, Mariano ....Casa 3666 Calle El Puerto Puerto Caimito/Panama
1995-187 ....Rivera, Roberto Diaz ....Old Add: Bayamon PR 00988
1995-188 ....Rivera, Ruben Moreno ....Old Add: Chorrea Panama
1970-114 ....Rivers, John Milton 'Mickey' ....Old Add: 350 Nw 48th Street Miami FL 33127
1921-088 ....Riviere, Arthur Bernard 'Tink' ....D. September 27, 1965 Liberty, Tex.
1912-165 ....Rixey, Eppa ....D. February 28, 1963 Terrace Park, O.
1938-082 ....Rizzo, John Costa ....D. December 4, 1977 Houston, Tex.
1941-095 ....Rizzuto, Philip Francis ....912 Westminster Avenue/Hillside NJ 7205
1995-189 ....Roa, Joseph Rodger ....%Ralph Roa 677 E. Brickley Avenue Hazel Park MI 48030
1953-076 ....Roach, Melvin Earl ....4131 Southaven Road/Richmond VA 23235
1910-127 ....Roach, Wilbur Charles 'Roxy' ....D. December 26, 1947 Bay City, Mich.
1961-090 ....Roarke, Michael Thomas ....11 Roseview Dr/Cranston RI 2910
1979-095 ....Robbins, Bruce Duane ....Old Add: 3813 Chadam Lane #1c Muncie IN 47304
1933-055 ....Robello, Thomas Vardasco 'Toby' ....D. December 25, 1994 Fort Worth, Texas
1979-096 ....Roberge, Bertrand Roland ....267 Sunderland Drive/Auburn Me 4210
1941-096 ....Roberge, Joseph Albert 'Skip' ....D. June 7, 1993 Lowell, Mass.
1993-152 ....Roberson, Kevin Lynn ....1565 East North Port Road/Decatur IL 62526
1995-190 ....Roberson, Sidney Dean ....332 Gleneagles Drive/Oarnge Park FL 32073
1943-116 ....Roberts, Charles Emory ....2027 Maple Street/Carrollton GA 30117
1913-149 ....Roberts, Clarence Ashley 'Skipper' ....D. December 24, 1963 Long Beach, Calif.
1954-090 ....Roberts, Curtis Benjamin ....D. November 14, 1969 Oakland, Calif.
1967-089 ....Roberts, Dale ....206 Berry Ave/Versailles KY 40383
1969-148 ....Roberts, David Arthur ....14007 Woodsedge Road/Fort Ashley WV 26719
1962-114 ....Roberts, David Leonard ....17510 Mayall Street/Northridge CA 91234
1972-090 ....Roberts, David Wayne ....17050 Nw Stoller Drive/Portland OR 97229
1924-089 ....Roberts, James Newsom ....D. June 24, 1984 Columbus, Miss.
1986-130 ....Roberts, Leon Joseph Bip ....17943 Highlands Ranch Place/Poway CA 92064
1974-113 ....Roberts, Leon Kauffman ....PO Box 170299/Arlington TX 76003
1919-069 ....Roberts, Raymond ....D. January 30, 1962 Cruger, Miss.
1948-085 ....Roberts, Robin Evan ....504 Terrace Hill Drive/Temple Terrace FL 33617
1954-091 ....Robertson, Alfred James 'Jim' ....5944 Corazon Drive/Las Vegas NV 89103

1981-106	Robertson, Andre Levett	2229 Cross Ln St/Orange TX 77360
1919-070	Robertson, Charles Culbertson	D. August 23, 1984 Fort Worth, Tex.
1962-115	Robertson, Daryl Berdine	755 Princton Dr/Midvale UT 84047
1912-166	Robertson, Davis Aydelotre	D. November 5, 1970 Virginia Beach, Va.
1954-092	Robertson, Donald Alexander	8325 South Dead Bear Draw/Hereford AZ 85615
1919-099	Robertson, Eugene Edward	D. October 21, 1981 Fallon, Nev.
1969-149	Robertson, Jerry Lee	D. March 24, 1996 Topeka, Kan.
1996-159	Robertson, Michael Francis	Old Add: Las Vegas NV 89101
1913-150	Robertson, Preston	D. October 2, 1944 New Orleans, La.
1966-075	Robertson, Richard Paul	12175 Saratoga-Sunnyvale Road/Saratoga CA 95070
1993-153	Robertson, Richard Wayne	PO Box 653/Waller TX 77484
1967-090	Robertson, Robert Eugene	Rr 1 Shinnamon Dr/Lavale MD 21502
1940-075	Robertson, Sherrard Alexander	D. October 23, 1970 Houghton, S. D.
1985-099	Robidoux, William Joseph	2 King George Drive/Ware MA 1082
1943-117	Robinson, Aaron Andrew	D. March 9, 1966 Lancaster,O.
1955-099	Robinson, Brooks Calbert	PO Box 1168/Baltimore MD 21203
1978-113	Robinson, Bruce Phillip	3968 San Augustine Way/San Diego CA 92130
1972-091	Robinson, Craig George	Old Add: PO Box 814 Pulaski VA 24301
1970-115	Robinson, David Tanner	6140 Camino Del Rinson/San Diego CA 92120
1979-097	Robinson, Dewey Everett	1388 Cottonwood Trail/Sarasota FL 34232
1978-114	Robinson, Don Allen	2209 87th Street Nw/Bradenton FL 34209
1958-076	Robinson, Earl John	6895 Oakwood Drive/Oakland CA 94611
1960-087	Robinson, Floyd Andrew	5843 MI King Way/San Diego CA 92114
1956-073	Robinson, Frank	15557 Aqua Verde Dr/Los Angeles CA 90077
1955-100	Robinson, Humberto Valentino	1695 Brooklyn Ave/Brooklyn NY 11210
1947-073	Robinson, Jack Roosevelt	D. October 24, 1972 Stamford, Conn.
1984-094	Robinson, Jeffrey Daniel	Old Add: 23726 Via Roble Mission Viejo CA 92679
1987-127	Robinson, Jeffrey Mark	5317 West 158th Place/Overland Park KS 66224
1949-074	Robinson, John Edward	210 Florida Shore Blvd/Daytona Beach Shores FL 32018
1911-145	Robinson, John Henry 'Hank'	D. July 3, 1965 North Little Rock, Ark.
1995-191	Robinson, Kenneth Neal	460 Moore Road/Akron OH 44319
1984-095	Robinson, Ronald Dean	473 Pine St/Woodlake CA 93286
1942-086	Robinson, William Edward 'Eddie'	6104 Cholla/Fort Worth TX 76112
1966-076	Robinson, William Henry	165 Pittman Downer Road/Sewell NJ 8080
1969-150	Robles, Rafael Radames	D. August 13, 1998 New York, N. Y.
1972-092	Robles, Sergio	Cerro Chiquihuite #148 C.Churubusco Mexico 21 Mexico
1974-114	Robson, Thomas James	611 East Alameda Dr/Tempe AZ 85282
1943-118	Rocco, Michael Dominick 'Mickey'	D. June 1, 1997 St. Paul, Minn.
1945-086	Roche, Armando Baez	Old Add: Avenue Los Pinos Havana Cuba
1914-178	Roche, John Joseph	D. March 31, 1983 Peoria, Ariz.
1914-179	Rochefort, Bennett Harold	D. April 2, 1981 Red Bank, N. J.
1944-112	Rochelli, Louis Joseph	D. October 3, 1992 Victoria, Texas
1988-112	Rochford, Michael Joseph	1802 Brand Farm Drive/South Burlington VT 5403
1936-079	Rock, Lester Henry	D. September 9, 1991 Davis, Calif.
1976-082	Rockett, Patrick Edward	1335 Viewridge/San Antonio TX 78213
1983-123	Rodas, Richard Martin Rick	6877 Bergano Place/Alta Loma CA 91701
1957-074	Rodgers, Kenneth Andre Ian 'Andre'	Box N386 Nassau/Bahamas
1961-091	Rodgers, Robert Leroy	5181 West Knoll Dr/Yorba Linda CA 92686
1915-137	Rodgers, Wilbur Kincaid	D. December 24, 1978 Goliad, Tex.
1944-113	Rodgers, William Sherman	1433 Naudain/Harrisburg PA 17104
1954-093	Rodin, Eric Chapman	D. January 4, 1991 Somerville, N. J.
1994-090	Rodriguez, Alexander Emmanuel	Old Add: Miami FL
1967-091	Rodriguez, Aurelio Huarte	Old Add: 4617 East Eastland St Tucson AZ 85711
1991-149	Rodriguez, Carlos	2929 Princeville Drive/Pickerington OH 43147
1973-100	Rodriguez, Eduardo	Urb. Catalina Calle 4 #E34/Barceloneta PR 617
1982-105	Rodriguez, Edwin	7901 30th Avenue North/Saint Petersburg FL 33710
1968-087	Rodriguez, Eliseo C. 'Ellie'	Old Add: Box 188 Bayamon PR 00619
1995-192	Rodriguez, Felix Antonio	Old Add: Montecristy Dominican Rep.
1958-077	Rodriguez, Fernando Pedro 'Freddy'	Old Add: 555 Mayia Rodriguez/Havana Cuba
1995-193	Rodriguez, Francisco 'Frank'	1017 Pond Apple Court/Oviedo FL 32765
1952-086	Rodriguez, Hector Antonio	Old Add: %A.Canizares,Cert. 99a "Col. Postal,Mexico City Mex."
1992-122	Rodriguez, Henry Anderson	295 Wadsworth Avenue #3f/New York NY 10040
1991-150	Rodriguez, Ivan/Pudge	E3 Calle 3/Vega Baja PR 693
1916-071	Rodriguez, Jose	D. March 23, 1948 Havana, Cuba
1996-160	Rodriguez, Luis Antonio 'Tony'	Old Add: Cidra PR 00739
1996-161	Rodriguez, Nerio	Old Add: Santo Domingo Dom. Rep.
1986-131	Rodriguez, Ricardo	5014 Proctor Road/Castro Valley CA 94546
1990-134	Rodriguez, Richard Anthony	2164 Amber Avenue/El Monte CA 91733
1967-092	Rodriguez, Roberto Munoz	Cortijito Desarrias, 8 Cjn Recobe 30 Caracas Venezuela
1989-105	Rodriguez, Rosario Isabel	Old Add: Los Mochis Sinaloa Mexico
1986-132	Rodriguez, Ruben Dario	10 #17 Ensanche Luperon Santo Domingo Dominican Rep.
1995-194	Rodriguez, Steven James	10430 Orchard Lane/Riverside CA 92503
1984-096	Rodriguez, Victor Manuel	Old Add: Villa Carolina Cle 23 #19 B15 Carolina PR 00985
1938-083	Roe, Elwin Charles 'Preacher'	204 Wildwood Terrace/West Plains MO 65775
1923-110	Roe, James Clay	D. April 3, 1956 Cleveland, Miss.
1955-101	Roebuck, Edward Jack	3434 Warwood Rd/Lakewood CA 90712
1976-083	Roenicke, Gary Steven	14152 Greenwood Court/Nevada City CA 95959
1981-107	Roenicke, Ronald Jon	2212 Avenida Las Ramblas/Chino Hills CA 91709
1989-106	Roesler, Michael Joseph	2760 East Paulding Road/Fort Wayne IN 46816

1923-111 ....Roettger, Oscar Frederick Louis.....................D. July 4, 1986 St. Louis, Mo.
1927-075 ....Roettger, Walter Henry ....D. September 14, 1951 Champaign, Ill.
1929-089 ....Roetz, Edward Bernard ....D. March 16, 1965 Philadelphia, Pa.
1938-084 ....Rogalski, Joseph Anthony ....D. November 20, 1951 Ashland, Wis.
1925-088 ....Rogell, William George ....4542 Garnet Drive #206/Newport Richey FL 34652
1992-123 ....Rogers, Charles Kevin Kevin ....204 Ashley Street/Cleveland MS 38732
1995-195 ....Rogers, James Randall ....Old Add: Tulsa OK 74101
1914-180 ....Rogers, Jay Louis ....D. July 18, 1964 Carlisle, Pa.
1989-1071 ....Rogers, Kenneth South ....6314 Maclaurin Drive/Tampa FL 33647
1938-085 ....Rogers, Lee Otis ....D. November 23, 1995 Little Rock, Ark.
1935-094 ....Rogers, Orlin Woodrow 'Buck' ....3145 Snake Path Road/Blairs VA 24527
1938-086 ....Rogers, Stanley Frank 'Packy' ....964 Walnut Street/Elmira NY 14901
1973-101 ....Rogers, Stephen Douglas ....3746 South Madison Avenue/Tulsa OK 74105
1917-071 ....Rogers, Thomas Andrew ....D. March 7, 1936 Nashville, Tenn.
1915-138 ....Rogge, Francis Clinton ....D. January 6, 1969 Mount Clemens, Mich.
1963-099 ....Roggenburk, Garry Earl ....18828 Canyon Road/Cleveland OH 44126
1973-102 ....Rogodzinski, Michael George ....1 Emlyn Court/Laurel Springs NJ 8021
1949-075 ....Rogovin, Saul Walter ....D. January 23, 1995 New York, N. Y.
1990-135 ....Rohde, David Grant ....1707 Port Barmouth/Newport Beach CA 92660
1983-124 ....Rohn, Daniel Jay ....526 West 14th Street #237/Traverse City MI 49684
1967-093 ....Rohr, Leslie Norvin ....1340 Wicks Lane/Billings MT 59105
1967-094 ....Rohr, William Joseph ....Old Add: 120 West 5th/Santa Ana CA 92701
1997-142 ....Rohrmeier, Daniel ....4240 West Ford Road/Cincinnati OH 45247
1921-089 ....Rohwer, Ray ....D. January 24, 1988 Davis, Calif.
1953-077 ....Roig, Anton Ambrose ....24125 East Lakeridge Drive/Liberty Lake WA 99019
1990-136 ....Rojas, Melquiades (Medrano) ....Km 12 #41 Prol. Indepencia Santo Domingo Dominican Rep.
1966-077 ....Rojas, Minervino Alejandro 'Minnie' ....7101a Plaska/Huntington Park CA 90255
1962-116 ....Rojas, Octavio 'Cookie' ....19195 Mystic Pointe Drive Bldg 100 #Lp2 Miami FL 33180
1942-087 ....Rojek, Stanley Andrew ....D. July 9, 1997 North Tonawanda, N. Y.
1962-117 ....Roland, James Ivan ....823 East Marion Street #1/Shelby NC 28150
1996-162 ....Rolen, Scott Bruce ....1883 South Highland Street/Jasper IN 47546
1931-074 ....Rolfe, Robert Abial 'Red' ....D. July 8, 1969 Gilford, N. H.
1912-167 ....Rollings, Raymond Copeland ....D. August 25, 1966 St.Paul, Minn.
1927-076 ....Rollings, William Russell 'Red' ....D. December 31, 1964 Mobile, Ala.
1961-092 ....Rollins, Richard John 'Rich' ....6822 Chaffee Court/Cleveland OH 44141
1984-097 ....Roman, Jose Rafael ....Vista Alegre #10 Sanches Luperon Puerto Plata Dominican Rep.
1964-095 ....Roman, William Anthony ....1720 Yale Court/Lake Forest IL 60045
1984-098 ....Romanick, Ronald James ....16028 East Sunflower Drive #203/Fountain Hills AZ 85268
1950-083 ....Romano, James King ....D. September 12, 1990 Deer Park, N. Y.
1958-078 ....Romano, John Anthony ....7 Tanglewood Hollow/Upper Saddle River NJ 7458
1987-128 ....Romano, Thomas Michael ....1266 Penora Street/Depew NY 14043
1954-094 ....Romberger, Allen Irving ....D. May 26, 1983 Weikert, Pa.
1997-143 ....Romero, Armando 'Mandy' ....Old Add: 1305 Nw 46th Street Miami FL 33142
1977-121 ....Romero, Edgardo ....1380 Wood Row Way/West Palm Beach FL 33414
1984-099 ....Romero, Roman ....Cle Ulises Espaillot #60 San Pedro De Macoris Dominican Rep.
1985-100 ....Romine, Kevin Andrew ....8750 Rogue River Ave/Fountain Valley CA 92708
1920-100 ....Rommel, Edwin Americus ....D. August 26, 1970 Baltimore, Md.
1977-122 ....Romo, Enrique ....Avenida Sn, Carlos #923 Torreon Coahuila/Mexico
1968-088 ....Romo, Vicente ....Old Add: Gmo Prieto 116 Ote Cd. Obregon Sonora Mexico
1953-078 ....Romonosky, John ....5090 Bixby Road/Groveport OH 43125
1993-154 ....Ronan, Edward Marcus 'Marc' ....3103 Northgate Drive/Opelika AL 36801
1913-151 ....Rondeau, Henri Joseph ....D. May 28, 1943 Woonsocket, R.I.
1976-084 ....Rondon, Gilbert ....Old Add: 339 Bleaker Street #2l/339 Bleaker Street #2l
1981-108 ....Roof, Eugene Lawrence ....175 Spring Valley Drive/Paducah KY 42001
1961-093 ....Roof, Phillip Anthony ....7350 Us Highway 45/Boaz KY 42047
1968-089 ....Rooker, James Philip ....1684 Citation Dr/Library PA 15129
1988-113 ....Roomes, Rolando Audley ....Old Add: 330 South Beck Ave Tempe AZ 85281
1914-181 ....Rooney, Frank ....D. April 6, 1977 Bessemer, Mich.
1981-109 ....Rooney, Patrick Eugene ....251 Bristol Street/Northfield IL 60093
1923-112 ....Root, Charles Henry ....D. November 5, 1970 Hollister, Calif.
1993-155 ....Roper, John Christopher ....519 Grant Avenue/Raeford NC 28376
1970-116 ....Roque, Jorge ....Old Add: Bo. San Anton #135 Ponce PR 00731
1996-163 ....Rosado, Jose Antonio ....Old Add: Dorado PR 00646
1977-123 ....Rosado, Luis (Robles) ....Calle 508 B-213 #13 5th/Carolina PR 630
1939-098 ....Rosar, Warren Vincent 'Buddy' ....D. February 13, 1994 Rochester, N. Y.
1971-089 ....Rosario, Angel Ramon ....Calle 1 #421 Hernandes Davila/Bayamon PR 619
1997-144 ....Rosario, Melvin Gregorio ....Old Add: Miami FL 33101
1965-092 ....Rosario, Santiago ....Hc1 Buzon #7982/Guayanilla PR 656
1990-137 ....Rosario, Victor Manuel ....Ave. Circum Valacion #36 San Pedro De Macoris Dominican Republic
1990-137 ....Rosario, Victor Manuel ....Ave. Circum Valacion #36 San Pedro De Macoris Dominican Rep.
1997-145 ....Rose, Brian Leonard ....Old Add: 5 Harbor Street South Dartmouth MA 02748
1971-090 ....Rose, Donald Gary ....1133 Huntingdon/San Jose CA 95129
1963-100 ....Rose, Peter Edward ....6584 Villa Sonrisa Drive #1121/Boca Raton FL 33433
1997-146 ....Rose, Peter "Edward, Jr." ....5948 Bridgeview Court/Cincinnati OH 45248
1989-108 ....Rose, Robert Richard ....2406 Costa Del Sol/Laverne CA 91750
1957-075 ....Roseboro, John Junior ....957 Airole Way/Los Angeles CA 90077
1995-196 ....Roselli, Joseph Donald ....Old Add: 6281 Lesage Ave Woodland Hills CA 91367
1955-102 ....Roselli, Robert Edward ....1548 Hemlock Ave/San Mateo CA 94401
1972-093 ....Rosello, David ....Paz 160 - Bo Paris/Mayaguez PR 708

1947-074	Rosen, Albert Leonard	15 Mayfair Drive/Rancho Mirage CA 92270
1937-091	Rosen, Goodwin George	D. April 6, 1994 Toronto, Ontario
1930-068	Rosenberg, Harry	D. April 13, 1997 San Mateo, Calif.
1923-113	Rosenberg, Louis	D. September 8, 1991 San Francisco, Calif.
1988-114	Rosenberg, Steven Allen	8425 Forest Hills Dr/Coral Springs FL 33065
1931-075	Rosenfeld, Max	D. March 10, 1969 Miami, Fla.
1936-080	Rosenthal, Lawrence John	D. March 4, 1992 Woodbury, Minn.
1925-089	Rosenthal, Simon	D. April 7, 1969 Boston, Mass.
1991-151	Rosenthal, Wayne Scott	734 East 80th Street/Brooklyn NY 11236
1944-114	Roser, Emerson Corey	210 Camp Road/Clayville NY 13322
1922-118	Roser, John Joseph 'Bunny'	D. May 6, 1979 Rocky Hill, Conn.
1924-090	Ross, Chester Franklin 'Buster'	D. April 24, 1982 Mayfield, Ky.
1939-099	Ross, Chester James	D. February 21, 1989 Buffalo, N.Y.
1954-095	Ross, Clifford David	2581 Rosewood/Roslyn PA 19001
1938-087	Ross, Donald Raymond	D. April 4, 1996 Arcadia, Calif.
1950-084	Ross, Floyd Robert 'Bob'	2010 West San Marcos Blvd #19/San Marcos CA 92069
1968-090	Ross, Gary Douglas	Old Add: 7985 Labrusca Way Carlsbad CA 92008
1918-063	Ross, George Sidney	D. April 22, 1935 Amityville, N. Y.
1936-081	Ross, Lee Ravon 'Buck'	D. November 23, 1978 Charlotte, North . C.
1982-106	Ross, Mark Joseph	1761 North Ranch Drive/Tucson AZ 85715
1952-087	Rossi, Joseph Anthony	934 Stannage Avenue/Albany CA 94706
1944-115	Rosso, Francis James	D. January 26, 1980 Springfield, Mass.
1991-152	Rossy, Elam Jose Rico	Atenas Street A#7 Rpto Flamingo/Bayamon PR 619
1948-086	Rotblatt, Marvin	8510 Mango Avenue/Morton Grove IL 60053
1914-182	Roth, Robert Frank 'Braggo'	D. September 11, 1936 Chicago, Ill.
1945-087	Rothel, Robert Burton	D. May 21, 1984 Huron, O.
1925-090	Rothrock, John Houston	D. February 2, 1980 San Bernardino, Calif.
1981-110	Rothschild, Lawrence Lee	4508 West Culbreath Avenue/Tampa FL 33609
1970-117	Rounsaville, Virl Gene 'Gene'	2901 Lone Tree Way #A/Antioch CA 94509
1913-152	Roush, Edd	D. March 21, 1988 Bradenton, Fla.
1911-146	Rowan, David	D. July 30, 1955 Toronto, Ont.
1984-100	Rowdon, Wade Lee	230 Crooked Tree Trail/Deland FL 32724
1963-101	Rowe, Donald Howard	19791 Scenic Bay Ln/Huntington Beach CA 92648
1916-072	Rowe, Harland Stimson	D. May 26, 1969 Springvale, Me.
1963-102	Rowe, Kenneth Darrell	708 Greenleaf Drive/Norcross GA 30092
1933-056	Rowe, Lynwood Thomas 'Schoolboy'	D. January 8, 1961 El Dorado, Ark.
1939-100	Rowell, Carvel William 'Bama'	D. August 16, 1993 Citronelle, Ala.
1923-114	Rowland, Charles Leland	D. January 21, 1992 Raleigh, N. C.
1915-139	Rowland, Clarence Henry 'Pants'	D. May 17, 1969 Chicago, Ill.
1980-113	Rowland, Michael Evan	15757 North 90th Place #2171/Scottsdale AZ 85260
1990-138	Rowland, Richard Garnet	Old Add: 91 Clark Street Cloverdale CA 95425
1933-057	Roy, Emile Arthur	D. January 5, 1997 Crystal River, Fla.
1946-090	Roy, Jean Pierre	202 Northwest 53rd Street/Pompano Beach FL 33064
1924-091	Roy, Luther Franklin	D. July 24, 1963 Grand Rapids, Mich.
1950-085	Roy, Norman Brooks	2 Autumn Leaf Drive #15/Nashua/NH/3060
1991-153	Royer, Stanley Dean	5718 Holly Hills Avenue/Saint Louis MO 63109
1973-103	Royster, Jeron Kennis	9 Sheldrake Lane/Palm Beach Gardens FL 33418
1981-111	Royster, Willie A.	229 55th Street Northeast/Washington Dc 20019
1950-086	Rozek, Richard Louis	57-188 Merion/La Quinta CA 92253
1977-124	Rozema, David Scott	4331 Heritage Drive/Georgetown Twp. MI 49426
1964-096	Roznovsky, Victor Joseph	1686 West Bullard/Fresno CA 93711
1940-076	Rubeling, Albert William	D. January 28, 1988 Baltimore, Md.
1969-151	Ruberto, John Edward 'Sonny'	13208 Laurel Lake Court/Saint Louis MO 63131
1966-078	Rubio, Jorge Jesus	Old Add:1001 Lerdo Ave/Mexicali Baja California
1927-077	Ruble, William Arthur	D. November 1, 1983 Maryville, Tenn.
1981-112	Rucker, David Michael	PO Box 559/Pinion Hills CA 92372
1940-077	Rucker, John Joel	D. August 7, 1985 Moultrie, Ga.
1967-095	Rudi, Joseph Oden	PO Box 425/Baker City OR 97814
1945-088	Rudolph, Ernest William	711 Alder/Black River Falls WI 54615
1957-076	Rudolph, Frederick Donald 'Don'	D. September 12, 1968 Encino, Calif.
1969-152	Rudolph, Kenneth Victor	939 South 48th Street #212/Tempe AZ 85281
1910-128	Rudolph, Richard	D. October 20, 1949 Bronx, N.Y.
1996-164	Ruebel, Matthew Alexander	3128 SW 45th Street/Oklahoma City OK 73119
1915-140	Ruel, Herold Dominic 'Muddy'	D. November 13, 1963 Palo Alto, Calif.
1993-156	Rueter, Kirk Wesley	42 Hickory Street/Nashville IL 62263
1917-072	Ruether, Walter Henry 'Dutch'	D. May 16, 1970 Phoenix, Ariz.
1949-083	Rufer, Rudolph Joseph	649 Cornwell Avenue/Malverne NY 11565
1993-157	Ruffcorn, Scott Patrick	2137 Barton Hills Drive/Austin TX 78704
1986-133	Ruffin, Bruce Wayne	15610 Fern Basin/Houston TX 77084
1993-158	Ruffin, Johnny Renando	314 South Church Street/Adams TN 37016
1924-092	Ruffing, Charles Herbert 'Red'	D. February 17, 1986 Mayfield Heights, O.
1974-115	Ruhle, Vernon Gerald	3188 Skinner Mill Road #16/Augusta GA 30909
1964-097	Ruiz, Hiraldo Sablon 'Chico'	D. February 9, 1972 San Diego, Calif.
1978-115	Ruiz, Manuel/Chico	Tapia 267/Santurce PR 912
1943-119	Rullo, Joseph Vincent	D. October 28, 1969 Philadelphia, Pa.
1914-183	Rumler, William George	D. May 26, 1966 Lincoln, Neb.
1981-113	Runge, Paul William	618 Sabal Avenue/Clewiston FL 33440
1985-101	Runnells, Thomas William	4322 Todd Drive/Sylvania OH 43560
1951-082	Runnels, James Edward 'Pete'	D. May 20, 1991 Pasadena, Texas

1997-147	Rusch, Glendon James	Old Add: Seattle WA 98101
1925-091	Rush, Jess Howard 'Andy'	D. March 16, 1969 Fresno, Calif.
1948-087	Rush, Robert Ransom	1358 East First Place/Mesa AZ 85203
1990-139	Ruskin, Scott Drew	53 Troon Trace/Ponte Vedra Beach FL 32082
1915-141	Russell, Allan E.	D. October 20, 1972 Baltimore, Md.
1910-129	Russell, Clarence Dickson 'Lefty'	D. January 22, 1962 Baltimore, Md.
1913-153	Russell, Ewell Albert 'Reb'	D. September 30, 1973 Indianapolis, Ind.
1939-101	Russell, Glen David 'Rip'	D. September 26, 1976 Los Angeles Cal.
1914-184	Russell, Harvey Holmes	D. January 8, 1980 Alexandria, Va.
1926-072	Russell, Jack Erwin	D. November 3, 1990 Clearwater, Fla.
1942-088	Russell, James William	D. November 24, 1987 Pittsburgh, Pa.
1983-125	Russell, Jeffrey Lee	2325 Oak Knoll Drive/Colleyville TX 76034
1917-073	Russell, John Albert	D. November 19, 1930 Ely, Nev.
1984-101	Russell, John William	2088 Coves/Afton OK 74331
1938-088	Russell, Loyd Opal	D. May 24, 1968 Waco, Tex.
1969-153	Russell, William Ellis	7206 East 90th Street/Tulsa OK 74133
1939-102	Russo, Marius Ugo	27 Norfolk Drive East/Elmont NY 11003
1966-079	Rusteck, Richard Frank	PO Box 5623/Ketchikan AK 99901
1944-116	Ruszkowski, Henry Alexander	12235 Valley Lane Drive/Cleveland OH 44125
1914-185	Ruth, George Herman 'Babe'	D. August 16, 1948 New York, N.Y.
1910-130	Rutherford, James Hollis	D. September 18, 1956 Lakewood, O.
1952-088	Rutherford, John William	911 Henrietta/Birmingham MI 48009
1973-104	Ruthven, Richard David	Old Add: 825 Cold Harbor Dr Woodstock GA 30188
1947-075	Rutner, Milton Mickey	14 Shotgun Lane/Levittown NY 11756
1982-107	Ryal, Mark Dwayne	506 East Garfield/Ralston OK 74650
1942-089	Ryan, Cornelius Joseph 'Connie'	D. January 3, 1996 New Orleans, La.
1912-168	Ryan, John Budd	D. July 9, 1956 Sacramento, Calif.
1930-069	Ryan, John Collins 'Blondy'	D. November 28, 1959 Swampscott, Mass.
1929-090	Ryan, John Francis	D. September 2, 1967 Rochester, Minn.
1992-124	Ryan, Kenneth Frederick	45 Tanager Road/Seekonk MA 2771
1966-080	Ryan, Lynn Nolan 'Nolan'	PO Box 670/Alvin TX 77512
1964-098	Ryan, Michael James	126 Main Street/Newton NH 3858
1919-071	Ryan, Wilfred Patrick Dolan 'Rosy'	D. December 10, 1980 Phoenix, Ariz.
1935-095	Ryba, Dominic Joseph 'Mike'	D. December 13, 1971 Springfield, Mo.
1931-076	Rye, Eugene Rudolph	D. January 21, 1980 Park Ridge, Ill.
1972-094	Ryerson, Gary Lawrence	1059 Terrace Court/El Cajon CA 92019
1984-102	Saberhagen, Bret William	1735 SW Mockingbird Drive/Port Saint Lucie FL 34986
1936-082	Sabo, Alexander	816 Anchor Drive/Forked River NJ 8731
1988-115	Sabo, Christopher Andrew	15003 Grandville/Detroit MI 48223
1951-083	Sacka, Frank	D. December 7, 1994 Dearborn, Mich.
1996-165	Sackinsky, Brian Walter	1820 Edward Drive/Library PA 15129
1960-088	Sadecki, Raymond Michael	4237 East Clovis Avenue/Mesa AZ 85206
1973-105	Sadek, Michael George	3015 Canal Drive/Stockton CA 95204
1960-089	Sadowski, Edward Ramon	D. November 6, 1993 Garden Grove, Calif.
1974-116	Sadowski, James Michael	537 Fieldcrest Drive/Pittsburgh PA 15209
1963-103	Sadowski, Robert	26 Barrington Court/Sharpsburg GA 30277
1960-090	Sadowski, Robert Frank	1050 Dodge Street/Fenton MO 63026
1960-091	Sadowski, Theodore	D. July 18, 1993 Shaler Twp., Pa.
1994-091	Saenz, Olmedo (Sanchez)	Aminta Burgos Amado #2027 Chitre Herrera/Panama
1949-077	Saffell, Thomas Judson	1503 Clower Creek Drive #262/Sarasota FL 33581
1994-092	Sager, Anthony Joseph 'A. J.'	235 North Fourth/Kirkersville OH 43033
1997-148	Sagmoen, Marc Richard	13607 18th Avenue Sw/Seattle WA 98166
1911-147	Saier, Victor Sylvester	D. May 14, 1967 East Lansing, Mich.
1942-090	Sain, John Franklin	2 South 707 Avenue Latour/Oakbrook IL 60523
1951-084	Saintclaire, Edward Joseph 'Ebba'	D. August 22, 1982 Whitehall, N. Y.
1984-103	Saintclaire, Randy Anthony	174 Cooper Street/Lake George NY 12845
1977-125	Sakata, Lenn Haruki	467 Halemaumau Street/Honolulu HI 96821
1984-104	Salas, Mark Bruce	330 Barca Ave/Lapuente CA 91744
1983-126	Salazar, Argenis Antonio	Rodriguez Domingues Manzana G#7 Varina Venezuela
1980-114	Salazar, Luis Ernesto	Old Add: 9974 Boca River Circle Boca Raton FL 33433
1924-093	Sale, Frederick Link	D. May 27, 1956 Hermosa Beach, Calif.
1993-159	Salkeld, Roger William	251 East Baylor Lane/Gilbert AZ 85296
1945-089	Salkeld, William Franklin	D. April 22, 1967 Los Angeles, Calif.
1912-169	Salmon, Roger Elliott	D. June 17, 1974 Belfast, Me.
1964-099	Salmon, Rutherford Eduardo 'Chico'	Almirante, Bocas Del Toro Panama/City Panama
1992-125	Salmon, Timothy James	1265 East Friess Drive/Phoenix AZ 85022
1932-072	Saltzgaver, Otto Hamlin 'Jack'	D. February 2, 1978 Keokuk, Ia.
1933-058	Salveson, John Theodore	D. December 28, 1974 Norwalk, Calif.
1939-103	Salvo, Manuel	D. February 7, 1997 Vallejo, Calif.
1976-085	Sambito, Joseph Charles	400 Randal Way #106/Spring TX 77388
1951-085	Samcoff, Edward William	8153 Madeira Port Lane/Fair Oaks CA 95628
1954-096	Samford, Ronald Edward	1325 West Canterbury Court/Dallas TX 75208
1990-140	Sampen, William Albert	11 Carnaby Court/Brownsburg IN 46112
1978-116	Sample, William Amos	10 Pascack Road/Westwood NJ 7675
1962-118	Samuel, Amado Ruperto	1931 Yale Dr/Louisville KY 40205
1983-127	Samuel, Juan Milton	700 Cypress Point West/Pembroke Pines FL 33027
1930-070	Samuels, Joseph Jones	D. October 28, 1996 Bath, N. Y.
1988-116	Samuels, Roger Howard	4865 Tampico Way/San Jose CA 95118
1923-115	Sanberg, Gustave E.	D. February 3, 1930 Los Angeles, Calif.

1982-108	Sanchez, Alejandro	Boca Chica Gatey Gautir Santo Domingo Dominican Rep.
1989-109	Sanchez, Alejandro Anthony	2100 Fuente Court/Antioch CA 94509
1972-095	Sanchez, Celerino (Perez)	D. May 1, 1992 Leon, Guanajunto, Mexico
1988-117	Sanchez, Israel	5444 North Spaulding Avenue/Chicago IL 60625
1981-114	Sanchez, Luis Mercedes Esco	Quinta Normadelyn #10881 El Cordon Cariaco Venezuela
1981-115	Sanchez, Orlando	Old Add: Box San Isodro P52 Canovanos PR 00629
1952-089	Sanchez, Raul Guadalupe	17821 Nw 56th Avenue/Coral City FL 33054
1991-154	Sanchez, Rey Francisco	Old Add: 4399 Willow Grove Rd Charlotte Harbour FL 33980
1923-116	Sand, John Henry 'Heinie'	D. November 3, 1958 San Francisco, Calif.
1981-116	Sandberg, Ryne Dee	3630 East Coconino Court/Phoenix AZ 85044
1945-090	Sanders, Dee Wilma	1312 Country Club Road/McAlester OK 74501
1989-110	Sanders, Deion Luwynn	Old Add: 125 West Meadows CT Alpharetta GA 30201
1965-093	Sanders, John Frank	12810 Sagamore Road/Leawood KS 66209
1964-100	Sanders, Kenneth George	12141 Parkview Ln/Hales Corners WI 53130
1942-091	Sanders, Raymond Floyd	D. October 28, 1983 Washington, Mo.
1974-117	Sanders, Reginald Jerome	5281 Newport/Detroit MI 48213
1991-155	Sanders, Reginald Laverne	PO Box 15273/Quinby SC 29506
1917-054	Sanders, Roy Garvin	D. January 17, 1950 Kansas City, Mo.
1918-064	Sanders, Roy Lee	D. July 8, 1963 Louisville, Ky.
1993-160	Sanders, Scott Gerald	13795 Camino Del Suelo/San Diego CA 92129
1978-117	Sanderson, Scott, Douglas	945 Newcastle Drive/Lake Forest IL 60033
1942-092	Sandlock, Michael Joseph	18 Rock Land Place/Old Greenwich CT 6870
1967-096	Sands, Charles Duane	3 Nottingham Way/Haines City FL 33844
1975-102	Sandt, Thomas James	Old Add: 15789 Murwood CT Lake Oswego OR 97035
1940-078	Sanford, John Doward	1001 Kenan Street West/Wilson NC 27893
1943-120	Sanford, John Frederick 'Fred'	1046 West 600 North/Salt Lake City/Ut 84116
1956-074	Sanford, John Stanley 'Jack'	105 Greenbrier Lane/Daniels WV 25832
1991-156	Sanford, Meredith Leroy 'Mo'	2800 Hwy 389/Starkville MS 39759
1967-097	Sanguillen, Manuel Dejesus	Old Add: 661 Woodcrest Drive/Pittsburgh PA 15205
1949-078	Sanicki, Edward Robert	D. July 6, 1998 Old Bridge, N. J.
1929-091	Sankey, Benjamin Turner	443 Wrightsboro Road/Washington GA 30673
1990-141	Santana, Andres Confesor (Belonis)	Calle 1 327 Quisqueya San Pedro De Macoris Dominican Rep.
1997-149	Santana, Julio Franklin	Old Add: San Pedro De Macoris D. R.
1983-128	Santana, Rafael Francisco	Villa Pereyra Calle Ira #99 Laromana Dominican Rep.
1995-197	Santangello, Frank Paul 'F.P.'	Old Add: El Dorado CA 95623
1986-134	Santiago, Benito	12503 Nw 23rd Street/Pembroke Pines FL 33028
1954-097	Santiago, Jose Guillermo	56-Se-No. 1167/Rio Piedras PR 921
1997-150	Santiago, Jose Rafael	Old Add: Loiza PR 00772
1963-104	Santiago, Jose Rafael	Yagrumo Street Z-12 Valle Arriba Heights Carolina PR 893
1960-092	Santo, Ronald Edward	1721 Meadow Lane/Bannockburn IL 60015
1979-098	Santodomingo, Rafael	PO Box 21/Orocovis PR 720
1968-091	Santorini, Alan Joel	Rr 2, Arthur Rd/Belle Meade NJ 8502
1987-129	Santovenia, Nelson Gil	Old Add: 12350 SW 185th St Miami FL 33177
1921-090	Sargent, Joseph Alexander	D. July 5, 1950 Rochester, N. Y.
1976-086	Sarmiento, Manuel Eduardo	Sabana Larga #70 Aragua Venezuela
1951-086	Sarni, William Florine	D. April 15, 1983 Creve Coeur, Mo.
1987-130	Sasser, Mack Daniel	712 Adkinson Road/Newton AL 36352
1961-094	Satriano, Thomas Victor	11661 San Vicente Blvd #615/Los Angeles CA 90049
1951-087	Saucier, Francis Field	1615 Bryan Place #9/Amarillo TX 79102
1978-118	Saucier, Kevin Andrew	2316 Silversides Loop/Pensacola FL 32526
1943-121	Sauer, Edward	D. July 1, 1988 Thousand Oaks, Calif.
1941-097	Sauer, Henry John	207 Vallejo Court/Millbrae CA 94030
1997-151	Saunders, Anthony Scott	Old Add: Severn MD 21144
1970-118	Saunders, Dennis James	Old Add: 19971 Ave Del Rey/Rowland Heights CA
1993-161	Saunders, Douglas Long	5791 Mountain View/Yorba Linda CA 92686
1927-078	Saunders, Russell Collier 'Rusty'	D. November 24, 1967 Dover Twp.,Ocean Co,N.J.
1986-135	Sauveur, Richard Daniel	3312 47th Avenue East/Bradenton FL 34203
1944-117	Savage, Donald Anthony	D. December 25, 1961 Montclair, N. J.
1912-170	Savage, James Harold	D. June 26, 1940 New Castle, Pa.
1987-131	Savage, John Joseph	2501 Clearbrook Drive/Louisville KY 40220
1942-093	Savage, John Robert 'Bob'	12 Raycrest Drive/Randolph/Nh 3570
1962-119	Savage, Theodore Ephesian	1510 Mallard Landing Court/Chesterfield MO 63017
1959-070	Saverine, Robert Paul	228 Slice Dr/Stamford CT 6907
1929-092	Savidge, Donald Snyder	D. March 22, 1983 Santa Barbara, Calif.
1954-098	Savransky, Morris 'Moe'	3745 Manhattan Street #65/Las Vegas NV 89109
1948-088	Sawatski, Carl Ernest	D. November 24, 1991 Little Rock, Ark.
1915-142	Sawyer, Carl Everett	D. January 17, 1957 Los Angeles, Calif.
1948-089	Sawyer, Edwin Milby	D. September 22, 1997 Phoenixville, Pa.
1974-118	Sawyer, Richard Clyde	1316 Crawford Street/Bakersfield CA 93301
1982-109	Sax, David John	Old Add: 120 Hart Ave West Sacramento CA 95691
1928-079	Sax, Erik Oliver 'Ollie'	D. March 21, 1982 Newark, N. J.
1981-117	Sax, Stephen Louis	201 Wesley Court/Roseville CA 95661
1939-104	Sayles, William Nisbeth	D. November 20, 1996 Lincoln City, Ore.
1948-090	Scala, Gerard Michael	D. December 14, 1993 Fallston, Md.
1939-105	Scalzi, Frank Joseph	D. August 25, 1984 Pittsburgh, Pa.
1931-077	Scalzi, John Anthony	D. September 27, 1962 Port Chester, N. Y.
1991-157	Scanlan, Robert Guy	3190 Black Hills Court/Westlake Village CA 91362
1974-119	Scanlon, James Patrick 'Pat'	7400 Portland Ave South/Richfield MN 55423
1956-075	Scantlebury, Patricio Athelstan	D. May 24, 1991 Glen Ridge, N.J.

1979-099	Scarbery, Randy James	5010 East Lewis/Fresno CA 93727
1942-094	Scarborough, Ray Wilson	D. July 1, 1982 Mount Olive Nc
1972-096	Scarce, Guerrant McCurdy 'Mac'	1708 Broadmoor Dr/Richmond VA 23221
1929-093	Scarritt, Stephen Russell Mallory	D. December 4, 1994 Pensacola, Fla.
1935-096	Scarsella, Leslie George	D. December 16, 1958 San Francisco, Calif.
1992-126	Scarsone, Steven Wayne	803 Freedom Circle/Harleysville PA 19438
1964-101	Schaal, Paul	17520 South Cody Street/Olathe KS 66062
1919-072	Schacht, Alexander	D. July 14, 1984 Waterbury, Conn.
1950-087	Schacht, Sidney	D. March 30, 1991 Fort Lauderdale, Fla.
1945-091	Schacker, Harold	4609 North Matanzas Avenue/Tampa FL 33614
1989-111	Schaefer, Jeffrey Scott	20 Brightwood Street/Patchogue NY 11772
1991-158	Schaefer, Robert Walden	9070 Old Hickory Circle/Fort Myers FL 33912
1952-090	Schaeffer, Harry Edward	412 Wheatland Avenue/Shillington PA 19607
1972-097	Schaeffer, Mark Philip	18261 Parthenia St/Northridge CA 91324
1961-095	Schaffer, Jimmie Ronald	655 Birch Ter/Coopersburg PA 18036
1959-071	Schaffernoth, Joseph Arthur	20 Marian Ave/Berkley Heights NJ 7922
1958-079	Schaive, John Edward	8000 Wilson Terrace/Springfield IL 62707
1932-073	Schalk, Leroy John	D. March 11, 1990 Gainesville, Texas
1912-171	Schalk, Raymond William	D. May 19, 1970 Chicago, Ill.
1995-198	Schall, Eugene David	2702 Dillie Circle/Jamison PA 18929
1911-148	Schaller, Walter 'Biff'	D. October 9, 1939 Emeryville, Calif.
1951-088	Schallock, Arthur Lawrence	749 Crocus Drive/Sonoma CA 95476
1914-186	Schang, Robert Martin	D. August 29, 1966 Sacramento, Calif.
1913-154	Schang, Walter Henry	D. March 6, 1965 St. Louis, Mo.
1944-118	Schanz, Charles Murrell	D. May 28, 1992 Sacramento, Calif.
1911-149	Schardt, Wilburt	D. July 20, 1964 Vermilion, O.
1932-074	Scharein, Arthur Otto	D. July 3, 1969 San Antonio, Tex.
1937-092	Scharein, George Albert	D. December 22, 1981 Decatur, Ill.
1981-118	Schattinger, Jeffery	PO Box 134/Lake Arrowhead CA 92352
1977-126	Schatzeder, Daniel Ernest	416 East North Broadway St/Lombard IL 60148
1913-155	Schauer, Alexander John 'Rube'	D. April 15, 1957 Minneapolis, Minn.
1913-156	Scheer, Allan G.	D. May 6, 1959 Logansport, Ind.
1922-119	Scheer, Henry 'Heinie'	D. March 21, 1976 New Haven, Conn.
1914-187	Scheeren, Frederick 'Fritz'	D. June 17, 1973 Oil City, Pa.
1943-122	Scheetz, Owen Franklin	D. September 28, 1994 Pickerington, O.
1941-098	Scheffing, Robert Boden	D. October 26, 1985 Phoenix, Ariz.
1912-172	Schegg, Gilbert Eugene Price 'Lefty'	D. February 27, 1963 Niles, O.
1943-123	Scheib, Carl Alvin	2922 Old Ranch Road/San Antonio TX 78217
1992-127	Scheid, Richard Paul	One Hancock Court/East Windsor NJ 8520
1965-094	Scheinblum, Richard Alan 'Richie'	Old Add: PO Box 7245 Northridge CA 91327
1954-099	Schell, Clyde Daniel 'Danny'	D. May 11, 1972 Mayville, Mich.
1939-106	Schelle, Gerard Anthony 'Jim'	D. May 4, 1990 Weymouth, Mass.
1923-117	Schemanske, Frederick George	D. February 18, 1960 Detroit, Mich.
1945-092	Schemer, Michael 'Lefty'	D. April 22, 1983 Miami, Fla.
1913-157	Scheneberg, John Bluford	D. September 7, 1950 Huntington, W. Va.
1946-091	Schenz, Henry Leonard 'Hank'	D. May 12, 1988 Cincinnati, O.
1919-073	Schepner, Joseph Martin	D. July 25, 1959 Mobile, Ala.
1950-088	Scherbarth, Robert Elmer	Hc 1 Box 37/Presque Isle WI 54557
1969-154	Scherman, Frederick John	5019 Lausanne Drive/Dayton OH 45458
1982-110	Scherrer, William Joseph	Old Add: 1149 Concord Avenue Spring Hill FL 34606
1931-078	Schesler, Charles 'Dutch'	D. November 19, 1953 Harrisburg, Pa.
1910-131	Schettler, Louis Martin	D. May 1, 1960 Youngstown, O.
1917-075	Schick, Maurice Francis	D. October 25, 1979 Hazel Crest, Ill.
1961-096	Schilling, Charles Thomas	5 Carlisle Road/Miller Place NY 11764
1988-118	Schilling, Curtis Montague	Old Add: 3935 East Willow Avenue Phoenix AZ 85032
1922-120	Schillings, Elbert Isaiah 'Red'	D. January 7, 1940 Oklahoma City, Okla.
1920-101	Schindler, William Gibbons	D. February 6, 1979 Perryville, Mo.
1984-105	Schiraldi, Calvin Drew	10915 Crown Colony Drive/Austin TX 78747
1914-188	Schirick, Harry Ernest 'Dutch'	D. November 12, 1968 Kingston, N.Y.
1965-095	Schlesinger, William Cordes	5708 Abelia Court/Cincinnati OH 45213
1923-118	Schliebner, Frederick Paul 'Dutch'	D. April 15, 1975 Toledo, O.
1971-091	Schlueter, Jayd	5232 East Shaw Butte Drive/Scottsdale AZ 85254
1938-089	Schlueter, Norman John	4211 Gull Cove/New Smyrna Beach FL 32069
1915-143	Schmandt, Raymond Henry	D. February 1, 1969 St. Louis, Mo.
1952-091	Schmees, George Edward	D. October 30, 1998 San Jose, Calif.
1967-098	Schmelz, Alan George	4638 East Desert Cove/Phoenix AZ 85028
1995-199	Schmidt, Curtis Allen	PO Box 2372/Miles City MT 59301
1981-119	Schmidt, David Frederick	Old Add: 26636 Portales Mission Viejo 92675
1981-120	Schmidt, David Joseph	17173 Rayen Street/Northridge CA 91325
1944-119	Schmidt, Frederick Albert	Old Add: PO Box 711 Emmaus PA 18049
1913-158	Schmidt, Herman Frederick 'Pete'	D. November 11, 1973 Pembroke, Ont.
1995-200	Schmidt, Jason David	%Ray Schmidt 134 Alameda Drive Kelso WA 98626
1996-166	Schmidt, Jeffrey Thomas	3409 Leonard Street/Lacrosse WI 54601
1972-098	Schmidt, Michael Jack	373 Eagle Drive/Jupiter FL 33477
1958-080	Schmidt, Robert Benjamin	9 Hardwood St/St Charles MO 63301
1916-073	Schmidt, Walter Joseph	D. July 4, 1973 Ceres, Calif.
1952-092	Schmidt, Willard Raymond	3726 N. Country Club Drive/Newcastle OK 73065
1941-099	Schmitz, John Albert	526 East Union Avenue/Wausau WI 54401
1943-124	Schmulbach, Henry Alrives	29 Dale Allen Drive/Belleville IL 62223

1914-189 ....Schmutz, Charles Otto ....D. June 27, 1962 Seattle, Wash.
1972-099 ....Schneck, David Lee ....3891 Lehigh Dr/Northampton PA 18067
1910-132 ....Schneiberg, Frank Frederick....................D. May 18, 1948 Milwaukee, Wis.
1963-105 ....Schneider, Daniel Louis ....PO Box 2421/Tubac AZ 85646
1981-121 ....Schneider, Jeffery Theodore....................321 East Park Street/Geneseo IL 61254
1914-190 ....Schneider, Peter Joseph ....D. June 1, 1957 Los Angeles, Calif.
1922-121 ....Schnell, Karl Otto ....D. May 31, 1992 Palo Alto, Calif.
1968-092 ....Schoen, Gerald Thomas ....Old Add: 1835 East Jasmine Drive/Tempe AZ 85284
1945-093 ....Schoendienst, Albert Fred 'Red'............1105 Jo Carr Drive/Town And Country MO 63017
1953-079 ....Schofield, John Richard 'Dick' ....138 Circle Dr/Springfield IL 62703
1983-129 ....Schofield, Richard Craig ....18606 Charlvoix Lane/Chesterfield MO 63005
1988-119 ....Schooler, Michael Ralph ....3964 Camino Lindo/San Diego CA 92122
1955-103 ....Schoonmaker, Jerald Lee ....8343 Schreider Ave/Munster IN 46321
1915-144 ....Schorr, Edward Walter................................D. September 12, 1969 Atlantic City, N.J.
1935-097 ....Schott, Arthur Eugene ....D. November 16, 1992 Sun City Center, Fla.
1991-159 ....Schourek, Peter Alan ....2343 Dale Drive/Falls Church VA 22043
1953-080 ....Schramka, Paul Edward............................13111 West Lucille Lane/Butler WI 53007
1911-150 ....Schreiber, David Henry 'Barney'...........D. October 6, 1964 Chillicothe, O.
1914-191 ....Schreiber, Henry Walter ....D. February 23, 1968 Indianapolis, Ind.
1922-122 ....Schreiber, Paul Frederick ....D. January 28, 1982 Sarasota, Fla.
1963-106 ....Schreiber, Theodore Henry ....144 Jerome Road/Staten Island NY 10305
1965-096 ....Schroder, Robert James ....7783 East Lorenzo Lane/Yuma AZ 85365
1983-130 ....Schroeder, Alfred William Bill ....10025 West Edgerton Avenue/Hales Corner WI 53130
1958-081 ....Schroll, Albert Bringhurst ....10427 Clearwater Road/Ocean Springs MS 39565
1980-115 ....Schrom, Kenneth Marvin ....713 Rosinante/El Paso TX 79922
1984-106 ....Schu, Rick Spencer ....11862 Marjon Ave/Nevada City CA 95959
1927-079 ....Schuble, Henry George 'Heine' ....D. October 2, 1990 Baytown, Texas
1972-100 ....Schueler, Ronald Richard ....10750 Churchill Drive/Orland Park IL 60462
1979-100 ....Schuler, David Paul ....406 Waters Edge Drive/Newark DE 19702
1994-093 ....Schullstrom, Erik Paul ....Old Add: Rural Route Ss Alameda CA 94501
1931-079 ....Schulmerich, Edward Wesley 'Wes'.....D. June 26, 1985 Corvallis, Ore.
1953-081 ....Schult, Arthur William ....231 East Lantana Rd/Lantana FL 33462
1927-080 ....Schulte, Fred William ....D. May 20, 1983 Belvidere, Ill.
1940-079 ....Schulte, Herman Joseph ....D. December 21, 1993 Saint Charles, Mo.
1923-119 ....Schulte, John Clement.............................D. June 28, 1978 St. Louis, Mo.
1944-120 ....Schulte, Leonard William ....D. May 6, 1986 Orlando, Fla.
1975-103 ....Schultz, Charles Budd ....6510 North 59th Street/Paradise Valley AZ 85253
1955-104 ....Schultz, George Warren 'Barney' ....790 Woodlane Rd/Beverly NJ 8010
1943-125 ....Schultz, Howard Henry ....1333 McKusick Road Lane West/Stillwater MN 55082
1939-107 ....Schultz, Joseph Charles ....D. January 10, 1996 Saint Louis, Mo.
1912-173 ....Schultz, Joseph Charles, Sr. ....D. April 13, 1941 Columbia, S.C.
1951-089 ....Schultz, Robert Duffy ....D. March 31, 1979 Nashville, Tenn.
1924-094 ....Schultz, Webb Carl ....D. July 26, 1986 Delavan, Wisc.
1947-076 ....Schultz, William Michael 'Mike' ....502 Roby Avenue/East Syracuse NY 13057
1912-174 ....Schulz, Albert Christopher ....D. December 13, 1931 Toledo, O.
1989-112 ....Schulz, Jeffrey Alan ....1167 South Stockwell Road/Evansville IN 47715
1920-102 ....Schulz, Walter Frederick ....D. February 27, 1928 Prescott, Ariz.
1983-131 ....Schulze, Donald Arthur ....Old Add: PO Box 287 West Chicago IL 60186
1931-080 ....Schumacher, Harold Henry ....D. April 21, 1993 Cooperstown, N. Y.
1913-159 ....Schupp, Ferdinand Maurice ....D. December 16, 1971 Los Angeles, Calif.
1964-102 ....Schurr, Wayne Allen ....10030 West 500 South/Hudson IN 46747
1937-093 ....Schuster, William Charles ....D. June 28, 1987 El Monte, Calif.
1996-167 ....Schutz, Carl James ....313 East 14th/Gramercy LA 70052
1989-113 ....Schwabe, Michael Scott ....Old Add: Orange CA
1961-097 ....Schwall, Donald Bernard ....2000 Lake Marshall Drive/Gibsonia PA 15044
1948-091 ....Schwamb, Ralph Richard ....D. December 21, 1989 Lancaster, Calif.
1965-097 ....Schwartz, Douglas Randall 'Randy' ....757 El Rancho Dr/El Cajon CA 92019
1993-162 ....Schwarz, Jeffrey William ....2310 Sweetwater Drive/Fort Pierce FL 33481
1914-192 ....Schwarz, William Dewitt ....D. June 24, 1949 Jacksonville Beach, Fla.
1913-160 ....Schwenk, Harold Edward ....D. September 3, 1955 Kansas City, Mo.
1914-193 ....Schwert, Pius Louis ....D. March 11, 1941 Washington, D.C.
1912-175 ....Schwind, Arthur Edwin ....D. January 13, 1968 Sullivan,Ill.
1955-105 ....Schypinski, Gerald Albert ....28014 Shadowood Lane/Selfridge MI 48045
1980-116 ....Scioscia, Michael Lorri ....1911 Falling Star Avenue/Westlake Village CA 91362
1936-083 ....Scoffic, Louis ....D. August 28, 1997 Herrin, Ill.
1913-161 ....Scoggins, James Lynn ....D. August 16, 1923 Columbia, S.C.
1981-122 ....Sconiers, Daryl Anthony ....Old Add: 16 Wilderness Place Pomona CA 91766
1955-106 ....Score, Herbert Jude ....% Wknr Radio 9446 Broadview Road Cleveland OH 44147
1973-106 ....Scott, Anthony ....PO Box 1893/Spartanburg SC 29304
1993-163 ....Scott, Darryl Nelson ....105 Estates Drive/Chico CA 95928
1983-132 ....Scott, Donald Malcolm ....6042 114th Terrace North/Pinellas Park FL 34666
1926-073 ....Scott, Floyd John 'Pete'.........................D. May 3, 1953 Daly City, Calif.
1991-160 ....Scott, Gary Thomas ....50 Linden Avenue/Pelham NY 10803
1966-081 ....Scott, George ....1316 Goodrich Street/Greenville MS 38701
1920-103 ....Scott, George William ....Old Add: Corsicana TX 75110
1914-194 ....Scott, James Walter ....D. May 12, 1972 South Pasadena, Fla.
1974-120 ....Scott, John Henry ....Old Add: 1756 E. 111th Place Los Angeles CA 90059
1916-074 ....Scott, John William ....D. November 30, 1959 Durham, N. C.
1939-108 ....Scott, Legrant Edward ....D. November 12, 1993 Birmingham, Ala.

1914-195	Scott, Lewis Everett	D. November 2, 1960 Fort Wayne, Ind.
1945-094	Scott, Marshall 'Lefty'	D. March 3, 1964 Houston, Tex.
1979-101	Scott, Michael Warren	28355 Chat Drive/Laguna Niguel CA 92677
1972-101	Scott, Ralph Robert 'Mickey'	1134 Vestal Ave/Binghamton NY 13903
1989-114	Scott, Richard Edward	Old Add: 56 Pine Street Ellsworth Me 04605
1963-107	Scott, Richard Louis	PO Box 525/Thomasville GA 31799
1975-104	Scott, Rodney Darrell	4206 Priscilla/Indianapolis IN 46226
1991-161	Scott, Timothy Dale	Old Add: 822 Mulberry Drive Hanford CA 93230
1984-107	Scranton, James Dean	18207 Brightman/Lake Elsinore CA 92530
1975-105	Scrivener, Wayne Allison	1766 Hazel/Birmingham MI 48009
1991-162	Scruggs, Anthony Raymond	Old Add: 890 Rengshorft Ave Mountain View CA 94043
1989-115	Scudder, William Scott Scott	PO Box 6/Blossom TX 75416
1980-117	Scurry, Rodney Grant	D. November 5, 1992 Reno, Nev.
1964-103	Seale, Johnnie Ray	1941 County Rd 207/Durango CO 81301
1979-102	Seaman, Kim Michael	3106 Canty Street/Pascagoula MS 39567
1989-116	Seanez, Rudy Caballero	1029 Jennifer Street/Brawley CA 92227
1981-123	Searage, Raymond Mark	9737 Pine Lake Trail/Saint Petersburg FL 33708
1988-120	Searcy, William Stephen Steve	4113 Fulton Drive/Knoxville TN 37918
1943-126	Sears, Kenneth Eugene	D. July 17, 1968 Bridgeport, Tex.
1912-176	Seaton, Thomas Gordon	D. April 10, 1940 Elpaso, Tex.
1940-080	Seats, Thomas Edward	D. May 10, 1992 San Ramon, Calif.
1967-099	Seaver, George Thomas 'Tom'	PO Box 4660/Avon CO 81620
1985-102	Sebra, Robert Bush	20 Misners Trail/Ormond Beach FL 32174
1940-081	Secory, Frank Edward	D. April 7, 1995 Port Huron, Mich.
1969-155	Secrist, Donald Laverne	5851 Park Road/Pinckneyville IL 62274
1921-091	Sedgewick, Henry Kenneth 'Duke'	D. December 4, 1982 Clearwater, Fla.
1919-074	See, Charles Henry	D. July 19, 1948 Bridgeport, Conn.
1986-136	See, Ralph Laurence Larry	1913 West Remington Drive/Chandler AZ 85248
1930-071	Seeds, Ira Robert 'Bob'	D. October 28, 1993 Erick, Okla.
1971-092	Seelbach, Charles Frederick	17896 Captains Cove/Cleveland OH 44107
1943-127	Seerey, James Patrick 'Pat'	D. April 28, 1986 Jennings, Mo.
1995-201	Sefcik, Kevin John	Old Add: Tinley Park IL 60477
1982-111	Segelke, Herman Neils	Old Add: 384 Heather Way South San Francisco CA 94080
1952-093	Segrist, Kal Hill	3813 55th Street/Lubbock TX 79413
1990-142	Segui, David Vincent	2740 North 131st Street/Kansas City KS 66109
1962-120	Segui, Diego Pablo	13421 Leavenworth Rd/Kansas City KS 66109
1988-121	Segura, Jose Altagracia	Calle Colon #8 Fundacion,/Barahona Dominican Rep.
1979-103	Seibert, Kurt Elliott	6518 Allview Drive/Columbia MD 21046
1915-145	Seibold, Harry 'Socks'	D. September 21, 1965 Philadelphia, Pa.
1980-118	Seilheimer, Ricky Allen	355 Old Burton Road/Brenham TX 77833
1986-137	Seitzer, Kevin Lee	409 Holly Drive/Lincoln IL 62656
1996-168	Selby, William Frank	5772 Ashford Drive/Walls MS 38680
1993-164	Sele, Aaron Helmer	Old Add: PO Box 543 Suquamish WA 98392
1934-090	Selkirk, George Alexander	D. January 19, 1987 Fort Lauderdale, Fla.
1922-123	Sell, Elwood Lester 'Epp'	D. February 20, 1961 Reading, Pa.
1985-103	Sellers, Jeffrey Doyle	Old Add: 5823 Clark Ave Lakewood CA 90712
1910-133	Sellers, Oliver 'Rube'	D. January 14, 1952 Pittsburgh, Pa.
1972-102	Sells, David Wayne	Old Add: 3233 East Greenleaf Brea CA 92621
1965-098	Selma, Richard Jay	1493 North Delmar Avenue/Fresno CA 93728
1929-094	Selph, Carey Isom	D. February 24, 1976 Houston, Tex.
1977-127	Sember, Michael David	PO Box 811804/Boca Raton FL 33481
1965-099	Sembera, Carroll William	Box 1103/Shiner TX 77984
1992-128	Seminara, Frank Peter	8029 Harbor View Terrace/Brooklyn NY 11209
1943-128	Seminick, Andrew Wasil	110 Peelskill Place/Melbourne FL 32901
1958-082	Semproch, Roman Anthony 'Ray'	4220 Buechner Ave/Cleveland OH 44109
1952-094	Senerchia, Emanuel Robert 'Sonny'	513 Passaic Avenue/Spring Lake NJ 7762
1982-112	Senteney, Stephen Leonard	D. June 19, 1989 Colusa, Calif.
1977-128	Seoane, Manuel Modesto	8912 Southern Drive/Tampa FL 33615
1942-095	Sepkowski, Theodore Walter	128 Inverness Road/Severna Park MD 21146
1996-169	Serafini, Daniel Joseph	2501 Bennington Drive/San Bruno CA 94066
1949-079	Serena, William Robert	D. April 17, 1996 Hayward, Calif.
1981-124	Serna, Paul David	1375 Camino Verde/Holtville CA 92250
1977-129	Serum, Gary Wayne	13996 Wellington Drive/Eden Prairie MN 55344
1991-163	Servais, Scott Daniel	508 Providence Drive/Castle Rock CO 80104
1988-122	Service, Scott David	1619 Vandalia/Cincinnati OH 45223
1941-100	Sessi, Walter Anthony	D. April 18, 1998 Mobile, Ala.
1928-080	Settlemire, Edgar Merle	D. June 12, 1988 Russell Point, O.
1965-100	Sevcik, John Joseph	3518 Barrington Street/San Antonio TX 78217
1911-151	Severaid, Henry Levai	D. December 17, 1968 San Antonio, Tex.
1969-156	Severinsen, Albert Henry	133 Warren Avenue/Mystic CT 6355
1970-119	Severson, Richard Allen	1036 North 145th Circle/Omaha NE 68154
1943-129	Seward, Frank Martin	117 Larchmont Road/Elmira NY 14905
1921-092	Sewell, James Luther 'Luke'	D. May 14, 1987 Akron, O.
1920-104	Sewell, Joseph Wheeler	D. March 3, 1990 Mobile, Ala.
1927-081	Sewell, Thomas Wesley	D. July 30, 1956 Montgomery, Ala.
1932-075	Sewell, Truett Banks 'Rip'	D. September 3, 1889 Plant City, Fla.
1948-092	Sexauer, Elmer George	826 Hancock Bridge Pkwy/Cape Coral FL 33990
1997-152	Sexson, Richmond Lockwood 'Richie'	18816 NE 130th Circle/Brush Prairie WA 98606
1977-130	Sexton, Jimmy Dale	2680 Baxter Road/Wilmer AL 36587

1963-108 ....Seyfried, Gordon Clay ....216 South Ponderosa Way/Evergreen CO 80439
1914-196 ....Shafer, Ralph Newton ....D. February 5, 1950 Akron, O.
1965-101 ....Shamsky, Arthur Lewis ....PO Box 1400/Grand Central Station New York NY 10017
1973-107 ....Shanahan, Paul Gregory 'Greg' ....PO Box 6428/Eureka CA 95502
1923-120 ....Shaner, Walter Dedaker ....D. November 13, 1992 Las Vegas, Nev.
1970-120 ....Shank, Harvey Tillman ....3123 East Vermont/Phoenix AZ 85016
1912-177 ....Shanks, Howard Samuel ....D. July 30, 1941 Monaca, Pa.
1912-178 ....Shanley, Henry Root 'Doc' ....D. December 14, 1934 St. Petersburg, Fla.
1920-105 ....Shanner, Wilfred William 'Bill' ....D. December 18, 1986 Evansville, Ind.
1915-146 ....Shannon, Joseph Aloysius ....D. July 28, 1955 Jersey City, N.J.
1915-147 ....Shannon, Maurice Joseph 'Red' ....D. April 12, 1970 Jersey City, N.J.
1962-121 ....Shannon, Thomas Michael 'Mike' ....% Kmox Radio 1 South/Memorial Drive Saint Louis MO 63102
1959-072 ....Shannon, Walter Charles 'Wally' ....D. February 8, 1992 Creve Couer, Mo.
1949-080 ....Shantz, Robert Clayton ....152 Mount Pleasant Avenue/Ambler PA 19002
1954-100 ....Shantz, Wilmer Ebert ....D. December 13, 1993 Lauderhill, Fla.
1917-076 ....Sharman, Ralph Edward ....D. May 24, 1918 Camp Sheridan, Ala.
1973-108 ....Sharon, Richard Louis ....PO Box 349/Dillon MT 59725
1973-109 ....Sharp, William Howard ....2244 Thornwood/Wilmette IL 60091
1987-132 ....Sharperson, Michael Tyrone ....D. May 26, 1996 Las Vegas, Nev.
1922-124 ....Shaute, Joseph Benjamin ....D. February 21, 1970 Scranton, Pa.
1993-165 ....Shave, Jonathan Taylor ....5045 Crowne Chase Pkwy/Birmingham AL 35244
1988-123 ....Shaver, Jeffrey Thomas ....25016 Molokai Drive/Tega Cay SC 29815
1917-077 ....Shaw, Benjamin Nathaniel ....D. March 16, 1959 Aurora, O.
1967-100 ....Shaw, Donald Wellington ....12228 Poggemoeller/Saint Louis MO 63138
1913-162 ....Shaw, James Aloysius ....D. January 27, 1962 Washington, D.C.
1990-143 ....Shaw, Jeffrey Lee ....419 Eastern Avenue/Washington Court Hou OH 43160
1957-077 ....Shaw, Robert John ....222 Us Hwy One #208/Tequesta FL 33469
1913-163 ....Shawkey, James Robert 'Bob' ....D. December 31, 1980 Syracuse, N.Y.
1916-075 ....Shay, Arthur Joseph 'Marty' ....D. February 20, 1951 Worcester, Mass.
1947-077 ....Shea, Francis Joseph 'Spec' ....72 Johnson/Naugatuck CT 6770
1928-081 ....Shea, John Michael Joseph ....D. November 30, 1956 Malden, Mass.
1927-082 ....Shea, Mervyn David John ....D. January 27, 1953 Sacramento, Calif.
1918-065 ....Shea, Patrick Henry ....D. November 17, 1981 Stafford, Conn.
1968-093 ....Shea, Steven Francis ....8 Grove Street/Exeter NH 3833
1987-133 ....Sheaffer, Danny Todd ....123 Savannah Lane/Mount Airy NC 27030
1928-082 ....Shealy, Albert Berley ....D. March 7, 1967 Hagerstown, Md.
1957-078 ....Shearer, Ray Solomon ....D. February 21, 1982 York, Pa.
1912-179 ....Shears, George Penfield ....D. November 12, 1978 Loveland, Colo.
1936-084 ....Sheehan, James Thomas ....107 Robert Drive/East Haven CT 6512
1920-106 ....Sheehan, John Thomas ....D. May 29, 1987 West Palm Beach, Fla.
1915-148 ....Sheehan, Thomas Clancy ....D. October 29, 1982 Chillicothe, O.
1921-093 ....Sheely, Earl Homer ....D. September 16, 1952 Seattle, Wash,
1951-090 ....Sheely, Hollis Kimball 'Bud' ....D. October 17, 1985 Sacramento, Calif.
1936-085 ....Sheerin, Charles Joseph ....D. September 27, 1986 Valley Stream, N. Y.
1996-170 ....Sheets, Andrew Mark ....Old Add: Saint Amant LA 70774
1984-108 ....Sheets, Larry Kent ....1413 Lyle Avenue/Staunton VA 24401
1988-124 ....Sheffield, Gary Antonian ....6731 30th Street South/St. Petersburg FL 33712
1981-125 ....Shelby, John T. ....2232 Broadhead Lane/Lexington KY 40515
1974-121 ....Sheldon, Bob Mitchell ....25370 Lacebark Drive/Murrietta CA 92362
1961-098 ....Sheldon, Roland Frank ....614 NE Coronado/Lees Summit MO 64063
1997-153 ....Sheldon, Scott Patrick ....Old Add: Houston TX 77001
1918-066 ....Shellenback, Frank Victor ....D. August 17, 1969 Newton, Mass.
1966-082 ....Shellenback, James Philip ....482 Homestead Avenue North/Palm Bay FL 32907
1935-098 ....Shelley, Hubert Leneirre 'Hugh' ....D. June 16, 1978 Beaumont, Tex.
1915-149 ....Shelton, Andrew Kemper 'Skeeter' ....D. January 9, 1954 Huntington, W. Va.
1993-166 ....Shelton, Benjamin Davis ....530 South Humphrey/Oak Park IL 60304
1944-121 ....Shemo, Stephen Michael ....D. April 13, 1992 Eden, N. C.
1945-095 ....Shepard, Bert Robert ....8014 Bangor Avenue/Hesperia CA 92345
1953-082 ....Shepard, Jack Leroy ....D. December 31, 1993 Atherton, Calif.
1968-094 ....Shepard, Lawrence William 'Larry' ....5610 Pioneers Blvd #294/Lincoln NE 68506
1924-095 ....Shephardson, Raymond Francis ....D. November 8, 1975 Little Falls, N.Y.
1992-129 ....Shepherd, Keith Wayne ....242 Gladstone Street/Wabash IN 46992
1984-109 ....Shepherd, Ronald Wayne ....Rr 2 Box 53x/Kilgore TX 75662
1918-067 ....Sherdel, William Henry ....D. November 14, 1968 McSherrystown, Pa.
1929-095 ....Sherid, Royden Richard ....D. February 28, 1982 Parker Ford, Pa.
1918-068 ....Sheridan, Eugene Anthony 'Red' ....D. November 25, 1975 Queens Village, N. Y.
1948-093 ....Sheridan, Neill Rawlins ....150 Chaucer Drive/Pleasant Hill CA 94523
1981-126 ....Sheridan, Patrick Arthur ....31654 Taft/Wayne MI 48184
1924-096 ....Sherling, Edward Creech ....D. November 16, 1965 Enterprise, Ala.
1930-072 ....Sherlock, John Clinton 'Monk' ....D. November 26, 1985 Buffalo, N. Y.
1935-099 ....Sherlock, Vincent Thomas ....D. May 11, 1997 Cheektowaga, N. Y.
1993-167 ....Sherman, Darrell Edward ....3576 Magnolia Avenue/Lynwood CA 90262
1915-150 ....Sherman, Joel Powers ....D. December 21, 1987 Cape Coral, Fla.
1914-197 ....Sherman, Lester Daniel 'Babe' ....D. September 16, 1955 Highland Park, Mich.
1978-119 ....Sherrill, Dennis Lee ....1691 Tolley Terrace SE/Palm Bay FL 32909
1990-144 ....Sherrill, Timothy Shawn ....PO Box 812/Harrison AR 72601
1911-152 ....Sherry, Fred Peter ....D. July 27, 1975 Honesdale, Pa.
1958-083 ....Sherry, Lawrence ....27181 Arena Ln/Mission Viejo CA 92675
1959-073 ....Sherry, Norman Burt ....4383-89 Nobel Drive/San Diego CA 92122

1959-074	Shetrone, Barry Stevan	34 Hampton Road/Linthicum Heights MD 21090
1930-073	Shevlin, James Cornelius	D. October 30, 1974 Fort Lauderdale, Fla.
1924-097	Shields, Benjamin Cowan	D. January 24, 1982 Woodruff, S. C.
1915-151	Shields, Francis Leroy 'Pete'	D. February 11, 1961 Jackson, Miss.
1985-104	Shields, Stephen Mack	4969 Leonard Drive/Gadsden AL 35903
1992-130	Shields, Thomas Charles	6700 Clark Road/Sarasota FL 34241
1924-098	Shields, Vincent William	D. November 24, 1952 Plaster Rock, Neb.
1957-079	Shifflett, Garland Jessie	1095 Cody/Lakewood CO 80215
1992-131	Shifflett, Steven Earl	24004 East 172nd Street/Pleasant Hill MO 64080
1939-109	Shilling, James Robert	D. September 12, 1986 Tulsa, Okla.
1993-168	Shinall, Zakary Sebastian	16605 Sell Circle/Huntington Beach CA 92649
1921-094	Shinault, Enoch Erskine 'Ginger'	D. December 29, 1930 Denver, Colo.
1983-133	Shines, Anthony Raymond 'Razor'	Old Add: PO Box 4669 Charleston WV 25304
1922-125	Shinners, Ralph Peter	D. July 23, 1962 Milwaukee, Wis.
1985-105	Shipanoff, David Noel	3 Salina Drive Saint Albert/Alberta Canada
1986-138	Shipley, Craig Barry	52 Beamish Road Northmead New South Wales 2152 Australia
1958-084	Shipley, Joseph Clark	23 Park Drive/Saint Charles MO 63303
1928-083	Shires, Charles Arthur 'Art'	D. July 13, 1967 Italy, Tex.
1920-107	Shirey, Clair Lee 'Duke'	D. September 1, 1962 Hagerstown, Md.
1941-101	Shirley, Alvis Newman 'Tex'	D. November 7, 1993 Desoto, Texas
1964-104	Shirley, Barton Arvin	3110 Crest Valley/Corpus Christi TX 78415
1924-099	Shirley, Ernest Raeford 'Mule'	D. August 3, 1955 Goldsboro, N. C.
1977-131	Shirley, Robert Charles	9641 South Sandusky Street/Tulsa OK 74137
1982-113	Shirley, Steven Brian	9200 James Place NE/Albuquerque NM 87111
1931-081	Shiver, Ivey Merwin	D. August 31, 1972 Savannah, Ga.
1916-076	Shocker, Urban James	D. September 9, 1928 Denver, Colo.
1964-105	Shockley, John Costen	405 Walter St/Georgetown DE 19947
1961-099	Shoemaker, Charles Landis	D. May 31, 1990 Mount Penn, Pa.
1929-096	Shoffner, Milburn James 'Milt'	D. January 19, 1978 Madison, O.
1947-078	Shofner, Frank Strickland 'Strick'	D. October 10, 1998 Crawford, Texas
1941-102	Shokes, Edward Christopher	222 Spring Street/Winchester VA 22601
1916-077	Shook, Raymand Curtis	D. September 16, 1970 South Bend, Ind.
1959-075	Shoop, Ronald Lee	Box 92/Rural Valley PA 16249
1967-101	Shopay, Thomas Michael	9600 Nw 38th Street #300/Miami FL 33178
1912-180	Shore, Ernest Grady	D. September 24, 1980 Winston-Salem, N.C.
1946-092	Shore, Raymond Everett	D. August 13, 1996 Saint Louis, Mo.
1928-084	Shores, William David	D. February 19, 1984 Purcell, Okla.
1959-076	Short, Christopher Joseph	D. August 1, 1991 Wilmington, Del.
1940-082	Short, David Orvis	D. November 22, 1983 Shreveport, La.
1960-093	Short, William Ross	2975 57th St/Sarasota FL 33580
1915-152	Shorten, Charles Henry 'Chick'	D. October 23, 1965 Scranton, Pa.
1935-100	Shoun, Clyde Mitchell	D. March 20, 1968 Mountain Home, Tenn.
1993-169	Shouse, Brian Douglas	1520 West Circle Road/Peoria IL 61604
1911-153	Shovlin, John Joseph	D. February 16, 1976 Bethesda, Md.
1981-127	Show, Eric Vaughn	D. March 16, 1994 Dulzura, Calif.
1992-132	Showalter, William Nathaniel 'Buck'	6730 East Exeter Blvd/Scottsdale AZ 85251
1922-126	Shriver, Harry Graydon	D. January 21, 1970 Morgantown, W. Va.
1948-094	Shuba, George Thomas 'Shotgun'	3421 Bent Willow Lane/Youngstown OH 44511
1994-094	Shuey, Paul Kenneth	8561 Acadia Drive/Sagamore Hills OH 44067
1911-154	Shultz, Wallace Luther 'Toots'	D. January 30, 1959 McKeesport, Pa.
1942-096	Shuman, Harry	D. October 25, 1996 Philadelphia, Pa.
1990-145	Shumpert, Terrance Darnell	1515 North 12th Street/Paducah KY 42001
1945-096	Shupe, Vincent William	D. April 5, 1962 Canton, O.
1916-078	Sicking, Edward Joseph	D. August 30, 1978 Cincinnati, O.
1993-170	Siddall, Joseph Todd	2785 Sierra Drive/Windsor Ontario N9E 2Y9 Canada
1956-076	Siebern, Norman Leroy	4089 Tamiami Trail North #A203/Naples FL 33940
1974-122	Siebert, Paul Edward	1711 Acker Street/Orlando FL 32837
1932-076	Siebert, Richard Walther	D. December 9, 1978 Minneapolis, Minn.
1964-106	Siebert, Wilfred Charles 'Sonny'	2555 Brush Creek/Saint Louis MO 63129
1963-109	Siebler, Dwight Leroy	11565 South 204th/Gretna NE 68028
1925-092	Siemer, Oscar Sylvester	D. September 5, 1959 St. Louis, Mo.
1986-139	Sierra, Ruben Angel	Old Add:/Ed. 25 #2501, Jard. Selles Rio Piedras PR 00924
1988-125	Sierra, Ulisses 'Candy'	Old Add: Bo. Torrecilla, Baja Buz. 108 Loiza PR 00672
1949-081	Sievers, Roy Edward	11505 Bellefontaine Road/Spanish Lake MO 63138
1926-074	Sigafoos, Francis Leonard	D. April 12, 1968 Indianapolis, Ind.
1914-198	Siglin, Wesley Peter 'Paddy'	D. August 5, 1956 Oakland, Calif.
1929-097	Sigman, Wesley Triplett 'Tripp'	D. March 8, 1971 Augusta, Ga.
1943-130	Signer, Walter Donald Aloysius	D. July 23, 1974 Greenwich, Conn.
1937-094	Silber, Edward James	D. October 26, 1976 Dunedin, Fla.
1919-075	Silva, Daniel James	D. April 4, 1974 Hyannis, Mass.
1996-171	Silva, Jose Leonel	Old Add: San Diego CA 92101
1955-107	Silvera, Aaron Albert 'Al'	723 North Sierra Dr/Beverly Hills CA 90210
1948-095	Silvera, Charles Anthony Ryan	1240 Manzanita Drive/Millbrae CA 94030
1978-120	Silverio, Luis Pascual	Calle 5 Casa #21, El Dorado Santiago Dominican Rep.
1970-121	Silverio, Tomas Roberto	Calle 9#14 Colinas Santo Domingo Dominican Rep.
1992-133	Silvestri, David Joseph	344 Buckhurst Drive/Ballwin MO 63021
1939-110	Silvestri, Kenneth Joseph	D. March 31, 1992 Tallahassee, Fla.
1950-089	Sima, Albert	D. August 17, 1993 Suffern, N. Y.
1995-202	Simas, William Anthony	6715 South Cherry/Fresno CA 93725

1924-100	Simmons, Aloysius Harry	D. May 26, 1956 Milwaukee, Wis.
1947-079	Simmons, Curtis Thomas	200 Park Road/Prospectville PA 19002
1910-134	Simmons, George Washington 'Hack'	D. April 26, 1942 Arverne, N.Y.
1949-082	Simmons, John Earl	9 Lee Drive/Farmingdale NY 11735
1984-110	Simmons, Nelson Bernard	209 Cedaridge Dr/San Diego CA 92114
1928-085	Simmons, Patrick Clement	D. July 3, 1968 Albany, N. Y.
1968-095	Simmons, Ted Lyle	PO Box 26/Chesterfield MO 63006
1990-146	Simms, Michael Howard	Old Add: 5951 Summit Yorba Linda CA 92686
1997-154	Simon, Randall Carlito	Old Add: Willemstad Curacao
1923-121	Simon, Sylvester Adam	D. February 28, 1973 Chandler, Ind.
1991-164	Simons, Douglas Eugene	552 Laurenburg Alne/Ocoee FL 34761
1931-082	Simons, Melbern Ellis	D. October 11, 1974 Paducah, Ky.
1951-091	Simpson, Harry Leon	D. April 3, 1979 Akron, O.
1975-106	Simpson, Joe Allen	4681 Jefferson Twp Lane/Marietta GA 30066
1962-122	Simpson, Richard Charles	696 San Juan Ave/Venice CA 90291
1972-103	Simpson, Steven Edward	D. November 2, 1989 Omaha, Neb.
1953-083	Simpson, Thomas Leo	100 West Broadway #1250/Glendale CA 91210
1970-122	Simpson, Wayne Kirby	330 Collamer Dr/Carson CA 90744
1915-153	Sims, Clarence 'Pete'	D. December 2, 1968 Dallas, Tex.
1964-107	Sims, Duane B. 'Duke'	10509 Shoalhaven Drive/Las Vegas NV 89134
1966-083	Sims, Gregory Emmett	6700 Rancho Pico Way/Sacramento CA 95828
1981-128	Sinatro, Matthew Stephen	21065 North 74th Way/Scottsdale AZ 85255
1964-108	Singer, William Robert	4572 Arrowhead Drive Se/Decatur Al 35603
1945-097	Singleton, Bert Elmer	D. January 5, 1996 Ogden, Utah
1994-095	Singleton, Duane Earl	Old Add: 16 Bond Street Staten Island NY 10302
1922-127	Singleton, John Edward	D. October 23, 1937 Dayton, O.
1970-123	Singleton, Kenneth Wayne	10 Sparks Farm Road/Spsrks MD 21152
1934-091	Sington, Frederic William	3238 Cornwall Drive/Birmingham AL 35226
1945-098	Sipek, Richard Francis	1611 Jackson Street/Quincy IL 62301
1969-157	Sipin, John White	328 Herman Ave/Watsonville CA 95076
1995-203	Sirotka, Michael Robert	15403 Misty Forest Court/Houston TX 77066
1982-114	Sisk, Douglas Randall	1408 Beach Drve NE/Tacoma WA 98422
1962-123	Sisk, Tommie Wayne	15 North 100 East #20/Provo UT 84606
1956-077	Sisler, David Michael	11 Hacienda Dr/Saint Louis MO 63124
1915-154	Sisler, George Harold	D. March 26, 1973 St. Louis, Mo.
1946-093	Sisler, Richard Allen	3704 Estes Road/#O/Nashville TN 37215
1939-111	Sisti, Sebastian Daniel 'Sibby'	38 Clifford Heights/Eggertsville NY 14226
1936-086	Sivess, Peter	531 Snow Hill Road/Franklin NC 28734
1982-115	Siwy, James Gerard	5721 Manito Circle/Las Vegas NV 89130
1969-158	Sizemore, Ted Crawford	Old Add: 1059 Fruit Tree Ln Creve Coeur MO 63141
1935-101	Skaff, Francis Michael	D. April 12, 1988 Towson, Md.
1977-132	Skaggs, David Lindsey	Old Add: 911 Dougherty Rd Norco CA 91760
1989-117	Skalski, Joseph Douglas	6423 Nevada Avenue/Hammond IN 46323
1957-080	Skaugstad, David Wendall	16222 Monterey Lane #274/Huntington Beach CA 92649
1910-135	Skeels, David	D. December 2, 1926 Spokane, Wash.
1942-097	Sketchley, Harry Clement 'Bud'	D. December 19, 1979 Los Angeles, Calif.
1970-124	Skidmore, Robert Roe	815 South Stone/Decatur IL 62521
1921-095	Skiff, William Franklin	D. December 25, 1976 Bronxville, N. Y.
1922-128	Skinner, Elisha Harrison 'Camp'	D. August 4, 1944 Douglasville, Ga.
1983-134	Skinner, Joel Patrick	24310 Lake Drive/Bay Village OH 44140
1954-101	Skinner, Robert Ralph	1576 Diamond St/San Diego CA 92109
1956-078	Skizas, Louis Peter	2101 West White/Champaign IL 61821
1973-110	Skok, Craig Richard	981 Slash Pine Way Nw/Lawrenceville GA 30243
1954-102	Skowron, William Joseph 'Moose'	1118 Beachcomber Dr/Schaumburg IL 60193
1982-116	Skube, Robert Jacob	6790 West Marco Polo Avenue/Glendale AZ 85308
1930-074	Slade, Gordon Leigh	D. January 2, 1974 Long Beach, Calif.
1979-104	Slagle, Roger Lee	7550 George Nash Road/White House TN 37188
1910-136	Slagle, Walter Jennings	D. June 17, 1974 San Gabriel, Calif.
1911-155	Slapnicka, Cyril Charles	D. October 20, 1979 Cedar Rapids, Ia.
1920-108	Slappey, John Henry	D. June 10, 1957 Marietta, Ga.
1971-093	Slaton, James Michael	41734 Misha Drive/Palmdale CA 93551
1915-155	Slattery, Philip Ryan	D. March 2, 1968 Long Beach, Cal9f.
1982-117	Slaught, Donald Martin	27 Middleridge Lane South/Rolling Hills CA 90274
1910-137	Slaughter, Byron Atkins 'Barney'	D. May 17, 1961 Philadelphia Pa.
1938-090	Slaughter, Enos Bradsher 'Country'	959 Lawson Chapel Church Road/Roxboro NC 27573
1964-109	Slaughter, Sterling Feore	742 East Ave Sierra Madre/Gilbert AZ 85234
1926-075	Slayback, Elbert 'Scottie'	D. November 30, 1979 Cincinnati, O.
1972-104	Slayback, William Grover	41421 Sandalwood Place/Lancaster CA 93536
1928-086	Slayton, Foster Herbert 'Steve'	D. December 20, 1984 Manchester, N. H.
1950-090	Sleater, Louis Mortimer	12 Bandon Court #102/Timonium MD 21093
1944-122	Sloan, Bruce Adams	D. September 24, 1973 Oklahoma City, Okla.
1913-164	Sloan, Yale Yeastman 'Tod'	D. September 12, 1956 Akron, O.
1948-096	Sloat, Dwain Clifford	2101 East 5th Street/Saint Paul MN 55119
1969-159	Slocum, Ronald Reece	Old Add: 5715 Baltimore Dr #82 Lamesa CA 92041
1991-165	Slocumb, Heath	130-14 97th Avenue/Richmond NY 11419
1991-166	Slusarski, Joseph Anthony	2904 Biscayne Drive/Springfield IL 62707
1988-126	Smajstrla, Craig Lee	4006 Elmwood/Pearland TX 77584
1994-096	Small, Aaron James	1427 West Badillo/West Covina CA 91790
1930-075	Small, Charles Albert	D. January 14, 1953 Lewiston, Me.

1978-121	Small, George Henry Hank	PO Box 763/Mount Pleasant SC 29464
1955-108	Small, James Arthur	9420 Taylors Turn/Stanwood MI 49346
1996-172	Small, Mark Allen	Old Add: Seattle WA 98101
1948-097	Smalley, Roy Frederick	256 Timber Trace Drive/Saint Albans MO 63073
1975-107	Smalley, Roy Frederick Iii	6319 Timber Trail/Edina MN 55439
1917-078	Smallwood, Walter Clayton	D. April 29, 1967 Baltimore, Md.
1946-094	Smaza, Joseph Paul	D. May 30, 1979 Royal Oak. Mich.
1986-140	Smiley, John Patrick	208 West Third Avenue/Trappe PA 19426
1934-092	Smith, Alfred John	D. April 28, 1977 Brownsville, Tex.
1926-076	Smith, Alfred Kendricks	D. August 11, 1995 San Diego, Calif.
1953-084	Smith, Alphonse Eugene	8440 Indiana 3rd Floor/Chicago IL 60619
1912-182	Smith, Armstrong Frederick 'Klondike'	D. November 15, 1959 Springfield, Mass.
1932-077	Smith, Arthur Laird	D. November 22, 1995 Norwalk, Conn.
1975-108	Smith, Billy Ed	Old Add: 5439 Timber Post San Antonio TX 78250
1981-129	Smith, Billy Lavern	8407 Neff/Houston TX 77036
1957-081	Smith, Bobby Gene	Old Add: 11808 Woodbine Lane Tacoma WA 98499
1987-134	Smith, Brick Dudley	4743 Amity Place/Charlotte NC 28212
1981-130	Smith, Bryn Nelson	1239 Highway 1/Santa Maria CA 93455
1970-125	Smith, Calvin Bernard 'Bernie'	Box 513/Lutcher LA 70071
1966-084	Smith, Carl Reginald 'Reggie'	6186 Coral Pink Circle/Woodland Hills CA 91367
1960-094	Smith, Charles William	D. November 29, 1994 Reno, Nev.
1981-131	Smith, Christopher William	Old Add: 237 Lajolla Drive Newport Beach CA 92663
1913-165	Smith, Clarence Ossie	D. February 16, 1924 Sweetwater, Tex.
1938-091	Smith, Clay Jamieson	1909 Loomis Street/Winfield KS 67156
1992-134	Smith, Daniel Scott	1617 Corvallis Trail/Arlington TX 76006
1990-147	Smith, Daryl Clinton	3319 Fieldview Road/Baltimore MD 21207
1938-092	Smith, David Merwin	D. April 1, 1998 Whiteville, N. C.
1980-119	Smith, David Stanley	1560 Cormorant Drive/Carlsbad CA 92009
1984-111	Smith, David Wayne	16330 Jersey Dr/Houston TX 77040
1912-181	Smith, Douglass Weldon	D. September 18, 1973 Greenfield, Mass.
1955-109	Smith, Earl Calvin	2764 North Leonard/Fresno CA 93727
1916-079	Smith, Earl Leonard	D. March 14, 1943 Portsmouth, O.
1919-076	Smith, Earl Sutton	D. June 8, 1963 Little Rock, Ark.
1936-087	Smith, Edgar	D. January 2, 1994 Willingboro, N. J.
1945-099	Smith, Edward Mayo	D. November 24, 1977 Boynton Beach, Fla.
1914-199	Smith, Elmer John	D. August 3, 1984 Columbia, Ky.
1926-077	Smith, Elwood Hope 'Mike'	D. May 31, 1981 Chesapeake, Va.
1923-122	Smith, Emanuel Carr	D. April 14, 1989 Miami, Fla.
1930-076	Smith, Ernest Henry	D. April 6, 1973 Brooklyn, N. Y.
1950-091	Smith, Frank Thomas	PO Box 724/Malone FL 32445
1913-166	Smith, Frederick Vincent	D. May 28, 1961 Cleveland, O.
1916-080	Smith, George Allen	D. January 7, 1965 Greenwich, Conn.
1963-110	Smith, George Cornelius	D. June 15, 1987 St. Petersburg, Fla.
1926-078	Smith, George Selby	D. May 26, 1981 Richmond, Va.
1989-118	Smith, Gregory Alan	PO Box 233/Harrington WA 99134
1932-078	Smith, Harold Laverne	D. September 27, 1992 Fort Lauderdale, Fla.
1956-079	Smith, Harold Raymond	PO Box 1247/Hilltop Lakes TX 77871
1955-110	Smith, Harold Wayne	613 Travis/Columbus TX 78934
1912-183	Smith, Harrison	D. July 26, 1964 Dunbar, Neb.
1910-138	Smith, Henry Joseph 'Hap'	D. February 26, 1961 San Jose, Calif.
1962-124	Smith, Jack Hatfield	5628 Shadowrock Drive/Lithonia GA 30038
1911-156	Smith, Jacob 'Big Jake'	D. November 7, 1948 East McKeesport, Pa.
1911-157	Smith, James Carlisle 'Red'	D. October 11, 1966 Atlanta, Ga.
1914-200	Smith, James Harry	D. April 1, 1922 Charlotte, N.C.
1914-201	Smith, James Lawrence	D. January 1, 1974 Pittsburgh, Pa.
1982-118	Smith, James Lorne	Old Add: 4452 Misty Way Yorba Linda CA 92686
1915-156	Smith, John	D. May 2, 1972 Westchester, Ill.
1989-119	Smith, John Dwight Dwight	PO Box 98/Varnville SC 29944
1931-083	Smith, John Marshall	D. May 9, 1982 Silver Spring, Md.
1913-167	Smith, John William 'Chick'	D. October 11, 1935 Dayton, Ky.
1977-133	Smith, Keith Lavarne	Old Add: 522 11th St North/Palmetto FL 33561
1981-132	Smith, Kenneth Earl	100 Landsdowne Blvd/Youngstown OH 44506
1920-109	Smith, Lawrence Patrick	D. December 2, 1990 New Rochelle, N. Y.
1980-120	Smith, Lee Arthur	Old Add: 4170 N. Marine Dr #4I Chicago IL 60613
1984-112	Smith, Leroy Purdy 'Roy'	472 Gramaton Ave/Mount Vernon NY 10552
1978-122	Smith, Lonnie	9085 Fairforest Road #D2/Spartanburg SC 29301
1983-135	Smith, Mark Christopher	Old Add: 711 South 19th St Arlington VA 22202
1994-097	Smith, Mark Edward	713 West Durate Road G105/Arcadia CA 91007
1925-093	Smith, Marvin Harold 'Red'	D. February 19, 1961 Los Angeles, Calif.
1984-113	Smith, Michael Anthony	3226 Livingston Road/Jackson MS 39213
1989-120	Smith, Michael Anthony Texas	7605 Antique Oak/San Antonio TX 78233
1955-111	Smith, Milton	D. April 11, 1997 San Diego, Calif.
1962-125	Smith, Nathaniel Beverly 'Nate'	6365 Tahoe Drive/Atlanta GA 30349
1978-123	Smith, Osborne Earl Ozzie	PO Box 8787/Saint Louis MO 63102
1984-114	Smith, Patrick Keith 'Keith'	Old Add: 1520 S. Galena Way #1322 Denver CO 80231
1953-085	Smith, Paul Leslie	711 Trevino Lane/Conroe TX 77302
1916-081	Smith, Paul Stoner	D. July 3, 1958 Decatur, Ill.
1987-135	Smith, Peter John	108 Newlanders Drive/Powder Springs GA 30073
1962-126	Smith, Peter Luke	124 Blackberry Drive/Brewster NY 10509

1981-133	Smith, Raymond Edward	Rural Route 6 Box 520/Johnson City TN 37601
1963-111	Smith, Richard Arthur	2252 Table Rock Road #143/Medford OR 97501
1951-092	Smith, Richard Harrison	1926 Norwood Lane/State College PA 16803
1969-160	Smith, Richard Kelly	2615 Gates Road/Lincolnton NC 28092
1927-083	Smith, Richard Paul 'Red'	D. March 8, 1978 Toledo, O.
1913-169	Smith, Robert Ashley	D. December 27, 1965 West Los Angeles, Calif.
1923-123	Smith, Robert Eldridge	D. July 19, 1987 Waycross, Ga.
1955-112	Smith, Robert Gilchrist	4003 Soundpointe Drive/Gulf Breeze FL 32561
1958-085	Smith, Robert Walkay 'Riverboat'	Rr 1 Box 21/Clarence MO 63437
1927-084	Smith, Rufus Frazier	D. August 21, 1984 Aiken, S. C.
1913-168	Smith, Salvatore Giuseppe 'Joe'	D. January 12, 1974 Yonkers, N. Y.
1911-158	Smith, Sherrod Malone	D. September 12, 1949 Reidsville, Ga.
1973-111	Smith, Tommie Alexander	1299 East Cannon Ave/Albemarie NC 28001
1941-103	Smith, Vincent Ambrose	D. December 14, 1979 Virginia Beach, Va.
1911-159	Smith, Wallace H.	D. June 10, 1930 Florence, Ariz.
1917-079	Smith, Willard Jehu 'Red'	D. July 17, 1972 Noblesville, Ind
1958-086	Smith, William Garland	D. March 30, 1997 Clinton, Md.
1963-112	Smith, Willie	Old Add: 607 Bradford Street Hobson City AL 36201
1994-098	Smith, Willie Everett	1330 East 68th Street/Savannah GA 31404
1984-115	Smith, Zane William	Old Add: Rr 2 Ogalalla NE 69153
1993-171	Smithberg, Roger Craig	Old Add: 21 White Oak Lane Elgin IL 60123
1982-119	Smithson, Billy Mike	Box 204/Centerville TN 37033
1940-083	Smoll, Clyde Hetrick	D. August 31, 1985 Quakertown, Pa.
1988-127	Smoltz, John Andrew	5950 State Bridge Road #H303/Duluth GA 30097
1912-184	Smoyer, Henry Neitz	D. February 28, 1958 Dubois, Pa.
1916-082	Smykal, Frank John	D. August 11, 1950 Chicago, Ill.
1944-123	Smyres, Clarence Melvin	11470 Orcas Avenue/San Fernando CA 91342
1915-157	Smyth, James Daniel 'Red'	D. April 14, 1958 Inglewood, Calif.
1929-098	Smythe, William Henry 'Harry'	D. August 28, 1980 Augusta, Ga.
1912-185	Snell, Charles Anthony	D. April 4, 1988 Reading, Pa.
1984-116	Snell, Nathaniel	7299 Old State Road/Holly Hill SC 29059
1913-170	Snell, Walter Henry	D. July 23, 1980 Providence, R. I.
1947-080	Snider, Edwin Donald 'Duke'	3037 Lakemont Drive/Fallbrook CA 92028
1988-128	Snider, Van Voorhees	Old Add: 621 19th Avenue South Birmingham AL 35205
1923-124	Snipes, Wyatt Eure 'Dutch'	D. May 1, 1941 Fayetteville, N.C.
1973-112	Snook, Frank Walter	167 Jenkins Road/Statesville NC 28625
1995-204	Snopek, Christopher Charles	103 Bradford Drive/Cynthiana KY 41031
1919-077	Snover, Colonel Lester	D. April 30, 1969 Rochester, N. Y.
1992-135	Snow, Jack Thomas 'J.T.'	401 Purdue Circle/Seal Beach CA 90740
1935-102	Snyder, Bernard Austin	2415 Waverly/Philadelphia PA 19146
1985-106	Snyder, Brian Robert	14834 Wood Home Road/Centerville VA 22020
1912-186	Snyder, Frank Elton	D. January 5, 1962 San Antonio, Tex.
1959-077	Snyder, Gene Walter	D. June 2, 1996 York, Pa.
1986-141	Snyder, James Cory 'Cory'	195 North 800 East/Mapleton UT 84664
1961-100	Snyder, James Robert	8613 Barkwood/Tampa FL 33615
1952-095	Snyder, Jerry George	2420 Gulfcrest Blvd/Pearland TX 77581
1914-202	Snyder, John William	D. December 13, 1981 Redstone Twp., Pa.
1959-078	Snyder, Russell Henry	PO Box 264/Nelson NE 68961
1919-078	Snyder, William Nicholas	D. October 8, 1934 Vicksburg, Mich.
1937-095	Sodd, William	D. May 14, 1998 Fort Worth, Tex.
1971-094	Soderholm, Eric Thane	10 South 360 Hampshire Ln West/Hinsdale IL 60521
1996-173	Soderstrom, Stephen Andrew	301 North Faith Home/Turlock CA 95380
1995-205	Sodowsky, Clint Rea	180 22nd Avenue NE/Norman OK 73071
1986-142	Soff, Raymond John	9015 Rodesiler Highway/Riga MI 49276
1979-105	Sofield, Richard Michael	18811 Big Cypress Drive/Jupiter FL 33458
1990-148	Sojo, Luis Beltran (Sojo)	Old Add: Barquisimeto Venezuela
1968-096	Solaita, Tolia Tony	D. February 10, 1990 Tafuna, American Samoa
1983-136	Solano, Julio Cesar	Villa Espana C.O. 31 Laromana Dominican Rep.
1958-087	Solis, Marcelino	Old Add: Calle Vidrea 8370/Monterrey Nuevo Leon Mex.
1973-113	Solomon, Eddie Buddy	D. January 12, 1986 Macon, Ga.
1923-125	Solomon, Moses Hirsch	D. June 25, 1966 Miami, Fla.
1934-093	Solters, Julius Joseph 'Moose'	D. September 28, 1975 Pittsburgh, Pa.
1910-139	Somerlott, John Wesley 'Jock'	D. April 21, 1965 Butler, Ind.
1912-187	Sommers, Rudolph	D. March 18, 1949 Louisville,Ky.
1950-092	Sommers, William Dunn	2550 SW Bobolink Court/Palm City FL 34990
1924-101	Songer, Don	D. October 3, 1962 Kansas City, Mo.
1977-134	Sorenson, Lary Alan	44769 Ford Way Drive/Novi MI 48375
1928-087	Sorrell, Victor Garland	D. May 4, 1972 Raleigh, N.C.
1965-102	Sorrell, William	12897 Abra/San Diego CA 92128
1922-129	Sorrells, Raymond Edwin 'Chick'	D. July 20, 1983 Terrell, Texas
1989-121	Sorrento, Paul Anthony	14470 Mark Drive/Largo FL 34644
1972-105	Sosa, Elias	7210 Petal Court/Charlotte NC 28227
1975-109	Sosa, Jose Ynocencio	Haina Km12 Carretera Sanchez Santo Domingo Dominican Rep.
1989-122	Sosa, Samuel	Mello Centro San Pedro De Macoris Dominican Rep.
1926-079	Sothern, Dennis Elwood	D. December 7, 1977 Durham, N. C.
1914-203	Sothoron, Allen Sutton	D. June 17, 1939 St. Louis, Mo
1977-135	Soto, Mario Melvin	Joachs Lachaustegui #42 Sur Bani Dominican Rep.
1946-095	Souchock, Stephen	441 Southwest 55th Terrace/Plantation FL 33317
1911-160	Southwick, Clyde Aubra	D. October 14, 1961 Freeport, Ill.

1964-110 .... Southworth, William Frederick .... 320 Dobben Rd/Webster Groves MO 63119
1913-171 .... Southworth, William Harrison .... D. November 15, 1969 Columbus, O.
1980-121 .... Souza, Kenneth Mark Mark .... 4214 208th Avenue NE/Redmond WA 98053
1942-098 .... Spahn, Warren Edward .... Rural Route 2/Hartshorne Ok/74547
1927-085 .... Spalding, Charles Harry 'Dick' .... D. February 3, 1950 Philadelpha, Pa.
1959-079 .... Spangler, Albert Donald .... 27202 Afton Way/Huffman TX 77336
1964-111 .... Spanswick, William Henry .... 183 West Bass Lane/Suffield CT 6078
1995-206 .... Sparks, Steven William .... PO Box 112 814 Nelson Crosby TX 77532
1964-112 .... Sparma, Joseph Blase .... D. May 14, 1986 Columbus, O.
1955-113 .... Speake, Robert Charles .... 4742 SW Urish Rd/Topeka KS 66604
1986-143 .... Speck, Robert Clifford Cliff .... 823 South Nueva Vista Dr/Palm Springs CA 92264
1924-102 .... Speece, Byron Franklin .... D. September 29, 1974 Elgin, Ore.
1975-110 .... Speed, Horace Arthur .... 1301 Bankers Drive/Carson CA 90746
1943-131 .... Speer, Ernie Floyd .... D. March 22, 1969 Little Rock, Ark.
1991-167 .... Spehr, Timothy Joseph .... 8524 Briar Grove Drive/Waco TX 76712
1971-095 .... Speier, Chris Edward .... 5100 North Placita Del Lazo/Tucson AZ 85750
1969-161 .... Spence, John Robert 'Bob' .... 2521 San Marcos/San Diego CA 92104
1940-084 .... Spence, Stanley Orville .... D. January 9, 1983 Kinston, N. C.
1952-096 .... Spencer, Daryl Dean .... 2740 Larkin Drive/Wichita KS 67216
1912-188 .... Spencer, Fred Calvin .... D. February 5, 1969 St. Anthony, Minn.
1950-093 .... Spencer, George Elwell .... 8160 Hickory Avenue/Galena OH 43021
1928-088 .... Spencer, Glenn Edward .... D. December 30, 1958 Binghamton, N. Y.
1978-124 .... Spencer, Hubert Thomas 'Tom' .... 2021 East Conner Strav/Tucson AZ 85716
1968-097 .... Spencer, James Lloyd .... 6403 Candlewicke CT Sykesville MD 21784
1913-172 .... Spencer, Lloyd Benjamin .... D. September 1, 1970 Finksburg, Md.
1925-094 .... Spencer, Roy Hampton .... D. February 8, 1973 Port Charlette, Fla.
1920-110 .... Spencer, Vernon Murray .... D. June 3, 1971 Wixom, Mich.
1920-111 .... Speraw, Paul Bachman .... D. February 22, 1962 Cedar Rapids, Ia.
1924-103 .... Sperber, Edwin George .... D. January 5, 1976 Cincinnati, O.
1974-123 .... Sperring, Robert Walter .... 13302 Chriswood Drive/Cypress TX 77429
1936-088 .... Sperry, Stanley Kenneth .... D. September 27, 1962 Evansville,Wis.
1955-114 .... Spicer, Robert Oberton .... 423 McPhee Dr/Fayetteville NC 28305
1989-123 .... Spiers, William James .... Rural Route 2 Box 108/Cameron SC 29030
1964-113 .... Spiezio, Edward Wayne .... 5620 N. Barrington Road/Morris IL 60450
1996-174 .... Spiezio, Scott Edward .... 5620 North Barrington Road/Morris IL 60450
1972-106 .... Spikes, Leslie Charles 'Charlie' .... 531 North Border Drive/Bogalusa LA 70427
1974-124 .... Spillner, Daniel Ray .... 111 Southwest 307th Street/Federal Way WA 98003
1978-125 .... Spilman, William Harry 'Harry' .... 4423 St. Phillips Road/Mount Vernon IN 47620
1939-112 .... Spindel, Harold Stewart .... 216 Del Cabo/San Clemente CA 92673
1969-162 .... Spinks, Scipio Ronald .... 14730 Earlswood Drive/Houston TX 77083
1970-126 .... Splittorff, Paul William .... 4204 Hickory Ln/Blue Spring MO 64015
1932-079 .... Spognardi, Andrea Ettore .... 4394 Washington Street/Roslindale MA 2131
1928-089 .... Spohrer, Alfred Ray .... D. July 21, 1972 Carmel, N. Y.
1994-099 .... Spoljaric, Paul Nikola .... Old Add: 1060 East Genesee St #6502 Syracuse NY 13210
1954-103 .... Spooner, Karl Benjamin .... D. April 10, 1984 Vero Beach, Fla.
1930-077 .... Spotts, James Russell .... D. June 15, 1964 Medford, N. J.
1993-172 .... Spradlin, Jerry Carl .... 2824 East Diana Avenue/Anaheim CA 92806
1947-081 .... Spragins, Homer Frank .... PO Box 113/Minter City Ms/38944
1968-098 .... Sprague, Edward Martin .... 19015 North Davis Road/Lodi CA 95242
1991-168 .... Sprague, Edward Nelson .... 4677 Pine Valley Circle/Stockton CA 95219
1911-161 .... Spratt, Henry Lee 'Jack' .... D. July 3, 1969 Washington, Pa.
1965-103 .... Spriggs, George Herman .... 75 West Bayfront Road/Lothian MD 20711
1955-115 .... Spring, Jack Russell .... PO Box 118/Colbert WA 99005
1925-095 .... Springer, Bradford Louis .... D. January 4, 1970 Birmingham, Mich.
1995-207 .... Springer, Dennis Leroy .... %Je Springer 4354 North 9th Street Fresno CA 93726
1992-136 .... Springer, Russell Paul .... PO Box 185/Pollock LA 71467
1990-149 .... Springer, Steven Michael .... 6091 Jade Street/Huntington Beach CA 92647
1930-078 .... Sprinz, Joseph Conrad .... D. January 11, 1994 Fremont, Calif.
1945-100 .... Sproull, Charles William .... D. January 13, 1980 Rockford, Ill.
1961-101 .... Sprout, Robert Samuel .... 148 Sunnyslope Lane/Manheim PA 17545
1978-126 .... Sprowl, Robert John .... Old Add: 4711 Leonard Avenue Northport AL 35476
1924-104 .... Spurgeon, Fred .... D. November 5, 1970 Kalamazoo, Mich.
1975-111 .... Squires, Michael Lynn .... 9548 Autumnwood Circle/Kalamazoo MI 49009
1980-122 .... Stablein, George Charles .... 8 Delaware/Irvine CA 92720
1910-140 .... Stack, William Edward .... D. August 28, 1958 Chicago, Ill.
1964-114 .... Staehle, Marvin Gustave .... 570 Checker Drive/Buffalo Grove IL 60089
1960-095 .... Stafford, Bill Charles .... 6108 Courtland Drive/Canton MI 48187
1916-083 .... Stafford, Henry Alexander 'Heinie' .... D. January 29, 1972 Lake Worth, Fla.
1977-136 .... Staggs, Stephen Robert .... 3113 SW 93rd Street/Oklahoma City OK 73159
1964-115 .... Stahl, Larry Floyd .... 1506 East Main Street #A/Belleville IL 62221
1993-173 .... Stahoviak, Scott Edmund .... 353 North Allegheny Rd/Grayslake IL 60030
1975-112 .... Staiger, Roy Joseph .... 641 South Main #1/Springfield MO 65806
1934-094 .... Stainback, George Tucker 'Tuck' .... D. November 29, 1992 Camarillo, Calif.
1992-137 .... Stairs, Matthew Wade .... Rural Route 1/Stanley New Bruns. E0M 1T0 Canada
1925-096 .... Staley, George Gaylord 'Gale' .... D. April 19, 1989 Walnut Creek, Calif.
1947-082 .... Staley, Gerald Lee .... 2517 NE 100th Street/Vancouver WA 98686
1960-096 .... Stallard, Evan Tracy 'Tracy' .... 13516 Herald Road/Coeburn VA 24230
1947-083 .... Stallcup, Thomas Virgil 'Virgil' .... D. May 2, 1889 Greenville, S. C.
1943-132 .... Staller, George Walborn .... D. July 3, 1992 Harrisburg, Pa.

1941-104 ....Stanceu, Charles ....D. April 3, 1969 Canton, O.
1925-097 ....Standaeart, Jerome John ....D. August 4, 1964 Chicago, Ill.
1911-162 ....Standridge, Alfred Peter ....D. August 2, 1963 San Francisco, Calif.
1963-113 ....Stanek, Al ....96 Allyn Street/Holyoke MA 1040
1979-106 ....Stanfield, Kevin Bruce ....7565 Newcomb St/San Bernardino CA 92410
1961-102 ....Stange, Albert Lee 'Lee'..........................11228 Villas On The Green Dr/Riverview FL 33569
1972-107 ....Stanhouse, Donald Joseph ....1315 Pecos Drive/Southlake TX 76092
1987-136 ....Stanicek, Peter Louis ....118 Chestnut/Park Forest IL 60466
1987-137 ....Stanicek, Stephen Blair ....118 Chestnut/Park Forest IL 60466
1997-155 ....Stanifer, Robert Wayne ....102 Luke Court/Easley SC 29640
1959-080 ....Stanka, Joe Donald ....32718 Weymouth Court/Fulshear TX 77441
1992-138 ....Stankiewicz, Andrew Neal ....1807 East Commerce Avenue/Gilbert AZ 85234
1943-133 ....Stanky, Edward Raymond ....PO Box 812/Fairhope AL 36532
1969-163 ....Stanley, Fredrick Blair ....Old Add: 8133 E Conquistadores St Scottsdale AZ 85255
1914-204 ....Stanley, James F. ....Old Add: Chicgao Il
1911-163 ....Stanley, John Leonard 'Buck' ....D. August 13, 1940 Norfolk, Va.
1964-116 ....Stanley, Mitchell Jack 'Mickey' ....Old Add: 4763 S. Old Us Hwy 23 Brighton MI 48116
1986-144 ....Stanley, Robert Michael ....1108 Northeast 10th Avenue/Fort Lauderdale FL 33304
1977-137 ....Stanley, Robert William ....19 William Fairfield Drive/Wenham MA 1984
1918-069 ....Stansbury, John James ....D. December 26, 1970 Easton, Pa.
1931-084 ....Stanton, George Washington 'Buck' ....D. January 1, 1992 San Antonio, Texas
1970-127 ....Stanton, Leroy Bobby ....1751 Norwood Ln/Florence SC 29501
1975-113 ....Stanton, Michael Thomas ....Old Add: Box 134/Phenix City AL 36867
1989-124 ....Stanton, William Michael ....Old Add: 16102 Rill Lane Houston TX 77062
1987-138 ....Stapleton, David Earl ....PO Box 702/Claypool AZ 85532
1980-123 ....Stapleton, David Leslie ....PO Box 1467/Daphne AL 36526
1962-127 ....Stargell, Wilver Dornel 'Willie'.................813 Tarpon Drive/Wilmington NC 28409
1987-139 ....Stark, Matthew Scott ....Old Add: 3641f Oak Creek Dr/Ontario CA 91761
1932-080 ....Starr, Raymond Francis ....D. February 9, 1963 Bayliss, Ill.
1947-084 ....Starr, Richard Eugene ....613 North Crescent Drive/Kittanning PA 16201
1935-103 ....Starr, William 'Chick' ....D. August 12, 1991 Lajolla, Calif.
1963-114 ....Starrette, Herman Paul ....152 Blueberry Hill Drive/Statesville NC 28625
1993-174 ....Staton, David Allen.....................................17381 Village Drive/Tustin CA 92680
1972-108 ....Staton, Joseph ....PO Box 28582/Seattle WA 98118
1919-079 ....Statz, Arnold John 'Jigger' ....D. March 16, 1988 Corona Del Mar, Calif.
1963-115 ....Staub, Daniel Joseph 'Rusty' ....% Wwor Radio 9 Broadcast Plaza Secaucus NJ 7094
1923-126 ....Stauffer, Charles Edward 'Ed' ....D. July 2, 1979 St Petersburg, Fla.
1974-125 ....Stearns, John Hardin ....7107 Cedarwood Circle/Boulder CO 80301
1916-084 ....Steele, Robert Wesley ....D. January 27, 1962 Ocala, Fla.
1910-141 ....Steele, William Mitchell ....D. October 19, 1949 Overland, Mo.
1987-140 ....Steels, James Earl ....712 West Polk Street/Santa Maria CA 93454
1912-189 ....Steen, William John ....D. March 13, 1979 Signal Hill, Calif.
1924-105 ....Steengrafe, Milton Henry ....D. June 2, 1977 Oklahoma City, Okla.
1962-128 ....Steevens, Morris Dale Moe'......................14465 Cadillac Drive/San Antonio TX 78248
1983-137 ....Stefero, John Robert ....529 Michelle Road/Odenton MD 21113
1978-127 ....Stegman, David William ....3234 Simmons Drive/Grove City OH 43123
1932-081 ....Stein, Irvin Michael ....D. January 7, 1981 Covington, La.
1938-093 ....Stein, Justin Marion ....D. May 1, 1992 Creve Coeur, Mo.
1972-109 ....Stein, William Allen ....2433 Le Gay Street/Cocoa FL 32926
1978-128 ....Stein, William Randolph ....1540 Palmer Street/Pomona CA 91766
1986-145 ....Steinbach, Terry Lee ....750 Boone Avenue North/Golden Valley MN 55427
1937-096 ....Steinbacher, Henry John ....D. April 3, 1977 Sacramento, Calif.
1912-190 ....Steinbrenner, William Gass ....D. April 25, 1970 Pittsburgh, Pa.
1931-085 ....Steinecke, William Robert ....D. July 20, 1986 Saint Augustine, Fla.
1923-127 ....Steineder, Raymond ....D. August 25, 1982 Vineland, N. J.
1945-101 ....Steiner, Benjamin Saunders ....D. October 27, 1988 Venice, Fla.
1945-102 ....Steiner, James Harry 'Red' ....17700 Southwestern Ave #93/Gardena CA 90248
1982-120 ....Steirer, Ricky Francis ....1015 Haverhill Road/Baltimore MD 21229
1916-085 ....Stellbauer, William Jennings ....D. February 16, 1974 Houston, Tex.
1971-096 ....Stelmaszek, Richard Francis.......................2734 East 97th St/Chicago IL 60617
1980-124 ....Stember, Jeffrey Alan ....3k Nobhill/Roseland NJ 7068
1912-191 ....Stengel, Charles Dillon 'Casey'.................D. September 29, 1975 Glendale, Calif.
1962-129 ....Stenhouse, David Rotchford ....70 Woodbury Rd/Cranston RI 2905
1982-121 ....Stenhouse, Michael ....70 Woodbury Rd/Cranston RI 2905
1971-097 ....Stennett, Renaldo Antonio 'Rennie' ....PO Box 810304/Boca Raton FL 33428
1968-099 ....Stephen, Louis Roberts 'Buzz' ....503 North Sunnyside Street/Porterville CA 93257
1947-085 ....Stephens, Bryan Maris...............................D. November 21, 1991 Santa Ana, Calif.
1990-150 ....Stephens, Carl Ray ....1065 Council Road NE/Charleston TN 37310
1952-097 ....Stephens, Glen Eugene 'Gene' ....9804 Hefner Village Place/Oklahoma City OK 73162
1941-105 ....Stephens, Vernon Decatur ....D. November 4, 1968 Long Beach, Calif.
1971-098 ....Stephenson, Chester Earl ....Old Add: Rr 1 Box 295d/Angier NC 27501
1996-175 ....Stephenson, Garrett Charles ....503 Gem Drive/Kimberly ID 83341
1921-096 ....Stephenson, Jackson Riggs ....D. November 15, 1985 Tuscaloosa, Ala.
1963-116 ....Stephenson, Jerry Joseph ....1425 Marelen Dr/Fullerton CA 92635
1964-117 ....Stephenson, John Herman ....17448 Bellewood Drive/Hammond LA 70401
1943-134 ....Stephenson, Joseph Chester ....822 Jade Way/Anaheim CA 92805
1989-125 ....Stephenson, Phillip Raymond......................3921 Sweet Bay/Wichita KS 67226
1955-116 ....Stephenson, Robert Loyd ....1518 Brookhaven Blvd/Norman OK 73072
1935-104 ....Stephenson, Walter McQueen......................D. July 4, 1993 Shreveport, La.

1974-126	Sterling, Randall Wayne	2516 Linda Ave/Key West FL 33040
1912-192	Sterrett, Charles Hurlbut 'Dutch'	D. December 9, 1965 Baltimore, Md.
1941-106	Stevens, Charles Augustus	12062 Valley View #211/Garden Grove CA 92645
1994-100	Stevens, David James	2630 Candlewood Way/Lahabra CA 90631
1990-151	Stevens, Dewain Lee 'Lee'	Old Add: 8611 Greenbriar Drive Overland Park KS 66212
1945-103	Stevens, Edward Lee	6211 South Braeswood/Houston TX 77096
1914-205	Stevens, James Arthur	D. September 25, 1966 Baltimore, Md.
1958-088	Stevens, R. C.	1405 Mound St/Davenport IA 52803
1931-086	Stevens, Robert Jordan	803 Roxboro Road/Rockville MD 20850
1995-208	Steverson, Todd Anthony	109 West Glenhaven Drive/Phoenix AZ 85045
1997-156	Stewart, Andrew David	2109 Giles Street/Wilmington DE 19805
1913-173	Stewart, Charles Eugene 'Tuffy'	D. November 18, 1934 Chicago, Ill.
1978-129	Stewart, David Keith	17762 Vineyard Lane/Poway CA 90264
1941-107	Stewart, Edward Perry	5501 West 119th Street/Inglewood CA 90304
1927-086	Stewart, Frank	1450 Triangle Drive/Houlton WI 54082
1940-085	Stewart, Glen Weldon	D. February 11, 1997 Memphis, Tenn.
1963-117	Stewart, James Franklin	16147 Craigend Place/Odessa FL 33556
1916-086	Stewart, John Franklin 'Stuffy'	D. December 30, 1980 Lake City, Fla.
1913-174	Stewart, Mark	D. January 17, 1942 Memphis, Tenn.
1978-130	Stewart, Samuel Lee	107 Scenic View Dr/Swannanoa NC 28778
1995-209	Stewart, Shannon Harold	18460 Southwest 78th Place/Miami FL 33157
1952-098	Stewart, Veston Goff 'Bunky'	514 26th Street/Columbus GA 31904
1921-097	Stewart, Walter Cleveland 'Lefty'	D. September 26, 1974 Knoxville, Tenn.
1940-086	Stewart, Walter Nesbitt	D. June 8, 1990 London, Ohio
1944-124	Stewart, William Macklin 'Mack'	D. March 21, 1960 Macon, Ga.
1955-117	Stewart, William Wayne	302 Rumford Road/Lititz PA 17543
1994-101	Stidham, Phillip Wayne	5025 Malabar Blvd/Melbourne Beach FL 32951
1979-107	Stieb, David Andrew	10860 Shay Lane/Reno NV 89511
1929-099	Stiely, Fred Warren	D. January 6, 1981 Valley View, Pa.
1960-097	Stigman, Richard Lewis	12914 5th Ave South/Burnsville MN 55337
1930-079	Stiles, Rolland Mays	3601 Lemay Ferry Road #C129/Saint Louis MO 63125
1975-114	Stillman, Royle Eldon	45847 Highway 6/Glenwood Springs CO 81601
1986-146	Stillwell, Kurt Andrew	1417 Dover Avenue/Thousand Oaks CA 91360
1961-103	Stillwell, Ronald Roy	1417 Dover/Thousand Oaks CA 91360
1980-125	Stimac, Craig Steven	Old Add: 1603 Robinhood Lane Lagrange IL 62525
1923-128	Stimson, Carl Remus	D. November 9, 1936 Omaha, Neb.
1934-095	Stine, Lee Elbert	1939 Calle Pasito/Hemet CA 92545
1994-102	Stinnett, Kelly Lee	35 North 35th Street/Lawton OK 73505
1969-164	Stinson, Gorrell Robert 'Bob'	14408 130th Avenue NE/Kirkland WA 98034
1943-135	Stirnweiss, George Henry 'Snuffy'	D. September 15, 1958 Newark, N. J.
1947-086	Stobbs, Charles Klein 'Chuck'	1731 Riviera Circle/Sarasota FL 34232
1913-175	Stock, Milton Joseph	D. July 16, 1977 Montrose, Ala.
1959-081	Stock, Wesley Gay	PO Box 1309/Allyn WA 98524
1993-175	Stocker, Kevin Douglas	Old Add: East 13108 22nd Spokane WA 99216
1981-134	Stoddard, Robert Lyle	15760 Sunnyside Ave/Morgan Hill CA 95037
1975-115	Stoddard, Timothy Paul	% Northwestern U. 1501 Central Street Evanston IL 60208
1925-098	Stokes, Albert John	D. December 10, 1986 Grantham, N. H.
1925-099	Stokes, Arthur Melton	D. June 3, 1962 Titusville, Pa.
1945-104	Stone, Charles Richard 'Dick'	D. February 18, 1980 Oklahoma City, Okla.
1953-086	Stone, Darrah Dean 'Dean'	407 15th Avenue/Moline IL 61244
1913-176	Stone, Dwight Ely	D. July 3, 1976 Glendale, Calif.
1923-129	Stone, Edwin Arnold 'Arnie'	D. July 29, 1948 Hudson Falls/N. Y.
1969-165	Stone, Eugene Daniel	6928 Plaza Street/Othello WA 99344
1967-102	Stone, George Heard	230 Fairfield Drive/Ruston LA 71270
1966-085	Stone, Harry Ronald 'Ron'	11720 Nw Lovejoy/Portland OR 97229
1983-138	Stone, Jeffrey Glen	Rural Route 2 Box 392/Portageville MO 63873
1928-090	Stone, John Thomas	D. November 30, 1955 Shelbyville, Tenn.
1943-136	Stone, John Vernon 'Vern'	D. November 12, 1986 Fountain Valley, Calif.
1971-099	Stone, Steven Michael	% Wgn-Tv 435 North Michigan Blvd Chicago IL 60611
1923-130	Stone, William Arthur 'Tige'	D. January 1, 1960 Jacksonville, Fla.
1933-059	Stoneham, John Andrew	7418 North 122nd East Place/Owasso OK 74055
1967-103	Stoneman, William Hambly	PO Box 500, Station M/Montreal Quebec H1V 3P2 Canada
1922-130	Stoner, Ulysses Simpson Grant 'Lil'	D. June 26, 1966 Enid, Okla.
1931-087	Storie, Howard Edward	D. July 27, 1968 Pittsfield, Mass.
1930-080	Storti, Lindo Ivan	D. July 24, 1982 Ontario, Calif.
1964-118	Stottlemyre, Melvin Leon	Old Add: 9 North 6th Avenue Yakima WA 98902
1990-152	Stottlemyre, Melvin "Leon, Jr."	Unlv Baseball 4505 South Maryland Pkwy Las Vegas NV 89154
1988-129	Stottlemyre, Todd Vernon	26004 SE 27th Street/Issaquah WA 98029
1931-088	Stout, Allyn McClelland	D. December 22, 1974 Sikeston, Mo.
1938-094	Stoviak, Raymond Thomas	D. February 23, 1998 Nicoya, Costa Rica
1960-084	Stowe, Harold Rudolph	1361 Union New Hope Road/Gastonia NC 28052
1970-128	Strahler, Michael Wayne	320 Foxglove Place/Oxnard CA 93030
1954-104	Strahs, Richard Bernard	D. May 26, 1988 Las Vegas, Nev.
1979-108	Strain, Joseph Allen	8668 East Otero Circle/Englewood CO 80112
1987-141	Straker, Lester Paul	Urb. Mario Briceno Irragary Calle Boceno #28 Maracay Venezuela
1972-110	Strampe, Robert Edwin	South 24720 Lance Hill Road/Cheney WA 99004
1913-177	Strand, Paul Edward	D. July 2, 1974 Salt Lake City, Ut.
1915-158	Strands, John Lawrence	D. January 19, 1957 Forest Park, Ill.
1934-096	Strange, Alan Cochrane	D. June 27, 1994 Seattle, Wash.

1989-126	Strange, Joseph Douglas Doug	7 Pebble Creek Way/Taylors SC 29687
1934-097	Stratton, Monty Franklin Pierce	D. September 29, 1982 Greenville, Texas
1983-139	Strawberry, Darryl Eugene	1419 Red Bluff Court/San Dimas CA 91773
1928-091	Strelecki, Edward Harold	D. January 9, 1968 Newark, N. J.
1954-105	Streuli, Walter Herbert	1107 Westminster/Greensboro NC 27410
1950-094	Strickland, George Bevan	6328 Constance Street/New Orleans LA 70118
1971-100	Strickland, James Michael	2139 Equestrian Road/Paso Robles CA 93446
1937-097	Strickland, William Goss	1001 Carpenters Way #J1117/Lakeland FL 33809
1959-082	Striker, Wilbur Scott 'Jake'	3170 Samaritan Way/Prescott AZ 86301
1940-087	Strincevich, Nicholas Mihailovich	1308 Camelot Manor/Portage IN 46368
1941-108	Stringer, Louis Bernard	23442 El Toro #E112/El Toro CA 92630
1928-092	Stripp, Joseph Valentine	D. June 10, 1989 Orlando, Fla.
1970-129	Strohmayer, John Emery	1825 Crosby Lane/Redding CA 96003
1972-111	Strom, Brent Terry	6115 East San Cristobal Street/Tucson AZ 85715
1939-113	Stromme, Floyd Marvin	D. February 7, 1993 Wenatchee, Wash.
1929-100	Stroner, James Melvin	D. December 6, 1975 Tarboro, N. C.
1966-086	Stroud, Edwin Marvin	1696 Oak St/Warren OH 44485
1910-142	Stroud, Ralph Vivian 'Sailor'	D. April 11, 1970 Stockton, Calif.
1982-122	Stroughter, Stephen Louis	323 NE 2nd/Visalia CA 93277
1934-098	Struss, Clarence Herbert 'Steamboat'	D. September 12, 1985 Grand Rapids, Mich.
1924-106	Stryker, Sterling Alpa 'Dutch'	D. November 5, 1964 Red Bank, N. J.
1922-131	Stuart, John Davis	D. May 13, 1970 Charleston, W. Va.
1921-098	Stuart, Luther Lane 'Luke'	D. June 15, 1947 Winston-Salem, N. C.
1949-083	Stuart, Marlin Henry	D. June 16, 1994 Paragould, Ark.
1958-089	Stuart, Richard Lee	926 Woodside Road/Redwood City CA 94061
1984-117	Stubbs, Franklin Lee	743 East Broadway #255/Louisville KY 40202
1967-104	Stubing, Lawrence George 'Moose'	10821 South Laconia Drive/Villa Park CA 92861
1921-099	Stueland, George Anton	D. September 9, 1964 Onawa, Ia.
1950-095	Stuffel, Paul Harrington	2381 Ansley Street/Alliance OH 44601
1997-157	Stull, Everett James	1667 Fieldgreen Overlook/Stone Mountain GA 30088
1957-082	Stump, James Gilbert	939 Weston/Lansing MI 48906
1931-089	Stumpf, George Frederick	D. March 6, 1993 Metairie, La.
1912-193	Stumpf, William Fredrick	D. February 14, 1966 Crownsville, Md.
1982-123	Stuper, John Anton	Yale Baseball PO Box 208216 New Haven CT 6520
1955-118	Sturdivant, Thomas Virgil	1324 SW 71st/Oklahoma City OK 73159
1927-087	Sturdy, Guy R.	D. May 4, 1965 Marshall, Tex.
1940-088	Sturgeon, Robert Harwood	5404 Signac Court/Chino Hills CA 91709
1914-206	Sturgis, Dean Donnell	D. June 4, 1950 Uniontown, Pa.
1941-109	Sturm, John Peter Joseph	3840 French Court/Saint Louis Mo/63116
1995-210	Sturtze, Tanyon James	%Earl Sturtze 6 Cheshire Road Worcester MA 1606
1926-080	Stutz, George	D. December 29, 1930 Philadelphia, Pa.
1919-080	Styles, William Graves 'Lena'	D. March 14, 1956 Huntsville, Ala.
1995-211	Stynes, Christopher Desmond	%Desmond Stynes 261 SW 13th Place Boca Raton FL 33432
1966-087	Suarez, Kenneth Raymond	2800 Avenue E East/Arlington TX 76011
1944-125	Suarez, Luis Abelardo	D. June 5, 1991 Havana, Cuba
1970-130	Such, Richard Stanley	PO Box 1741/Sanford NC 27330
1938-095	Suche, Charles Morris	D. February 11, 1984 San Antonio, Texas
1950-096	Suchecki, James Joseph	3392 Clinton Avenue #1f/Berwyn IL 60402
1968-100	Sudakis, William Paul	Old Add: 4190 East Palm Canyon Dr Palm Springs CA 92264
1941-110	Suder, Peter	903 Roosevelt Avenue/Aliquippa PA 15001
1992-139	Suero, Williams	D. November 30, 1995 Santo Domingo, Dominican Rep.
1930-081	Suhr, August Richard 'Gus'	341 Hazel Avenue/Millbrae CA 94030
1926-081	Sukeforth, Clyde Leroy	Rural Route 3 Box 123/Waldoboro Me 4572
1964-119	Sukla, Edward Anthony	16 Perch/Irvine CA 92714
1980-126	Sularz, Guy Patrick	10818 North 83rd Street/Scottsdale AZ 85260
1936-089	Sulik, Ernest Richard	D. May 31, 1963 Oakland, Calif.
1944-126	Sullivan, Carl Manuel 'Jack'	D. October 15, 1992 Dallas, Texas
1928-093	Sullivan, Charles Edward	D. May 28, 1935 Maiden, N. C.
1953-087	Sullivan, Franklin Leal	Box 1873/Lihue HI 96766
1955-119	Sullivan, Haywood Cooper	Fenway Park/Boston MA 2215
1921-100	Sullivan, James Richard	D. February 12, 1972 Burtonsville, Md.
1935-105	Sullivan, Joe	D. April 8, 1985 Sequim, Wash.
1919-081	Sullivan, John Jeremiah	D. July 7, 1958 Chicago, Ill.
1920-112	Sullivan, John Lawrence	D. April 1, 1966 Union Co., Pa.
1942-099	Sullivan, John Peter	2301 183rd Street #403a/Homewood IL 60430
1963-118	Sullivan, John Peter	24 Highland St/Dansville NY 14437
1982-124	Sullivan, Marc Cooper	Old Add: 9808 Ensign CT Fort Myers FL 33919
1939-114	Sullivan, Paul Thomas 'Lefty'	D. November 1, 1988 Scottsdale, Ariz.
1951-093	Sullivan, Russell Guy H	1701 Hill-N-Dale Drive/Fredericksburg VA 22401
1922-132	Sullivan, Thomas Augustin	D. September 23, 1962 Boston, Mass.
1925-100	Sullivan, Thomas Brandon	D. August 16, 1944 Seattle, Wash.
1931-090	Sullivan, William Joseph, Jr.	D. January 4, 1994 Sarasota, Fla.
1995-212	Sullivan, William Scott	Rural Route 1 Box 24a/Carrollton AL 35447
1920-113	Summa, Homer Wayne	D. January 29, 1966 Los Angeles, Calif.
1974-127	Summers, John Junior	2091 Trevino/Oceanside CA 92056
1928-094	Sumner, Carl Ringdahl	24 Winterset Drive/Chatham MA 2633
1974-128	Sundberg, James Howard	Old Add: 4610 Riverforest Drive Arlington TX 76017
1956-080	Sundin, Gordon Vincent	19510 Lost Creek Drive/Fort Myers FL 33912
1936-090	Sundra, Stephen Richard	D. March 23, 1952 Cleveland, O.

1937-098	Sunkel, Thomas Jacob	1238 Tucker Beach Road/Paris IL 61944
1995-213	Suppan, Jeffrey Scot	%Larry Suppan 24207 Archwood Canoga Park CA 91307
1985-107	Surhoff, Richard Clifford	1389 White Oak Drive/Reading PA 19608
1987-142	Surhoff, William James 'B.J.'	221 Oakland Beach Avenue/Rye NY 10580
1949-084	Surkont, Matthew Constantine 'Max'	D. October 8, 1986 Largo, Fla.
1929-101	Susce, George Cyril Methodius, Sr.	D. February 25, 1986 Sarasota, Fla.
1955-120	Susce, George Daniel	2852 Velma Street/Matlacher FL 33909
1934-099	Susko, Peter Jonathan	D. May 22, 1978 Jacksonville, Fla.
1938-096	Sutcliffe, Charles Inigo	D. March 2, 1994 Fall River, Mass.
1976-087	Sutcliffe, Richard Lee	25911 99th Street/Lees Summit MO 64063
1964-120	Sutherland, Darrell Wayne	1011 Nw Jeffrey Place/Beaverton OR 97006
1966-088	Sutherland, Gary Lynn	338 North Oak Cliff/Monrovia CA 91016
1921-101	Sutherland, Harvey Scott 'Suds'	D. May 11, 1972 Portland, Ore.
1949-085	Sutherland, Howard Alvin 'Dizzy'	D. August 26, 1979 Washington, D. C.
1980-127	Sutherland, Leonardo Cantin	12082 Nieto Drive/Garden Grove CA 92640
1990-153	Sutko, Glenn Edward	PO Box 46/Cumming GA 30130
1976-088	Sutter, Howard Bruce	1368 Hamilton Rd/Kennesaw GA 30144
1966-089	Sutton, Donald Howard	1145 Mountain Ivy Drive/Roswell GA 30075
1977-138	Sutton, Johnny Ike	1909 Elm Street/Glenn Heights TX 75154
1997-158	Sutton, Larry James	932 South Easthills Drive/West Covina CA 91791
1996-176	Suzuki, Makoto 'Mac'	Old Add: Kobe Japan
1986-147	Sveum, Dale Curtis	13483 East Estrella Avenue/Scottsdale AZ 85259
1983-140	Swaggerty, William David	4421 Old Hanover Road/Westminster MD 21158
1973-114	Swan, Craig Steven	25 Long Meadow Road/Riverside CT 6878
1914-207	Swan, Harry Gordon 'Ducky'	D. May 9, 1946 Pittsburgh, Pa.
1989-127	Swan, Russell Howard	785 SE Ridgeview Street/Pullman WA 99163
1955-121	Swanson, Arthur Leonard	1139 Chippenham Drive/Baton Rouge LA 70808
1929-102	Swanson, Ernest Evar	D. July 17, 1973 Galesburg, Ill.
1928-095	Swanson, Karl Edward	212 Hillcrest Drive/Avon Park FL 33825
1971-101	Swanson, Stanley Lawrence	Old Add: 235 Antigone Drive Hamilton MT 59840
1914-208	Swanson, William Andrew	D. October 14, 1954 New York, N.Y.
1947-087	Swartz, Sherwin Merle	D. June 24, 1991
1920-114	Swartz, Vernon Monroe 'Dazzy'	D. January 13, 1980 Germantown, O.
1995-214	Swartzbaugh, David Theodore	%A.Swartzbaugh 811 Baler Court Middletown OH 45044
1914-209	Sweeney, Charles Francis	D. March 13, 1955 Pittsburgh, Pa.
1944-127	Sweeney, Henry Leon	D. May 6, 1980 Columbia, Tenn.
1995-215	Sweeney, Mark Patrick	32 Hemlock Street/Holliston MA 1746
1995-216	Sweeney, Michael John	2802 Tam O'Shanter/Ontario CA 91761
1928-096	Sweeney, William Joseph	D. April 18, 1957 San Diego, Calif.
1978-131	Sweet, Richard Joe 'Rick'	7402 Michigan Street/Vancouver WA 98664
1927-088	Sweetland, Lester Leo	D. March 4, 1974 Melbourne, Fl.
1922-133	Swentor, August William	D. November 10, 1969 Waterbury, Conn.
1929-103	Swetonic, Stephen Albert	D. April 22, 1974 Canonsburg, Pa.
1940-089	Swift, Robert Virgil	D. October 17, 1966 Detroit, Mich.
1985-108	Swift, William Charles	5880 East Sapphire Lane/Paradise Valley AZ 85253
1932-082	Swift, William Vincent	D. February 23, 1969 Bartow, Fla.
1939-115	Swigart, Oadis Vaughn	D. August 8, 1997 St. Joseph, Mo.
1917-080	Swigler, Adam William	D. February 5, 1975 Philadelphia, Pa.
1986-148	Swindell, Forest Gregory 'Greg'	5639 East Sanna Street/Paradise Valley AZ 85253
1911-164	Swindell, Joshua Ernest	D. March 19, 1969 Fruita, Colo.
1993-176	Swingle, Paul Christopher	2732 West Obispo Circle/Mesa AZ 85202
1974-129	Swisher, Steven Eugene	1905 Washington Avenue/Parkersburg WV 26101
1965-104	Swoboda, Ronald Alan	315 Alonzo Street/New Orleans LA 70115
1977-139	Sykes, Robert Joseph	509 West Main St/Carmi IL 62821
1953-088	Szekely, Joseph	3260 Allen/Paris TX 75460
1970-131	Szotkiewicz, Kenneth John	205 Bruce Drive/Statesboro GA 30058
1994-103	Tabaka, Jeffrey Jon	Old Add: 5360 Longwoods Drive Indianapolis IN 46254
1976-089	Tabb, Jerry Lynn	8500 Nw 89th/Oklahoma City OK 73132
1926-082	Taber, Edward Timothy 'Lefty'	D. November 5, 1983 Lincoln, Neb.
1981-135	Tabler, Patrick Sean	11814 Spiral Pass/Cincinnati OH 45249
1987-143	Tabor, Gregory Stephen	29317 Whale Bone Way/Hayward CA 94544
1938-097	Tabor, James Reubin	D. August 22, 1953 Sacramento, Calif.
1991-169	Tackett, Jeffery Wilson	3119 Belair Court/Camarillo CA 93010
1913-178	Taff, John Gallatin	D. May 15, 1961 Houston, Tex.
1928-097	Taitt, Douglas John	D. December 12, 1970 Portland, Ore.
1963-119	Talbot, Frederick Lealand	7701 Lunseford Lane/Falls Church VA 22043
1953-089	Talbot, Robert Dale	608 West Kaweah/Visalia CA 93277
1943-137	Talcott, Leroy Everett	5060 Southwest 82nd Avenue/Miami FL 33155
1966-090	Talton, Marion Lee 'Tim'	130 Hardy Talton Road/Pikeville NC 27863
1976-090	Tamargo, John Felix	5810 Silver Moon Avenue/Tampa FL 33625
1934-100	Tamulis, Vitautis Casimirus	D. May 5, 1974 Wethersfield, Conn.
1973-115	Tanana, Frank Daryl	28492 South Harwich/Farmington Hills MI 48334
1925-101	Tankersley, Lawrence William 'Leo'	D. September 18, 1980 Dallas, Texas
1985-109	Tanner, Bruce Matthew	1 East Hazelcroft Avenue/New Castle PA 16105
1955-122	Tanner, Charles William	34 Maitland Ln East/New Castle PA 16101
1989-128	Tapani, Kevin Ray	7232 Paulsen Drive/Eden Prairie MN 55346
1954-106	Tappe, Elvin Walter	D. October 10, 1998 Quincy, Ill.
1950-097	Tappe, Theodore Nash	500 North Emerson #603/Wenatchee WA 98801
1914-221	Tappen, Walter Van Dorn	D. December 19, 1967 Lynwood, Calif.

1993-177	Tarasco, Anthony Giacinto	1950 Cloverfield #12/Santa Monica CA 90404
1927-089	Tarbert, Wilber Arlington 'Arlie'	D. November 27, 1946 Cleveland, O.
1984-118	Tartabull, Danilo	16840 Northwest 79th Place/Hialeah FL 33016
1962-130	Tartabull, Jose	16840 Nw 79th Place/Hialeah FL 33016
1986-149	Tarver, Laschelle	1148 Second Street/Clovis CA 93612
1958-090	Tasby, Willie	1486 12th St/Oakland CA 94607
1946-096	Tate, Alvin Walter	D. May 8, 1993 Bountiful, Utah
1924-107	Tate, Henry Bennett 'Bennie'	D. October 27, 1973 Frankfort, Ill.
1958-091	Tate, Lee Willie	6905 Pratt/Omaha NE 68131
1975-116	Tate, Randall Lee	8550 County Road 33/Killen AL 35645
1989-129	Tate, Stuat Douglas	695 Liberty Hill Road/Toney AL 35773
1997-159	Tatis, Fernando	Old Add: San Pedro De Macoris D. R.
1997-160	Tatis, Ramon Francisco	Old Add: Guayabin Dominican Rep.
1992-140	Tatum, James Ray	7433 Indian Wells Cove/Littleton CO 80124
1968-101	Tatum, Jarvis	PO Box 1506/Moreno Valley CA 92556
1969-166	Tatum, Kenneth Ray	19 Oakdale Road/Montevallo AL 35115
1941-111	Tatum, Thomas Vee Tee	D. November 7, 1989 Oklahoma City, Okla.
1991-170	Taubensee, Edward Kenneth	2600 Lake Grassmere Circle/Zellwood FL 32798
1935-106	Tauby, Fred Joseph	D. November 23, 1955 Concordia, Calif.
1928-098	Tauscher, Walter Edward	D. November 27, 1992 Winter Haven, Fla.
1958-092	Taussig, Donald Franklin	910 Stuart Avenue #4h/Mamaroneck NY 10543
1994-104	Tavarez, Jesus Rafael	Calle Yz #39 Los Minas Santo Domingo Dominican Rep.
1993-178	Tavarez, Julian	Calle 17 #56, Buenas Aires Santiago Dominican Rep.
1921-102	Tavener, John Adam	D. September 14, 1969 Ft. Worth, Tex.
1976-091	Taveras, Alejandro Antonio 'Alex'	Calle 7b #18, Reparto Perello Santiago Dominican Rep.
1971-102	Taveras, Franklin Crisostomo	Calle 31 #16 Los Colinos Santiago Dominican Rep.
1969-167	Taylor, Charles Gilbert 'Chuck'	1535 Georgetown Lane/Murfreesboro TN 37129
1958-093	Taylor, Antonio 'Tony'	334 East Lake Road #124/Palm Harbor FL 34685
1921-103	Taylor, Arlas Walter	D. September 10, 1958 Dade City, Fla.
1912-194	Taylor, Benjamin Harrison	D. November 3, 1946 Martin County, Ind.
1977-140	Taylor, Bruce Bell	8 Highland Park Rd/Rutland MA 1543
1925-102	Taylor, C. L. 'Chink'	D. July 7, 1980 Temple, Texas
1968-102	Taylor, Carl Means	2356 Riviera Drive/Sarasota FL 34232
1926-083	Taylor, Daniel Turney	D. October 11, 1972 Latrobe, Pa.
1987-144	Taylor, Donald Clyde Dorn	1645 Franklin Avenue/Willow Grove PA 19090
1986-150	Taylor, Dwight Bernard	Old Add: 1230 North Park Ave #103 Tucson AZ 85721
1926-084	Taylor, Edward James	D. January 30, 1992 Chula Vista, Calif.
1951-094	Taylor, Eugene Benjamin 'Ben'	1813 West Main Street/Clarksville AR 72830
1950-098	Taylor, Frederick Rankin	3144 Derby Road/Columbus OH 43221
1969-168	Taylor, Gary William	Old Add: 827 North Martha Dearborn MI 48128
1957-083	Taylor, Harry Evans	2125 Cooks Lane/Fort Worth TX 76120
1932-083	Taylor, Harry Warren	D. April 27, 1969 Toledo, O.
1946-097	Taylor, James Harry 'Harry'	8571 Us Highway 150/West Terre Haute IN 47885
1920-115	Taylor, James Wren 'Zack'	D. September 19, 1974 Orlando, Fla.
1954-107	Taylor, Joe Cephus	D. March 18, 1993 Pittsburgh, Pa.
1993-179	Taylor, Kerry Thomas	506 6th Street NE/Roseau MN 56751
1923-131	Taylor, Leo Thomas	D. May 20, 1982 Seattle, Wash.
1911-165	Taylor, Philip Wiley	D. July 9, 1954 Topeka, Kan.
1957-084	Taylor, Robert Dale 'Hawk'	Rr 5 Box 897/Murray KY 42071
1970-132	Taylor, Robert Lee	27 Sunnybrook Rd/Springfield MA 1109
1992-141	Taylor, Rodney Scott Scott	926 Indian Branch Lane/Defiance OH 43512
1962-131	Taylor, Ronald Wesley	19 Alvin Avenue/Toronto Ontario M4T 2A7 Canada
1958-094	Taylor, Samuel Douglas	PO Box 812/Simpsonville SC 29681
1995-217	Taylor, Scott Michael	1461 Woodale Street/Wichita KS 67230
1988-130	Taylor, Terry Derrell	743 West Walnut Avenue/Crestview FL 32536
1924-108	Taylor, Thomas Livingstone Carlton	D. April 5, 1956 Greenville, Miss.
1952-099	Taylor, Vernon Charles 'Pete'	Old Add: 823 Cedarcroft Drive Millersville MD 21108
1991-171	Taylor, Wade Eric	6 Sleepy Hollow Cove/Longwood FL 32750
1994-105	Taylor, William Howell	140 Covington Place/Thomasville GA 31792
1954-108	Taylor, William Michael	Old Add: PO Box 146/Acton CA 93510
1930-082	Teachout, Arthur John 'Bud'	D. May 11, 1985 Laguna Beach, Calif.
1936-091	Tebbetts, George Robert 'Birdie'	1078 Oak Avenue/Anna Maria FL 33501
1914-211	Tedrow, Allen Seymour	D. January 23, 1958 Westerville, O.
1953-090	Teed, Richard Leroy	45 Taylor Street/Windsor CT 6095
1997-161	Tejada, Miguel Ordalis Martinez	Old Add: Bani Dominican Republic
1986-151	Tejada, Wilfredo Aristides	Calle Prinera #12,Manzana 3947 Santo Domingo Dominican Rep.
1974-130	Tekulve, Kenton Charles	1531 Sequoia/Pittsburgh PA 15241
1996-177	Telemaco, Amaury Regalado	Old Add: La Romana Dominican Rep.
1990-154	Telford, Anthony Charles	2733 Scottsdale Drive/San Jose CA 95148
1993-180	Telgheder, David William	58 Orchard Crest Drive/Westtown NY 10998
1979-109	Tellmann, Thomas John	271 Yankee Bush Road/Starbrick PA 16365
1952-100	Temple, John Ellis	D. January 9, 1994 Anderson, S. C.
1955-123	Templeton, Charles Sherman	D. October 9, 1997 Irving, Texas
1976-092	Templeton, Garry Lewis	13552 Del Poniente Road/Poway CA 92064
1969-169	Tenace, Fury Gene 'Gene'	2650 Cliff Hawk Court/Redmond OR 97756
1929-104	Tennant, James McDonnell	D. April 16, 1967 Trumbull, Conn.
1912-195	Tennant, Thomas Francis	D. February 16, 1955 San Carlos, Calif.
1967-105	Tepedino, Frank Ronald	95 Davis St/Hauppauge NY 11787
1946-098	Tepsic, Joseph John	Rural Route 3 Box 164/Tyrone PA 16686

1972-112	Terlecki, Robert Joseph	923 Rowantree Circle/Morrisville PA 19067
1975-117	Terlecky, Gregory John	2130 Camino Laurel/San Clemente CA 92673
1974-131	Terpko, Jeffrey Michael	Rr 1 Box 156/Sayre PA 18840
1982-125	Terrell, Charles Walter Walt	2188 Rice Pike/Union KY 41091
1973-116	Terrell, Jerry Wayne	1301 Sunny Creek Ln/Blue Springs MO 64015
1940-090	Terry, Lancelot Yank	D. November 4, 1979 Bloomington, Ind.
1956-081	Terry, Ralph Willard	801 Park Street/Larned KS 67550
1986-152	Terry, Scott Ray	3009 Stony Ridge Court/Saint Louis MO 63129
1923-132	Terry, William Harold	D. January 9, 1989 Jacksonville, Fla.
1916-087	Terry, Zebulon Alexander	D. March 14, 1988 Los Angeles, Calif.
1932-084	Terwilliger, Richard Martin	D. January 21, 1969 Greenville, Mich.
1949-086	Terwilliger, Willard Wayne 'Wayne'	2945 Cambridge/Mound MN 55364
1915-160	Tesch, Albert John	D. August 3, 1947 Jersey City, N.J.
1912-196	Tesreau, Charles Monroe 'Jeff'	D. September 24, 1946 Hanover, N.H.
1958-095	Testa, Nicholas	4324 Kepler Avenue/Bronx NY 10470
1955-124	Tettelbach, Richard Morley	D. January 26, 1995 East Harwich, Mass.
1984-119	Tettleton, Mickey Lee	52 Royal Oak Road/Pauls Valley OK 73075
1983-141	Teufel, Timothy Shawn	Old Add: 411 Santa Marina Court Escondido CA 92029
1986-153	Tewksbury, Robert Alan	63 Ridge Road/Concord NH 3301
1914-212	Textor, George	D. March 11, 1954 Massillon, O.
1958-096	Thacker, Morris Benton 'Moe'	D. November 13, 1997 Louisville, Ky.
1978-132	Thayer, Gregory Allen	1000 3rd St North/Sauk Rapids MN 56379
1920-116	Theis, John Louis	D. July 6, 1941 Georgetown, O.
1977-141	Theiss, Duane Charles	236 East Walnut Street/Waterville OH 43081
1971-103	Theobald, Ronald Merrill	319 West Jacaranda/Fullerton CA 92632
1973-117	Theodore, George Basil	1388 Princeton Avenue/Salt Lake City UT 84105
1944-128	Thesenga, Arnold Joseph 'Jug'	3907 Countryside Plaza/Wichita KS 67218
1924-109	Thevenow, Thomas Joseph	D. July 28, 1957 Madison, Ind.
1952-101	Thiel, Maynard Bert	Rural Route 2/Marion WI 54950
1963-120	Thies, David Robert	6140 Arctic Way/Minneapolis MN 55436
1954-109	Thies, Vernon Arthur 'Jake'	4 Cornflower Court/Florissant MO 63033
1986-154	Thigpen, Robert Thomas	PO Box 87/Monticello FL 32344
1995-218	Thobe, John Joseph 'J. J.'	9531 Panacea Drive/Huntington Beach CA 92646
1995-219	Thobe, Thomas Neal	9531 Panacea Drive/Huntington Beach CA 92646
1967-106	Thoenen, Richard Crispin	51 North Peach St/Medford OR 97501
1926-085	Thomas, Alphonse Thomas 'Tommy'	D. April 27, 1988 York County, Pa.
1985-110	Thomas, Andres Peres	35 Duarte #35 Boca Chica Dominican Rep.
1911-166	Thomas, Blaine M.	D. August 21, 1915 Payson, Ariz.
1960-099	Thomas, Carl Leslie	4525 North 66th Street #99/Scottsdale AZ 85251
1912-197	Thomas, Chester David 'Pinch'	D. December 24, 1953 Modesto, Calif.
1925-103	Thomas, Clarence Fletcher 'Lefty'	D. March 21, 1952 Charlottesville, Va.
1916-088	Thomas, Claude Alfred	D. March 6, 1946 Sulphur, Okla.
1976-093	Thomas, Danny Lee	D. June 12, 1980 Mobile, Ala.
1971-104	Thomas, Derrel Osbon	7908 Wisteria Court/Highland CA 92346
1927-090	Thomas, Fay Wesley	D. August 16, 1990 Chatsworth, Calif.
1990-155	Thomas, Frank Edward	3649 Dunhill Drive/Columbus GA 31906
1951-095	Thomas, Frank Joseph	118 Doray Drive/Pittsburgh PA 15237
1918-070	Thomas, Frederick Harvey	D. January 15, 1986 Rice Lake, Wisc.
1957-085	Thomas, George Edward	927 Wallace Drive/Amery WI 54001
1924-110	Thomas, Herbert Mark	D. December 4, 1991 Starke, Fla.
1973-118	Thomas, James Gorman	759 Tallwood Rd/Charleston SC 29412
1961-104	Thomas, James Leroy 'Lee'	14260 Manderleigh Woods Dr/Chesterfield MO 63017
1951-096	Thomas, John Tillman 'Bud'	2607 Stephenson Street/Sedalia MO 65301
1952-102	Thomas, Keith Marshall	D. January 7, 1995 Rocky Mount, N. C.
1995-220	Thomas, Larry Wayne	1003 Louise Avenue/Mobile AL 36609
1950-099	Thomas, Leo Raymond	Old Add: 2024 Sandcreek Way Alameda CA 94501
1932-085	Thomas, Luther Baxter 'Bud'	56 Morningside Court/Ruckersville VA 22968
1995-221	Thomas, Michael Steven	Old Add: 350 Windwood Loop Cabot AR 72023
1926-086	Thomas, Myles Lewis	D. December 12, 1963 Toledo, O.
1938-098	Thomas, Raymond Joseph	D. December 6, 1993 Wilson, N. C.
1921-104	Thomas, Robert William 'Red'	D. March 29, 1962 Fremont, O.
1977-142	Thomas, Roy Justin	6514 West Robin Lane/Glendale AZ 85310
1974-132	Thomas, Stanley Brown	23 Middle Avenue/Mexico Me 4257
1957-086	Thomas, Valmy	Box 9184/Santurce PR 908
1910-143	Thomasen, Arthur Wilson	D. May 2, 1944 Kansas City, Mo.
1974-133	Thomason, Melvin Erskine 'Erskine'	Rural Route 7 Box 738/Laurens SC 29360
1972-113	Thomasson, Gary Leah	Old Add: 4515 E. Onyx St Phoenix AZ 85028
1991-172	Thome, James Howard	1827 South Crest Drive/Peoria IL 61605
1978-133	Thompson, Bobby Larue	Old Add: 3106 Capitol Dr #2 Charlotte NC 28208
1954-110	Thompson, Charles Lemoine	536 Summit Drive/Lewistown PA 17044
1970-133	Thompson, Danny Leon	D. December 10, 1976 Rochester, Minn.
1948-098	Thompson, David Forrest	D. February 26, 1979 Charlotte, N. C.
1949-087	Thompson, Donald Newlin	87 East Euclid Pkwy/Asheville NC 28804
1939-116	Thompson, Eugene Earl	7934 East Crestwood Way/Scottsdale AZ 85250
1920-117	Thompson, Frank E.	D. June 27, 1940 Jasper Co., Mineral Twp., Mo.
1911-167	Thompson, Fuller Weidner	D. February 19, 1972 Los Angeles, Calif.
1919-082	Thompson, Harold	D. February 14, 1951 Reno, Nev.
1947-088	Thompson, Henry Curtis	D. September 30, 1969 Fresno, Calif.
1914-213	Thompson, James Alfred	D. January 7, 1990 Black Mountain, N. C.

1976-094 ....Thompson, Jason Dolph ....1358 Forest Bay Drive/Waterford MI 48328
1996-178 ....Thompson, Jason Michael ....25141 Buckboard Lane/Laguna Hills CA 92653
1921-105 ....Thompson, John Dudley 'Lee' ....D. February 17, 1965 Santa Barbara, Calif.
1948-099 ....Thompson, John Samuel 'Jocko' ....D. February 3, 1988 Olney, Md.
1996-179 ....Thompson, Justin Willard ....Old Add: 510 Enchanted Hollow Dr Spring TX 77388
1925-104 ....Thompson, Lafayette Fresco ....D. November 20, 1968 Fullerton, Calif.
1994-106 ....Thompson, Mark Radford ....146 Nature Drive/Russellville KY 42276
1971-105 ....Thompson, Michael Wayne ....7565 Turner Dr/Denver CO 80221
1984-120 ....Thompson, Milton Bernard ....1404 Heath Court/Williamstown NJ 8094
1985-111 ....Thompson, Richard Neil ....7 Chambers Court/Huntington Station NY 11746
1986-155 ....Thompson, Robert Randall ....4438 Gun Club Road/West Palm Beach FL 33406
1933-060 ....Thompson, Rupert Luckhart 'Tommy' ....D. May 24, 1971 Auburn, Calif.
1992-142 ....Thompson, Ryan Orlando ....918 Woodcrest Drive/Dover DE 19904
1912-198 ....Thompson, Thomas Carl ....D. January 16, 1963 Lajolla, Calif.
1912-199 ....Thompson, Thomas Homer ....D. September 19, 1957 Atlanta, Ga.
1978-134 ....Thompson, Vernon Scot ....110 Beacon Rd/Renfrew PA 16053
1997-162 ....Thomson, John Carl..........................1414 East Kent Street/Sulphur La/70663
1946-099 ....Thomson, Robert Brown ....122 Sunlit Drive/Watchung NJ 7060
1979-110 ....Thon, Richard William 'Dickie' ....3022 West Hickory Park Circle/Sugarland TX 77479
1917-081 ....Thormahlen, Herbert Ehler 'Hank' ....D. February 6, 1955 Los Angeles, Calif.
1977-143 ....Thormodsgard, Paul Gayton ....Old Add: 6531 E. Cypress Scottsdale AZ 85257
1973-119 ....Thornton, Andre ....Box 395/Chagrin Falls OH 44022
1985-112 ....Thornton, Louis ....115 McLean Road/Hope Hull AL 36043
1973-120 ....Thornton, Otis Benjamin ....410 7th Street/Docena AL 35060
1951-097 ....Thorpe, Benjamin Robert ....D. October 30, 1996 Waveland, Miss.
1913-179 ....Thorpe, James Francis ....D. March 28, 1953 Lomita, Calif.
1955-125 ....Thorpe, Robert Joseph ....D. March 17, 1960 San Diego, Calif.
1916-089 ....Thrasher, Frank Edward 'Buck' ....D. June 12, 1938 Cleveland, Tenn.
1955-126 ....Throneberry, Marvin Eugene ....D. June 23, 1994 Fisherville, Tenn.
1952-103 ....Throneberry, Maynard Faye 'Faye' ....12016 Macon Road/Collierville TN 38017
1975-118 ....Throop, George Lynford ....239 Windwood Lane/Sierra Madre CA 91024
1939-117 ....Thuman, Louis Charles Frank ....6117 Edlynne Rd/Baltimore MD 21212
1987-145 ....Thurman, Gary Montez ....6814 Equestrian Court/Indianapolis IN 46260
1997-163 ....Thurman, Michael Richard ....Old Add: Philomath OR 97370
1955-127 ....Thurman, Robert Burns ....D. October 31, 1998 Wichita, Kan.
1983-142 ....Thurmond, Mark Anthony ....Old Add: 4706 Misty Shadows Dr Houston TX 77041
1923-133 ....Thurston, Hollis John 'Sloppy' ....D. September 14, 1973 Los Angeles, Calif.
1964-121 ....Tiant, Luis Clemente ....14 Steeple Run Way/Savannah GA 31405
1984-121 ....Tibbs, Jay Lindsey ....Old Add: 1451 Annapolis Way Grayson GA 30221
1972-114 ....Tidrow, Richard William ....324 NE Warrington Court/Lees Summit MO 64064
1952-104 ....Tiefenauer, Bobby Gene ....700 Poplar/Desloge MO 63601
1962-132 ....Tiefenthaler, Verle Wayne ....1852 Quint Ave/Carroll IA 51401
1920-118 ....Tierney, James Arthur 'Cotton' ....D. April 18, 1953 Kansas City, Mo.
1933-061 ....Tietje, Leslie William ....D. October 2, 1996 Rochester, Minn.
1957-087 ....Tighe, John Thomas 'Jack' ....145 Southeast 28th Avenue/Pompano Beach FL 33062
1915-161 ....Tillman, John Lawrence ....D. April 7, 1964 Harrisburg, Pa.
1962-133 ....Tillman, John Robert 'Bob' ....403 Waderbrook Dr/Gallatin TN 37066
1982-126 ....Tillman, Kerry Jerome Rusty ....130 Jackson Rd/Atlantic Beach FL 32233
1967-107 ....Tillotson, Thaddeus Asa ....2025 Finch Court/Atwater CA 95301
1969-170 ....Timberlake, Gary Dale ....1975 Banner Avenue/Corydon IN 47112
1991-173 ....Timlin, Michael August ....1801 Palm Valley Blvd #1812/Round Round TX 78864
1969-171 ....Timmermann, Thomas Henry ....11369 Centennial Drive/Whitmore Lake MI 48189
1995-222 ....Timmons, Osborne Llewellyn 'Ozzie' ....4901 83rd Street/Tampa FL 33619
1914-214 ....Tincup, Austin Ben ....D. July 5, 1980 Claremore, Ok.
1982-127 ....Tingley, Ronald Irvin ....Old Add: 1830 Greenbrae Sparks NV 89431
1932-086 ....Tinning, Lyle Forrest 'Bud' ....D. January 17, 1961 Evansville, Ind.
1993-181 ....Tinsley, Lee Owen ....237 Tenor Street/Shelbyville KY 40065
1915-162 ....Tipple, Daniel ....D. March 26, 1960 Omaha, Neb.
1939-118 ....Tipton, Eric Gordon ....125 Nina Lane/Williamsburg VA 23185
1948-100 ....Tipton, Joseph John ....D. March 1, 1994 Birmingham, Ala.
1969-172 ....Tischinski, Thomas Arthur ....2607 NE 68th Ter/Gladstone MO 64119
1936-092 ....Tising, Johnnie Joseph ....D. September 5, 1967 Leadville, Colo.
1978-135 ....Tobik, David Vance ....Old Add: 1243 Coryden Road Cleveland OH 44124
1937-099 ....Tobin, James Anthony..........................D. May 19, 1969 Oakland, Calif.
1932-087 ....Tobin, John Martin ....D. August 8, 1983 Rhinebeck, N. Y.
1945-105 ....Tobin, John Patrick ....D. January 18, 1982 Oakland, Calif.
1914-215 ....Tobin, John Thomas ....D. December 10, 1969 St. Louis, Mo.
1941-112 ....Tobin, Marion Brooks 'Pat' ....D. January 21, 1975 Shreveport, La.
1932-088 ....Todd, Alfred Chester ....D. March 8, 1985 Elmira, N. Y.
1977-144 ....Todd, Jackson ....Oklahoma Sooners Baseball 401 West Inhoff Norman OK 73019
1974-134 ....Todd, James Richard ....Old Add: 8630 East Pawne Dr Parker CO 80134
1924-111 ....Todt, Philip Julius ....D. November 15, 1973 St. Louis, Mo.
1947-089 ....Toenes, William Harrell 'Hal' ....5119 Branch Avenue/Tampa FL 33603
1965-105 ....Tolan, Robert ....804woodstock Street/Bellaire TX 77401
1991-174 ....Tolentino, Jose Franco ....PO Box 351/Seminole OK 74868
1984-122 ....Toliver, Freddie Lee ....27470 Stratford Street/Highland CA 92346
1981-136 ....Tolleson, Jimmy Wayne Wayne ....313 Massycup Oak Court/Spartanburg SC 29306
1981-137 ....Tolman, Timothy Lee ....6828 Dechelly Loop/Tucson AZ 85741
1925-105 ....Tolson, Chester Julius 'Chick' ....D. April 16, 1965 Washington, D. C.

1953-091	Tomanek, Richard Carl	165 Duff Dr/Avon Lake OH 44012
1949-088	Tomasic, Andrew John	677 Maryland Street/Whitehall PA 18052
1993-182	Tomberlin, Andy Lee	7411 Crooked Creek Road/Monroe NC 28110
1913-180	Tomer, George Clarence	D. December 15, 1984 Perry, Iowa
1997-164	Tomko, Brett Daniel	4805 Grainary Avenue/Tampa FL 33624
1972-115	Tomlin, David Allen	2020 Clayton Road/Manchester OH 45144
1990-156	Tomlin, Randy Leon	110 Ridgeview Lane/Madison Heights VA 24572
1912-200	Tompkins, Charles Herbert	D. September 20, 1975 Prescott, Ark.
1965-106	Tompkins, Ronald Everett	25072 Leucadia #G/Aliso Viejo CA 92656
1975-119	Toms, Thomas Howard	Old Add: 1707 Roxbury Drive/Wilson NC 27893
1911-168	Toney, Fred Alexandra	D. March 11, 1953 Nashville, Tenn.
1911-169	Tonneman, Charles Richard 'Tony'	D. August 7, 1951 Prescott, Ariz.
1911-170	Tooley, Albert	D. August 17, 1976 Marshall, Mich.
1921-106	Toporcer, George 'Specs'	D. May 17, 1989 Huntington Station, N.Y.
1962-134	Toppin, Ruperto	3124 Shadow Pond Terrace/Winter Garden FL 34787
1964-122	Torborg, Jeffrey Allen	5208 Ciesta Cove Drive/Sarasota FL 34242
1947-090	Torgeson, Clifford Earl 'Earl'.	D. November 8, 1990 Everett, Wash.
1917-082	Torkelson, Chester Leroy 'Red'	D. September 22, 1964 Chicago, Ill.
1920-119	Torphy, Walter Anthony 'Red'.	D. February 11, 1980 Fall River, Mass.
1956-082	Torre, Frank Joseph	% Torre Ent. 11985 Ushwy 1 #204 West Palm Beach FL 33408
1960-100	Torre, Joseph Paul	20 Lawrence Lane/Harrison NY 10528
1975-120	Torrealba, Pablo Arnoldo	El Manantial,Apt L.Cordones "Piso 5, Aptos 52, Barquisimeto Venezuela/"
1977-145	Torres, Angel Rafael	Seccim Lacienga Casa 40 Azua Dominican Rep.
1995-223	Torres, Dilson Dario	1009 1/2 38th Street/Kansas City MO 64111
1940-091	Torres, Don Gilberto (Nunez) 'Gil'	D. January 10, 1983 Regla, Havana Cuba
1962-135	Torres, Felix	Hc01 Box 6424/Santa Isabel PR 757
1968-103	Torres, Hector Epitacio	662 Lexington Street/Dunedin FL 34698
1920-120	Torres, Ricardo J.	D. April 17, 1960 Regla, Havana, Cuba
1971-106	Torres, Rosendo 'Rusty'	250 North Cedar Street/Massapequa NY 11758
1993-183	Torres, Salomon Ramirez	Prol. Carlos Ordonez 53 San Pedro De Macoris Dominican Rep.
1967-108	Torrez, Michael Augustine	56 Mansfield Road/White Plains NY 10605
1988-131	Torve, Kelvin Curtis	18701 Hammock Lane/Davidson NC 28036
1942-100	Tost, Louis Eugene	D. February 22, 1967 Santa Clara, Calif.
1962-136	Toth, Paul Louis	3540 West 214th Street/Cleveland OH 44126
1928-099	Touchstone, Clayland Maffitt	D. April 28, 1949 Beaumont, Tex.
1965-107	Tovar, Cesar Leonardo	D. July 14, 1994 Caracas, Venezuela
1920-121	Townsend, Ira Dance	D. July 21, 1965 Schulenberg, Tex.
1920-122	Townsend, Leo Alphonse	D. December 3, 1976 Mobile, Ala.
1984-123	Traber, James Joseph	11674 Little Patuxent #203/Columbia MD 21044
1962-137	Tracewski, Richard John	5 Flora Dr/Peckville PA 18452
1993-184	Trachsel, Stephen Christopher	4141 Ricardo Drive/Yorba Linda CA 92686
1980-128	Tracy, James Edwin	3535 Arlington Avenue/Hamilton OH 45015
1913-181	Tragesser, Walter Joseph	D. December 14, 1970 Lafayette, Ind.
1940-092	Tramback, Stephen Joseph 'Red'.	D. December 28, 1979 Buffalo, N. Y.
1977-146	Trammell, Alan Stuart	641 North Old Woodward Ave #9/Birmingham MI 48009
1997-165	Trammell, Thomas Bubba 'Bubba'	Old Add: Knoxville TN 37901
1915-163	Trautman, Frederick Orlando	D. February 15, 1964 Bucyrus, O.
1988-132	Trautwein, John Howard	452 West Oakwood Drive/Barrington IL 60010
1912-201	Travers, Aloysius Joseph Allan	D. April 21, 1968 Philadelphia, Pa.
1974-135	Travers, William Edward	10 Shoreline Dr/Foxboro MA 2035
1933-062	Travis, Cecil Howell	2260 Highway 138/Riverdale GA 30296
1990-157	Traxler, Brian Lee	363 Sutton Avenue/San Antonio TX 78228
1920-123	Traynor, Harold Joseph 'Pie'	D. March 16, 1972 Pittsburgh, Pa.
1930-083	Treadaway, Edgar Raymond 'Ray'	D. October 12, 1935 Chattanooga, Tenn.
1987-146	Treadway, Hugh Jeffery 'Jeff'	116 Stillwater Trace/Griffin GA 30223
1944-129	Treadway, Thadford Leon 'Red'	D. May 26, 1994 Atlanta, Ga.
1986-156	Trebelhorn, Thomas Lynn	4344 SE 26th Avenue/Portland OR 97202
1937-100	Trechock, Frank Adam	D. January 16, 1989 Minneapolis, Minn.
1913-182	Trekell, Harry Roy	D. November 4, 1963 Spokane, Wash.
1934-101	Tremark, Nicholas Joseph	1906 Laurel Drive/Harlingen TX 78550
1954-111	Tremel, William Leonard	315 East 23rd Ave/Altoona PA 16601
1995-224	Tremie, Christopher James 'Jim'	2442 Rodney/Houston TX 77034
1927-091	Tremper, Carlton Overton 'Overton'	D. January 8, 1996 Clearwater, Fla.
1938-099	Tresh, Michael	D. October 1, 1966 Detroit, Mich.
1961-105	Tresh, Thomas Michael	4256 East Wing Road/Mount Pleasant MI 48858
1978-136	Trevino, Alejandro	Alondra #103,Cuachtemoc Monterrey Nuevo Leon Mexico
1968-104	Trevino, Carlos Castro 'Bobby'	Alondra #102, Cuauhtemoc Monterrey Nuevo Laredo Mexico
1953-092	Triandos, Constandin Gus 'Gus'	PO Box 5642/San Jose CA 95150
1953-093	Trice, Robert Lee	D. September 16, 1988 Weirton, W. Va.
1973-121	Trillo, Jesus Manuel 'Manny'.	Calle 724 Ave 3am Ed. Everest #14 Maracaibo Venezuela
1955-128	Trimble, Joseph Gerard	14 Fair Oaks Drive/Lincoln RI 2865
1943-138	Trinkle, Kenneth Wayne	D. May 10, 1976 Paoli, Ill.
1938-100	Triplett, Herman Coaker 'Coaker'	D. January 30, 1992 Boone, N. C.
1992-143	Trlicek, Richard Alan	20818 Park Canyon Drive/Katy TX 77450
1973-122	Troedson, Richard Lamonte	899 Bowen Avenue/San Jose CA 95123
1992-144	Trombley, Michael Scott	942 Fairfield Way/Minnetonka MN 55305
1958-097	Trosky, Harold Arthur	1414 NE Curtis Bridge Road/Swisher IA 52338
1933-063	Trosky, Harold Arthur, Sr.	D. June 18, 1979 Cedar Rapids, Iowa
1937-101	Trotter, William Felix	D. August 26, 1984 Arlington, Mass.

1952-105 ....Trouppe, Quincy Thomas ....D. August 10, 1993 Creve Coeur, Mo.
1939-119 ....Trout, Paul Howard 'Dizzy' ....D. February 28, 1972 Harvey, Ill.
1978-137 ....Trout, Steven Russell...............................919 Riverview Drive/South Holland IL 60473
1956-083 ....Trowbridge, Robert ....D. April 3, 1980 Hudson, N. Y.
1912-202 ....Troy, Robert 'Bun' ....D. October 7, 1918 Meuse, France
1941-113 ....Trucks, Virgil Oliver 'Fire' ....36 Santarem Circle/Punta Gorda FL 33983
1910-144 ....Truesdale, Frank Day ....D. August 27, 1943 Albuquerque, N. M.
1985-113 ....Trujillo, Michael Andrew ....2636 South Stuart Way/Denver CO 80219
1993-185 ....Tsamis, George Alex ....3234 Hyde Park Drive/Clearwatr FL 34621
1957-088 ....Tsitouris, John Philip ....5207 Austin Road/Monroe NC 28110
1993-186 ....Tubbs, Gregory Alan ....114 Hunter/Cookeville TN 38501
1992-145 ....Tucker, Eddie Jack 'Scooter' ....Old Add: 2556 Cricket Ridge Dr Cantonment FL 32533
1995-225 ....Tucker, Michael Anthony ....Old Add: Highway 600 Chase City VA 23924
1927-092 ....Tucker, Oscar Dinwiddie ....D. July 13, 1940 Radiant, Va.
1942-101 ....Tucker, Thurman Lowell ....D. May 7, 1993 Oklahoma, Okla.
1979-111 ....Tudor, John Thomas ....31 Upton Hills Lane/Middleton MA 1949
1918-071 ....Tuero, Oscar Monzon................................D. October 21, 1960 Houston, Texas
1981-138 ....Tufts, Robert Malcolm ....67-38 108th Street #A27/Forest Hills NY 11375
1982-128 ....Tunnell, Byron Lee 'Lee' ....36 Stillmeadow/Round Rock TX 78664
1993-187 ....Turang, Brian Craig ....3014 McNab Avenue/Long Beach CA 90808
1935-107 ....Turbeville, George Elkins ....D. October 5, 1983 Salisbury, N. C.
1943-139 ....Turchin, Edward Lawrence ....D. February 8, 1982 Brookhaven, N. Y.
1923-134 ....Turgeon, Eugene Joseph 'Pete' ....D. January 24, 1977 Wichita Falls, Tex.
1922-134 ....Turk, Lucas Newton ....D. January 11, 1994 Homer, Ga.
1951-098 ....Turley, Robert Lee ....15470 Thorntree Run/Alpharetta Ga/30004
1993-188 ....Turner, Christopher Wan ....211 Schwarzkopf/Bowling Green KY 42104
1948-101 ....Turner, Earl Edwin ....18 Reservoir Road/Fort Edward NY 12828
1937-102 ....Turner, James Riley ....1004 Woodmont Blvd/Nashville TN 37204
1974-136 ....Turner, John Webber 'Jerry' ....1935 18th Street #B/Santa Monica CA 90404
1967-109 ....Turner, Kenneth Charles ....Old Add: 4913 Neblina Drive Carlsbad CA 92008
1977-162 ....Turner, Robert Edward 'Ted' ....1050 Techwood Avenue/Atlanta GA 30318
1988-133 ....Turner, Shane Lee ....13104 Glenn Court #20/Chino Hills CA 91709
1920-124 ....Turner, Theodore Holtop ....D. February 4, 1958 Lexington, Ky.
1915-164 ....Turner, Thomas Lovatt 'Tink' ....D. February 25, 1962 Philadelphia, Pa.
1940-093 ....Turner, Thomas Richard ....D. May 14, 1986 Kennewick, Wash.
1993-189 ....Turner, William Matthew 'Matt' ....829 Della Drive/Lexington KY 40504
1952-106 ....Tuttle, William Robert ....D. July 27, 1998 Anoka, Minn.
1911-171 ....Tutweiler, Guy Isbell ....D. August 15, 1930 Anniston, Ala.
1928-100 ....Tutwiler, Elmer Strange ....D. May 3, 1976 Pensacola, Fla.
1916-090 ....Twining, Howard Earle 'Twink' ....D. June 14, 1973 Lansdale, Pa.
1970-134 ....Twitchell, Wayne Lee ....5719 SW Bruggr Street/Portland OR 97219
1980-129 ....Twitty, Jeffrey Dean ....New Orleans Baseball Lakefront Arena New Orleans LA 70148
1920-125 ....Twombly, Clarence Edward 'Babe'.........D. November 22, 1974 San Clemente, Calif.
1921-107 ....Twombly, Edwin Parker 'Cy' ....D. December 3, 1974 Savannah, Ga.
1914-216 ....Twombly, George Frederick ....D. February 17, 1975 Lexington, Mass.
1943-140 ....Tyack, James Fred ....D. January 3, 1995 Bakersfield, Calif.
1914-217 ....Tyler, Frederick Franklin ....D. October 14, 1945 Derry, N.H.
1910-145 ....Tyler, George Albert 'Lefty' ....D. September 29, 1953 Lowell, Mass.
1934-102 ....Tyler, John Anthony.................................D. July 11, 1972 Mount Pleasant, Pa.
1914-218 ....Tyree, Earl Carlton ....D. May 17, 1954 Rushville, Ill.
1962-138 ....Tyriver, David Burton ....D. October 28, 1988 Oshkosh, Wis.
1972-116 ....Tyrone, James Vernon ....107 Encinal Street/Alice TX 78332
1976-095 ....Tyrone, Oscar Wayne 'Wayne' ....107 Encinal Street/Alice TX 78332
1926-087 ....Tyson, Albert Thomas 'Ty' ....D. August 16, 1953 Buffalo, N. Y.
1944-130 ....Tyson, Cecil Washington ....713 East Church Street/Elm City NC 27822
1972-117 ....Tyson, Michael Ray ....479 Thunderhead Canyon Dr/Baldwin MO 63011
1926-088 ....Uchrinscko, James Emerson 'Emerson' ....D. March 17, 1995 Mount Pleasant, Pa.
1962-139 ....Uecker, Robert George ....31n7867 North Country Lane/Menomonee Falls WI 53051
1934-103 ....Uhalt, Bernard Bartholomew ....1160 Leisure Lane #1/Walnut Creek CA 94595
1965-108 ....Uhlaender, Theodore Otto ....703 Filmore Street/McGregor TX 76657
1919-083 ....Uhle, George Ernest.................................D. February 26, 1985 Lakewood, O.
1938-101 ....Uhle, Robert Edward ....D. August 21, 1990 Santa Rosa, Calif.
1914-219 ....Uhler, Maurice William ....D. May 4, 1918 Baltimore Md.
1934-104 ....Uhlir, Charles Karel ....D. July 9, 1984 Spirit Lake, Iowa
1980-130 ....Ujdur, Gerald Raymond ....112 Riveness Road/Duluth MN 55811
1945-106 ....Ulisney, Michael Edward ....1481 Purita Street/Deltona FL 32725
1983-143 ....Ullger, Scott Matthew ....4232 West Cambridge/Visalia CA 93277
1944-131 ....Ullrich, Carlos Santiago Castello ....3671 Nw 15th Street/Miami FL 33125
1925-106 ....Ulrich, Frank W. 'Dutch' ....D. February 11, 1929 Baltimore, Md.
1964-123 ....Umbach, Arnold William ....760 Moores Mill Road/Auburn AL 36830
1975-121 ....Umbarger, James Harold ....421 Marwood Drive/Mansfield OH 44904
1959-083 ....Umbricht, James.......................................D. April 8, 1964 Houston, Tex.
1953-094 ....Umphlett, Thomas Mullen ....Rr 2 Box 17c/Ahoskie NC 27910
1927-093 ....Underhill, Willie Vern ....D. October 26, 1970 Bay City, Texas
1979-112 ....Underwood, Patrick John ....708 Riverview Drive/Kokomo IN 46901
1974-137 ....Underwood, Thomas Gerald ....13549 83rd Lane North/West Palm Beach FL 33412
1995-226 ....Unroe, Timothy Brian ....Old Add: 1112 W. Columbia Ave Chicago IL 60626
1942-102 ....Unser, Albert Bernard ....D. July 7, 1995 Decatur, Ill.
1968-105 ....Unser, Delbert Bernard ....115 Spyglass Drive/Blue Bell PA 19422

1935-108	Upchurch, Jefferson Woodrow 'Woody'	D. October 23, 1971 Buies Creek, N. C.
1967-110	Upham, John Leslie	1502 Pierre Avenue Windsor Ontario Canada
1915-165	Upham, William Lawrence	D. September 14, 1959 Newark, N.J.
1953-095	Upright, Roy T. 'Dixie'	D. November 13, 1986 Concord, N. C.
1966-091	Upshaw, Cecil Lee	D. February 7, 1995 Lawrenceville, Ga.
1978-138	Upshaw, Willie Clay	193 Osborne Lane/Southport CT 6490
1950-100	Upton, Thomas Herbert	306 May Street/Bishop CA 93514
1954-112	Upton, William Ray	D. January 2, 1987 San Diego, Calif.
1957-089	Urban, Jack Elmer	8607 Fowler/Omaha NE 68134
1927-094	Urban, Louis John 'Luke'	D. December 7, 1980 Somerset, Mass.
1993-190	Urbani, Thomas James	1680 Pinoak Lane/Carson City NV 89703
1931-091	Urbanski, William Michael	D. July 12, 1973 Perth Amboy, N. J.
1995-227	Urbina, Ugueth Urtain	Rojas Conj Res Las Aca Lias #2 Ocumare Del Toy Venezuela
1984-124	Uribe, Jose Altagracia	Cie D #9 Sab.Grande De Palenque Juan Dominican Rep.
1977-147	Urrea, John Godby	19426 Sequoia Avenue/Cerritos CA 90701
1946-100	Usher, Robert Royce	1022 North Fifth Street/San Jose CA 95112
1925-107	Ussat, William August 'Dutch'	D. May 29, 1959 Dayton, O.
1925-108	Vache, Ernest Lewis 'Tex'	D. June 11, 1953 Los Angeles, Calif.
1975-122	Vail, Michael Lewis	3859 Lake Shore Drive/Palm Harbor FL 34684
1994-107	Valdes, Ismael	Old Add: Victoria Tamaulipas Mexico
1995-228	Valdes, Marc Christopher	7519 Paula Drive/Tampa FL 33615
1996-180	Valdes, Pedro Jose Manzo	Old Add: Loiza PR 00773
1957-090	Valdes, Rene Gutierrez	Avenida 7a,14511 Alturas "Manana, Havana Cuba"
1944-132	Valdes, Rogelio Lazaro 'Roy'	241 Ponce De Leon Blvd/Coral Gables FL 33134
1965-109	Valdespino, Hilario Sandy	17920 Nw 43rd Ave/Carol City FL 33055
1995-229	Valdez, Carlos Luis Lorenzo	Old Add: Nizao Bani Dominican Rep.
1990-158	Valdez, Efrain Antonio	K Num 118 En Nizao De Bani Bani Dominican Rep.
1980-131	Valdez, Julio Julian Castillo	Maximo Gomez #3 Nizao Bani Dominican Rep.
1997-166	Valdez, Mario Antonio	7155 West 14th Court/Hialeah FL 33014
1990-159	Valdez, Rafael Emilio (Diaz)	Maximo Gomez #5 Nizao De Bani Dominican Rep.
1986-157	Valdez, Sergio Sanchez	Old Add: Cal La Paz #14,Herrera/Santo Domingo Dominican Rep.
1955-129	Valdivielso, Jose Lopez	14 Rita Dr/Mount Sinai NY 11766
1992-146	Valentin, John William	Old Add: 239 16th Street Jersey City NJ 07310
1992-147	Valentin, Jose Antonio (Rosario)	Urb. Flamboyan Asui 31/Manati PR 701
1997-167	Valentin, Jose Javier Rosario 'Javier'	Old Add: Manati PR 00674
1975-123	Valentine, Ellis Clarence	43931 40th Street East/Lancaster CA 93535
1959-084	Valentine, Fred Lee	4838 Blagden Ave Nw/Washington Dc 20011
1954-113	Valentine, Harold Lewis 'Corky'	Rural Route 1 Freehome Road/Canton GA 30114
1969-173	Valentine, Robert John	4102 Flower Garden Court/Arlington TX 76016
1954-114	Valentinetti, Vito John	271 Summit Ave/Mount Vernon NY 10552
1958-098	Valenzuela, Benjamin Beltran	Bahia San Esteban #267 Sur Los Mochis Sinaloa/Mexico
1980-132	Valenzuela, Fernando	3004 N. Beachwood Dr/Hollywood CA 90068
1990-160	Valera, Julio Enrique	Old Add: 9-H-12 Sebastian PR 00755
1984-125	Valle, David	Old Add: 27735 SE 56th St Issaquah WA 98029
1965-110	Valle, Hector Jose	PO Box 5909 College Station/Mayaguez PR 708
1940-094	Valo, Elmer William	D. July 19, 1998 Palmerton, Pa.
1927-095	Vanalstyne, Clayton Emery	D. January 5, 1960 Hudson, N. Y.
1933-064	Vanatta, Russell	D. October 10, 1986 Andover, N. J.
1954-115	Vanbrabant, Camille Oscar 'Ossie'	1206 North Lakeshore Road/Port Sanilac MI 48464
1993-191	Vanburkleo, Tyler Leo	320 Galena Pines Road/Reno NV 89511
1928-101	Vancamp, Albert Joseph	D. February 2, 1981 Davenport, Iowa
1915-166	Vance, Clarence Arthur 'Dazzy'	D. February 16, 1961 Homosassa Springs, Fla.
1970-135	Vance, Gene Covington 'Sandy'	Old Add: 953 Foye Drive/Lafayette CA 94549
1935-109	Vance, Joseph Albert	D. July 4, 1978 Devine, Texas
1950-101	Vancuyk, Christian Gerald	D. November 3, 1992 Hudson, Fla.
1947-091	Vancuyk, John Henry	15 11th Avenue Northwest/Rochester MN 55901
1914-220	Vandagrift, Carl William	D. October 9, 1920 Fort Wayne, Ind.
1982-129	Vandeberg, Edward John	12435 6th Street #703/Yucaipa CA 92399
1935-110	Vandenburg, Harold Harris 'Hy'	D. July 31, 1994 Bloomington, Minn.
1937-103	Vandermeer, John Samuel	D. October 6, 1997 Tampa, Fla.
1991-175	Vanderwal, John Henry	PO Box 454/Jenison MI 49428
1955-130	Vandusen, Frederick William	826 Rockrimmon Rd/Stamford CT 6903
1994-108	Vanegmond, Timothy Layne	Old Add: 463 Seavy Street Senola GA 30276
1919-084	Vangilder, Elam Russell	D. April 30, 1977 Cape Girardeau, Mo.
1982-130	Vangorder, David Thomas	2712 West Calle Arandas/Tucson AZ 85745
1994-109	Vanlandingham, William Joseph	3023 Old Hillsboro Road/Franklin TN 37064
1913-183	Vann, John Silas	D. June 10, 1958 Shreveport, La.
1951-099	Vannoy, Jay Lowell	1092 North 1700 East/Logan UT 84321
1991-176	Vanpoppel, Todd Matthew	PO Box 142/Meridian TX 76665
1939-120	Vanrobays, Maurice Rene	D. March 1, 1965 Detroit, Mich.
1996-181	Vanryn, Benjamin Ashley	16226 Jackson Hole Court/Eagle River AK 99577
1983-144	Vanslyke, Andrew James	16316 Wilson Creek Court/Chesterfield Nymo 63005
1950-102	Varga, Andrew William	D. November 4, 1992 Orlando, Fla.
1982-131	Vargas, Hediberto	Box 1172/Guanica PR 653
1955-131	Vargas, Robert Enrique	Old Add: Brisaida St. No. 24/Guaynabo PR 00657
1925-109	Vargus, William Fay	D. February 12, 1979 Hyannis, Mass.
1997-168	Varitek, Jason A.	321 Cypress Landing Drive/Longwood FL 32779
1952-107	Varner, Glen Gann	1737 East Varner Road/Hixson TN 37343
1973-123	Varney, Richard Fred 'Pete'	Brandeis Baseball 415 South Street Waltham MA 2254

1988-134 ....Varsho, Gary Andrew ....11921 Lindsey Drive/Chili WI 54420
1979-113 ....Vasquez, Rafael (Santiago) ....Calle Julio A Jarsia #29/La Romana Dominican Rep.
1990-161 ....Vatcher, James Ernest.............................16039 Northfield Street/Pacific Palisades CA 90272
1940-095 ....Vaughan, Cecil Porter 'Porter' ....9201 Forest Hill Avenue #105/Richmond VA 23235
1966-092 ....Vaughan, Charles Wayne ....500 Santa Ana Avenue/Rancho Viejo TX 78575
1963-121 ....Vaughan, Glenn Edward ....2700 Post Oak Blvd #1300/Houston TX 77056
1932-089 ....Vaughan, Joseph Floyd 'Arky' ....D. August 30, 1952 Eagleville, Calif.
1934-105 ....Vaughn, Clarence Leroy ....D. March 1, 1937 Martinsville, Va.
1988-135 ....Vaughn, Dewayne Mathew ....5501nw 37th Street/Oklahoma City OK 73122
1944-133 ....Vaughn, Frederick Thomas ....D. March 2, 1964 Lake Wales, Fla.
1989-130 ....Vaughn, Gregory Lamont ....6309 Thresher Court/Elk Grove CA 95758
1991-177 ....Vaughn, Maurice Samuel 'Mo'.............7971 Park Drive/Fair Oaks CA 95628
1935-111 ....Veach, Alvis Lindell ....D. September 6, 1990 Charlotte, N. C.
1912-203 ....Veach, Robert Henry ....D. August 7, 1945 Detroit, Mich.
1958-099 ....Veal, Orville Inman 'Coot' ....1258 Timberlane/Macon GA 31204
1962-140 ....Veale, Robert Andrew ....2833 Bush Blvd/Birmingham AL 35208
1920-126 ....Vedder, Louis Edward ....D. March 9, 1990 Lake Placid, Fla.
1979-114 ....Vega, Jesus Antonio ....Old Add: Magoly Central Nh22 Levittown PR 00632
1939-121 ....Veigel, Allen Francis ....1907 Dover Avenue/Dover OH 44622
1997-169 ....Velandia, Jorge Luis Macias ....Old Add: Caracas Venezuela
1987-147 ....Velarde, Randy Lee ....1302 South Windy Ridge Court/Anaheim CA 92808
1992-148 ....Velasquez, Guillermo ....1137 Milpitas Drive/Calexico CA 92231
1973-124 ....Velazquez, Carlos ....Old Add: Bo Medina Alta Luiza Aldea PR 00672
1969-174 ....Velazquez, Federico Antonio ....Jose Amado Soler No. 70/Santo Domingo Dominican Rep.
1973-125 ....Velez, Otoniel Otto ....Old Add: Los Caobos Calle #35 T2 Ponce PR 00731
1926-089 ....Veltman, Arthur Patrick ....D. October 1, 1980 San Antonio, Texas
1979-115 ....Venable, William McKinley 'Mac' ....107 Clark Street/San Rafael CA 94901
1989-131 ....Ventura, Robin Mark ....2755 Coast View Drive/Arroyo Grande CA 93420
1945-107 ....Ventura, Vincent ....3595 Birdie Drive #106/Lake Worth FL 33467
1996-182 ....Veras, Dario Antonio ....Old Add: Villa Vasquez Dom. Rep.
1995-230 ....Veras, Quilvio Alberto Perez ....Old Add: Santo Domingo Dom.Rep.
1944-134 ....Verban, Emil Matthew 'The Antelope' ....D. June 8, 1989 Quincy, Ill.
1966-093 ....Verbanic, Joseph Michael ....85462 Lorane Hwy/Eugene OR 97405
1951-100 ....Verble, Gene Kermit...............................1096 Old Charlotte Hwy/Concord NC 28025
1944-135 ....Verdel, Albert Alfred ....D. April 16, 1991 Sarasota, Fla.
1953-096 ....Verdi, Frank Michael ....10961 Peppertree Lane/Port Richey FL 34668
1915-167 ....Vereker, John James ....D. April 2, 1974 Baltimore, Md.
1994-110 ....Veres, David Scott ....1488 NE Vista Way/Gresham OR 97030
1989-132 ....Veres, Randolph Ruhland ....Old Add: 9469 Fort Worth Rancho Cordova CA 95670
1931-092 ....Vergez, John Louis ....D. July 15, 1991 Davis, Calif.
1976-096 ....Verhoeven, John C. ....8401 Tepic Drive/Paramount CA 90723
1939-122 ....Vernon, James Barton 'Mickey' ....100 East Rose Valley Road/Wallingford PA 19086
1912-204 ....Vernon, Joseph Henry ....D. March 13, 1955 Philadelphia, Pa.
1959-085 ....Versalles, Zoilo Zorro ....D. June 9, 1995 Bloomington, Minn.
1973-126 ....Veryzer, Thomas Martin ....41 Union Ave/Islip NY 11751
1980-133 ....Veselic, Robert Michael ....D. December 26, 1995 Los Angeles, Calif.
1922-135 ....Vick, Henry Arthur 'Ernie' ....D. July 16, 1980 Ann Arbor, Mich.
1917-083 ....Vick, Samuel Bruce ....D. August 17, 1986 Memphis, Tenn.
1948-102 ....Vico, George Steve ....D. January 13, 1994 Redondo Beach, Calif.
1966-094 ....Vidal, Jose Nicolas.................................Old Add: Juan Erazo 152 Santo Domingo Dom Rep
1997-170 ....Vidro, Jose/Angel Cetty ....Old Add: Sabana Grande PR 00637
1990-162 ....Villanueva, Hector (Balasquide) ....2 Ambese 156 R.P.H./Rio Piedras PR 926
1995-231 ....Villone, Ronald Thomas.........................Old Add: 87 Spring Valley Rd Montvale NJ 07645
1993-192 ....Vina, Fernando ....5637 Gearny Drive/Sacramento CA 95823
1924-112 ....Vines, Robert Earl ....D. October 18, 1982 Orlando, Fla.
1964-124 ....Vineyard, David Kent ....Rr 2 Box 83b/Left Hand WV 25251
1966-095 ....Vinson, Charles Anthony.......................3821 Walters Ln/Forestville MD 20747
1982-132 ....Viola, Frank John ....844 Sweetwater Island Cir/Longwood FL 32779
1912-205 ....Viox, James Henry ....D. January 6, 1969 Erlanger, Ky.
1955-132 ....Virdon, William Charles ....1311 River Rd/Springfield MO 65804
1980-134 ....Virgil, Osvaldo Jose ....5444 West Creedance Blvd/Glendale AZ 85310
1956-084 ....Virgil, Osvaldo "Jose, Sr." 'Ozzie' ....4316 West Mescal St/Glendale AZ 85301
1944-136 ....Vitelli, Antonio Joseph 'Joe' ....D. February 7, 1967 Pittsburgh, Pa.
1995-232 ....Vitiello, Joseph David ....4 Waverly Drive/Stoneham MA 2180
1992-149 ....Vitko, Joseph John ....113 Parkside Avenue #1/Mount Lebanon PA 15228
1912-206 ....Vitt, Oscar Joseph ....D. January 31, 1963 Oakland, Calif.
1989-133 ....Vizcaino, Jose Luis ....Duarte #107 Palenque De San Cris Dominican Rep.
1989-134 ....Vizquel, Omar Enrique ....Blvd Del Cafetel,R.Adriana 6 Pisa 6a Caracas Venezuela
1923-135 ....Vogel, Otto Henry ....D. July 19, 1969 Iowa City, Ia.
1992-150 ....Voigt, John David Jack ....1274 Reserve Drive/Venice FL 34292
1924-113 ....Voigt, Olen Edward ....D. April 7, 1970 Scottsdale, Ariz.
1942-103 ....Voiselle, William Symnes ....105 Lowell Street/Ninety Six SC 29666
1942-104 ....Vollmer, Clyde Frederick ....PO Box 3321/Cincinnati OH 45201
1965-111 ....Vonhoff, Bruce Kenneth ....423 River Hills Drive/Temple Terrace FL 33617
1914-222 ....Vonkolnitz, Alfred Holmes 'Fritz' ......D. March 18, 1948 Mount Pleasant, S.C.
1983-145 ....Vonohlen, David ....Old Add: 1106 128th Street College Point NY 11356
1986-158 ....Vosberg, Edward John ....5671 East 12th Street/Tucson AZ 85711
1930-084 ....Vosmik, Joseph Franklin ....D. January 27, 1962 Cleveland, O.
1965-112 ....Voss, William Edward ....Old Add: 5882 Sierra Siena Irvine CA 92650

1929-105 ....Voyles, Philip Vance ....D. November 3, 1972 Marlboro, Mass.
1975-124 ....Vuckovich, Peter Dennis ....309 Keiper Lane/Conemaugh PA 15909
1980-135 ....Vukovich, George Stephen ....615 Summer Grass Lane/Roswell GA 30076
1970-136 ....Vukovich, John Christopher ....6 Knottingham Drive/Voorhees NJ 8043
1917-084 ....Wachtel, Paul Horine ....D. December 15, 1964 San Antonio, Tex.
1984-126 ....Waddell, Thomas David ....Old Add: 47 Fifth Street Closter NJ 07624
1931-093 ....Waddey, Frank Orum ....D. October 21, 1990 Knoxville, Tenn.
1948-103 ....Wade, Benjamin Styron ....1165 Medford Road/Pasadena CA 91107
1955-133 ....Wade, Galeard Lee ....Rr 1 Box 766/Nebo NC 28761
1995-233 ....Wade, Hawatha Terrell 'Terrell' ....%Hattie Wade 6380 Dinkins Mill Rembert SC 29128
1936-093 ....Wade, Jacob Fields ....316 Wildwood Road/Newport NC 28570
1923-136 ....Wade, Richard Frank ....D. June 16, 1957 Duluth, Minn.
1938-102 ....Wagner, Charles Thomas ....1523 Linden Street/Reading PA 19604
1965-113 ....Wagner, Gary Edward ....5315 Hagerstown Road/Baton Rouge LA 70817
1937-104 ....Wagner, Harold Edward ....D. August 7, 1979 Riverside Nj
1990-163 ....Wagner, Hector Raul ....Segunda Casa #114,Los Mameye/Santo Domingo Dominican Rep.
1915-168 ....Wagner, Joseph Bernard.............................D. November 15, 1948 Bronx, N.Y.
1958-100 ....Wagner, Leon Lamar ....% Abdullah 2795 Tola Avenue Altadena CA 91001
1976-097 ....Wagner, Mark Duane ....1346 Eleanor Drive/Ashtabula OH 44004
1996-183 ....Wagner, Matthew William ....1112 Lilac Drive/Cedar Falls IA 50613
1992-151 ....Wagner, Paul Alan ....623 Ellys Way/Slinger WI 53086
1995-234 ....Wagner, William Edward ....2607 Iris Court/Pearland TX 77584
1913-184 ....Wagner, William George 'Bull' ....D. October 2, 1967 Muskegon, Mich.
1914-223 ....Wagner, William Joseph ....D. January 11, 1951 Waterloo, Ia.
1944-137 ....Wahl, Kermit Emerson ....D. September 16, 1987 Tucson, Ariz.
1991-178 ....Wainhouse, David Paul ....6101 85th Place Southeast/Mercer Isla ND 98040
1941-114 ....Waitkus, Edward Stephen ....D. September 15, 1972 Boston, Mass.
1973-127 ....Waits, Michael Richard 'Rick' ....2001 Klondike Road/Tucson AZ 85749
1991-179 ....Wakamatsu, Wilbur Donald 'Don' ....2407 East Silverwood Drive/Phoenix AZ 85048
1941-115 ....Wakefield, Richard Cummings ....D. August 26, 1985 Redford Twp., Wayne Co., Mich.
1992-152 ....Wakefield, Timothy Stephen ....2827 Choctaw Drive/Melbourne FL 32935
1964-125 ....Wakefield, William Sumner ....250 29th Avenue/San Francisco CA 94121
1993-193 ....Walbeck, Matthew Lovick ....4127 H Street/Sacramento CA 95819
1923-137 ....Walberg, George Elvin 'Rube' ....D. October 27, 1978 Tempe, Ariz.
1945-108 ....Walczak, Edwin Joseph ....D. March 10, 1998 Norwich, Conn.
1917-085 ....Waldbauer, Albert Charles 'Doc'...................D. July 16, 1969 Yakima, Wash.
1912-207 ....Walden, Thomas Fred ....D. September 27, 1955 Jefferson Barracks, Mo.
1987-148 ....Walewander, James ....5133 North Octavia Street/Harwood Heights IL 60656
1980-136 ....Walk, Robert Vernon ....%C.Shields,Box 954/Frazier Park CA 93225
1948-104 ....Walker, Albert Bluford 'Rube' ....D. December 12, 1992 Morganton, N.C.
1986-159 ....Walker, Anthony Bruce ....Old Add: 4024 Peterlynn Way San Diego CA 92154
1917-086 ....Walker, Charles Franklin ....D. September 16, 1974 Bristol, Tenn.
1911-172 ....Walker, Clarence William 'Tilly'..................D. September 21, 1959 Unicoi, Tenn.
1980-137 ....Walker, Cleotha/Chico ....5344 South Emerald Avenue/Chicago IL 60609
1982-133 ....Walker, Duane Allen ....2509 Georgia Avenue/Deer Park TX 77536
1913-185 ....Walker, Ernest Robert ....D. April 1, 1965 Pell City, Ala.
1931-094 ....Walker, Fred Dixie ....D. May 17, 1982 Birmingham, Ala.
1910-146 ....Walker, Frederick Mitchell ....D. February 1, 1958 Oak Park, Ill.
1931-095 ....Walker, Gerald Holmes 'Gee' ....D. March 20, 1981 Whitfield, Miss.
1982-134 ....Walker, Gregory Lee ....Forest Circle Drive/Douglas GA 31533
1940-096 ....Walker, Harry William 'The Hat' ....2120 Montevallo Road Sw/Leeds/AL 35094
1931-096 ....Walker, Harvey Willos 'Hub' ....D. November 26, 1982 San Jose, Calif.
1965-114 ....Walker, James Luke ....316 Loma Linda/Wake Village TX 75501
1912-208 ....Walker, James Roy ....D. February 10, 1962 New Orleans, La.
1997-171 ....Walker, Jamie Ross ....1125 Hunting Creek Court/Clarksville TN 37042
1957-091 ....Walker, Jerry Allen ....2015 Collins Blvd/Ada OK 74820
1919-085 ....Walker, John Miles ....D. August 19, 1976 Hollywood, Fla.
1923-138 ....Walker, Joseph Richard.............................D. June 20, 1959 West Mifflin, Pa.
1989-135 ....Walker, Larry Kenneth Robert ....21642 River Road/Maple Ridge British Col. V2X 2B7 Canada
1928-102 ....Walker, Martin Van Buren ....D. April 24, 1978 Philadelphia, Pa.
1992-153 ....Walker, Michael Aaron ....Old Add: 4301 Bissonet #89 Bellaire TX 77401
1988-136 ....Walker, Michael Charles ....23195 Tankersley Road/Brooksville FL 34601
1995-235 ....Walker, Peter Brian ....33 Pattagansett Drive/East Lyme CT 6333
1972-118 ....Walker, Robert Thomas 'Tom'.......................Whippoorwill Hill Road/Gibsonia PA 15044
1996-184 ....Walker, Todd Arthur ....527 Glenwood Street/Bossier City LA 71111
1919-086 ....Walker, William Curtis 'Curt' ....D. December 9, 1955 Beeville, Tex.
1927-096 ....Walker, William Henry ....D. June 14, 1966 East St. Louis, Ill.
1934-106 ....Walkup, James Elton ....D. February 7, 1997 Danville, Ark.
1927-097 ....Walkup, James Huey ....D. June 12, 1990 Duncan, Okla.
1995-236 ....Wall, Donnell Lee 'Donne' ....%Cecil Wall 1450 State Road Aa Festus MO 63028
1950-103 ....Wall, Murray Wesley ....D. October 8, 1971 Lone Oak, Texas
1975-125 ....Wall, Stanley Arthur ....9907 E. 80th St/Raytown MO 64138
1915-169 ....Wallace, Clarence Eugene 'Jack' ....D. October 15, 1960 Winnfield, La.
1973-128 ....Wallace, David William ....101 South Avenue #38/Attleboro MA 2703
1996-185 ....Wallace, Derek Robert ....Old Add: Oxnard CA 93030
1967-111 ....Wallace, Donald Allen ....23 Kris Ln/Manitou Springs CO 80829
1919-087 ....Wallace, Frederick Renshaw 'Doc' ....D. December 31, 1964 Haverford Twp, Pa.
1912-209 ....Wallace, Harry Clinton 'Huck' ....D. July 9, 1951 Cleveland, O.
1942-105 ....Wallace, James Harold 'Lefty'.....................D. July 28, 1982 Evansville, Ind.

1997-172	Wallace, Jeffrey Allen	PO Box 23/Paris OH 44669
1973-129	Wallace, Michael Sherman	12483 Elk Run Road/Midland VA 22728
1980-138	Wallach, Timothy Charles	10762 Holly Drive/Garden Grove CA 92640
1940-097	Wallaesa, John	D. December 27, 1986 Easton, Pa.
1945-109	Wallen, Norman Edward	Old Add: 3429 North Weil Milwaukee WI 53212
1980-139	Waller, Elliott Tyrone 'Tye'	318 59th Street/San Diego CA 92114
1975-126	Walling, Dennis	Box 1312/Waynesboro VA 22980
1975-127	Wallis, Harold Joseph 'Joe'	410 Humes Lane/Florissant MO 63031
1952-108	Walls, Raymond Lee 'Lee'	D. October 11, 1993 Los Angeles, Calif.
1927-098	Walsh, August Sothley	D. November 12, 1985 San Rafael, Calif.
1914-224	Walsh, Austin Edward	D. January 26, 1955 Glendale, Calif.
1990-164	Walsh, David Peter	613 Rolling Hills Terrace/Edmond OK 73034
1928-103	Walsh, Edward Arthur	D. October 31, 1937 Meriden, Conn.
1912-210	Walsh, James Charles	D. July 3, 1962 Syracuse, N.Y.
1946-101	Walsh, James Gerald	D. November 12, 1990 Olyphant, Pa.
1921-108	Walsh, James Thomas	D. May 13, 1967 Boston, Mass.
1910-147	Walsh, Joseph Francis	D. January 6, 1967 Buffalo, N.Y.
1938-103	Walsh, Joseph Patrick	D. October 5, 1996 Boston, Mass.
1913-186	Walsh, Leo Thomas 'Dee'	D. July 14, 1971 St. Louis, Mo.
1910-148	Walsh, Michael Timothy 'Jimmy'	D. January 21, 1947 Baltimore, Md.
1920-127	Walsh, Walter William	D. January 15, 1966 Neptune, N. J.
1985-114	Walter, Gene Winston	6042 South Monitor/Chicago IL 60638
1930-085	Walter, James Bernard 'Bernie'	D. October 30, 1988 Nashville, Tenn.
1915-170	Walters, Alfred John 'Roxy'	D. June 3, 1956 Alameda, Calif.
1969-175	Walters, Charles Leonard	12387 Paseo Verano/Yuma AZ 85365
1992-154	Walters, Daniel Gene	Old Add: 9456 Domer Road Santee CA 92071
1945-110	Walters, James Frederick 'Fred'	D. February 1, 1980 Laurel, Miss.
1960-101	Walters, Kenneth Rogers	9545 Belle Meade Dr/San Ramon CA 94583
1983-146	Walters, Michael Charles	Old Add: 80119 Palm Circle Drive Indio CA 92201
1931-097	Walters, William Henry 'Bucky'	D. April 20, 1991 Abington, Pa.
1991-180	Walton, Bruce Kenneth	5711 Bayberry Avenue/Bakersfield CA 93308
1968-106	Walton, Daniel James	1130 Sunkist Avenue/Lapuente CA 91746
1989-136	Walton, Jerome O'Terrell	459 Country Club Road/Newnan GA 30263
1980-140	Walton, Reginald Sherard	1142 South Carson Ave/Los Angeles CA 90019
1914-225	Wambsganss, William Adolph	D. December 8, 1985 Lakewood, O.
1927-099	Waner, Lloyd James	D. July 22, 1982 Oklahoma City, Okla.
1926-090	Waner, Paul Glee	D. August 29, 1965 Sarasota, Fla.
1925-110	Wanninger, Paul Louis 'Pee Wee'	D. May 7, 1981 North Augusta, S. C.
1965-115	Wantz, Richard Carter	D. May 13, 1965 Inglewood, Calif.
1990-165	Wapnick, Steven Lee	8557 Aqueduct Avenue/Sepulveda CA 91343
1917-087	Ward, Aaron Lee	D. January 30, 1961 New Orleans, La.
1917-088	Ward, Charles William	D. April 4, 1969 St. Petersburg, Fla.
1972-119	Ward, Chris Gilbert	Old Add: 365 Burchett Street #214 Glendale CA 91203
1985-115	Ward, Colin Norval	Old Add: 242 South Olive Mesa AZ 85204
1979-116	Ward, Gary Lamell	PO Box 20038/Riverside CA 92516
1963-122	Ward, John Francis 'Jay'	5271 Beach Drive SE #B/Saint Petersburg FL 33705
1912-211	Ward, Joseph Nicholas 'Hap'	D. September 13, 1979 Elmer, N. J.
1991-181	Ward, Kevin Michael	133 F Avenue/Coronado CA 92118
1962-141	Ward, Peter Thomas	575 Southwest/G/Lake Oswego OR 97034
1948-105	Ward, Preston Meyer	Old Add: 4371 De Silva Place Las Vegas NV 89121
1934-107	Ward, Richard Ole	D. June 1, 1966 Freeland, Wash.
1990-166	Ward, Robert Colby	1601 East Hobblecreek/Springville UT 84663
1986-160	Ward, Roy Duane Duane	4505 Pacific Street/Farmington NM 87401
1990-167	Ward, Turner Max	232 Autumn Drive/Saraland AL 36571
1968-107	Warden, Jonathan Edgar	9573 Loveland Madeira Road/Loveland OH 45140
1984-127	Wardle, Curtis Ray	2290 Hillside/Norco CA 91760
1995-237	Ware, Jeffrey Allen	4861 Ridgemoore Circle/Palm Harbor FL 34685
1913-187	Wares, Clyde Ellsworth 'Buzzy'	D. May 26, 1964 South Bend, Ind.
1916-091	Warmoth, Wallace Walter 'Cy'	D. June 20, 1957 Mount Carmel, Ill.
1930-086	Warneke, Lonnie	D. June 23, 1976 Hot Springs, Ark.
1912-212	Warner, Edward Emory	D. February 2, 1954 Fitchburg, Mass.
1916-092	Warner, Hoke Hayden 'Hooks'	D. February 19, 1947 San Francisco, Calif.
1962-142	Warner, Jack Dyer	5938 West Calle Lejos/Glendale AZ 85310
1966-096	Warner, John Joseph	649 Crestview Drive/Glendora CA 91740
1925-111	Warner, John Ralph 'Jack'	D. March 13, 1986 Mount Vernon, Ill.
1935-112	Warnock, Harold Charles	D. February 8, 1997 Tucson, Ariz.
1939-123	Warren, Bennie Louis	D. May 11, 1994 Oklahoma City, Okla.
1983-147	Warren, Michael Bruce	12281 Diane Street/Garden Grove CA 92640
1944-138	Warren, Thomas Gentry	D. January 2, 1968 Tulsa, Okla.
1914-226	Warren, William Hackney	D. January 28, 1960 Whiteville, Tenn.
1930-087	Warstler, Harold Burton 'Rabbit'	D. May 31, 1964 North Canton,O.
1975-128	Warthen, Daniel Dean	3933 Southwest Wapato Avenue/Portland OR 97201
1961-106	Warwick, Carl Wayne	14102 Bonney Brier/Houston TX 77069
1921-109	Warwick, Firman Newton 'Bill'	D. December 19, 1984 San Antonio, Texas
1937-105	Wasdell, James Charles	D. August 6, 1983 Newport Richey, Fla.
1995-238	Wasdin, John Truman	1897 Shady Oaks Drive/Tallahassee FL 32303
1937-106	Wasem, Lincoln William	D. March 6, 1979 South Laguna, Calif.
1941-116	Washburn, George Edward	D. January 5, 1979 Baton Rouge, La.
1969-176	Washburn, Gregory James	1685 E. Stellon St/Coal City IL 60416

1961-107	Washburn, Ray Clark	19001 131st Drive SE/Snohomish WA 98290
1974-138	Washington, Claudell	845 Lime Avenue/Long Beach CA 90813
1974-139	Washington, Herbert	642 East Austin Street/Flint MI 48505
1978-139	Washington, Larue	4122 Gundry Avenue/Long Beach CA 90807
1977-148	Washington, Ronald	7365 Perth Street/New Orleans LA 70126
1935-113	Washington, Sloan Vernon 'Vern'	D. February 17, 1985 Linden, Texas
1977-149	Washington, U. L.	Box 164/Stringtown OK 74569
1986-161	Wasinger, Mark Thomas	265 Caribe Circle/El Paso TX 79927
1967-112	Waslewski, Gary Lee	McKenzie Dr/Southington CT 6489
1976-098	Waterbury, Steven Craig	710 N. Garfield/Marion IL 62958
1955-134	Waters, Fred Warren	D. August 28, 1989 Pensacola, Fla.
1976-099	Wathan, John David	1401 Deer Run Trail/Blue Springs MO 64015
1969-177	Watkins, David Roger	1502 Roosevelt Rd/Owensboro KY 42301
1930-088	Watkins, George Archibald	D. June 1, 1970 Houston, Tex.
1969-178	Watkins, Robert Cecil	4417 West 58th Place/Los Angeles CA 90043
1995-239	Watkins, Scott Allen	%C.Watkins Rural Route 7 Box 252 Sand Springs OK 74063
1997-173	Watkins, William Patrick 'Pat'	1205 Fowler Drive/Garner NC 27529
1953-097	Watlington, Julius Neal	Box 418/Yanceyville NC 27379
1993-194	Watson, Allen Kenneth	61-44 65th Street/Middle Village NY 11379
1914-227	Watson, Arthur Stanhope	D. May 9, 1950 Buffalo, N. Y.
1913-188	Watson, Charles John 'Doc'	D. December 30, 1949 San Diego, Calif.
1918-072	Watson, John Reeves 'Mule'	D. August 25, 1949 Shreveport, La.
1930-089	Watson, John Thomas	D. April 29, 1965 Huntington, W. V.
1916-093	Watson, Milton Wilson	D. April 10, 1962 Pine Bluff, Ark.
1966-097	Watson, Robert Jose	13164 Memorial Drive #121/Houston TX 77079
1920-128	Watt, Albert Bailey	D. March 15, 1968 Norfolk, Va.
1966-098	Watt, Eddie Dean	PO Box 7/North Bend NE 68649
1931-098	Watt, Frank Marion	D. August 31, 1956 Glen Cove, Md.
1929-106	Watwood, John Clifford	D. March 1, 1980 Goodwater, Ala.
1952-109	Waugh, James Elden	3109 Oakridge/Corsicana TX 75110
1927-100	Way, Robert Clinton	D. June 20, 1974 Pittsburgh, Pa.
1924-114	Wayenberg, Frank	D. April 16, 1975 Zanesville, O.
1989-137	Wayne, Gary Anthony	Old Add: 521 Centralia Dearborn Heights MI 48127
1936-094	Weafer, Kenneth Albert	66 Ryckman Avenue/Albany NY 12208
1936-095	Weatherly, Cyril Roy 'Roy'	D. January 19, 1991 Woodville, Texas
1991-182	Weathers, John David 'Dave'	Old Add: 25 Second Creek Road Leoma TN 38468
1962-143	Weaver, David Floyd	Rr 1 Box 579/Powderly TX 75473
1968-108	Weaver, Earl Sidney	501 Cypress Pointe Drive West/Pembroke Pines FL 33027
1912-213	Weaver, George Daniel 'Buck'	D. January 31, 1956 Chicago, Ill.
1915-171	Weaver, Harry Abraham	D. May 30, 1983 Rochester, N. Y.
1967-113	Weaver, James Brian	276 Rhoda Dr/Lancaster PA 17601
1928-104	Weaver, James Dement	D. December 12, 1983 Lakeland, Fla.
1985-116	Weaver, James Francis	212 77th Street/Holmes Beach FL 33510
1931-099	Weaver, Monte Morton	D. June 14, 1994 Orlando, Fla.
1910-149	Weaver, Orlie Forest	D. November 28, 1970 New Orleans, La.
1980-141	Weaver, Roger Edward	Box 15/Saint Johnsville NY 13452
1910-150	Webb, Cleon Earl 'Lefty'	D. January 12, 1958 Circleville, O.
1972-120	Webb, Henry Gaylon	Old Add: 38 Harbor Oaks Cir/Safety Harbor FL 33572
1932-090	Webb, James Leverne 'Skeeter'	D. July 8, 1986 Meridian, Miss.
1948-106	Webb, Samuel Henry	D. February 7, 1996 Hyattsville, Md.
1925-112	Webb, William Earl	D. May 22, 1965 Jamestown, Tenn.
1943-141	Webb, William Franklin	D. June 1, 1994 Mableton, Ga.
1917-089	Webb, William Joseph	D. January 12, 1943 Chicago, Ill.
1942-106	Webber, Lester Elmer	D. November 13, 1986 Santa Maria, Calif.
1989-138	Webster, Leonard Irell Lenny	323 Weil Street (PO Box 811)/Lutcher LA 70071
1983-148	Webster, Mitchell Dean	4935 Quail Creek Drive/Great Bend KS 67530
1967-114	Webster, Ramon Alberto	PO Box 6-5790 El Dorado/Panama
1959-086	Webster, Raymond George	311 5th Street/Marysville CA 95901
1991-183	Wedge, Eric Michael	345k Bolivar Street/Canton MA 2021
1911-173	Weeden, Charles Albert	D. January 7, 1939 Northwood, N.H.
1962-144	Weekly, John	D. November 24, 1974 Walnut Creek, Calif.
1969-179	Wegener, Michael Denis	Old Add: PO Box 634/Broomfield CO 80020
1985-117	Wegman, William Edward	1458 Cliffmont Circle/Lawrenceburg IN 47025
1930-090	Wehde, Wilbur 'Biggs'	D. September 21, 1970 Sioux Falls,S.D.
1945-111	Wehmeier, Herman Ralph	D. May 21, 1973 Dallas, Tex.
1991-184	Wehner, John Paul	2368 Rochester Road/Sewickley PA 15143
1976-100	Wehrmeister, David Thomas	4216 Dubbe CT Concord CA 94521
1946-102	Weigel, Ralph Richard	D. April 15, 1992 Memphis, Tenn.
1948-107	Weik, Richard Henry	D. April 21, 1991 Harvey, Ill.
1940-098	Weiland, Edwin Nicholas	D. July 12, 1972 Chicago, Ill.
1928-105	Weiland, Robert George	D. November 9, 1988 Chicago, Ill.
1912-214	Weilman, Carl Woolworth	D. May 25, 1924 Hamilton, O.
1919-088	Weinert, Phillip Walter 'Lefty'	D. April 17, 1973 Rockledge, Fla.
1945-112	Weingartner, Elmer William	13604 Lorain/Cleveland OH 44111
1933-065	Weintraub, Philip	D. June 21, 1987 Palm Springs, Calif.
1936-096	Weir, William Franklin	D. September 30, 1989 Anaheim, Calif.
1962-145	Weis, Albert John	902 South Poplar/Elmhurst IL 60126
1922-136	Weis, Arthur John	D. May 4, 1997 Saint Louis, Mo.
1915-172	Weiser, Harry Budson 'Bud'	D. July 31, 1961 Shamokin, Pa.

1980-142	Weiss, Gary Lee	Rural Route 1 Box 83/Brenham TX 77833
1915-173	Weiss, Joseph Harold	D. July 7, 1967 Cedar Rapids, Ia.
1987-149	Weiss, Walter William	7200 South Flanders/Aurora CO 80016
1939-124	Welaj, John Ludwig	1519 College Street #103/Arlington TX 76010
1914-228	Welch, Floyd John	D. January 6, 1943 Great Bend, Kan.
1919-089	Welch, Frank Tiguer	D. July 25, 1957 Birmingham, Ala.
1925-113	Welch, Herbert M.	D. April 13, 1967 Memphis, Tenn.
1926-091	Welch, John Vernon	D. September 2, 1940 St. Louis, Mo.
1945-113	Welch, Milton Edward	2860 Taylor Street/Eugene OR 97405
1978-140	Welch, Robert Lynn	10800 East Cactus Road #33/Scottsdale AZ 85259
1982-135	Welchel, Donald Ray	21518 Patton Avenue/Leander TX 78645
1911-174	Welchonce, Harry Monroe	D. February 26, 1977 Arcadia, Calif.
1916-094	Welf, Oliver Henry	D. June 25, 1967 Cleveland, O.
1982-136	Wellman, Brad Eugene	733 Graham Court/Dabville CA 94526
1948-108	Wellman, Robert Joseph	D. December 20, 1994 Villa Hills, Ky.
1987-150	Wells, David Lee	1640 Lago Vista Blvd/Palm Harbor FL 34685
1923-139	Wells, Edwin Lee	D. May 1, 1986 Birmingham, Ala.
1981-139	Wells, Gregory Dewayne Boomer	Rr 1 Box 98/McIntosh AL 36553
1944-139	Wells, John Frederick	D. October 23, 1993 Olean, N. Y.
1942-107	Wells, Leo Donald	1322 Alton Avenue #315/Saint Paul MN 55116
1994-111	Wells, Robert Lee	Old Add: 916 South 34th Avenue Yakima WA 98902
1990-168	Wells, Terry	Old Add: 411 East Healey #1 Champaign IL 61820
1981-140	Welsh, Christopher Charles	12640 Huey Lane/Walton KY 41094
1925-114	Welsh, James Daniel	D. October 30, 1970 Oakland, Calif.
1948-109	Welteroth, Richard John	122 Eldred Street/Williamsport PA 17701
1926-092	Welzer, Anton Frank	D. March 18, 1971 Milwaukee, Wis.
1915-174	Wendell, Lewis Charles	D. July 11, 1953 Bronx, N. Y.
1993-195	Wendell, Steven John 'Turk'	1053 South Street/Dalton MA 1226
1995-240	Wengert, Donald Paul	%Wj Wengert 3822 Vine Avenue Sioux City IA 51106
1943-142	Wensloff, Charles William 'Butch'	8 Ryan Avenue/Mill Valley CA 94941
1945-114	Wentzel, Stanley Aaron	D. November 28, 1991 St. Lawrence, Pa.
1968-109	Wenz, Frederick Charles	1 Circle Dr/Somerville NJ 8876
1927-101	Wera, Julian Valentine	D. December 12, 1975 Rochester, Minn.
1930-091	Werber, William Murray	Villa 5732a 5800 Old Providence Road Charlotte NC 28226
1964-126	Werhas, John Charles	7420 Stone Creek Lane/Anaheim CA 92807
1949-089	Werle, William George	833 West 28th Avenue/San Mateo CA 94403
1956-085	Werley, George William	1374 Clarkson Clayton Cir/Ballwin MO 63011
1975-129	Werner, Donald Paul	2204 Briarwood/Arlington TX 76013
1963-123	Wert, Donald Ralph	647 Saw Mill Road/Mechanicsburg PA 17051
1979-117	Werth, Dennis Dean	Old Add:/PO Box 802 Lincoln IL 62656
1914-229	Wertz, Dwight Lyman Moody	D. May 26, 1958 Sarasota, Fla.
1926-093	Wertz, Henry Levi 'Johnny'	D. August 24, 1990 Newberry, S. C.
1947-092	Wertz, Victor Woodrow	D. July 7, 1983 Detroit, Mich.
1993-196	Wertz, William Charles	Old Add: 6634 Boston Avenue Cleveand OH 44127
1979-118	Wessinger, James Michael	4275 Altair Course/Liverpool NY 13090
1988-137	West, David Lee	5159 Fernleaf Avenue/Memphis TN 38134
1938-104	West, Max Edward	4040 Piedmont Drive #125/Highland CA 92346
1938-105	West, Richard Thomas	D. March 13, 1996 Fort Wayne, Ind.
1927-102	West, Samuel Filmore	D. November 23, 1985 Lubbock, Texas
1928-106	West, Walter Maxwell 'Max'	D. April 25, 1971 Houston, Tex.
1944-140	West, Weldon Edison 'Lefty'	D. July 23, 1979 Hendersonville, N. C.
1955-135	Westlake, James Patrick	909 Seamas Avenue/Sacramento CA 95822
1947-093	Westlake, Waldon Thomas	3800 61st/Sacramento CA 95820
1929-107	Weston, Alfred John	D. November 13, 1997 San Diego, Calif.
1989-139	Weston, Michael Lee 'Mickey'	819 Lydia Street/Warsaw IN 46580
1947-094	Westrum, Wesley Noreen	Rural Route 1 Box 114/Leonard MN 56652
1989-140	Wetherby, Jeffrey Barrett	10263 Gandy Blvd North #2410/Saint Petersburg FL 33702
1989-141	Wetteland, John Karl	PO Box 884/Cedar Crest NM 87008
1927-103	Wetzel, Charles Edward 'Buzz'	D. March 7, 1941 Globe, Ariz.
1920-129	Wetzel, Franklin Burton 'Buzz'	D. March 5, 1942 Burbank, Calif.
1982-137	Wever, Stefan Matthew	7 Corte Sombras/Greenbrae CA 94904
1923-140	Whaley, William Carl	D. March 3, 1943 Indianapolis, Ind.
1913-189	Whaling, Albert James	D. January 21, 1965 Los Angeles, Calif.
1954-116	Wheat, Leroy William	4010 Galt Ocean Drive #609/Fort Lauderdale FL 33308
1915-175	Wheat, McKinley Davis 'Mack'	D. August 14, 1979 Los Banos, Calif.
1912-215	Wheatley, Charles	D. December 10, 1982 Tulsa, Okla.
1943-143	Wheaton, Elwood Pierce 'Woody'	D. December 11, 1995 Lancaster, Pa.
1949-090	Wheeler, Donald Wesley	8127 Colfax Avenue South/Minneapolis MN 55420
1945-115	Wheeler, Edward Raymond	D. August 4, 1983 Centralia, Wash.
1921-110	Wheeler, Floyd Clark 'Rip'	D. September 18, 1968 Marion, Ky.
1910-151	Wheeler, George Harrison	D. June 14, 1918 Clinton, Ind.
1918-073	Wheeler, Richard	D. February 12, 1962 Lexington, Mass.
1976-101	Wheelock, Gary Richard	8557 North 110th Avenue/Peoria AZ 85345
1913-190	Whelan, James Francis	D. November 29, 1929 Dayton, O.
1920-130	Whelan, Thomas Joseph	D. June 26, 1957 Boston, Mass.
1971-107	Whillock, Jack Franklin	2118 River Ridge Road/Arlington TX 76017
1997-174	Whisenant, Matthew Michael	Old Add: La Canada CA 91011
1952-110	Whisenant, Thomas Peter 'Pete'	D. March 22, 1996 Port Charlotte, Fla.
1977-150	Whisenton, Larry	2507 Slattery St/Saint Louis MO 63106

1977-151	Whitaker, Louis Rodman	803 Pipe/Martinsville VA 24112
1966-099	Whitaker, Steve Edward	10127 Filbert Southwest/Tacoma WA 98499
1964-127	Whitby, William Edward	13926 Huntersville Concord Rd/Huntersville NC 28078
1945-116	Whitcher, Robert Arthur	D. May 8, 1997 Akron, Ohio
1937-107	White, Adel 'Abe'	D. October 1, 1978 Atlanta, Ga.
1940-099	White, Albert Eugene 'Fuzz'	Ruiral Route 1 Box 1049/Branson MO 65616
1954-117	White, Charles	D. May 26, 1998 Seattle, Wash.
1993-197	White, Derrick Ramon	Old Add: San Rafael CA
1985-118	White, Devon Markes	Old Add: 1156 N. Date Palm Dr Gilbert AZ 85234
1948-110	White, Donald William	D. June 15, 1987 Carlsbad, Calif.
1955-136	White, Edward Perry	D. September 28, 1982 Lakeland, Fla.
1962-146	White, Elder Lafayette	919 Colony Ave/Ahoskie NC 27910
1940-100	White, Ernest Daniel	D. May 22, 1974 Augusta, Ga.
1973-130	White, Frank	Old Add: 13950 Switzer Road Shawnee Mission KS 66221
1994-112	White, Gabriel Allen	2121 Fairfax Avenue #16/Nashville TN 37212
1941-117	White, Harold George	612 Bird Bay Drive #113c/Venice FL 34292
1974-140	White, Jerome Cardell	PO Box 43130/Oakland CA 94624
1927-104	White, John Peter	D. June 19, 1971 Flushing, N. Y.
1932-091	White, Joyner Clifford 'Jo-Jo'	D. October 9, 1986 Tacoma, Wash.
1963-124	White, Joyner Michael 'Mike'	1820 284th East/Roy WA 98580
1983-149	White, Larry David	12601 Van Nuys Blvd #210/Pacoima CA 91331
1978-141	White, Myron Alan	3814 South Flower #E/Santa Ana CA 92707
1994-113	White, Richard Allen 'Rick'	Old Add: 2521 Chelsey Court Cranberry Twp. PA 16066
1993-198	White, Rondell Bernard	PO Box 534/Gray GA 31032
1951-101	White, Samuel Charles	D. August 4, 1991 Hanalei, Hawaii
1919-090	White, Samuel Lambeth	D. November 11, 1929 Philadelphia, Pa.
1912-216	White, Stephen Vincent	D. January 29, 1975 Braintree, Mass.
1945-117	White, William Barney	3721 Darrell Lane/Tyler TX 75701
1956-086	White, William Dekova	% National League 350 Park Avenue New York NY 10022
1989-142	Whited, Edward Morris	22 Yorktown Road/Bordentown NJ 8505
1933-066	Whitehead, Burgess Urquhart 'Whitey'	D. November 25, 1993 Windsor, N. C.
1935-114	Whitehead, John Henderson	D. October 20, 1964 Bonham, Tex.
1923-141	Whitehill, Earl Oliver	D. October 22, 1954 Omaha, Neb.
1914-231	Whitehouse, Charles Evis	D. July 19, 1960 Indianapolis, Ind.
1912-217	Whitehouse, Gilbert Arthur	D. February 14, 1926 Brewer, Me.
1981-141	Whitehouse, Leonard Joseph	300 Shore Road/Burlington VT 5401
1989-143	Whitehurst, Walter Richard	186 Ardmore/Shreveport LA 71105
1990-169	Whiten, Mark Anthony	1374 Rule Street/Pensacola FL 32514
1995-241	Whiteside, David Sean 'Sean'	PO Box 1177/Haleyville AL 35565
1992-155	Whiteside, Matthew Christopher	713 South Main/Charleston MO 63834
1962-147	Whitfield, Fred Dwight	Rr 1 Box 91/Vandiver AL 35176
1974-141	Whitfield, Terry Bertland	Old Add:793 Ninantic Drive/Foster City CA 94404
1946-103	Whitman, Dick Corwin	20114 North 92nd Avenue/Peoria AZ 85382
1946-104	Whitman, Walter Franklin 'Frank'	D. February 6, 1994 Maryville, Ill.
1980-143	Whitmer, Daniel Charles	823 Robinhood Ln/Redlands CA 92373
1993-199	Whitmore, Darrell Lamont	301 East 15th Street/Front Royal VA 22630
1928-107	Whitney, Arthur Carter	D. September 2, 1987 Center, Texas
1977-152	Whitson, Eddie Lee	Old Add: Tipton Hill Road Bakersville NC 28705
1976-102	Whitt, Ernest Leo	37370 Moravian/Clinton Township MI 48036
1916-095	Whittaker, Walter Elton	D. August 7, 1965 Pembroke, Mass.
1912-218	Whitted, George Bostic 'Possum'	D. October 16, 1962 Wilmington, N.C.
1989-144	Wickander, Kevin Dean	4128 West Kimberly Way/Glendale AZ 85308
1968-110	Wicker, Floyd Euliss	1758 West G Bro Chapel Hill Rd/Snow Camp NC 27349
1936-097	Wicker, Kemp Caswell	D. June 11, 1973 Kernersville, N. C.
1960-102	Wickersham, David Clifford	9118 West 104th Ter/Overland Park KS 66204
1913-191	Wickland, Albert	D. March 14, 1980 Port Washington, Wisc.
1992-156	Wickman, Robert Joe	PO Box 105/Abrams WI 54101
1995-242	Widger, Christopher Jon	42 Oliver Avenue/Pennsville NJ 8070
1947-095	Widmar, Albert Joseph	3919 South Oswego Avenue/Tulsa OK 74135
1958-101	Wieand, Franklin Delano Roosevelt 'Ted'	216 Walnut St/Slatington PA 18080
1934-108	Wiedemeyer, Charles John	D. October 27, 1979 Lake Geneva, Fla.
1979-119	Wiedenbauer, Thomas John	135 Mill Spring Place/Ormond Beach FL 32174
1981-142	Wieghaus, Thomas Robert	9724 East 800 North Road/Grant Park IL 60940
1921-111	Wieneke, John	D. March 16, 1933 Pleasant Ridge, Mich.
1951-102	Wiesler, Robert George	2325 Indian Cup Drive/Florissant MO 63031
1939-125	Wietelmann, William Frederick 'Whitey'	7712 Golfcrest Drive/San Diego CA 92119
1981-143	Wiggins, Alan Anthony	D. January 6, 1991 Los Angeles, Calif.
1946-105	Wight, William Robert	6247 Meadow Vista Drive/Carmichael CA 95608
1923-142	Wigington, Frederick Thomas	D. May 8, 1980 Mesa, Ariz.
1979-120	Wihtol, Alexander Ames 'Sandy'	195 South San Antonio Road/Los Altos CA 94022
1946-106	Wilber, Delbert Quentin	513 Woodleaf Court/Kirkwood MO 63122
1940-101	Wilborn, Calude Edward	D. November 13, 1992 Roxboro, N. C.
1979-121	Wilborn, Thaddeaus Iglehart Ted	6429 Surfside Way/Sacramento CA 95831
1970-137	Wilcox, Milton Edward	Old Add: 50906 Jefferson Avenue New Baltimore MI 48047
1977-153	Wiles, Randall	108 Nancy Court/Belle Chasse LA 70037
1975-130	Wiley, Mark Eugene	22273 Vista Logo Drive/Boca Raton FL 33428
1977-154	Wilfong, Robert Donald 'Rob'	2905 Hollybrook Drive/West Covina CA 91791
1953-098	Wilhelm, Charles Ernest 'Spider'	D. October 20, 1992 Venice, Fla.
1952-111	Wilhelm, James Hoyt 'Hoyt'	8206 Timber Lake Lane/Sarasota FL 34243

1978-142 ....Wilhelm, James Webster ....73 Locust Avenue/Mill Valley CA 94941
1916-096 ....Wilhoit, Joseph William ....D. September 25, 1930 Santa Barbara, Calif.
1911-175 ....Wilie, Denney Earnest ....D. June 20, 1966 Hayward, Calif.
1927-105 ....Wilke, Harry Joseph ....D. June 21, 1991 Hamilton, Ohio
1983-150 ....Wilkerson, Curtis Vernon ....2407 Wildrose Court/Arlington TX 76006
1941-118 ....Wilkie, Aldon Jay ....D. August 5, 1992 Tualatin, Ore.
1989-145 ....Wilkins, Dean Allan ....8580 Hydra Lane/San Diego CA 92126
1979-122 ....Wilkins, Eric Lamoine ....2233 East Miller/Seattle WA 98112
1996-186 ....Wilkins, Marc Allen ....Old Add: Mansfield OH 44901
1991-185 ....Wilkins, Richard David Rick ....12766 Longview Drive West/Jacksonville FL 32223
1944-141 ....Wilkins, Robert Linwood ....357 Janie Lane/Shreveport La/71106
1911-176 ....Wilkinson, Edward Henry ....D. April 9, 1918 Tucson, Ariz.
1918-074 ....Wilkinson, Roy Hamilton ....D. July 2, 1956 Louisville, Ky.
1985-119 ....Wilkinson, William Carl ....4400 South Quebec St #X205/Denver CO 80237
1944-142 ....Wilks, Teddy ....D. August 21, 1989 Houston, Texas
1957-092 ....Will, Robert Lee ....PO Box 1476/Banner Elk NC 28604
1984-128 ....Willard, Gerald Duane ....806 Thayer Lane/Port Hueneme CA 93041
1958-102 ....Willey, Carlton Francis ....Box 64/Cherryfield Me 4622
1963-125 ....Willhite, Jon Nicholas 'Nick' ....Old Add: 5329 South 580 East #F Salt Lake City UT 84107
1980-144 ....Williams, Albert Hamilton ....Pearl Lagoon, Depot Zeloya Nicaragua/Nicaragua
1937-108 ....Williams, Almon Edward ....D. July 19, 1969 Groves, Tex.
1911-177 ....Williams, Alva Mitchel 'Rip' ....D. July 23, 1933 Keokuk, Ia.
1911-178 ....Williams, August Joseph ....D. April 16, 1964 Sterling, Ill.
1991-186 ....Williams, Bernabe (Figueroa) ....PO Box 203/Vega Alta PR 762
1970-138 ....Williams, Bernard ....1919 Manchester Road #123/San Leandro CA 94578
1959-087 ....Williams, Billy Leo ....586 Prince Edward Road/Glen Ellyn IL 60137
1991-187 ....Williams, Bryan O'Neal ....Old Add: Fort Lawn Sc
1971-108 ....Williams, Charles Prosek ....5898 Kendrew Drive/Port Orange FL 32127
1913-192 ....Williams, Claud Preston 'Lefty' ....D. November 4, 1959 Laguna Beach, Calif.
1981-144 ....Williams, Dallas McKinley ....7638 Allenwood Circle/Indianapolis IN 46208
1989-146 ....Williams, Dana Lamount ....1544 Marlboro Avenue/Pittsburgh PA 15221
1949-091 ....Williams, David Carlous ....14802 Enterprise Drive #30c/Farmer's Branch TX 75234
1913-193 ....Williams, David Carter 'Mutt' ....D. March 30, 1962 Fayetteville, Ark.
1996-187 ....Williams, David Keith 'Keith' ....Old Add: Bedford PA 15522
1944-143 ....Williams, Dewey Edgar ....720 13th Street West/Williston ND 58801
1958-103 ....Williams, Donald Fred ....2114 Christiansburg Pike NE/Floyd VA 24091
1963-126 ....Williams, Donald Reid ....D. December 20, 1991 Lajolla, Calif.
1928-108 ....Williams, Earl Baxter ....D. March 10, 1958 Knoxville, Tenn.
1970-139 ....Williams, Earl Craig ....61 Winston Drive/Somerset NJ 8873
1986-162 ....Williams, Edward Laquan ....10221 Caminito Covewood/San Diego CA 92131
1930-092 ....Williams, Edwin Dibrell 'Dib' ....D. April 2, 1992 Searcy, Ark.
1921-112 ....Williams, Evon Daniel ....D. March 23, 1929 San Clemente, Calif.
1984-129 ....Williams, Frank Lee ....Old Add: 2470 Valleyview Drive Clarkston WA 99403
1912-219 ....Williams, Frederick 'Cy' ....D. April 23, 1974 Eagle River, Wis.
1945-118 ....Williams, Frederick 'Pap' ....D. November 2, 1993 Meridian, Miss.
1961-108 ....Williams, George ....4267 Tyler St/Detroit MI 48238
1995-243 ....Williams, George Erik ....N 5250 County Road M/West Salem WI 54669
1992-157 ....Williams, Gerald Floyd ....PO Box 47/Laplace LA 70068
1993-200 ....Williams, Gregory Scott ....137 Live Oak/Alvin TX 77511
1913-194 ....Williams, Harry Peter ....D. December 20, 1963 Haywood, Calif.
1969-180 ....Williams, James Alfred ....Old Add: 1200 S. Highland Ave #142/Fullerton CA 92632
1966-100 ....Williams, James Francis 'Jimy' ....1630 Honey Bear Ln/Dunedin FL 33528
1914-232 ....Williams, John Brodie ....D. September 8, 1963 Long Beach, Calif.
1915-176 ....Williams, Kenneth Roy ....D. January 22, 1959 Grants Pass, Ore.
1986-163 ....Williams, Kenneth Royal ....3255 Selva Drive/San Jose CA 95148
1926-094 ....Williams, Leon Theo ....D. November 20, 1984 Atlanta, Ga.
1977-155 ....Williams, Mark Westley ....119 Third Street #2/Ithaca NY 14850
1916-097 ....Williams, Marshall McDiarmid ....D. February 22, 1935 Tucson, Ariz.
1987-151 ....Williams, Matthew Derrick ....9393 North 90th Street #129/Scottsdale AZ 85258
1983-151 ....Williams, Matthew Evan ....120 Jupiter Street/Lake Jackson TX 77566
1992-158 ....Williams, Michael Darren ....107 Riverview Street/Pembroke VA 24136
1986-164 ....Williams, Mitchell Steven ....2332 Riverton Road/Cinnaminson NJ 8077
1914-233 ....Williams, Rees Gephardt 'Steamboat' ....D. June 29, 1979 Deer River, Minn.
1992-159 ....Williams, Reginald Bernard ....10 Perry Street/Charleston SC 29403
1985-120 ....Williams, Reginald Dewayne ....7185 Crestridge Road/Memphis TN 38119
1978-143 ....Williams, Richard Allen ....1217 Wessmith/Madera CA 93638
1951-103 ....Williams, Richard Hirschfield ....146 Tyler Court/Henderson NV 89014
1914-234 ....Williams, Rinaldo Lewis ....D. April 24, 1966 Cottonwood, Ariz.
1911-179 ....Williams, Robert Elias ....D. August 6, 1962 Nelsonville, O.
1940-102 ....Williams, Robert Fulton ....Old Add: 57 Atlantic Ave Rye NH 03870
1996-188 ....Williams, Shad Clayton ....4682 East Cornell/Fresno CA 93703
1958-104 ....Williams, Stanley Wilson ....4702 Hayter Ave/Lakewood CA 90712
1939-126 ....Williams, Theodore Samuel ....2448 North Essex Avenue/Hernando FL 34442
1995-244 ....Williams, Todd Michael ....Old Add: 300 Highland Ave East Syracuse NY 13057
1964-128 ....Williams, Walter Allen ....2417 Monterey Dr/Brownwood TX 76801
1969-181 ....Williams, William ....Old Add: 3227 Randolph Ave Oakland CA 94602
1938-106 ....Williams, Woodrow Wilson ....D. February 24, 1995 Appomattox, Va.
1997-175 ....Williamson, Anthony Joseph 'Antone' ....Old Add: Tempe AZ 85282
1987-152 ....Williamson, Mark Alan ....1415 Chippendale Road/Lutherville MD 21093

1928-109 ....**Williamson, Nathaniel Howard 'Howie'** ....D. August 15, 1969 Texarkana, Ark.
1928-110 ....**Williamson, Silas Albert**.........D. November 29, 1978 Hot Springs, Ark.
1930-093 ....**Willingham, Thomas Hugh** ....D. June 15, 1988 El Reno, Okla.
1984-130 ....**Willis, Carl Blake** ....6811 Lipscomb Drive/Durham NC 27712
1925-115 ....**Willis, Charles William 'Lefty'** ....D. May 10, 1962 Bethesda, Md.
1963-127 ....**Willis, Dale Jerome**.........2801 Spaniel Lane/Seffner FL 33584
1953-099 ....**Willis, James Gladden** ....Box 35/Boyce LA 71409
1911-180 ....**Willis, Joseph Denk** ....D. December 3, 1966 Ironton, O.
1947-096 ....**Willis, Lester Evans** ....D. January 22, 1982 Jasper, Texas
1977-156 ....**Willis, Michael Henry** ....Old Add: 201 Wilcrest #2305 Houston TX 77042
1966-101 ....**Willis, Ronald Earl** ....D. November 21, 1977 Memphis, Tenn.
1925-116 ....**Willoughby, Claude William** ....D. August 14, 1973 McPherson, Kan.
1971-109 ....**Willoughby, James Arthur**.........PO Box 143/Pollock Pines CA 95726
1977-157 ....**Wills, Elliott Taylor 'Bump'** ....4226 Glen Pines Court/Arlington TX 76016
1983-152 ....**Wills, Frank Lee** ....733 Gen. Pershing St/New Orleans LA 70115
1959-088 ....**Wills, Maurice Morning** ....1000 Elysian Park Avenue/Los Angeles CA 90012
1959-089 ....**Wills, Theodore Carl**.........2204 Indianapolis/Clovis CA 93611
1918-075 ....**Willson, Frank Hoxie 'Kid'** ....D. April 17, 1964 Union Gap, Wash.
1989-147 ....**Wilmet, Paul Richard** ....226 North 6th Street/Depere WI 54115
1934-109 ....**Wilshere, Vernon Sprague 'Whitey'** ....D. May 23, 1985 Cooperstown, N. Y.
1973-131 ....**Wilshusen, Terry Wayne** ....1839 West 255th Street/Lomita CA 90717
1951-104 ....**Wilson, Archie Clifton** ....1620 Woodland Street SE/Decatur AL 35601
1951-105 ....**Wilson, Arthur Lee** ....2226 NE 10th Avenue/Portland OR 97212
1931-100 ....**Wilson, Charles Woodrow** ....D. December 19, 1970 Rochester, N. Y.
1989-148 ....**Wilson, Craig**.........22 Parole Street/Annapolis MD 21401
1992-160 ....**Wilson, Daniel Allen** ....1933 East Blaine Street/Seattle WA 98112
1996-189 ....**Wilson, Desi Bernard** ....Old Add: Glen Cove NY 11542
1966-102 ....**Wilson, Donald Edward** ....D. January 5, 1975 Houston, Tex.
1958-105 ....**Wilson, Duane Lewis** ....525 Greenfield Street/Valley Center KS 67147
1959-090 ....**Wilson, Earl Lawrence** ....16277 West Murray Road/Ponchatoula LA 70454
1936-098 ....**Wilson, Edward Francis** ....D. April 11, 1979 Hamden, Conn.
1997-176 ....**Wilson, Enrique Martes** ....Old Add: Santo Domingo Dom. Rep.
1914-235 ....**Wilson, Finis Elbert** ....D. March 9, 1959 Coral Gables, Fla.
1924-115 ....**Wilson, Francis Edward** ....D. November 25, 1974 Leicester, Mass.
1995-245 ....**Wilson, Gary Morris** ....1021 Glendale Drive/Arcata CA 95521
1979-123 ....**Wilson, Gary Steven** ....Old Add: PO Box 644 Camden AR 71701
1911-181 ....**Wilson, George Francis 'Squanto'** ....D. March 26, 1967 Winthrop, Me.
1934-110 ....**Wilson, George Peacock 'Icehouse'**.........D. October 13, 1973 Moraga, Calif.
1952-112 ....**Wilson, George Washington** ....D. October 29, 1974 Gastonia, N.C.
1982-138 ....**Wilson, Glenn Dwight** ....Old Add: 1 Wood Estates Drive Conroe TX 77304
1924-116 ....**Wilson, Gomer Russell 'Tex'** ....D. September 15, 1946 Sulphur Springs, Tex.
1923-143 ....**Wilson, James** ....D. June 1, 1947 Palmetto, Fla.
1945-119 ....**Wilson, James Alger** ....D. September 2, 1986 Newport Beach, Calif.
1985-121 ....**Wilson, James George** ....2400 Nw 88th Street/Vancouver WA 98665
1934-111 ....**Wilson, John Francis 'Black Jack'** ....D. April 19, 1995 Edmonds, Wash.
1913-195 ....**Wilson, John Nicodemus**.........D. September 23, 1954 Annapolis, Md.
1927-106 ....**Wilson, John Samuel** ....D. August 27, 1980 Chattanooga, Tenn.
1911-182 ....**Wilson, Lester Wilbur** ....D. April 4, 1969 Edmonds, Wash.
1923-144 ....**Wilson, Lewis Robert 'Hack'** ....D. November 23, 1948 Baltimore, Md.
1940-103 ....**Wilson, Max** ....D. January 2, 1977 Greensboro, N. C.
1983-153 ....**Wilson, Michael 'Tack'** ....1089 Olde Hinge Way/Snellville GA 30078
1993-201 ....**Wilson, Nigel Edward** ....110 Burchr Road/Ajax Ontario L1S 2R2 Canada
1996-190 ....**Wilson, Paul Anthony** ....2215 Barksdale Drive/Orlando FL 32822
1958-106 ....**Wilson, Robert** ....D. April 23, 1985 Dallas, Texas
1951-106 ....**Wilson, Robert James 'Red'** ....806 Cabot Lane/Madison WI 53711
1928-111 ....**Wilson, Roy Edward** ....D. December 3, 1969 Clarion, Ia.
1960-103 ....**Wilson, Sammy Oneil 'Neil'** ....4300 Highway 412 West/Lexington TN 38351
1921-113 ....**Wilson, Samuel Marshall 'Mike'** ....D. May 16, 1978 Boynton Beach, Fla.
1988-138 ....**Wilson, Stephen Douglas** ....Old Add: 8446 Aqua Drive Vancouver B.C. Can. V5p 4s2
1914-236 ....**Wilson, Thomas C.** ....D. March 7, 1953 San Pedro, Calif.
1988-139 ....**Wilson, Trevor Kirk** ....16665 South Annette Drive/Oregon City OR 97045
1945-120 ....**Wilson, Walter Wood** ....D. April 17, 1994 Bremen, Ga.
1920-131 ....**Wilson, William Clarence 'Mutt'** ....D. August 31, 1962 Wildwood, Fla.
1950-104 ....**Wilson, William Donald** ....Old Add: 17126 Woodruff Ave #A Bellflower CA 90706
1969-182 ....**Wilson, William Harlan** ....D. August 11, 1993
1980-145 ....**Wilson, William Hayward 'Mookie'** ....1111 Heyward Wilson Road/Eastover SC 29044
1976-103 ....**Wilson, Willie James** ....3905 West 110th Terrace/Leawood KS 66211
1926-095 ....**Wiltse, Harold James** ....D. November 2, 1983 Bunkie, La.
1956-087 ....**Winceniak, Edward Joseph** ....10828 South Avenue O/Chicago IL 60617
1997-177 ....**Winchester, Scott J.** ....4705 Oakridge Drive/Midland MI 48640
1959-091 ....**Windhorn, Gordon Ray** ....145 Bent Creek Rd/Danville VA 24540
1928-112 ....**Windle, Willis Brewer** ....D. December 8, 1981 Corpus Christi Tx.
1986-165 ....**Wine, Robert "Paul, Jr." 'Robbie'** ....Oklahoma State Baseball Allie Reynolds Stadium Stillwater OK 74078
1960-104 ....**Wine, Robert "Paul, Sr/"** ....2612 Woodland Ave/Norristown PA 19401
1929-108 ....**Wineapple, Edward** ....D. July 23, 1996 Delray Beach, Fla.
1930-094 ....**Winegarner, Ralph Lee** ....D. April 14, 1988 Wichita, Kan.
1973-132 ....**Winfield, David Mark** ....14970 Hickory Greens Court/Fort Myers FL 33912
1932-092 ....**Winford, James Head**.........D. December 16, 1970 Miami, Okla.

1924-117 ....Wingard, Ernest James ....D. January 17, 1977 Prattville, Ala.
1923-145 ....Wingfield, Frederick Davis 'Ted' ....D. July 18, 1975 Johnson City, Tenn.
1919-091 ....Wingo, Absalom Holbrook 'Al' ....D. October 9, 1954 Detroit, Mich.
1920-132 ....Wingo, Edmond Armand ....D. December 5, 1964 Lachine, Que.
1911-183 ....Wingo, Ivey Brown ....D. March 1, 1941 Norcross, Ga.
1973-133 ....Winkles, Bobby Brooks ....78452 Calle Huerta/Laquinta CA 92253
1919-092 ....Winn, George Benjamin ....D. November 1, 1969 Roberta, Ga.
1983-154 ....Winn, James Francis ....%Corn County Cement Co. 510 Sherman Parkway Springfield MO 65802
1984-131 ....Winningham, Herman Son ....360 Fishburne Street/Charleston SC 29403
1930-095 ....Winsett, John Thomas 'Tom' ....D. July 20, 1987 Memphis, Tenn.
1997-178 ....Winston, Darrin Alexander ....Old Add: Fords NJ 08863
1933-067 ....Winston, Henry Rudolph ....D. February 7, 1974 Jacksonville, Fla.
1924-118 ....Winters, Clarence John ....D. June 29, 1945 Detroit, Mich.
1919-093 ....Winters, Jesse Franklin 'Buck' ....D. June 5, 1986 Abilene, Texas
1989-149 ....Winters, Matthew Littleton.............................1201 Foxfire Drive/Greensboro NC 27410
1978-144 ....Wirth, Alan Lee ....1012 West Mountain View/Mesa AZ 85201
1921-114 ....Wirts, Elwood Vernon 'Kettle' ....D. July 12, 1968 Sacramento, Calif.
1932-093 ....Wise, Archibald Edwin ....D. February 2, 1978 Waxahachie, Tex.
1930-096 ....Wise, Hugh Edward ....D. July 21, 1987 Plantation, Fla.
1957-093 ....Wise, Kendall Cole 'Casey' ....1325 7th Street South #4b/Naples FL 33940
1964-129 ....Wise, Richard Charles ....8235 SW 184th Avenue/Beaverton OR 97007
1944-144 ....Wise, Roy Ogden 'Ogden' ....123 Ninth Street #2/Huntington Beach CA 92648
1919-094 ....Wisner, John Henry ....D. December 15, 1981 Jackson, Mich.
1964-130 ....Wissman, David Alvin ....Hawk Hill Road/Shelbrooke Falls MA 1370
1934-112 ....Wistert, Francis Michael 'Whitey' ....D. April 23, 1985 Painesville, Ohio
1914-230 ....Wisterzil, George John 'Tex' ....D. June 27, 1964 San Antonio, Tex.
1996-191 ....Witasick, Gerald Alphonse 'Jay' ....923 East Broadway/Bel Air MD 21014
1940-104 ....Witek, Nicholas Joseph 'Mickey' ....D. August 24, 1990 Kingston, Pa.
1920-133 ....Withrow, Frank Blaine ....D. September 5, 1966 Omaha, Neb.
1963-128 ....Withrow, Raymond Wallace 'Corky' ....1112 Buford Drive/Utica KY 42376
1991-188 ....Witmeyer, Ronald Herman..............................Ath. Dept.,Stanford Univ./Stanford CA 94305
1957-094 ....Witt, George Adrian ....2209 Catalina St/Laguna Beach CA 92651
1916-098 ....Witt, Lawton Walter 'Whitey' ....D. July 14, 1988 Salem County, N. J.
1981-145 ....Witt, Michael Atwater ....Old Add: 8042 San Leon Circle Dr Buena Park CA 90620
1986-166 ....Witt, Robert Andrew ....4601 Winewood Court/Colleyville TX 76034
1946-107 ....Witte, Jerome Charles ....7515 Oak Vista/Houston TX 77087
1938-107 ....Wittig, John Carl ....17136b Big Road/Bloxom VA 22306
1974-142 ....Wockenfuss, John Bilton ....Old Add: 428 North Street/Elkton MD 21921
1923-146 ....Woehr, Andrew Emil ....D. July 24, 1990 Fort Wayne, Ind.
1991-189 ....Wohlers, Mark Edward ....1265 Stuart Ridge/Alpharetta GA 30022
1972-121 ....Wohlford, James Eugene ....240 East Parkview Avenue/Visalia CA 93277
1995-246 ....Wojciehowski, Steven Joseph ....Old Add: 1033 Burnham 3304 Calumet City IL 60409
1962-148 ....Wojcik, John Joseph ....1072 Eastern Parkway/Louisville KY 40217
1954-118 ....Wojey, Peter Paul ....D. April 23, 1991 Mobile, Ala.
1985-122 ....Wojna, Edward David.....................................53 South Jeffery Street/Beverly Hills FL 34465
1995-247 ....Wolcott, Robert William ....1374 Bonita Avenue/Medford OR 97520
1912-220 ....Wolf, Ernest...D. May 23, 1964 Atlantic Highlands, N.J.
1927-107 ....Wolf, Raymond Bernard ....D. October 6, 1979 Fort Worth, Texas
1969-183 ....Wolf, Walter Beck ....7 Beachcomber/Corona Del Mar CA 92625
1921-115 ....Wolf, Walter Francis 'Lefty' ....D. September 25, 1971 New Orleans, La.
1923-147 ....Wolfe, Charles Henry ....D. November 27, 1957 Schellsburg, Pa.
1952-113 ....Wolfe, Edward Anthony ....Old Add: 5615 Kermit Lane Stockton CA 95207
1917-090 ....Wolfe, Harold ....D. July 28, 1971 Fort Wayne, Ind.
1977-158 ....Wolfe, Laurence March ....2325 Hartford Court/El Dorado Hills CA 95762
1912-221 ....Wolfe, Roy Chamberlain 'Polly' ....D. November 21, 1938 Morris, Ill.
1941-119 ....Wolff, Roger Francis ....D. March 23, 1994 Chester, Ill.
1914-237 ....Wolfgang, Meldon John ....D. June 30, 1947 Albany, N.Y.
1993-202 ....Womack, Anthony Darrell ....7101 Halifax Road/Chatham VA 24531
1966-103 ....Womack, Horace Guy 'Dooley' ....209 Weeping Cherry Lane/Columbia SC 29212
1926-096 ....Womack, Sidney Kirk ....D. August 28, 1958 Jackson, Miss.
1930-097 ....Wood, Charles Asher 'Spades' ....D. May 18, 1986 Wichita, Kan.
1923-148 ....Wood, Charles Spencer 'Doc' ....D. November 3, 1974 New Orleans, La.
1991-190 ....Wood, Edward Robert 'Ted' ....Old Add: New Orleans La
1961-109 ....Wood, Jacob ....851 Magnolia Ave/Elizabeth NJ 7201
1944-145 ....Wood, Joe Frank ....PO Box 53/Clinton CT 6413
1943-144 ....Wood, Joseph Perry ....D. March 25, 1985 Houston, Texas
1913-196 ....Wood, Roy Winton ....D. April 6, 1974 Fayetteville, Ark.
1961-110 ....Wood, Wilbur Forrester ....3 Elmsbrook Road/Bedford MA 1730
1920-134 ....Woodall, Charles Lawrence 'Larry'.............D. May 6, 1963 Cambridge, Mass.
1994-114 ....Woodall, David Bradley 'Brad' ....303 Old Course Loop/Blythewood SC 29016
1978-145 ....Woodard, Darrell Lee ....1227 East 69th Street/Los Angeles CA 90001
1985-123 ....Woodard, Michael Cary ....PO Box 35/Maywood IL 60153
1997-179 ....Woodard, Steven Larry ....1219 Chickasaw/Hartselle AL 35640
1911-184 ....Woodburn, Eugene Stewart............................D. January 18, 1961 Sandusky, O.
1944-146 ....Woodend, George Anthony ....D. February 6, 1980 Hartford, Conn.
1956-088 ....Woodeshick, Harold Joseph ....803 Wycliffe Dr/Houston TX 77079
1943-145 ....Woodling, Eugene Richard ....926 Remsen Road/Medina OH 44256
1914-239 ....Woodman, Daniel Courtenay ....D. December 14, 1962 Topsfield, Mass.
1977-159 ....Woods, Alvis ....2518 60th Ave/Oakland CA 94605

1914-238 ....Woods, Clarence Cofield ....D. July 2, 1969 Rising Sun, Ind.
1976-104 ....Woods, Gary Lee ....Old Add: 2621 North Swan Tucson AZ 85712
1943-146 ....Woods, George Rowland 'Pinky' ....D. October 30, 1982 Los Angeles, Calif.
1957-095 ....Woods, James Jerome ....1222 Dawson Drive/Reno NV 89523
1924-119 ....Woods, John Fulton ....D. October 4, 1946 Norfolk, Va.
1969-184 ....Woods, Ronald Lawrence ....Old Add: 1002 7th Street Los Angeles CA 90017
1969-185 ....Woodson, Richard Lee ....Old Add: 3203 Villa Addlee Spring Valley CA 91978
1987-153 ....Woodson, Tracy Michael ....10204 Riverstone Place/Raleigh NC 27614
1992-161 ....Woodson, Walter Browne Kerry ....1144 Kay Ellen Court/San Jose CA 95125
1918-076 ....Woodward, Frank Russell ....D. June 11, 1961 New Haven, Conn.
1985-124 ....Woodward, Robert John ....Hcr 63 Box 43a Eastman Hill/Lebanon NH 3766
1963-129 ....Woodward, William Frederick 'Woody' ....5404 Lk Washington Blvd NE #A/Kirkland WA 98033
1955-137 ....Wooldridge, Floyd Lewis ....214 Barber St/Greenfield MO 65661
1947-097 ....Wooten, Earl Hazell ....702 Williams Street/Williamston SC 29697
1914-240 ....Worden, Frederick Bamford ....D. November 9, 1941 St. Louis, Mo.
1938-108 ....Workman, Charles Thomas ....D. January 3, 1953 Kansas City, Mo.
1924-120 ....Workman, Harry Hall 'Hoge' ....D. May 20, 1972 Fort Myers, Fla.
1950-105 ....Workman, Henry Kilgariff ....307 19th Street/Santa Monica CA 90402
1993-203 ....Worrell, Timothy Harold ....515 Santa Maria Road/Arcadia CA 91007
1985-125 ....Worrell, Todd Roland ....Old Add: 515 Santa Maria Rd Arcadia CA 91007
1978-146 ....Wortham, Richard Cooper ....10247 Missel Thrush Drive/Austin TX 78750
1953-100 ....Worthington, Allan Fulton ....734 12th Street Nw/Alabaster AL 35007
1988-140 ....Worthington, Craig Richard ....9431 Van Allen/Pico Rivera CA 90660
1931-101 ....Worthington, Robert Lee 'Red' ....D. December 8, 1963 Los Angeles, Calif.
1916-099 ....Wortman, William Lewis 'Chuck' ....D. August 19, 1977 Las Vegas, Nev.
1983-155 ....Wotus, Ronald Allan ....1902 Strayhorn Road/Pleasant Hill CA 94523
1933-068 ....Wright, Albert Edgar ....Old Add: 4030 Panama CT #213 Oakland CA 94611
1935-115 ....Wright, Albert Owen 'Ab' ....D. May 23, 1995 Muskogee, Okla.
1916-100 ....Wright, Ceylon ....D. November 7, 1947 Hines, Ill.
1966-104 ....Wright, Clyde ....528 Jeanine Avenue/Anaheim CA 92806
1924-121 ....Wright, Forest Glenn ....D. April 6, 1984 Olathe, Kan.
1982-139 ....Wright, George Dewitt ....4228 NE 18th Street/Oklahoma City OK 73121
1945-121 ....Wright, Henderson Edward 'Ed' ....D. November 19, 1995 Dyersburg, Tenn.
1927-108 ....Wright, James ....D. April 12, 1963 Oakland, Calif.
1978-147 ....Wright, James Clifton ....PO Box 199/Baldwinsville NY 13027
1981-146 ....Wright, James Leon ....2822 South 29th/Saint Joseph MO 64503
1982-140 ....Wright, James Richard 'Ricky' ....2502 Clark Lane/Paris TX 75460
1996-192 ....Wright, Jamey Alan ....1424 SW 93rd/Oklahoma City OK 73159
1997-180 ....Wright, Jaret Samuel ....528 Jeanine Avenue/Anaheim CA 92806
1970-140 ....Wright, Kenneth Warren ....1651 Ora Drive/Pensacola FL 32506
1954-119 ....Wright, Melvin James ....D. May 16, 1983 Houston, Tex.
1915-177 ....Wright, Robert Cassius ....D. July 30, 1993 Carmichael, Calif.
1956-089 ....Wright, Roy Earl ....331 Pinehurst Cir/Chickamauga GA 30707
1938-109 ....Wright, Taft Shedron ....D. October 22, 1981 Orlando, Fla.
1948-113 ....Wright, Thomas Everett ....1116 Poplar Springs Ch Road/Shelby NC 28152
1917-091 ....Wright, Wayne Bromley 'Rasty' ....D. June 12, 1948 Columbus, O.
1915-178 ....Wright, Willard James 'Dick' ....D. January 24, 1952 Bethlehem, Pa.
1920-135 ....Wrightstone, Russell Guy ....D. March 1, 1969 Harrisburg, Pa.
1988-141 ....Wrona, Richard James ....7514 E. 17th Street/Tulsa OK 74112
1929-109 ....Wuestling, George 'Yats' ....D. April 26, 1970 St. Louis, Mo.
1944-147 ....Wurm, Frank James ....D. September 19, 1993 Glens Falls, N. Y.
1961-111 ....Wyatt, John ....D. April 6, 1998 Omaha, Neb.
1929-110 ....Wyatt, John Whitlow 'Whit' ....PO Box 56/Buchanan GA 30113
1924-122 ....Wyatt, Loral John 'Joe' ....D. December 5, 1970 Oblong, Ill.
1913-197 ....Wyckoff, John Weldon ....D. May 8, 1961 Sheboygan Falls, Wis.
1976-105 ....Wynegar, Harold Delano ....PO Box 915811/Longwood FL 32791
1939-127 ....Wynn, Early ....6151 Jack Street/Venice FL 34293
1963-130 ....Wynn, James Sherman ....8181 El Mundo #2054/Houston TX 77054
1983-156 ....Wynne, Marvell ....15811 Bent Tree Road/Poway CA 92064
1967-115 ....Wynne, William Vernon ....7722 Greenwich Court West/Jacksonville FL 32216
1942-108 ....Wyrostek, John Barney ....D. December 12, 1986 St.Louis, Mo.
1942-109 ....Wyse, Henry Washington ....1105 South Karen Street/Pryor OK 74361
1930-098 ....Wysong, Harlin 'Biff' ....D. August 8, 1951 Xenia, O.
1996-193 ....Yan, Esteban Luis ....Old Add: La Higuera Dominican Rep.
1972-122 ....Yancy, Hugh ....Box 9064/Sarasota FL 33578
1942-110 ....Yankowski, George Edward ....164 Chapman Street/Watertown MA 2172
1912-222 ....Yantz, George Webb ....D. February 26, 1967 Louisville, Ky.
1926-097 ....Yarnall, Waldo Ward 'Rusty' ....D. October 9, 1985 Lowell, Mass.
1922-137 ....Yarrison, Byron Wardsworth 'Rube' ....D. April 22, 1977 Williamsport, Pa.
1921-116 ....Yaryan, Clarence Everett 'Yam' ....D. November 16, 1964 Birmingham, Ala.
1961-112 ....Yastrzemski, Carl Michael ....4621 South Ocean Blvd/Highland Beach FL 33487
1971-110 ....Yates, Albert Arthur ....Old Add: 27705 98th Camp Lake WI 53109
1924-123 ....Yde, Emil Ogden ....D. December 4, 1968 Leesburg, Fla.
1919-095 ....Yeabsley, Robert Watkins 'Bert' ....D. February 8, 1961 Philadelphia, Pa.
1972-123 ....Yeager, Stephen Wayne ....PO Box 34184/Granada Hills CA 91394
1922-138 ....Yeargin, James Almond ....D. May 8, 1937 Greenville, S. C.
1989-150 ....Yelding, Eric Girard ....PO Box 325/Montrose AL 36559
1917-092 ....Yelle, Archie Joseph ....D. May 2, 1983 Woodland, Calif.
1963-131 ....Yellen, Lawrence Allen ....3886 Toccoa Falls Drive/Duluth GA 30097

Coaches With No Playing Experience From 1910 To 1997

C1935-01 ....Abbott, Spencer Arthur ....D. December 18, 1951 Washington, D. C.
C1992-01 ....Adair, Michael Richard 'Rick' ....141 Bennett Circle/Spartanburg SC 29302
C1997-01 ....Alejo, Robert Kevin ....7767 Oakport Street #200/Oakland CA 94621
C1992-02 ....Alfonso, Carlos ....1171 Royal Drive/Naples FL 33940
C1994-01 ....Arsenault, Pierre Jean ....17942 Amalfi Pierrefonds Quebec/H9k 1m2 Canada
C1973-01 ....Auferio, Anthony Patrick 'Tony' ....35 Beech Terrace/Wayne NJ 7470
C1989-01 ....Berardino, Richard J. ....37 Emmeline Avenue/Waltham MA 2154
C1967-01 ....Beringer, Carroll James 'C.B.' ....4917 Granite Shoals/Fort Worth TX 76103
C1996-01 ....Berteotti, Gerald ....000 Elysian Park Avenue/Los Angeles CA 90012
C1992-03 ....Biagini, Gregory Peter ....111 Lady Di Drive/Winterville NC 28590
C1994-02 ....Bialas, David Bruce ....14080 North Bayshore Drive/Madeira Beach FL 33708
C1996-02 ....Billmeyer, Michael Frederick 'Mick' ....% Display Memory 8 Sturgis Drive Hagerstwon MD 21740
C1964-01 ....Blackburn, Wayne Clark ....1414 Offnere Street/POrtsmouth OH 45662
C1974-01 ....Bloomfield, Gordon Leigh 'Jack' ....1310 Iris/Mcallen TX 78501
C1992-04 ....Bolek, Kenneth ....304 South Street/Chardon OH 44024
C1996-03 ....Bombard, Marc ....8612 Barkwood Court/Tampa FL 33615
C1967-02 ....Bragan, James Alton ....1055 Martinwood Lane/Birmingham AL 35235
C1986-01 ....Breeden, Harold Scott ....12123 Riverhills Drive/Tampa FL 33617
C1995-01 ....Breeden, Joseph Thomas ....1305 Bonaventure/Melbourne FL 32940
C1994-03 ....Butterfield, Brian James ....4521 East Morning Vista Lane/Cave Creek AZ 85331
C1969-01 ....Camacho, Joseph Gomes ....48 Massasoit Avenue/Fairhaven MA 2719
C1997-02 ....Carey, Paul Jerome 'P.J.' ....5051 East Tano Blvd/Phoenix AZ 85044
C1996-04 ....Carlucci, David Mario ....4 Yawkey Way/Boston MA 2215
C1970-01 ....Carnevale, Daniel Joseph ....161 Dorchester Road/Buffalo NY14213
C1988-01 ....Carrion, Leonel Santiago ....San Jacinto, Sec 7, Ver 5#1 Maracaibo Venezuela
C1959-01 ....Carter, Richard Joseph ....D. September 11, 1969 Philadelphia, Pa.
C1991-01 ....Chiti, Harry Dominic 'Dom' ....3582 Thistle Valley Lane/Memphis TN38135
C1991-02 ....Ciccantelli, Patrick Richard ....3133 Cambridge Drive/Cuyahoga Falls OH 44224
C1977-01 ....Clear, Elwood Robert 'Bob' ....120 East 234th Street/Carson CA 90745
C1979-02 ....Cluck, Robert Alton ....6192 Baltimore Drive/Lamesa CA 92042
C1985-01 ....Connor, Mark Peter ....7252 East Whistling Wind Way/Scottsale AZ 85255
C1953-01 ....Crandall, James Mark 'Jimmie ....D. February 1, 1983 Bullhead City, Ariz.
C1977-02 ....Cresse, Mark Emery ....3840 Goldenrod Street/Seal Beach CA 90740
C1995-02 ....Dearmas, Rolando Jesus 'Roly' ....2840 Valencia Lane West/Palm Harbor FL 34684
C1989-02 ....Demerritt, Martin Gordon ....8317 Lakeland Drive/Granite Bay CA 95746
C1979-01 ....Dews, Robert Walter ....423 Audubon/Albany GA 31707
C1980-01 ....Donnelly, Richard Francis ....7921 Nw 6th Street/Plantation FL 33324
C1961-01 ....Douglas, Otis Whitfield ....D. March 21, 1989 Kilmarnock, Pa.
C1988-02 ....Down, Richard John 'Rick' ....3148 Rowland/Las Vegas NV 89106
C1969-02 ....Dunlop, Harry Alexander ....PO Box 4606/Helena MT59604
C1983-01 ....Dusan, Eugene Paul ....61174 Conco Street/Bend OR97701
C1983-02 ....Ezell, Glenn Wayne ....2416 West 137th Street/Leawood KS 66224
C1996-05 ....Fischer, Bradley James ....7767 Oakport Street/ Oakland CA 94621
C1947-01 ....Fitzgerald, Joseph Patrick ....D. August 29, 1967 Orlando, Fla.
C1953-02 ....Fitzpatrick, John Arthur ....D. November 19, 1990
C1985-02 ....Galante, Matthew Joseph ....11008 Hammerly/Houston TX 77043
C1994-04 ....Glynn, Eugene Patrick ....9 Tecoma Circle/Littleton CO 80127
C1992-06 ....Gomez, Juan Alejandro 'Orlando' ....C-1 Urb. Las Flores/Juana Diaz PR 795
C1981-01 ....Guerrero, Epifanio Obdulio (Abud) 'Epy' ....Res. La Rotonda #19,Arroyo Hondo Santo Domingo Dominican Rep.
C1991-03 ....Hansen, Guy Christopher ....3876 Red Rock Street/Las Vegas NV 89103
C1992-07 ....Hansen, Roger Christian ....6175 West Blackhawk Drive/Glendale AZ 85038
C1982-01 ....Harmon, Thomas Harold ....6101 Bon Terra Drive/Austin TX 78731
C1993-01 ....Hernandez, Carlo Amado 'Chuck' ....3113 West River Cove Drive/Tampa FL 33614
C1993-02 ....Hill, Perry Wendell ....2507 Westpark Way Circle/Euless TX 76040
C1984-01 ....Hines, Benjamin Thortan ....2709 Second Street/Laverne CA 91750
C1991-04 ....Hines, Bruce Edwin ....5345 East Mclellan Road #98/Mesa AZ 85205
C1994-05 ....Holmberg, Dennis Nels ....2086 Swan Lane/Palm Harbor FL 34683
C1984-02 ....Holmquist, Douglas Leonard ....D. February 27, 1988 Altamonte Springs, Fla.
C1948-01 ....Holt, Golden Desmond 'Goldie' ....D. June 11, 1991 Sherman Oaks, Calif.
C1968-01 ....Hoscheit, Vernard Anthony ....PO Box 36/Plainview Ne 68769
C1993-03 ....Hubbard, John H. 'Jack' ....508 Fayette Circle North/Safety Harbor FL 34695
C1988-04 ....Isaac, Luis (Aponte) ....PO Box 1167/Carolina PR 979
C1990-01 ....Jaramillo, Rudolph ....3853 Echo Brook Lane/Dallas TX 75229
C1997-03 ....Jauss, David Patrick ....77 Presentation Road/Brighton MA 2135
C1987-01 ....Jones, Joseph Carmack ....2411 Carlisle Place/Sarasota FL 34231
C1955-01 ....Kahn, Louis ....916 Tift Street/Albany GA 31701
C1930-01 ....Kelly, Bernard Francis ....D. October 23, 1968 Indianapolis, Ind.
C1989-03 ....Kim, Wendell Kealohapauole ....5804 East Fox Street/Mesa AZ 85205
C1969-03 ....Kissell, George Marshall ....658 Mount Oak Avenue NE/Saint Petersburg FL 33702
C1971-01 ....Kittle, Hubert Milton 'Hub' ....3801 Richey Road/Yakima Wa 98902
C1970-02 ....Koenig, Fred Carl ....D. January 12, 1993 Choteau, Okla.
C1995-03 ....Lachemann, William Charles ....208 Riverview Lane/Great Falls MT59404
C1988-05 ....Lett, James Curtis ....Star Route 34 Box 5751/Winfield WV 25213
C1957-01 ....Levy, Leonard Howard ....D. February 2, 1993 Palm Desert, Calif.
C1994-06 ....Linares, Julio Marienu (Rijo) ....PO Box 62 San Pedro De Macoris Dominican Rep./

C1996-06 ....Liska, Tony ....600 Stadium Circle/ Pittsburgh/ PA 15212
C1996-07 ....Little, William Grady 'Grady' ....PO Box 3157/Pinehurst NC 28374
C1951-01 ....Lobe, William Charles ....D. January 7, 1969 Cleveland, O.
C1997-05 ....Lopez, Juan ....Rural Route 1 Box 12690/Toa Alta PR 953
C1972-01 ....Lowe, Q. V. ....Dozier Road/Wetumpka AL 36092
C1964-03 ....Macko, Joseph John ....2219 Templeton Court/Arlington TX 76006
C1995-04 ....Maddon, Joseph John ....2560-32 North Lindsay Road/Mesa AZ 85213
C1989-04 ....Majtyka, Leroy Walter 'Roy' ....Rural Route 1 Box 767/Wagoner OK 74467
C1990-02 ....Maloof, Jack Garth ....3140 South Vista Drive/Chandler AZ 85248
C1991-05 ....Mansolino, Douglas ....2813 Carolina Avenue/Clovis CA 93611
C1995-05 ....Mathews, Rick Ray ....837 Drake Avenue/Centerville IA 52544
C1996-08 ....Maulding, Todd ....912 Springer Drive/Griffin GA 30224
C1985-03 ....Mazzone, Leo David ....16410 Lakewood Drive/Rawling Heights MD 21557
C1951-02 ....McDonnell, Robert A. 'Maje' ....7423 Revere Street/Philadelphia PA 19152
C1986-02 ....MClaren , John Lowell ....Old Add: 2828 Hayes Rd #711 Houston TX 77082
C1993-04 ....Miley, David Allen ....9304 Forest Hills Drive/Tampa FL 33612
C1977-03 ....Mozzali, Maurice Joseph 'Mo' ....D. March 2, 1987 Lakeland, Fla.
C1985-05 ....Mull, Jack Leroy ....2361 Mccleary/Chambersburg PA 17221
C1983-03 ....Napoleon, Edward George ....1312 73rd Street Northwest/Bradenton FL 34209
C1983-04 ....Nottle, Edward William ....3417 South Hennepin Avenue/Sioux City IA 51106
C1958-01 ....Oceak, Frank John ....D. March 19, 1983 Johnstown, Pa.
C1994-07 ....Oliveras, Max ....16th Street Nn #8 Jardines Caparra Bayamon PR 959
C1962-01 ....Oneil, John Jordan 'Buck' ....3409 East 32nd Street/Kansas City MO 64128
C1963-01 ....Osborn, Donald Edwin ....D. March 23, 1979 Torrance, Calif.
C1974-02 ....Pacheco, Antonio Aristides 'Tony' ....D. March 23, 1987 Miami, Fla.
C1961-02 ....Paepke, Jack ....4560 Trieste Drive/Carlsbad CA 92008
C1946-01 ....Patkin, Max O. ....211 Mitchell Road/Exton PA 19341
C1985-06 ....Pavlick, Gregory Michael ....936 Pinellas Bayway South #T8/Tierra Verde FL 33715
C1997-06 ....Pentland, Jeff ....437 East Bluebelle Lane/Tempe AZ 85281
C1984-04 ....Peterson, Eric Harding 'Rick' ....2308 89th Street West/Bradenton FL 34209
C1969-04 ....Plaza, Ronald Charles ....2050 68th Avenue South/Saint Petersburg FL 33712
C1993-05 ....Radison, Daniel John ....116 Se 20th Avenue/Deerfield Beach FL 33441
C1950-01 ....Redys, Edward ....4105 John Paul Court/Warren MI 48091
C1966-01 ....Resinger, Grover S. ....D. January 11, 1986 St. Louis, Mo.
C1981-02 ....Reyes, Benjamin (Chavez) 'Cananea' ....D. December 10, 1991 Hermosillo, Sonora, Mexico
C1995-06 ....Riggins, Mark Alan ....1636 Oxford Drive/Murray KY 42071
C1996-09 ....Rigoli, Joseph M. ....94 Championship #2/Augusta NJ 7822
C1992-09 ....Roberts, Melvin Henry ....PO Box 16683/Greeneville SC 29606
C1966-02 ....Robinson, Warren Grant 'Sheriff' ....5 Kiowa Road/Cambridge MD 21613
C1973-02 ....Rosenbaum, Glen Otis ....PO Box 1/Union Mills IN 46382
C1972-02 ....Rowe, Ralph Emanuel ....D. February 29, 1996 Newberry, S.C.
C1976-02 ....Saul, James Allen ....2405 Osborne Street/Bristol VA 23201
C1970-03 ....Scherger, George Richard ....701 Sain T Julien/Charlotte NC 28205
C1987-02 ....Slider, Rachel W. 'Rac' ....Rural Route 4 Box 64e/Dekalb TX 75559
C1984-05 ....Smith, Billy Franklin ....PO Box 204/Jamestown NC 27282
C1996-10 ....Smith, Steven J. ....2224 Village Center Drive/Encinitas CA 92024
C1985-07 ....Snitker, Brian Gerald ....3148 Pine Needle Court/Lilburn/GA 30241
C1977-04 ....Sommers, Dennis James ....PO Box 133/Hortonvile WI 54944
C1979-03 ....Sparks, Joseph Everett ....3915 East Cholla Street/Phoenix AZ 85028
C1996-11 ....Suba, Stretch ....PO Box 288/ Houston TX 77001
C1997-07 ....Suplizio, Sam ....145 North Fourth Street/Grand Junction CO 81501
C1922-01 ....Thomas , Ray
C1985-08 ....Torchia, Anthony Louis 'Tony' ....5229 Sw 11th Avenue/Cape Coral FL 33904
C1995-07 ....Treuel, Ralph Martin ....516 East Beacon Road/Lakeland FL 33803
C1992-10 ....Turner , Richard Arthur ....
C1981-03 ....Vanornum, John Clayton ....40193 Road 222/Bass Lake CA 93604
C1943-01 ....Vincent, Albert Linder ....260 Manor Avenue/Beaumont TX 77706
C1961-03 ....Walker, Verlon Lee 'Rube' ....D. March 24, 1971 Chicago, Ill.
C1973-03 ....Walton, James Robert ....PO Box 787/Shattuck OK 73858
C1977-05 ....Warner, Harry Clinton ....Jackson Heights/Reeders PA 18352
C1995-08 ....Williams, Daniel Lawrence ....3440 West 151st Street/Cleveland OH 44111
C1977-06 ....Williams, Donald Ellis ....5597 Greene Road #125/Paragould Ar 72450
C1994-08 ....Williams, Donald Ray 'Spin' ....257 Moreland Drive/Pittsburgh PA 15237
C1981-04 ....Williams, James Bernard ....4 Old Sound Road/Joppatowne MD 21085
C1995-09 ....Williams, Richard Anthony ....1 Tropicana Drive/Saint Petersburg FL 33705
C1997-08 ....Witt, Doug ....PO Box 90111/Arlington TX 76011
C1932-01 ....Wolgamot, Clifton Earl ....D. April 25, 1970 Independence, Ia.
C1976-03 ....Zimmer, Thomas Jeffrey ....4219 28th Avenue North/Saint Petersburg FL 33713

Umpires Debuting From 1910 To 1997

U1914-01	Anderson, Oliver	D. July 7, 1945 Los Angeles, Calif.
U1969-01	Anthony, George Merlyn 'Merlyn'	D. February 2, 1993 Yuba City, Calif.
U1965-01	Ashford, Emmett Littleton	D. March 1, 1980 Marina Del Rey, Calif.
U1969-02	Avants, Nick	5805 Woodlawn/Little Rock AR 72205
U1936-01	Ballanfant, Edward Lee 'Lee'	D. July 15, 1987 Dallas, Texas
U1940-01	Barlick, Albert Joseph	D. December 27, 1895 Springfield, Ill.
U1990-01	Barnes, Ronald	12860 North Meadview Way/Tucson AZ 85737
U1968-01	Barnett, Lawrence Robert	6464 Hughes Road/Prospect OH 43342
U1931-01	Barr, George Mckinley	D. July 26, 1974 Sulphur, Okla.
U1994-01	Barrett, Ted	6664 East Villeroy/Mesa AZ 85205
U1992-01	Barron, Mark	585 Clearwater Place/Lawrenceville/GA 30244
U1928-01	Barry, Daniel	D.
U1936-02	Basil, Stephen John	D. June 24, 1962 Gilchrist, Tex.
U1994-02	Bean, Eddie	1827 Third Court Southeast/Winter Haven FL 33880
U1992-02	Bell, Wally	418 Glenwoods Court/Youngstown OH 44512
U1942-01	Berry, Charles Francis	D. September 6, 1972 Evanston, Ill.
U1976-01	Betcher, Ralph	153 Parkfel Avenue/Pittsburgh PA 15237
U1970-01	Blandford , Fred	Old Add: 246 1/2 Allen St Elmira NY14904
U1944-01	Boggess, Lynton Ross 'Dusty'	D. July 8, 1968 Dallas, Tex.
U1984-01	Bonin, Gregory	403 Cobblestone Road/Lafayette LA 70508
U1944-02	Boyer, James Murry	D. July 25, 1959 Finksburg, Md.
U1917-01	Bransfield, William Edward 'Kitty'	D. May 1, 1947 Worcester, Mass.
U1973-01	Bremigan, Nicholas Gregory	D. March 29, 1989 Garland, Texas
U1915-01	Brewer ,	
U1973-02	Brinkman, Joseph Norbert	1021 Indian River Drive/Cocoa FL 32922
U1979-01	Brocklander, Fred William	123-40 83rd Avenue #10J/Kew Gardens NY11415
U1996-01	Bucknor, C. B.	46 Midwood Street/Brooklyn NY11225
U1957-01	Burkhart, William Kenneth 'Ken'	3708 Splendor Drive Rural Route 7 Knoxville TN 37918
U1911-01	Bush, Garnet C.	D. December 30, 1919 St. Louis, Mo.
U1913-01	Byron, William J. 'Lord'	D. December 27, 1955 Ypsilanti, Mich.
U1928-02	Campbell , William	Old Add: 676 South Belvedere Memphis TN
U1961-01	Carrigan , Herve Samuel 'Sam'	Old Add: 651 Mckinstry Ave Chicopee Falls MA 01020
U1989-01	Cederstrom, Gary L.	2910 2nd Avenue Southwest/Minot ND 58701
U1914-02	Chill , Oliver P. 'Ollie'	Old Add: Majestic Hotel Kansas City Mo
U1954-01	Chylak, Nestor	D. February 17, 1982 Dunmore, Pa.
U1976-02	Clark, Alan Marshall	16 Independence Place/Newtown PA 18940
U1930-01	Clarke , Robert	
U1982-01	Coble, George Drew 'Drew'	3554 Boy Wood Road/Graham NC 27253
U1915-02	Cockill, George	D. November 2, 1937 Steeltown, Pa.
U1976-03	Cohen, Alfred	7207 Beacon Hill Drive/Pittsburgh PA 15221
U1910-01	Colliflower, James Harry	D. August 14, 1961 Washington, D. C.
U1968-02	Colosi, Nicholas	68-17 54th Avenue/Maspeth NY11378
U1941-01	Conlan, John Bertrand 'Jocko'	D. April 16, 1989 Scottsdale, Ariz.
U1975-01	Cooney, Terrance Joseph	3205 Filbert Avenue/Clovis CA 93612
U1996-02	Cooper, Eric R.	2417 51st Street/Des Moines IA 50310
U1914-03	Corcoran, Thomas William	D. June 25, 1960 Plainfield, Conn.
U1983-01	Costello, Perry	406 Rosadell/Lansing MI 48910
U1979-02	Cousins, Derryl	78136 Desert Mountain Circle/Indio CA 92201
U1975-02	Crawford, Gerald Joseph	1 Pinzon Avenue/Havertown PA 19083
U1956-01	Crawford, Henry Charles 'Shag'	1530 Virginia Avenue/Havertown PA 19083
U1914-04	Cross, Montford Montgomery	D. June 21, 1934 Philadelphia, Pa.
U1993-01	Culbreth, Fieldin	804 Southfield Street/Inman NC 29349
U1991-01	Cuzzi, Philip	108 Passaic #C23/Nutley NJ 7110
U1970-02	Dale , Jerry Parker	Old Add: 428 West Huntington Dr #4 Arcadia CA 91006
U1991-02	Danley , Kerwin	3211 West Frankfort Drive/Chandler AZ 85226
U1986-01	Darling, Gary Richard	16422 South 36th Place/Phoenix AZ 85044
U1948-01	Dascoli, Frank	D. August 11, 1990 Danielson, Conn.
U1969-03	Davidson, David Leroy 'Satch'	2400 Westheimer Street #209W/Houston TX 77098
U1982-02	Davidson, Robert Allan	91 Deerwood Drive/Littleton CO 81027
U1982-03	Davis , Gerald	Old Add: 616 Camellia Appleton WI 54915
U1970-03	Deegan, William Edward John	8392 77th Avenue/Largo FL 34647
U1956-02	Delmore, Victor	D. June 10, 1960 Scranton, Pa.
U1983-02	Demuth, Dana Andrew	1156 West Wagner Drive/Gilbert AZ 85234
U1968-03	Denkinger, Donald Anton	3505 Kingswood Place/Waterloo IA 50701
U1966-01	Dezelan, Frank John	1314 Wood Street/Pittsburgh PA 15221
U1995-01	Diaz , Lazaro	Old Add: 2851 Nw 189th Street Opa Locka FL 33056
U1963-01	Dimuro, Louis John	D. June 7, 1982 Arlington, Tex.
U1997-01	Dimuro, Michael	1048 West Swan Drive/Chandler AZ 85248
U1996-03	Dimuro, Ray	770 North Nantucket Street/Chandler AZ 85225
U1953-01	Dixon, Hal Hayworth	D. July 28, 1966 Churnee, S. C.
U1950-01	Donatelli, August Joseph 'Augie'	D. May 24, 1990 St. Petersburg, Fla.
U1931-02	Donnelly, Charles	D. December 13, 1968 Lake Worth, Fla.
U1930-02	Donohue, Michael	D. August 7, 1968 St. Louis, Mo.
U1911-02	Doyle, John Joseph 'Dirty Jack'	D. December 31, 1958 Holyoke, Mass.
U1963-02	Doyle, Walter James	D. March 2, 1988 Tampa, Fla.
U1996-04	Dreckman, Bruce M.	110 North Maple/Marcus IA 51035

U1960-01	Drummond, Calvin Troy 'Troy'	D. May 2, 1970 Des Moines, Iowa
U1951-01	Duffy, James Francis	20-32 Indian Avenue #15/Portsmouth RI2871
U1939-01	Dunn, Thomas Patrick	D. January 20, 1976 Prince Georges Co., Md.
U1914-05	Eldridge , Clarence	
U1965-02	Engel, Robert Allen	3500 Harmony Lane/Bakersfield CA 93306
U1952-01	Engeln, William Raymond	D. April 17, 1968 Palo Alto, Calif.
U1971-01	Evans, James Bremond	PO Box 2142/Littleton CO 80161
U1996-05	Everitt, Mike	821 East Boston Street/Chandler AZ 85225
U1913-02	Ferguson, Charles Augustus	D. May 17, 1931 Sault Sainte Marie, Mich.
U1979-03	Fields, Stephen	5941 Queenston Street/Springfield VA22152
U1911-03	Finneran, William	D. July 30, 1961 Erie, Pa.
U1979-04	Fitzpatrick, Michael	262 Lodge Lane/Kalamazoo MI 49009
U1953-02	Flaherty, John Francis 'Red'	9 Fowler Lane/Falmouth MA 2540
U1975-03	Ford, Robert Dale 'Dale'	220 Charlie Avenue/Piney Flats TN 37686
U1961-02	Forman, Allen Sanford	219b West Tateway/Kitty Hawk NC 27949
U1996-06	Foster, Martin	319 West 5th Avenue/Denver CO 80204
U1968-04	Frantz, Arthur Frank	3052 North Marmosa Avenue/Chicago IL 60634
U1911-04	Frary, Ralph	D. November 10, 1925 Aberdeen, Wash.
U1920-01	Friel, William Edward	D. December 24, 1959 St. Louis, Mo.
U1971-02	Froemming, Bruce Neal	702 West Haddonstone Place/Thiensville WI 53092
U1952-02	Froese, Grover	D. July 20, 1982 Bay Shore, N.Y.
U1915-03	Fyfe , Louis	
U1975-04	Garcia, Richard Raul	PO Box 3276/Clearwater FL 33767
U1925-01	Geisel, Harry Christian	D. February 20, 1966 Indianapolis, Ind.
U1994-03	Gibbons, Brian	1238 Academy Place/South Bend IN 46616
U1997-02	Gibson, Greg	3628 Briarwood Drive/Catletsburg KY41129
U1914-06	Goeckel, Edward	D. March 19, 1963
U1936-03	Goetz, Lawrence John	D. October 31, 1962 Cincinnati, O.
U1968-05	Goetz, Russell Lewis	937 Fawcett Avenue/Mckeesport PA 15132
U1946-01	Gore, Arthur Joseph 'Artie'	D. September 29, 1986 Wolfeboro, N. H.
U1991-03	Gorman, Brian	PO Box 1208/Somis CA 93066
U1951-02	Gorman, Thomas David	D. August 11, 1986 Closter, N. J.
U1976-04	Gregg, Eric Eugene	2635 Mimi Circle/Philadelphia PA 19131
U1938-01	Grieve, William Turner	D. August 17, 1979 Yonkers, N. Y.
U1970-04	Grimsley, John William	D. October 23, 1992
U1983-03	Grinder , Scott	Old Add: 128 Northview Drive Zelienople PA 16063
U1914-07	Groom, Robert	D. February 19, 1948 Belleville, Ill.
U1970-05	Grygiel , George R.	Old Add: PO Box 31633 Tucson AZ 85751
U1952-03	Guglielmo, Angelo Augie	D. December 28, 1996 Waterbury, Conn.
U1913-03	Guthrie, William	D. March 6, 1950 Chicago, Ill
U1961-03	Haller, William Edward	Rural Route 2 Box 82c/Brownstown IL 62418
U1985-01	Hallion, Thomas Francis	4040 Ormond Road/Louisville KY40207
U1979-05	Harris, Lanny Dean	D. June 16, 1991
U1916-01	Harrison, Peter	D. March 9, 1921 Saranac Lake, N. Y.
U1912-01	Hart, Eugene	D. May 10, 1937 Lowell, Mass.
U1962-01	Harvey, Harold Douglas 'Doug'	16081 Mustang Drive/Springville CA 93265
U1977-01	Hendry, Eugene/'Ted'	14740 North 90th Place/Scottsdale AZ 85260
U1945-01	Henline, Walter John 'Butch'	D. October 9, 1957 Sarasota, Fla.
U1993-02	Henrichs , Jeff	Old Add: 1901 Morningstar Dr Lincoln NE 68506
U1991-04	Hernandez , Angel	Old Add: 9701 Sw 14th Court Pembroke Pines FL 33025
U1990-02	Hickox, Edwin W.	2001 Steamboat Ridge Court/Daytona Beach Fl/32124
U1912-02	Hildebrand, George Albert	D. May 30, 1960 Woodland Hills, Calif.
U1983-04	Hirschbeck, John Francis	8730 Raintree Run/Poland OH 44514
U1987-01	Hirschbeck, Mark	15 Blackberry Lane/Shelton CT 6484
U1987-02	Hohn , William John	Old Add: 134 Lafayette Court Collegeville PA 19426
U1997-03	Holbrook, Sam	3861 Grassy Creek Drive/Lexington KY40514
U1923-01	Holmes, Howard Elbert 'Ducky'	D. September 18, 1945 Dayton, O.
U1949-01	Honochick, George James 'Jim'	D. March 10, 1994 Allentown, Pa.
U1915-04	Howell, Henry/'Handsome Harry'	D. May 22, 1956 Spokane, Wash.
U1936-04	Hubbard, Robert Cal 'Cal'	D. October 16, 1977 St Petersburg, Fla.
U1983-05	Humphrey , Richard	Old Add: 1476 Brownleaf Richmond VA23225
U1947-01	Hurley, Edwin Henry	D. November 12, 1969 Boston, Mass.
U1912-03	Hyatt, Robert Hamilton 'Ham'	D. September 11, 1963 Liberty Lake, Wash.
U1952-04	Jackowski, William Anthony	D. July 29, 1996 Springfield, Vt.
U1914-08	Johnson, Harry	D. February 20, 1951 Memphis, Tenn.
U1984-02	Johnson , Mark Stephen	Old Add: 666 Prospect Rd Honolulu HI 96813
U1936-05	Johnston, Charles Edward	D.
U1944-03	Jones, Nicholas Ittner 'Red'	D. March 19, 1987 Miami, Fla.
U1927-01	Jorda, Louis De Larond	D. May 27, 1944 Largo, Fla.
U1989-03	Joyce, James A.	7440 Sw Hart Place/Beaverton OR 97005
U1977-02	Kaiser, Kenneth John	56 Holly Sue Lane/Rochester NY14626
U1910-02	Kecher, W. H.	D.
U1991-05	Kellogg, Jeffrey	22900 Cherry Hill Court/Mattawan MI 49071
U1963-03	Kibler, John William	3046 Sonia Court/Oceanside CA 92056
U1960-02	Kinnamon, William Ervin	8240 Brentwood Road/Largo FL 33543
U1933-01	Kolls, Louis Charles	D. February 23, 1941 Hoopple, Ill.
U1976-06	Kosc, Gregory John	3465 Hunting Run Road/Medina OH 44256
U1968-06	Kunkel, William Gustave James	D. May 4, 1985 Red Bank, N. J.
U1955-01	Landes, Stanley Albert	D. January 23, 1994 Peoria, Ariz.

U1915-05 ....Langevin, Joseph ....D. March 18, 1953 Binghamton, N. Y.
U1979-06 ....Lawson , William ....Old Add: 7228 East Eastview Dr Tucson AZ 85710
U1989-04 ....Layne, Jerry Blake ....2323 Cypress Garden Blvd/Winter Haven FL 33884
U1985-02 ....Lepperd, Thomas ....121 South 49th Street/West Des Moines IA 50265
U1914-09 ....Lincoln , Frederick ....
U1961-04 ....Linsalata, Joseph ....4017 Washington Street/Hollywood FL 33021
U1968-07 ....Luciano, Ronald Michael ....D. January 18, 1995 Endicott, N. Y.
U1928-02 ....Magee, Sherwood Robert 'Sherry' ....D. March 13, 1929 Philadelphia, Pa.
U1929-01 ....Magerkurth, George Levi 'Major' ....D. October 7, 1966 Rock Island, Ill.
U1970-06 ....Maloney, George Patrick ....600 Nw 93rd Avenue/Pembroke Pines FL 33024
U1935-01 ....Marberry, Fred/'Firpo' ....D. June 30, 1976 Mexia, Texas
U1981-01 ....Marsh, Randall Gilbert ....3023 Winterborne Road/Covington KY41017
U1914-10 ....Maxwell, James Albert 'Bert'......................D. December 10, 1961 Brady, Tex.
U1983-06 ....McClelland, Timothy Reid ....5405 Woodland Avenue/West Des Moines IA 50265
U1914-11 ....McCormick, William J. 'Barry' ....D. January 28, 1956 Cincinnati, O.
U1970-07 ....McCoy, Larry Sanders ....Rural Route 1/Greenway AR 72450
U1910-03 ....McGinnis, ...D.
U1925-02 ....McgGowan, William Aloysius ....D. December 9, 1954 Silver Spring, Md.
U1912-04 ....McGreevy, Edward ....D.
U1930-03 ....McGrew, Harry Hancock 'Ted'......................D. June 29, 1969 Bedford, Va.
U1974-01 ....McKean, James Gilbert ....740 Sand Pike Drive Ne/Saint Petersburg FL 33703
U1946-02 ....McKinley, William Francis ....D. August 1, 1980 Mount Pleasant, Pa.
U1929-02 ....McLaughlin, Edward.....................................D. November 28, 1965 Philadelphia, Pa.
U1924-01 ....McLaughlin, Peter ....D. March 1, 1972 Saint Joseph, Mo.
U1971-03 ....McSherry, John Patrick ....D. April 1, 1996 Cincinnati, Ohio
U1992-04 ....Meals, Gerald ....2195 Southeast Blvd/Salem OH 44460
U1988-01 ....Meriwether, Julius/'Chick' ....2409 Seifried Street/Nashville TN 37208
U1977-03 ....Merrill, Edwin Durwood 'Durwood'...............PO Box 115/Hooks TX 75561
U1997-04 ....Miller, William ....371 Baltusrol Drive/Aptos CA 95003
U1974-02 ....Montague, Edward Michael ....1521 Cherrywood Drive/San Mateo CA 94402
U1917-02 ....Moran, Charles Barthel ....D. June 13, 1949 Horse Cave, Ky.
U1970-08 ....Morgenweck, Henry Charles ....33 Bogert Street/Teaneck NJ 7666
U1917-03 ....Moriarty, George Joseph ....D. April 8, 1964 Miami, Fla.
U1983-07 ....Morrison, Daniel G. ....14220 Sunshine Court/Largo FL 34644
U1915-06 ....Mullaney, Dominic ....D. August 21, 1964 Jacksonville, Fla.
U1914-12 ....Murray , J. A. ....Old Add: 95 Malcolm Street Minneapolis Mn
U1915-07 ....Nallin, Richard ....D. September 7, 1956 Frederick, Md.
U1951-03 ....Napp, Larry Albert ....D. July 7, 1993 Plantation, Fla.
U1995-02 ....Nauert, Paul..3102 Meadow Wood Court Nw/Lawrenceville GA 30244
U1997-05 ....Nelson, Jeff ....8335 Hyde Court/Cottage Grove Mn 55016
U1979-07 ....Nelson, Richard ....Rural Route 2 Box 129e/Perryville AR 72126
U1965-03 ....Neudecker, Jerome/'Jerry'..........................D. January 11, 1997 Fort Walton Beach, Fla.
U1922-01 ....O'Sullivan , John ....
U1912-05 ....Obrien, Joseph ....D. November 5, 1925 Troy, N. Y.
U1914-13 ....Oconnor , Arthur ....
U1964-01 ....Odom, James Cecil ....D. January 18, 1989 Bennettsville, S. C.
U1966-02 ....Odonnell , James Michael ....Old Add: 204 North Diamond St Clifton Heights Pa
U1915-08 ....Ohara , ...
U1968-08 ....Olsen, Andrew Holger ....451 93rd Avenue North/Saint Petersburg FL 33702
U1992-05 ....Onora, Brian ....4294 Maureen Drive/Youngstown OH 44511
U1923-02 ....Ormsby, Emmett T. 'Red'.............................D. October 11, 1962 Chicago, Ill.
U1977-04 ....Palermo, Stephen Michael ....7921 West 118th/Overland Park Ks 66210
U1979-08 ....Pallone , David Michael ....Old Add: 1318 Beacon Street #12 Brookline Ma
U1946-03 ....Paparella, Joseph James..............................D. October 17, 1994 Sebastian, Fla.
U1911-05 ....Parker, Harley ....D.
U1979-09 ....Parks , Dallas Finney ....Old Add: 10700 Coastal Hwy #405 Ocean City Md 21842
U1941-02 ....Passarella, Arthur Matthew ....D. October 12, 1981 Hemet, Calif.
U1960-03 ....Pelekoudas, Christos George ....D. November 30, 1984 Sunnyvale, Calif.
U1922-02 ....Pfirman, Charles H. 'Cy'.............................D. May 16, 1937 New Orleans, La.
U1912-06 ....Phelps, Edward Jaykill.................................D. January 31, 1942 East Greenbush, N. Y.
U1970-09 ....Phillips, David Robert ....29 Hlloway Drive/Lake Saint Louis Mo 63367
U1935-02 ....Pinelli, Ralph Arthur 'Babe' ....D. October 22, 1984 Daly City, Calif.
U1938-02 ....Pipgras, George William ....D. October 19, 1986 Gainesville, Fla.
U1985-03 ....Poncino, Larry ....2954 North Calle Ladera/Tucson AZ 85715
U1991-06 ....Potter, Scott A. ....2916 Carriage Drive/Daytona Beach FL 32119
U1923-03 ....Powell, Cornelius Joseph ....D. July 25, 1971 Lynwood, Calif.
U1961-05 ....Pryor, John Paul 'Paul' ....D. December 15, 1995 St. Petersburg, Fla.
U1972-01 ....Pulli, Frank Victor ....1981 Downing Place/Palm Harbor FL 34683
U1976-07 ....Puskaric, Joseph ....429 35th Avenue/Mckeesport PA 15132
U1974-03 ....Quick, James Edward ....PO Box 12760/Scottsdale AZ 85267
U1935-03 ....Quinn, John Aloysius ....D. July 4, 1968 Philadelphia, Pa.
U1914-14 ....Quisser , Arthur ....
U1990-03 ....Rapuano, Edward ....3412 Palladian Circle/Deerfield Beach FL 33442
U1926-01 ....Reardon, John Edward 'Beans' ....D. July 31, 1984 Long Beach, Calif.
U1979-10 ....Reed, Rick Alan ....1648 Kilburn/Rochester Hills MI 48306
U1977-05 ....Reilly, Michael Eugene................................131 Smithfield Road/Battle Creek/MI 49015
U1989-05 ....Reliford, Charles Harold ....1505 Cypress Road/Ashland KY41101
U1973-03 ....Rennert, Laurence Harvey ....Walkers Glen 2560 46th Road Vero Beach FL 32966
U1955-02 ....Rice, John LA Claire ....2666 East 73rd Street #A12w/Chicago IL 60649

U1992-06	Rieker, Richard	5805 Potomac/Saint Louis Mo 63139
U1983-08	Rippley, Thomas Steven	9100 Park Blvd #8/Largo FL 34647
U1947-02	Robb, Douglas W. 'Scotty'	D. April 10, 1969 Montclair, N.J.
U1953-03	Roberts , Leonard Wyatt	Old Add: 5505 Spruce View Dallas TX 75232
U1974-04	Rodriguez , Armando Humberto	Old Add: Indepencia 1375 Veracruz Ver Mex
U1980-01	Roe, John/'Rocky'	8552 Summerville Place/Orlando FL 32819
U1938-03	Rommel, Edwin Americus	D. August 26, 1970 Baltimore, Md.
U1923-04	Rowland, Clarence Henry 'Pants'	D. May 17, 1969 Chicago, Ill.
U1938-04	Rue, Joseph William	D. December 1, 1984 Laguna Hills, Calif.
U1954-02	Runge, Edward Paul	4949 Cresita Drive/San Diego CA 92115
U1972-02	Runge, Paul Edward	649 Calle De LA Sierra/El Cajon CA 92021
U1946-04	Ryan, Walter	D. June 16, 1981
U1961-06	Salerno, Alex Joseph	1913 Tilden Avenue/New Hartford NY13413
U1970-10	Satchell , Darold	Old Add: 1613 North Duke St Durham NC 27701
U1997-06	Schrieber, Paul	9805 Phoenix Trail/Louisville KY40223
U1960-04	Schwarts, Harry Clark	D. February 22, 1963 Cleveland, O.
U1985-04	Scott, Dale Allan	1283 Sw Cardinell Drive/Portland OR 97201
U1930-04	Scott, James/'Death Valley Jim'	D. April 7, 1957 Palm Springs, Calif.
U1934-01	Sears, John William 'Ziggy'	D. December 16, 1956 Houston, Tex.
U1952-05	Secory, Frank Edward	D. April 7, 1995 Port Huron, Mich.
U1914-15	Shannon, William Porter 'Spike'	D. May 16, 1940 Minneapolis, Minn.
U1979-11	Shulock, John Richard	185 13th Avenue/Vero Beach FL 32962
U1957-02	Smith, Vincent Ambrose	D. December 14, 1979 Virginia Beach, Va.
U1960-05	Smith, William Alaric 'Al'	609 Delhi Street/Bossier City LA 70111
U1950-02	Soar, Albert Henry 'Hank'	60 Conch Road/Narragansett RI2882
U1977-06	Spenn, Frederick Charles	PO Box 127/Royal IL 61871
U1966-03	Springstead, Martin John	5164 Flicker Field Circle/Sarasota FL 33581
U1928-03	Stark, Albert D. 'Dolly'	D. August 28, 1968 New York, N. Y.
U1961-07	Steiner, Melvin James	11296 Linda Way/Los Alamitos CA 90720
U1968-09	Stello, Richard Jack	D. November 18, 1987 Lakeland, Fla.
U1948-02	Stevens, John William	D. September 9, 1981 Philadelphia Pa.
U1941-03	Stewart , Ernest Draper	Old Add: 107 San Marcos Del Rio Tx
U1959-01	Stewart, Robert William	D. December 1, 1981 Woonsocket, R. I.
U1933-02	Stewart, William Joseph	D. February 18, 1964 Jamaica Plain, Mass.
U1915-09	Stockdale , M. J.	Old Add: 314 West 42nd St New York Ny
U1957-03	Sudol, Edward Lawrence	415 Revilo Blvd PO Box 5486 Daytona Beach FL 32108
U1933-03	Summers, William Reed	D. September 12, 1966 Upton, Mass.
U1924-02	Sweeney, James	D. January 29, 1950 Tyler, Tex.
U1956-03	Tabacchi, Frank Tule	D. October 26, 1983 Hoboken, N. J.
U1972-03	Tata, Terry Anthony	300 Village Drive/Cheshire CT 6410
U1970-11	Tremblay, Richard Henry	D. June 12, 1987 Littleton, N. H.
U1985-05	Tschida, Timothy	274 15 1/2 Avenue/Turtle Lake WI 54889
U1954-03	Umont, Frank William	D. June 20, 1991 Fort Lauderdale, Fla.
U1963-04	Valentine, William Terry	15 Blue Ridge Circle/Little Rock/AR 72207
U1927-02	Van Graflan, Roy	D. September 4, 1953 Rochester, N. Y.
U1914-16	Van Sickle, Charles	D. May 4, 1909
U1991-07	Vanover, Larry W.	801 Glenn Court/Owensboro KY42303
U1960-06	Vargo, Edward Paul	101 Freedom Road/Butler PA 16001
U1957-04	Venzon, Anthony	D. September 20, 1971 Pittsburgh,Pa.
U1977-07	Voltaggio, Vito Henry 'Vic'	1049 Florian Way/Spring Hill/FL 34609
U1922-03	Walsh, Edward Augustin 'Big Ed'	D. May 26, 1959 Pompano Beach, Fla.
U1961-08	Walsh, Francis D. 'Frank'	D. July 1, 1985
U1949-02	Warneke, Lonnie	D. June 23, 1976 Hot Springs, Ark.
U1943-01	Weafer, Harold Leon	D. August 23, 1978 Richmond, Va.
U1983-09	Welke, Timothy James	7790 Doubletree Court/Kalamazoo MI 49009
U1966-04	Wendelstedt, Harry Hunter	88 South St Andrews/Ormond Beach FL 32074
U1976-08	West, Joseph Henry	114 North Eastern Street/Greenville NC 27834
U1911-06	Westervelt, Frederick	D. May 4, 1955 Drexel Hill, Pa.
U1961-09	Weyer, Lee Howard	D. July 4, 1988 San Mateo, Calif.
U1990-04	Wickham, Daniel	3221 East Mountain Vista Drive/Phoenix AZ 85044
U1972-04	Williams, Arthur	D. February 8, 1979 Bakersfield, Calif.
U1963-05	Williams, William George 'Billy'	D. September 22, 1998 Deerfield Beach, Fla.
U1921-01	Wilson, Frank	D. June 1, 1928 Brooklyn, N. Y.
U1994-04	Winans, Matthew	86 Dunrobin Lane/Watertown/CT 6795
U1988-02	Winters, Michael John	15843 Prairie Vista Road/Poway CA 92064
U1983-10	Young, Larry Eugene	PO Box 255/Roscoe IL 60173

Glossary

The definitions presented in this glossary are definitions as they are interpreted by autograph collectors. For example, **PHOTO** refers to an autographed photo and **HOFer** refers to the autograph of a Hall of Famer. Some of the definitions may appear self-explanatory and hence unnecessary; however, they are included for completeness.

ALL-STAR BALL
A ball autographed by most or all members of a particular baseball all-star game.

AUTOPEN
A mechanical device used to affix a signature on a document, letter or other paper medium. Autopen autographs are not considered collectible.

BALL POINT
A type of pen through which the ink is delivered by means of a revolving ball tip.

BASEBALL COMMEMORATIVE ENVELOPE
A stamped envelope postmarked on the date of a significant event in baseball history. The envelope contains some graphic or illustrative identification of the event.

CARD
A card autographed by the player portrayed on the card. Cards are normally autographed on the front; however, cards autographed on the back still qualify under this definition.

CHECK
A cancelled check or bank note containing the autograph of a ballplayer. Checks are quite often obtained from the estate of deceased ballplayers. Official ballclub checks in many cases contain more than one autograph.

CLUB ISSUED POSTCARDS
Postcard size pictures of ballplayers, the older ones normally being in black and white, with modern postcards being predominantly in color. There are usually blank backed, sold at ballparks and make excellent autograph media. Many players send autographed copies of these postcards to fans requesting autographs.

CONTRACT
A legal document, for any purpose, including agreements concerning players and management, equipment or other product manufacturers, or personal agreements signed by the sports personality.

CUT
An autograph that has been "cut" from a larger piece of paper, photo, letter or other written or printed matter.

DATED
An autograph which contains both the signature and the date when the signature was written.

DEBUT YEAR
The year in which a player first appeared in a game in the big leagues. For a manager or coach with no player experience, the debut year refers to the year he first appeared as manger or coach.

DEBUT YEAR NUMBER
Within a particular debut year the number for a player obtained by placing in alphabetical order all players who debuted that particular year and placing a number on each, from 1 to "the total number of players debuting that year," based on this alphabetical order.

FACSIMILE
A copy of an original signature. Facsimile autographs are not considered collectible.

FELT TIP
A type of pen which has a felt tip and which provides a smooth unbroken signature.

HOFer
The autograph of a member of baseball's Hall of Fame.

LETTER
A typed or handwritten communication with a heading listing to whom the letter is written and a closing autographed by a sports personality.

ORIGINAL ART
A unique drawing, painting or other piece of artwork portraying a personality or an event and bearing the signature of a participant of the event or the personality portrayed.

PENCIL
A signature in pencil by a sports personality. Pencil signatures predominated during the early parts of the century and are sometimes the only types of signatures available of certain sports personalities. Care should be taken with pencil signatures as they smear quite easily.

PLAQUE
Postcard pictures of the bronzed plaques of Hall of Fame baseball players in the Baseball Hall of Fame in Cooperstown, NY. Through the years there have been several different color plaques issues by the Hall of Fame, including black and white types.

PERSONALIZED

An autograph which contains a reference to the person for whom the autograph was written.

PHOTO

A glossy picture, normally 5" X 7" or 8" X 10", which contains an autograph of the player portrayed on the photo.

SASE

Self-addressed stamped envelope. When requesting autographs, SASEs should be sent to ensure that returned autographs will be sent to the proper place and to provide the autograph giver a convenient means of returning autographed material.

SHARPIE

A brand of ink pen very popular with autograph collectors because if its broad stroke and its rapid drying characteristics on almost any surface.

STAMP

A signature affixed by means of a rubber or wooden device which contains a facsimile of the sports personality's autograph. Stamped signatures are not considered collectible.

TEAM BALL

A ball autographed by most or all members of a particular team.

TEAM SHEET

A single sheet of paper containing the autographs of most or all members of a particular team during a particular year. Many team sheets are on club stationery.

3 X 5

An index card, either lined or unlined, which many collectors use for obtaining autographs. The 3 X 5 refers to the approximate dimensions of the card. 3 X 5s usually contain only one signature.

Margaret Smalling (1942-1997)

The past fourteen months haven't been kind to the Smalling family. A year ago, my wife, Marge, experienced some pain in her side while on vacation in Northern Minnesota. Upon our return home, we moved as quickly as possible with surgery resulting at the Mayo Clinic in late August. The prognosis wasn't good however, gall bladder cancer had spread to her liver. The evident malignancy had been

removed. The chance for re-occurrence was nearly 100%. Although chemotherapy couldn't stop it, we had four months with a number of good days of quality life. But she lost her battle on December 18, 1997. She passed away with dignity and grace at home with thirteen of her family at her side. We miss her very much and still mourn her loss.

Marge and I met in 1962 at Kee Nee Moo Sha resort on Woman Lake near Longville, Minnesota. We married two years later and have since raised four sons. We continued to vacation at the resort for two weeks almost every year since.

Marge was a vital participant in our family autograph business. She filled many of the orders, was often the only one home to answer the phone and filed away thousands of autographs. Our last price list was November 1997. She filled some of the orders that came in early December.

Those of us that remain, my four sons, daughter-in-law, and I determined that we will go on, hold the family together and be strong. We all vacationed together on Woman Lake in August.

Ray, the oldest, is married, lives in Kansas City and works for Transsystems. He has a Civil Engineering Degree from Iowa State, A.P.E. designations and will get his Master's Degree from Kansas State this December.

Matt took his Iowa State Marketing Degree to California and works in sales for Montgomery Kone elevators in Hermosa Beach.

David has moved back home while he finishes his Civil Engineering Degree at Iowa State.

Robbie is a Freshman at Luther College, a liberal arts school in Decorah, Iowa.

David, at home for now, has taken over a lot of the household chores, and continues to be a tremendous help with the autographs.

It's been over two years since the last Address List. We'd prefer the interval to be two years or less. When life deals you a tough hand, you adjust and go on. It's taken a while to change habits, daily duties and life in general. I still have two children to raise. They come first. The New Handbook had to wait. I thank all of you who have been kind and thoughtful to us this past year.

Sincerely,

Jim Smalling

Autographs

Autographs

Autographs

Autographs

Autographs